Holy Trinity Pric
City of London

An archaeological reconstruction and history

MoLAS Monograph Series

1 Excavations at the priory and hospital of St Mary Spital, London, Christopher Thomas, Barney Sloane and Christopher Phillpotts
ISBN 1 901992 00 4

2 The National Roman Fabric Reference Collection: a handbook, Roberta Tomber and John Dore
ISBN 1 901992 01 2

3 The Cross Bones burial ground, Redcross Way, Southwark, London: archaeological excavations (1991–8) for the London Underground Limited Jubilee Line Extension Project, Megan Brickley and Adrian Miles with Hilary Stainer
ISBN 1 901992 06 3

4 The eastern cemetery of Roman London: excavations 1983–90, Bruno Barber and David Bowsher
ISBN 1 901992 09 8

5 The Holocene evolution of the London Thames: archaeological excavations (1991–8) for the London Underground Limited Jubilee Line Extension Project, Jane Sidell, Keith Wilkinson, Robert Scaife and Nigel Cameron
ISBN 1 901992 10 1

6 The Limehouse porcelain manufactory: excavations at 108–116 Narrow Street, London, 1990, Kieron Tyler and Roy Stephenson, with J Victor Owen and Christopher Phillpotts
ISBN 1 901992 16 0

7 Roman defences and medieval industry: excavations at Baltic House, City of London, Elizabeth Howe
ISBN 1 901992 17 9

8 London bridge: 2000 years of a river crossing, Bruce Watson, Trevor Brigham and Tony Dyson
ISBN 1 901992 18 7

9 Roman and medieval townhouses on the London waterfront: excavations at Governor's House, City of London, Trevor Brigham with Aidan Woodger
ISBN 1 901992 21 7

10 The London Charterhouse, Bruno Barber and Christopher Thomas
ISBN 1 901992 23 3

11 Medieval 'Westminster' floor tiles, Ian M Betts
ISBN 1 901992 24 1

12 Settlement in Roman Southwark: archaeological excavations (1991–8) for the London Underground Limited Jubilee Line Extension Project, James Drummond-Murray and Peter Thompson with Carrie Cowan
ISBN 1 901992 28 4

13 Aspects of medieval and later Southwark: archaeological excavations (1991–8) for the London Underground Limited Jubilee Line Extension Project, Heather Knight
ISBN 1 901992 30 6

14 The prehistory and topography of Southwark and Lambeth, Jane Sidell, Jonathan Cotton, Louise Rayner and Lucy Wheeler
ISBN 1 901992 31 4

15 Middle Saxon London: excavations at the Royal Opera House 1989–99, Gordon Malcolm and David Bowsher with Robert Cowie
ISBN 1 901992 32 2

16 Urban development in north-west Roman Southwark: excavations 1974–90, Carrie Cowan
ISBN 1 901992 33 0

17 Industry in north-west Roman Southwark: excavations 1984–8, Friederike Hammer
ISBN 1 901992 34 9

18 The Cistercian abbey of St Mary Stratford Langthorne, Essex: archaeological excavations for the London Underground Limited Jubilee Line Extension Project, Bruno Barber, Steve Chew, Tony Dyson and Bill White
ISBN 1 901992 38 1

19 Material culture in London in an age of transition: Tudor and Stuart period finds *c* 1450–*c* 1700 from excavations at riverside sites in Southwark, Geoff Egan
ISBN 1 901992 39 X

20 Excavations at the priory of the Order of the Hospital of St John of Jerusalem, Clerkenwell, London, Barney Sloane and Gordon Malcolm
ISBN 1 901992 20 9

21 Roman and medieval Cripplegate, City of London: archaeological excavations 1992–8, Elizabeth Howe and David Lakin
ISBN 1 901992 42 X

22 The royal palace, abbey and town of Westminster on Thorney Island: archaeological excavations for the London Underground Limited Jubilee Line Extension Project, Christopher Thomas, Robert Cowie and Jane Sidell
ISBN 1 901992 50 0

23 A prestigious Roman building complex on the Southwark waterfront: excavations at Winchester Palace, London, 1983–90, Brian Yule
ISBN 1 901992 51 9

24 Holy Trinity Priory, Aldgate, City of London: an archaeological reconstruction and history, John Schofield and Richard Lea
ISBN 1 901992 45 4

Holy Trinity Priory, Aldgate, City of London

An archaeological reconstruction and history

John Schofield and Richard Lea

MoLAS Monograph 24

Museum of London Archaeology Service

Published by the Museum of London Archaeology Service

A CIP catalogue record for this book is available from the British Library

Production and series design by Tracy Wellman
Typesetting and design by Sue Cawood
Reprographics by Andy Chopping
Copy editing by Simon Burnell
Series editing by Sue Hirst/Susan M Wright
Post-excavation and series management by Peter Rowsome

Printed by the Lavenham Press

Front cover: reconstructed three-dimensional view of the priory at its fullest monastic extent in c 1500, from the north-east; ground-floor plan of the priory by John Symonds, c 1585; view of the south transept and interior of chapel 1, from the west

Back cover: tin-glazed plate in the Museum of London, attributed to the Aldgate workshop, dated 1600 or 1602 (see Fig 159 for inscription); the south side of St James's Place (the former monastic great court) in 1884, watercolour by John Crowther; 16th-century stove tile (crest tile) with classical portrait

CONTRIBUTORS

Principal authors	John Schofield, Richard Lea
Stratigraphic records (site A)	Richard Bluer
Architectural context of the priory	Malcolm Thurlby
Building material	Ian M Betts, Mark Samuel
Continental tile-stoves	David R M Gaimster
Pottery	Lyn Blackmore
Non-ceramic finds	Geoff Egan
Animal remains	Alan Pipe
Human remains	Janice Conheeney
Photography	Jon Bailey, Edwin Baker, Andy Chopping, Maggie Cox, Trevor Hurst, Jan Scrivener
Graphics	Susan Banks, Peter Hart-Alison, Lyn Blackmore (pottery), Alison Hawkins (finds), Richard Lea (3-D modelling)
Editors	Laura Schaaf, Susan M Wright

CONTENTS

Specialist appendices 8

FIGURES

TABLES

SUMMARY

The priory of Holy Trinity Aldgate (founded in 1107 or 1108) lay just inside Aldgate in the eastern part of the City of London, north of Leadenhall Street. This report, the first to reconstruct the development of the Augustinian priory and its buildings, is based on a variety of evidence: principally archaeological observations and excavations of 1908, 1953 and 1977–90, but also two plans of all the main priory buildings, drawn at ground-floor and first-floor levels by John Symonds in *c* 1585, and antiquarian observations of 1790–1825 as parts of the priory were uncovered and gradually demolished.

A church had been established by the late 11th century, and a cemetery found on several sites in the study area may have functioned with it or with the new priory church, which was built in the first half of the 12th century. Much of the architecture of the eastern arm of the priory church can be reconstructed, and something of the other priory buildings at this time. Two of the children of King Stephen were buried near the high altar in the years shortly before 1147; there seems to have been a connection with the royal family, and possibly with Henry of Blois, the king's brother. A Lady chapel was constructed in 1197–1221, and a period of concerted rebuilding from the late 12th century to about 1350 is indicated by a combination of the documentary and archaeological evidence. The cloister lay to the north of the church and the canons probably had a latrine or reredorter, of the late 13th century, over the city ditch on the north side of the precinct, and a doorway through the city wall; but both these features were removed, probably when the wall was reinforced with brick arches by the City in 1477. The artefactual evidence from the priory was slight, but included pieces of silk from vestments (the fabric made in Islamic Spain), pottery, glass urinals, metalwork and items of leather and wood. There were also architectural fragments which have helped to reconstruct the priory buildings.

Two areas of external cemetery were also excavated. The larger lay on the south side of the priory church; the other comprised a smaller number of inhumations north of the north-west corner of the church, in the space later taken over for the great tower and the widening of the western claustral range to the west. No differentiation could be made, based on ceramic dating, between the groups of burials, and the whole cemetery is dated to a span beginning in the 11th or 12th century, with some burials probably continuing into the early 13th century. From the presence of men, women and children in the graves on the two sites it is probable that both burial areas included lay people. It is not possible to say whether the canons had their own exclusive cemetery at the priory, though one is likely; it might have lain in the area north-east of the church, although no burials were located during the admittedly limited observations there. One mature man buried on the south side of the church had a silver pectoral cross on his shoulder. The skeletons presented a variety of osteological conditions consistent with their probable high status.

Holy Trinity Priory was dissolved in 1532, three years before the general Dissolution. The site passed to Thomas Audley, who built a house by adapting the extensive priory buildings before his death in 1544. The precinct then passed via his daughter to the Duke of Norfolk, who entertained Queen Elizabeth there. The house, with its adaptation of the large church building as a gallery, banqueting house and garden, can be partly reconstructed from the Symonds plans of about 1585. The precinct was sold to the City in 1592. By the 1560s, however, the grand house was skirted about within the former precinct by smaller houses and industrial premises. Documented among the latter in 1571 were those of Jacob Jansen, a Dutch immigrant potter who is credited with introducing the manufacture of 'delftware' pottery to London, and the area soon attracted other potters. Although their workshops have not been found, there are wasters from several sites around the former priory; and one pit containing pottery and tile wasters, possibly of the 1570s, which according to the Symonds plans would have been dug in the floor of the undercroft of the western claustral range, was found below the former hall of Audley and Norfolk.

In 1657 the Jews were officially allowed to return to England and, through the efforts of a small number of Jews already here, they settled in the precinct and the adjacent parish of St Katherine Cree. One of their synagogues was built on the site of the prior's kitchen, adjacent to the grand house which seems to have gradually slipped into decay; indeed, it fell down in 1822. The archaeology of the Jewish community is briefly considered.

Reconstruction of the buildings, based on a combined study of the architectural fragments and documentary evidence, forms a major element of the publication. The pottery analysis links the different phases of the site and summarises the various local, non-local and imported wares found, which range in date from the 10th to 18th centuries, and there is a detailed discussion of the evidence for the earliest tin-glazed pottery production in London.

The evidence thus brought together forms an assessment of the place of Holy Trinity Priory in the history of the Augustinian movement, in the history of London's monasteries and, as far as possible from the evidence so far obtained, in the development of Romanesque architecture in Britain. It also fills an important gap in our understanding of the social and technological changes taking place in London during the 16th to 18th centuries.

ACKNOWLEDGEMENTS

The excavation sites or observations of 1953, 1972 and 1977–90 were variously supervised by Sue Rivière (sites A and E), Hugh Chapman (site C), Chris Goode and Sarah Jones (site D), John Schofield (site F), Brian Pye (site G), John Maloney (site H), Ivor Noël Hume (site I) and Geoff Egan (site J). Negotiations for access to the excavated sites of 1977–90 were conducted by Brian Hobley, John Schofield, John Maloney and Hal Bishop. We thank the developers of the sites who, in almost every case, provided funds for the excavation and assistance during the work: Speyhawk (sites A and E), P&O Properties (site D), International Stores (site F), and the Corporation of London (site H). This report has been produced with the financial support of the City of London Archaeological Trust, English Heritage and generous grants from Swiss Re Insurance Ltd. We are grateful to various present and former colleagues at the Museum of London and at English Heritage and its predecessors for encouragement, support and criticism: Glyn Coppack, Brian Davison, Tony Dyson, Hazel Forsyth, Richard Halsey and David Robinson. The criticism of Christopher Wilson on an early draft of the text was much appreciated. The project was monitored for English Heritage by Gill Chitty, Gill Andrews and Brian Kerr; assistance at various points was given by Barney Sloane and Gordon Malcolm of the Museum of London Archaeology Service (MoLAS).

Several illustrations are reproduced by kind permission of the following institutions and individuals: the Guildhall Library; the City of London Record Office; English Heritage; the London Metropolitan Archives; the Ashmolean Museum; Sir John Soane's Museum; the Conway Library, Courtauld Institute of Art; the Bodleian Library, Oxford; the Marquis of Salisbury; and Lord Braybrooke.

The finds from the sites excavated in 1977 to 1984 were initially spot-dated and selectively quantified by members of the Department of Urban Archaeology (DUA) of the Museum of London (Julie Edwards, Beverley Nenk, Jacqui Pearce, Lucy Whittingham and Alan Vince) as part of specific ware studies, which have also involved scientific analyses; their records may be consulted, together with those of the Roman material, at the Museum of London's London Archaeological Archive and Research Centre (LAARC). Lyn Blackmore wishes to thank Jacqui Pearce, Roy Stephenson and Nigel Jeffries of the Museum of London Specialist Services (MoLSS), and also Hugo Blake, Julie Edwards, Michael J Hughes and Johann Veeckman.

The two main authors thank the specialists for their reports, which form Chapter 8, as well as Dick Bluer and Malcolm Thurlby (contributors to Chapter 4), and for discussion of their results. Bill White kindly edited the human bone report. Richard Lea wrote the reports on the conservation of the arch at Mitre Street (Chapter 8.1) and on the architectural fragments (Chapter 8.2); he also produced the original versions of all the maps and plans which replot the Symonds plans, and the reconstructions based on them. Otherwise, John Schofield and Richard Lea together wrote Chapters 3 and 4, while John Schofield also wrote Chapters 1–2 and 5–7 and melded together the various contributions into a single publication text.

The summary was translated into French by Elisabeth Lorans and into German by Friederike Hammer. The index was compiled by Ann Hudson.

1

Introduction

1.1 The circumstances of excavation at Holy Trinity Priory

'After their coming to England', wrote William of Malmesbury in the 1120s, 'the Normans revived the rule of religion which had grown lifeless. You might see great churches rise in every village, and, in the towns and cities, monasteries built after a style unknown before' (Douglas and Greenaway 1953, 291). This was the time of the rebuilding of large churches at Canterbury (*c* 1070), Norwich (1086), Ely (1087), St Paul's in London (1087), Winchester (1090) and Durham (1093). By 1100 what might be called mainstream Anglo-Norman monasticism, having produced so many large churches in the four decades since the Conquest, had attained its fullest expansion. In the first half of the 12th century there were a number of other developments, notably the arrival and spread of establishments of regular canons (most of them Augustinian) and the introduction of the Cistercians into the south of England at Waverley, Surrey (1128), and in the north at Rievaulx, Yorkshire North Riding (1132); both these developments enjoyed the encouragement of the king, Henry I (1100–35).

It is generally accepted that St Botolph's, Colchester was the first house of the regular canons in England. The community of priests there, which existed by 1093 x 1100, was uncertain which rule to adopt, and two of their number, Norman and Bernard, equipped with a letter of recommendation from Archbishop Anselm, went to Beauvais and Chartres to study. They returned to Colchester, perhaps around 1104, and it is here that in all likelihood the Rule of St Augustine was first embraced in Britain (Dickinson 1950, 102–8; Robinson 1980, 6–15; Burton 1994, 46). In 1107 Norman was released to found the priory of Holy Trinity, Aldgate.

Holy Trinity Priory (otherwise called Christchurch) is of particular interest for being the earliest post-Conquest monastery within the walls of the City of London; the richest of London's monastic houses; the premier Augustinian house in the London area; and, in 1532, the first religious house in the country to be dissolved or secularised in the manner which was shortly after applied to the whole country (that is, its assets taken, not to be transferred to the foundation or support of another religious institution, but for general secular purposes). Despite these distinctions, topographical and archaeological evidence for the priory has never been brought together, and that is the purpose of the present volume.

There is now a growing literature concerning the origins, development and demise of urban monasteries in Britain and other European countries. As in the case of Holy Trinity, this has arisen partly because of archaeological excavations ahead of modern redevelopments on parts of their vanished or built-over sites in towns, particularly in the 1970s and 1980s. In the case of central London, archaeologists of the Museum of London are now producing a series of monographs, each on one of the monastic houses in and around the City: St Mary Spital (Thomas et al 1997), Charterhouse (Barber and Thomas 2002),

St Mary Stratford Langthorne (Barber et al 2004), St John Clerkenwell (Sloane and Malcolm 2004), the present volume on Holy Trinity Aldgate, St Mary Clerkenwell (Sloane in prep), Merton Priory (Miller et al in prep), Bermondsey Abbey (Steele in prep) and St Mary Graces (Grainger and Phillpotts in prep). Major excavations or architectural studies of monastic sites in other British and Irish towns have now been reported from, among others, Beverley, Yorkshire East Riding (Armstrong et al 1991; Foreman 1996), Chester (Ward 1990), Cirencester, Gloucestershire (Wilkinson and McWhirr 1998), Cork, Ireland (Hurley and Sheehan 1995), Gloucester (Heighway and Bryant 1999), Hexham, Northumberland (Cambridge and Williams 1995), Leicester (Mellor and Pearce 1981), Norwich (Fernie 1993a), Oxford (Blair 1990), Peterborough (Reilly 1997), Romsey, Hampshire (Scott 1996), Waltham Abbey, Essex (Huggins and Bascombe 1992; Fernie 1985) and York (Kemp and Graves 1996). There have been modern archaeological investigations of rural Augustinian houses, notably at Norton, Cheshire (Greene 1989) and Kirkham, Yorkshire East Riding (Coppack et al 1995). National reviews of the archaeology of monastic houses have also appeared (Coppack 1990; Greene 1992; Keevill et al 2001), as well as two shorter surveys (Butler 1987; 1993). At the same time there have been new studies of monastic life by historians (eg Harvey 1993; Burton 1994) or by archaeologists studying aspects of monasticism over the whole country (eg Gilchrist and Mytum 1993; Gilchrist 1994), and publication of cartularies (charter-collections) of Augustinian houses (Walker 1998 for St Augustine, Bristol; the Holy Trinity Priory cartulary was edited by G A J Hodgett in 1971, and is hereafter cited as *Cartulary*).

The modern archaeological sites and observations reported here include four from the period 1908–72, but principally comprise investigations in 1977–90 by the Department of Urban Archaeology (DUA) of the Museum of London. These later sites were excavated ahead of redevelopment as the area to the north-west of Aldgate in the eastern part of the City of London, consisting predominantly of 19th-century buildings, underwent radical change (Fig 1; Fig 2). The combination of economic pressures for redevelopment and a road widening scheme for Duke's Place has meant that a picture of the priory can be pieced together from a number of sites (Table 1).

A medieval stone arch encased in brickwork, south of Mitre Street, had been known since the end of the 19th century (Norman 1897–8); this was to figure in the main excavation at 71–77 Leadenhall Street (site A). A small number of observations had been made on the site of Sir John Cass Primary School, on the north side of Mitre Street, by P Norman and F Reader, with photographs by A E Henderson, in 1908 (site B), and what seems to have been one of the priory drains was observed in Duke's Place in 1953 (site I). A large new building, International House, was constructed in 1969–75 on the northern part of what can be identified as the western claustral range, including the site of the main priory kitchen, but this site was not observed by the Guildhall Museum, and whether any Roman or medieval strata remain beneath this building is not known. In 1972 the site of 20–30 Aldgate, in the eastern part of the former precinct, was excavated ahead of development (site C; Chapman in Chapman and Johnson 1973), but little of the medieval period was recorded apart from pits. Further remains of the priory were identified at Duke's Place in

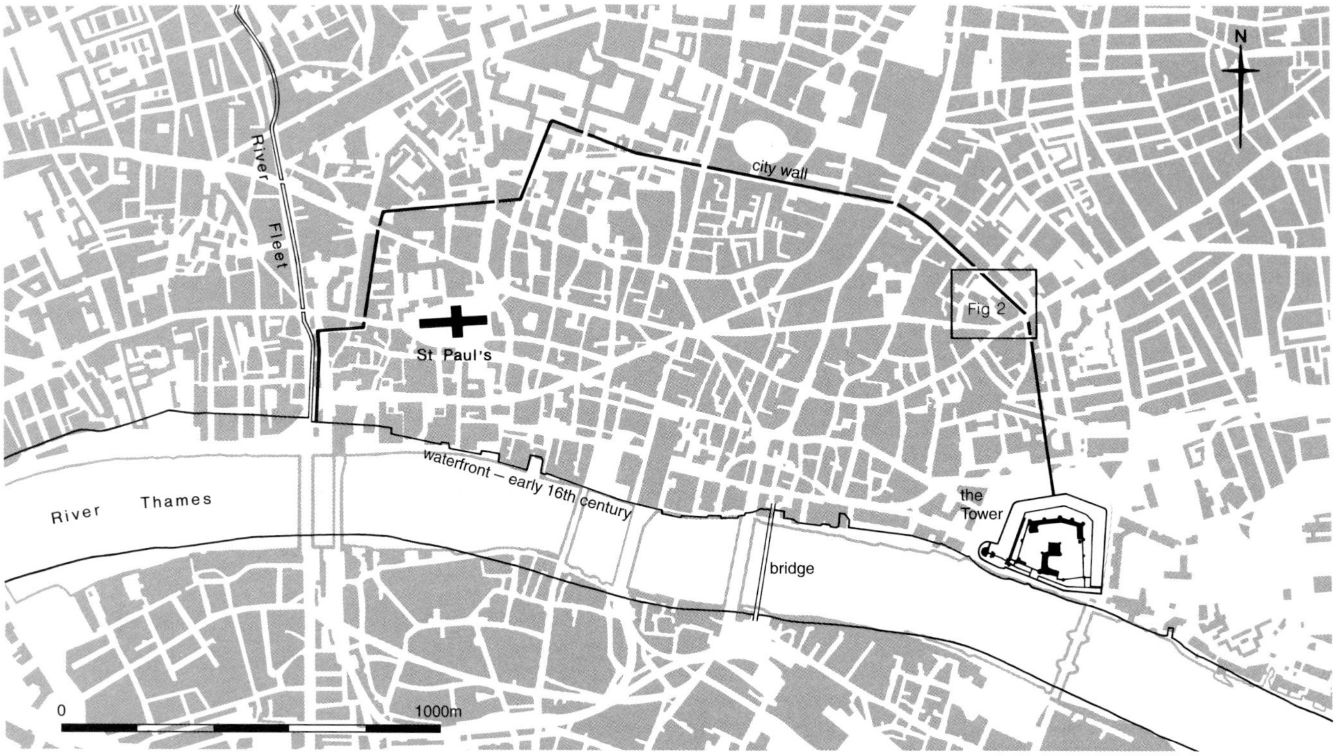

Fig 1 Map of the modern City of London, showing the general position of the priory (scale 1:20,000). The base map is the modern street plan; on it are shown the Tower of London, the site of medieval London Bridge, the medieval form of St Paul's Cathedral and the medieval city wall

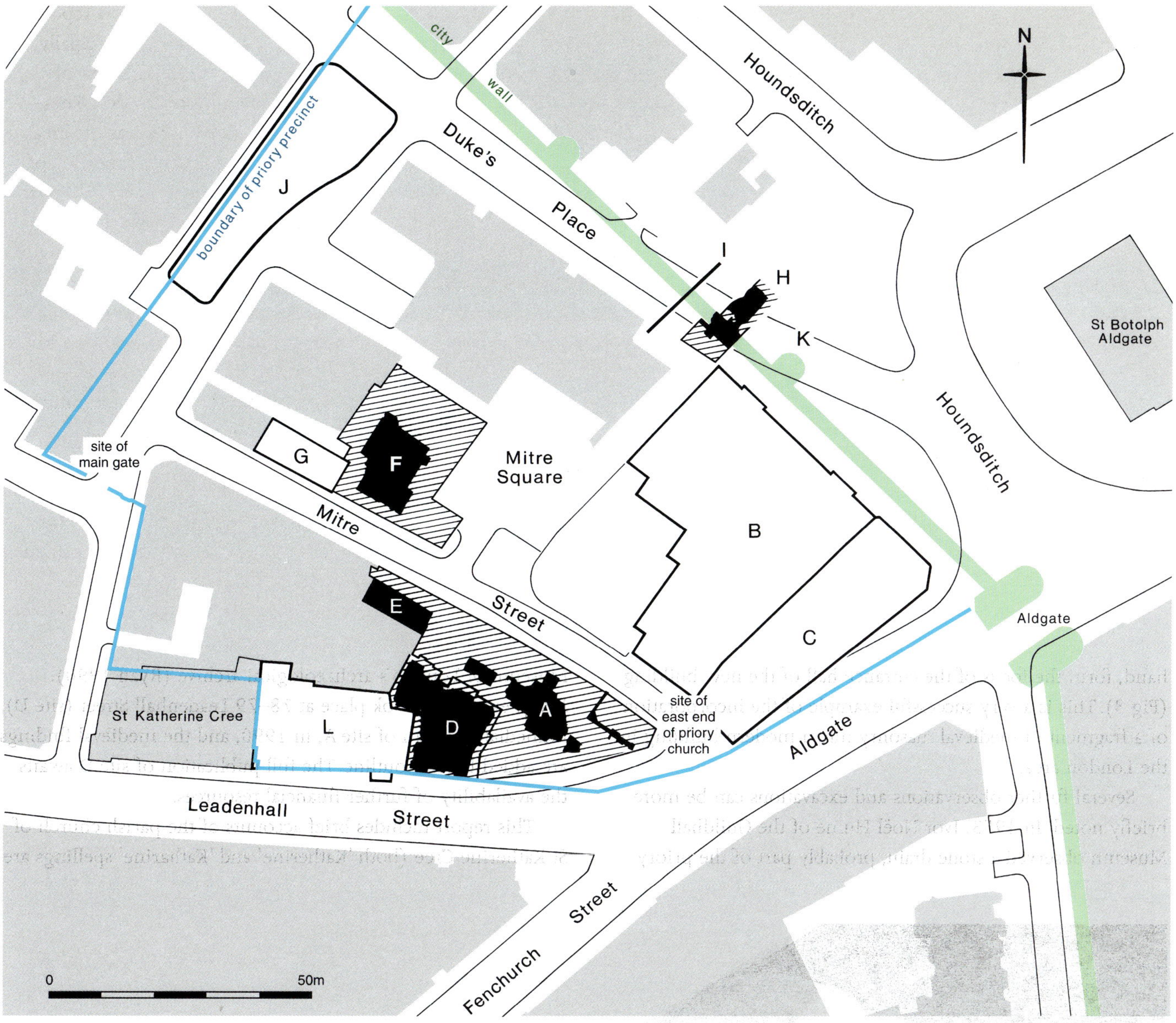

Fig 2 The area of the former priory precinct today, with sites (A–L) of excavations and observations 1908–90 (for key see Table 1) (scale 1:1250)

1977 (site H) when excavation originally designed to obtain a section across the Roman and medieval defences, in advance of a pedestrian subway under Duke's Place, located a door in the medieval city wall and adjacent medieval foundations.

Table 1 Sites described in this volume (see Fig 2)

	Address	Site code	Site type
A	71–77 Leadenhall Street, 32–40 Mitre Street	LEA84	excavation
B	Sir John Cass Primary School, Mitre Street	-	1908 observations
C	20–30 Aldgate	CASS72	excavation
D	78–79 Leadenhall Street	LHN89	excavation
E	32–34 Mitre Street (west part of site A)	MIT86	watching brief
F	west side of Mitre Square	HTP79	excavation
G	12–14 Mitre Street	MIR84	watching brief
H	St James's Passage and 2–7 Duke's Place (subway)	DUK77	excavation
I	Duke's Place (opposite 32–38)	GM53	watching brief
J	33 Creechurch Lane, 16a Bevis Marks	CRE79	watching brief
K	bastion 6, Duke's Place	GM55	excavation
L	80–84 Leadenhall Street	LAH88	excavation

Plans by John Symonds of the majority of the buildings in the priory, at both ground- and first-floor levels (HH, CPM I/10, I/19), had long been published (Lethaby 1900: dated there to 1592 but here to c 1585), but rarely commented upon. The plans suggested that the medieval foundations found at Duke's Place in 1977 were of the north end of the priory dormitory range (north of the church), and that the newly discovered door would originally have led from the passage north out of the cloister (now represented by Mitre Square) through the city wall to the priory's extramural garden; or, as suggested in this study, additionally to the lower part of a building immediately outside the city wall which may have been the canons' latrine block.

Further excavations took place in following years on the west side of Mitre Square (site F), and on three sites in Mitre Street: 71–77 Leadenhall Street and 32–40 Mitre Street (site A) and a thin westward appendage of this site which had the former street-numbers 32–34 (site E), both on the south side of the street, and a watching brief at 12–14 Mitre Street (site G) on the north side. There was also a watching brief on a small site at the north-west corner of the great court of the priory (33 Creechurch Lane and 16a Bevis Marks; site J). The main Leadenhall Street–Mitre Street excavation (site A) was the largest of the series of excavations in the priory area, and had two special features. At the same time as the excavation, restoration works proceeded on the standing medieval arch, which occupied part of the narrow site. Second, during the initial part of the excavation, a stone structure was revealed beneath post-medieval stone paving; this was identified as the remarkable survival of a transept chapel of the priory church. After discussion with English Heritage, the Museum of London and the Corporation of London, the developer took the imaginative step of preserving the chapel by removing it temporarily, constructing foundations, and swinging the chapel back into place in approximately its original location, though somewhat lower (Chapter 8.1). The chapel is now within a basement room at Swiss Re House, and is generally not accessible by the public. The arch and its surrounding masonry, on the other hand, form the focus of the entrance hall of the new building (Fig 3). This is a very successful example of the incorporation of a fragment of medieval masonry into a modern building in the London area.

Several further observations and excavations can be more briefly noted. In 1953, Ivor Noël Hume of the Guildhall Museum observed a stone drain, probably part of the priory water system, in Duke's Place (site I). In 1971, Peter Marsden, also of the Guildhall Museum, excavated the site of bastion 6 on the Roman wall in Duke's Place and the adjacent city ditches of Roman and medieval date (site K; the Roman period sequence is summarised in Marsden 1980, 172). The site of this small excavation fell within the larger site of the work a few years later at the 'Duke's Place' site (site H), though the 1971 trenches were not re-excavated. Since this report is about the priory and not about the Roman and medieval city defences, site K is not described in detail here, except for one feature: post-medieval pottery and kiln waste, including a kiln trivet, were found in the backfill of the medieval ditch. This pottery and kiln waste is described in outline as it is relevant to the finding of similar material at the Mitre Square site (site F), and may represent part of the important developments in pottery manufacture by alien immigrants such as Jacob Jansen in the late 16th and early 17th centuries.

Another excavation on the southern edge of the precinct at 80–84 Leadenhall Street took place in 1988 (site L), but its findings were almost all of the Roman period. It was decided not to include analysis of the excavation records for the present project. In the meantime, an archive report exists in the Museum of London's archaeological archive (Ryan 1990). Lastly, excavation took place at 78–79 Leadenhall Street (site D), immediately south of site A, in 1990, and the medieval findings are added here in outline. The full publication of site D awaits the availability of further financial resources.

This report includes brief accounts of the parish church of St Katherine Cree (both 'Katherine' and 'Katharine' spellings are

Fig 3 The arch of chapel 2 of the church of Holy Trinity Priory in its indoor setting within Swiss Re House, 2001

found in the records and on maps, but 'Katherine' is preferred here), in its medieval and 17th-century building phases. The church still stands in Leadenhall Street, at the south-west corner of the precinct. It contains fragments of stained glass which might be from the priory.

1.2 Organisation of the report

This study may appear, more than usually with an archaeological report, to resemble a detective story in that many kinds of evidence are considered, and some pieces of evidence are looked at from different points of view, being brought forward again and again as the discussion proceeds. Partly for this reason, this introduction contains three overall plans or maps of the priory which place the excavations in their medieval and modern settings, and which anticipate the attempted overall reconstruction of the priory which is one of the main objectives of the report. These maps should help the reader with orientation and to find specific excavations or parts of the priory. Fig 2 shows the present street plan (1998), with the sites of the excavations and observations of 1908 to 1990; Fig 4 shows the precinct as drawn by John Symonds in *c* 1585, harmonised as best it can be with the modern map (the largest 'rectifications' being argued for at their individual places in the text), with sites of excavations indicated to show where they lie within the priory complex; and Fig 5 depicts the buildings of the priory, as shown by Symonds, in relation to the present street plan, according to the results of this study.

Documentary and cartographic evidence for the history of the priory precinct, in both the medieval and post-medieval periods, is comparatively plentiful and is summarised in Chapter 3. The cartulary of Holy Trinity, compiled in 1425–7

Fig 4 The priory precinct as drawn by John Symonds c 1585, rectified according to the modern map, with sites of excavations (A–L) indicated (scale 1:1250) (cf Fig 2)

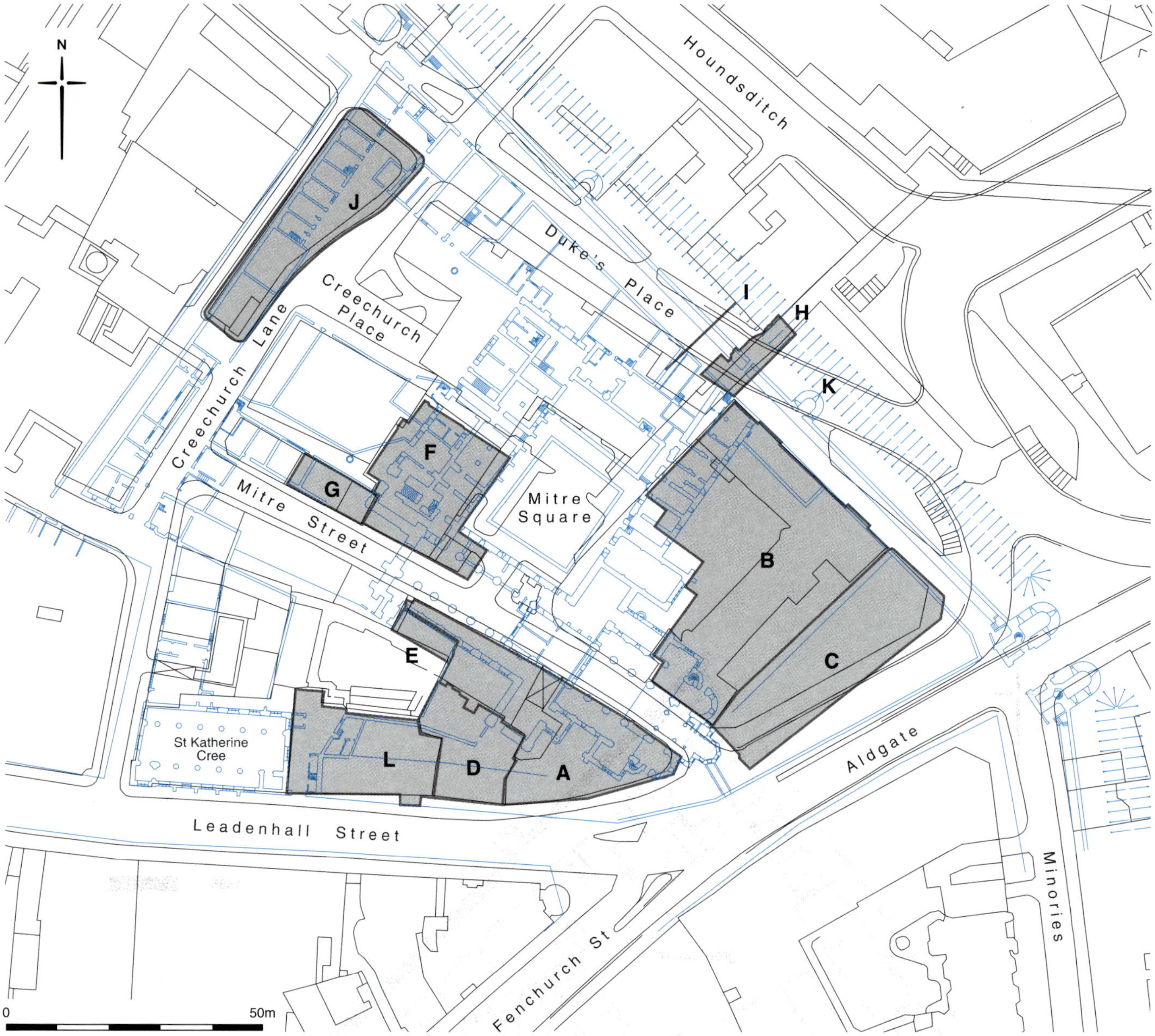

Fig 5 The plan of the priory, as surveyed by Symonds, in relation to the modern street-plan as proposed in this study (scale 1:1250) (cf Fig 2)

but including the official early history of the priory (GUL, Hunter MS U.2.6), was published in 1971 and is hereafter cited as *Cartulary*. Much of the priory site passed to the City in 1592, and thus a number of lease plans from the beginning of the 18th century – including several showing priory buildings or fragments of them – survive in Corporation records. A number of drawings of the priory buildings have been published since 1795, and other unpublished plans and drawings have now been located. In Chapter 3 we consider the relevant evidence from documents, maps, plans and topographical drawings, up to the end of the 17th century. This provides an overview of the main phases in the priory's development and demise, as it might have been written before the investigations forming this project started in the late 1970s.

To describe the excavations, the priory precinct is divided into six areas or 'zones': 1) the east end and south side of the priory church, and the area between the church and Leadenhall Street; 2) the west end of the church, the great tower, and the west range of the cloister; 3) the cloister itself, chapter house, dormitory, and adjacent city wall; 4) the area east of the dormitory and probable site of the infirmary; 5) the refectory and kitchen; and 6) the main ('great') court and main gate. In treating each of these six areas within the priory, we have found it easiest to call the antiquaries of the 1790s archaeologists, as indeed they were, and therefore to place their evidence, all of it graphic, alongside the material evidence of the modern excavations. Chapter 4 deals with the medieval period up to the dissolution of Holy Trinity Priory in 1532.

We have attempted to make a fine distinction between reconstruction of details from the fabric itself or from detailed parallels for individual features (in Chapter 4), and reconstruction from speculation, wider parallels or contextual evidence, which is reserved for a discussion of the priory architecture in Chapter 5. This chapter places Holy Trinity Priory, as a building of the Augustinian canons, in its setting among the major 12th-century buildings of London, and within the context of English medieval ecclesiastical architecture.

Chapter 6 presents the archaeological and documentary evidence for the priory site at its dissolution and afterwards, down to the present: principally as a late 16th-century noble town house of the most powerful personage in the land apart from the queen herself, namely the Duke of Norfolk; and in great contrast, by the 1580s, as an area of immigrant industries. Chapter 7 forms the conclusions to the whole project and the report. Thereafter specialist appendices, brought together in Chapter 8, describe the incorporation of two pieces of the medieval fabric into the present building at 71–77 Leadenhall Street; the moulded or carved stones which have been recovered from the various priory sites since 1908; pottery and other archaeological artefacts from the excavations; and human skeletal remains found on several of the priory sites.

The comparative wealth of cartographic, plan and antiquarian sources for the reconstruction of the medieval priory and its adaptation for secular use after the Dissolution is the chief reason why the structure of this monograph differs somewhat from those previously published in this series on the monasteries of medieval London (Thomas et al 1997; Barber and Thomas 2002; Barber et al 2004; Sloane and Malcolm 2004). Those studies arranged the history of the religious house in question into broad historical periods covering first the medieval and then the post-medieval developments, presenting first the documentary evidence and then the archaeological evidence for each of the individual periods. The present study describes all the main graphic sources first, in Chapter 3, because many of the features of the medieval priory, and the post-Dissolution developments, can only be reconstructed from the graphic evidence, which extends to the late 19th century. Much of the fabric of the priory can be discerned within 18th-century and later buildings, as shown in lease plans and illustrated by engravings. Apart from this difference, however, the authors have endeavoured to make this study comparable in its themes, scope and treatment to the others in the series. In the general discussions in Chapters 5 and 6, an attempt is made to summarise the development and dissolution of Holy Trinity Priory in terms of priory-wide periods: periods M1–M3 for the medieval era to 1532, and periods P1–P2 for the post-Dissolution centuries to about 1900 (below, 1.4).

One topic of analysis not extensively undertaken for this report is that of environmental remains such as animal bones, molluscs and seeds (this approach has also been taken in the report on excavations at St Oswald's Priory, Gloucester: Heighway and Bryant 1999, 108). Only very small amounts of these materials were recovered, and many of the specimens could be residual from the Roman period. The preferred course is to leave analysis of the environmental remains, with the exception of the human bones and a short note on a dog skeleton of the 12th or 13th century, to future studies of the area.

1.3 Textual and graphical conventions

The excavations of 1977 and later are reported with metric measurements (metres). The documentary evidence and excavations before 1977 are reported with imperial measurements (yards, and feet and inches, the latter abbreviated to ft and in), along with conversions when appropriate (1ft = 0.305m; 12in to 1ft, 3ft to 1 yard). The discussion sections use either system, as appropriate.

Sums of money are quoted in the text as cited in £ s d, where 12 pence (d) made one shilling (s) and 20 shillings (or 240d) a pound (£), and one mark equals 13s 4d, since modern equivalents would be misleading. An approximation to current values may be gained from, for example, the wages of a skilled building worker who earned 2d per day in 1250, 4d per day in 1400 and 6d in 1500, while a cow could be bought for between 6s and 11s in the Middle Ages, after *c* 1200 (Dyer 1989, xv; 2002, x). Weights and measures are also sometimes quoted in the text in the units used before metrication in the late 20th century. Cloth was measured by the yard (3 feet) or the ell which was often as long as 45 inches (1.1m). Grain was measured by volume, in bushels (36 litres) and quarters (290 litres; 8 bushels made a quarter), and other dry goods by the pound (abbreviated to lb) (1lb equals 0.45kg), which comprises 16 ounces (1oz equals 28g). County names in the text refer to historic counties.

Two dates separated by 'x' (eg '1107 x 1108') means that the event described happened at a point some time in the span of years shown, but further certainty is not possible. The use of the term 'ragstone' is as recorded on site by the excavators.

Some traditional terms for monastic buildings have been replaced by the generally accepted modern terms. Thus, although John Symonds in his survey of the priory of *c* 1585 mentions the 'frater' and the 'dorter', these will be rendered whenever possible by the terms 'refectory' and 'dormitory'. The term 'reredorter' is sometimes dismissed as a 19th-century invention, but actually occurs as a term around 1450 (OED 1967); the present study, however, avoids it in favour of the plainer term 'latrine block'. The eastern arm of the church was occupied, in the central space, by the presbytery, and beyond it to the east was an ambulatory; beyond that was the Lady chapel. The monastic choir was below the crossing of the church, west of the presbytery. Symonds uses the term 'chancel', which strictly speaking is not appropriate for a monastic church, and which demonstrates his post-Reformation thinking, sympathetic to but not completely informed about the monastery he was surveying.

The buildings found on each site are labelled within each site sequence. The report on site F, being based on the archive report written at intervals during 1980–5, uses letters (A onwards) for the buildings; the other sites use numbers, reflecting a change in post-excavation methods in the mid 1980s to the scheme used generally by the Museum of London today. There is no other significance in the difference. The graphical conventions for the site plans are given in Fig 6.

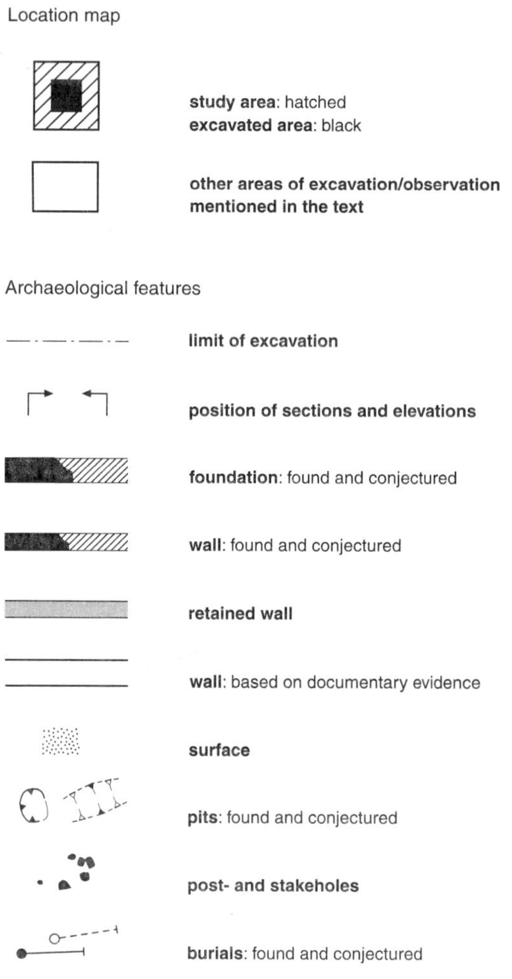

Fig 6 Graphical conventions used in this report

The sites in this report have been given letter codes from A to L (Table 1). An individual context (layer, pit, cut, skeleton) within each site is given in square brackets with the site letter, for example A[100]. The only exception to this is site K where the original Guildhall Museum context numbers in the ER (Excavation Register) series are shown. During post-excavation analysis on sites A, F and H, contexts were ordered in stratigraphic groups, which sometimes had subdivisions, for example group A31 or group A36.1 (abbreviated as gpA31, gpA36.1). The other sites are not divided into groups and the contexts (where numbers have been given) are referenced directly, for example D[557]. The other excavations were either considered too small to apply the group structure (sites B, C, E, G, I and J) or have not been analysed completely for this project for financial or other reasons (sites D, K and L). These last three sites are susceptible to detailed analysis in the future, which may affect the interpretations offered here.

The archive reports for the three main sites (A, F and H) have internal period structures which are given in Roman numerals, for example period III, period IV. These have been retained in the present report for correlation with the archive reports, but only have relevance within each site sequence. A concordance table for the whole site, relating these periods to the project-wide periods, is given as Table 2.

Certain conventions are used for reporting the pottery and finds. Catalogue numbers have a find category prefix letter inside angled brackets; thus, <P1> denotes an illustrated (P)ot and <A1> denotes an illustrated (A)rchitectural fragment reconstituted from loose moulded stones. The individual moulded stones, and all forms of registered or small finds, are given accession numbers prefixed by their site code letter outside angled brackets, so that A<218> is a moulded stone from site A, and D<222> is a fragment of antler comb from site D. The relatively few fragments of floor and wall tiles discussed here are only referred to by accession numbers, and not by catalogue numbers. Abbreviations used in the catalogues are as follows: Diam (diameter), H (height), L (length), Th (thickness), W (width), Wt (weight).

The ceramic dating of stratigraphic groups is presented in the reports on the excavations (Chapter 4). For computerisation purposes and the sake of brevity, the many different wares found on London sites are generally identified by acronyms of established ware names (eg ANDE, Andenne-type ware). These pottery codes are listed at the beginning of the pottery report (Chapter 8.5), in Table 18 (medieval wares) and Table 19 (post-medieval wares).

It should be emphasised that only a small fraction of the area of the priory has been investigated by archaeological excavation. A portion has no doubt been lost for ever through redevelopment in the 19th and 20th centuries, but a considerable part of the priory precinct does remain beneath streets and beneath buildings with light foundations or only single basements. It is therefore likely that any future study would augment the present report, and conduct complementary analyses in ways not attempted here for lack of information.

The archive reports and finds of all the excavations reported here are held in the Museum of London and may be consulted by prior arrangement at the Museum's London Archaeological Archive and Research Centre (LAARC), Mortimer Wheeler House, 46 Eagle Wharf Road, London N1 7ED.

1.4 Summary of the medieval and post-medieval archaeological phases and periods

The history of the priory and its site has been divided into three medieval and two post-Dissolution periods, as shown in Table 2. Period M1, *c* AD 900 to 1108, concerns the nature of previous occupation on the site and in the area, and the church associated with Syredus and its graveyard. Period M2, from 1108 to *c* 1350, comprises the establishment and main first building period of the priory. Period M3, from *c* 1350 to 1532, includes the various late medieval building phases which can be discerned, and the reinforcing of the city wall along the side of the precinct in 1477. The immediately post-Dissolution period in the 16th century (P1) covers the time of Sir Thomas Audley

Table 2 Correlation of stratigraphic periods on the four main sites and documentary evidence

Overall period	Site A (LEA84)	Site E (MIT86)	Site F (HTP79)	Site H (DUK77)	Other observations	Conclusions from archaeological evidence	Main documentary evidence
M1 c 900–1108	demolition and levelling, after c 1020 (period II, gpA18–A20, gpA27)	dark earth (residual Roman pottery only, period II, gpE3)	sunken feature, pits, late Saxon (period II, gpF1, gpF6–F9)	Roman city wall still standing		scattered late Saxon activity, perhaps along Aldgate Street	
	burials c 1040–c 1100+ (period III, gpA21–A26)	burials, undated (period III, gpE4)	burials (period III, gpF11)		burials also at site D	?pre-priory cemetery, 11th century; probably also start of construction of church by Syredus	church of Syredus founded before 1108
M2 1108–c 1350	S transept of priory church, 12th century (period IV, gpA28, gpA34, gpA37); jambs of chapel 2 (period IV, gpA54)	S wall of priory church, undated (period IV, gpE5)	Building B, W range of cloister, 12th to mid 13th century (period III.1, gpF10)	Building 2, ?N end of the dormitory, not accurately dated (period I, gpH7, gpH14)		construction of priory church, W range of cloister and N end of dormitory, 12th century	foundation of priory 1108; donation of St Botolph's 1125; ?fire 1132
	use of and burials outside S transept, early 12th to mid 13th century (period V, gpA29–A30, gpA33, gpA35, gpA51); tile floors in S transept (gpA32)		Building C, NW corner of a large building (?church), ?late 12th century (period III.2, gpF12) Building C robbed (period III.3, gpF14) Building D, tower, ?late 12th century (period III.3, gpF16)		drain at site I	rebuilding of church, some late 12th century but continuing into 14th century	
	construction of S side of chapel 2, after c 1270; restyling of arch leading into chapel (period VI, gpA31, gpA36, gpA55)	buttresses and further burials, medieval (period V, gpE6–E7)		postern in city wall and foundations ? of latrine block, late 13th century (period II, gpH15.1–15.2, gpH18–H19)		building of latrine block over city ditch and connecting door in wall, late 13th century	enclosure of lane by Prior Eustace in 1260s; church apparently being built in two decades before c 1350; probably included rebuilding of chapel 2
M3 c 1350–1532			Building E, doubling of cloister to W, 14th century or later (period III.4, gpF18–F19)	reinforcement of city wall and blocking of period II postern, probably in 1477 (period III, gpH15.3, gpH21, gpH25–H26); backfilling of city ditch begins c 1480–c 1500 (period III, gpH12)		doubling of cloister to W, 14th century or later; blocking of postern by Mayor Jocelyn, 1477	
P1 1532–92	Dissolution phase robbing of walls, scaffolding and dumps, 16th century (period VII, gpA38–A41, gpA50, gpA52)	brick wall and further burials, 16th to 20th centuries (period VI, gpE8–E10)	post-Dissolution foundation and wasters, 16th century (period IV, gpF21–F22)	post-Dissolution well, dumps, 16th century (period IV, gpH22, gpH27, gpH36–H37)		gradual disappearance of monastic buildings; establishment of small industries (pottery manufacture, baking, sugar baking)	Dissolution, 1532; sale of precinct to City, 1592
	post-Dissolution reuse (period VIII, gpA42.1–A42.5, gpA43–A44); blocking of arch and later adaptation, late 16th century (after c 1585) (period VIII, gpA56–A57)						

Table 2 (cont)

Overall period	Site A (LEA84)	Site E (MIT86)	Site F (HTP79)	Site H (DUK77)	Other observations	Conclusions from archaeological evidence	Main documentary evidence
P2 1592–*c* 1900	19th-century sewer trench (gpA45) and mid 17th-century cesspit (gpA46); refacing of cellar in brick (gpA47); other cellars (gpA48–A49); 19th-century foundations (gpA53)	graveyard of St Katherine Cree, 17th century and later (gpE9–E10)	a foundation of brick and rubble (gpF20, undated)	backfill of ditch 17th century to *c* 1680 (gpH12.1–12.5); brick surface sealing ditch *c* 1630–*c* 1700 (gpH30.1); pits from houses along Houndsditch, *c* 1720–40 (gpH23.1–23.2)	Jewish plate of *c* 1720 in cesspit on site G; 17th- to 19th-century brick cesspits on Aldgate frontage at site C; 17th- to 19th-century pottery also in city ditch studied on site K	priory buildings largely obscured and partly replaced by *c* 1750, but fragments observed by antiquaries in 1790 and 1800; Jewish community in the area by *c* 1700	establishment of Jews in area from 1657; city ditch area filled in as gardens and yards of houses along Houndsditch; city wall almost obscured by *c* 1700

and the Duke of Norfolk in 1532–64, and the subsequent period of 1564 to 1592, the date of the sale of the precinct to the City of London. The Symonds plans of *c* 1585 illustrate the state of the buildings at the end of this period (Chapter 3.3). The final period P2 covers the early modern developments, from 1592 to *c* 1900.

2

Geology and Roman and Saxon activity on the priory sites: a summary

2.1 Geology and general levels of strata

The top of the geological strata in this area is formed by brickearth, up to 1.7m thick where undisturbed (which is very rare), on sand and gravel. Boreholes undertaken in the northern part of the precinct area in 1969, supplemented by the findings of the subsequent excavations, suggest that the top of the brickearth generally lies between 11.00m above Ordnance Datum (hereafter OD) and 13.00m OD; due to many forms of human intrusion into this layer, especially pits and foundations, it is not really possible to construct with confidence any slope or local aberrations.

The modern topography is fairly flat, but rises slightly from 16.00m OD in Duke's Place (street) at its junction with St James's Passage, on the north side of the precinct, to 16.20m OD in Leadenhall Street near its junction with Fenchurch Street, on the south side of the precinct; and there is a similar small rise from west to east across the area of the precinct. Although much damaged by 19th-century basements, the total depth of strata in this area is, therefore, between 3.0m and 5.0m from street level.

Some approximations can be made about the gradual rising of the ground levels over the centuries. Roman strata in the excavations reported here were generally about 1.0m deep, and Roman ground level would by the end of the period have been at about 12.50m OD (as observed at site A). By the middle of the 12th century, when the south transept chapel was erected on site A, the external ground level was at about 14.10m OD; the late Saxon and medieval graveyard in this area had resulted in a definite build-up of strata.

Within the priory church, levels were slightly higher. The first floor screed or finished level of construction at the entrance to the south transept chapel (chapel 1) discovered on site A was at 14.31m OD; after several refloorings, some with tiles, this reached 14.64m OD. The internal floor level in the eastern arm or presbytery of the priory church, as reconstructed from the standing fragment of arch now in Swiss Re House, Leadenhall Street, and other observations, would have been at about 14.75m OD. As suggested below in the detailed description (Chapter 4.3), it is likely that there were two steps from the crossing and transepts into the presbytery, and a further step in at least the south aisle further east.

2.2 Roman and Saxon activity to *c* AD 900

In the Roman period the future site of the priory lay on the north-east edge of the main area of occupation, and was enclosed by the city wall of the early 3rd century AD. This wall, and the gate at Aldgate, formed the basis of the medieval wall and gate in this area, and were not superseded until the 18th century. The character of Roman occupation in this zone at the edge of the town is not well known (Perring 1991). The Roman topography of the area will be the subject of a separate study (Williams in prep). A major road from eastern England entered the city at Aldgate. South of the extramural road lay a large Roman cemetery, in use from the end of the 1st to the 4th centuries AD (Barber and Bowsher 2000). So far, in the study of this cemetery, no objects or practices with Christian connotations have been noticed.

During the early and middle Saxon periods, the gate at Aldgate was probably maintained sporadically, but there is no archaeological evidence. This part of the Roman city was again a backwater, and from the 7th to the 9th centuries AD the focus of London was west of the city, along the Strand. In 886 Alfred ousted the Vikings from a temporary occupation of the city, and the old Roman wall was reused to define the new centre which would become the medieval metropolis (Vince 1990; Cowie 2000).

Because the priory had some kind of late Saxon predecessor, the church of Syredus (Chapter 5.2), a division has been made here between the period up to *c* AD 900 and that after it. What follows here are brief references to archive information on the main features on the priory sites that can be dated to before *c* AD 900.

On site A, the natural stratum preceding all human activity was an orange brickearth, heavily truncated but surviving to a maximum height of 12.34m OD. This was cut by a beamslot and many postholes prior to the whole area being sealed by a layer of redeposited brickearth. There followed considerable activity represented by further beamslots, stakeholes, dumps and pits, the latter category including a possible fish-tank. A row of five paired postholes was probably for a post-and-plank wall, and there was a possible well. The top of the Roman strata was at between 12.50m OD and *c* 12.80m OD.

A total of seven structures were identified, although most of these were ephemeral and consisted of little more than a truncated beamslot. With one exception these elements used the same north-west to south-east building line, but none of them provided the complete ground-plan of a building. The pottery and small finds suggest that occupation continued throughout the Roman period, the area apparently lacking well-defined topography, with a rapid succession of flimsy timber buildings, possibly outhouses. The bulk of the pottery is of 1st- to 2nd-century AD date, with a small amount of 3rd-century material, and a slightly larger amount of 4th-century AD date. Post-Roman finds are limited to three sherds, all of which may be intrusive. Roman coins were also found in post-Roman contexts; they comprised 1st- to 4th-century AD types, the latter including a coin of Constantius II (AD 337–61) from group A23)

Immediately to the west on site E, the natural material was a dark orange brickearth recorded at 11.06m OD, sealed by a loose sandy silt, probably make-up for two phases of well-compacted brickearth surface (gpE1). A deep cut (gpE2) made into this was probably a quarry pit. This activity would have been broadly contemporary with Roman-period activity on site A (period I). The group E1 make-up produced five fabric types of Hadrianic date, with a *terminus post quem* of AD 120.

3

Documentary and cartographic sources for the reconstruction of the priory and Duke's Place

3.1 Introduction

In this chapter an outline history of the priory and its precinct from the early 12th century to the later 17th century is given to provide a framework for the detailed investigations and analyses which are presented afterwards. This introduces and assesses the main cartographic and pictorial sources for the reconstruction of the medieval and post-Dissolution phases of the priory buildings, in particular two plans of the majority of the precinct, drawn at ground-floor and first-floor levels of all the main buildings, by John Symonds in *c* 1585 (HH, CPM I/10, I/19). The Symonds plans form the chief reference point for all the individual building reconstructions, and they are studied here in detail for the first time. It is necessary to describe the main documentary and graphic sources for the post-Dissolution use of the monastery, particularly as the residence in 1532–64 of Thomas Audley and later the Duke of Norfolk, because a large amount of information about the medieval buildings of the priory is contained in the post-Dissolution documentation, principally the Symonds plans.

The chief source of documentary evidence for the establishment and development of the priory is its cartulary, compiled in 1425–7, which is now in Glasgow University Library (GUL, Hunter MS U.2.6). Fig 7 illustrates that part of the text (transcribed in *Cartulary*, appendix nos 1–6) which describes the establishment of the priory by Queen Matilda, and its support by Henry I.

3.2 The founding of the priory and its history to 1532

The priory was founded in 1107 x 1108 by Queen Matilda, the wife of Henry I (*VCH* 1909, 464–75, the account of the priory's history by Miss M Reddan). Besides the site of the priory, on which there was or had previously been a church, the queen gave the canons the nearby gate of Aldgate with its soke, which included the nearby churches of St Augustine Papey, St Edmund Lombard Street and All Hallows on the Wall; and two thirds of the farm of Exeter. After Matilda's death in 1118, Henry I allowed the priory to enclose a lane between their conventual buildings and the wall of the city (which runs beneath the present Duke's Place) and granted them the soke of the *cnihtengild*, Portsoken ward, in 1125 (*Cartulary*, xiv–xv, no. 113). This grant included the churches of St Botolph Aldgate and All Hallows or St Gabriel Fenchurch, which lay in the middle of Fenchurch Street; both churches had belonged to the *cnihtengild*, an organisation of local leaders (Fig 8; for the churches, Schofield 1994).

Two widespread fires in London in the 1130s or 1140s should now be considered. In 1132, according to the cartulary, 'the church and nearly all the conventual buildings were burnt out' in a disastrous fire which started in the house of Gilbert

Fig 7 An extract, describing the establishment of the priory by Queen Matilda and its support by Henry I, from the beginning of the Holy Trinity Priory cartulary (GUL, Hunter MS U.2.6), fos 1v and 2r (by courtesy of Glasgow University Library)

Becket (*Cartulary*, no. 13). This fire allegedly ravaged much of the city, and Gilbert's house was on the other side of London from Holy Trinity. The chronicler later describes a second widespread fire, in the time of the second prior, Ralph (1147–67), which started at the house of Ailward by London Stone in Cannon Street, and apparently reached nearly to Aldgate but not specifically the priory (ibid, no. 31). In 1598 John Stow, apparently quoting from the chronicle, then in his possession, asserted that the fire which began in Ailward's house (ie the second one) occurred in 1135 (Stow 1603, i, 22) or 1136 (ibid, i, 224, 'the first [year] of King Stephen'); Stephen was crowned on about 22 December 1135 (Davis 1967, 18). If Stow is right, the fire cannot have taken place in Prior Ralph's time, as the chronicle claims, since Ralph's priorate started in 1147. Since only the first fire is said to have damaged the priory, we need only take account of that first fire in 1132. As will be shown at the end of this study (Chapter 5.4), the date of this fire is important for the early history of the priory buildings, even though no evidence of it has been found on the archaeological sites excavated so far.

Around the time of the beginning of the tenure of Ralph, two of King Stephen's children, Baldwin and Matilda, were buried in the church; Baldwin on the north side of the altar and Matilda on the south side (*Cartulary*, appendix no. 14). This must have taken place in or shortly before 1147–8, when Stephen granted 100s of land in Hertfordshire to the priory for the souls of his two children buried there (ibid, no. 973). This special connection between the priory and Stephen's family, including perhaps his brother, the great churchman Henry of Blois, is explored in Chapter 5.4. Other eminent persons buried in the priory included Geoffrey de Mandeville (d 1215) and London's first mayor, Henry FitzAilwin (d 1212), who had the distinction of being buried in the entrance to the chapter house.

Ralph, a friend of Thomas Becket, is said to have doubled the revenues of the priory (*Cartulary*, no. 14). As just noted, the cartulary maintains that the church and nearly all the conventual buildings were badly damaged by the fire of 1132, and great funds would have been required for their reconstruction. Ralph initiated a policy of selling quitrents from the priory's very large city estate, which in the papal *Taxatio* of 1291 was found to be spread among 72 parishes. Surviving documentation about the city estate, including rentals which survive from the late 14th century, is calendared by Keene and Harding (1985, 79). The priory also possessed many rural manors in Middlesex (eg at Edmonton and Tottenham: *VCH*

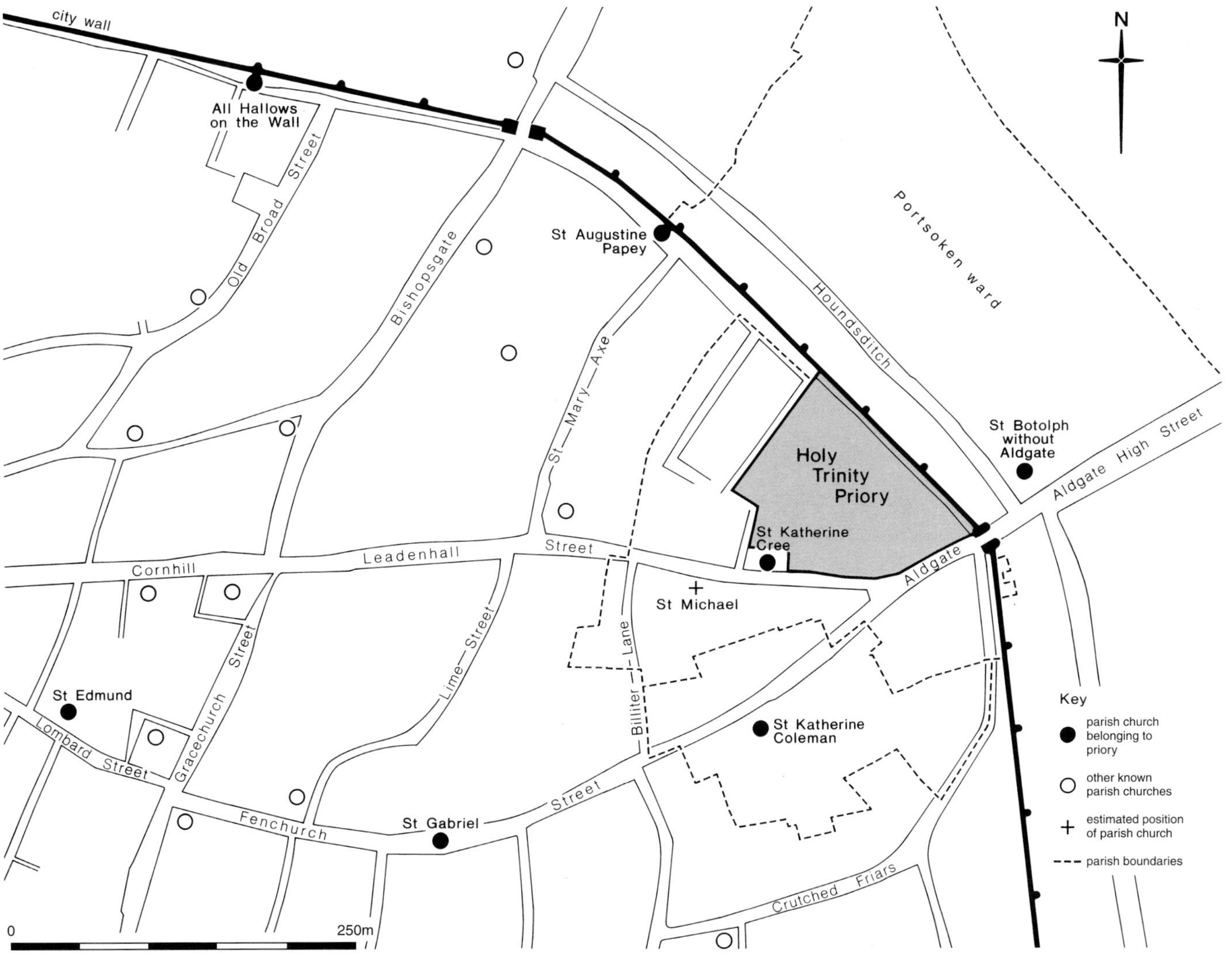

Fig 8 *Map of the eastern part of the medieval city of London, showing the priory precinct and the surrounding topography (scale 1:5000)*

1976, 153, 328, 348), Essex and Kent; and several mills in the countryside immediately east of the City (eg in *Crassenielane*, Stepney: HMC 1883, 49, no. 1761). During the 12th century it acquired several churches, which would generate income through tithes and other charges, in the countryside north of London and in Essex, for instance at Tottenham (1131 x 1134), Shoreditch (1141 x 1148, though lost to older rights of the king in the 1180s), Walthamstow (probably 1141 x 1148), Broomfield (1141 x 1150), Layston and Black Notley (both 1163 x 1174) (Neininger 1999, 29, 37–8, 89).

A grant of the church of St Mary, Bixley (Kent), to the priory by Thomas Becket between 1162 and 1170 furnishes striking artefactual evidence of the priory's status at the highest level. The charter survives in the Public Record Office (PRO, E40/4913), complete with its seal in a silk seal bag (Fig 9) (Robinson and Urquhart 1934, 164, n 2). The following description has been provided by Frances Pritchard. The bag, which measures 63 x 90mm, is made from cloth of gold patterned with lobed ogival medallions enclosing a lotus palmette surrounded by flowers and leaves. The weave is a type of lampas with the pattern bound in 1.2 twill on a 3.1 twill ground. Both the main warp and the binding warp are made from fine, Z-twisted silk thread used singly, and there are four main warp ends to each binding warp end. The ground weft is dark pink silk (which was probably originally red) without appreciable twist and the pattern weft is a flat strip of gilded animal substrate (ie gut). The bag is lined in lightweight red, tabby-woven silk cloth, and the two textiles are bound together with a green silk tablet-woven band which terminated in a tassel with a 'Turk's head' knop.

The pattern of this luxurious cloth of gold and the use of flat metal thread indicates that it was woven in Central Asia to the east of the River Oxus. A study of Eastern Islamic silks woven with gold and silver thread, often referred to in medieval inventories as *panni tartarici*, has been made by Anne Wardwell; the fabric for the bag belongs to the first of her eight categories of classification (Wardwell 1988–9, 97–102). Other examples of this type of textile have been recovered from the tombs of Blanche of Portugal (d 1321), Pedro son of Sancho (d 1319) and Alfonso de la Cerda (d 1333), in the mausoleum of the Castilian royal family at the monastery of Las Huelgas, Burgos, and from the tomb of Can Grande della Scala, overlord of Verona (d 1329). Inventories of St Paul's Cathedral and Canterbury Cathedral, dated 1295 and 1315 respectively,

Fig 9 The seal bag made from cloth of gold accompanying a charter of Thomas Becket, between 1162 and 1170, giving the church of St Mary, Bixley (Kent), to the priory (PRO, E40/4913) (Public Record Office)

include eight references to tartar cloths used for vestments (ibid, 101, 144, figs 11–18). The closest to the seal bag according to its description is a Canterbury chasuble patterned with gold pine nuts (*Casula una de rubeo panno de Tharse, cum nucibus pini auratis*). A considerable quantity of *panni de Tars* was purchased for the coronation of Edward III in 1327, when it was draped around a specially erected ceremonial pulpitum (ie platform) in Westminster Abbey (Monnas 2001, 4–6, 13). The evidence, therefore, points to the cloth being manufactured much later than the date of sealing of the document, in the second half of the 13th century or the early 14th century, when the cloth was used as a status symbol by magnates of the highest rank in Europe. A second silk seal bag in the Public Record Office houses the seal of a confirmation of privileges by Henry III to the priory in 1227. The silk, of the kind called cloth of aresta, may have been manufactured in France, possibly at workshops in Languedoc (Desrosiers 1999, 115).

In 1155 the first son of Henry II and Eleanor of Aquitaine, also called Henry, was baptised in the church; in the following year their daughter Matilda was also baptised there (*Cartulary*, appendix no. 14). This presumably reflects the fact that the priory was a royal foundation, and, therefore, that Henry II would have inherited the role and privileges of patron from his predecessors.

The fourth prior, Peter of Cornwall (1197–1221), was a well-known and prolific theological writer, whom the cartulary calls 'in his time the chief teacher among all the English teachers' (*Cartulary*, no. 16; Dickinson 1950, 187), though Christopher Brooke has described him as 'without a trace of originality of mind' and his writings as 'ponderous' (Brooke 1975, 324). Fitzstephen, writing of London in the 1170s, says that 'the three principal churches [of the city] possess, by privilege and ancient dignity, celebrated schools' (Wheatley 1956, 503); John Stow, writing in 1598, took the three mentioned by Fitzstephen to be St Paul's, Westminster Abbey and Bermondsey Priory, since, as he pointed out, all the Augustinian houses were of later foundation (Stow 1603, i, 72–3). These houses, he added, also had their schools, though ones not as famous as the first three. It is possible that here Stow was mistaken. A writ of Henry of Blois, acting as administrator of the see of London during an episcopal vacancy in 1134–41, sought to excommunicate those who taught in unlicensed schools, with the exception of the schools at St Mary le Bow and St Martin le Grand, and by implication St Paul's (Neininger 1999, 31). It is, therefore, probable that Fitzstephen's three schools of the 12th century were these three, and that the churches involved (St Paul's, St Martin's and St Mary le Bow) were thus considered to be 'the three principal churches' of London.

The priory and its priors continued to enjoy prominence in both royal and City circles during the 13th and 14th centuries (*VCH* 1909, 468–9). In the early 14th century the inquisitors sent by the Pope to enquire into the charges against the Templars sat several times at Holy Trinity, presumably partly on account of the size and importance of its buildings; and one of the knights of the Order, following its dissolution, was sent there. Like most monasteries, the priory was used by nobles as a repository for their charters and other valuables; during riots in 1326 the house was attacked and the treasure of the Earl of Arundel carried off. In times of scarcity (such as in 1315) it was a focus for civic processions, and in times of crisis the wardmotes assembled in the priory to discuss the City defences. The prior was an alderman of Portsoken ward (presumably from the area being donated to the priory by the *cnihtengild*), thus symbolising the intimate connection between the priory and the City.

Eustace, prior in 1264–80, took advantage of the disgrace which the City suffered after the battle of Evesham (1265) to enclose within the priory part of the high road from Aldgate to Bishopsgate (*Rot Hund*, i, 407, 412, 418). This must refer to the same lane or highway inside the city wall which was the subject of Henry I's grant in 1122. From at least 1250, corrodians (lay people who purchased annuities or accommodation from the priory) both brought endowments to the priory and in some cases had to be housed in it: in that year Master Richard de Wendover gave 30 marks to the priory, and the prior and canons agreed to receive him into their community, also promising him an anniversary and a place in their martyrology (HMC 1883, 27, nos 1748–50). A period of great building from about 1339 is implied by continual acknowledgement of debts by the prior up to at least 1345; in 1368, £100 was given to relieve the debt incurred by erecting and rebuilding the church (*Rot Hund*, i, 470). In the late 14th century grants of further corrodies were accepted to raise money, perhaps for the building works. In 1379 the priory had a prior, 17 canons and seven clerks, making 25 members in all (McHardy 1977, no. 3). In terms of numbers, among the religious houses of London, it was slightly behind St Martin le Grand with a total of 30 and the Minoresses with 27, but was a larger community than the 23 of St Bartholomew Smithfield (Webb 1921, i, 3, 171).

The 15th century was evidently a time of lax and inefficient direction, crippling debts and waste. The priory staggered into the 16th century, and the ostensible reasons for its surrender to the king in February 1532, its deterioration and debts, seem to be near the truth. At its dissolution there were 18 canons, virtually the same number as in 1379.

There are few references to the main parts of the priory church in the documentary record. A Lady chapel was constructed in the time of the fourth prior, Peter (1197–1221), who was buried in the middle of the chapel of the Virgin Mary which he himself had built (*Cartulary*, appendix no. 16); however, the cartulary does not say where the Lady chapel was within the priory church. By about 1300 a belfry had been built, since in 1312 a second bell weighing 2820lb (1279kg) was required from Richard de Wymbishe, 'potter' (ie bell-founder); this was to ring in tune with the greater bell he had already made for the church (Riley 1868, 100). Details of the interior of the church known from documentary evidence are largely of burials (discussed in greater detail in Chapter 5.4–5.5). The south door of the priory church is mentioned in 1375 (*Cal Husting Wills*, ii, 184), and an almonry is implied in a surviving account of internal expenditure dating to 1514–15, which is summarised below (Chapter 5.6). Along Aldgate Street to the south (what is now the eastern part of Leadenhall Street) were tenements in the *atrium* of the priory, including a gate to the street, in 1349 (CLRO, HR 75/201). Presumably this was on the site of the later gateway from the street to the churchyard of St Katherine Cree, at the east end of that church as shown by Symonds (Figs 13–16).

The church of St Katherine Cree, which still stands in Leadenhall Street, was probably originally a chapel in the churchyard of the priory; the churchyard of the parish was a separate entity within this larger burial ground by 1365 (*Cal Husting Wills*, i, 594; ii, 88; Schofield 1994, 108–9). The parish of St Katherine is mentioned in City records in 1280 (*Cal Husting Wills*, i, 50); but this parish evidently required further specification or definition, since the church and its parish were the subject of a *compositio*, an agreement between the priory and the residents sanctioned or perhaps arranged by the Bishop of London, in 1414 (Strype 1720, i.ii, 57–8). Even so, part of the nave of Holy Trinity Priory was given over to parochial use, as in similar London cases at the religious houses of St Helen Bishopsgate and St Mary Clerkenwell; this is discussed below, when the known characteristics of the nave are described (Chapter 4.3). Presumably the priory church continued to have a local parochial function (that is, within the precinct itself) after 1414 until the Dissolution, since the parish of St Katherine never claimed jurisdiction over the majority of the priory site, and a new parish, St James Duke's Place, had to be created to fill this vacuum in 1622. There was, furthermore, at least one craft association connected with the priory: the Shearmen, and later the Clothworkers (who were formed from a union of the Shearmen and Fullers in 1528) comprised a brotherhood of the Assumption of the Virgin Mary, and went to the priory church on several occasions as part of the solemnities accompanying the election of the wardens.

The cloister and refectory were evidently laid out early in the priory's building history, for on one occasion before the fire of 1132 the citizens of London, joining in procession around the cloister in their accustomed manner, noticed the refectory tables carefully set out but lacking bread, and after enquiring made good the deficiency (Dickinson 1950, 110, n 4). Other conventual buildings mentioned in the 13th and early 14th centuries include the buttery in *c* 1252–60 (*Cartulary*, no. 90) and infirmary in 1270–1 and 1277–8 (ibid, nos 684, 1007). A record of an archbishop's visitation in 1303 stipulates that the prior was to eat dinner with one third of the convent in his room, the other two thirds dining in the refectory (*VCH* 1909, 468); this shows that the prior had a personal room by that date. There must also have been a library or book store in the priory, though exactly where is unknown; Peter of Cornwall's writings reveal an encyclopedic knowledge of theological works.

The priory had a great extramural garden north-east of Houndsditch, mentioned in 1255–6, which comprised 7 acres (2.83 hectares) and included a dovecot at the Dissolution; a lane with a great gate led to it from Houndsditch (*Cartulary*, no. 893; Strype 1720, i.ii, 23). This will be termed the 'extramural garden' in this volume, to distinguish it from the other 'great garden', the term given by Symonds to an area east of the main complex of priory buildings and up to Aldgate, the area now covered by Sir John Cass Primary School.

3.3 The Dissolution and Duke's Place, 1532–1603: 16th-century views and the drawings by Symonds and Thorpe

The Dissolution phase, 1532–64

Because Chapter 6 is devoted to a detailed history of the post-Dissolution break-up of the priory site, only an outline is given here, with a concentration on the evidence of the main plans, panoramas and documents which furnish information concerning the medieval priory.

In February 1532 Nicholas Hancock, the last prior, and 18 canons signed a deed giving the king their monastery and all its possessions (Jeffries Davies 1925, 9). The precinct of Holy Trinity Priory, Aldgate, was granted by Henry VIII to Sir Thomas Audley in 1534. Audley partly demolished the church and steeple, rebuilt other parts of the priory and died there in 1544 (Stow 1603, i, 142). The priory then passed via Audley's elder daughter Margaret to her husbands, the second of whom was Thomas Howard, 4th Duke of Norfolk; the main house was thereafter known as Duke's Place. Since the name Duke's Place can be identified with the western range of the cloister from at least the time of Ogilby and Morgan's map (Ogilby and Morgan 1676; Fig 18), it is likely that the portion rebuilt and lived in by Audley was also the west range of the cloister, the customary site for the prior's lodging in the medieval period.

Audley, according to Stow, wanted to extend his mansion, based around the great court, towards Leadenhall Street in the south by exchanging the parish church of St Katherine Cree (originally part of the priory and now in the way) for the monastic church, but the parishioners refused. He then began a radical alteration of the monastic church. By about 1585 (the proposed date of the plans of the former priory buildings by John Symonds, to be discussed later in this section) the roofs of both presbytery and nave had been removed, a way had been knocked into the presbytery through the Lady chapel, the north transept had fallen or had been knocked down, and two suites of rooms occupied the church on the first floor: one suite over the Lady chapel, and a second called the 'Ivy chamber', formed out of the crossing of the church and looking down on the one side into the former presbytery and on the other side into the ruins of the nave. A gallery led from this apartment to the grand house. We cannot say from this evidence alone how much of this building can be attributed to Audley; some suggestions are made below (Chapter 6.2), after all the available cartographic and excavated evidence has been presented. In 1564 the Duke of Norfolk acquired another London house at Charterhouse, across the City, and seems to have left the house at Aldgate. He was executed in 1572 for complicity in the plots surrounding Mary Queen of Scots. The main period of post-Dissolution alterations which produced the grand house will be taken in this study to be the years 1534–64.

From the mid 16th century, pictorial evidence begins to fill out the documentary record, and each picture or plan must be carefully analysed. The first group of illustrations are panoramas and map-views of the 16th-century city, all from the south.

The earliest is Wyngaerde's panorama of London (the original now in the Ashmolean Museum, Oxford, and reproduced in its entirety most recently in Colvin and Foister 1996), of which the relevant portion is shown in Fig 10. This shows the priory church west of Aldgate, which is depicted with traitors' heads on poles above it; the church outside the gate to the east (right) is St Botolph Aldgate. This section of the panorama appears to have been drawn from a point on the south bank of the river opposite the Tower. The two arms of the priory church shown in the view can, therefore, be identified as most likely representing the south transept and presbytery. The transept (left) is shorter than the presbytery and has a higher roof; both arms have corner turrets. The drawing is intrinsically undated, but is dated 1543–4 by Colvin and Foister (1996, 6). Since part of the argument for its dating to this year concerns the appearance of Holy Trinity Aldgate on the panorama, and the degree to which Audley may have torn down the crossing tower when the drawing was made, the date of this panorama will be considered further in Chapter 6.2.

The second 16th-century source is the copperplate map of c 1559; two plates from this originally 15-sheet map are in the Museum of London (Margary 1979) and a third plate was rediscovered in a German museum in 1997 (all three now published in Saunders and Schofield 2001). The two Museum plates together comprise a bird's-eye view of the eastern half of the city, and show the western half of the priory precinct after the Dissolution (Fig 11). The western half of the church appears divided into two distinct façades, both crenellated and

Fig 10 Detail from *Wyngaerde's panorama of London, c 1540, showing the priory church (centre); to the right of it are shown Aldgate (with criminals' heads on poles) and St Botolph Aldgate (© Ashmolean Museum, Oxford; reproduced from Colvin and Foister 1996, ix)*

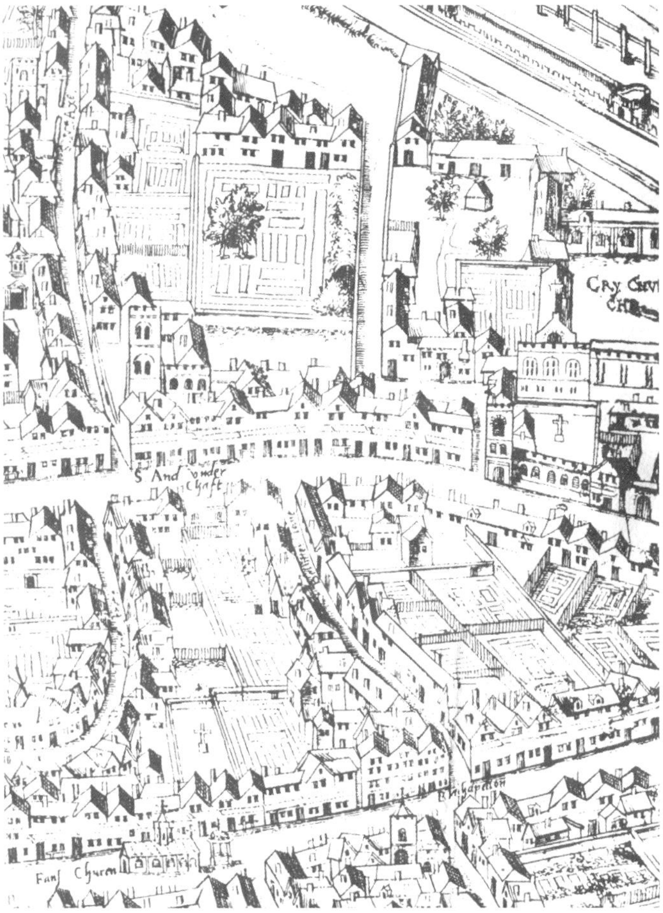

Fig 11 Detail from a copperplate map of c 1559, showing the priory in the top right. Also shown here is the church of St Gabriel (or All Hallows) Fenchurch Street (bottom, left) (Guildhall Library)

both pierced by three windows above a lower storey. The windows in the western half are set within arches. The gable of the west range of the cloister is shown as rising above the church and is pierced by a window. The north range of the cloister features four windows set between buttressing. At the western side of the precinct, the south gate of the priory leads to the great court, in which are a well and two gardens which also figure in the Symonds plan. St Katherine Cree is shown crenellated, with six windows in its south wall and a three-storey tower with a door onto Leadenhall Street, in contrast to Symonds (Fig 13; Fig 14), who shows a door in the south aisle.

Next in the sequence of illustrations is the 'Agas' woodcut map (Fig 12; Margary 1979). Cruder than the copperplate map and almost certainly derived from it, this woodcut shows the western half of the precinct very much as in the copperplate map. Though the spire of St Paul's, destroyed in 1561, does not appear and the map has been amended to include the Royal Exchange, opened in 1570, which means that it must date from between 1561 and 1570, the information on the woodcut must be regarded as the same as that on the copperplate. Because the individual sheets of the woodcut cover slightly different areas, however, it shows the eastern half of the precinct not included in the surviving sheets of the copperplate. The treatment of the buildings occupying the fabric of the church suggests that they are constructed within the elevation of the north arcade of the nave, since this would produce the effect of windows set within large round-headed arches. We know that by about 1585 something like this was the case, with a gallery running along the north side of the nave but the south wall of the nave largely demolished.

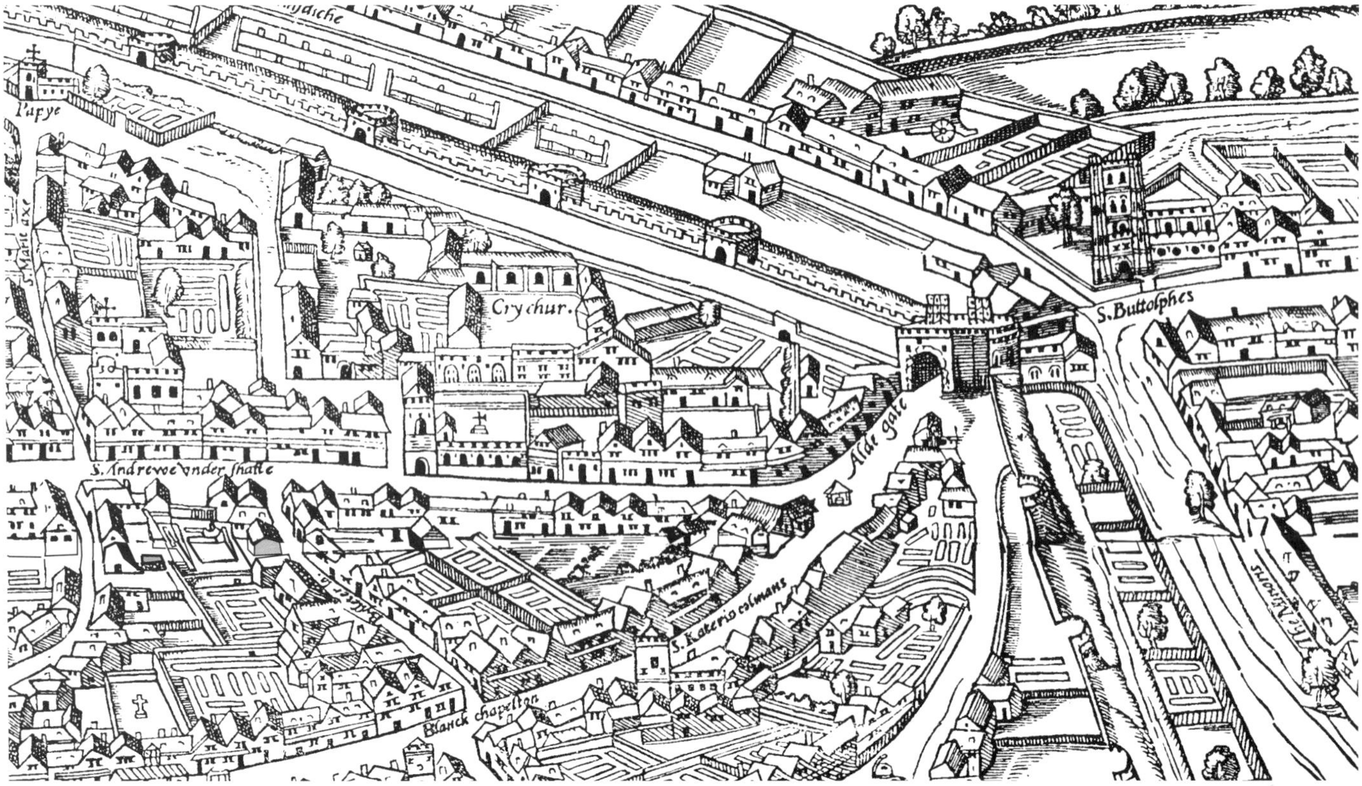

Fig 12 Detail of the 'Agas' woodcut view, based on the copperplate map of c 1559 redrawn and amended between 1561 and 1570, showing the whole precinct (Guildhall Library)

The sale of the precinct to the City and the drawings by Symonds and Thorpe, 1579–1603

In 1579 the City began discussions with appointees of the Lord Chancellor, Sir Thomas Bromley, about his lease of 'Creechurch' from Lord Howard; this presumably refers to the mansion (CLRO, CCPR Aldgate within, 1579). In 1586 City representatives were talking to Lord Thomas Howard himself about the possible purchase of the priory, which occurred in 1592 (CLRO, Repertory 21, fo 422b; 22, fo 379). It is to this period of negotiation that the plans by John Symonds (HH, CPM I/10, I/19, here as Fig 13; Fig 15), redrawn by Lethaby (1900, here as Fig 14; Fig 16), which are intrinsically undated, are usually assigned. John Symonds, a joiner by trade but evidently also skilled in masonry, made several surveys of mansions, including the royal manor house at Havering, Essex, in 1578 (Colvin et al 1982, 152); he died in 1597. Lord Burghley seems to have patronised him from 1577, and he made drawings of Theobalds and Burghley House. He also produced plans for remodelling Robert Cecil's house in Chelsea, and a John Symons (*sic*) is said to have been the architect of an extension to Lincoln's Inn Hall in 1583, which produced the two southern bay windows still extant there (Clapham and Godfrey 1913, 77–104; Cherry and Pevsner 1998, 286). In 1592 he provided 'platts' or designs for a house at Kyre Park, Worcestershire (Girouard 1983, 14).

Symonds's survey of Holy Trinity comprises ground-floor and first-floor plans in ink and wash. The drawings are framed by black ink wash borders about 17mm wide. The first-floor plan within the borders measures 505 x 535mm, and the ground-floor plan 505 x 540mm. The correspondence between the two floor plans is very good overall, with only one or two anomalies, and it seems likely that the first-floor plan was largely traced from the ground-floor plan. The plans were not drawn to one consistent scale. Four measurements are written on the first-floor plan: the length (50ft, 15.25m) and breadth (24ft, 7.32m) of the 'Ivy chamber' which occupies the crossing of the church, and the length of the 'haule' (43ft, 13.12m) and of the 'parlor' (32ft, 9.76m) in the west range of the cloister. The lack of consistency in scale across the drawings is illustrated by the comparisons in Table 3.

From the degree of variation in the use of scales, it seems reasonable to assume that the plans were based on freehand sketch-plans drawn in the field and possibly using pacing as an approximate indication of measurement. Inside the precinct, the buildings are drawn to conform to a regular rectangular grid, which our own replotting shows to be inaccurate. Symonds may have had an idealised plan of a priory and its claustral buildings in mind; certainly he was aware of the original functions of the buildings, since he names several of them. The plans show the priory precinct, church, and claustral buildings, the city wall and the north-western half of Aldgate. The original drawings are tinted in different colours according to tenancies. The presbytery, the north transept ('where the Great Tower fell down') and the nave are apparently open spaces and not roofed. The central area in the nave at the crossing has become a two-storey building incorporating 'The Ivy chamber'. 'Tenyments' have been built at first-floor level over the vaults of the north aisle of the nave, the presbytery aisles, and over the eastern chapels.

Some of the tenements, for example those along the Aldgate frontage, are drawn only in outline. Presumably they were outside the scope of the survey. In other respects, however, the survey extends beyond the limit of what might be expected to have been Symonds's brief, since it includes the church of St Katherine Cree, a length of the city wall and one of the towers of Aldgate. Symonds's interest in the monastic plan is demonstrated by annotations such as 'The Body of the Church', 'The Chapter House' and 'The Fratrye'. Furthermore, he uses dotted lines to complete the monastic plan; the west wall of the north transept, presumably ruinous, the south transept wall lines and the cloister are all dotted in.

The way the Symonds plans have been used to reconstruct the phases of the priory is summarised near the end of this study (Chapter 5.3), when their reliability has been tested against modern archaeological and cartographic evidence (Chapter 4).

A test of accuracy and a source for further inference is to overlay the two plans one above the other. Jettying of structures becomes apparent in the west face of the west claustral range and around the east end of the church. By correlating the two plans it is also possible to divide the tenements around the east end and in the west claustral range into separate household units. The drawing of stairs is accurate in the sense that they link one floor plan to the other. We should note the convention used, whereby stairs ascend into light and descend into darkness. There is one apparent exception: in the south transept is a staircase at first-floor level for which there is no corresponding stair on the ground-floor plan. It could be that the stairs were entirely above ground level, but it seems unlikely that a staircase of this size would not have had a supporting substructure at ground-floor level.

Further comparison of the two plans reveals at least four apparent anomalies. In the north end-wall of the dormitory are two doors one above the other, both apparently giving access via separate stairs or sets of steps to the lane. 'The great tower' at the west end of the church is hard to define since it is difficult to find a rectangular structure appearing in the same position in both plans. Set against the west front and the south wall of the great tower is a small structure with an angle buttress which appears on the first-floor plan only. The spacing between the buttresses against the east wall of the west range of the cloister is not consistent between the two floors. There are four steps at each end of the passage through the west range, implying that the floor is either four steps above or below ground level, although one can return to ground level via the doors in the north and south walls of the passage without recourse to any steps. The floor of the lower storey of the dormitory is also four steps above or below ground level. In both cases all other relevant evidence (engravings, inference from archaeological findings and the overall histories of the buildings concerned) suggests that the steps were down into

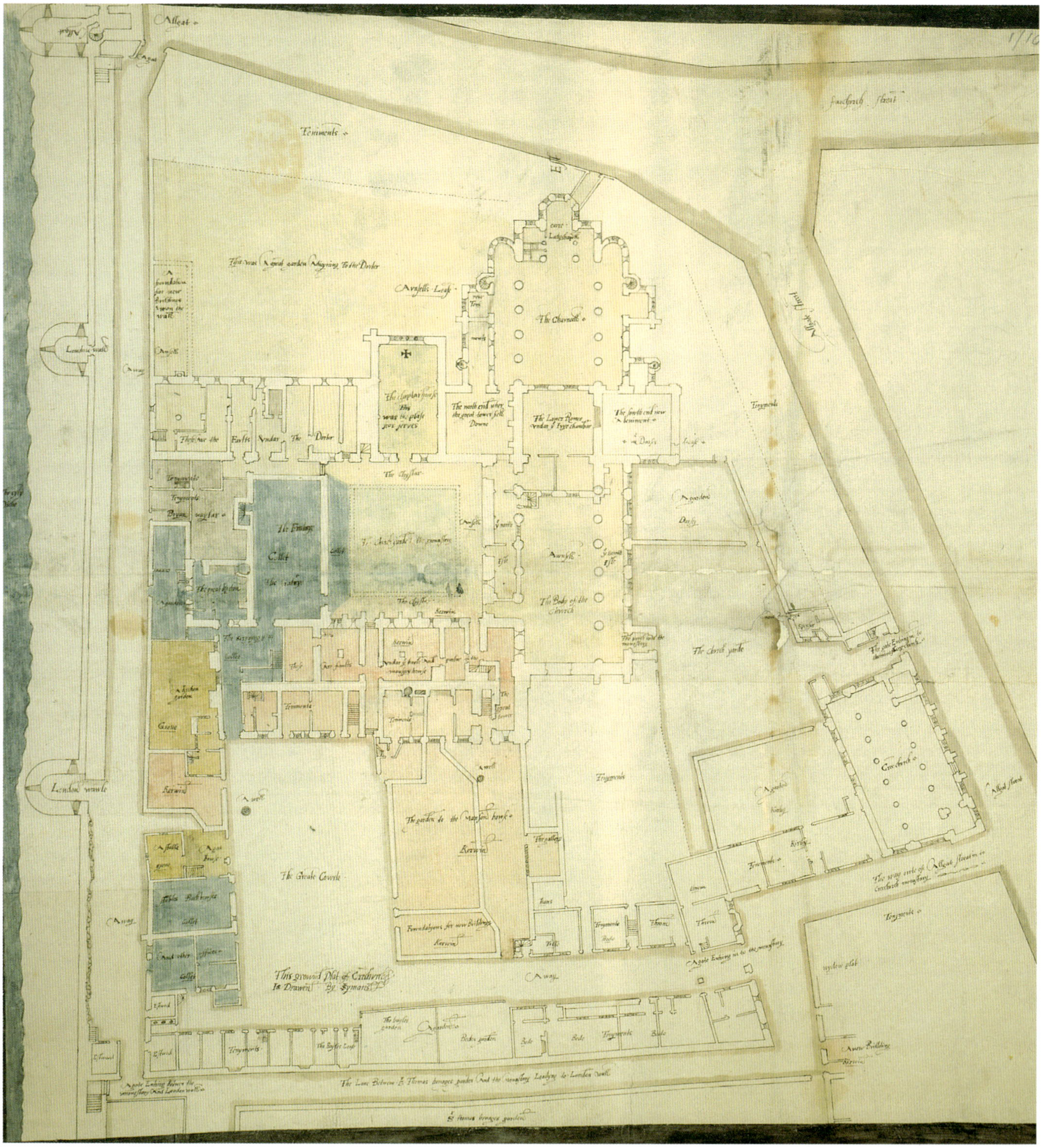

Fig 13 John Symonds, ground-floor plan of the priory c 1585 (HH, CPM I/10; reproduced by permission of the Marquis of Salisbury) (measures 505 x 540mm within the border)

the range. The lower, ground floors of these old buildings would be slowly 'sinking' in relation to the accumulation of surrounding stratification.

The circles used to represent the piers in the Symonds plans are a simple shorthand device; they are contradicted in a plan of the east end by John Thorpe of c 1600 (see Fig 17) and by later drawings and engravings of 1790–1800 (see Fig 21; Fig 22). The Thorpe plan shows the piers of the presbytery arcades as symmetrical compound piers with round shafts attached to the four faces of a central square pier. The first-floor Symonds plan implies that large drum-like elements were carried up through the first floor either as responds or as a gallery arcade. The substantial reuse of the fabric of the church suggests that the first-floor plan represents the medieval presbytery arcade at first-floor level, implying a two-storey elevation with a gallery. The bay system shown at the east end on the Symonds plans is

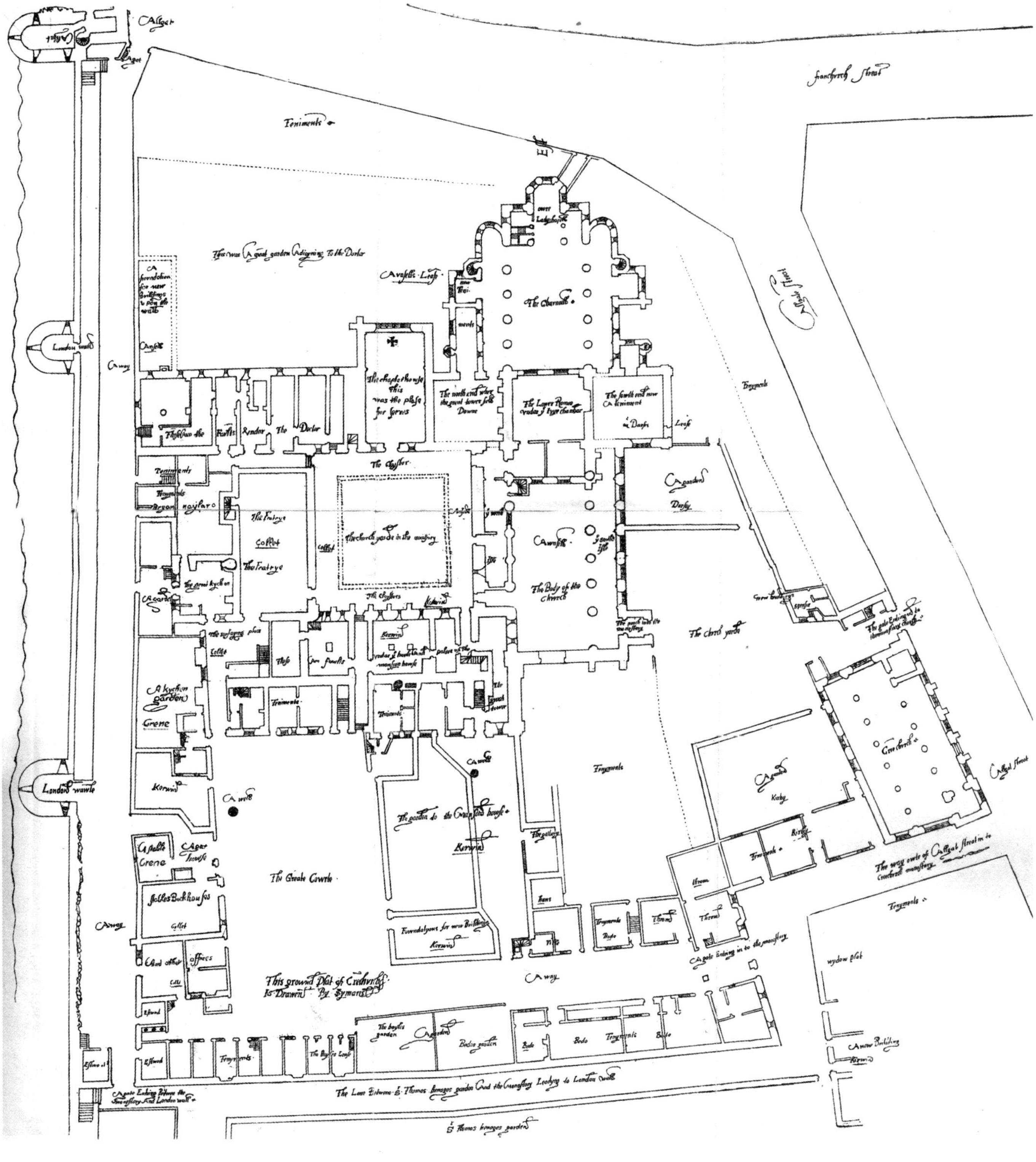

Fig 14 Symonds's ground-floor plan, redrawn by Lethaby (1900, opposite 46)

irregular; the arcade piers do not correspond with the openings into the chapels flanking the aisles. Comparison between this plan and a plan of c 1790 (see Fig 22) suggests that this unlikely arrangement is a draughting error.

The window jambs and splays are treated with a single sweep of the pen which does not accurately represent the detail form of the window mouldings, but the size and number of the lights per window can be taken as an approximate guide for dating purposes. The windows in the presbytery aisles appear as single lights, suggesting a 12th-century date, but given the likelihood of prominent monuments in the presbytery and patronage of it from the 12th century onwards, it would be extraordinary if the presbytery had nothing but 12th-century windows by the 16th century. At the east end, the two-light windows and octagonal plan of the Lady chapel might suggest a 13th-century date, but an earlier date is

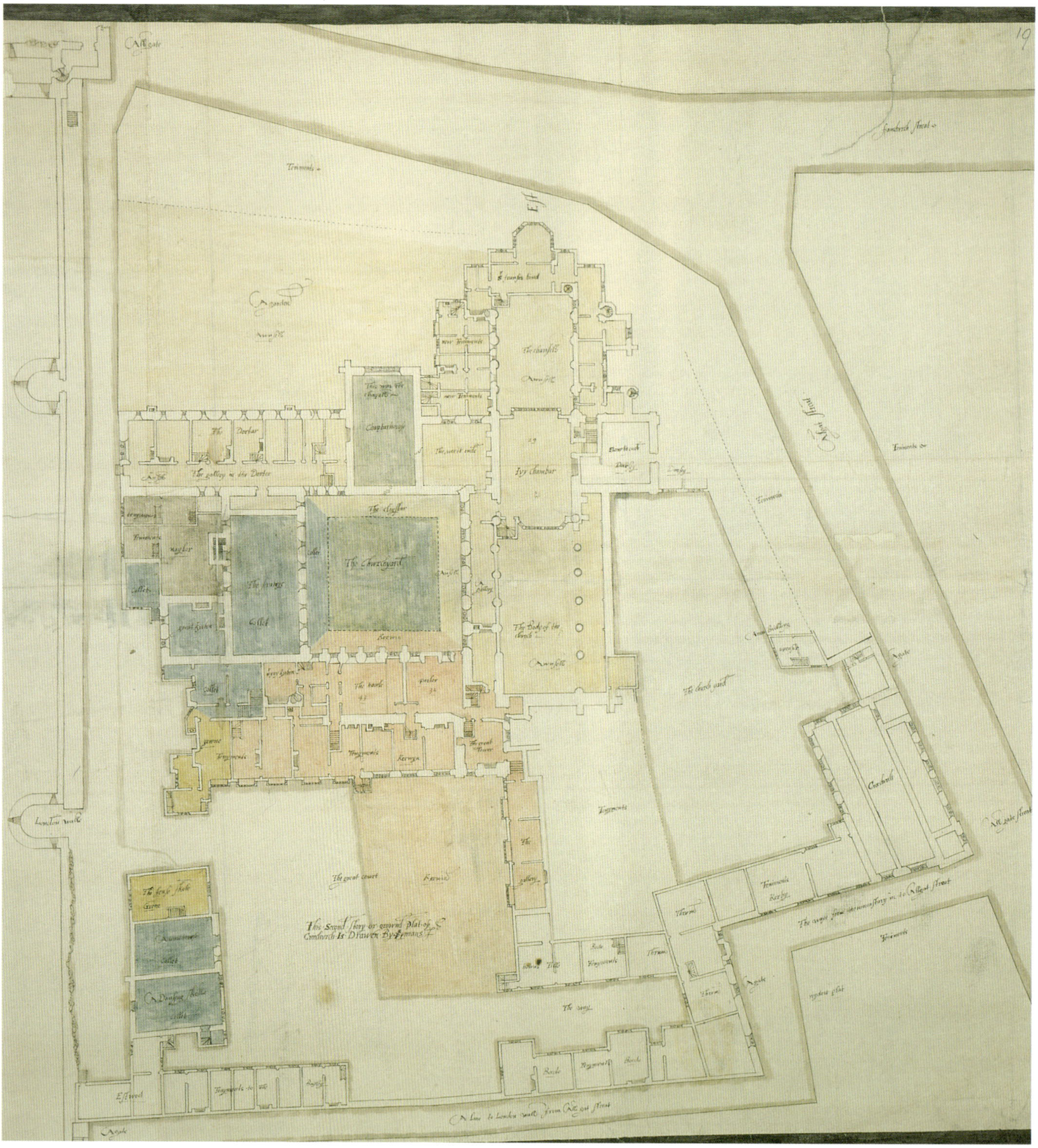

Fig 15 John Symonds, first-floor plan of the priory c 1585 (HH, CPM I/19; reproduced by permission of the Marquis of Salisbury) (measures 505 x 535mm within the border)

suggested in this volume. The windows in the nave aisle walls appear to be of three or four lights, and could, therefore, date anywhere from the later 13th to the early 16th centuries.

The buttress forms and proportions of the west end of the church appear to be of 13th-century date, contrasting with the clasping buttresses of the great tower, which are here suggested to be of late 12th-century date (see overall discussion in Chapter 5.4).

Documentary evidence can be adduced to help date the plans. It is clear that the precinct, like others in London, was subject to fragmentation from shortly after its sale to Audley in 1534. Counterparts of leases issued by Audley and the Duke of Norfolk were included with the documents when most of the priory site was sold to the City by Lord Thomas Howard in 1592 (CLRO, Letter Book AB, 106d; Repertory 22, fo 379), and they were listed at the time of sale (they cannot now be traced

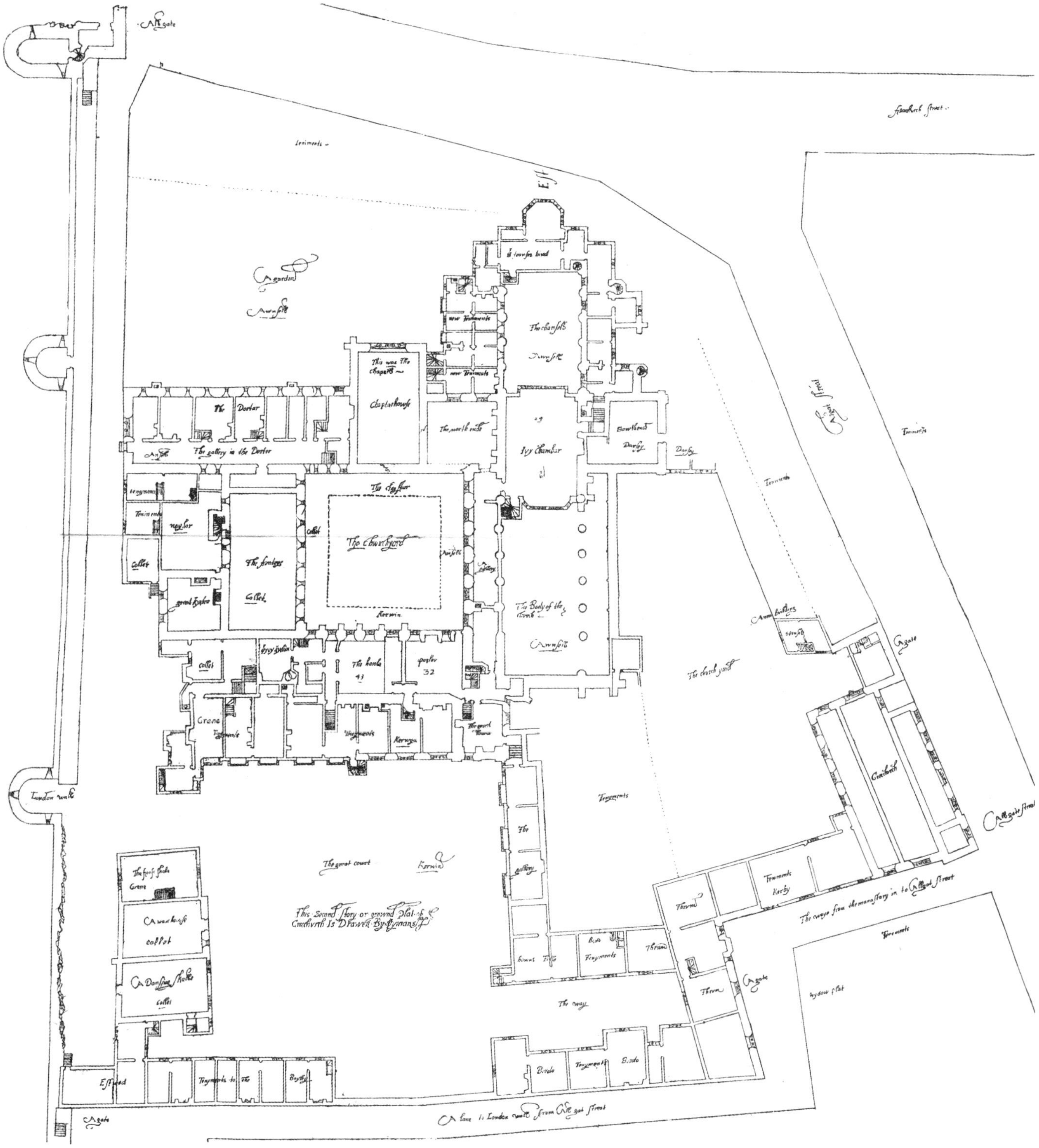

Fig 16 *Symonds's first-floor plan, redrawn by Lethaby (1900, opposite 50)*

in Corporation records). Six leases date from Audley's time (1540–4); lists of leases, probably incomplete, also date from 1564–5, 1582–3, 1586–7 and 1591–2. Of the tenants shown in the Symonds plan, Edmond Auncell appears on the list of 1582–3 and two others, Richard Bedoe and Bryan Nayler, in 1591–2. But since the three tenants Auncell, Bedoe and Nayler could have held leases for years both before and after the drawing of the plans, the leases suggest only that the plans could be from the 1580s or 1590s.

Something is known of one of the tenants named on the Symonds plan. William Kerwin occupied most of the west range of the cloister (the part most likely to have been the house of Audley and Howard), the west walk of the cloister, and the garden occupying the southern half of the great court, in which he was erecting new buildings (Fig 13; Fig 14). Apart from the outline of their foundations shown by Symonds, the nature of

Table 3 Dimensions, annotations and implied scales of buildings on the Symonds first-floor plan (see Fig 15)

Building measured	Dimension on plan (mm)	Annotation (ft)	Implied scale
Ivy chamber, width	32.5	24	1:224.9
Ivy chamber, length window to window	54.0	50	1:282.2
Ivy chamber, length wall to wall	46.0	50	1:331.3
Hall, length	34.9	43	1:375.6
Hall, length excluding gallery	28.6	43	1:458.4
Parlour	26.2	32	1:372.1

these buildings is unknown; but by 1676, as shown on Ogilby and Morgan's map (see Fig 18), the alley to the south of them was known as Sugar Baker's Yard. Kerwin was Master of the Masons' Company in 1579 (GL, MS 4318) and the City Mason who rebuilt Ludgate in 1585–6 (Masters 1984, xix, 23, 38–9, 179, 181). He was buried in St Helen's in 1594, and his tomb survives (RCHME 1929, 23). It can, therefore, be suggested that the Symonds plans date from before 1594, the year of Kerwin's death.

Lethaby (1900, 46) suggested that the date of the Symonds plans was about 1592, the date of the sale of most of the priory site to the City by Lord Thomas Howard. Symonds was then in the employ of Lord Burghley, the Lord Treasurer, and Burghley may have ordered the plans to be drawn since Howard applied to the Crown for licence to alienate the property (CLRO, Repertory 22, fos 414b–416).

A refinement to this dating is, however, suggested by a number of further documentary references. First, the 1582 subsidy roll for London mentions, in the listing for St Katherine Cree parish, Sir Francis Hinde, Sir Henry Darcey, and Edward Darcey, but none of the other English tenants shown by Symonds (Lang 1993, no. 185); an Edmund Ansell, who appears both on the list of tenants in 1582–3 and on the Symonds plan, is assessed under the parishes of St George Botolph Lane and St Margaret Bridge (ibid, no. 207). Second, in 1590 Lord Thomas Howard sold part of the priory to Henry Billingsley, alderman, for the sum of £140 (GL, MS 7329/1). This was the great messuage or tenement formerly in the tenure of Nicholas Darc(e)y, and currently in the tenure of Billingsley, which can be reconstructed as occupying the former south transept and land to the south. (This grant is transcribed in Chapter 6.2 as part of the detailed discussion of the post-Dissolution development of the priory site.) Since 'Darsey' is the tenant of the south transept on the Symonds plans, they must have been drawn at some date before 1590, when Darcey's tenancy was sold to Billingsley. A date before 1591 is also suggested by the fact that Brian Naylor, baker, became tenant of the great kitchen by that year (LMA, Acc/2712/I/A/64 no. 1); on the Symonds plan the kitchen is held by a certain Collett. The Symonds plans, therefore, seem to date from shortly after 1582 (the reference to Hinde) to shortly before 1590 (the sale to Billingsley); therefore, a date of 'about 1585' is adopted here.

A sketch-plan by John Thorpe (c 1565–?1655) (Fig 17) should also be noted. This drawing, which now forms a page in a bound volume of Thorpe's drawings held at the Sir John Soane's Museum (vol 101/145), shows the east end of Holy Trinity Priory very much as portrayed by Symonds. Its reliability, however, is in question, since its appears to be, in part at least, either a tracing from the Symonds plan (Fig 13) or derived from Symonds's survey notes. This is evident in the replication of the inaccurate ratio of nave to aisle width and the locations of piers in relation to the side chapels: the nave and aisle widths have been established through antiquarian evidence and archaeological excavation. Thorpe must, however, have had some direct knowledge of or access to another source of information for the site because there are some notable differences between his drawing and that of Symonds, which indicate that Thorpe was not merely making a blind copy. The differences are as follows.

1) In the Thorpe drawing, there is a door in the south choir aisle next to the spiral staircase. This door was recorded during excavation of the site (see below, site A) but does not appear on the plan by Symonds.
2) Thorpe shows the piers as rectangular in plan with half-round attached shafts, which corresponds with some of the later antiquarian evidence (see below); Symonds drew round piers.
3) Thorpe shows attached vault shafts in the central eastern chapel; Symonds omitted them.
4) Thorpe shows responds with attached shafts either side of the entrance into the eastern projecting chapel, but Symonds shows these as half-round responds.

Otherwise, the Thorpe drawing appears to be either a design in which the east end of the priory was to be integrated into a long north–south structure, never built, or an attempt to show the structures as the south transept of a church aligned north-east to south-west. Antiquaries who visited the site around 1790 interpreted the site in this way.

The drawing, therefore, provides details that are important to the discussion of the original form of the east end in two respects. First, the inclusion of the shafts in the eastern chapel indicates that the chapel was probably vaulted. And second, the attached shaft on the north face of the first free-standing pier in the south choir arcade suggests that – if this pier stood on the line of the gable wall of the main eastern vessel – the wall was pierced by an arch immediately north of this pier. This last piece of evidence suggests that the gable wall was articulated either in tripartite or bipartite fashion.

3.4 The priory site in the middle of the 17th century

At the conclusion of this survey of the main documentary and cartographic sources, we may consider the area as shown on the map of the City by Ogilby and Morgan of 1676 (Fig 18). From the map, it would seem that all traces of the priory had

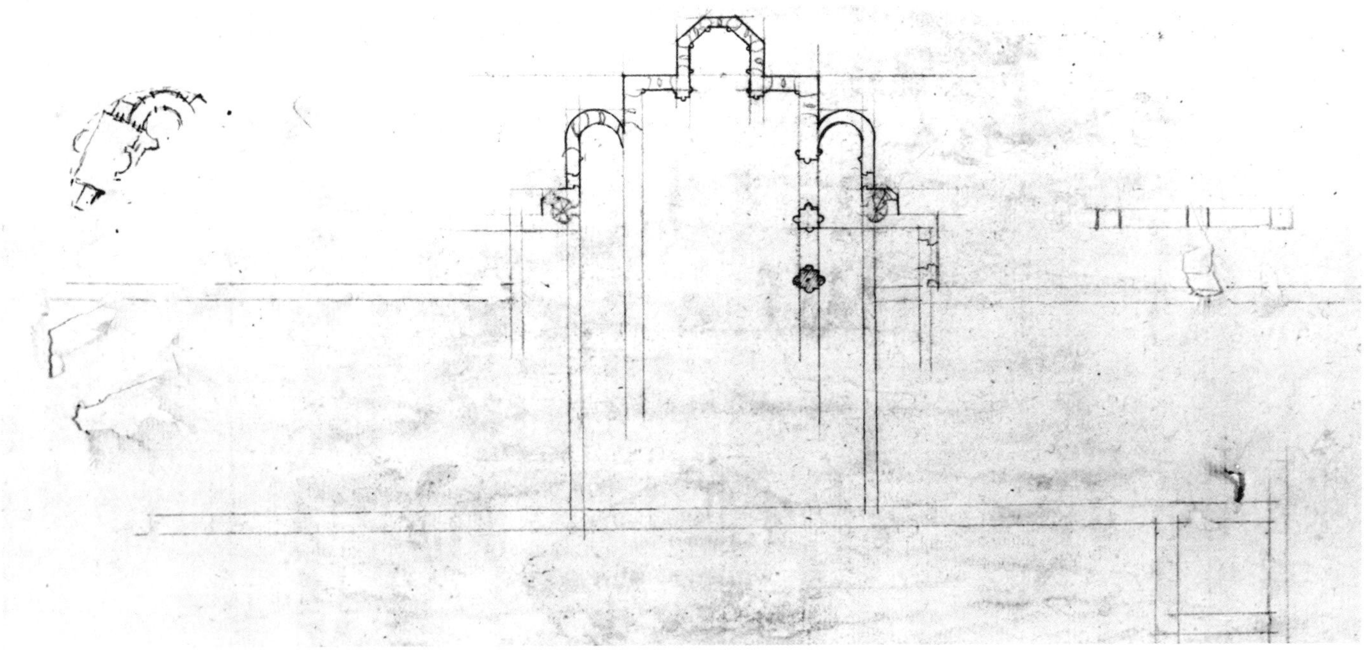

Fig 17 East end of the priory church: a sketch in the book of drawings by John Thorpe (Sir John Soane's Museum, vol 101/145)

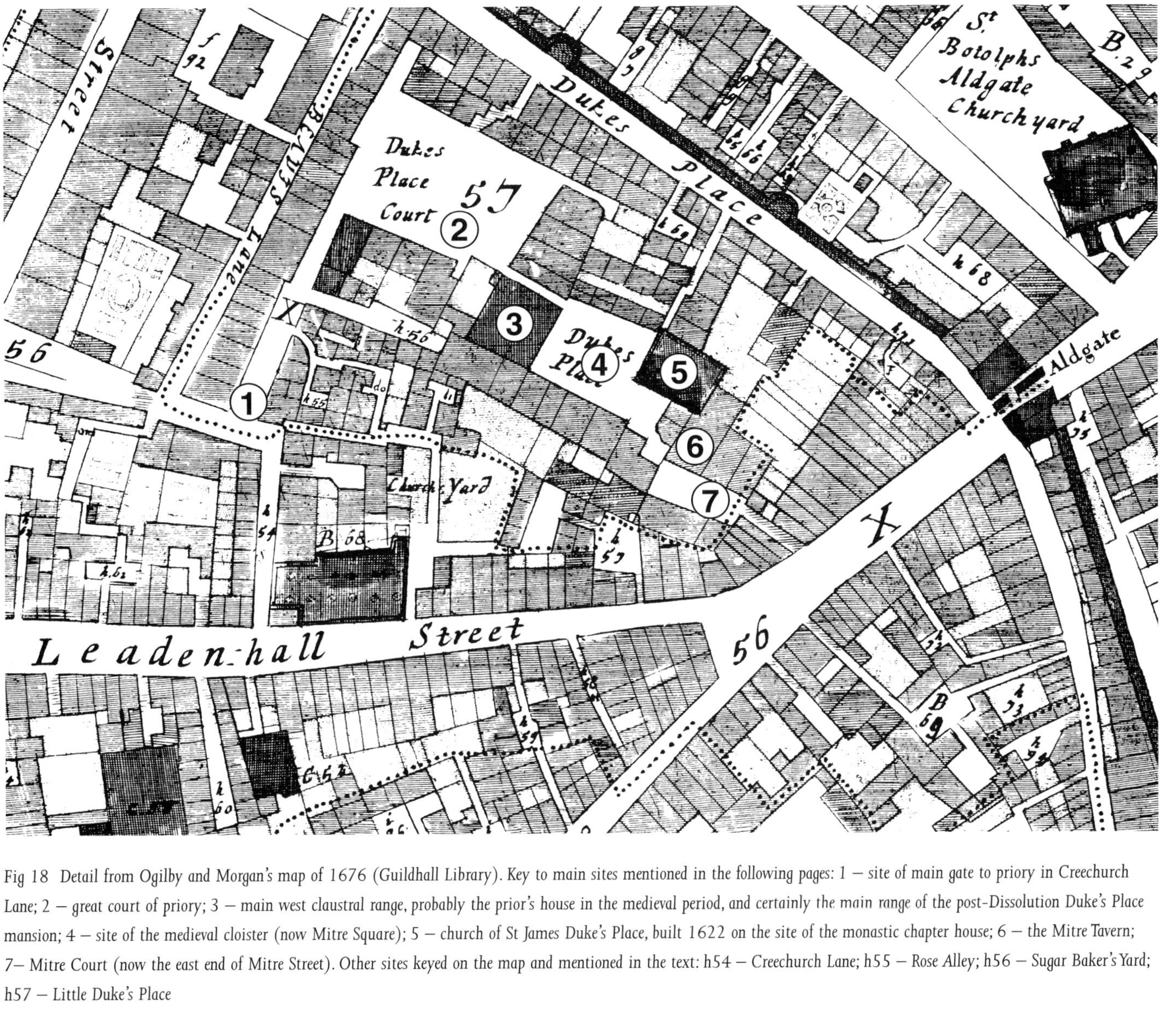

Fig 18 Detail from Ogilby and Morgan's map of 1676 (Guildhall Library). Key to main sites mentioned in the following pages: 1 – site of main gate to priory in Creechurch Lane; 2 – great court of priory; 3 – main west claustral range, probably the prior's house in the medieval period, and certainly the main range of the post-Dissolution Duke's Place mansion; 4 – site of the medieval cloister (now Mitre Square); 5 – church of St James Duke's Place, built 1622 on the site of the monastic chapter house; 6 – the Mitre Tavern; 7– Mitre Court (now the east end of Mitre Street). Other sites keyed on the map and mentioned in the text: h54 – Creechurch Lane; h55 – Rose Alley; h56 – Sugar Baker's Yard; h57 – Little Duke's Place

been removed. But the underlying topography is still that of the large precinct and its component parts. Duke's Place Court is the former great court of the priory and Duke's Place to the east of it the site of the monastic cloister. The shaded building west (left) of this space is the former mansion of the Duke of Norfolk; the shaded building east (right) of it is the new church of St James Duke's Place, built in 1622. The rebuilt St Katherine Cree in Leadenhall Street is shown in the bottom left. This map is also shown here to explain the setting of a number of surveyed plans and antiquarian drawings of 1734–1825 which are used in Chapters 4 and 5, where it becomes evident that the buildings shown by Ogilby and Morgan, in many cases, contained pieces of medieval masonry from the priory.

4

The archaeological sequence: the medieval period, *c* AD 900–1532

4.1 Introduction

In this report, the site of the priory is divided into six areas or 'zones', and the 12 excavations and watching briefs of 1908–90 (see Fig 2) are situated in those areas. Ten of the excavations are treated in detail and there are brief mentions of the remaining two, the records of which remain in the archive. For each area, because of the weight of evidence, the drawing and plan evidence (in effect, archaeological recording from the 1790s) is presented first, and the modern archaeological findings afterwards. Then, at the end of each area account, a synthesis drawing together all the evidence and citing parallels is attempted.

The areas (zones 1–6) are as follows.

ZONE 1: THE EAST END AND SOUTH SIDE OF THE PRIORY CHURCH, AND THE AREA BETWEEN THE SOUTH SIDE OF THE CHURCH AND LEADENHALL STREET

71–77 Leadenhall Street, 32–40 Mitre Street, 1984 (site A)
Sir John Cass Primary School, Mitre Street, 1908 (site B)
20–30 Aldgate, 1972 (site C)
78–79 Leadenhall Street, 1989–90 (site D); with a note on 80–84 Leadenhall Street, 1988 (site L)
32–34 Mitre Street, 1986 (site E)

ZONE 2: THE WEST END OF THE CHURCH, THE GREAT TOWER, AND THE WEST RANGE OF THE CLOISTER

West side of Mitre Square, 1979 (site F)
12–14 Mitre Street, 1984 (site G)

ZONE 3: THE CLOISTER, CHAPTER HOUSE, DORMITORY AND THE ADJACENT CITY WALL

St James's Passage and 2–7 Duke's Place, 1977 (site H); with a note on bastion 6, Duke's Place, 1971 (site K)

ZONE 4: THE AREA EAST OF THE DORMITORY AND SITE OF THE INFIRMARY

There have been no excavations here, but what is known of the area is outlined.

ZONE 5: THE REFECTORY AND KITCHEN

Duke's Place sewer, opposite 32–38, 1953 (site I)

ZONE 6: THE GREAT COURT AND GATEHOUSE TO CREECHURCH LANE

33 Creechurch Lane, 16a Bevis Marks, 1979 (site J).

An extended discussion concerning the reconstruction of the priory church, first by the two authors (below, 4.3) and then with a commentary by Malcolm Thurlby (below, 4.4), follows the section on zone 1.

4.2 Zone 1: the east arm of the priory church, the transepts and the south side of the nave of the church, and the area between the south side of the church and Leadenhall Street

Documentary and antiquarian evidence

For this area, the Symonds plans can be supplemented by later drawings, engravings and surveys. The east arm of the priory church can be partly reconstructed from surviving 18th-century lease plans and antiquarian drawings of fragments of medieval work found within later buildings. These later drawings fall into three groups: 1) two ground-plans of properties on the site of the church in the middle of the 18th century; 2) drawings resulting from a visit to the site by antiquaries and their draughtsman John Carter in 1790; and 3) drawings and plans by surveyors and antiquaries after a fire in Mitre Court in 1800 exposed large fragments of the presbytery. The north transept was also surveyed in 1670, and its internal dimensions can be roughly reconstructed to compare with Symonds; this detail is reported where it is most relevant, in the discussion section concerning the possible form of the transepts (below, 4.3).

A number of 18th-century property plans in the Corporation of London Records Office have provided a framework for a measured reconstruction of the precinct (CLRO, Comptroller's City Lands Plans 24B, 120, 540A; Comptroller's Deeds Box 11, 20; City Lands (Bridge House) Properties Plan Book, ii, 23v, 26, 33, 44); two are illustrated here (Fig 19; Fig 20), and are discussed individually. When compass points are mentioned in the following discussion, they refer to the liturgical north or south, since the post-medieval buildings were erected in the shell of the monastic church, which was aligned about 35° down from a strict east–west alignment (ie pointing almost south-east).

On 31 March 1743 the City leased to John Boover, poulterer, the Mitre Tavern in Duke's Place. An attached plan by George Dance (Fig 19) shows that the front room of the tavern had stone walls or piers marking its south-east, south-west and north-east corners; the first two were rounded, suggesting that they were originally piers. The site of the Mitre Tavern can be identified from the appearance of its front in the drawings of antiquaries of 1790–1800 (see Fig 28) and thus it can be shown that these stone piers originally formed a bay in the north aisle of the presbytery of the priory church. There had been a Mitre Tavern here from at least the 1650s, and in 1666 the Pewterers' Company held meetings there (Rogers 1928, 119–21).

On 16 December 1755 the Corporation leased to Edmund Smith, clothworker, and Peregrine Cust, mercer, the executors of Sir William Smith, property near Aldgate which the City had granted to Sir William in August 1754; a plan of the property attached to the lease of 1755 had been drawn by George Dance slightly earlier, in October 1753. The lease plan has been redrawn as Fig 20 to explain its features, and the letters A–D added to four of the areas on it. These are letters used in a plan of the same site in 1790, probably by John Carter, which is described below (see Fig 22).

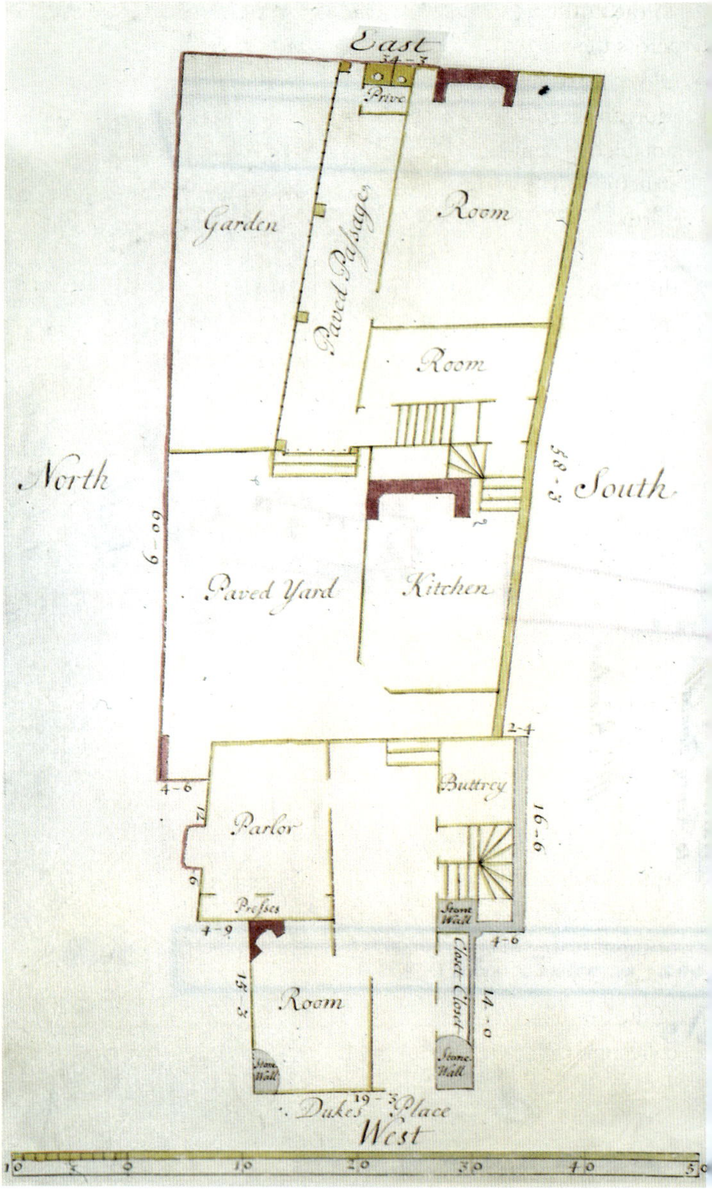

Fig 19 Lease plan of the Mitre Tavern, 1743 (CLRO, City Lands (Bridge House) Properties Plan Book, ii, 44); this is to be fitted at D on Fig 20

Comparison of the ground-plan of the tenancy (Fig 20) with the plans of Symonds (Figs 13–16) shows that Smith was tenant of a great part of the presbytery and nave of the church, and of a second property at right angles and on the north side of the court which comprised the former monastic presbytery. In essence the combined tenancy approximated to that of Edmund Auncell around 1585, and was presumably derived from it. What can be recognised as the timber façade of the former Ivy chamber (the crossing of the priory church) still stood at the inner end of the court; behind it to the west lay a mansion, with a particularly thick brick wall on its south side, and an open space beyond where the nave had been. The ground floor of the Ivy chamber was occupied by an alehouse.

To the north of the house, a diagonal passage took the same line across the site of the north transept as that surveyed by John Oliver in 1670 (below, 4.3) and on the map of Ogilby and Morgan in 1676 (Fig 18). The other, subsidiary property is notable for being entered through a square brick or masonry structure ('The Porch'), which can be shown to be a bay of the north aisle. The Mitre Tavern (Fig 19) would have fitted into the space immediately west of the 'Porch', as shown in Fig 20. Both the 'Porch' and the Mitre Tavern are shown in one of the views made after 1800 (see Fig 27).

The next group of pieces of graphic evidence comes from 1790, and it merits presentation and analysis in some detail. In notebook 26 of J C Brooke (1746–94), a pencil sketch-plan (Fig 21) was made 'on a perambulation in the city, 9 June 1790 with 2 men and Carter their draughtsman' (Bodleian, MS Top. Gen. E. 1 19, fo 36; note on fo 30). The plan shows one bay ('A') on the 'west' side and three bays ('B' to 'D') on the 'east' side of a court entered from Aldgate, near the pump which stood at the junction of Leadenhall Street and Fenchurch Street. This must be Mitre Court, which actually ran north-west to south-east and was the predecessor of the eastern end of the present Mitre Street. Brooke's plan includes remains which would later be covered by the buildings of Sir John Cass Primary School on the north side ('east' to Brooke), and, therefore, by the archaeological site B (below) and by 32–40 Mitre Street on the south side ('west'), later the excavated site A.

An anonymous drawing entitled 'The plan and sections of the remains of the Priory of the Holy Trinity, called Christchurch within Aldgate, as they would appear if divested of the present modern buildings', was formerly in the collection of J E Gardner, sold at Sotheby's in 1923, but its exact location today is unknown; it is only recorded as a photograph in the English Heritage London Region collection (Fig 22). It can be dated to about 1790, and from the handwriting is most probably by John Carter (1748–1817). It will be called 'Carter's plan' here. The use of the same letters and their assignment to the same bays suggests that the two plans (Fig 21; Fig 22) date from the same visit, though presumably Fig 21, in Brooke's notebook, is by Brooke. The labelling of the bays 'A' to 'D' was common to Brooke and Carter; and from all the other cartographic and archaeological evidence we can say that they mistook the surviving remains for part of the south transept

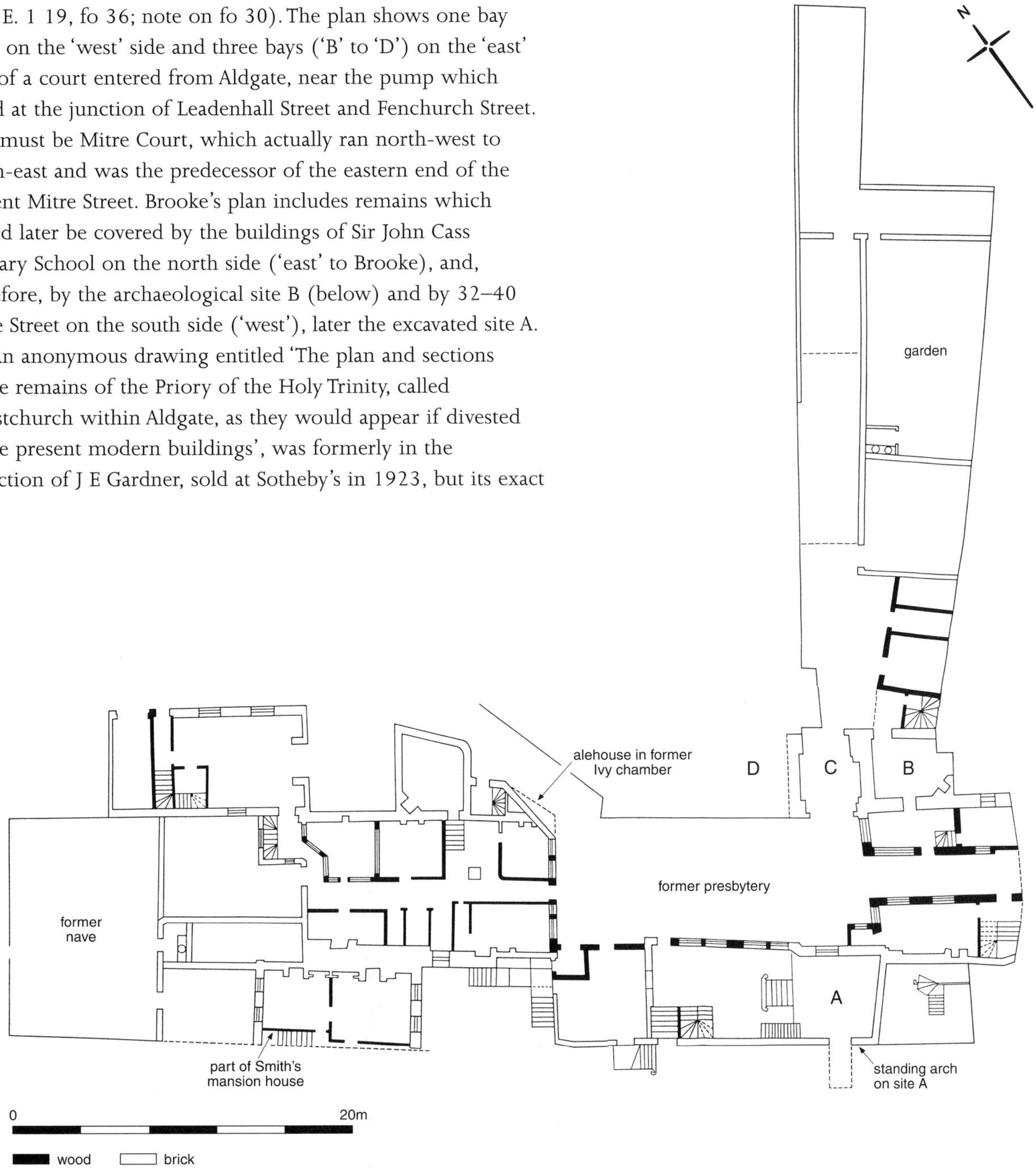

Fig 20 Plan of property leased to Edmund Smith and Peregrine Cust, 1755 (CLRO, Comptroller's City Lands Deeds Box 11, 20), redrawn and oriented with north towards the top; the letters A–D are those given to bays of the monastic presbytery as identified by John Carter in 1790 (see Fig 22) (scale 1:400)

instead of the presbytery. They were probably misled by the orientation of the church which, as already noted, is 35° down from an east–west alignment.

Carter's plan of the east end of the church shows three and a half bays, the half apparently apsidal, with a fourth coaligned and set at a distance from the centre bay. The arrangement corresponds to the three eastern bays of the presbytery north aisle and the bay immediately north of the rectangular chapel attached to the south wall of the south aisle (the bay immediately north of the surviving arch) as all shown in the plan by Symonds. A scale is included on the plan and the width of the presbytery accords with the same dimension recorded by Symonds as 24ft. However, the piers are roughly sketched in plan and are exaggerated in size. The four bays are labelled 'A' to 'D' and the annotation states that they are occupied by: 'A, leathersellers; B, greengrocers; C, carpenters; D, public house' (ie the Mitre Tavern). This naming of the bays A–D will be followed in the interpretation of the drawings. It should, however, be noted that the more detailed plan in Fig 22, which is followed here, places bay A opposite bay C, whereas the sketch-plan in Brooke's notebook (Fig 21) places bay A opposite bay B. All the other map and structural evidence suggests that Carter was correct.

Fig 21 J C Brooke's sketch-plan, 1790 (Bodleian, MS Top. Gen. E. 1 19, fo 36)

Carter's plan (Fig 22) includes a small-scale elevation through bays A and C looking east. This elevation hints at an asymmetrical arch between bay A north of the surviving arch and the next bay east, possibly with a flat pilaster respond against the south wall and a round or half-round shaft to the north. Also shown is the 'profile and front [view] of the moulding of the rib to the groins to the arch of A', that is the vault in the south aisle. This then provides the form of the vault rib in the bay immediately north of the standing arch.

The drawing of Fig 22 includes a detail of the chevron moulding around the arch at C which corresponds with Carter's plate XXI (see Fig 25), and a detail elevation of the 'cluster of capitals to pier No 2', that is the east face of the west arcade pier of bay C. Although it is not stated which face of the pier is drawn, the profile of the arch moulding, a soffit roll between two hollow chamfers, clearly matches the profile of the ribs shown in another illustration, of 1802 (see Fig 27; the ribs are broken off at the top of the vault). Although this elevation appears to show a pier composed of rectangular elements and round shafts, it probably also includes a large-diameter cylindrical drum pier which was recorded by Carter. This discrepancy is probably due to an inexact use of light and shade in Fig 27.

John Carter published the two volumes which comprise *The ancient architecture of England* over a period of 19 years. The first volume contains engraved plates from 1795 through to 1806, the second from 1807 through to 1814. Plate XVI, first published in 1797 and collated with others in 1806, includes details of St Botolph's Priory in Colchester, Gloucester Cathedral and 'Christ Church Priory, Aldgate' (Fig 23). Those of Holy Trinity Priory clearly correspond to bay A in Carter's plan (Fig 22). They are accompanied by the following text on page 17 (Carter 1806).

> Y Section of half a division of the west aile of the remains of the south transept of the priory church of the Holy Trinity, called Christ Church, without Aldgate, erected by *Maud*, queen of *Henry* I, early in the twelfth century. This division now belongs to the habitation of a leather-seller, and is but part of the west aile of the transept: on the north side are three divisions, mostly perfect, and parcelled out into tenements; no other vestige of this once famous church is visible.
>
> The base of the column is buried in the ground. The capital is like the preceding but has some different mouldings: the ribs of the groins have their mouldings ornamented with pateras, and between them large beads.
>
> Z Plan.
>
> A2 Capital, with part of the rib.
>
> B2 Soffit of the ribs, taken from the centre of them.

The mention of the leatherseller confirms the connection with bay A in Carter's plan (Fig 22) which we have identified as the bay immediately north of the surviving arch. The mistake in the orientation of the plan of the church accords with Brooke's error and strongly suggests that Carter made his notes during his visit to the site with Brooke in 1790.

It seems, however, that Carter made a further drawing of bay A, which was not translated into publication. Many of his

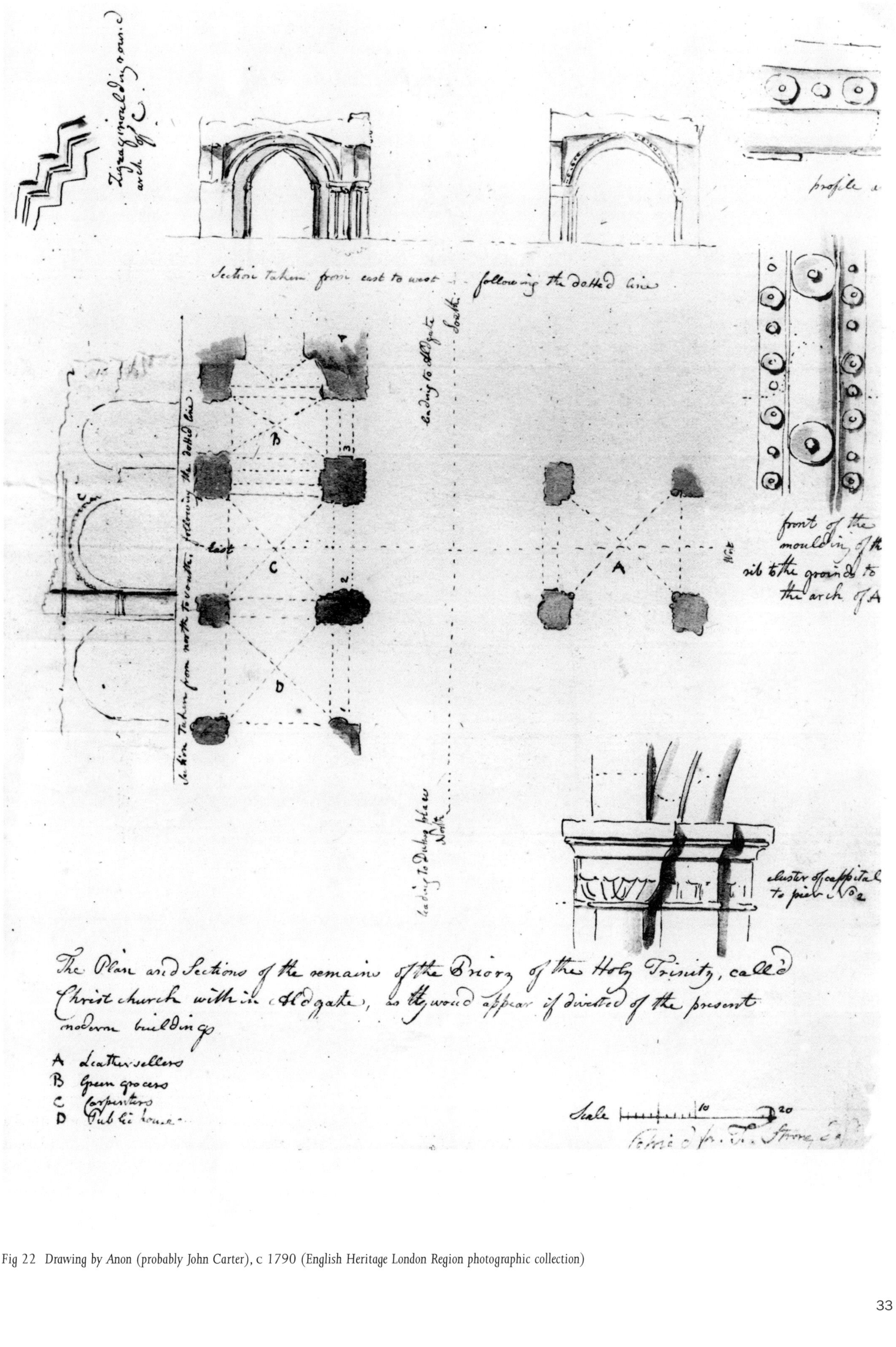

Fig 22 Drawing by Anon (probably John Carter), c 1790 (English Heritage London Region photographic collection)

Fig 23 *John Carter,* The ancient architecture of England, Vol 1 *(1806), pl XVI (first published in 1797)*

site drawings are preserved in 20 bound volumes in the British Library (BL, Add MSS 29925–44). On fo 242 in the second volume of this set is a pencil drawing incorrectly titled by Carter himself as the 'Inside view of a Saxon building at Canterbury now the counting house of a Leathersellers' (Fig 24) but which, on examination, is unmistakably a perspective drawing of the interior of bay A, viewed from the south-west looking north-east. The mention of the leatherseller confirms the identification. Although sketchy in detail other than for the vault, it strongly suggests that the pier in the north-east corner of the bay was of the compound or clustered type. Both this drawing and the plan appear to have attracted the interest of a Mr T Strong. The plan is annotated 'Copied for T. Strong Esq.' and the perspective similarly 'drawn fair for T. Strong Esq.'

Thus there is a full record of bay A, immediately north of the surviving arch, with its very unusual and distinctive vault. A single example of this type of vault rib was found in 17th- or 18th-century brickwork in the south face of the arch (A[83]).

Fig 24 *Drawing by John Carter entitled 'Inside view of a Saxon building at Canterbury...', but identified here as bay A at Holy Trinity Priory. The view is looking east (liturgically north-east) (BL, Add MS 29926, fo 242)*

Carter also published details from bay C in the north presbytery aisle. Plate XXI from the first volume of his *Ancient architecture* illustrates details from Gloucester Cathedral, St Peter's Northampton, Sherborne Castle, Rochester Castle and Christ Church Priory (Fig 25). The Holy Trinity details are explained by the following text taken from pages 20 and 21, but note the continuing error in his understanding of the orientation of the church.

> W The first storey of one of the divisions of the remains of the east side of the north transept of the priory church of the Holy Trinity, called Christ Church without Aldgate, London. This division with similar ones on each side, (now parcelled out into habitations) formed the east side of the transept. A flat column, or sweeping buttress, is placed between this division and that on its left side: there are no traces of a correspondent buttress on the right side. Clusters of columns (the centre one being in the return of the archway), support an arch with many sweeps; the outer sweep appears as an architrave, the half of which on the right side appears with the diagonals. The bases of the columns are buried in the ground. Above the arch runs a torus string moulding. So small a part of the remains of the second storey, that no idea can be formed of its structure.
>
> X The Plan. Clusters of columns on each side are diversified.
>
> Y Half of the capitals, to the cluster of columns on the right side.
>
> Z Half of the capitals, to the cluster of columns on the left side.
>
> A2 Architrave to the arch on the left side.
>
> B2 Architrave to the arch on the right side.

Comparison between this drawing and Carter's plan shows that the plan and elevation labelled 'X' illustrate the presbytery arcade across bay C. The pier between bays C and D is clearly shown with its large cylindrical element passing through the first-floor string, described as a 'torus string'. The elevations 'Z' and 'Y' of the pier capitals illustrate the west and east piers respectively, 'Z' shows the east face of the western pier and 'Y' the west face of the eastern pier. Above the arch, the outermost moulding appears to change from a plain half-round moulding (torus) to a chevron halfway across its span.

One can speculate here on the possibility that Carter may have made a mistake in his translation of site notes to publication. There is some evidence for inconsistency since according to his site notes (incorporated into Fig 22) bay A was opposite bay C, but the published text puts bay A in the west aisle of the south transept and bay C in the east aisle of the north transept. Even if we allow him compensation for an error in the orientation of the church, the two statements are not consistent.

This point is especially significant for the discussion of the change from chevron ornament to torus moulding above bay C in the published elevation (Fig 25); but can we rely on this as an accurate record for a change or break in moulding design mid-way across an arch? According to his own site notes there was no such break: the chevron is shown across the full span of the arch and the note attached to the detail reads 'Zigzag moulding arch of C'. It is only in the published drawing that the break is introduced. It therefore seems more likely that the published elevation is a schematic representation of arches from two sides of the presbytery, with the chevron above bay C in the north arcade and the torus moulding above bay A in the south arcade. If this is an error, then it could be due to confusion in the use of the terms 'left' and 'right'. He is consistent in describing the capitals either side of bay C, but perhaps his use of left and right in the description of the architrave mouldings

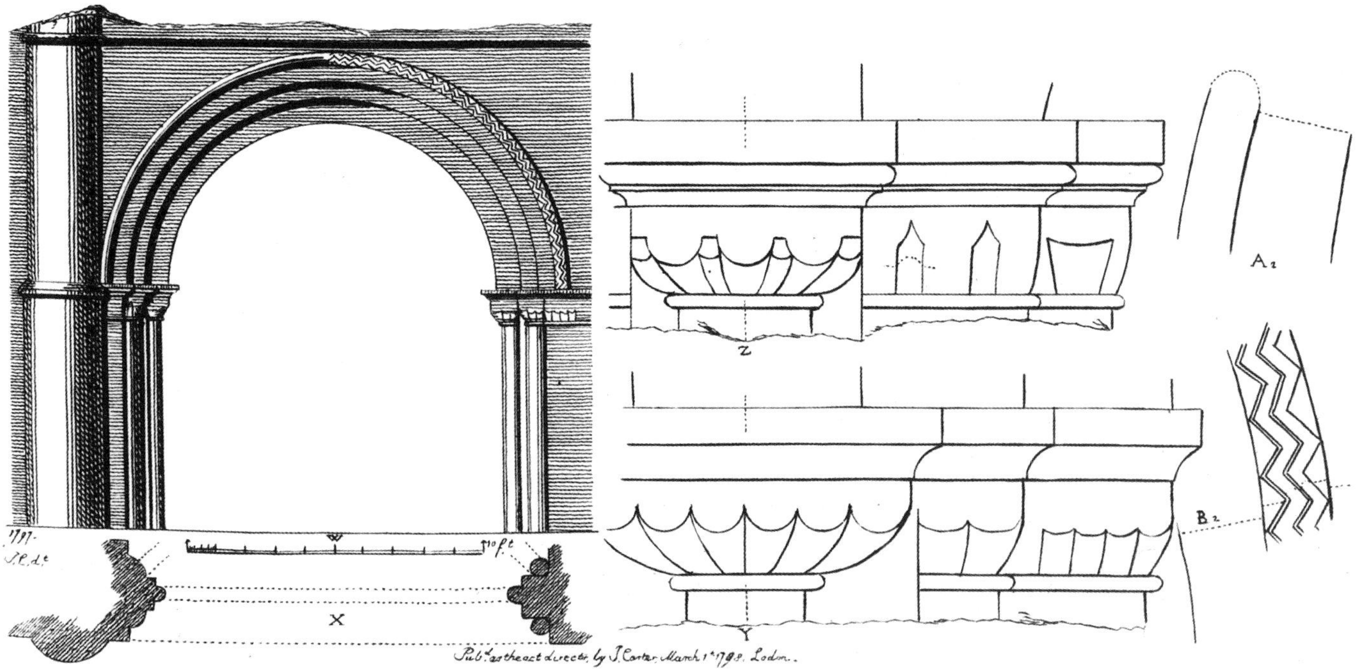

Fig 25 John Carter, The ancient architecture of England, Vol 1 (1806), pl XXI (first published in 1798)

should be taken as referring to the two main arcades. We therefore propose that in this bay only, chevron was used on the north arcade, facing the central vessel, and that it was matched on the south arcade by a torus moulding.

A third group of illustrations dates from about ten years later. In November 1800 a fire occurred in Mitre Court, which, though unroofed, was still in essence the interior of the former presbytery of the church; a City surveyor made a plan of the damaged area (Fig 26). This shows that four property units at the junction of Mitre Court and Aldgate were burnt down, and two adjacent properties damaged. The damage was viewed by the City Lands Committee on 14 November 1800 (CLRO, City Lands Journal 92, 171). They subsequently arranged with the tenants, by a process of payments or exchange of lands, for a widening of Mitre Court, and ordered that when the improvements were completed, 'a stone be affixed in some conspicuous part of the new buildings denoting the same' (ibid, 171v–172, 217). The materials of the old work were sold off (ibid, 234v). The wall between 'Mr Hardcastle' and the property alongside the gateway of the court in the plan must be the wall containing the standing arch; hence we can expect a building phase in the arch and its surrounding brickwork of shortly after 1800.

The fire revealed remains of Romanesque arches, which we identify with the presbytery of the priory church, within the burnt down or damaged buildings. They were visited by several topographical artists, either during the post-fire demolition or shortly afterwards. The naming of bays A–D in 1790 can be used to describe the details the antiquaries found then, and to identify the bays in subsequent drawings.

An engraving in the *European Magazine* for September 1802 (Fig 27) shows the two bays B and C, viewed from the south-east, partially demolished next to bay D which was still occupied as the Mitre Tavern. As in Carter's plan (Fig 22), bay B appears narrower east–west than bay C. The vault rib in bay C is recognisable as a soffit roll between two hollow chamfers.

An undated line and wash drawing by the antiquary David Thomas Powell (?1773–1848), called 'The last scene of the Holy Trinity Priory Aldgate' (Fig 28), evidently drawn at this time, appears to show two bays of an arcade of compound piers. The label 'Mitre Tavern' in the lower left part of the drawing locates the viewpoint somewhere in the eastern half of the church. The annotation appears to apply to the building in the background, whose façade is shown behind the large

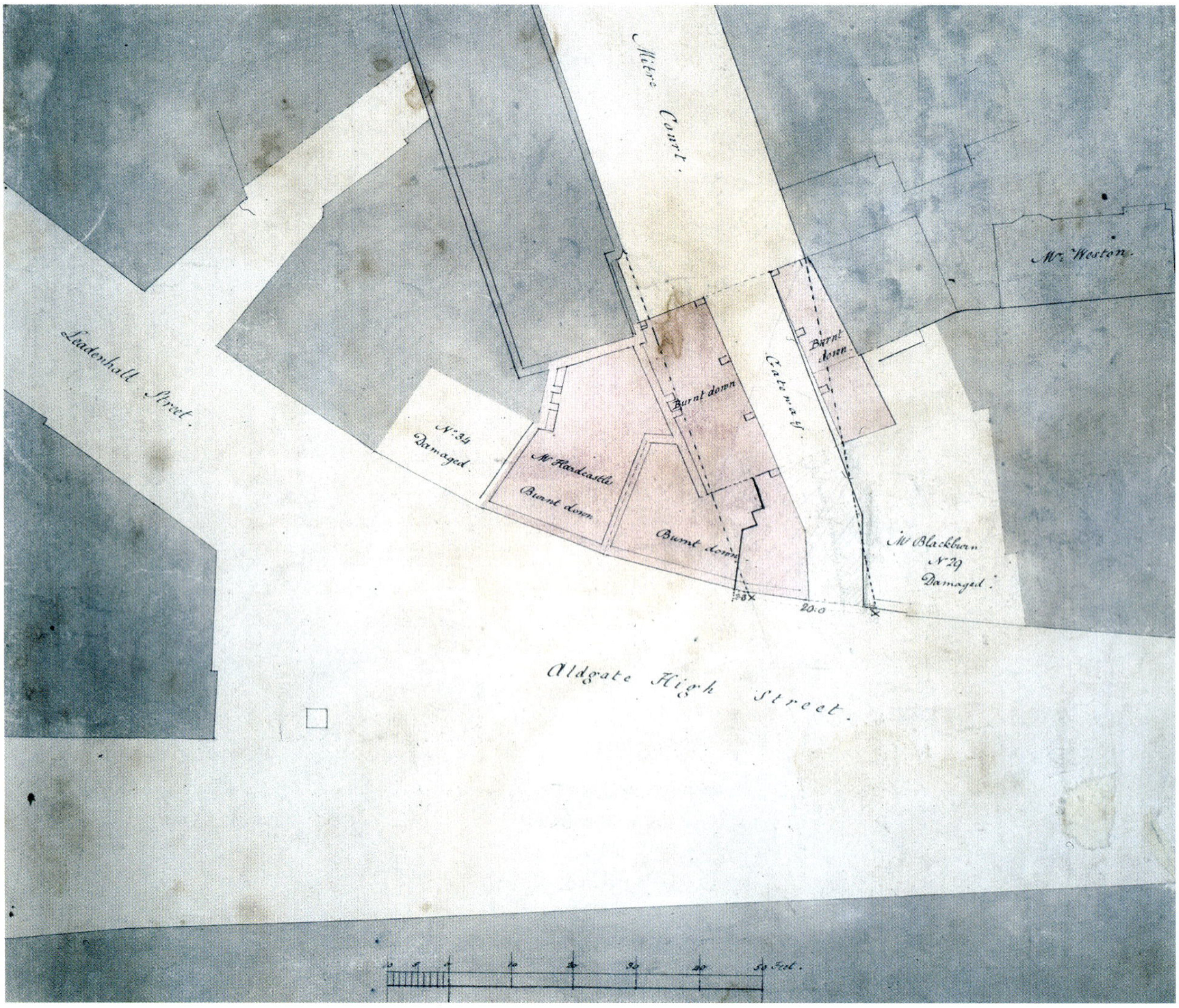

Fig 26 Plan of the extent of damage of the fire in Mitre Court in 1800 (CLRO, Comptroller's City Lands Plan 540A)

Fig 27 *'Part of AUDLEY HOUSE ... after the Fire in 1800'* (European Magazine, *September 1802, opposite 169*)

diagonal timber stay supporting the wall above the 'arcade'. Since transverse and diagonal ribs are shown springing towards the viewer from the piers in the foreground, we must assume that the view is taken from somewhere within a presbytery aisle, and not from within the presbytery itself.

This would seem to imply that the view is of the presbytery south arcade, on the south side of Mitre Court, with the bays B, C and D in the background, including the Mitre Tavern, on the north side of the street. The absence of a respond and nook shaft, or similar detail, on the south face of the western (left) bay, together with the large pilaster-like projection to the left, suggests that the arcade may have been interrupted at this point (not confirmed by the Symonds plan: see Fig 13; Fig 14), or that some reworking has taken place. But it should be noted that a string conforming with the level of the abaci of the arcade capitals continues across this length of the wall. The unlikely alignment of arches seen through and to the right of these two bays, however, leads one to suspect a carelessness in perspective, and the following discussion leads to the conclusion that the perspective is entirely misleading.

A second drawing by Powell (Fig 29) shows various architectural details which fit with bay C as recorded by Carter and as they appear both in Carter's plan (Fig 22) and the *European Magazine* illustration (Fig 27). The more finished drawing to the right, an elevation of a respond, capitals and vault rib, together with the superimposed sketch-plan of a pier, also correspond to Carter's record of the east face of the west arcade pier from the same bay, labelled 'Z' in his drawing (Fig 23). The depicted state of demolition of bay C suggests that Powell's drawings are contemporary with the drawing of Fig 27.

It seems very unlikely that a substantial portion of the south presbytery arcade, as apparently shown by Powell, could have survived to this date and escaped the attentions of John Carter, the *European Magazine* illustrator and the author of the plan in Fig 22, who was probably also Carter; another explanation seems more plausible. The appearance of the tenement above bay C, together with the tall drum pier or pilaster and the annotation 'Mitre Tavern' in Powell's main sketch (Fig 28), resemble the tenement above the 'arcade' and the pilaster-like feature with the string at abacus height in the more finished drawing (Fig 29). Also in the more finished drawing, the presence of demolition workmen above the arcade in front of the tenement wall suggests a greater depth than the thickness of an arcade wall would allow. It is, therefore, more likely that the main drawing of Fig 28 is misleading in its perspective and is in fact simply another representation of the bays B and C as they appear in the *European Magazine*. The left side of the left arch with the tall pilaster-like projection formed part of the north presbytery arcade to the west of bay C, and the two 'piers' to the right are the responds against the north wall of the north aisle either side of bay B. This accounts for the ribs springing towards the viewer in the right side of the drawing and their absence from the left. The presence of shafts and capitals in the left-hand bay C is compatible with access to the chapel to the

Fig 28 Drawing by David Powell showing the north arcade during demolition, shortly after 1800 (GL, MS 3776, fo 2)

north as shown on the Symonds plan, and originally may have been paralleled in the surviving arch before it was reworked with a hollow chamfered pointed arch (the main arch on the surviving fragment). However, their appearance in the bay B to the east is not compatible with the Symonds plan since this should be a blank wall. Inaccuracies of this kind suggest that Powell completed the finished parts of the drawings away from site.

The *Gentleman's Magazine* (1803, 417) also published an engraving of an 'Arch at ALDGATE, taken 1801' (Fig 30). This engraving shows a vaulted bay with diagonal ribs seen through an arch between two tall drum-like piers with moulded strings at capital and first-floor levels. The left-hand pier rises above the first-floor level. These piers conform with those drawn earlier in Carter's plan (Fig 22) and by Carter between bays C and D (Fig 25); but Carter states that he found no trace of a flat column or sweeping buttress on the pier to the east. Either all traces of a corresponding pier had been removed or there never was a corresponding pier at this point.

The masonry above the left-hand pier in Fig 30 conforms in outline with the masonry shown above the pier between the bays C and D in drawings by C J M Whichelo (see below), suggesting that the engraving depicts bay C viewed from the south. The pier to the left is, therefore, either a reconstruction based on evidence not recorded by Carter or, more likely, based on principles of symmetry and an absence of contrary evidence.

C John M Whichelo (1784–1863) visited the site in 1803 and produced three drawings, the first two entitled 'Outside of the gate of part of the chapel, Mitre Court, Aldgate' and 'Part of the chapel near the gate, Mitre Court, Aldgate' respectively and jointly annotated 'Now destroyed' (Fig 31). This pair of drawings shows the remains of the first three bays of the north aisle of the presbytery. The left-hand drawing shows the arcade piers either side of bay D viewed from the south-east, with the large cylindrical element rising through the gallery floor to the right (compare Carter, Fig 22). This drawing was apparently done following the demolition of the Mitre Tavern which formerly occupied bay D. The right-hand view is harder to locate within the context of the priory. The two views do not appear to show the same fragments of masonry. Comparison with the *European Magazine* illustration (Fig 27), however, suggests that the right-hand view shows bay B viewed from the south.

A third drawing by Whichelo survives (Fig 32), entitled 'Inside of the gate of part of the chapel, Mitre Court, Aldgate,

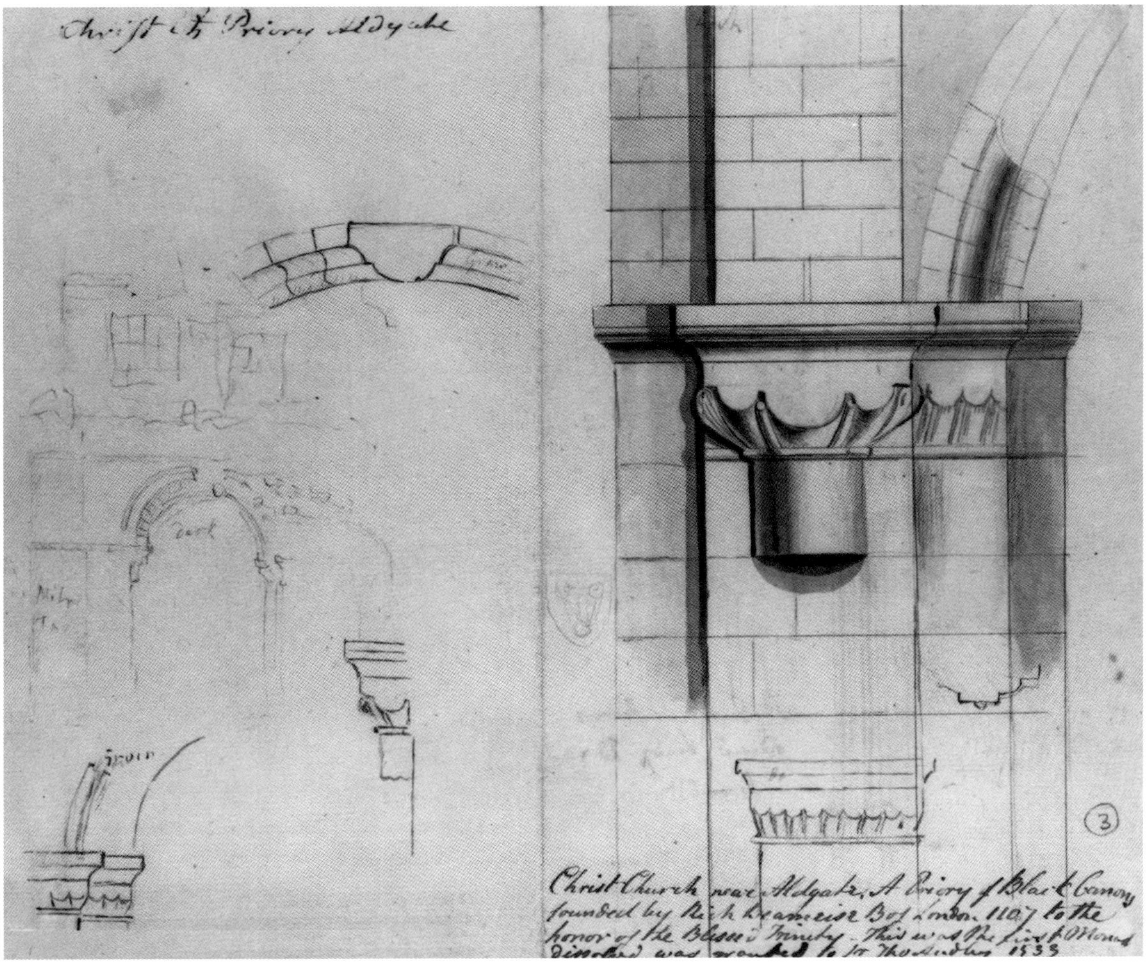

Fig 29 *Drawing by David Powell of architectural details (GL, MS 3776, fo 3)*

within Mitre Court', signed and dated 1803, and annotated in another hand 'Christs Church or Trinity Priory Aldgate. As it appeared after the Fire 1800, see European Mag 1802, Bought at the Baker Sale, June 1826 JB[?]'. The present whereabouts of this drawing are not known. The photograph of the drawing used here is in the English Heritage London Region photographic collection, filed under 'Holy Trinity Aldgate, City, pre-1946'; it dates from 1908 and is annotated 'Gardner Collection', so presumably it was part of the former Gardner Collection of London drawings. Fig 32, like Fig 31 (left), shows piers either side of bay D, viewed from the north-east in a similar state of demolition. Both bays C and D clearly had torus-moulded diagonal vault ribs. Fig 32 shows the distinction between the piers to either side of bay D.

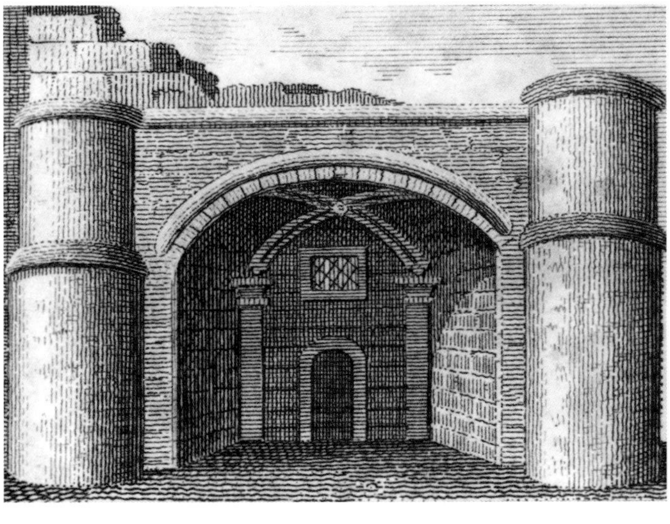

Fig 30 *'Arch at ALDGATE, taken 1801'* (Gentleman's Magazine 1803, 417)

Finally, three drawings investigated the interior of some of the surviving bays. An anonymous and undated watercolour (LMA, BC15010) shows a view similar to the Whichelo view of bay B (Fig 31, left) with a similar arrangement of a window above a door; but the details of the capitals differ in such a way as to be not easily accounted for, say, by different stages of demolition. It is almost as likely to represent the bay east of the surviving arch. An anonymous engraving (Fig 33) in R Kemp's *Notes on the ward of Aldgate* (Kemp 1904, 10), although there wrongly said to have come from J P Malcolm's *Londinium Redivivum* (1803–7), shows probably the interior of bay C with the arcade arch of bay A on the other side of Mitre Court. The form of the pier matches that recorded by Carter on the east side of bay C. The reliability of this engraving is, however, in question since it does not show the diagonal vault ribs shown in bay C in the other views. Third, an engraving (Fig 34) actually in Malcolm's *Londinium Redivivum* shows one of the bays on the north side of Mitre Court, probably bay C, although

Fig 31 Two drawings made within Mitre Court, by C J M Whichelo, 1803: left, 'Outside of the gate of part of the chapel, Mitre Court, Aldgate'; right, 'Part of the chapel near the gate, Mitre Court, Aldgate' (Sir John Soane's Museum, Soane's copy of Some account of London *by Thomas Pennant, 4 edn (1805), inserted drawings 231 and 232)*

Fig 32 A third drawing made within Mitre Court, by C J M Whichelo, 1803 (whereabouts of original unknown; from a photograph held by English Heritage London Region photographic collection)

Malcolm, like Brooke and Carter, assumes this to have been part of one of two aisles in the south transept (Malcolm 1803–7, iv, pl facing 1). The Whichelo drawings show large-diameter shafts for the responds between bays C and D as opposed to flat pilasters.

The antiquaries of 1790–1803 described bays B, C and D, forming the liturgical north aisle, and bay A, in the south aisle, of the presbytery of the priory church. Bay B was the last full bay and apsidal termination of the north aisle, and C the bay which led to the northern chapel. On the south side, bay A originally led to the southern chapel (chapel 2 in the excavation on site A: see below) through what is now the only surviving arch. In 1753 the east and west sides of bay C were thick walls of brick, and no doubt this is why several of the antiquaries, around forty years later, thought this bay was a porch or gate to the 'chapel' of Holy Trinity, wherever that could be located (and for which there is no separate documentary evidence, so that it is not clear what they were thinking of). These two walls coincide with 'chalk walls' found on the site of Sir John Cass Primary School, Mitre Street, in 1908 (below, site B), which were presumably medieval foundations for those post-medieval brick walls. The presbytery of the church was 24ft (7.32m) wide, pier centre to pier centre.

Two significant decorative details have been identified from these drawings. Bay A on the south side had vault ribs enriched with ornamental medallions (which we call 'rosettes') and

Fig 33 Anonymous engraving (c 1800) of the interior of a surviving bay within Mitre Court (probably bay C), reproduced in Kemp 1904, 10

Fig 34 J P Malcolm, 'Remains of the Holy Trinity Aldgate', Londinium Redivivum *(Malcolm 1803–7, iv, pl facing 1)*

beadwork; this was evidently not present in bay C on the north side. On the arcade arch of bay C, however, two different outer mouldings were noticed by Carter. The eastern half of the arch was decorated with chevrons, whereas the western half, from the middle of the crown, had a plain half-round moulding. If this were to be accepted (and the reasons for not accepting it are set out above), then it might indicate a break in construction.

The 35° deviation of the axis of the church from a true east–west alignment to the south-east confused nearly all the early observers, who assumed that the arches they recorded around 1800 were the relics of an unusually long south transept. Plotting of the outline of the church from the Symonds plans, 18th-century lease plans and the excavated fragments, however, makes it clear that Mitre Street now bisects the church along its entire length from south-east to north-west, and that the arches exposed on either side of the street (then Mitre Court, Fig 26) were those of the presbytery. In the following pages the normal liturgical compass points will be used for the sake of clarity. Mitre Square, on the north side of Mitre Street, now lies on the site of the cloister, which was on the north side of the church.

Excavations and standing masonry

Observations of 1908 and four excavations of 1972–90 (sites A–E) are relevant to the east end and south side of the priory church and the area south of the church towards Leadenhall Street. The largest excavation is presented first, in two parts: the excavation, and the simultaneous recording of a medieval arch encased in later brickwork which stood on the site (site A), known beforehand to be part of the eastern arm or presbytery.

71–77 Leadenhall Street, 32–40 Mitre Street, 1984 (LEA84; slte A): the excavation

Richard Bluer and John Schofield

INTRODUCTION

Excavation took place in 1984 on vacant land in the angle between Leadenhall Street and Mitre Street (Fig 35). The following summary, which is based on the archive report (Rivière 1986a), incorporates a report by Richard Lea on the recording of the standing medieval arch on the site. Though the site is known conventionally as 'Leadenhall Street/Mitre Street' in all the archive records, the areas of excavation lay along the south side of Mitre Street over the south part of the presbytery of the monastic church and the site of most of the south transept.

The excavation was divided by modern intrusions into three areas: a large central area subdivided by unexcavated medieval masonry into area A (to the south-east) and area C, while small peripheral areas (B and D) lay to the north-west and south-east respectively (see Fig 37). The site produced 1444 contexts, which were divided during post-excavation analysis into 58 groups (in brackets, abbreviated to gpA1, gpA2 etc). Some of these groups were further divided into subgroups, referred to as A1.1, A1.2 and so on, by one of the authors of this summary (Bluer) when parts of a group were physically separated though clearly related. In the archive report for the site, the groups were assigned to nine periods I–IX which are retained here (for a summary of periods II onwards see Table 2).

Period I (Roman), which comprised activity pre-dating the

Fig 35 View of Mitre Street and site A from the north-west in 1979. Key: 1 – brick masonry incorporating (in the far wing) the surviving arch on site A; 2 – Little Duke's Place, later Pound's Buildings; 3 – site of the high altar of the priory church, beneath Mitre Street; 4 – wall along the south side of the nave; 5 – present extent of churchyard of St Katherine Cree; 6 – future site of excavation on site E; 7 – site of priory chapter house; 8 – location of excavations then in progress (1979) on site F

scope of this report, is not considered here. Periods II–VIII (gpA18–A51, gpA53) comprised a late Saxon/early Norman graveyard, the construction of substantial masonry structures of the church of Holy Trinity Priory, and the use, dismantling and reuse of those structures. Groups A54–A56 comprise the standing arch of the church which was stratigraphically independent of the main archaeological sequence; it is not assigned a discrete period, as its phases span those of periods IV–VIII.

Thus the medieval masonry recorded on site A comprised two separate parts of the priory church: first, the south transept (identified principally from its character and its representation on the Symonds plans) and an associated eastern chapel (chapel 1); and second, the remains of an arch encased in post-Dissolution brickwork which originally led from the south aisle of the presbytery into a second chapel (chapel 2), the south-west corner of which was found by excavation. Both parts survive within the new building on the site, though the transept chapel was moved during construction of Swiss Re House (Chapter 8.1).

A group and land-use diagram for site A is given in Fig 36 as a guide to the stratigraphic relationships of the structures recorded.

DEMOLITION AND LEVELLING ACTIVITY, AFTER *c* AD 900 (PERIOD II, gpA18–A20, gpA27)

The latest Roman (period I) activity (gpA5) in area A was sealed by an area-wide horizon (gpA18) which raised the ground level some 0.35m to 13.45m OD. The deposits were of clayey silt but included fragments of a wide variety of Roman building materials including painted plaster, suggesting an element of demolition debris. Cutting into the top of this horizon were two pits (gpA20), the fills of which contained fragments of *opus signinum* and tesserae as well as painted plaster (Fig 37).

Also intruding into the top of the group A18 deposits was a deep and substantial subrectangular cut (gpA19), adhering to the sides of which were two patches of mortar, suggesting that the cut had contained masonry which was robbed some time after the deposition of the group A18 material. In the bottom of the cut were 12 voids arranged in three rows, the remains of a group of driven timber piles supporting an inferred masonry foundation. The south side of this cut was beyond the limit of excavation, so it could have been the north end of a north–south wall, but it might equally have been an isolated foundation pier. Situated 4.9m to the south-east in area B was a similar feature (gpA27), though here the cut was linear, and the pile impressions were larger and randomly distributed.

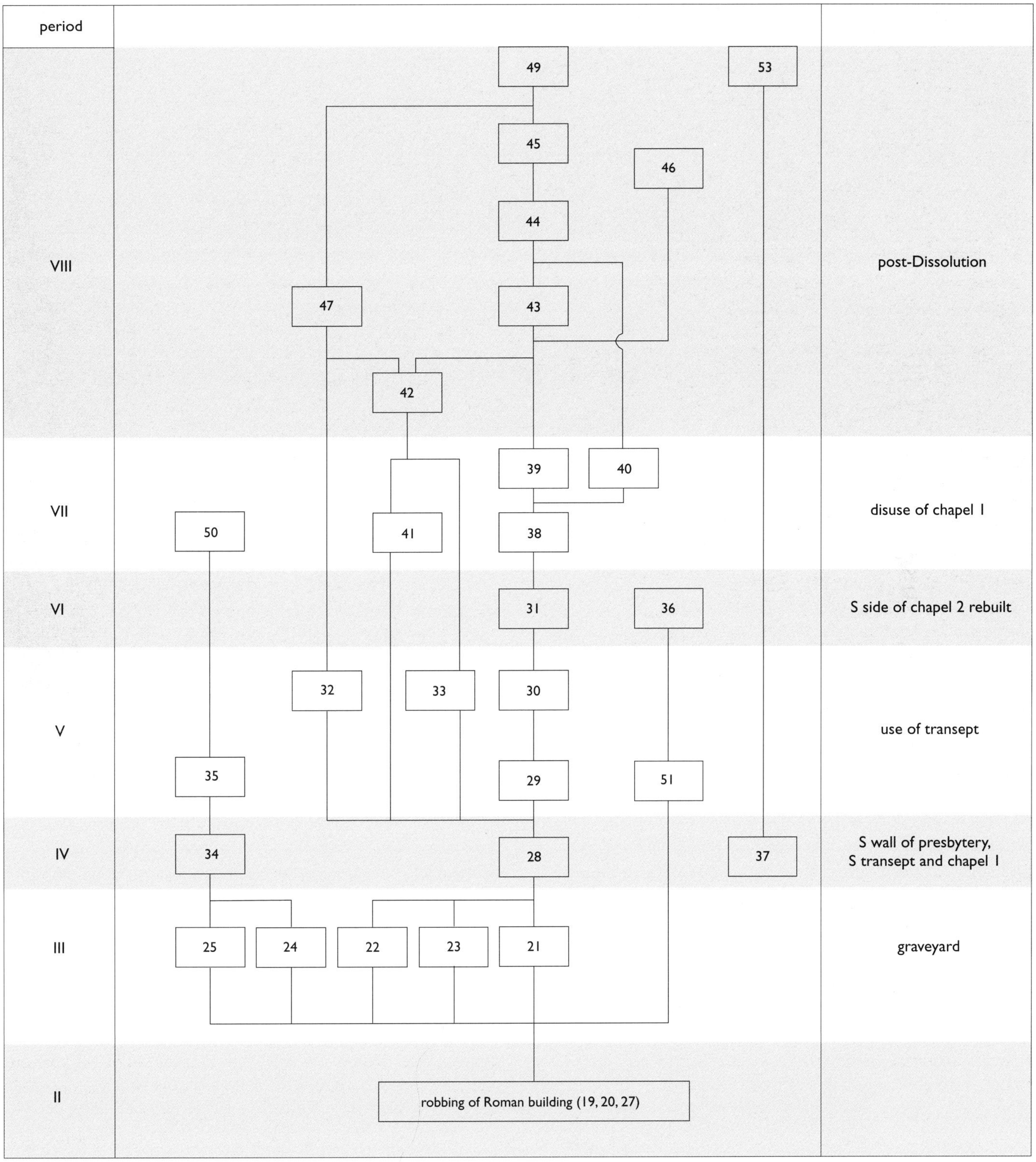

Fig 36 Site A: group sequence and land-use diagram (excludes the recording of the standing arch (gpA54–A56) and subgroups)

In neither feature was the original construction level apparent, so it cannot be categorically asserted that they were contemporary, nor did enough survive to conjecture in any detail the form of the superstructure of any building these robbed masonry foundations might have supported. It can be suggested, however, that the building was a high-status one since the tesserae and painted plaster found in the group A18 dumps and group A20 pits probably derived from it. The painted plaster would have been from the superstructure, and its presence amongst the demolition debris suggests that some upstanding wall survived until the period II activity. It is likely from all the fragmentary evidence that this was a late Roman building.

Both groups A20 and A27 cuts contained mainly 3rd- and 4th-century AD material, with a lesser amount of 1st- to 2nd-century AD date. Medieval pottery was limited. Ipswich-/

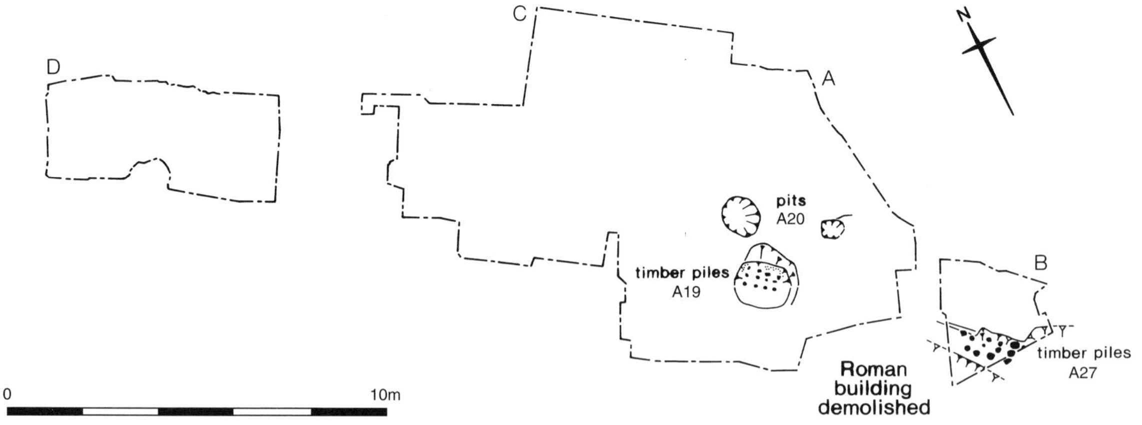

Fig 37 Plan of robbing of Roman buildings on site A (period II, gpA19–A20, gpA27) (scale 1:200)

Thetford-type ware (THET, *c* 900–*c* 1100) was recorded in A[851] (gpA20). The group A27 robber trench contained four sherds of early medieval flint-tempered ware (EMFL), early medieval grog-tempered ware (EMGR), early medieval sand- and shell-tempered ware (EMSS) and coarse London-type ware with shell inclusions (LCOAR SHEL), from A[145], and one of EMSS from A[115] (total 43g). These features can be broadly dated to *c* 1080–*c* 1150.

To summarise, period II began with the deposition of the group A18 clayey silts, though whether these were dumped or accumulated naturally was not clear. There followed the cutting of two pits and the demolition and robbing of the masonry foundations of part of a well-decorated Roman building in the period *c* 1080–*c* 1150, leaving a level ground surface prepared for the period III activity. It is therefore likely that period II lasted for some time, and comprised two separate demolition programmes, the intervening time represented by the group A18 silts. It is possible that the robbing of underlying Roman buildings, and any parts of them which still protruded above the ground, was carried out or at least completed as the first part of the period III activity on site; but equally possible is that the graveyard to be described next, with a date range of ?1000 to 1140, was in use before the Roman building was finally robbed out in the decades after *c* 1080.

A SAXO-NORMAN GRAVEYARD, *c* 1000–*c* 1100+ (PERIOD III, gpA21–A26)

In period III an extensive graveyard covered the whole excavated site, though burials survived only in some parts (Fig 38). Sixty-one grave-cuts were identified, of which 33 still contained skeletons in varying states of articulation; graves 16 and 39 each contained two skeletons. Where sufficient remained to judge, the skeleton was invariably supine and fully extended with head to the west. Arms were outstretched beside the trunk, with hands beside or tucked below the pelvis. Most of the graves were oriented close to true east–west, but a few were skewed round close to east-south-east/west-north-west. Some of the graves were lined with cists of stone and tile, and others lined with crushed chalk or charcoal.

The graveyard was divided by later masonry intrusions into five discrete areas. These were termed areas A–E in the archive report, and A and C were contiguous. The burials were recorded in areas A, C and D (Fig 38). As there was considerable variation between the areas in terms of spatial configuration of the burials, the burials will be discussed by area. Details of the burials, including the age and stature of individual skeletons, are given in Table 4. Further discussion of this cemetery in the context of the development of the whole priory can be found in Chapter 5.2 and 5.4. The specialist appendix in Chapter 8.8 discusses pathology and other aspects of the skeletons.

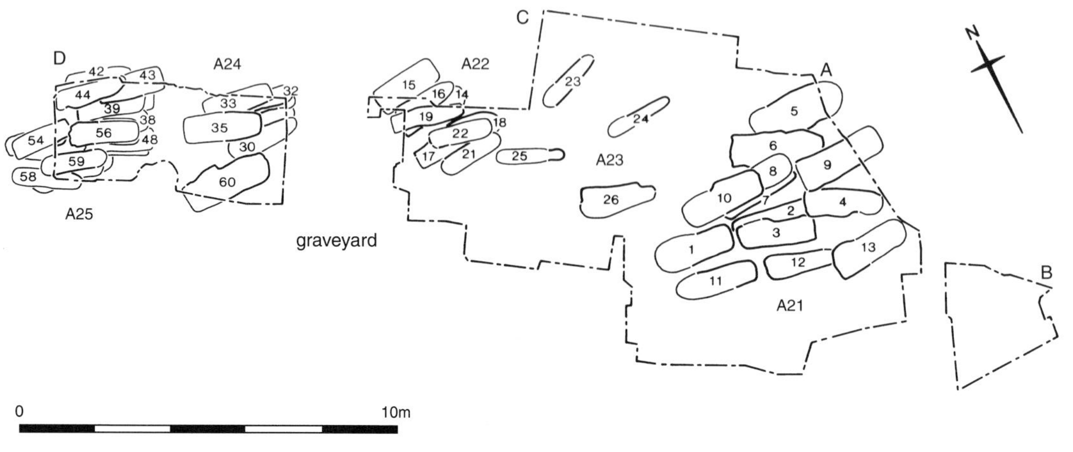

Fig 38 Plan of Saxo-Norman graveyard on site A (period III, gpA21–A25) (scale 1:200)

Table 4 Graves on site A, periods III–V, groups A21, A22, A23, A24, A25, A26, A29 and A35 (groups A21–A26 form the main period III Saxo-Norman graveyard; groups A29 and A35 are probably later and are reported separately in the text)

Grave no.	Context no. of skeleton	Sex	Age (yrs)	Stature (m)	Comments
Period III					
Area A, group A21					
1	-				no skeleton; cist wall of ragstone and tile, floor covered with thin layer of mortar
2	-				no skeleton; cist wall of ragstone, Reigate stone and tile, floor covered with crushed chalk
3	A[833]	f	33–35	1.54	cist wall of Reigate stone and tile, layer of crushed sandstone and chalk on floor
4	A[782]	m	adult		thin spread of charcoal below tibia
5	A[747]	f	18	1.60	cist wall of tile, ragstone and sandstone, chalk and mortar on floor
6	A[677]	m	adult 23+	1.75	cist wall of tile, ragstone and sandstone, head set between two blocks of Reigate stone (Fig 39)
7	-				no skeleton; sides lined with crushed chalk
8	A[685]	m	24–25	1.75	floor and sides lined with crushed chalk
9	A[609]	m	24	1.69	cist wall of tile, ragstone and chalk, wall and floor lined with mortar, two blocks of rag pillowing head, chicken bone between teeth and silver cross A<60> on shoulder (Fig 40)
10	-				no skeleton but fill contained disturbed bones
11	A[674]	m	30–35	1.83	cist of tile, chalk, ragstone and fragments of *opus signinum*
12	-				no skeleton, no lining; interpreted as a grave because of shape and dimensions
13	-				no skeleton; as grave 2, depth of 0.89m as opposed to general depth within range 0.22–0.4m
Area C, group A22					
14	A[1065]	m	24	1.69	floor and side lined with thin (5mm) layer of 'charcoal', probably a coffin; cover also traced
15	-				no lining, no skeleton but skull in fill
16	A[774]	m	adult 17+	1.69	floor lined with 2mm thick layer of purple silt; two skeletons, one on top of the other
	A[766]	m	25–29	1.64	
17	A[1163]	-	6–8		child, skeleton sealed with charcoal; probable coffin with nails
18	-				floor lined with crushed chalk, skull in fill
19	A[655]	m	adult 18+	1.73	floor lined with mortar, sealed with purple-brown sandy silt
20	A[613]	m	adult 18+	1.69	floor covered with dark purple silt, four nails along north edge and three along south
21	-				no skeleton; no lining
22	-				no skeleton, lining (12mm thick) of crushed chalk
Area C, group A23					
23	A[899]	m	20–24	1.63	floor and vertical sides lined with thin layer of 'charcoal', probably traces of a coffin
24	A[658]				heavily truncated, only 50mm deep
25	-				no skeleton, bottom lined with crushed chalk
26	A[611]	m			floor lined with mortar and crushed chalk
Area D, group A24					
27	A[617]	m	16–18	1.80	sides lined with grey-brown clay; traces of possible coffin
28	-				no skeleton, no lining
29	A[539]	f	18	1.64	sides lined with mid-brown clay
30	A[497]	m	25–34	1.69	sides lined with dark brown clay with lens of charcoal on surface
31	A[481]	m	18–23	1.81	sides lined with dark brown clay with flecks of charcoal on surface, lower legs of skeleton detached at knee, apparently at interment, and replaced beside femurs
32	-				no skeleton, sides and floor lined with dark brown clay; possible trace of coffin in base
33	-				no skeleton, side lined with dark brown clay
34	A[415]	f	17–23	1.59	sides lined with dark brown clay
35	-				no skeleton but cist; ? wooden box (Fig 42)
Area D, group A25					
36	A[898]	m	25–35	1.67	skull supported in grave by small piece of tile
37	-				no skeleton, no lining
38	-				no skeleton, no lining
39	A[760]	f	40–50	1.69	two skeletons directly on top of each other, probably buried at the same time; upper one possibly
	A[761]	f	19–25	1.76	decomposed before burial; lower skeleton had head supported with a small piece of ragstone on each side (Fig 43)
40	-				no skeleton, floor lined with mortar mixed with silt
41	A[366]				cist wall of ragstone and tile
42	A[841]				no lining
43	-				no skeleton, cist wall of ragstone and tile
44	-				no skeleton, cist wall of ragstone and tile in sandy yellow mortar
45	A[205]				no lining
46	-				no skeleton, no lining
47	-				no skeleton, no lining
48	A[1010]				skull and part of skeleton only
49	A[976]	m	adult 18+	1.62	
50	A[469]	m	adult 18+	1.85	

Table 4 (cont)

Grave no.	Context no. of skeleton	Sex	Age (yrs)	Stature (m)	Comments
51	-				no skeleton, no lining
52	A[441]				no lining
53	-				no skeleton, no lining
54	A[454]				no lining
55	A[410]				skeleton heavily truncated, cist wall of chalk and tile, floor of crushed chalk
56	-				no skeleton, cist wall of ragstone tile and chalk, floor of crushed chalk; apparently an emptied grave
57	A[500]	m	adult 18+	1.83	cist wall of tile and ragstone, top and sides of wall and floor lined with crushed chalk mixed with mortar; depth of cut 0.82m; floor of creamy-buff mortar
58	-				no skeleton, no lining
59	-				no skeleton, no lining
60	A[1068]				possible traces of coffin; grave is deep at 1.05m; perhaps part of group A24
Area A, group A26					
61	-				no skeleton; floor and sides lined with crushed chalk (seen in north-facing section)
Periods III–V					
Area A, group ?A21					
62	A[563]	f	35–45	1.67	floor lined with crushed chalk
Period V					
Area A, group A29					
63	A[492]	f	50–60	1.60	cist wall of chalk, tile, sandstone, Reigate stone and slate (Fig 56)
64	A[504]	m	41–50	1.79	unlined
Periods III–V					
Area D, group A35					
65	A[193]	-			cist of ragstone, tile, chalk and Reigate stone, charcoal on floor and part of north face; sealing the primary
	A[189]	-	10–12	1.54–1.60	extended burial A[193] (unsexed due to survival of legs only) was a thin layer of brown silt, sealed in turn by another layer of charcoal which ran up the south face of the cut and included a row of four nails; on this was the skeleton of a 10- to 12-year-old juvenile A[189] (Fig 57)
66	A[157]				sealed grave 65
67	-				no skeleton; grave lined with charcoal

Area A

Area A (Fig 38) contained 13 graves (gpA21), with seven skeletons surviving (Table 4). The cist for grave 6 (Fig 39) had a layer of broken Roman tiles around its top, probably signifying the top of the grave lining and perhaps the seating for a grave cover (Chapter 5.4).

Grave 9 (Fig 40) is noteworthy in two respects. The skeleton, a male of about 24 years, had a small piece of chicken bone in his mouth and a small silver cross pendant (Fig 41) on his shoulder. Among the crudely lined graves, his was of a better quality, in that the stones of the cist were carefully squared and the standard of finish was higher. The nearest analogy for the pectoral cross is in the grave of a 13th-century bishop in Denmark (Chapter 8.6). Presumably this skeleton was

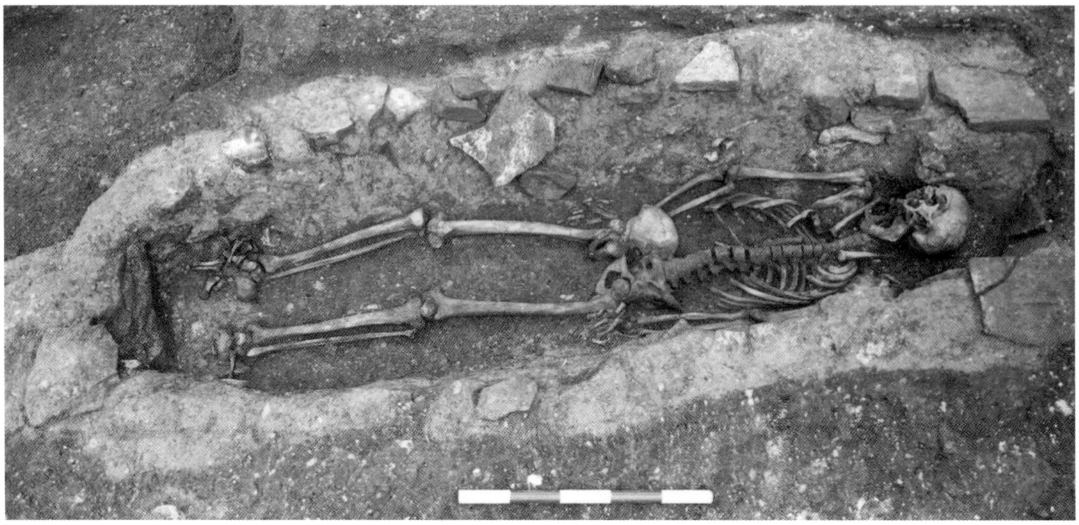

Fig 39 Saxo-Norman graveyard (site A): cist-burial, grave 6, skeleton A[677], from the north (0.5m scale)

Fig 40 Saxo-Norman graveyard (site A): cist-burial, grave 9, skeleton A[609], from the south (0.2m scale)

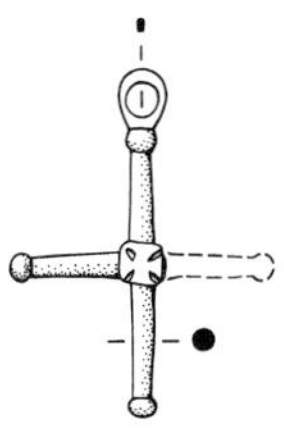

Fig 41 Silver pectoral cross A<60> from grave 9, site A (scale 1:1)

of an important ecclesiastical personage of the 11th or possibly 12th century.

The graves appear to form three north–south rows, with the position of each grave apparently chosen within the context of its predecessors, so that graves were dug either adjacent in their row and end-to-end or directly on top of a previous one, almost obliterating it; in the latter cases the earlier grave was usually empty of bones. The careful placement of these burials suggests that individual graves were marked, possibly by the low mound of earth over the interment or by a headstone. Five layers of clayey silts formed the soil between the graves.

Area C

Area C to the west (Fig 38) was divided into two distinct areas by a later masonry intrusion (12th-century, period IV). The easternmost area (gpA23) was at a minimum distance of 1.0m from the area A (gpA21) burials. There were fewer burials than in area A, with only four graves (Table 4), but there was more activity associated with them, represented by eight layers and three cut features. One of these cuts was 2.6m by at least 1.4m in plan and at least 1.7m deep; it may have been a well, but no lining survived and the fills were undiagnostic. At one interface between fills in the pit was the skeleton of a dog (Chapter 8.7).

Grave 23 probably contained a coffin, which survived as dark traces. This was the earliest recorded coffin (if such it was) on the site.

There were too few graves for any arrangement in rows to be discernible. The paucity of burials may have been due to the entire area having been truncated by a post-Dissolution (period VIII) cellar at 13.50m OD, though all but one of the graves in area A survived to a substantially lower level, and it seems probable that the low burial density was real.

The much smaller western part of area C (gpA22) contained nine graves (Table 4) heavily intercutting and interwoven with 33 loamy layers and ten small pits. The highest stratification in this group lay at 13.40m OD. This must represent a considerable level of graveside activity, though none of the layers had a sufficiently compacted surface to have been trodden for very long. The pits were distributed throughout the sequence, and might represent the removal of headstones. The graves cut each other to provide a sequence of – from earliest to latest – graves 14, 15, 16, 18 and 19, and then 20.

This group of graves is notable in several respects. Grave 14 contained a layer of what was described as 'charcoal', up to 5mm thick, surviving over the bottom and south side of the grave; a similar layer of probably decayed wood was recorded in the top of the grave. This was probably a coffin, but no metal fittings were recorded. Grave 16 contained two skeletons, both male, one on top of the other. The lower burial (skeleton A[774]) may have been in a shroud, a trace of which was detected by the excavator. Grave 17 also contained traces of what may have been the coffin, this time with three nails.

The spatial arrangement of these burials resembles area A (gpA21) in so far as the graves were either discrete in plan or almost completely truncated a predecessor, suggesting that the position of the graves may have been marked. However, no clear arrangement in rows was discernible, although this may be due to the smallness of the area (2.0m x 1.4m).

Area D

Area D (Fig 38) was divided into two separate areas by a 12th-century (period IV) masonry intrusion (the foundations of the west side of the south transept of the priory church). The eastern area (gpA24) was very small (1.8m x 1.2m) but nevertheless contained nine graves (Table 4), interspersed with 11 loamy layers and six cut features. The graves in this group were connected stratigraphically, so that they formed a succession of nine in numerical sequence, from grave 27 (the earliest) to grave 35 (the latest). The top of the strata of this group lay at 13.20m OD; since the first grave in this group (grave 27) was cut from a level of 12.60m OD, this means that the dumps which were interspersed with the graves in this group raised the ground level by about 0.6m.

Grave 35 (Fig 42) was sufficiently unusual to merit detailed description. The primary fills of the cut contained a number of human bone fragments; these were sealed by a cist wall of ragstone and tile, incorporated into which were a human pelvis, mandible, femur and other bones. The internal face of the wall was smoothly rendered with mortar, which was further faced with crushed chalk. The grave survived to a depth of 0.32m. The floor was lined with a layer of crushed chalk and mortar, in the centre of which was a well-defined rectangular (300 x 100mm) layer of wood, badly decayed but still fibrous, overlain by two small pieces of roundwood. In the centre of the wood layer was a square spread of powdered chalk mixed with ash. These organic deposits are interpreted as the remains of a wooden box, apparently burnt. It appeared to be secondary in as much as it was contained within a full-length cut designed for an extended inhumation. The large quantity of bone in the primary fills of the cut was presumably from a previous inhumation, as would be the bones in the cist wall.

Fig 42 Saxo-Norman graveyard (site A): empty cist-grave 35 (with the traces of a ? wooden box removed) (0.1m scale)

The spatial arrangement of the burials in the eastern part of area D (gpA24) was different from the groups so far described. Each burial heavily truncated its predecessor, and no grave was isolated in plan from its neighbours. However, all the skeletons seemed to be truncated at the same places, the neck and ankles, suggesting that the graves were positioned in a constant place on an east–west axis. There may, therefore, have been an arrangement into north–south rows.

Grave 60 (Fig 38) was separate from the other groups, to the south-east of the group A25 burials, having survived truncation by the 12th-century (period IV) masonry by virtue of its great depth, 1.05m. On the floor was a small area of charcoal mixed with clay, beneath a heavily truncated skeleton (A[1068]).

The western part of area D (gpA25) was 2.7m north–south by 2.2m east–west (Fig 38). It contained 25 graves or possible graves (Table 4); eight (37, 38, 46, 47, 51, 53, 58 and 59) were not lined and contained no skeleton, and are interpreted as graves only by virtue of their orientation and shape in plan. Grave 48 was truncated and contained only a skull and part of a shoulder. There were only two cut features interspersed with the graves, and the absence of any horizontal stratification in this area might suggest a very low level of graveside activity. This group of burials, if the less certain grave-cuts are counted, included up to 11 in a single stratigraphic sequence: graves 46 to 56 inclusive, in numerical order. Grave 56 appeared to be intentionally empty. Grave 39 contained two skeletons, both adult females, though one – the upper – was significantly older than the other (Fig 43). The lower individual A[761] had her head supported by a small piece of ragstone on either side. The upper burial A[760], which was missing most of its right side due to later truncation, was turned slightly to the left side.

The burials in the southern part of this area looked very similar in plan to those of group A24 situated 2.0m to the east, with each grave almost obliterating its predecessor. It may be noted that the six graves lined with stone cists were all near the top of the stratigraphic sequence of the graves, showing that the practice was adopted late in the use of this area (though there were also unlined graves high in the sequence).

Grave 61 (gpA26; Fig 38) was seen in the north-facing section at the limit of excavation of area A; it is given a separate stratigraphic group number only because it was separate from the other burials. The floor and sides were lined with crushed chalk, but no skeleton was present.

Dating evidence

The great majority of the pottery from this period is of Roman date (474 of the original 501 pottery spot-date records), with only one small intrusive post-medieval sherd. Late Saxon and early medieval material amounts to 26 sherds (412g, 0.42 EVEs), of which ten sherds are from burials (137g, 0.18 EVEs). The earliest pottery is from area C, grave 23 (gpA23, A[908]), which contained a single sherd of late Saxon shelly ware (LSS,

Fig 43 Saxo-Norman graveyard (site A): grave 39, showing adult female skeleton A[760] lying directly on top of second adult female skeleton A[761], from the south (0.2m scale)

7g), dating to *c* AD 900–*c* 1050. Grave 26 (gpA23, A[602]), which contained the rim of a cooking pot in London-type ware (LOND) and a sherd of early medieval sand- and shell-tempered ware (EMSS, 43g, 0.11 EVEs), dates to after *c* 1000, and possibly to before *c* 1100.

Grave 11 (gpA21, A[624]), and graves 5 and 8 (gpA21, A[697] and A[630]) in area A all contained pottery which was in use between *c* 1050 and *c* 1150. Grave 11 contained a single sherd of EMSS (7g), while the rim of a cooking pot in early Surrey ware (ESUR), and a sherd of yellow-glazed Andenne-type ware (ANDE) pitcher were found in grave 5 (20g, 0.07 EVEs). Grave 8 also contained four sherds (60g, 0.07 EVEs) together with two residual Roman sherds; one is from a pitcher in Stamford-type ware (STAM), two are of early medieval shell-tempered ware (EMSH), while one is from a cooking pot with thumbed rim in ESUR, part of which was also found in dump A[526] (gpA23).

Small amounts of post-Roman pottery were recovered from the dumped deposits in areas A and C (assigned to gpA21, gpA22 and gpA23; 16 sherds, 275g, 0.17 EVEs, of which ten sherds are from gpA23). The earliest sherds are from group A22, which contained two fragments of LOND (A[550] and A[1046]); some disturbance of this area is, however, indicated by the sherd of coarse Surrey-Hampshire border ware (CBW) from A[535]. Groups A21 and A23 contained some late Saxon material (early medieval sandy ware (EMS), LOND), but are dated to after *c* 1050 by sherds of ESUR, one of which is from a vessel also represented in grave 8 (see above). Context A[595] (gpA23) contained a possible sherd of coarse London-type ware (LCOAR), which would date this layer to after *c* 1080. Other fabrics comprise EMSS and Ipswich-/Thetford-type ware (THET) (gpA23, A[635]). A sherd of EMSS was found in the fill of a pit (gpA23, A[649]). It is possible, therefore, that some graves pre-date the foundation of the priory, but equally likely that they contain residual pottery.

The Saxo-Norman graveyard: summary

This was a graveyard measuring at least 19m east–west by 14.6m north–south; in the absence of any structures at this level the graveyard is assumed to be external. Area A (gpA21) to the east and area D (gpA24 and gpA25) to the west represent two areas of dense burials, with area C between being a zone of less density (Fig 38). Area C tended more towards the area A pattern of discrete graves; so if there was a formal separation, such as a fence, between two areas of different density, it would probably have been between areas C and D. There was, however, no evidence for a fence or any other kind of structure. A possible explanation of the varying burial density is that the earliest burials took place in area D, continuing until that area became full, with the graveyard then spreading to the south-east. According to this hypothesis, the adoption of masonry cists late in the area D sequence coincided with the spreading of the graveyard to area A, where the demolition and robbing of the Roman building (period II) provided the structural materials for the cists. An extension of this argument would be that a church associated with the graveyard would be to the north-west of area D. Alternatively, however, it could be that area A was reserved from the outset for high-status burials, with the less prestigious burials consigned to the crowded area D. It is notable that grave 9, the burial with a pectoral cross, lay in area A and might have formed a focus for this part of the cemetery. Grave 9, however, also cut two other graves (4 and 6), so it was not the first in the area.

Many of the burials had been disturbed. Even in the better-organised area A, six out of the 13 graves had no occupant, and elsewhere the skeletons were heavily truncated or disturbed, with little sign of formal reburial of disturbed bones. The stone cist in grave 35 incorporated human bones, and one of the layers of 'graveyard' soil (ie dark grey-black silty soil) in group A22 contained two skulls.

CONSTRUCTION OF THE PRIORY CHURCH SOUTH TRANSEPT AND CHAPEL 1, 12TH CENTURY (PERIOD IV, gpA28, gpA34, gpA37)

The stratification both inside and outside the south transept is described in this and the following two sections, before the detailed history of the standing arch and chapel 2, though the periods of construction overlap. Fig 44 reconstructs the relationship of these parts in plan, and Fig 58 is a photograph showing their relation to each other.

The main surviving features of the combined transept and chapel structure can be divided into foundations, superstructure (walling) and internal features. All the features of the first construction period (which included both transept and chapel) were originally one large stratigraphic group (gpA28), later subdivided into seven subgroups (A28.1–A28.7, some now amalgamated). At foundation level, parts survived in other small areas of excavation, namely areas D, E and a tiny area between areas C and D (Fig 45); these other parts were described as groups A34.1–A34.4 and A37.

A substantial masonry foundation (gpA28.1) in area C, in conjunction with further foundation elements (gpA34.1–A34.3)

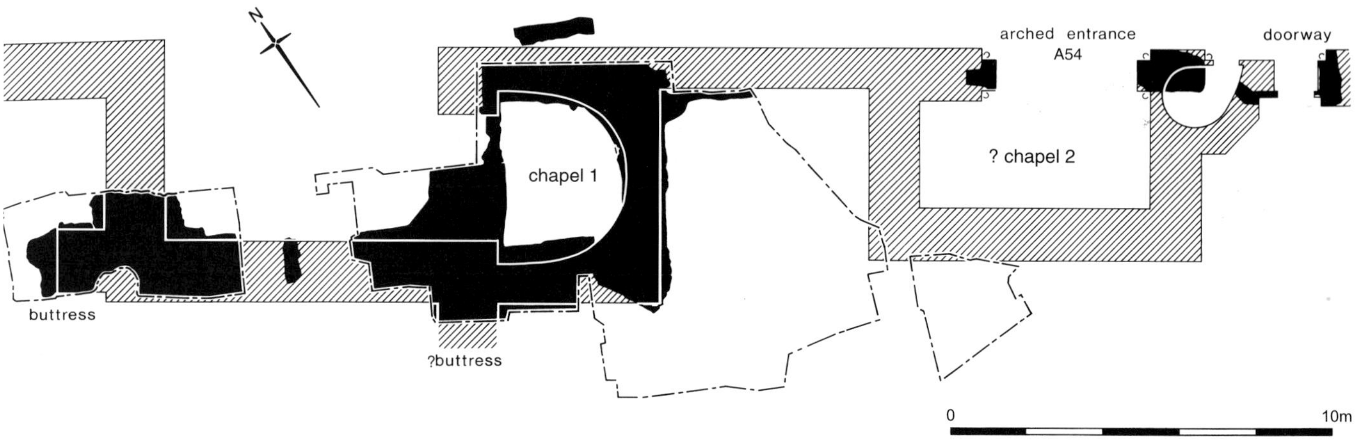

Fig 44 Plan of the priory church south transept and chapels 1 and 2 (site *A*), showing principal features in the 12th century (period *IV*) (scale 1:200)

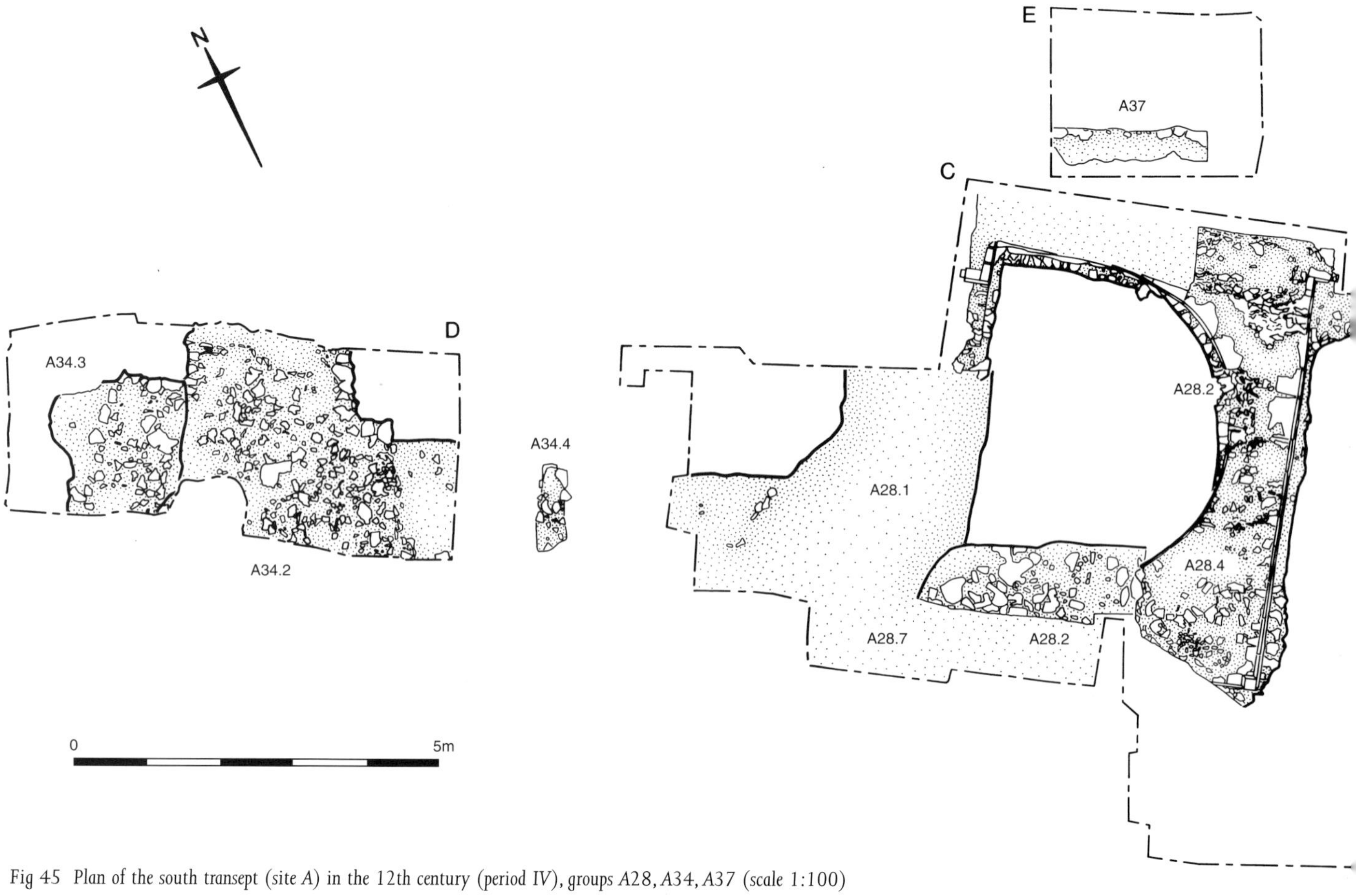

Fig 45 Plan of the south transept (site *A*) in the 12th century (period *IV*), groups *A28*, *A34*, *A37* (scale 1:100)

Fig 46 View of the south transept chapel 1 (site A), from the east (1.0m scale)

in area D to the west, represented the east, west and south walls of the south transept of the priory church (Figs 45–8). The foundation trench was at least 2.21m deep; a layer of large squared blocks of ragstone was sealed by seven rough courses

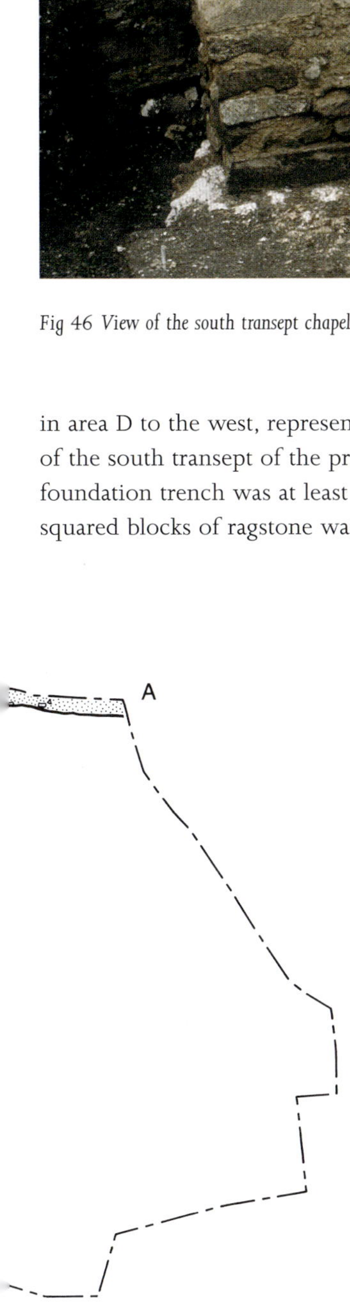

of chalk and ragstone (gpA28.1). In general, ragstone blocks made up less than 10% of the foundation, but in the south-east corner this proportion was significantly higher at 80% and there was also a large fragment of *opus signinum*. Both these measures presumably demonstrate a concern for greater load-bearing strength at the corner. Thin layers of silty trample between the courses suggested that each course was laid individually from within the trench. A similar foundation lay in area D, forming the internal angle of the south-west corner of the transept (gpA34.2). Like the foundation in area C, this also cut through the Saxo-Norman (period III) burials. Between the two parts of the foundation (ie between areas C and D) was a small area of chalk blocks (gpA34.4; Fig 45), surviving between later intrusions, which formed part of a further foundation either of the south wall of the transept or of a wall which crossed it from east to west (discussed further below).

Continuing to the west from the south-east corner of the transept was a further chalk foundation (gpA28.2). This seemed to overlie the transept foundation but again may be a later phase in a single construction project. There were seven courses, mostly of chalk, but with significant proportions of Reigate stone, tile and flint. As with the transept foundation, the bottom course was of ragstone, and the similarity in construction technique with the transept foundation confirms the view that this projection was broadly contemporary. A 2.5m length of linear east–west foundation was excavated but to the east of this

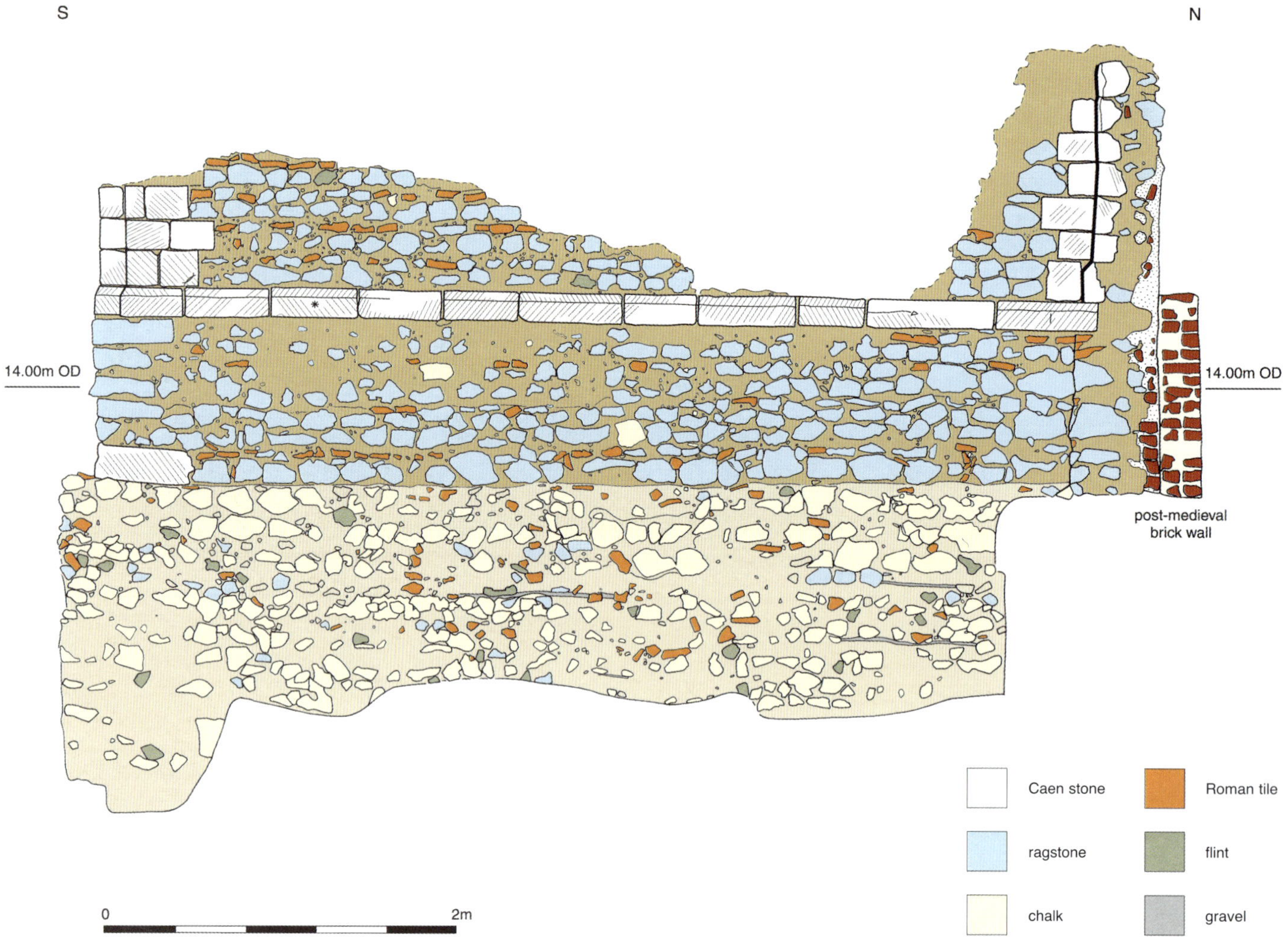

Fig 47 The east elevation of the remains of chapel 1 (site A) (scale 1:40)

the foundation supported the standing superstructure and was not excavated. Nevertheless, it could be seen to consist of chalk blocks in courses 0.18m deep, with the general depth of the foundation being 1.5m but reaching a maximum of 2.0m (Fig 47). The top of the foundation was at a uniform 13.67m OD.

The foundation for the south wall of the south transept was only partly exposed in the excavation, and lay under a later brick wall which formed the limit of excavation on practical grounds. As the plan in Fig 45 shows, the width of the foundation of the south wall is not known; groups A28.1, A28.2 and A28.7 are all probably part of this foundation. The transept was buttressed on the outside of the south-west corner, where there were eight courses of large chalk blocks (gpA34.3; Fig 45) which were probably part of the same building phase. Since this corner also lay partly under the boundary of the excavation site, it is equally possible that this foundation was for a corner feature on both the west and south sides of the transept, such as a stair turret with foundations protruding from both sides of the corner.

At the north end of the east wall of chapel 1, the corner with the south aisle of the presbytery consisted of ashlar quoins above plinth level; here the presbytery wall had a chamfered plinth one stone higher than that of the transept chapel (Fig 49). Nothing of the superstructure of the presbytery wall survived east of the quoins. A linear foundation continued for 2.5m west of the corner, however, and this is interpreted as the south wall of the presbytery (Fig 45). To the north of the north wall of chapel 1, an isolated fragment of chalk foundation of similar character (gpA37) was observed, which implied that the presbytery wall foundation was at least 1.76m wide at this point.

Above this foundation, parts of the superstructure also survived, but only of an apsidal chapel which originally protruded east from the east side of the transept; no walls of the transept itself were recorded. The chapel 1 superstructure (gpA28.4; Fig 46; Fig 47; Fig 50) stood to a further height of 2.5m at the highest point, 16.24m OD. The surviving wall, of randomly coursed undressed ragstone with fragments of Roman tile, contained seven lifts or horizontal divisions, varying from 0.2m to 0.55m in height (observed in section). The mortar was a heavily compacted light buff yellow silt with sand, being finer and smoother than the mortar of the foundation. At approximately 0.8–0.9m above the foundation, and laid through the whole wall, was a chamfered plinth of Caen stone. The Caen blocks were uniformly 0.16m high, and up to 0.74m long. The top of the plinth was at about 14.71m OD. The south-east corner of the chapel was recessed (Fig 50).

Fig 48 *View of the south transept and interior of chapel 1 (site A), from the west (1.0m scale)*

Fig 49 *Detail of the north-east corner of chapel 1 at its junction with the south wall of the presbytery (site A), from the south-east (0.2m scale)*

Fig 50 *Detail of the south-east corner of chapel 1, exterior (site A), from the south-east (0.2m scale)*

The inner face of the wall formed a stilted semicircle in plan, with the stones in the plinth shaped to form the curve of the semicircle (Fig 48). There were two rectangular notches on the internal plinth, the northern one 0.1m and the southern one 0.08m in diameter, both cutting into the angled face of the plinth. It is possible that the notches housed timbers, which could have been part of a bench or other fitting around the curved internal side of the wall, and so they are described here; but they are equally and perhaps more likely to be post-Dissolution intrusions into the fabric, when the lowest part of the chapel was used as a cellar.

The blocks forming the plinth and the ashlar blocks which formed the corners (Figs 49–51) were carefully finished and several retained incised marks. These are probably masons' marks, inscribed on the stones before erection (Alexander 1996). On one of the plinth stones in the east (external) face of the wall was a star (Fig 51, upper); two identical marks were also identified on two ashlar blocks in the south face of the wall between the transept and the chapel, forming its entrance. There was also a further mark on an ashlar block on the east face immediately above the external plinth of the chapel, consisting of two superimposed arcs and resembling compass marks (Fig 51, lower).

In the north wall of the chapel, above plinth level, was a vertical jamb or possibly pilaster of ashlar, 0.25m wide and surviving about 1.5m high (Fig 52; see Fig 48). To east and west of this feature the walling was (and is) a mixture of brick covered with plaster. This was not investigated and remains as part of the surviving fragment. However, a discussion of the jamb and brickwork follows later (below, 4.3), where it is suggested that the blocking is of a doorway from the chapel into the adjacent south aisle of the presbytery.

The north respond of the chapel arch was truncated on its west side, though its length was determined as 0.55m (Fig 53; see Fig 46). The south and east faces were neatly faced in ashlar both above and below the plinth. The ashlar of the south face of this stub implies that it formed the north jamb of an entrance

Fig 51 Detail of tooling and masons' marks immediately above or on external plinth of chapel 1 (site *A*): (upper) star; (lower) compass mark (0.1m scales)

Fig 52 Jamb or pilaster of ashlar on the north side of chapel 1 (site *A*), from the south (0.2m scale)

Fig 53 Detail of the east side of the northern stub of walling forming the north jamb of the entrance to chapel 1 (site A), looking north-west (0.2m scale)

from the south transept into the semicircular chapel to the east; the other jamb did not survive, so that the size of the entrance can only be conjectured. If, as is likely, the arch was symmetrical about the central east–west axis through the chapel, it would have been 3.35m wide. The foundations of the east transept wall continued beneath the entrance, and consideration of the evidence for floor levels hereabouts suggests that there was a single step into the chapel.

Correspondence with the Symonds plans shows that this structure (chapel 1) was a chapel protruding east from the south transept of the priory church (see Fig 55; the full correspondence is shown on Fig 76, after evidence for the south side of the nave on site E has been presented). It should be noted, however, that Symonds depicts a chapel with straight walls, not circular within, and with a stair turret at its south-east corner. No trace of a stair turret was found in excavation of this corner.

To the east of chapel 1 were two dumps of material (gpA28.5, not illustrated) dug out of the foundation trench. One of these contained an articulated fragment of Roman building material: a wall tile attached to which was a wedge of white mortar surmounted by two tegulae roof tiles, capped with an imbrex. The fragment was from the interface between the wall and roof of a Roman building, and showed that the pitch of the roof was about 1 in 3. There was pink painted plaster on the internal face of the wall tile (ie at the top of the internal side of the wall in the original Roman building). This articulated piece may have been robbed, in period II, from the Roman building postulated as having been removed to make way for the graveyard (above, gp A19, gpA27).

Dating evidence

The dating of the first form of the transept and chapel 1, which share the same phase of construction, depends on the type of foundation construction and on parallels for the plan in other large churches. The latest, and only medieval, pottery from group A28.5, part of the first dumping of soil against the east side of the chapel, is a single sherd from a cooking pot in south Hertfordshire-type greyware (SHER) which probably dates to the late 12th or earlier 13th century.

The technique of foundation construction can be broadly dated. A distinction first proposed in 1990 (Schofield et al 1990, 164–7) is followed here between three different techniques for constructing foundations on large stone buildings in the City of London; only the first of the three techniques is employed in this phase. Late Saxon and medieval stone buildings before *c* 1250 in London generally have foundations of layered stone, sometimes with Roman building material, interleaved with gravel. These foundations have no mortar, and in some cases are supported with timber piles. On the Holy Trinity Priory site this technique was used for the south transept (where the stones were both chalk and ragstone) on site A and for the spine-wall of the west claustral range on site F (where only chalk was used). The technique of layered unmortared foundations, sometimes supplemented by piles, is found throughout London and its environs in religious structures in the Saxon and early medieval period, and on secular sites from the 12th century. On religious sites, it is used in the first, probably 11th-century, church of St Nicholas Shambles (Schofield 1997); in the first (?11th-century) church at St Bride's Fleet Street (Grimes 1968, 185); in St Nicholas Acon (Schofield 1994, 123); and in larger conventual churches (eg Bermondsey Abbey, *c* 1082–7: Gem 1990, 50; Steele in prep). Secular analogies include buildings on the waterfront, at Seal House, Upper Thames Street (Building A, early to mid 12th century: Schofield 1975) and New Fresh Wharf, Lower Thames Street (Buildings A–D, mid 12th to early 13th century: Schofield 1977). One of the earliest secular examples is a stone building at Milk Street, excavated in 1977, which is possibly of early 12th-century date (Schofield et al 1990, 164). In the City of London there are no examples independently dated to later than the early 13th century; the duration of the technique is placed on present evidence in the 11th to early 13th centuries, though instances in Saxon churches outside London would suggest that the technique is as old as the 8th century AD (Salzman 1967, 83).

The plan form of an unaisled transept, with one protruding

eastern chapel, is widespread among larger English churches of the late 11th and 12th centuries (for example, the cathedrals of Norwich and Gloucester). However, the plan of chapel 1, with its square outside but apsidal or rounded form within, is less usual. This form is sometimes used to terminate the eastern end of choir or presbytery aisles, east of the main altar, as at Old Sarum I (1075–8: Clapham 1934, 22) and Peterborough (1117 or possibly 1107: Reilly 1997).

On archaeological grounds, therefore, the construction of the transept and chapel 1 can only be placed in the late 11th or 12th centuries. On documentary grounds it should be after 1108, unless this structure is part of the church of Syredus (Chapter 5.2), which is unlikely. So far, no structure recorded in London using ragstone in its lower foundations and with Caen stone details dates to before 1070, though by 1100 Caen stone was much employed in St Paul's Cathedral and at the Tower.

USE OF THE TRANSEPT AND CHAPEL 1, 12TH TO MID 13TH CENTURY (PERIOD V, gpA29–A30, gpA32–A33, gpA35, gpA51)

The period (period V) immediately following the construction of the south transept and chapel 1 (period IV) left traces both outside and inside the transept (see Fig 55). The internal features are considered first.

Evidence for the interior aspect of chapel 1 was not abundant. An area of just over 1.0m^2 of the face of the internal wall above plinth level bore three superimposed layers of plaster (gpA33). The primary render was of a fine-sandy pale buff mortar, whose surface was coloured with black, red and orange paint in a pattern of horizontal strips at the top corner. This primary surface had been pecked to key-in the next layer, a similar mortar faced with a 2mm thick skim of white chalky plaster. This had been painted in patches of orange, red, black and cream, but no pattern was discernible. The surface was smoother and presented a better-quality finish than its predecessor. The third coat, however, was very badly eroded, and indeed may have been only a repair to the second. It was a cream-coloured chalk plaster with three small areas of black paint. Although too little survived to permit any detailed reconstructions, it is clear that the interior of chapel 1 was decorated.

Butting up to the south side of the north jamb of the entrance from the transept into the chapel was a sequence of 16 superimposed surfaces (gpA32; see Fig 55), surviving over an area of only 0.7m x 0.3m (Fig 54). Twelve of these were composed of buff or orange mortar, with the general tendency being towards alternating layers of loose make-up and compacted surface. Many of these layers were only 5–10mm thick, and the 16 together only raised the level by 0.33m. The latest surface (A[322]; Fig 54, lower right) included three fragments of glazed tile, one of which is a plain glazed floor tile of probable 'Westminster' type, but otherwise there were no impressions of tiles within the sequence of layers. The lowest surface was at 14.31m OD and the highest at 14.67m OD.

In the south-east corner of area A, and outside the chapel, a grave (grave 62; Fig 55) was cut from the same level as the chapel 1 foundation, its floor lined with crushed chalk. Although it was aligned closer to the chapel foundation than the Saxo-Norman (period III, gpA21) burials (Fig 38), and could, therefore, post-date the chapel construction, it could just as easily belong to the period III graveyard, which was immediately below stratigraphically. Grave 62 and its skeleton A[563] (Table 4) are added to the relevant tables as being from 'group ?A21', but have been kept separate in the analysis.

Post-dating the construction spreads (gpA28.5) to the east of chapel 1 was an extensive dump of clayey silt (gpA29; Fig 55). It sealed grave 62 and covered the whole of area A to a depth of 0.2m, raising the ground level to 13.90m OD. The top of this material was not sufficiently even or compacted to suggest that it had been used as a surface, but two graves (grave 63 (Fig 56) and grave 64, gpA29) were cut into it (Table 4; Fig 55).

Both the graves contained extended inhumations, the head to the west, and were aligned close to the north-west to south-east alignment of the period IV masonry. The materials used in the cist-grave 63, including chalk but no ragstone, reflect the adoption of chalk in the foundations of the period IV masonry, rather than the Roman-derived building materials of the period III graveyard. Pottery from grave 64 includes a sherd dated to after 1200 (see below, 'Dating evidence'). Also cut from this level in area A were three pits with non-diagnostic fills.

Further east, in the western side of area B, was a deep (at least 0.78m) cut (gpA51; Fig 55), the latest fill of which contained frequent fragments of human bone. Cutting this was a smaller rectangular cut whose long axis was parallel to graves 63 and 64, and whose fill contained three human skulls, two long bones and many disarticulated small bones.

The activity in area A immediately east of chapel 1 was sealed by a further sequence of four deposits of clayey silt or silty clay (gpA30), which raised the ground level here to 14.30m OD. Although the dumps were not compacted, the presence of four cuts (including a possible posthole) shows some level of activity.

Three burials in area D were grouped together (gpA35; Fig 55) in the archive report (Table 4). These lay immediately west of the south transept. The cist-grave 65, which proved to contain two burials (Fig 57), abutted the masonry of the west wall of the transept, and was interpreted by the excavator as cutting the latter. However, the grave alignment was that of the Saxo-Norman (period III) graveyard, and it could be that the foundation respected the pre-existing grave. Grave 66 was defined as a later and narrower cut within the area of grave 65. Grave 67 was within the area or outline of the transept, but the alignments of grave and transept differed by 30°, and it seems possible that this burial also belongs to the period III graveyard which preceded the transept. It survived only as a grave-cut lined with charcoal, with no skeleton present.

Dating evidence

As in period IV, most of the pottery from this period is Roman (43 of the 63 original spot-date records). The medieval pottery amounts to *c* 27 sherds (*c* 400g, 0.25 EVEs), of which eight sherds were found in grave 64 (48g, A[484], gpA29). These comprise 12th-century cooking pots (early medieval chalk-tempered ware (EMCH), coarse London-type ware (LCOAR), coarse London-type ware with shell inclusions (LCOAR SHEL) and shelly-sandy ware (SSW)) and a few jug sherds in LCOAR (including the strap handle of an early-style jug), and slipped Earlswood-type ware (EARL); the latter dates to after 1200. The nine sherds (160g, 0.25 EVEs) from the dumped deposits outside the chapel (gpA30 A[437], gpA29 A[488]) are probably residual; they comprise cooking pots in late Saxon shell-tempered ware (LSS), early medieval shell-tempered ware (EMSH), early medieval chalk-tempered ware (EMCH), early Surrey ware (ESUR) and LCOAR SHEL, and part of a bowl in early medieval sand- and shell-tempered ware (EMSS) from A[437] (<P2>, Fig 199). Joining sherds of Ipswich-/Thetford-type ware (THET) were found in A[488] and A[629] (gpA29). An overall date for this group would, therefore, be the end of the 12th and beginning of the 13th century.

The eight sherds (102g) from the fill of the possible graves or charnel/reburial pits dug south of the presbytery (gpA51, A[122] and A[133]) include six of late Saxon/early medieval date (LOND, EMSS, St Neots ware (NEOT), Stamford-type ware (STAM)), but also two sherds of Kingston-type ware (KING, one in each context), one of which is from a jug with applied pellets/scales. These indicate a date of after about 1230 for these features. It seems probable, therefore, that the period V activity, following the construction of the chapel in the 12th century and

Fig 54 Details of surfaces in the entrance from the transept into chapel 1 (gpA32, site A), from the south (0.1m scales): upper right – earliest (A[344]); lower left – intermediate (A[325]); lower right – latest (A[322])

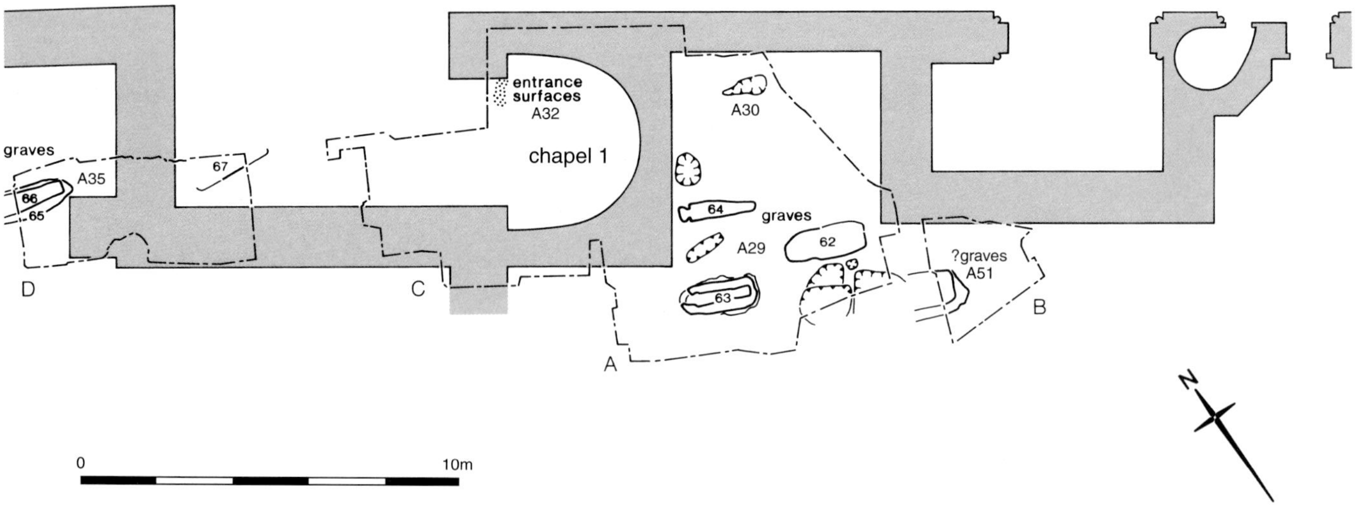

Fig 55 Plan of the south transept and chapel 1 (site A) in the 12th to mid 13th century (period V), and graves (periods III–V), groups A29–A30, A35, A51 (scale 1:200)

Fig 56 13th-century grave 63 (site A) during excavation, from the south-east, showing the relation of the cist to the corner of the transept and chapel 1 (right)

continuing at least until the middle of the 13th century, included burials both east and west of the south transept. Much of the ground within the transept, however, was disturbed by later activity, and no medieval floor levels survived, so it is unclear whether or not burials took place there in period V.

CONSTRUCTION OF THE SOUTH SIDE OF CHAPEL 2, AFTER c 1270–PRE-DISSOLUTION (PERIOD VI, gpA31, gpA36)

About 5.0m to the east of the south transept and its chapel (chapel 1) was the standing medieval arch on site A; the location of the arch in relation to the transept chapel is shown in Fig 58. Archaeological excavation confirmed that this was an arch leading into a rectangular chapel (chapel 2) protruding south from the south aisle of the presbytery. The masonry stratigraphy of the standing arch, however, suggests an earlier arch (Fig 44, gpA54; see below, '71–77 Leadenhall Street, 32–40 Mitre Street, 1984 (LEA84; site A): the standing arch'), presumably leading into a 12th-century chapel. This would also have protruded from the presbytery south aisle; its form is not known, but it has been reconstructed here as rectangular.

The first archaeologically observed part of chapel 2, however, was the foundation of its south-west corner and part of what we consider to be a rebuilding of this chapel (Fig 59). Cutting into the period V silts (gpA30) at the south-east corner of area A and about 5.0m east of the transept was a substantial piece of masonry (gpA31) measuring 1.6m north–south by 1.4m east–west, and at least 2.1m deep (it was not bottomed) (Fig 60). It consisted of at least 15 courses of unworked chalk blocks with 5% each of tile and ragstone, in a creamy-buff mortar; the top of the foundation lay at 14.45m OD. It appeared to have been constructed in two phases (gpA31.1 and gpA31.2), as there was a north–south vertical butt joint within it. The western of the two parts (gpA31.2) was later, and had a face to the north, south and west.

The south-west corner of the later phase (gpA31.2) was surmounted by two masonry courses, of ragstone and Reigate stone, with fair faces to the south and west (the offset is shown in Fig 60, at the top). It incorporated three reused stones: two ashlar and one with a hollow chamfer and roll arch moulding, of the first half of the 12th century, later recut as a plain chamfer (<A69>, Fig 195).

The depth of these foundations shows that they must have borne a considerable load. It is suggested that the earlier phase (gpA31.1) was the south-west corner of a chapel, chapel 2, entered from the presbytery of the priory church by the arch which has remained standing to the present day. The second phase of the foundation, plus its superstructure (gpA31.2), had three fair sides and can only be a buttress, attached at a later

Fig 57 Saxo-Norman or 12th/13th-century grave 65 (site A), showing skeleton of 10- to 12-year-old child A[189] above adult skeleton A[193], from the north (0.2m scale)

Fig 58 Site A: view of the excavation in progress in 1984, from the south-west, showing the transept chapel (chapel 1) in the foreground and the arch into chapel 2 in scaffolding in the background (right). To the left is Mitre Street with, on the other side, Sir John Cass Primary School (1908) (site B in this report)

date. It is also possible that both these phases belonged within a single period of construction rather than being separated by a long expanse of time.

Immediately to the south-east of the group A31 masonry, in the north-west corner of area B, was another chalk foundation (gpA36.1), truncated at 13.30m OD, and with no superstructural elements surviving (Fig 59). It was located directly to the north of the group A51 (period V) pits and must post-date them, as the latter were cut from 12.23m OD and the chalk foundation must have been cut from above 13.30m OD. Sides were observed to the east and south, so the masonry is best interpreted as another buttress at least 1.3m long and 0.8–1.4m wide, and projecting south from the south-west corner of chapel 2. This could have been contemporary with either phase of the group A31 masonry nearby, and could, therefore, have been part of the original period VI south wall of chapel 2 or a later buttress.

To the east of the group A36.1 masonry, the southern edge of an east–west oriented chalk foundation (gpA36.2) was observed (Fig 59). This was probably the foundation of part of the south wall of the chapel.

Dating evidence

All the pottery from this period is from group A31. Again, most is Roman (26 out of 32 original spot-date records) but six sherds of medieval pottery were also found (35g), of which three are residual (early medieval sand- and shell-tempered ware (EMSS) and early Surrey ware (ESUR), from A[434] and A[489] respectively). Contemporary material comprises three jug sherds, two of Kingston-type ware (KING, A[429] and A[434]) and one of Mill Green ware (MG, A[438]); the latter indicates a date of after 1270 for the backfilling of the group A31 cut. This date would apply to the chapel 2 masonry whether the fills pre-dated the chapel or were construction backfills. The excavated evidence, therefore, suggests construction in the period after *c* 1270; the 14th century is the proposed construction date of the surviving arch into the chapel (gpA55, below). The masonry of the standing arch, however, suggests an earlier arch, presumably leading into a 12th-century chapel. It is possible that the moulded stone <A69> (Fig 195), of the first half of the 12th century and reused in the foundation of the south-east corner and its buttresses which formed part of the rebuilding after 1270, was from the original chapel (Chapter 8.2). Perhaps the rib

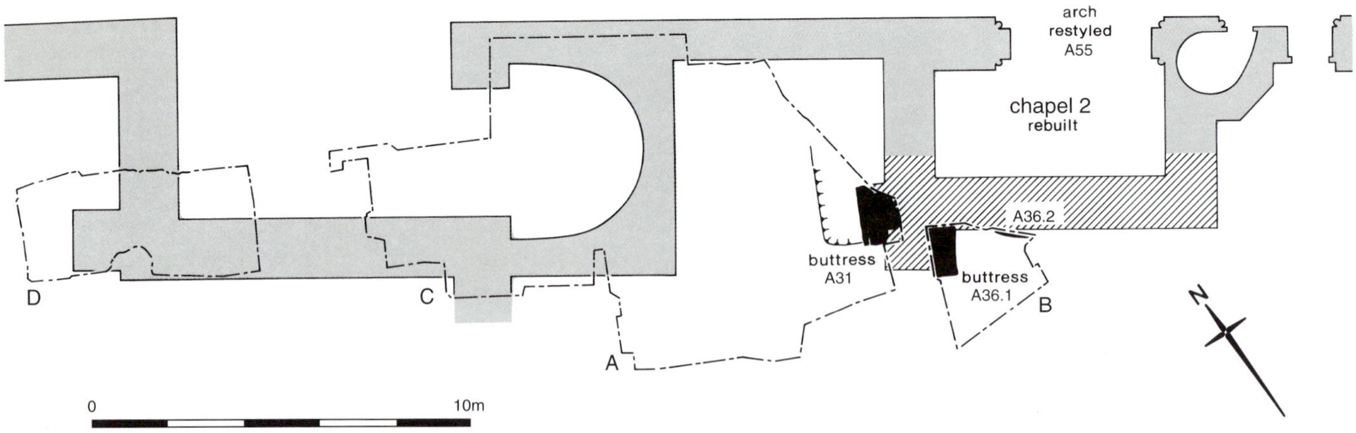

Fig 59 Plan of the rebuilding of chapel 2 (site A), groups A31, A36.1–A36.2, A55 (scale 1:200)

Fig 60 Detail of buttress for the south-west corner of chapel 2 (site A), group A31, looking east (0.5m scale)

Fig 61 View of the standing medieval and later arch on site A in 1984, before recording and conservation work began, from the north (1.0m scale)

indicated by this stone was originally used in the vault of chapel 2, and the vault altered when the existing arch was inserted into the presumed earlier arch between the south aisle and chapel 2.

71–77 Leadenhall Street, 32–40 Mitre Street, 1984 (LEA84; site A): the standing arch

The area of excavation included a standing medieval arch about 3.0m south of Mitre Street and parallel to the present street (Fig 61; see Fig 35, no. 1). By 1984, when recording work began, the arch had already been identified as forming the entrance to a chapel, itself projecting south from the south aisle of the presbytery, as shown in the Symonds plans (Figs 13–16). Six major periods of construction were identified in the masonry and brickwork of the standing arch, of which the first two are medieval. The chapel was called chapel 2, to distinguish it from chapel 1 which had been found projecting from the south transept.

Because of the complexity of the standing structure, the individual context numbers have been retained here for clarity. The structure had two medieval phases: group A54, probably 12th-century (Fig 44; Fig 62), and group A55, of the 14th century (Fig 66). All the dating evidence for the surviving arch is architectural, deriving from analysis of the masonry, and there is no ceramic dating.

CONSTRUCTION OF THE PRESBYTERY SOUTH AISLE AND CHAPEL 2, PROBABLY 12TH CENTURY (PERIOD IV, gpA54)

Except where noted below, the facing stones on both sides of the earliest presbytery wall had been removed. The core of the wall A[79] consisted of unworked or roughly shaped fragments of Reigate stone, rag, flint, chalk and pebbles in mortar (Fig 62, upper). The scar of a diagonal vault rib could be seen on the north side.

Twenty-one courses of ashlar work in Caen stone, including a chamfered plinth, formed the eastern respond of an opening through the south wall of the presbytery, and in the north elevation the ashlar was seen to continue for at least 1.85m to the east of the opening A[16] (Fig 63). The top four surviving courses of the east-facing ashlar bore traces of red paint forming two parallel horizontal lines.

Seventeen courses of similar ashlar work A[39] formed the western respond of the opening. The lowest course bore a mason's mark of intersecting lines (Fig 64) and the upper courses of the west face also bore marks. One of these included a group of four short parallel strokes which may be a construction mark; another was an elongated T-shape on its side, while a third stone bore an asterisk. Above this, the single stone in the topmost course bore a glyph of three intersecting segments of a circle, and a second example of one curved and two straight lines (not illustrated).

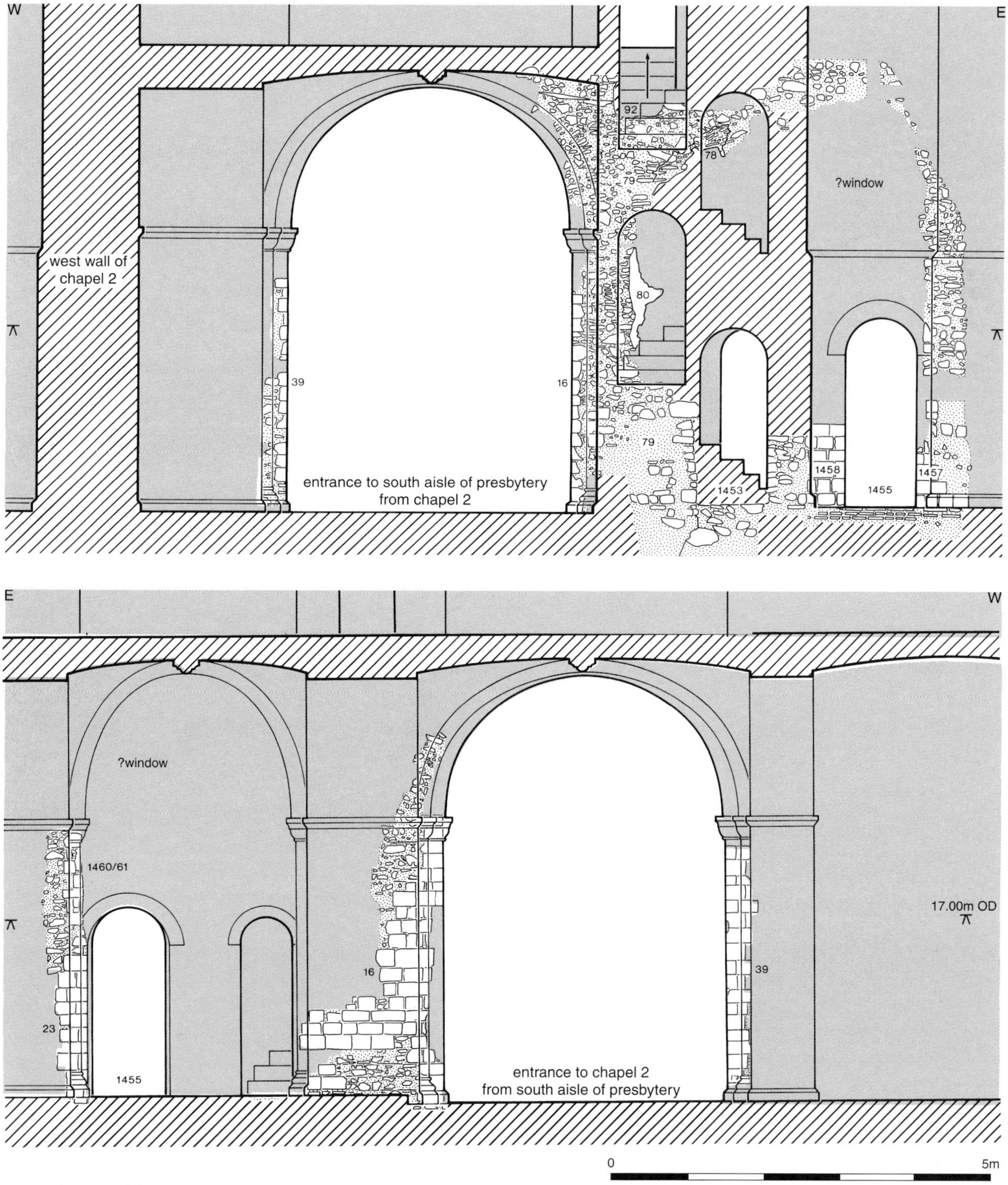

Fig 62 Elevations of the arch on site A, group A54 (original context numbers are shown, eg 39 = A[39]), drawing and interpretation: upper – south elevation; lower – north elevation (scale 1:80)

Fig 63 *Detail of the east jamb of the arch (site A), showing mortar lensing into the core, looking south-east*

Fig 64 *Detail of mason's mark on ashlar of the west jamb A[39] of the arch (site A) (0.1m scale)*

The jambs formed an opening in the wall 3.7m wide. The only evidence for the height or the form of the arch above was a relieving arch within the rubble core of the wall. Evidence for the presence of nook shafts on both sides of the arch was provided by an alternating pattern of broken-off nook shaft stems (Fig 65). The shafts were, therefore, three-quarter round. They were probably cut away after the fire of 1800. The shaft on the north side of the east jamb was recorded partially *in situ* by John Carter in 1790 (Fig 23). The shaft shown in Carter's drawing supported a cushion capital and a moulded diagonal vault rib. Physical evidence for the vault rib survived in the core of the wall as impressions formed in the mortar around the backs of the individual ribs. The surviving facework of the arch showed no signs of weathering, which is consistent with its interpretation as an internal arch opening into a chapel projecting from the south presbytery wall. The base of the ashlar on the north side of the eastern jamb at 14.55m OD, corresponding with the level of the plinth on the south side of the same jamb, establishes the internal floor level within the chapel.

Situated 1.67m east of the eastern respond of the arch, in the south elevation (Fig 62), an opening or doorway 0.95m wide and at least 1.1m high A[1453] ran at an angle through the wall. Above and to the west of the doorway in the south elevation, stones within the rubble core consistently set at angles to the horizontal implied an upward-spiralling tunnel vault A[78] which, taken together with the curving plaster face A[80], indicates the partial survival of a spiral stair. The stair probably linked the ground-floor doorway A[1453] with a second doorway A[92] at first-floor level, presumably into the presbytery gallery. This spiral stair is shown by Symonds (Figs 13–16) and by Thorpe (Fig 17).

One metre to the east of this opening in the south elevation was another doorway A[1455], 0.95m wide and at least 1.1m high. Unlike the opening A[1453], it was flanked by ashlar jambs A[1457] and A[1458]. Its sill was probably at 14.65m OD, providing one suggestion for the level of the floor of the presbytery south aisle inside the door. Weathering around the base indicates that this part of the elevation was external and that the surrounding ground level was at 14.47m OD. Both jambs rested on chamfered plinths. The eastern jamb A[1457] included an ashlar projection to the south of 0.22m, which indicates a buttress at this point.

On the north elevation most of the evidence for both these openings had been removed by later brickwork, but the north face of the eastern doorway survived as ten courses of ashlar 1.85m high (A[23]), suggesting this as a minimum height for the door A[1455]. Furthermore, given the break in the coursing at this point A[1460/61] and the absence of any evidence for a lintel, the head of the door was probably arched. The pattern of broken-off shaft stems in the facing stones A[23] and A[1460/61] indicates a nook shaft set in a rebate east of the implied door.

The masonry was not directly datable, other than by style and tooling which are consistent with a 12th-century date. No moulded stones were recovered *in situ*, and close dating is therefore not possible. The structures are consistent in alignment with the south presbytery wall, south transept and chapel foundations ascribed to period IV in the main excavation of site A.

The eastern doorway A[1455] with ashlar jambs appears to be an external door opening into the south aisle. The door is not shown on the Symonds ground-floor plan (Fig 13; Fig 14) but it is shown on the drawing by John Thorpe (Fig 17), though without the possible buttress next to it (he does not show any buttresses).

The western doorway appeared in the south face of the surviving masonry as an opening A[1453] associated with the spiral staircase to the west. In the north elevation its western jamb was obscured by ashlar, presumably of a slightly later date (shown to the east of the arch in Fig 62, upper; it is not clear if this affected the door and stair). Symonds shows a spiral stair entered from the south aisle and rising in an octagonal projection in the corner with the east wall of the projecting chapel 2 (Fig 13; Fig 14). It therefore seems likely that there was a doorway through the wall, a little to the east of the surviving ashlar A[16] in the north face.

The masonry of the arch is consistent with the nook shaft, cushion capital and decorated vault rib recorded by John Carter (Fig 22; Fig 23). These details, discussed later (below, 4.3), suggest a date of c 1140. The appearance of the decorated vault rib in the bay immediately north of the arch and chapel 2 signals some special significance attached to this part of the church. Furthermore, given that we know that the corresponding bay in the north aisle was not treated in the same way (below, 4.3), the chapel attached to the south aisle had greater significance than its northern counterpart. The offset aisle window, if primary, indicates that the stair turret was also a primary feature.

The correlation of excavated evidence for the two parts of site A (the excavated trenches and the standing arch) with the plans of John Symonds is shown in Fig 76.

The combined evidence from the fabric and Symonds plans alone is not sufficient to determine whether chapel 2 and, by analogy, its northern counterpart, were originally built as two-storey structures. The excavation revealed that the south-west corner of chapel 2 was buttressed but that the buttress was probably not primary. The need for a buttress may or may not have been due to stresses caused by a second storey. The staircase shown on the Symonds plan immediately east of chapel 2, and confirmed in observation of the standing remains, appears to be original, although the octagonal plan recorded by Symonds is probably a later modification (Fig 13; Fig 14). However, the existence of a staircase need not suggest that the chapel was of two storeys, since it might simply have provided access to the gallery above the south aisle. Symonds's first-floor plan (Fig 15; Fig 16) appears to show thin masonry walls above chapel 2, as opposed to even thinner, presumably timber-framed, walls around the chevet. Although this indicates a two-storey structure in the medieval period, it is not necessarily original to the 12th-century build. In fact, the three-light window in the south wall tends to suggest a later date. The question can, therefore, only be resolved through a consideration of the east end as a whole and its 12th-century context. This is discussed in the section on priory architecture (below, 4.4).

Fig 65 Detail of the east jamb A[16] of the arch (site A), showing alterations, from the north-west

A RESTYLING OF THE ARCH LEADING INTO CHAPEL 2, LATE 13TH OR 14TH CENTURY (PERIOD VI, gpA55)

The core was later cut (A[97]) for the insertion of the surviving arch, a two-centred arch of two orders with hollow chamfers A[18] (Fig 66). It was set on the earlier responds A[16] and A[39] by cutting, sometimes clumsily (cuts A[94]). Some filling of the gap between the new arch and the old took place with mortar and rubble A[82]. Two slots or cuts in each of the responds, A[1466] and A[1467] on the east, and A[1468] and A[1469] on the west (not illustrated), probably supported horizontal timbers across the new arch.

To the east of the arch, in the south elevation, were the remains of a round-headed arch of a window about 1.15m wide and 1.8m tall A[30], bonded in the same mortar as the new arch A[18]. Neither jamb nor sill survived. The Reigate stone voussoirs were not fair-faced, and probably represent the course above the actual window-head, forming a relieving arch.

The masonry was not directly datable. The large hollow chamfers of the new arch suggest a late 13th- or 14th-century date. The window arch A[30] was round-headed but its mortar was similar to that of the new arch. It was part of the window opening rather than a diagnostic face, the stones of which had been robbed. The window is presumably that shown in this

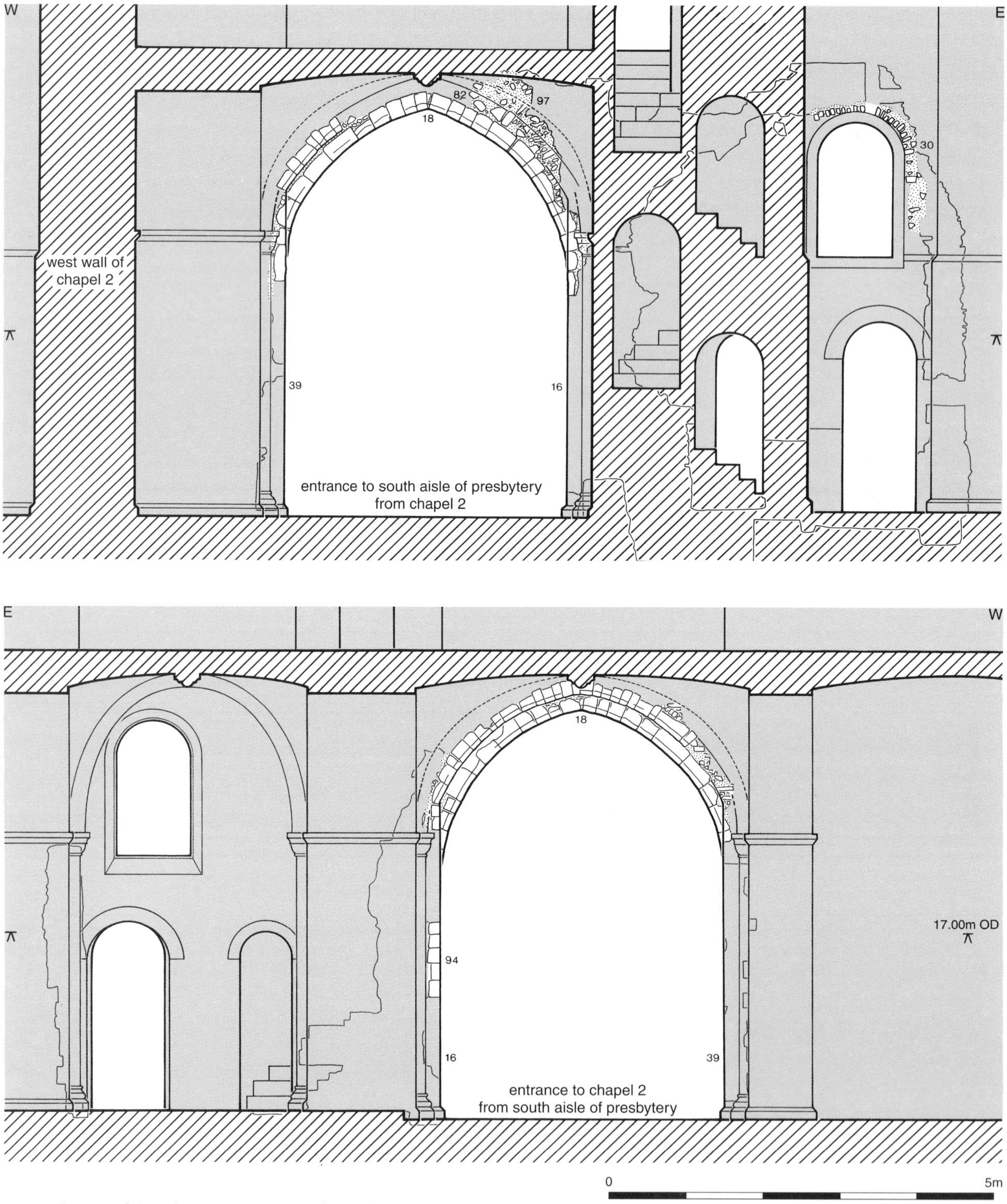

Fig 66 Elevations of the arch on site A, group A55 (original context numbers are shown, eg 39 = A[39]), drawing and interpretation: upper – south elevation; lower – north elevation (scale 1:80)

position, immediately east of the projecting chapel and spiral stair, by Symonds (Fig 13; Fig 14). The arch, a rebuild of the presumed previous 12th-century arch, spanned the entrance into chapel 2 which was recorded in the main site A excavations (see above, 'Construction of the south side of chapel 2, after *c* 1270–pre-Dissolution (period VI, gpA31, gpA36)') and is shown in plan by Symonds.

Excavation showed that buttresses were added to the south-west corner of the chapel sometime after 1270 (gpA31, gpA36.1, gpA36.2). This seems the most appropriate date for a rebuilding of the chapel with a refurbished entrance. The Symonds plans show that at a lower level this chapel had a four-light window in the south wall, and a smaller window (because of the adjacent stair) in the east wall (Fig 13; Fig 14); and, at first-floor level (in *c* 1585), a three-light window higher up in the south wall (Fig 15; Fig 16). These windows may have been contemporary with the alterations to the arch and the addition of the buttresses.

Sir John Cass Primary School extension site, Mitre Street, 1908 (site B)

A note on an excavation here (site B, Fig 2) was published by Norman and Reader (1912, 269). The note, which did not include a site plan, runs as follows.

> The site was that between no. 7 and the synagogue at the corner of Church Passage, extending to Mitre Street on the west. A large space was excavated, much of it being intersected by old walls for the most part of chalk and apparently of medieval construction. These occurred chiefly on the northern portion adjoining Duke Street.
>
> Over the space made earth had accumulated to a depth of 10ft to 17ft [3.05m–5.18m], when the original surface was found to consist of brickearth which ran very irregularly, having many pitlike hollows suggesting that at some early time it had been dug away for brick-making. In some places it was 6ft or 7ft [1.83m–2.14m] deep, while in some of the hollows it had been wholly removed.
>
> A carved stone of the Roman period was found, having three figures in relief, the meaning of which is not yet satisfactorily explained. This is now preserved in the Guildhall Museum. There were also many portions of amphorae and quantities of samian and other pottery. Several carved stones of medieval date were also found, probably they had belonged to the Priory of Holy Trinity. Fragments of later glazed pottery, delft, etc, were plentiful.

A copy of a drawing in the English Heritage (London Division) drawings collection appears to be the unpublished site plan from this excavation (redrawn here as Fig 67). It shows remains of walls, a ditch at the south end of the site, and a midden. On the original, but not reproduced in Fig 67, are drawings of several medieval moulded stones which correspond to photographs annotated by A E Henderson, Architect of the London County Council; the stones are redrawn for the specialist appendix on moulded stones from the priory (Chapter 8.2). The carved Roman stone recovered at the same time (*VCH* 1909, 86, fig 35; Ling 1993) is on display in the Roman gallery of the Museum of London. Though observed in 1908, there is no entry for this site in the current catalogue of Guildhall Museum excavations, which begins with notices of 1907 (Schofield 1998), as there are no archaeological records in the Museum of London except for copies of the photographs published in *Archaeologia* in 1912. The medieval stones appear to

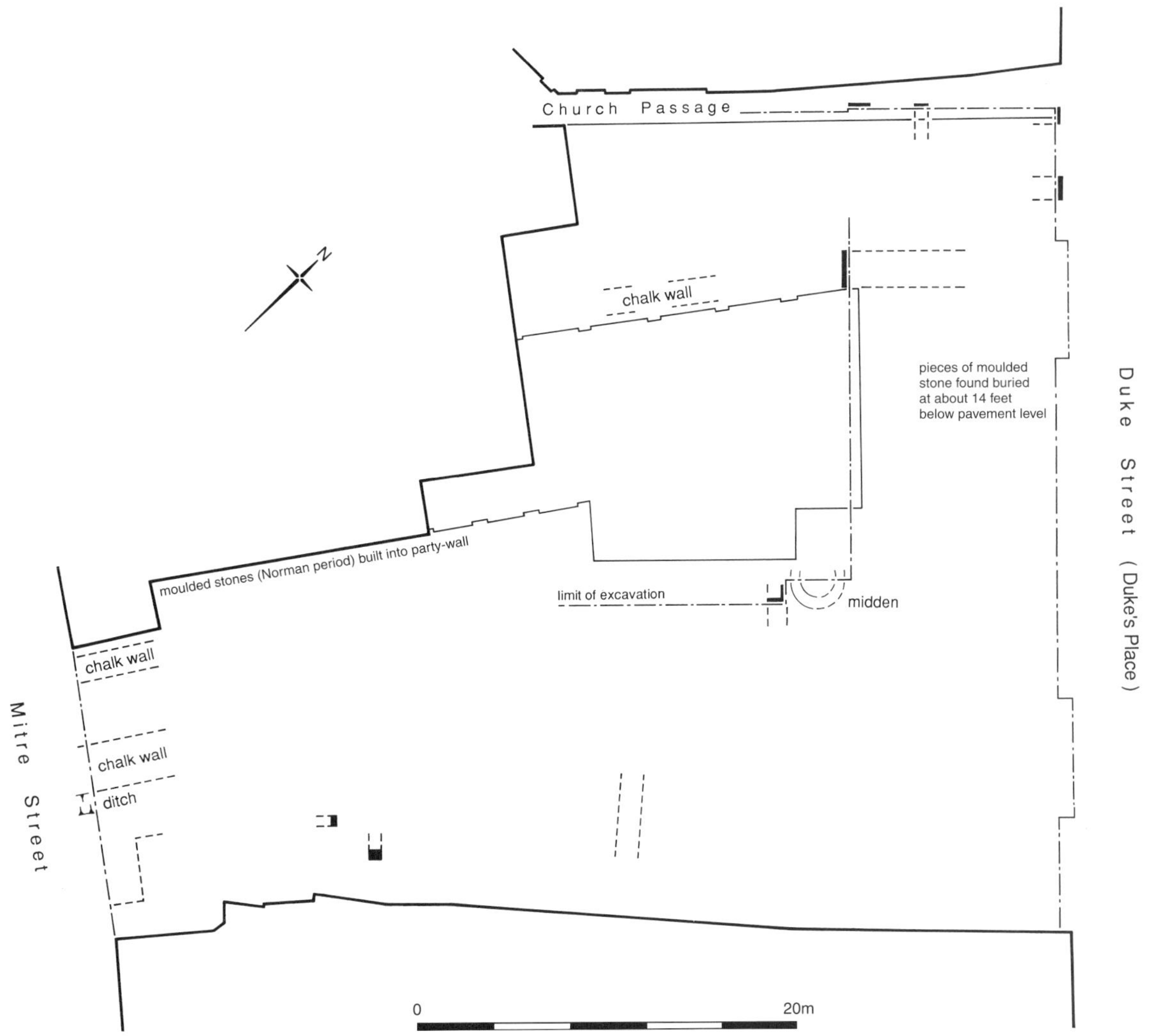

Fig 67 Plan of remains recorded in 1908 beneath Sir John Cass Primary School (site B) (redrawn from RCHME, LCC/GLC Collection, 96/05800 HB/10779/0008) (scale 1:400)

have been retained, but cannot at present be identified if they survive in Museum stores.

20–30 Aldgate, 1972 (CASS72; site C)

Demolition of these buildings took place for road widening in 1966–7, and a proposal to level the remaining area for a playground for the adjoining Sir John Cass Primary School led to an archaeological investigation in 1972 (site C, Fig 2; Chapman and Johnson 1973). Although much relating to the Roman period was found, very few post-Roman features were recorded: just one medieval pit and four post-medieval cesspits. The paucity of medieval pits was attributed to the site's being part of the priory's eastern garden (as shown by Symonds) in the medieval period (ibid, 3, 12).

The earliest post-Roman pit (P4) was subrectangular and 1.2m deep, containing dark brown organic material and sherds (besides Roman) of the late 11th or early 12th century, and including a sherd of glazed Stamford ware (Chapman and Johnson 1973, 40). Though an isolated feature, this pit suggests occupation along the street of Aldgate, immediately inside the gate, at this time.

The medieval pottery from pit P4 on this site was published in the site report (Clark 1973) but the post-medieval pottery from three other pits was not reported on (ibid, 12) and has not been examined for the present volume. The range of medieval wares found in pit P4 suggests that this feature dates to *c* 1100–50. The coarsewares include part of a spouted pitcher in early medieval chalk-tempered ware (EMCH) (<P3>, Fig 199; ibid, fig 19, no. 4), while the one glazed sherd was thought to be of Stamford ware (ibid, 41). A problematic find is a bag of pottery probably from C[140] found in the archaeological archive and marked 'ER1332 (Bastion 6)', but with a label 'CASS72 [140]' inside the bag. C[140] is described in the site archive as 'directly over natural – pre-Flavian', while ER1332 was a layer of green-grey earth over disturbed brickearth. The pottery comprises many small sherds from a small pitcher (not published in the 1973 report). This was probably assumed to be Roman, but the rim form is atypical for the Roman period, and is more in keeping with 'north French' imported wares from the middle Saxon emporium of Lundenwic, although the fabric is rather coarser than those found in the *wic*.

78–79 Leadenhall Street, 1990 (LHN89; site D)

In 1990 the Department of Urban Archaeology (DUA) of the Museum of London excavated a site directly to the south-west of the south transept of the monastic church (site D, Fig 2). Details are taken from the draft archive report (Goode and Jones 1990).

Sealing Roman horizons was a substantial number of burials, resembling the Saxo-Norman (period III) graveyard at site A (which lay contiguously to the north) both in the burial practices used and in the varying density of graves across the site (Fig 68). Twenty-one complete skeletons were recorded,

Fig 68 Plan of burials on site D (after Goode and Jones 1990) (scale 1:200)

including one child, and a further 34 incomplete ones; all were extended and supine with head to the west.

There was, as at the site A graveyard, a variability in burial density across the site. There was a similar distinction between a densely-packed area of heavily intercutting graves to the north-west, and a much sparser distribution on the eastern part of the site. The southern part of the site contained no burials at all, and this is presumed to mark the southern limit of the pre-priory graveyard. It presumably also marks a boundary with 11th- and 12th-century occupation (ie secular buildings) along this part of the north side of Leadenhall Street, but no positive evidence was recorded.

The most common burial practice here was the lining of the grave-cut with crushed chalk. Eighteen graves had a thin covering of this material on the floor, with three of these showing the chalk lining continuing up the sides of the grave-cut. In one example, the chalk was mixed with an equal proportion of ash, though this was spread along the length of the cut.

Ten graves had a floor lined with sandy or lime mortar, which again continued up the side of the cut in three cases. One grave had a brickearth floor. Seven graves were unlined; four of these were in a neat row, and might represent a single episode of less elaborate and presumably lower-status burials.

Four graves were lined with stone cists similar to those seen at site A (cf Table 4), constructed of ragstone, Roman tile, sandstone, chalk and mortar. Four graves contained pillow stones of ragstone, brickearth or mortar, situated either side of the skull, with another grave showing a fragment of hassock stone below the skull. No grave contained spreads of charcoal or other direct evidence for a coffin, although two contained an iron nail which may have derived from a coffin. One skeleton had a pin over the left side of the pelvis which may have come from a shroud. The considerable disturbance of the graves in the crowded north-west corner of the site produced an unusual burial: a skull, presumably from a disturbed skeleton, had been placed at each side of the skull of the primary burial, with a pelvis and other long bones deliberately laid at the other end of the grave. The human bones have been retained and are available for study in the Museum of London's archaeological archive (Chapter 1.3).

A scan of the pottery shows that the bulk of the assemblage is of Roman date, but that a few small sherds of 10th- to 12th-century coarsewares occur in a number of contexts, with larger pieces in D[550] (a large early medieval shell-tempered ware (EMSH) jar), D[958] (mainly early Surrey ware (ESUR)) and D[2030]; glazed wares are very rare but include part of a pitcher with broad applied thumbed strip in north French yellow-glazed ware (NFRY) (cf Vince and Jenner 1991, no. 286). Later medieval sherds are rare but occur in contexts D[960] (Kingston-type ware (KING)) and D[985] (a coarse Surrey-Hampshire border ware (CBW) jar). Individual finds of note include a late Saxon composite antler comb and case (Fig 69) from a pit pre-dating the burials, a coin of Edward the Confessor (1042–66) (Fig 70) and a Saxo-Norman bone skate (Fig 71) (see Chapter 8.6).

Fig 69 Saxon comb D<42> from site D, in its case, closed (length 121mm) (for the comb outside its case, see Fig 206)

Fig 70 Penny or halfpenny of Edward the Confessor (1042–66) D<52> from site D (scale 2:1)

Fig 71 Bone skate D<14> from site D (length 179mm)

For the present report, the precise context of the pottery and these objects has not been researched; future work on the site records and on this part of Leadenhall Street in the late Saxon and Norman periods may bring out their true significance.

Numerous fragments of masonry foundation were recorded, provisionally interpreted as deriving from two buildings. One was in the southern part of the site and was at least 11m long, with its long axis orientated north-east to south-west to within 5° of the period I Roman building alignment at site A. To its north was a building of apparently at least three rooms, on the same alignment as the priory church. However, projection of the walls beyond the north-east site boundary did not line up with the church south transept, which suggests that this building pre-dated the transept. It could be, therefore, that these masonry buildings are late Roman in date.

Virtually all later medieval and post-medieval activity was truncated by a Victorian basement. The site therefore produced nothing of direct relevance to the buildings of the priory, but added to knowledge of the extent of the graveyard before and during the early years of the priory, and provided artefactual evidence for probably secular occupation along the Leadenhall Street frontage in the late Saxon period.

32–34 Mitre Street, 1986 (MIT86; site E)

In the spring of 1986, a narrow trench measuring 15m north-west to south-east by 3.5m north-east to south-west was dug (site E, Fig 2), forming a continuation to the north-west of the area excavated as site A and summarised above ('71–77 Leadenhall Street, 32–40 Mitre Street, 1984 (LEA84; site A): the excavation'). This trench was dug by machine, and archaeological recording was therefore limited to drawing the north-facing section, the other three sides being formed by Victorian basement walls (Rivière 1986b; 1986c).

The archaeological sequence was divided into seven periods, which corresponded closely to the site A periods (Table 2; Fig 72). Because of the watching-brief conditions, collection of finds was very limited, and dating is correspondingly conjectural.

GRAVES, ? LATE SAXON OR EARLY MEDIEVAL (PERIOD III, gpE4)

This activity consisted of a sequence of eight graves, interspersed with six layers of loamy graveyard soil and a large cut feature (Fig 72, primary phase). The burials are described in Table 5 in the same format as for site A; however, the bones were not retrieved for examination, and so their sex and other skeletal details are not known.

It was difficult to assess the density of burials, although there was some intercutting, as might be expected from the proximity to the densely-packed burials of group A25 at site A. The correspondence of levels of the earliest burials in the respective sequences (12.26m OD for grave 1 here, 12.34m OD for grave 46 at site A, gpA25) suggests that this group of burials is a continuation to the north-west of the Saxo-Norman (period III) graveyard at site A. The repetition of the pattern of earlier unlined graves giving way to later cist-burials points towards the same conclusion. The skeletons had been heavily disturbed but all appeared to have been supine with head to the west. The burials were undated, but are presumed to form a continuation of the 11th/12th-century burials immediately to the east, on site A.

On the south side of the trench, a pit 2.5m wide east–west was observed in section, and is shown separately in Fig 72 (period III, secondary phase). It was recorded as cutting the early graveyard soil, but not the nearby burials. At most 0.9m deep, it was filled with silt and clay containing fragments of ragstone, flint and tile (either Roman or medieval). It probably represents the robbing of an unmortared foundation of some kind or a pit for the disposal of building debris.

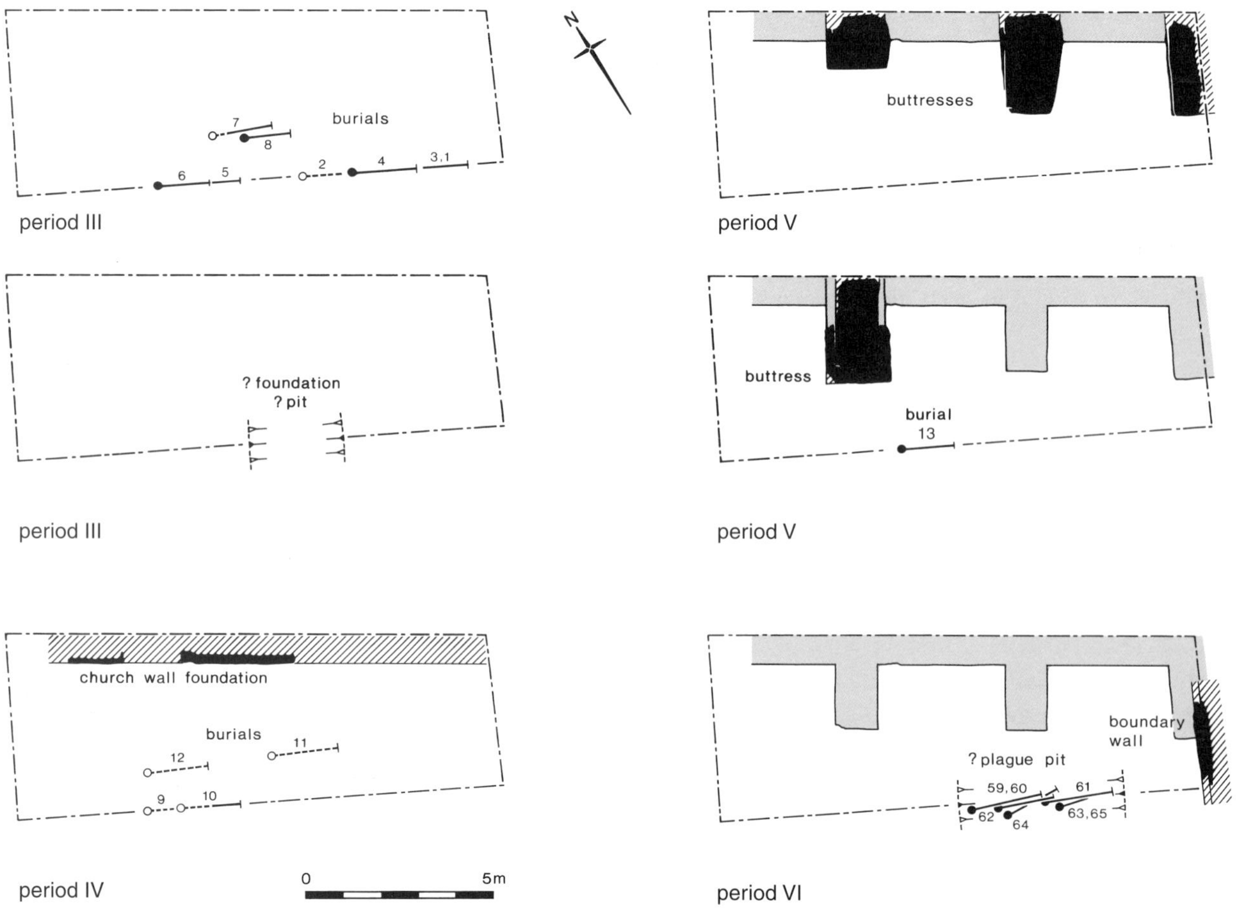

Fig 72 Plans of site E in periods III (two successive phases), IV, V (two successive phases) and VI (scale 1:200)

Table 5 Graves on site E, periods III–V, groups E4, E5 and E7

Grave no.	Context no. of skeleton	Comments
Period III, group E4		
1	E[109]	unlined
2	E[107]	no cut visible, apparently laid on period II horizon
3	E[102]	cist of four courses of ragstone and tile, walls and floor lined with crushed chalk
4	E[56]	non-masonry cist of very hard beige mortar, 'pillow' recess at head end, two drainage holes in floor
5	E[112], E[113]	two heavily disturbed skeletons in unlined cut
6	E[91]	cist of rag and tile, floor and sides lined with crushed chalk
7	E[47]	cist of rag, tile and flint, wall sealed with crushed chalk
8	-	cist of three courses of tile, mortar floor; disturbed bones in fill E[40]
Period IV, group E5		
9	-	cist wall of three courses of two tiles and one brick (180mm x 90mm), presumably Roman; disturbed bones in fill E[83]
10	E[86]	no cut, skeleton badly disturbed
11	-	floor lined with thick layer of sandy clay; disturbed bones in fill E[36]
12	-	floor lined with mortar, left open to silt up and then re-lined with crushed chalk; disturbed bones in fill E[30]
Period V, group E7		
13	E[75]	floor and lower part of sides lined with crushed chalk; extended skeleton sealed with further layer of chalk and second skeleton

FOUNDATION OF SOUTH NAVE WALL OF THE PRIORY CHURCH, ? 12TH OR 13TH CENTURY (PERIOD IV, gpE5)

This period opened with a deep (up to 1.1m) site-wide layer of graveyard soil (interpreted as a dump), which was cut by a further four graves (Table 5; Fig 72).

Also cutting into the graveyard soil were two lengths of chalk foundation (Fig 72). Only the vertical southern sides of these were seen, the remainder being truncated or obscured by later features. They were in alignment on a north-west to south-east axis, and were part of the same wall, whose length was at least 6.0m. The highest point recorded was at 10.40m OD (above was the 19th-century wall forming the south side of Mitre Street), and at least 0.4m height of the south side of the foundation was seen (the bottom could not be recorded). The masonry comprised large chalk blocks up to 0.3m across set randomly within a marginally compacted dark yellow-orange mortar.

Comparison with the Symonds plan (see Fig 76) shows that this foundation was of the south wall of the nave of the priory church. No further dating evidence was recovered.

BUTTRESSES AND FURTHER BURIALS, MEDIEVAL (LATE 12TH CENTURY OR LATER) (PERIOD V, gpE6–E7)

This period also opened with a site-wide horizon of graveyard soil, up to 0.6m deep. Cutting through this were three deep stone foundations (gpE6), interpreted as buttresses (Figs 72–4). These were all rectangular in plan, their long axis north–south, and up to 2.54m long, 1.6m wide and 4.4m deep. The construction level of the foundations was clearly marked by horizontal spreads, at 14.20m OD, of the same mortar used to bond the masonry. Thus, the external ground level at the time of construction, on the south side of the nave, was at about this level.

A wide variety of building materials was used in these foundations: uncoursed fragments of ragstone, reused moulded Reigate stone, chalk, flint, yellow sandstone and slate. The westernmost of the three appeared to have been constructed in two phases, the construction levels separated by some 0.3m depth of dumps of sandy silt with some mortar (gpE7). This two-part construction is shown in separate plans within Fig 72.

Each foundation was surmounted by a fair-faced superstructure of one or two courses surviving, inset by up to 0.3m from the foundation, and standing up to 0.64m high (the highest surviving to 15.14m OD). Several blocks of Caen stone with an ogee moulding formed a plinth for the easternmost of the three buttresses (Fig 74), and the middle buttress had a fragmentary plinth with a similar moulding formed in mortar (Fig 73, foreground). (The stones are not included in Chapter 8.2 as they were not recovered.) The moulding of the plinth stones is unusual in this external context because the quirk in the upper face of the stone retains water. Similar mouldings were used at Lesnes Abbey (Kent) in the crossing and transepts which probably date from *c* 1180 (Clapham 1915, 45, pls IX, XI, XII). Lesnes was founded in 1178 as an Augustinian house by Richard de Lucy (d 1179) who was also a benefactor of Holy Trinity Priory. Although the moulding does not appear to have been used externally at Lesnes, its use suggests that the date for period V here could be as early as the 1180s.

These three structures are interpreted as buttresses supporting the superstructure of the south wall of the nave, which did not survive. The buttresses post-date the foundation of the wall, there being 0.6m of graveyard soil between the two construction levels, and are probably associated with additions to the superstructure of the church. The depth of the buttress foundations, and the use of the more durable ragstone rather than the customary chalk, suggest that a load-bearing strength was required. They were placed at intervals of 4.4m (14ft 6in). On the Symonds plan (Fig 13; Fig 14) the buttresses line up with the piers of the south arcade of the nave, confirming the bay divisions.

Fig 73 General view looking east on site E, showing (foreground) the middle and (rear) the easternmost of the three buttress foundations (period V). Each foundation was surmounted by a layer of squared stone topped with a hollow moulding which was made of stone in the eastern buttress (see also Fig 74) but of mortar in the small fragment surviving on the middle buttress (2.0m scale)

Fig 74 Detail of the easternmost buttress on site E, showing reused coping stones, looking east (0.2m scale)

Cutting through the debris associated with the construction of the buttresses was another grave (gpE7; Table 5). Post-dating the later phase of the westernmost buttress was a further dump of graveyard soil, which raised the ground level by 0.65m to 15.30m OD.

Although some residual Roman pottery was found, no contemporary dating evidence was recovered for this period. It was, however, broadly contemporary with periods V and VI of site A (Table 2). The mouldings, based on the parallel at Lesnes, suggest a date in the late 12th century or later for the addition of the buttresses; but this could equally have been done during the 13th century.

From this site several moulded stones were recovered: a fragment of a 12th-century carved capital <A78> (Fig 75; below, 4.4; Chapter 8.2), a group of fragments from a late medieval glazed window, the head of a small blind traceried arch, possibly part of a piscina and other fragments. The capital and 14 other stones came from a post-medieval wall – evidently a post-Dissolution establishment of the churchyard of St Katherine Cree – overlying the easternmost of the three buttresses. Several blocks forming the plinth for the same buttress were originally a 12th-century string-course or cornice, reused in the buttress by being turned upside down (discussed above).

The suggested correspondence of the archaeological findings on both sites A and E with the Symonds survey is shown on Fig 76. This also shows the north end of the post-medieval east wall of the graveyard of St Katherine Cree, which formed the east end of the narrow site E at the time of excavation, and which lay on top of the easternmost of the three buttress foundations (Fig 73, rear).

<A78>

Fig 75 Capital <A78>, decorated with acanthus leaves and beads, here attributed to the third quarter of the 12th century, from site E (height 190mm)

The cemetery south of the church and the entrance from Leadenhall Street

A number of references already cited can be brought together to complete this part of the survey by giving an outline of the area between the priory church and Leadenhall Street.

Sites D and L lay on the north side of Leadenhall Street (Fig 2); their stratigraphic information did not form part of the post-excavation analysis project for the present study. Site D contained many burials (Fig 68), indicating that the early medieval cemetery of the priory, and possibly that of its predecessor church, extended up to the street. Immediately west of site L was the entrance from the street to the cemetery of the priory; this entrance, by *c* 1585, was at the east end of St Katherine Cree church, and St Katherine's probably originated as a chapel within the cemetery itself. This entrance was for the secular public, and was separate from the main priory gate in Creechurch Lane which led to the main courtyard and the prior's residence.

The entrance may, however, not have been precisely in this position in earlier times. In 1421 the prior and convent came to an agreement about rebuilding a stone wall which had collapsed into the highway. This wall stretched 40ft (12.2m) from the east end of St Katherine's church, enclosing the priory cemetery, to a tenement of the priory (presumably, though not certainly, on the north side of Leadenhall Street); for 20ft of the rebuilding, the wall was to be 4ft 4in (1.32m) wide (*Cartulary*, no. 421; it is not clear from this single reference why the two lengths are different, and one may be an error).

This entrance had a tavern nearby or possibly just inside it by 1349. On 8 January 1349 Walter of Costantyn of Croydon, citizen, and his wife Alice granted to Robert de Felstede, vintner, all their newly built tenement with cellar and new houses built thereupon with a certain *herbarium* (herb garden) adjacent, on the high street of Aldgate in the parish of St Katherine, and in the *atrium* of Holy Trinity. This lay between two other tenements east and west, so presumably had a frontage to Leadenhall Street. But the new building seems to have been back from the street, since the *herbarium* lay on its south side, and measured 16ft 10in by 13ft 1in (5.13 x 3.94m) including its walls. They also granted a small parcel of land only 27in (0.69m) wide with a gate built on it, and steps ascending to the solar in the newly built portion. The gate and steps were on the west side of the new building, 'and on the said street', which must be Leadenhall Street (CLRO, HR 72/201). In 1349 Felstede bequeathed a tavern and two shops here (*Cal Husting Wills*, i, 636).

Within the cemetery there would have been a path up to the south porch of the nave (shown on the Symonds plans, Figs 13–16) at least from the 14th century, which may be the date of the porch. Nearby, against the nave, medieval burials were excavated on site E (see above).

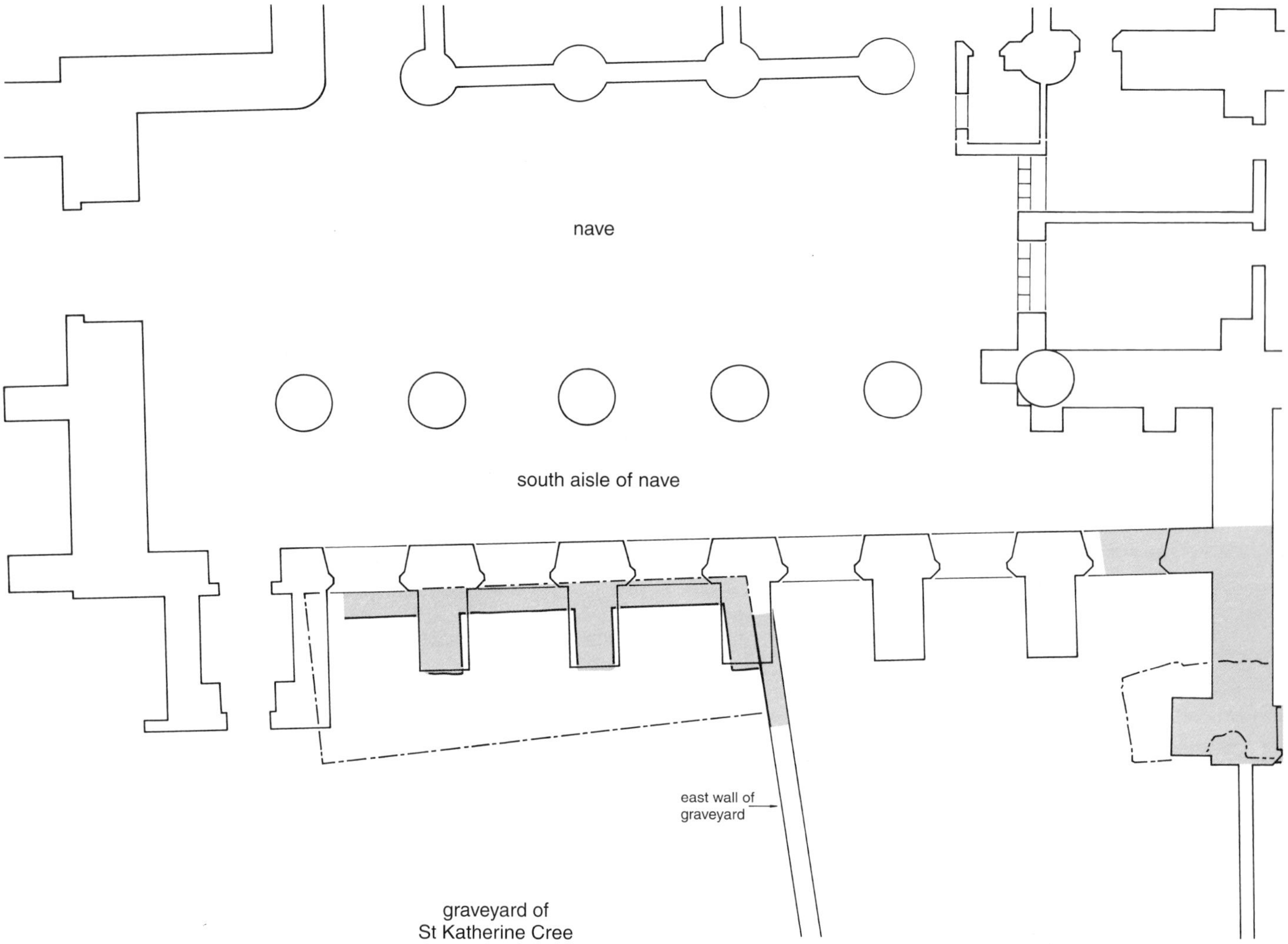

Fig 76 Correlation with the Symonds survey of the archaeological findings on sites A and E (scale 1:200)

4.3 Reconstructing the priory church (east end, transepts and crossing, and nave)

Introduction

This section deals with the reconstruction of the priory church in the 12th to 16th centuries, based on the evidence now recovered for the presbytery, south transept and south side of the nave. Because of the way in which the excavations are reported, discussion of the west end of the church is deferred until after description of site F (below, 4.5); but references to it are incorporated here. The next section (below, 4.4) comprises a commentary on the reconstruction of the east arm of the priory church by Malcolm Thurlby.

The east end of the church

In this report a possible reconstruction of the east end of the church is proposed using a variety of sources, but principally the surviving fabric, archaeological and antiquarian evidence, and the Symonds survey of *c* 1585. The existence of one of the side chapels is confirmed by the survival of the standing arch at the entry to chapel 2. The width of the presbytery and aisles is recorded by Symonds (Figs 13–16) and by Carter (Fig 22). The line of the east gable wall, it is suggested, is given by the line of the thick chalk foundation recorded in the site B excavation (Fig 67) and by Carter's plan.

The position of the east gable wall

The line of the east gable wall is a major structural element in the design and layout of the east end. In this report, it is argued that it stood on the line dividing the bays dubbed B and C by Carter on his plan (Fig 22). This interpretation is corroborated in the plan by the double order of transverse arches between the two bays, which, when compared with the single orders shown to the west, suggest a major structural division on this line. The pier is also in line with the eastern of the two chalk walls recorded in the excavation plan on site B (Fig 67). This wall, presumably a foundation, appears to be *c* 2.5m wide, and is comparable with the foundations of the south aisle and transept recorded in 1984 at site A (Fig 44; Fig 45). A

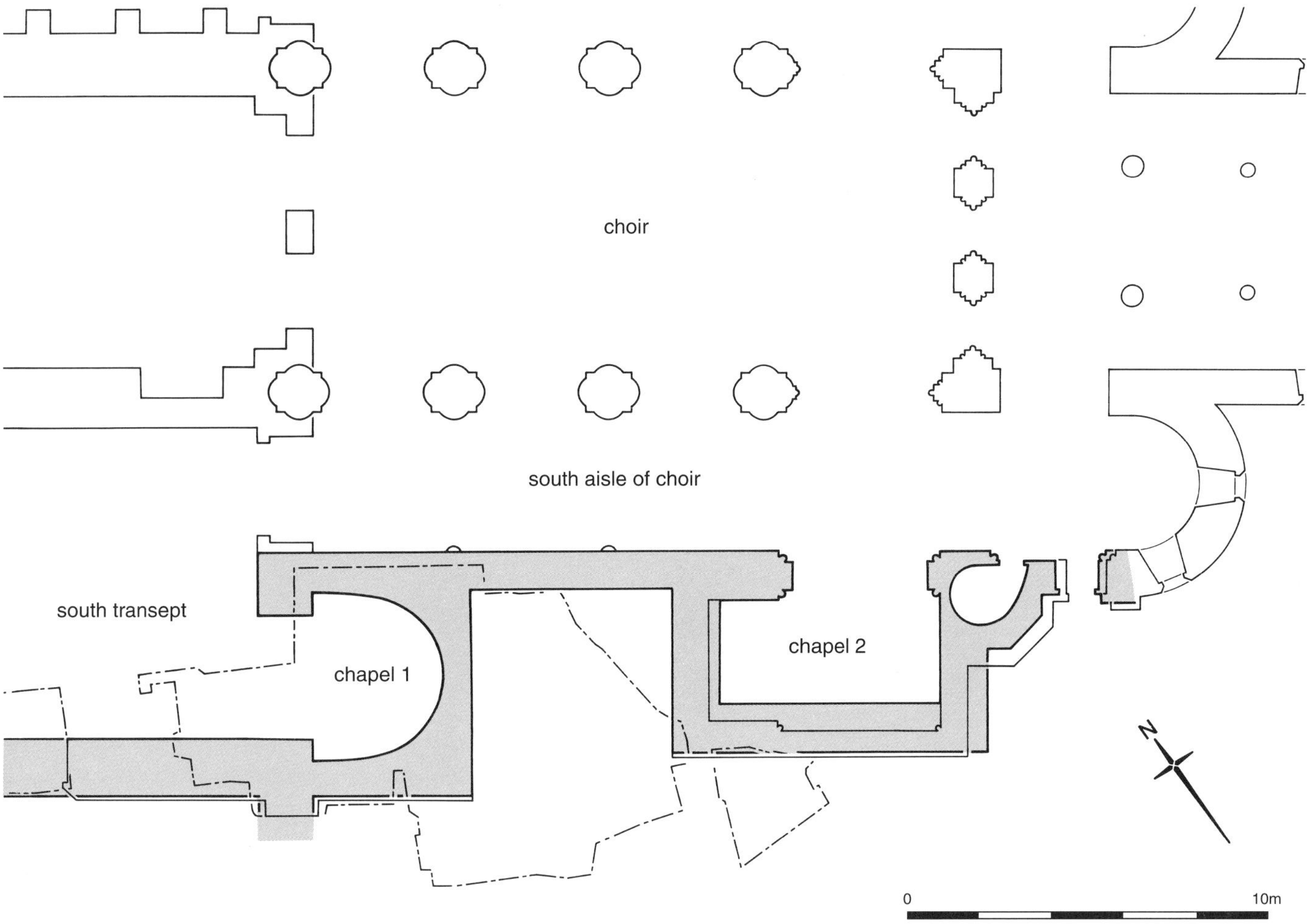

suggestion that the gable wall lay on this line requires a reassessment of Symonds's plans, which show bays of the arcade out of alignment with the rectangular chapels to the north and south. Symonds's skewed arrangement seems most improbable, especially when Carter's plan appears to show a rectilinear layout. The error must lie in Symonds's drawing. That he repeated the error in his first-floor plan is probably due to his use of the ground-floor plan as a basis for his first-floor drawing.

The location of the gable wall on this line implies a main vessel in the east arm of four bays and a rectangular ambulatory of the kind which still survives at Romsey Abbey, Hampshire (see Fig 87). In this layout, the north and south presbytery aisles return east of the gable wall to form a cross aisle from which the terminal chapels open eastwards. The spiral staircases east of the rectangular chapels are in line with the gable wall.

The line of the gable wall is a significant basis for the present interpretation; two further possible alignments have been considered but appear less plausible. The first is that the gable wall stood one bay further to the east, which would result in an east arm of five bays and no ambulatory. This interpretation, illustrated in a previous reconstruction published by the authors in 1980 (Schofield and Dyson 1980, 60; Schofield 1999, fig 32), was suggested by the post-Dissolution conversion of the east end into tenements recorded in the plans by Symonds (Figs 13–16).

Since 1980, however, our understanding of the fabric has benefited from new evidence from two sources: excavation, and the discovery of Carter's plan (Fig 22) (made known to us in 1984 by James Edgar, then of the GLC Historic Buildings Division). The excavation, which included the stripping and recording of the standing arch, the discovery of the south-west corner of chapel 2, the transept and chapel 1, provided more detail for interpretation of the Symonds plans, the 18th-century lease plans and antiquarian evidence. The resulting greater precision has also allowed a better understanding of the Sir John Cass Primary School (site B) excavation plan, which shows a thick foundation crossing the north presbytery aisle on the line of the gable wall (Fig 67).

Neither of the Symonds plans indicates the survival of a substantial wall on the line of a supposed gable wall five bays east of the crossing. Instead, the ground-floor plan shows two round piers which, by analogy with the arcade piers, were probably compound. These two piers are clearly distinguished from those in the arcades by their smaller diameter. This, in turn, suggests that the wall above was of lesser significance than those walls above the principal arcades. At first-floor level, Symonds shows the wall as thin and presumably of post-Dissolution timber-frame construction. If the medieval gable wall had stood on this line, it would have been possible to adapt it in the same way as the walls above the arcades to the north and south, but this was not done.

A second less likely possibility is that the gable wall stood above the rectangular termination of the axial chapel (Symonds's 'Lady chapel'). This implies a main vessel in the east arm of six or possibly seven bays. In this interpretation the small piers shown in the chapel by Symonds would probably date from the post-Dissolution period, although the possibility of a raised area for the altar above a crypt-like structure in a 12th-century church cannot be ruled out entirely. Neither this nor the previous alternative, however, are consistent with the double transverse arch and wide chalk foundation between bays B and C. Further consideration of the plan in the context of ecclesiastical architecture in England from the first half of the 12th century suggests that a rectangular ambulatory, as proposed here, may be the most likely arrangement.

The central eastern chapel

An interpretation of the Symonds plan as including a rectangular ambulatory was in fact first proposed by Clapham (1934, 46). He was, however, sceptical about a 12th-century date for the central projecting octagonal chapel and suggested that it was probably a later extension, no doubt partly due to the presence of two-light windows shown in the plan. Indeed, the fourth prior, Peter (1197–1221), is credited with the building of a chapel dedicated to the Virgin Mary, and the cartulary says that he himself was buried in the middle of the chapel: *et sepultus est in medio capelle beate Marie virginis quam ipse edificavit* (*Cartulary*, appendix no. 16). Symonds clearly identifies the central eastern chapel as the Lady chapel in his plan, but it might not always have been located in this part of the church, nor was it necessarily the only chapel on the site with a dedication to the Virgin.

In some larger churches, the Lady chapel was built on the north side of the presbytery. At Bristol (Gloucestershire), the Augustinian abbey founded in 1140 was enlarged by Abbot David in *c* 1210–20 through the addition of a Lady chapel alongside the north presbytery aisle (Paul 1912; Thurlby 1997c). Bristol is not only similar in date to Prior Peter's work at Holy Trinity Priory, but it also suggests an alternative location for the 13th-century Lady chapel at Holy Trinity. At Bristol, the dedication of this chapel remained even though a second larger Lady chapel was added to the east end by Edmund Knowle from 1298. At Binham Priory (Norfolk), founded in *c* 1091 for Benedictine monks, a Lady chapel on the site of the former north presbytery aisle formed part of the alterations to the east end in the 15th century. At Castle Acre Priory (Norfolk), a Cluniac foundation begun between 1080 and 1100, the north aisle of the presbytery was taken down and replaced by a large Lady chapel in the 15th century (Coad and Coppack 1998, 26). At Leicester Abbey, an Augustinian foundation of 1143, a long chapel running alongside the north presbytery aisle is identified as the Lady chapel, although Pevsner is sceptical about the validity of the plan as it is preserved today (Pevsner 1984, 249). Alternatively, the Lady chapel could be on the south side of the presbytery, though the two examples we cite are from the late 14th century. At Little Dunmow (Essex), an Augustinian priory founded in 1106, the south aisle of the presbytery was rebuilt and widened probably to form a Lady chapel in *c* 1370 (RCHME 1916, 175–9). At Lesnes Abbey (Kent) a Lady chapel built along the south side of the presbytery was apparently under construction in 1371 (Clapham 1915, 45).

At Holy Trinity Priory, the north aisle or chapel shown by Symonds in *c* 1585 (Fig 13; Fig 14) may have been an extension of an original 12th-century apsidal chapel on the north transept, which mirrored that found on the south transept (chapel 1). The Bristol analogy suggests that the reference to Prior Peter's 'building' of the Lady chapel could refer to this extension to the east of the north transept chapel, rather than to a new or rebuilt chapel at the east end of the church. In the present study, we therefore cannot be sure that the Lady chapel shown on the Symonds plan is the one described in the cartulary as having been rebuilt by Prior Peter.

However, we do know from the Symonds and Carter plans that the nave was 24ft (7.32m) wide and that the tripartite division of the eastern chapel must, therefore, have resulted in aisles of less than 8ft (2.44m) in width. The scale of this chapel thus seems more consistent with 12th-century architecture than that of the 13th century. The discussion here and in Chapter 5.4 leads to the conclusion that not only are there sufficient parallels and precedents to suggest that the plan of the east end recorded by Symonds was of 12th-century date, but that it was typical for large churches of the period.

The rectangular ambulatory plan in the context of contemporary architecture

In his analysis of the plans of the major English churches of the late 11th century, Clapham identified two main types which he distinguished on the basis of the treatment of the east ends (Clapham 1934, 18–50). They are characterised as 1) churches with apses without an ambulatory at the east end, which we will call type A (for example, Lanfranc's Canterbury Cathedral in Kent, Lincoln, and St Albans, Hertfordshire), and 2) those with both apse and ambulatory, which we will call type B (as at Battle Abbey (Sussex), St Augustine's at Canterbury, Winchester (Hampshire), Worcester and Gloucester) (Fig 77). He noted little significance in the geographical distribution of the two types. Moving on to the churches of the first half of the 12th century, Clapham noted that although both persisted, type A became less frequent. He also noted an early modification of the type A plan in which the central apse is squared off, which we can call type A1 (as at St Martin's in Dover, Kent).

Clapham then identified a variant of the church with ambulatory (our type B) which he suggested may 'almost be

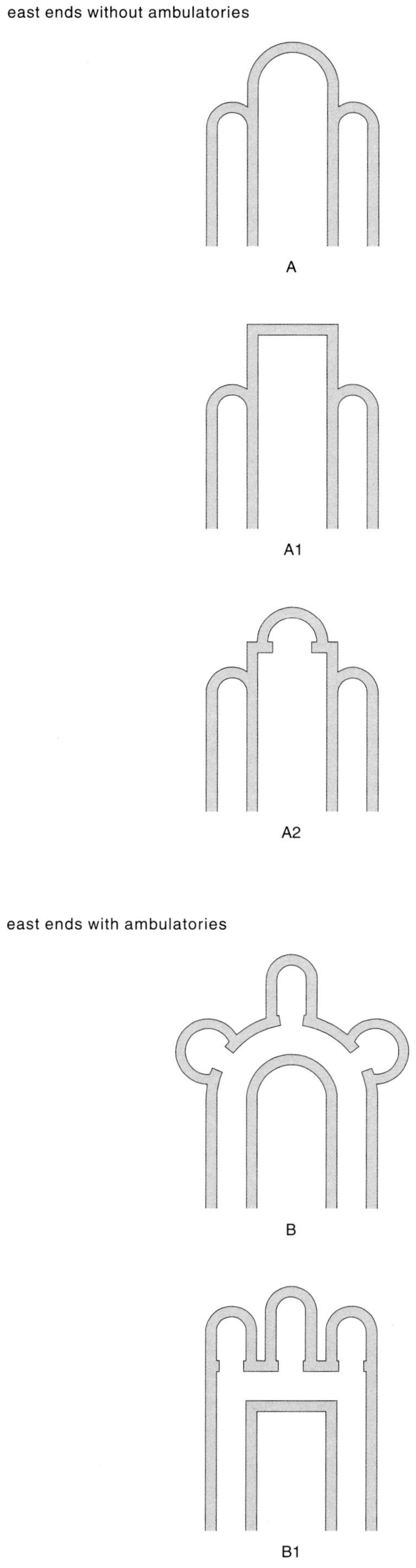

Fig 77 Various possibilities for the original plan of the eastern arm of the priory church, following groupings originally established by A W Clapham (1934)

regarded as a new type', and it is to this group that Holy Trinity Priory most clearly belongs. The type is characterised by a square east end to the main vessel with a rectangular ambulatory carried round it and chapels projecting eastwards. We can call this type B1. The three principal examples cited by Clapham are Chertsey (Surrey), Romsey (Hampshire) and Old Sarum II (Wiltshire). He also suggested an interpretation of Rochester (Kent) which would include it as a member of the group, and so the evidence for Rochester is also briefly summarised here.

From the excavation plan, Chertsey Abbey (Poulton 1988, 32) had a rectangular ambulatory from which opened three discrete apsidal chapels. The line of the gable wall of the main east arm was represented at foundation level, pierced by an opening approximately in line with the central eastern chapel which indicates a link in the architectural spaces formed by the main east vessel and the central eastern chapel. The transepts had apsidal chapels projecting eastwards.

At Romsey Abbey, much of the square east end and ambulatory from the period *c* 1120–*c* 1140/5 survives intact (Hearn 1975). The double central eastern chapel is known from excavation (Scott 1996, 79–84). The east wall of the main vessel was correspondingly divided into two bays. For the reconstruction of the gable wall at Holy Trinity Priory, this suggests that we might expect to see some degree of correspondence between the bay articulation of the eastern chapel and the gable wall.

Old Sarum II, the cathedral extended eastwards by Bishop Roger (1102–39), is known only from excavated foundation evidence, but from this it is clear that the east arm had a rectangular ambulatory and chapels projecting eastwards. The aisle chapels were apsidal within a squared exterior. The form of the central chapel is, however, more open to speculation. Clapham's published plan suggests an apsidal chapel with side aisles, but the Royal Commission on Historical Monuments (England) has since re-examined the excavation records and proposed an alternative interpretation (RCHME 1980, 15–24). The analysis is complicated by a later phase of 12th-century work. According to the RCHME, in the initial phase of the church a two-storey arrangement was constructed with an enclosed chapel below an apse equal in width to the main vessel of the east arm. This raises the question of how this two-storey structure related to the main vessel, but this is not dealt with in the reconstruction. In the later 12th century, according to the RCHME, the upper storey was removed.

In deference to W H St John Hope, Clapham included Rochester as an example of a three-apse type plan but he also proposed an alternative interpretation. The evidence for the treatment of the 12th-century east end was, and still is, very slight. St John Hope had suggested a square east end with a single small projecting rectangular chapel (St John Hope 1898) and this interpretation has been accepted more recently by Hearn (1971, 201) and Gem (1982, 11–12). Clapham, however, could not accept this because he could find no contemporary parallel (Clapham 1934, 45–6). Instead, he suggested a rectangular ambulatory above the 12th-century crypt, that the ambulatory occupied the eastern bays at ground level, and that the gable wall of the main vessel was set one bay back from the east end of the crypt. More recently, it has been argued that the excavation evidence cannot be relied on at all and that a three-apse plan without ambulatory is the most likely arrangement (McAleer 1999).

The following interpretation of Rochester, however, also seems to be possible. If the ambulatory crossed from north to south, one bay further to the west than that suggested by Clapham, then the eastern bays could have been used as chapels. In this arrangement, the gable wall would stand between the second and third bays. It is probably significant that it is this line which now separates the earlier work from the present 13th-century east end. In this interpretation, it would have been possible for the presbytery to remain in full use throughout the construction of the new work.

As mentioned above, Clapham noted that Holy Trinity Priory was probably of the rectangular ambulatory type (our type B1), although he qualified this by suggesting that the semi-octagonal apse shown by Symonds (the 'Lady chapel') was probably a later extension. He then went on to identify a second variant of the type A plan, which we shall call type A2, in which an apse projects from the square end of a type A1 plan, as at Hereford, St John's in Chester, and Llandaff (Glamorgan), all of the period *c* 1110–40. This final type is mentioned here only to complete the description of Clapham's grouping, since we follow his attribution of Holy Trinity Priory to the type B1 subgroup.

Since Clapham's analysis, M F Hearn (1971) has further explored the origins of the rectangular ambulatory of the type proposed for Holy Trinity Priory, type B1. He suggests that this development probably had its origins among 10th- and 11th-century Continental churches with external crypts and that the tradition continued into the 12th century, when Hearn suggests the English examples may have exerted some influence. He argues that the distinction between an external crypt and an ambulatory with chapels can sometimes be blurred and that, although in the majority of cases the crypts have different floor levels from the interior of the church and access between the crypt and main vessel is restricted, in some notable examples the arrangements bear a striking resemblance to the rectangular ambulatory plan, type B1, defined by Clapham. A further point of significance among these examples is that some of the axial spaces are treated as small aisled chapels. This characteristic suggests that the aisled axial chapel recorded by Symonds at Holy Trinity Priory could have been an original feature from the early 12th century. The sites in Hearn's analysis most relevant to Holy Trinity are St-Philibert de Grandlieu (Loire-Atlantique, France), probably dating to AD 836–53, St-Barthélemy, Liège (Belgium), St-Feuillen, Fosses (Belgium), St-Hubert, Andenne (Belgium), all of the 11th century, St-Bavo, Ghent (Belgium) of the 12th century, and St-Etienne, Beauvais (Oise, France), probably of *c* 1125–30.

St-Hubert, Andenne, had an aisled axial chapel in which the central aisle was separated from the side aisles by two-bay arcades which, as at Holy Trinity, featured both major and minor piers. At St-Philibert de Grandlieu, the plan of the external crypt bears a striking resemblance to that of Holy Trinity, with its aisled central chapel between two apsidal aisle chapels. At St-Feuillen, Fosses, the central projecting chapel was octagonal, like that at Holy Trinity. At St-Etienne, Beauvais, the surviving remains suggest a rectangular ambulatory rather than an external crypt; its date is not known with any certainty. Hearn includes it as an example in the group of rectangular ambulatory plans, suggesting that it was influenced by Romsey and consequently assigning it to the period *c* 1125–30.

Since Clapham's study (1934) and Hearn's survey (1971) the list of churches with rectangular ambulatories can now be augmented with some well-proven examples and conjectural reconstruction. The excavated plan of Lewes Priory (Sussex) is interesting in this context (Lyne 1997). At first sight, it appears to present a long east arm with an apse and ambulatory with chevet and side chapels analogous to those at Holy Trinity Priory. However, closer examination shows that the main vessel reduces in width east of the fourth bay to the east of the main crossing. This raises the question of the position of the high altar and the architectural relationship between the four bays east of the main crossing and those parts of the building further to the east. The combination of apsidal ambulatory and radiating chapels strongly suggests that the apse was two or three storeys high. Immediately west of the main apse there is what appears to be an eastern transept. In effect, the plan of the eastern termination is that of an apse with ambulatory and transept crossing built at a reduced scale from the main body of the church. There must have been altars in each of the apses but where was the main altar? If it was located in the fourth bay east of the main crossing, then the plan can be viewed as a variation on the rectangular ambulatory theme, the eastern transept providing a processional route across the church east of the main altar. In this arrangement the apse and chevet can be seen as providing a particularly elaborate central eastern chapel.

The published plan of the excavations at Faversham (Kent) in 1965 (Philp 1968) shows that the Cluniac abbey founded by King Stephen in 1147 can now be added to the rectangular ambulatory group. Chertsey is clearly its closest parallel. The extra-long east end at Faversham was required by the creation of a royal chapel intended, and used, for the burial of Stephen, his son Eustace and his queen Matilda.

Recent excavations at Bermondsey Abbey (Surrey) have led to a reassessment of the form of the east end, and the plan published by Richard Gem (Gem 1990, fig 1) has been shown to be incorrect (Steele in prep). Gem's error is perhaps due to a misreading of a drawing by Buckler of 1797, which records the major dimensions of the church itself (BL, Add MS 24433). An excavation in the area of the northern aisle of the east arm which was published in 1968 (Grimes 1968, 214) supplements Buckler's plan but the correlation between the two sets of evidence is not straightforward. The Buckler drawing clearly records a church with aisles, where the nave was 26ft (7.93m) wide between the centre lines of the arcade and the aisles were 13ft (3.96m) wide between the centre line of the arcade and the inner face of the aisle wall. From these two sets of dimensions the thickness of the arcades must also be subtracted. This clearly contradicts Gem's reconstruction in which the church is shown without aisles. Because the evidence is only in the form of records of foundations, it is not possible to reconstruct the detail of the east end. It seems likely, however, that the plan did include a rectangular ambulatory from which apsidal chapels projected eastwards. The Grimes plan clearly records an apse at the end of the north aisle. Abutting this foundation to the south was a second curving foundation for an apse east of the main vessel. However, the radius of this arc as recorded by Grimes is too tight for a single axial chapel. One possible interpretation of the arrangements east of the main vessel is that the axial chapel was aisled, with a central projecting apse between two shorter apsidal projections. With the chapels at the ends of the aisles, there would have been five apses *en échelon*. A further chapel was attached to the side of the north aisle in line with the ambulatory. From the plan of the foundations it is possible that this chapel, like those attached to the north transept, was apsidal internally and rectangular externally. If this chapel were mirrored on the south side of the church, then the east end would have presented seven chapels *en échelon*. The stylistic connection between Holy Trinity Priory and Bermondsey Abbey is further reinforced by stylistic similarities in the treatment of the scallop capitals.

A reappraisal of the excavated and standing fabric evidence at Lichfield Cathedral, Staffordshire (Rodwell 1989) has resulted in the identification of a distinct phase in the 12th-century alterations which resulted in the creation of a rectangular ambulatory from which projected four rectangular and equal-sized chapels in line. The piers used in this phase of alterations appear to have been the same as those suggested for the eastern arm of Holy Trinity Priory, that is, a compound pier formed by the merging of square and round forms. Again the bipartite division of the gable wall of the main east vessel relates to the plan of the chapels lying to the east. The date suggested by Rodwell for this phase is c 1170–5, but its similarity to Holy Trinity Priory suggests that this date could perhaps be pushed earlier.

On balance, therefore, the present analysis reinforces Clapham's suggestion that the original east end of the presbytery at Holy Trinity Priory contained a rectangular ambulatory east of the high altar, with projecting chapels; we have called this type B1 (Fig 77). It has been argued that the rectangular ambulatory is an English or Saxon variant of the Norman round ambulatory (Prior 1900). The origins of this group probably lie in the development of the outer crypt plan in northern Europe between the 9th and the 11th centuries, but, with the exception of St-Etienne, Beauvais, this group is exclusively English and can now be seen as a substantial tradition in its own right. The churches, apart from St-Etienne, are all located in south-east England and have royal connections. The more recent discoveries we can now add to the group, especially Holy Trinity Priory and Faversham, tend to reinforce this theory. It is not particularly 'Augustinian', but a feature of certain major English churches in the first half of the 12th century. The dates of the comparable churches – Romsey, Chertsey and Faversham – tend to fall within the second quarter of the 12th century. At Holy Trinity, at least some of the eastern arm must have been constructed by the time of the burial of the two royal children shortly before 1147–8.

The arcade piers in the presbytery

By considering the evidence contained within the various antiquarian records of c 1800, and combining this with the surviving fabric evidence from around the standing arch on the south side of the presbytery, it is possible to reconstruct each of the three eastern piers of the north arcade of the presbytery (Fig 78).

The first pier from the east between bays B and C (Fig 78, a) is shown in plan by Carter (Fig 22) and in his more finished drawing to scale (Fig 25). This drawing also includes its blank south face as part of the elevation of the arch spanning bay C. Carter's text accompanying Fig 25 which says 'there are no traces of a correspondent buttress on the right side' signals that there was no evidence for a large drum on the south side of this pier. Details of the west face of the pier at capital level are also drawn at a larger scale. From Carter's sketch-plan this is the largest pier of the three. Its relative size is underlined by the additional transverse arches shown between the two vaulted bays to the north. Its size and the additional arches are no doubt due to its location at the north-east corner of the presbytery, beneath the east gable wall.

The second pier, that between bays C and D, reconstructed here (Fig 78, b), is the best recorded. Its plan is included, albeit crudely, in Carter's sketch and again, in more detail and to scale, in his finished drawing. Powell (Fig 29) also records the east face of the same pier sketchily in plan. The south face is recorded in elevation in both of Carter's drawings and in perspective by Whichelo (Fig 31, left). All three drawings clearly show the large drum element passing up above gallery floor level. The east face of the pier is drawn in elevation by Carter (Fig 22; Fig 25) and Powell (Fig 29) and in perspective from the north-east, by Whichelo (Fig 31, left). The north face of the pier is not so well recorded. It is omitted from Carter's scale plan but it does appear in the perspective view by Whichelo (Fig 32) where it is shown with a round drum below a rectangular scalloped capital. Probably the best parallel for this pier is found in the nave of Peterborough Cathedral, probably of 1177–93 (Fig 79). The west face of the pier is not recorded in any of the drawings but it probably matched the opposing pier.

This third pier, on the west side of bay D (Fig 78, c), is shown in Carter's sketch-plan with a relatively large drum on its east face. The same face also appears in the two perspective views of bay D by Whichelo (Fig 31, left; Fig 32). The drawing of the drum and the treatment of the capital resembles that on the north face of the pier between bays C and D. Unfortunately, the south face of the pier is not recorded in any of the views by Carter, Whichelo or Powell. However, if the *Gentleman's Magazine* illustration (Fig 30) has any validity (see Chapter 3.4), it is to suggest that the large drum elements on the south side of the

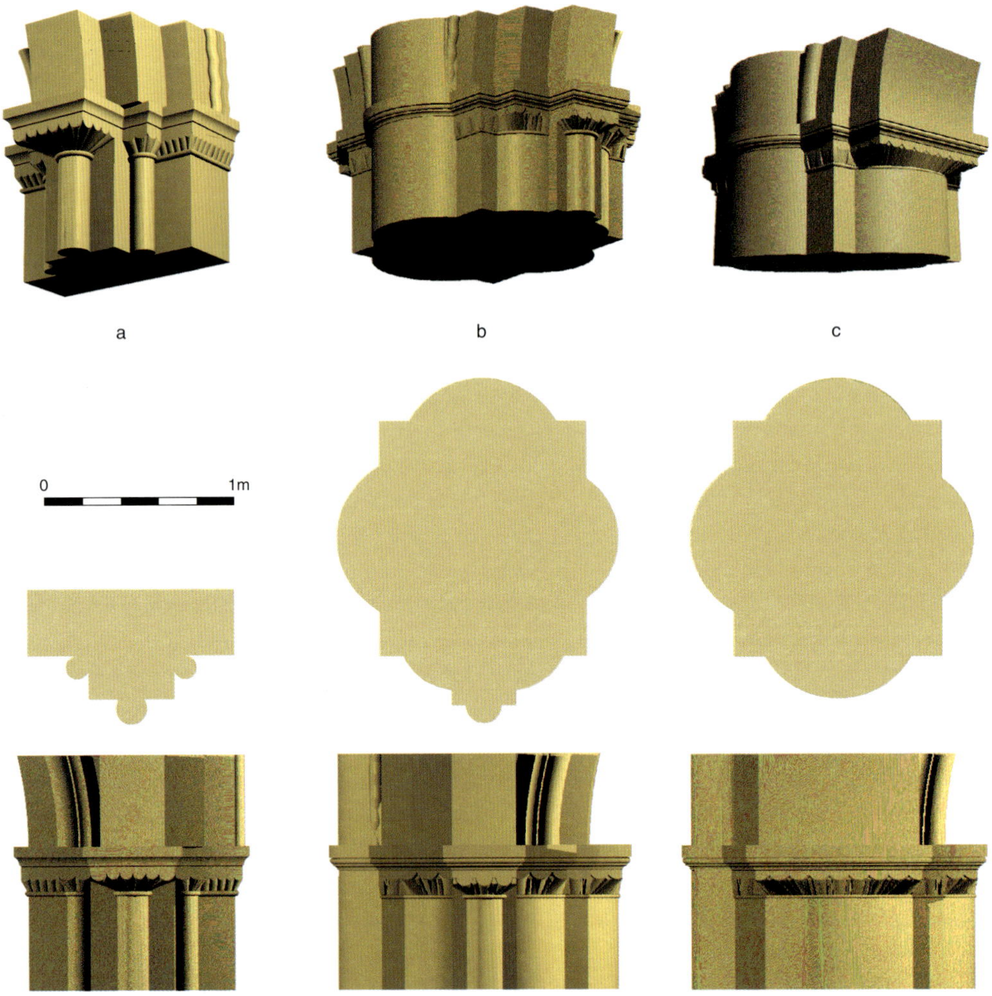

Fig 78 *Reconstructed sections, elevations and perspective drawings of three piers of the north arcade of the presbytery: a – pier between bays B and C; b – pier between bays C and D; c – pier on the west side of bay D (Richard Lea) (scale 1:40). The perspective drawings are included to enable comparison of the piers with the drawings of Carter and others*

pier between bays C and D may have been repeated. This is not entirely unreasonable since it allows the reconstruction of a simple compound pier in which elements from a large-diameter round pier are combined with a square pier. This reconstruction fits easily with Symonds's graphic representation of the piers using circles.

The use of compound pier design in London in the 12th century associates Holy Trinity with a regional school centred in the east of England. The principal members of this group identified by Bridget Cherry are the cathedrals of Ely (Cambridgeshire), Peterborough (Northamptonshire) and Norwich (Cherry 1978). The inclusion of large-diameter shafts in the composition of the pier is seen as one of the defining characteristics. Although not every building in the group has this feature, it can be seen in the east end of the nave at Norwich of 1096–1119, in piers facing along the line of the arcade in the nave at Thorney (Cambridgeshire) probably of 1098–1108, the east arm at Thetford (Norfolk) of 1107–14, the east arm of Bardney Abbey (Lincolnshire) probably of c 1115, the nave at Castle Acre (Norfolk) probably of 1125–50, the transepts at Peterborough probably of 1133–55, and in the nave at Rochester (Kent), probably of 1137–50/5 (McAleer 1999). The more specific use of a large-diameter shaft at Holy Trinity Priory – in conjunction with a half-round attached shaft and dosseret (ie a block above the capital) applied to its centre in line with the arcade – has parallels in the galleries of both the transepts and nave at Ely, probably of 1100–20 (Fig 80), the nave at Thorney probably of 1098–1108, at Peterborough, in the transept gallery arcades, probably of 1133–55, and in the nave arcades, probably of 1177–93 (Fig 81) (*VCH* 1906, 431–47), and in the nave at Denny Priory (Cambridgeshire), founded in c 1160. In the nave at Dunstable (Bedfordshire), of c 1150 (*VCH* 1912, 356–66), the same combination of elements is used facing into the nave as part of a giant order elevation (ie a column or pier going through two storeys).

At both Peterborough and Ely, the piers incorporating this last device are used as part of a regular system of alternating pier designs. In both systems, it is clear that the alternation is between a strong and a weak element, and the piers with the large-diameter shafts are used as the weaker form. The stronger piers are composed of clusters of attached shafts and nook shafts. At Holy Trinity Priory, although we have in the first and second piers the same combination of clustered shafts facing a large-diameter shaft with an attached shaft and dosseret, the design of the third pier clearly indicates that these piers did not form part of an alternating system. A system of alternation in the design of church arcades was not a prerequisite for the period. Even at Peterborough, four designs are used among the six piers in the eastern arm, although the overall impression is of matching pairs across the main vessel. At Rochester, similarly, no two adjacent piers in the nave are the same although they do match from one arcade to the other.

At Holy Trinity Priory, we have no evidence for the design of the fourth pier between the first and second bays east of the crossing, other than the plan by Symonds, which simply shows all piers as uniformly round. In our reconstruction, we have a square pier with large-diameter shafts on each face for both the third and fourth piers. This fits with what we do know of the third pier and is consistent with the design of the second pier. Similar piers can be found in the nave at Rochester, in the piers in both arcades between the fourth and fifth bays west of the crossing (Fig 82), probably of 1137–55 (McAleer 1999). Later, at Lichfield, the same form was used in the extension of the presbytery to create a rectangular ambulatory, in *c* 1170–5 (Rodwell 1989).

The plan forms of this pier and the first in the arcade (on the line of the gable wall) are both common in Romanesque architecture. The first in the arcade can be considered as one face of a 'cruciform pillar with engaged shafts' and the form suggested for the third and fourth piers has been termed a 'pier with engaged pillar'. In examples of the latter form, however, the shafts are more typically half-round, as in the nave at Conques (Aveyron, France) of 1050–1130, the transept of Santiago de Compostela (Galicia, Spain) of 1075–1125, and the nave of San Martin, Fromista (Palencia, Spain) of possibly before 1066 to after 1100. The heavier treatment of the form at Holy Trinity Priory and its parallels cited above is perhaps more peculiarly English in suggesting a single round pier rather than four separate shafts attached to the faces of a square pier.

A reconstruction of the presbytery from all this evidence is offered in Fig 83 and Fig 84. If a standard pier form was used at Holy Trinity Priory throughout the rest of the presbytery as shown in our reconstruction, then the proliferation of shafts around the end of the eastern arm could be seen as a conscious device to focus attention on the high altar.

Did Holy Trinity Priory have a giant order?

The compound design of the second pier in the presbytery recorded by Carter (Fig 22) is the product of the merging of circular and rectangular pier plans. Geographically, the closest parallel for this pier can be found in the Rochester Cathedral

Fig 79 Peterborough Cathedral: the third pier in the south nave arcade, probably of 1177–93, viewed from the south aisle (photograph: Malcolm Thurlby)

Fig 80 Ely Cathedral: the north nave arcade, probably of 1100–20, looking east (photograph: Malcolm Thurlby)

Fig 81 Peterborough Cathedral: the north nave arcade, probably of 1170–93, looking east (photograph: Malcolm Thurlby)

Fig 82 Pier in the south arcade of Rochester Cathedral, from the building period of Prior Ernulf, probably 1137–55 (photograph: Malcolm Thurlby)

nave, but there the drum is proportionally smaller in relation to the square section and there is a capital at the springing of the main arcade. Above the capital, the shaft diminishes in diameter. There is no hint of a giant order at Rochester. The main arcade and gallery elevations are treated entirely separately as two storeys, which happen to share the same bay articulation. At Holy Trinity Priory, however, the shaft represents a major vertical element in the treatment of the elevation and must have united the two storeys. It appears to have risen without diminution from the springing of the main arcade through the gallery floor, and the diameter of the shaft is large enough to suggest a giant order.

Clear examples of the use of the giant order in church architecture of the 12th century can be found at Romsey Abbey (Hampshire), in the first bays west of the crossing, built probably c 1140/5–60 (Hearn 1975); in the choir elevation at Jedburgh (Roxburghshire), founded by King David I of Scotland and Bishop John of Glasgow in c 1138 as an Augustinian house (Fawcett 1990), where the effect is of columnar piers rising without interruption to capitals at gallery level; and at St Frideswide, Oxford, another Augustinian foundation, in work probably dating from c 1160 onwards (Halsey 1990), where the giant order columns rise to capitals at gallery floor level and the tribune openings are set within the semicircle formed by the giant order arch.

Holy Trinity Priory is clearly not wholly analogous to these examples since the face of the shaft was broken by string-courses at the springing of the main arcade and at gallery floor level. In strict terms, however, even the piers at Romsey and Jedburgh are interrupted by capitals for the main arcade and aisle vaults throughout three quarters of their diameter. It is only the segment of the pier facing into the main vessel that is left free of horizontal interruptions. At Aldgate, it is only the abacus for the arcade capitals which was continued around the face of the pier. A distinction was therefore drawn in the creator's mind between the front of the pier and the remaining three quarters, but the problem remains as to whether or not it was treated merely as a vault shaft. The diameter of the shaft is a significant factor in this respect since it appears as a continuation of the cylindrical part of the arcade pier.

At Romsey, in the eastern arm, the substantial half-round vault shafts set against dosserets rising to roof level are interrupted only by decorated strings at both gallery floor level

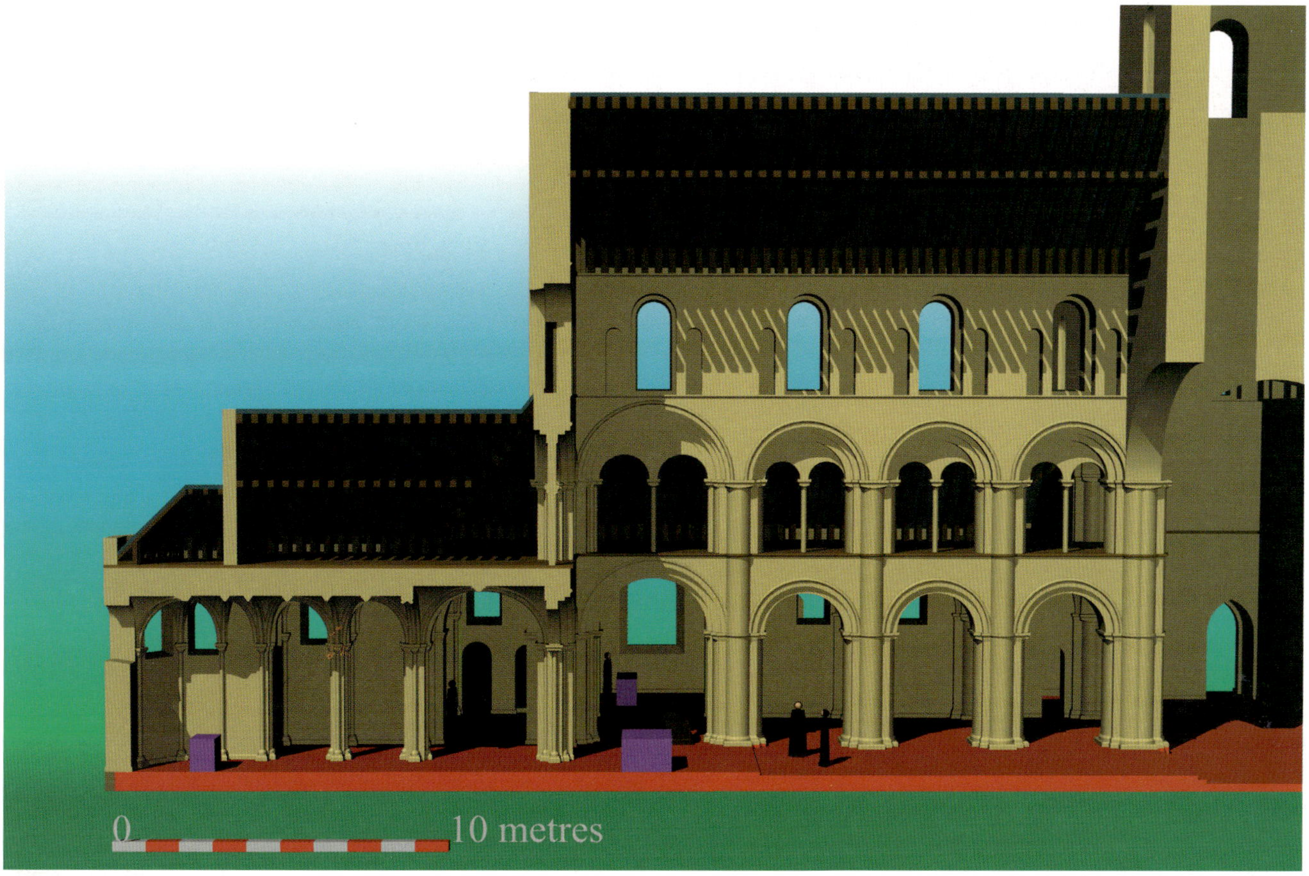

Fig 83 Reconstructed section through the eastern arm of the church of Holy Trinity in c 1300, looking south (the form of the clerestory is conjectural)

Fig 84 Reconstructed view eastwards down the presbytery of Holy Trinity in c 1300 (the form of the clerestory is conjectural)

and above the springing of the gallery arcade. In the nave, west of the giant order bays, the system reverts to that in the eastern arm except for a modification which preserves an important characteristic of the giant order system in the first two bays. The wall face above the main arcade is set back from the plane of the wall face above the gallery arcade. This feature is essential to the system of subordination of the lower to the upper arch. The upper wall face is supported by shafts with capitals only at gallery level. Thus, although the giant round piers were only used between the first two bays of the nave, the subordination of the main arcade to the gallery arcade was maintained.

If the large shaft at Holy Trinity Priory terminated in a capital at a high level, what did it support? If a Romsey-like system of subordination was adopted here, it may have been used in part to support the projecting wall face in a system in which the main arcade was subordinated. It is possible to reconstruct a capital for the shaft to support both the outer order of the gallery arcade and vault shaft.

A related system was employed at Dunstable Priory, founded for Augustinian canons in 1131 by Henry I, and colonised by Holy Trinity; the first prior at Dunstable was Bernard, brother of Prior Norman of Holy Trinity. There, a giant order system was created, in *c* 1150, which did not rely on the use of wholly round piers. As in the nave at Romsey, the wall face above the gallery is set in front of that above the main arcade and there is a greater proliferation of capitals at the springing of the gallery arcade than there is for the main arcade. Again it is worth noting that a string was carried around the face of the rising pier at gallery floor level. The design of the piers at Dunstable also has a significant affinity with Holy Trinity Priory: the combination of a half-round shaft set against a dosseret against a drum element is precisely that recorded by Carter at Aldgate, except that there the combination faced eastwards instead of into the main vessel.

So Holy Trinity Priory may not have had a fully developed giant order, but it does appear to have incorporated some design elements to suggest that the main arcade arches were subsumed under the gallery arches. This type of articulation was characterised by Prior (1900, 103) as 'Augustinian' bay design. The churches he cites as demonstrating this design are Romsey, Jedburgh, Dunstable, St Frideswide, Oxford, and Glastonbury (Somerset). In this respect, therefore, Holy Trinity appears to conform to Augustinian design in the second and third quarters of the 12th century. Richard Halsey has also added Reading (Berkshire) to the giant order group and stressed its royal connections (Halsey 1985). At this point, however, it does not seem possible to determine whether these characteristics are due to royal patronage, Augustinian ideas or a combination of both.

A cross-axis emphasis on the line of the altar

At Holy Trinity, there is some evidence to suggest that the design of the east end included a strong cross-axis with something of the feel of a crossing aisle. This was achieved by the location of rectangular chapels attached to the presbytery aisles either side of the main altar, wide arches in the principal arcades and elaboration in the design of the piers.

The surviving arch opening into the southern chapel, chapel 2, indicates the width of the arches into the side chapels. This dimension sits comfortably with the width of the first arch in the north arcade as recorded by Carter. These two arches were on either side of the high altar.

According to our interpretation of the east gable wall in relation to the Symonds plan, there were four bays in the main vessel of the eastern arm, an arrangement with parallels at Romsey (Hampshire) and Old Sarum II (Wiltshire). However, four arches of the span of the first arch in the arcade do not fit within the crossing, as given by the east wall of the transept, and the line of the east gable wall, discussed above. The solution is to invoke a further parallel at Romsey, where the first bay west of the east gable wall is wider than the three remaining bays (Scott 1996), and this interpretation has been adopted here in our reconstruction graphics (Fig 83; Fig 84). Thus the fourth bay of the presbytery, at the altar, was wider east–west than the others.

In our discussion of the piers of the presbytery arcade, we suggest that there may have been a standard pier with a variation in its design possibly confined to the first bay. If this was the case, then the variation around the altar area, which consists of a proliferation of shafts, can be seen as an increase in elaboration designed to give emphasis. Further emphasis was given to the aisle bay to the south of the main altar by the unique decoration applied to the vault ribs.

Decoration and the fire of 1132

One of Carter's published drawings (Fig 25) and his accompanying text describe two mouldings above the arcade in front of bay C. His drawing shows 'zigzag' or chevron decoration on the east side of the arch and a plain 'torus' moulding on the west side, and his notes are consistent with his drawing.

Chevron decoration by itself is only broadly datable. It is present at Lanfranc's dormitory at Christchurch, Canterbury, in the 1080s, and in quantity in the nave of Durham after 1110. It is also used in the presbytery at Peterborough, which is dated to 1117 by Peers (*VCH* 1906, 431–56) but to 1107 by a new history (Reilly 1997, 69), although the argument for the earlier dating is found unconvincing by Thurlby (1994b, 184, n 1); in the transept arms and on the arcades of the nave galleries at Norwich, of the building campaign before 1119 (Fernie 1993a, 145); and thereafter throughout much of the 12th century.

The two types of decoration on a single arch might suggest a break in construction, with the revised decoration being taken up after the break. If, however, it is assumed that the church was built from east to west, then this break is too close to the line of the presbytery gable wall to represent a natural point to interrupt building operations. An alternative interpretation is that the break represents a secondary phase in the works due to rebuilding or repairs. A likely date for such a break in construction might be the fire of 1132, which is said to have damaged the church. If the east gable and the ambulatory were damaged in the fire, then the chevron moulding could form part of the repair work and, therefore, post-date the work immediately to its west; so the apparent chronological order of the two mouldings – chevron then torus – would be reversed.

Apart from the change in the design of the arch moulding, no effect of a large fire has been discerned in the archaeological or topographical record. Though only small areas of 12th-century ground surfaces adjacent to the wall of the presbytery were excavated, there was no trace of a fire. This in itself is not remarkable; more extensive excavations at Canterbury Cathedral in 1994 also failed to find any evidence of the fire of 1067 (Blockley et al 1997, 22).

Further, it might be reasonable to question the veracity of Carter's record on this point since his site notes (Fig 22) do not wholly substantiate his published account. In his small-scale elevation of the north arcade, the arch above bay C appears with chevron carried across the full span and his note below the detail of the chevron at the top of the page reads 'Zigzag moulding round arch of C'. Could it be that Carter erred in translating his site notes into published drawings? Several possible explanations present themselves. Perhaps the torus moulding was found above another arch, either to the west of bay C or above the arch to bay A. In either case it would not be necessary to invent a building break to explain their existence. A third possibility, that the torus moulding was in fact a wall rib on the aisle side of the arcade (G Coppack, pers comm), is not supported by Whichelo's third drawing (Fig 32) which appears to show the web of the vault meeting the plain second order of the arch without any such elaboration. At present, this question cannot be resolved and in the meantime we must accept that, unusually, there is some reason to doubt Carter's reliability on this point.

To conclude, all the indications so far are that the eastern arm of the church post-dates 1132. This would imply that the fire may have been as destructive as the priory's cartulary suggests, and that what we are studying is a totally new church of the years after 1132. This matter is further considered in the general discussion (Chapter 5.4).

The roof of the presbytery

According to the Wyngaerde view of c 1540 (Fig 10) the roof of the presbytery was lower than that of the south transept. Unfortunately, we have no other archaeological or documentary evidence to indicate whether it was vaulted or covered with timber, since the roof had been removed by the time of the Symonds survey of c 1585. At St Bartholomew Smithfield, Webb suggested that in the 12th century there was a flat wooden ceiling over the presbytery (Webb 1921, ii, 7, 41). At Peterborough Cathedral, the straight section of the presbytery had a timber roof, and the eastern apse was probably vaulted in stone (Thurlby 1994b; Reilly 1997, 26). In our interpretation of the internal elevation in the eastern arm, we have suggested a large capital at gallery level, which could easily have been used to support a stone vault. We have no evidence, such as large-scale vault rib fragments, to indicate that such a vault was ever built.

The vaulting of the presbytery aisles

The surviving arch at site A provided the level for the springing of the vault in the south aisle, at 18.30m OD. The surviving core of the south wall contained evidence that bay A was vaulted with diagonal ribs. The unusual decorated form of the ribs was recorded by Carter (Fig 23). We have been unable to find direct parallels for the design of the rosettes or 'discs' on both the main rib and the sides of the rib. A vault boss in the form of a rosette, at the junction of ribs and in the centre of the bay, is found in two forms in the ground-floor stage of the water tower at Canterbury Cathedral, of 1153–67 (Kahn 1991, figs 172–3). But here the discs are not along the main rib or along the sides, only at the apex of the vault. In the hall of Wolvesey Palace, Winchester, erected by Henry of Blois, King Stephen's brother, in the second quarter of the 12th century (Fig 85), discs or rosettes are found on the hollow part of the moulding. Further examples of this latter form are widespread, from castles and churches in Britain, France (eg the north transept of St-Etienne, Beauvais, of c 1150: Henwood-Reverdot 1982, 132, figs 80–3), and in northern Spain (at Santa Maria, La Seu d'Urgell, Catalonia, the nave piers of 'before 1131' have chamfered edges with studded ball decoration: Barral I Altet

Fig 85 Wolvesey Palace, Winchester: discs or rosettes on the hollow part of the moulding, a parallel for the design of the vaulting over bay A of the presbytery aisle at Holy Trinity Priory (Conway Library, Courtauld Institute of Art)

1998, 159). Discs and disc-and-ball motifs are found on sunken mouldings on the south porch door of Iffley church (Oxfordshire) in *c* 1140; on the outer hollow moulding of the westernmost bay of blind arcading in the chapter house at Much Wenlock (Shropshire) of *c* 1150–60, and in the south porch of St Brendan's Cathedral, Clonfert (Galway, Ireland), probably after 1164 (R Halsey, pers comm). Stones about 8in or 9in square with stylised flowerheads either projecting from or cut into the stone, now removed from their original context, are found in the close wall at Salisbury (Wiltshire), and probably come from the former church at Old Sarum (RCHME 1993, 40–2); but, as they are fixed in the wall, it is not possible to determine what architectural features they came from.

The idea of using such flower or disc forms to emphasise a space or a doorway between spaces can be seen in other monastic houses. A possibly significant parallel is provided by the 'abbess's doorway' at Romsey Abbey, a house which may have been rebuilt also with the assistance of Henry of Blois (Scott 1996, 45, 69), where small ball-like rosettes are carved on the outer order of a processional doorway. This doorway has been dated to *c* 1140–5 on the basis of its similarities to the prior's door at Ely Cathedral of *c* 1135, the west doorway of Lincoln Cathedral of *c* 1145, and the west doorway of Castle Acre Priory (Norfolk) of *c* 1150 (Hearn 1975, n 17). A doorway in this position, the eastern of two from the nave into the cloister, was traditionally the more prestigious and the more decorated; it led from the church to the chapter house via the cloister. So the rosettes may have been a general device for indicating places, or entrances to spaces, of significance or status. A similar heightened significance may have been attached to the use of similar rosettes on both sides of the arch leading from a new parochial north aisle eastwards into the north transept at St Oswald's Priory, Gloucester; the arch is dated to *c* 1150–75 (Heighway and Bryant 1999, 88, figs 2.46–8). In this case the transition would be from the parochial space into the priory space of the transept. It should, therefore, be concluded that the elaborate decoration of the mouldings in the bay at Holy Trinity, though only in one bay in the south aisle of the presbytery, was drawing attention to something. Malcolm Thurlby suggests (below, 4.4) that it might have been an early Lady chapel; and whether or not that was the case, the burial of the princess Matilda south of the altar, and so in or near this bay, is probably connected.

In the corresponding bay C in the north aisle, Carter recorded a simpler vault rib (Fig 22). The basic profile of the rib recorded by Powell (Fig 29), a half-round between two hollows, was the same as that in bay A, but lacked the elaboration. Furthermore, the view by Whichelo from the north-east (Fig 32) shows that the vault ribs in bay D were similar to those in bay C. Examples of these ribs were recovered in the excavation of site B in 1908. This rib is clearly designed to match the diagonal ribs recorded in bays C and D.

The diagonal moulded ribs were supplemented by flat pilaster-like transverse arches between bays B and C, recorded by the *European Magazine* (Fig 27) and by Whichelo (Fig 31, right); and between bays C and D, also recorded by Whichelo (Fig 32). The presence of these wide transverse arches is confirmed by Carter's plan.

Of other large churches in the first quarter of the 12th century, the cathedrals of Norwich and Ely have choir aisles with groin vaulting only, whereas Peterborough Cathedral has rib vaults, from the initial period of construction now dated to 1107 rather than 1117 (Reilly 1997, 68). Whichever date is preferred for Peterborough, rib vaults for the aisles of the presbytery at Holy Trinity would be in order by 1132.

The presbytery galleries

From the views of around 1800 it is clear that after the Dissolution floors were inserted at least in some of the aisle bays around the east end. But it is important to determine whether these floors, as shown on Symonds's first-floor plan (Fig 15; Fig 16), lay at the level of the springing of the vaults or at gallery level, that is above the vaults.

In the Symonds ground-floor plan, there are no walls shown between the presbytery arcade piers and the aisle walls or between the piers themselves. This strongly suggests that when Symonds surveyed the site in *c* 1585, the presbytery aisle vaults were left exposed. Indeed, some of the vaults are known from antiquarian records to have survived until 1800. The walls of the 'new Teniments' shown by Symonds on the first-floor plan are too insubstantial to include the vaults or walls supporting vaults; they must, therefore, have been located above the vaults at gallery level. Furthermore, because there are no steps shown between the tenement rooms, it appears that the vaults above the presbytery aisles and eastern chapels were of uniform height. With the tenements above the arcade, the presbytery would have looked like the courtyard of a palazzo with loggias on the two long sides.

It can, therefore, be established that the presbytery had galleries; but their form, and that of any work above, is unknown. Other churches such as St Bartholomew Smithfield and those at Winchester (Hampshire), Gloucester or Tewkesbury (Gloucestershire), for instance, provide a range of possible forms. There is also no evidence at Holy Trinity that the galleries may have been decorated and thus possibly used for liturgical purposes, as at Ely or Peterborough (Maddison 2000, 33–4; Reilly 1997, 26).

The towers and stairs at the east end shown by Wyngaerde

The view by Wyngaerde of *c* 1540 (Fig 10) shows two towers or turrets either side of the gable at the east end of the main vessel of the eastern arm, as well as two more either side of the gable of the south transept, as already discussed above. All four towers appear to be capped with domical or onion-shaped roofs, which would appear to be of 16th-century date. The detail in the view is not sufficient to determine whether the towers are round or octagonal. Their distribution about the building and their appearance, apart from the onion-shaped roofs, are very similar to that at Peterborough Cathedral, as depicted in 1827 (Britton 1828, pl X). There, the towers are octagonal, have steeply pointed roofs and appear to date from the late 12th or early 13th century.

At Holy Trinity Priory, the Symonds evidence for the towers in the eastern arm is either missing or confused. In his ground-floor plan (Fig 13; Fig 14), spiral stair turrets are shown immediately east of the side chapels, and this corresponds with the evidence from the fabric for a 12th-century stair on the south side of the standing arch (above, 4.2). The parallel with Peterborough suggests that the octagonal form, normally associated with late medieval or even post-Dissolution stairs, could be original.

The first-floor plan (Fig 15; Fig 16) shows stairs either side of the main vessel, but there are problems in associating either of them with the turrets shown by Wyngaerde. The northern of the two is approximately on the line of the east gable wall, according to the argument given above. Its apparently flimsy construction, however, suggests that it is a post-Dissolution timber stair, dating from the construction of the jettied timber-framed tenements. The southern stair appears to be one bay further east and not on the gable line. Although it is more substantial than its northern counterpart, and probably of masonry or brick, it is shown without an entry. It might be either an original stair drawn in the wrong place, or a post-Dissolution construction in brick. It appears similar in scale to the stair at the south-east corner of the south transept chapel (chapel 1).

There is, therefore, no connection between the eastern turrets depicted by Wyngaerde and the stairs shown by Symonds, unless Symonds was mistaken about the southern one. The two eastern turrets shown by Wyngaerde, we would suggest, were medieval and probably communicated between the gallery and roof level, being attached to the gable.

The chapels north and south of the presbytery

The chapel on the south side of the presbytery, immediately south of Carter's bay A, was excavated as chapel 2 on site A (above, 4.2). The excavation revealed that its west wall did not align with the corresponding bay division within the presbytery but lay further to the west. This arrangement has a partial parallel at St Bartholomew Smithfield, where, although the corresponding chapels are rounded in plan, the opening from the aisle is positioned a short distance to the east of the west wall of the chapel.

From the style and tooling of stonework where it survived, chapel 2 was originally of the 12th century. The excavation also revealed that buttresses were added to its south-west corner and that a spiral staircase was located immediately to its east against the south aisle wall. The Symonds survey (Figs 13–16) shows the chapel as rectangular in plan. Although the east end of the chapel was not excavated, it must have been rectangular from the beginning, since the evidence from site A demonstrated that there was not enough space between the spiral stair and the east jamb of the arch opening into the chapel to accommodate an apse. The Symonds survey shows a matching chapel on the north side of the choir.

Symonds shows that by *c* 1585 the northern side of the presbytery had been rebuilt as tenements, with timber-framed rooms occupying the gallery above the arcade. Above chapel 2 on the south side, however, the thickness of the walls suggests that the pre-Dissolution work survived at gallery level. Moreover, the south chapel had a three-light window at ground level and a separate two-light window at first-floor level. Unfortunately, we cannot be sure that the upper window was medieval, and thus it remains uncertain whether chapel 2 had two floors in the medieval period.

The feature of a pair of square or rectangular chapels projecting north and south of the presbytery aisles in line with the altar is found at Cluny II (Saône-et-Loire, France), originally a 10th-century design, which served as a model for many Romanesque churches of the type we have termed type A in England and on the Continent (Zarnecki 1972, 61–3). The succeeding Cluny III had paired side chapels with apses, and these have been described as a second transept. An English derivative of Cluny III, Lewes Priory in Sussex (a Cluniac foundation of 1077) also had rectangular side chapels, but at both Cluny III and Lewes the position of the high altar is not known for certain.

The floor levels within the eastern arm, steps into the presbytery, and the possibility of a crypt

The first lime-based floor screed at the entrance to the south transept chapel (chapel 1) was at 14.31m OD; the latest, laid with probably 'Westminster' tiles, was at 14.64m OD. This, however, was about 0.12m lower than the base of the plinth course enclosing the chapel, and it suggests that the threshold to the chapel was level with the transept floor and that there was one step up into the chapel immediately east of the transept wall line. The earliest floor level of the south presbytery side chapel (chapel 2) and the adjacent area of floor in the aisle can be reconstructed at 14.55m OD from the remains of a plinth in the masonry around the base of the entrance. The threshold of the door into the south aisle to the east of chapel 2 was at 14.65m OD (above gpA54). This shows that in the 12th century there was a difference of 0.24m (about 9½in) in floor levels, suggesting two steps between the transept chapel floor and the south aisle of the choir (the transept chapel being the lower). Presumably these steps were at the entrance to the presbytery aisle from the transept, and they may have crossed the presbytery and the north aisle also, as in other large churches. At Norwich Cathedral, the floor of the choir is three steps higher than that of the transept, and was so by 1145 (Fernie 1993a, 31); there were also three steps in this position at Canterbury in the 'glorious choir' of 1174 (Salzman 1967, 371) and at Bath Abbey, Somerset (Davenport 1996, 23), and at least two at Lewes Priory, Sussex (Lyne 1997, 30).

It was also evident from the surviving masonry around the standing arch that there was a single step in the south aisle immediately east of the opening into chapel 2 (Fig 62). This would be in line with the east gable wall, as proposed here, and behind the high altar. Our reconstructions propose that this step would have been mirrored in the north aisle; but that the equivalent single step within the central nave would have been one bay further west, to provide a one-step three-sided podium for the altar, backing onto the gable wall and its arches.

No evidence, archaeological or documentary, has been recovered to suggest that there ever was a crypt under the east end of the church. Crypts were a feature of several larger Norman churches, for example St Augustine, Canterbury (1070–3) and the cathedrals of Winchester (1079), Worcester (1084) and Gloucester (1089). The first church of the Hospitallers in Clerkenwell has a surviving crypt beneath its choir, initially of *c* 1140 and expanded west, north and south in *c* 1180 (RCHME 1925, 17; Sloane and Malcolm 2004). Crypts could be used for housing relics and altars, though some (as was the case at Winchester) may never have been used at all (Crook 1989). There was a crypt beneath the south transept at St Botolph, Colchester (Colchester Archaeological Trust, pers comm). The possibility of a crypt at the east end of Holy Trinity seems extremely remote; for one thing, there would probably have been a need to elevate the presbytery floor, and provide something like the 12 steps from the crossing into the choir at St Paul's Cathedral; at Holy Trinity, as just described, there were probably only two.

Burials in the presbytery

The presbytery aisles, and the spaces between the columns of the presbytery arcade and up to the high altar, were often used for prestigious burials in major medieval churches. At Holy Trinity Priory the locations of some important burials are of significance for understanding both the architecture of the building and perhaps its early building history. In this section, the evidence for burials in the presbytery is presented, while in Chapter 5.4 the significance of the relationship between the priory and successive royal families is considered. The burials can be considered in two groups: those of two children of King Stephen, and those of the early priors.

The cartulary records that 'King Stephen and the queen greatly loved (*dilexerunt*) the said Prior Ralph and this church because they caused to be honourably buried in this church their son Baldwin and their daughter Matilda, sometime wife of the Count of *Medlinc* [Meulan, Seine-et-Oise], Baldwin on the north side of the altar (*ad aquilonem partem altaris*) and Matilda on the south [side] (*ad australem*)' (*Cartulary*, appendix no. 14; quoted in Dickinson 1950, 134, n 1).

Since Stephen gave 100s of land in *Brackyng*, Hertfordshire, to Holy Trinity for the repose of the souls of his children Baldwin and Matilda 'who lie in the church of Holy Trinity' in 1147–8 (*Cartulary*, no. 973), these burials must have taken place before that date. Nothing is known of the date of Baldwin's death, but Matilda was betrothed at the age of two to Waleran, Count of Meulan, early in 1136. She must have died in or before the autumn of 1141, when Waleran married Agnes, the elder sister of Count Simon of Evreux (Crouch 1986, 50, 52; S Priestley, pers comm).

A reconstructed plan of the east end of the church in the 13th century is suggested in Fig 86, showing the possible sites of the two royal burials. Such positions, flanking the altar and probably under the presbytery arcades, would be normal for burials of members of a royal family in the 12th century. In the reconstruction graphics (Fig 83; Fig 84) we have made both tombs look like the surviving 12th-century sarcophagus with a half-hipped roof at Winchester, traditionally believed to be the tomb of William Rufus, but now thought to be possibly that of Henry of Blois (d 1171) himself (Crook 1999). In this royal context, the unusual decoration of the ribs of the bay in the south aisle immediately south of the altar (Fig 25) is probably significant, but we cannot suggest how this was intended to reflect the tomb, unless – which would be unusual – the princess's tomb lay in the aisle, beneath the special vaulting.

At Holy Trinity, the high altar was also the focus for burials of at least two of the earliest priors and an eminent canon who went on to achieve high ecclesiastical office. Prior Norman was buried before the high altar in a new sarcophagus in 1147; in 1176 his body was translated to the north part or side of the altar (*Cartulary*, appendix no. 13). If the east end was new in 1147, Norman, as the founding prior, might well have lain west of the altar and on the central axis of the presbytery.

The body of the second prior, Ralph, who died in 1167, was translated, perhaps also in 1176, to the *latus exterius* (presumably the aisle) near the grave of Prior Norman (*Cartulary*, appendix no. 13). The precise word used in the cartulary is *transposuimus*, 'we transposed', which suggests that Ralph was initially buried elsewhere.

Thirdly, during Peter's priorate (1197–1221), Edmund, a canon, returned from being Bishop of Limerick and was buried in the north part of the church between two columns near the presbytery (*Cartulary*, appendix no. 13). Perhaps the north side of the presbytery was a usual place of burial for Augustinian priors; at St Bartholomew Smithfield, the founder Rahere and at least two other priors are buried either in the north arcade of the presbytery or in the north transept (Webb 1921, ii, 189–90).

The transepts and crossing

The reconstruction of the transepts and crossing is complicated by problems encountered when trying to reconcile the various forms of evidence. In this discussion the archaeological evidence is considered first, followed by the Symonds plans and then evidence from lease plans of the 18th century. Both sites A and D provide archaeological evidence for the plan of the south transept (though the evidence from site D is only negative). There is no archaeological evidence for the north transept.

The plan of the transepts

Substantial physical remains of the foundations for the east, south and west walls of the south transept were found on site A (in plan, Fig 44; Fig 45). The widths of the foundations for both the east and west walls were revealed as *c* 1.95m (6ft 5in) and 2.25m (7ft 5in) respectively. The walls above ground level would not have been as thick as the foundations, but their irregular and

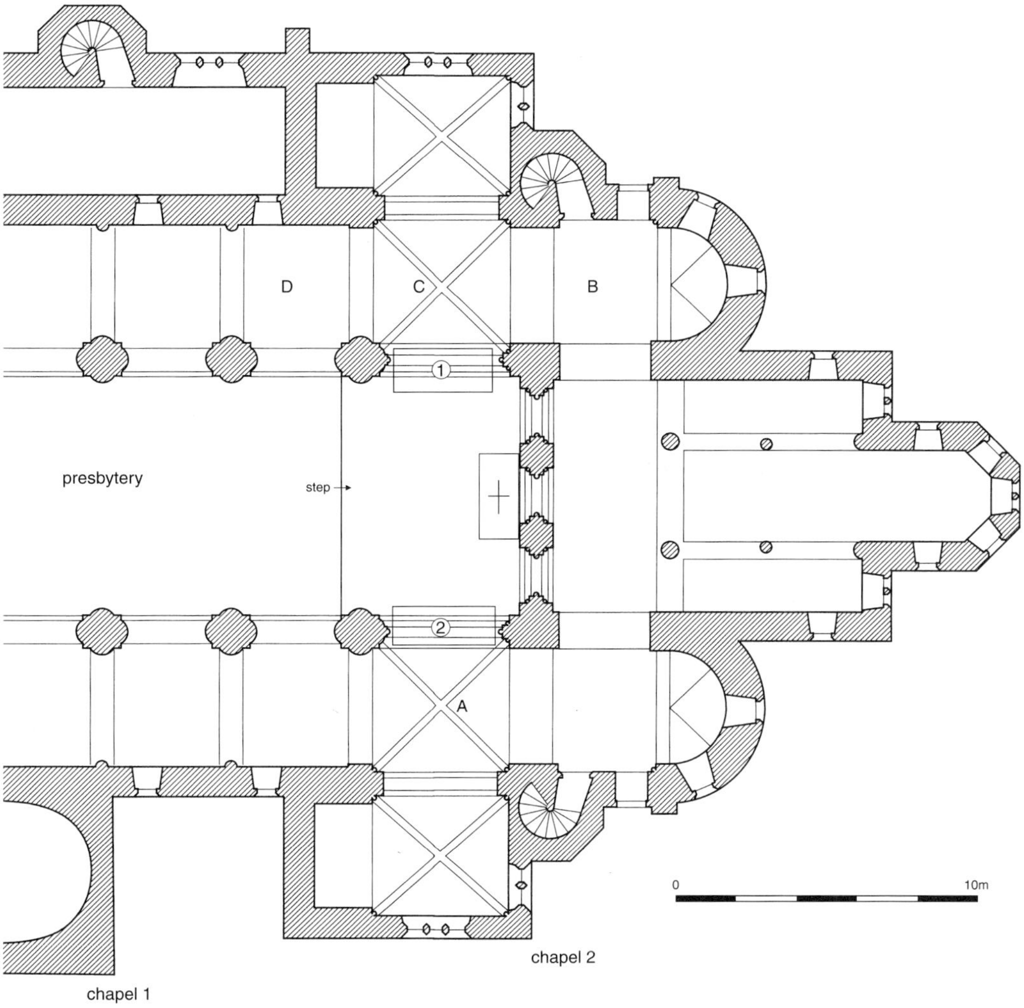

Fig 86 Reconstructed plan of the east end of the priory church in the 13th century, showing the possible sites of the two royal burials (1 – Baldwin; 2 – Matilda) (scale 1:250)

non-rectilinear plan means it is impossible to suggest a single dimension for the offset. A width of *c* 1.55m (5ft) for the thickness of both east and west walls, however, seems to offer the best fit with the available evidence and is comparable with the thickness of the piers of the presbytery arcades. Even though there is substantial variation in the thickness of the foundations, it would seem unlikely that the walls were of different thickness, given the structural requirements of the east and west transept walls. The internal width of the transept thus appears to have been *c* 7.2m (23ft 6in) which is very close to the dimension of 24ft recorded by Symonds for the internal width of the east arm. Thus the four arms of the cruciform plan were probably of the same width, producing a crossing with a square plan.

Unfortunately, the absence of evidence for the south face of the terminal wall of the south transept causes problems for interpretation. The wall probably lay under the southern boundary of the excavated part of site A in 1984, but its foundation could only be recorded on the north side. The widths of both foundation and terminal wall therefore remain unknown. Consideration of comparable sites also suggests the possibility of architectural features in this part of the building, which might have required foundations in addition to those of the south wall. Site D provides negative evidence for the extent of the south transept, since no fabric of the south transept wall was encountered. Thus, the terminal wall cannot have extended, in width, more than *c* 5.0m (16ft 5in) south of the north face of the south foundation seen on site A.

At its west end, east of the internal face of the west wall of the transept, the foundation measured *c* 1.9m (6ft 4in) north–south. At its east end, in line with the east wall of the transept, it extended at least another 0.8m (2ft 7in) to the south, but here it is likely that the foundations were thickened to support buttressing at the south-east corner of the transept. The south face of the south wall of the transept chapel (chapel 1), above ground, lay *c* 2.25m (7ft 5in) south of the north face of the terminal foundation. If the two walls were aligned, and allowing for an offset of *c* 0.25m, the terminal wall could have been up to 2.05m (6ft 9in) thick, which is thicker than the two side walls. Consideration of parallel sites, such as Peterborough Cathedral (Reilly 1997, 28), suggests that this would not have been unusual. The greater thickness was perhaps considered necessary to support the additional masonry forming the gable, or in addition to supply a basis for stairs at the corners.

Two other features observed on site A, however, have an

important bearing on the interpretation of the evidence for the location and design of the south end of the south transept. The relationship in plan between chapel 1 and the north face of the foundation of the terminal wall suggests that the interior volume of the chapel extended further south than that of the south transept. This is an unusual feature in design terms, but it would be even more unusual if the entrance from the transept into chapel 1 was not symmetrical about the central east–west axis through the chapel. Thus, in our reconstruction (Fig 86), we have aligned the south face of the terminal wall with the south face of the chapel and put the entrance into the chapel on axis. This results in a large offset, 0.6m on the north side of the terminal wall, giving it an overall thickness of *c* 1.66m (5ft 4in).

The second feature to be noted is the foundation (gpA34.3; Fig 45), presumably for a buttress, on the west side of the transept and approximately in line with the north face of the terminal wall foundation on the east side of the transept. Its location suggests that even if it did not relate directly to the south transept wall, there was a significant bay or structural division on this line. The significance of this buttress will emerge in the following discussion.

The archaeological information (Fig 45) is not easily reconciled with the Symonds plan evidence (Figs 13–16). Symonds shows a symmetrical arrangement of the two transepts, and it would be very unusual if the original 12th-century plan had been asymmetrical. The internal proportions of the two transepts shown by Symonds, that is the width compared with the distance between the terminal walls and the crossing, are shown slightly longer north–south than east–west, by a ratio of about 1.14:1. These proportions accord almost exactly with the plan of the south transept recovered by excavation, if the north face of the foundation is assumed to represent the line of the south wall. Thus, a transept terminal wall, flush with the south face of the transept chapel, fits with the internal proportions of the transept shown by Symonds.

In other respects, however, the archaeological evidence for the 12th-century transepts is not consistent with the Symonds plans, and it is suggested here that this correspondence in proportions is probably no more than coincidence. The transepts, by the time of Symonds's survey, were probably longer and narrower, extending beyond the excavated area (see Fig 135; Fig 136).

In the Symonds plans the south transept wall is shown offset by a considerable distance from the transept chapel south wall. This might be considered a slight error were it not for the following observations. A large window of four lights is shown in the west wall of the south transept whereas corresponding windows in the south aisle of the nave are shown with only three lights. This suggests that this section of the west wall of the south transept was longer than a single bay width in the nave. Furthermore, a pair of clasping buttresses is shown at the south-east corner of the transept and this appears wholly credible as an authentic 12th-century feature.

The probability of symmetry between north and south transepts is also relevant here. Symonds shows the north transept projecting beyond the north wall of the extended north transept chapel. Not only is there a clear space between the extended chapel and the chapter house south wall, which is one with the north transept terminal wall, but spiral staircases are shown occupying the gap at ground- and first-floor levels. If the terminal wall had been in line with the north wall of the north transept chapel, then there would have been no space in which these features could have been accommodated.

In 1670, the property on the site of the north transept, demised to Mr Thomas Yates in a survey by John Oliver, was described as occupying an area 37ft 6in (11.44m) north–south by 29ft 3in (8.92m) east–west:

> Demised to Mr Thomas Yates several intermixed dwellings formerly one house abutting East on the Church and in depth on that side from North to South 29 foot and a quarter little more or less and in front to Duke's Place North from East to West 37 foot and a half more or less including a cart way or passage at the North West passage of the Same 7 foot and a half, little more or less out of the Court or Way leading into Leadenhall Street. (Jones and Reddaway 1962–6, v, 90)

The church is St James Duke's Place (built in 1622 on the site of the chapter house: see Chapter 6.4), and the plot and the passage fit with later evidence to show that this was the site of the north transept of the priory church, which had either fallen down or been demolished in the period 1532–85; though the compass points reflect the skew of the buildings to the south-east ('east' to Oliver is in fact north-east, and the liturgical north).

In the Symonds survey the west wall of the north transept is shown as ruinous. The width of the transept recorded in this survey is consistent with the internal dimension of the transept, *c* 7.2m (23ft 6in) as recorded by excavation plus the thickness of one wall, *c* 1.55m (5ft 1in). By 1670, it is likely that the west wall had been rebuilt but probably less substantially. The north–south dimension, however, is harder to explain. The equivalent internal dimension for the south transept, that is between the crossing and the south terminal foundation, is 8.2m (26ft 10in), 3.2m (10ft 6in) shorter than that recorded in 1670. This discrepancy might be explained by the suggestion that a passage or a narrow room originally built between the transept and chapter house in the 12th century had been absorbed into the main volume of the transept by the time of the Symonds survey. Consideration of the date of the fabric Symonds shows in his plan seems to provide the key to the problem.

The plan of the south transept chapel (chapel 1), as drawn by Symonds, is consistent with the squaring of the interior represented by post-Dissolution brick walls (period VIII, gpA42.3 and gpA42.5), as reported below (Chapter 6.2). This rebuilding is dated through associated features to the period 1580–1600.

A presumed matching chapel on the north transept is shown in an extended form, which it probably assumed in the 13th century or later. It therefore seems reasonable to suggest that there were other features in the 12th-century plan which were not recorded by Symonds because they had either been altered or removed by the time of his survey.

The excavated remains of the south transept are part of the

original 12th-century plan. At this time the south terminal wall was probably aligned with the south wall of the apsidal chapel (see Fig 135). The north transept would have mirrored this plan but a slype passage was probably located between the north transept terminal wall and the chapter house. By the time of the Symonds survey, however, the north transept had perhaps been extended to include the slype. This measure may or may not have been contemporary with the eastern extension of the north transept chapel, which could well have been carried out by Prior Peter in *c* 1220 to create a Lady chapel (see Fig 136). Similarly, to maintain symmetry in plan, the south terminal wall was perhaps rebuilt *c* 3.0m (9ft 9in) to the south. If this is the case, then the clasping buttresses suggest that this alteration was made within the 12th century. But there is no archaeological evidence for such an extension of the south transept.

The superstructure of the transepts and crossing

Wyngaerde in *c* 1540 (Fig 10) clearly shows that the south transept had turrets at its external corners, and it would be natural to suppose that these enclosed newel staircases. But stairs in these positions are missing from both of the floor plans by Symonds (Figs 13–16), and he seems otherwise to be punctilious about showing stairs. It can only be assumed that he did not see or chose not to record any vestiges of these stairs at the external corners of the south transept. Neither of these corners could be totally investigated in the site A excavation. It is also the case, however, that such spirelets or turrets might not enclose stairs, or only sometimes: a reconstruction of Romanesque Durham Cathedral (Jarrett and Mason 1995, 193–4) shows turrets on both corners of the south transept, and there is only a stair in the one at the south-west corner. In this instance the square tower containing the stair is larger in bulk than the other turret or spirelet at the south-east corner.

The Wyngaerde view provides the only clear evidence for the roof of the transept. If we are to credit this view, the roof of the transept stood higher than the roof of the choir, which would be unusual. The Symonds plans give little detail for the south transept, probably because at the time of the survey it was occupied as a tenement. The clasping buttresses shown at the south end of the south transept are not necessarily an accurate representation of their actual form; the foundations excavated on site A suggest larger projections.

The south transept and chapel seem to have survived as an 'edifice built with stones' described in a lease to Henry Billingsley of 1590 (see Chapter 6.2), and the transept is probably shown on the 'Agas' woodcut panorama (Fig 12) of some twenty years earlier as a prominent, crenellated tower north of Leadenhall Street. The gable behind it must, therefore, represent the crossing in its post-Dissolution form as the upper part of the Ivy chamber.

The crossing supported a high tower, as shown by Wyngaerde. The structure appears to be consistent with a 12th-century date, with two storeys, windows in pairs, four corner turrets and no visible signs of a pitched roof. According to Symonds, the plan of the crossing was rectangular, being wider east–west than north–south, but this appears to be a drafting error since our excavation evidence indicates that since both the presbytery and the transepts were 24ft (7.32m) wide, the crossing was square. None of the crossing piers has yet been excavated, so precise dimensions are lacking. According to a note on the Symonds ground-floor plan, the tower fell down into the north transept, presumably when demolition took place after the Dissolution.

The form of the transept chapel(s)

The form of the recorded 12th-century south transept chapel (chapel 1), apsidal internally and square externally, has parallels at Lincoln, in the aisle chapels (1072–92), Old Sarum II (*c* 1125–30) and Hereford Cathedral (first half of the 12th century) (Clapham 1934, 21, 45, 49).

By the time of the Symonds survey, the south transept chapel had been altered; and if there was a corresponding chapel on the north transept, that had been extended as shown by Symonds, perhaps as the Lady chapel of Prior Peter. The excavated details of the post-Dissolution (period VIII) changes to chapel 1 on the south transept are described below (Chapter 6.2). The square interior of the chapel corresponds with the brick walls identified on site A (gpA42.3, gpA42.5) and with the brick facing (no group number) of the north wall of chapel 1. These elements correspond reasonably well with the plan of the chapel recorded by Symonds. The east wall group A42.3 (see Fig 152) even contains the window shown in plan. The level of the associated floor, 13.10m OD, means that earlier floors within the chapel were removed.

There is no evidence, archaeological or documentary, to indicate whether the original chapel(s) were of one or two storeys. The Symonds plans show a two-storey arrangement for the south chapel, but this was a brick structure, which from the excavation appears to have been created in the 16th century, probably after the Dissolution. There are several possibilities for the original appearance: 1) the chapels were of only one storey, that is single height; 2) they were of two storeys (as at Gloucester, for instance); 3) they were of double height, but still only one storey, with no intermediate floor. On balance the original arrangement was probably single-storey, since two-storey chapels in the 12th century are uncommon and there is nothing to suggest that Holy Trinity was unusual in this respect. The vertical ashlar feature in the north wall of the south transept chapel (chapel 1) (Fig 52) invites further investigation in the future, which is possible because the chapel has been saved and is now in the basement of Swiss Re House on the site. For the moment, this feature suggests an opening through the wall into the south aisle. The existing wall face immediately east of this feature appears to be plastered brick, but the chamfered plinth below gives the plane of the original face. The eastern edge of the ashlar feature is surprising because it is vertical and straight and appears not to have been quoined into the adjacent wall matrix, which otherwise seems to be the general pattern where ashlar is merged into an uncoursed face. It is clear from the south side of the chapel that the original interior wall face above plinth level was uncoursed ragstone finished with plaster.

The west side of the feature also forms a vertical edge. This is less surprising because it coincides with the western termination of the plinth, and the adjacent wall face, which consists of brick finished with plaster, occupies the space the size of a door opening. The coursing of the ashlar is regular, with stones occupying the full width of 0.3m alternating with two stones of approximately half that width. This pattern is similar to that presented by the remains of the nook shafts which survive on the fabric around the standing arch. Here it seems more likely that for those courses consisting of two stones, the western stone probably formed the tail for a nook shaft set within a rebate to the west. This suggests a door opening from the chapel into the south aisle framed by two shafts and presumably a round arch. The threshold of this opening cannot have been lower than *c* 14.55m OD, since the wall fabric survives to this level.

The surviving chamfered plinth on the north jamb of the entrance to the chapel from the transept is set at the same level as the others in the chapel. This one stone is set uniquely above ashlar, suggesting that there was a change in floor level at the entrance to the chapel. From the surviving floor surfaces adjacent to this jamb it seems reasonable to assume that the actual step up into the chapel lay on the line of the east face of the jamb. The accumulation of surfaces in this position could, therefore, relate to a westward movement of this step (above, 4.2; Fig 54).

St Bartholomew Smithfield probably had a similar apsidal chapel protruding from the east side of its south transept, and possibly a matching chapel on the north side. A pointed arch forming the entrance to the chapel on the south transept at St Bartholomew's is shown in an engraving of 1802 (Webb 1921, ii, pl XLIV).

The nave

The present-day alignment of Mitre Street splits the south side of the nave, and site E, from the north side of the nave, the north-west corner of which was excavated on site F and is described later (below, 4.5). The small amount of relevant information from site F concerning the west end of the nave can be summarised here: two successive foundations were found, in close proximity (buildings C and D). Neither could be accurately dated, but the second fits with the Symonds plan in being the (main, later) west end of the nave.

Symonds shows that the nave, by the time of the Dissolution, was seven bays long (Figs 13–16). The date of construction of the elements of the nave found or inferred on sites A and E can only be ascertained in very broad terms. The excavation at site E provided the location of the south wall of the nave. The foundation of the wall was of chalk and mortar, as opposed to the chalk with some tile and ragstone and without mortar which was used for the south transept and the south presbytery side chapel. In the London area, this suggests a date of *c* 1220 when foundations in larger buildings were mortared, as opposed to layered in sand and gravel. The mouldings on the buttress foundations at site E suggest the period 1180–1300. To anticipate the report on site F, a foundation which is taken to be a second west end for the priory church was dated by a single mortar-encrusted sherd to after 1150–1200. It therefore seems safest to suggest that the south wall of the nave on site E dates from *c* 1200, and that buttresses were added to the south side of the nave during the 13th century.

Assuming that the nave and presbytery were approximately the same width and that our interpretation of the correspondence between the excavated remains at site F and the Symonds plan is correct, it appears that there was a slight misalignment between the nave and eastern arm.

Three doorways are shown by Symonds in the north aisle wall opening into the cloister. The centre door probably dates from after the Dissolution. The north wall of the nave is shown as a very thick wall, and the windows appear to be higher; this would be expected as the cloister lay on this side. Symonds shows the south wall of the nave cut down to a lower level, with just the sills of the windows apparent. He did not draw the buttresses excavated at the west end of the south wall of the nave at site E; presumably by this time (*c* 1585) they had been demolished and covered with soil from the churchyard of St Katherine Cree.

The floor of the nave has never been recorded. Perhaps it was in part tiled, as in the 14th century at Waltham Abbey, Essex (Huggins and Bascombe 1992, 304) and elsewhere. The excavated portions of the nave and aisle floors at Merton Priory (Surrey) were of tiles and Reigate stone slabs (Miller et al in prep).

Between the first pair of piers west of the crossing, Symonds shows that the west end of the Ivy chamber was supported by a masonry wall. This is likely to have been based on, if not built to incorporate, the pulpitum which would have separated the monastic choir from that part of the nave conventionally called the ambulatory. A similar wall, its lower part faced in ashlar on its west side, was recorded at St Bartholomew Smithfield priory church in 1865 (Webb 1913, 166, fig 2), and dated by Webb to the mid 13th century; a decayed fragment of its base can still be seen. The wall at Holy Trinity, at ground-floor level, had two three-light windows (or possibly arched openings) in it, but we cannot say if these are medieval in date or post-medieval insertions.

It is probable that there were one or more parish altars, as well as other altars, in the nave or nave aisles. Parish altars were often in the nave of conventual churches, especially Augustinian houses (Dickinson 1950, 233), for instance at St Frideswide, Oxford (Halsey 1990, 135). At Holy Trinity, Simon de Hattefeld, potter, wished to be buried near the altar of St John the Baptist in the priory in 1372 (*Cal Husting Wills*, ii, 155). In 1376 John de Cantebrigge, fishmonger, elected for St Mary's chapel, where his son and two former wives were already buried (ibid, 197); a Fraternity of St Mary is mentioned in a will of 1380 (ibid, 227). The 18th-century historian John Strype records that there was a parish altar to St Mary Magdalen 'on the south part of the church' (Strype 1720, i.ii, 56), and it is likely this would be the south aisle, on the opposite site of the nave from the cloister (which lay on the north) and perhaps with direct access via the south door of the church to the major thoroughfare of

Leadenhall Street. It is possible that the parochial interests were confined to the south nave aisle. To allocate, and even build, one aisle for the parish is known in other monastic houses both in London and elsewhere: for instance at St Mary Clerkenwell, London, in *c* 1180 (Sloane in prep), and in 1150–70 at St Oswald's Priory, Gloucester (Heighway and Bryant 1999, 19). At St Helen Bishopsgate, London, in the early part of the 13th century (before 1216), the reverse occurred: the nave, choir and claustral buildings of a nunnery were attached to the north side of an existing parish church.

At Holy Trinity Priory, the parish font was in the priory church and presumably, therefore, in the nave by 1409, when as part of the definition or redefinition of the parish of St Katherine Cree, the Pope directed that the font should remain in the (priory) church (*Cal Pap Reg*, 1409). A similar function as the place for baptisms must have been enjoyed by St Bartholomew Smithfield, where the 15th-century font survives, though it is not known where it stood in the church in the medieval period. At St Bartholomew's the parish chapel seems to have been in the north transept, on the opposite site to the claustral buildings. The parish altar may even have been in the presumed apsidal east chapel of the transept (Webb 1921, ii, 95). If this arrangement is transposed to Holy Trinity, then a parish chapel would have been in the south transept, perhaps even in the apsidal chapel excavated as chapel 1; but this is pure speculation.

Symonds shows a porch protruding from the south aisle, in the first bay from the west end. There is no archaeological or antiquarian evidence for its date, and we have tentatively assigned the structure shown by Symonds to the 14th century. Whether there was an entrance here to the 12th- or 13th-century nave is unknown, but one seems likely and so has been included in the phase plans at the end of this study.

There has been no excavation within the area of the nave, and apart from the miniscule representations in the copperplate and 'Agas' maps (Fig 11; Fig 12), no graphic evidence apart from Symonds exists for the walls, arcades and roof of the nave. The different fates of the north and south galleries by *c* 1585 have already been outlined, by deduction from the Symonds plans. There is nothing in the plans themselves which allows any inferences to be drawn about the form or date of the nave arcades. The fact that there were seven bays in the nave argues against any arrangement of alternating pier designs (such as the alternating clustered columns and single columns of Jumièges or Durham). Presumably, if the nave was rebuilt in the 13th or early 14th century, some or all of the arcade piers and the work above would have been of that date in *c* 1585.

From the Symonds plans, we can try to ascertain whether the presbytery arcades and nave arcades rose to the same height. Although this is the case in some large Norman churches, for instance at Durham, Norwich and Peterborough, it was not universal. Where there was a crypt beneath the choir or presbytery, making it a podium, the tops of the choir or presbytery arcades were naturally higher than those of the nave, as at Winchester, where the difference in height is 2.2m (Crook 1996, 142). But in the Holy Trinity case we have concluded (above) that there is no evidence for a crypt beneath the presbytery. Symonds shows that the floor of the post-Dissolution first-floor Ivy chamber inserted in the crossing, and that of the 'gallery' which led from it along the north side of the ruined nave, were at the same level; but that 15 steps lay between the Ivy chamber and the tenements on the south side of the presbytery. It is not clear from the plan whether these steps are all in the same direction, or up and down either side of an apparent landing in the middle; so unfortunately the evidence of this stair is equivocal. It is, therefore, possible that the nave and presbytery ground-floor arcades of the church rose to approximately the same height; but since the nave was rebuilt in the 13th and early 14th centuries, it is equally likely that this later building produced different levels, as at St Bartholomew Smithfield, where the 13th-century north arcade of the nave is *c* 2.0m taller, as shown in the surviving bay of masonry now exposed on the north side of the church. This matter, therefore, remains unresolved.

The form of the roof and of any vaulting above the nave or nave aisles is not known. Although some large stone vaults were erected around 1100 in England and Normandy, most notably over the choir of Durham Cathedral in 1093 and possibly intended for the nave of St Paul's Cathedral in the 12th century (Gem 1990; Schofield in prep), the majority of large churches in England and northern France continued to have wooden roofs over their naves well into the 12th century (Kubach 1978, 85); an example is the reconstruction from reused rafters and the outline of a 12th-century truss preserved on the west tower at Ely Cathedral (Simpson and Litton 1996, 190). At Holy Trinity Priory, vaulting of the central vessel of the nave by the late 12th or during the 13th century is implied by the buttresses found on the south side of the nave at site E (Fig 73). These were at intervals of 4.4m (14ft 6in) and aligned, as far as can be ascertained, with the bay divisions of the south aisle as drawn by Symonds. The aisles were probably always vaulted, to assist in taking the thrust of the main vessel back to the exterior walls (as for instance at St Paul's and at Peterborough, both in the middle of the 12th century). Unfortunately, no moulded stones certainly or conjecturally from the nave piers or vaulting have so far been recovered. Any remaining information about these features lies buried under the present surface of Mitre Street.

4.4 The architecture of the eastern arm of Holy Trinity Priory in its wider context

Malcolm Thurlby

Introduction

Reconstruction of a lost building from limited antiquarian sources, partial excavation and a few fragments is never an easy task. The reader will already be well aware of the problems involved with interpretation of the evidence, and that, concomitantly, for many details a definitive answer is not possible. In such cases the parallels and analogues cited provide clues as to the appearance of elements of the church of Holy Trinity Priory, Aldgate, but only in certain cases is the evidence absolute. On the one hand, the basic plan of the eastern arm of the church is known, along with the formal elements of three of the north main arcade piers of the presbytery, one aspect of the vertical articulation and details of the rib vaults of the aisles. On the other hand, the form of the gallery and clerestory and other elements of the interior can only be surmised by analogy with other churches. For the exterior the evidence is scant; Wyngaerde (Fig 10) informs on the use of angle turrets to the presbytery, south transept and crossing tower, but on matters of detail there is nothing. As a whole, however, there is more than enough to allow analysis of the church in the context of English Romanesque architecture. In turn, it is possible to determine the aim of the patron, King Stephen, to create an appropriately 'royal' building, one that would vie with the finest churches in Norman England.

The four-bay eastern arm

The inclusion of a four-bay eastern arm at Holy Trinity Priory places the church amongst the most ambitious designs in Norman England. The tradition begins in 1077 with Abbot Paul of Caen's abbey church at St Albans (Hertfordshire) to provide a grand setting for the shrine of the patron saint and a longer presbytery than in Normandy, where two- and three-bay eastern arms were the norm (Thurlby 1997a). St Albans was soon followed at Winchester Cathedral (1079) (Crook 1993a), and the Benedictine abbey at Ely (1081, cathedral after 1106) (Fernie 1979; Ferguson 1986), with the shrines of St Swithin and St Etheldreda respectively. Bury St Edmunds (1081) (Fernie 1998) and possibly St Paul's Cathedral, London (1087) (Gem 1990), extend the presbytery to five bays, while Durham Cathedral (1093) (Bilson 1922; Thurlby 1994a), Norwich Cathedral (1096) (Fernie 1993a), and the Benedictine abbey (now cathedral) of Peterborough (1117–18) (*VCH* 1906, 431–56) all have four-bay eastern arms. Canterbury Cathedral after 1096 had a nine-bay eastern arm replacing the three-bay arrangement in the 1070 cathedral of Lanfranc (Woodman 1981, 45–76). The association of the long eastern arm with a shrine church may have been in the mind of King Stephen with regard to the burial of his children next to the high altar in Holy Trinity Priory.

The square east end

The plan of the east end of Holy Trinity Priory is unique but the constituent elements of its design evolve from late 11th- and early 12th-century major churches in England. For the arrangement of the eastern chapels the design ultimately evolves from the three-apse *en échelon* plan. In such churches where a shrine was placed in the main apse, it would make sense to provide an ambulatory in the form of a wooden screen, as proposed by Fernie (1993b, 150–1, fig 1) for the Romanesque cathedral at Durham. This type of 'furniture ambulatory' was also probably used at St Albans and Ely. Already at Winchester Cathedral and St Werbergh's at Chester a full architectural apse-ambulatory plan with a semicircular apse arcade was combined with three chapels facing east. Winchester is especially interesting for our purposes in that the central chapel was larger than the others, being four bays deep plus an apse, and was divided into two aisles at crypt level. Brooke (1993, 10) has suggested royal patronage for the nave of Winchester Cathedral and also at Romsey Abbey, Hampshire, *c* 1120 (Fig 87) where the plan of the eastern chapels is even closer to Holy Trinity in having a square termination to the presbytery and consequently a square ambulatory. At Romsey the central chapel was entered from the ambulatory through two arches that corresponded in size to those of the facing main arcade, and the chapel was divided into two aisles. The square ambulatory with three east-facing chapels was earlier used (1110) at Chertsey Abbey (Surrey), a Benedictine house founded in AD 666 by Erkenwald, afterwards Bishop of London. Here just one arch was used in the east wall of the presbytery that corresponded in width to the arch of the eastern chapel. Chertsey enjoyed strong royal patronage and Abbot Hugh, under whom the rebuilding commenced, was a relative of King Stephen (*VCH* 1905, 55, 58–9). The eastern extension of Old Sarum Cathedral undertaken by Bishop Roger (1102–39) also provides a parallel for the square ambulatory with three eastern chapels. Here it is possible and even likely that there were three arches in the east wall of the presbytery. Excavation did not reveal evidence for the rhythm of the arcade in the east wall, but the arrangement of the eastern chapels would have made it impossible to vault the ambulatory with a single large arch in the east wall of the presbytery (Stalley 1971, 73). This suggests that the division of the east wall of the presbytery would have matched the responds between the chapels to provide three arches. A reflection of this may also be in the early Gothic fabric of Salisbury Cathedral, where it is surely more than coincidence that the width of the presbytery, 39ft centre-to-centre of the main arcades, matches that of Bishop Roger's presbytery at Old Sarum Cathedral (Cocke and Kidson 1993).

While Chertsey, Romsey and Old Sarum provide analogues for the square ambulatory with eastern chapels at Holy Trinity Priory, their significance for the arrangement of the east wall of the presbytery and vaulting of the ambulatory at Holy Trinity cannot be determined absolutely. There are two possibilities: a three-bay or a two-bay division. The shafted respond on the north face of the easternmost pier in Thorpe's plan (Fig 17) indicates that an arch in the east wall must have sprung from this point. The three-aisled division of the central eastern chapel immediately suggests that a corresponding division would be appropriate for the east wall of the presbytery, in the manner of Salisbury Cathedral and probably Old Sarum Cathedral. This seems to be the most likely solution but the possibility of a two-bay scheme is worth considering.

Clearly the supports in the east wall of the presbytery would have to have been more substantial than those at the

Fig 87 The presbytery of Romsey Abbey, looking east (photograph: Malcolm Thurlby)

entrance to the chapel because they had to carry the tall gable wall. It is with this in mind that one might question the plausibility of the three-bay division of the east arcade of the presbytery at Holy Trinity. The latter was just 24ft (7.32m) wide as opposed to 39ft (11.89m) at Old Sarum and Salisbury. Therefore, the existence of just two arches in the main arcade of the east wall becomes a distinct possibility. It is true that this would lead to an eccentric vault in the ambulatory, given two bays to the west opposite three to the east. The result would be a central triangular vault flanked by trapezoidal, quadripartite rib vaults, an arrangement certainly within the repertoire of the English mason of the time. Such a design reads typologically as a fusion of the Romanesque ambulatory at Gloucester Cathedral (Clapham 1934, fig 10), where there were alternating square and triangular bays, with trapezoidal bays, as in the ambulatory of Norwich Cathedral (ibid, fig 11). And any idea that it would be unduly complicated is laid to rest through examination of the remarkable contortions of the vaults in the ambulatory of the crypt of Winchester Cathedral (ibid, fig 21). The very two-to-three-bay juxtaposition suggested here for Holy Trinity does occur in the early Gothic inner crypt of Glasgow Cathedral (Wilson 1998), and eccentricity in vault design is well known in the so-called crazy vault of St Hugh's choir of Lincoln Cathedral (1192–1200). Here it is worth recalling Peter Kidson's musings on the use of two keystones between each pair of transverse ribs in the nave vault of Durham Cathedral and that the vault added to the nave of Lincoln Cathedral by Bishop Alexander (1128–48) may have influenced St Hugh's choir vault. The Durham nave arrangement is also found in an Augustinian context in the vestibule of the chapter house at St Augustine's, Bristol (*c* 1160), so perhaps something a little more audacious might have happened in Augustinian London in the ambulatory of Holy Trinity Priory.

Eastern transeptal chapels on the presbytery

The inclusion of one-bay chapels outside the aisles of the presbytery and to the west of the ambulatory is unusual. The chapels may have been conceived as a reduced version of the eastern transepts of Anselm's choir of Canterbury Cathedral (1096–1130), or the third abbey church of Cluny (Saône-et-Loire, France), a house heavily patronised by King Henry I. Unlike these two examples the eastern 'transept' at Holy Trinity was not expressed in the main elevation of the presbytery, and in this regard the arrangement at Holy Trinity is formally closer to the great abbey church of Saint-Benoit-sur-Loire (Loiret, France).

Presbytery and transept turrets

Wyngaerde provides clear evidence for the existence of turrets at the angles of the presbytery and south transept and at the corners of the crossing tower. Eastern towers have been reconstructed at Winchester Cathedral (Crook 1989; 1993a), Durham Cathedral (Thurlby 1994a) and Hereford Cathedral. They may have existed at St Albans Abbey (Thurlby 1997a), and seem to have been intended at Kirkwall Cathedral (Orkney) on the model of those at Durham (Thurlby 1997b). Here the association is with the imperial grandeur of Speyer Cathedral (Rhineland-Palatinate, Germany) and possibly with Old St Peter's in Rome (Thurlby 1994b). Turrets also form part of this vertical accent as in the transept turrets at St Albans and subsequently at Winchester, Ely, Durham, Norwich, Peterborough and elsewhere. Angle turrets also appear in a secular setting on the White Tower of the Tower of London and other keeps such as Castle Hedingham (Essex) and Rochester (Kent). Turrets were used on the angles of the crossing tower at St Albans and have been restored on the crossing tower at Norwich Cathedral. They may be in part a reference to the symbolism of the church as the Heavenly City of Jerusalem (Smith 1956, 74–106, 186–8).

Pier forms

The compound pier is used in the Basilica Julia in Rome while the square pier articulated with an attached shaft on the outer face is a standard form in Roman amphitheatres. These forms are conceptually fused to create compound piers with attached shafts in the first half of the 11th century at the cathedral of Orléans (Loiret), St-Martin in Tours (Indre-et-Loire), in the cathedral crypts of Auxerre (Yonne) and Nevers (Nièvre), in the westblock of Saint-Benoit-sur-Loire (Loiret), and in Bernay (Eure) abbey church (all in France). In England, the compound pier with single attached shafts on the cardinal faces appears in Edward the Confessor's abbey church of Westminster. After the Conquest, a more complex pier with shafts on the cardinal faces and in the angles is introduced into England from St-Etienne at Caen (Calvados). Compound piers display great inventiveness and variety in Norman England (Hoey 1989b) and the three piers of which we have evidence in the north presbytery arcade at Holy Trinity have three different designs. The segmental east face of the west pier of bay D relates to the minor piers of the main arcades of Norwich Cathedral and the nave of Ely Cathedral (Fernie 1993a), the presbytery piers of Thetford Priory, Norfolk, and the faces of four piers in both arcades of the nave of Castle Acre Priory, Norfolk (Cherry 1978; Thurlby 1996). Of these the projection of the segmental element at Ely is greater than in the other examples; it is difficult to tell which is closer to Holy Trinity Priory.

The west face of the east pier of bay D is not recorded in any of the antiquarian evidence and has been reconstructed (Fig 78, b) to match the reconstructed pier face of the pier on the west side of the bay (Fig 78, c). This results in an asymmetrical pier, for there is clear evidence for a compound shafted arrangement on the east side in the drawings of both Carter (Fig 25) and Whichelo (Fig 31, left). Analogues for this detail are found in the minor piers of the nave gallery at Ely Cathedral and in the main arcade at Peterborough Cathedral (formerly Abbey). Seemingly closer to the face of the Holy Trinity pier is the face towards the nave of the Dunstable Priory (Bedfordshire) arcade piers (Fig 88). Asymmetrical pier

Fig 88 The nave of Dunstable Priory, looking east (photograph: Malcolm Thurlby)

design, combined with symmetry of the faces of the pier on either side of a particular bay, is the very arrangement used in the nave of Castle Acre Priory (Cherry 1978; Thurlby 1996). Its application in this instance at Holy Trinity seems assured because it appears from the evidence of the engraving in the *European Magazine* (Fig 27) and Whichelo's drawing (Fig 31, left) that the arch in bay D had two orders while in bay C there was a three-order arch.

In contrast to bay D, the faces of the piers to either side of bay C were asymmetrical, as clearly recorded by Carter (Fig 25). Here the compound plan with nook shafts supporting the second order of the arch evolves, along with many other piers in England, from the nave of St-Etienne at Caen. The change in pier design to either side of bay C relates to the nave of Rochester Cathedral. There the pier plans change from east to west but match across the nave north to south. This diversity in the piers of Holy Trinity is perhaps symptomatic of an Anglo-Saxon aesthetic as represented in the nave of Great Paxton (Huntingdonshire) which was possibly built for Edward the Confessor (Fernie 1983, 129–32).

The giant order

Evidence for a large segment of a cylinder continuing into the gallery pier from the front of the main arcade pier between bays C and D is provided by Carter and Whichelo (Fig 22; Fig 31, left). This continuation of the shaft on the front of the main arcade piers to carry the arches of the gallery is an adaptation of the giant order at the basilica at Fano (Italy) as described by Vitruvius in Book V of his *Ten books on architecture* (Vitruvius, 134–5), and seemingly first used after the Conquest at Tewkesbury, Gloucestershire (Halsey 1985; Thurlby 1985), and then at Romsey Abbey, Hampshire (Hearn 1975), Reading Abbey, Berkshire (Halsey 1985; Thurlby and Baxter 2001), Jedburgh Abbey, Roxburghshire (Thurlby 1995), Dunstable Priory, Bedfordshire (Halsey 1982) and St Frideswide, Oxford (Halsey 1990). The last four are all Augustinian foundations, and it has been suggested that the use of the giant order represents a house style for the Augustinians. Halsey added that the Dunstable nave may reflect Holy Trinity Aldgate (Halsey 1982). The suggestion is a good one for the giant order with cylinder at the front of the pier rising up to support the arches of the gallery, and the stepped shafted elements of the compound piers do recall Holy Trinity Priory. The pier design at Dunstable is uniform, however, in contrast to the change in pier design evident in Holy Trinity. It is significant that at Romsey, Reading and Dunstable we are dealing with the royal patronage of Henry I, and that the motif of the giant order was appropriated by King David I of Scotland in his foundation at Jedburgh Abbey.

Rib vaults

The introduction of the rib vault into English architecture is traditionally associated with Durham Cathedral (1093), although Christchurch Priory (Hampshire), Tewkesbury (Gloucestershire), Lincoln and Chepstow (Monmouthshire) may all have been earlier. The use of rib vaults in the aisles of major churches in England and Scotland became the norm for buildings commenced in the 12th century. Examples are, or were, at Winchester Cathedral as remodelled after the fall of the crossing tower in 1107, Exeter Cathedral (Devon), Peterborough Abbey (now Cathedral), Romsey Abbey (Hampshire), Dunfermline Abbey (Fife), Kirkwall Cathedral (Orkney), Jedburgh Abbey and Kelso Abbey (both Roxburghshire), Malmesbury Abbey (Wiltshire), Kirkstall Abbey (Yorkshire West Riding), Dunstable Priory (Bedfordshire) and St Frideswide, Oxford (now the cathedral). The profile of the ribs with a torus roll flanked by two hollow rolls is paralleled in a number of churches including Winchester Cathedral (after 1107), Exeter Cathedral (1112–14) (Thurlby 1991), Dunfermline Abbey (1128), the chancel and tower of Studland, Dorset (Lundgren and Thurlby 1999), and the chancel of Hemel Hempstead (Hertfordshire). This last parallel is interesting in an Augustinian context in that at some point in the 12th century the church of Hemel Hempstead seems to have been granted by the king to the canons of St Bartholomew Smithfield, London, for in 1201 they paid a fine of 200 marks for the confirmation of the grant (*VCH* 1908, 227; Webb 1921, i, 365).

The iconographic associations of the rib are significant for Holy Trinity. It has been suggested that the ribs of Durham should be allied with the free-standing ribs of the ciborium above the shrine of St Peter in Rome. More generally they are associated with altars, as at Christchurch, Tewkesbury, formerly at Peterborough (Thurlby 1994b), Ewenny, Glamorgan (Thurlby 1988), and Cormac's Chapel at Cashel (Tipperary), Ireland (Stalley 1981). Once again church furniture may be cited as a prototype, as in the ciborium of Sant'Ambrogio, Milan, where the ribs are fully integrated into the vault of the furniture above the high altar. At Speyer Cathedral the high rib vaults in the transepts have been read as signifiers of imperial burial in contrast to the groin vaults in the nave (Kidson 1996). The latter association may suggest that the highly elaborate ribs at Holy Trinity Priory should be read in connection with the royal burials, shortly before 1147, of the two children of King Stephen: Baldwin buried on the north side of the altar and Matilda on the south side. However, this seems unlikely because the richer ribs are only used in the south aisle, bay A, and not in the equivalent bay C on the north side. It is possible that the altar to the Virgin was in bay A, thus making the bay a Lady chapel, as possibly at the so-called Founder's Chapel off the south transept at Reading Abbey. At both Holy Trinity and Reading it is possible that the respective spaces had been intended for the royal burials, Matilda in bay A at Holy Trinity, and King Henry I in the Founder's Chapel at Reading. As it turned out, Henry was buried before the high altar, which suggests that there might have been a similar change in plan at Holy Trinity.

An iconographic reading is also appropriate for the arch mouldings: the richer design with the chevron ornament may be associated with the burial of King Stephen's two children to either side of the high altar. This interpretation may also apply to the more elaborate, or more shafted, eastern responds of the main arcades. This was the part seen by the viewer from the west.

Capital types

Scalloped capitals are used in St John's chapel of the Tower of London (*c* 1080), the crypt of Gloucester Cathedral, the dado arcades of the aisles of Durham Cathedral (1093–1133), and the crossing of North Newbald (Yorkshire East Riding), a prebendary church of York Minster. Especially close are parallels at Peterborough and Rochester.

The variety and the details of the multiscalloped capitals of Holy Trinity Priory suggest a date into the second quarter of the 12th century. A good parallel for the scalloped capital of the second pier in the north arcade of the eastern arm at Aldgate (Fig 78, a) is in the fifth pier from the west of the south arcade of the nave at Peterborough Cathedral, probably built in the time of Abbot Martin de Bec (1133–55). Also close to the Holy Trinity scalloped capital with fillets between the lower, segmental sections (Fig 25; Fig 29) are examples in the water tower of Canterbury Cathedral (1153–67), and in the chapter house and vestibule of St Augustine's, Bristol (1160–70), where there are many variants on the theme of this type of capital. This is not to say that the Holy Trinity capitals are contemporary with these Canterbury and Bristol examples, for it must be recognised that pointed wedges are used between the segmental sections of the scalloped capitals in the late 11th-century crypt of Gloucester Cathedral.

The foliage sculpture

A fragmentary capital with upright fleshy leaves from site E (<A78>, Fig 75; Fig 196) is closely related work of the third quarter of the 12th century in London. It may be compared to capitals of the dado arcade of the nave aisle of the Temple church, London, to a loose capital at Westminster Abbey and, perhaps most precisely, to a capital and voussoirs from St Bartholomew Smithfield. The broad, hollowed leaf topped with a heavy volute on the left of the capital would originally have been mirrored by a similar leaf to the right of the central leaf with the beaded central vein and trefoil top. This symmetrical design is paralleled in capitals 1, 6, 8, 25 and 36 in the dado arcade of the nave aisle of the Temple church, London, as recorded by Billings (1838) (Fig 89). The substantial angle volute is allied to Temple capitals 4, 7 and 61, while the beaded central leaf relates to Temple capital 34. An analogous design is encountered on a larger capital preserved in the cellar of 5 The Little Cloister, Westminster Abbey (Fig 90). Closer still is a capital from St Bartholomew Smithfield,

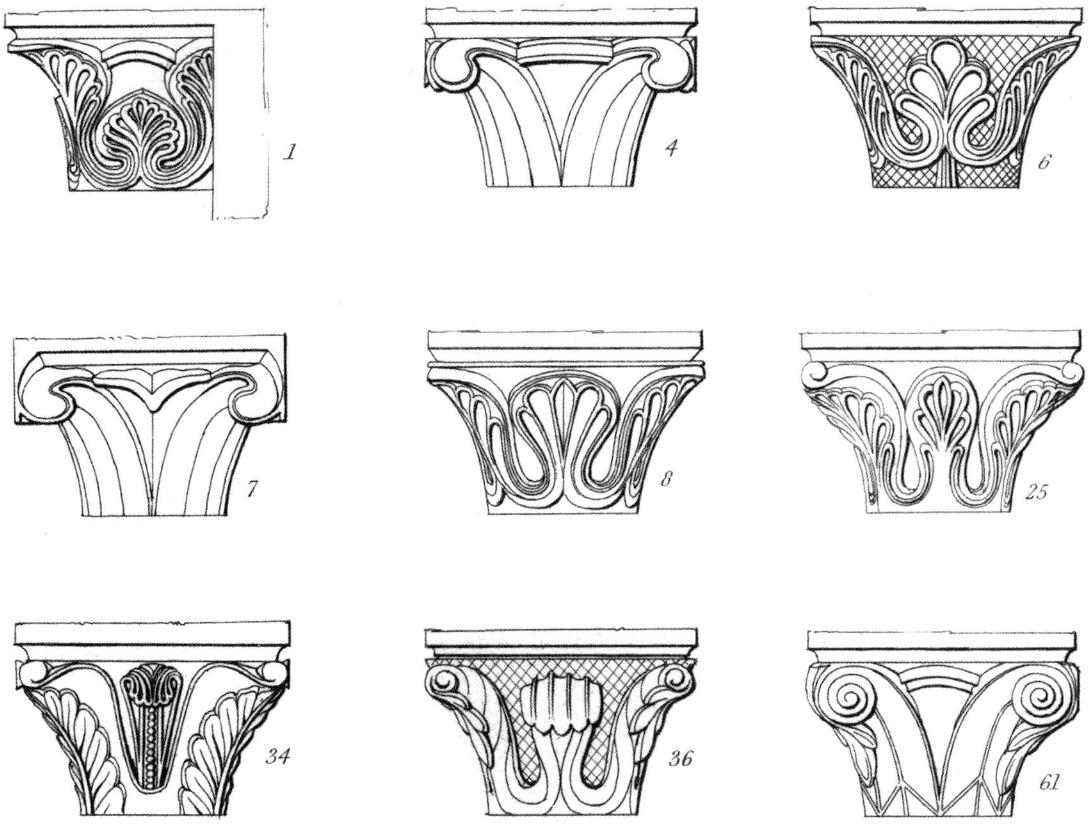

Fig 89 *Capitals from the nave of the Temple church, London (Billings 1838, pls XXII–XXIV)*

photographed in 1974 and now believed to be lost (Fig 91). Here is the same general disposition of the fleshy leaves, the beaded vein of the central leaf, and the volutes of the side leaves.

The Temple and St Bartholomew's parallels are important for dating the Holy Trinity capital. The Templars moved to the 'New Temple', the present church, in 1161, at which time it was probably completed. The Old Temple was built of Caen stone, and it is unlikely that the Templars would have moved from it into an unfinished building (Lees 1935, 158–60). The capital at St Bartholomew's belongs with other sculpture associated with the chapter house and east range of the cloister. The work is not documented but it is closely related to the great west doorway of the Augustinian priory of Dunstable which may be attributed to Prior Thomas (Marks 1970, 33–5; Thurlby 2001). A letter from Gilbert

Fig 90 *Capital preserved at Westminster Abbey (photograph: Malcolm Thurlby)*

Fig 91 *Capital from St Bartholomew Smithfield, London, now believed to be lost (photographed 1974, Malcolm Thurlby)*

Foliot, Bishop of London, to the prior and canons of St Bartholomew's supports the petition of the canons of Dunstable that T(homas), canon of St Bartholomew's, be released to become prior of Dunstable (Morey and Brooke 1967, 309, no. 236). The letter is datable to 1163–76 and perhaps more closely because it refers to the church – but not the Bishop – of Lincoln, which may suggest that the see of Lincoln was vacant, as was the case from late December 1166 until the election of Geoffrey in 1173. The St Bartholomew's sculpture is, therefore, likely to have been executed between 1150 and 1166–73. Concomitantly, the Holy Trinity capital may be attributed to the third quarter of the 12th century.

Three-storey elevation with thick wall

A full three storeys was essential for any great church in England, whether or not the galleries had any liturgical function. As reconstructed (Fig 83; Fig 84), the form of the clerestory is guesswork but it was the norm to have a wall passage at this level (Bony 1939; Hoey 1989a). Vertical articulation may have stopped at gallery level or have continued through to the top of the clerestory (Hoey1989b). It is surely significant that in the Dunstable nave the shaft continues into the spandrels of the gallery arcade and, therefore, on into the clerestory (Fig 88). The Holy Trinity Priory reconstruction (Fig 84) opts for a single opening at clerestory level, although parallels with other great churches in Norman England would suggest that a tripartite arrangement would be more likely, with a large arch in the centre facing the window flanked by two narrower arches (Hoey 1989a).

While rib vaults were used in the aisles there is no indication that there was a high vault at Holy Trinity. In Continental terms this is unusual, in that a high vault was considered as essential in most great churches, as at Speyer Cathedral, Sant'Ambrogio in Milan, St-Sernin in Toulouse, and Cluny III. This was not the case in England. High vaults were introduced in early post-Conquest churches at Chepstow, Lincoln, Gloucester and Tewkesbury. Rib vaults were planned from the first at Durham, but there was hesitancy in using them throughout the church (Thurlby 1993a; 1993b; 1994a; Fernie 1993b). Elsewhere, high vaults were used very selectively, as in the apse and forebay of Peterborough, possibly following Ely and Norwich (Thurlby 1994b). William of Malmesbury praised the painted ceiling of the choir of Canterbury Cathedral and it is interesting that this solution was taken up in the nave of Peterborough as finished by Abbot Baldwin (*VCH* 1906, 431–56). He had been prior at Canterbury before moving to Peterborough in 1177, and in spite of flirtation with a high vault the final decision was in favour of the painted ceiling that survives to this day.

In conclusion, the church at Holy Trinity Priory was therefore an ambitious essay in royal patronage, in which the eclectic approach to design aimed at the creation of a building that would vie with the greatest churches of Norman England and the rest of Europe.

4.5 Zone 2: the west end of the priory church, the great tower, and the west range of the cloister

Documentary and antiquarian evidence

There is virtually no documentary or antiquarian evidence for the west end of the priory church or the 'great tower' which Symonds shows at the north-west corner of the church (Figs 13–16). Shortly before 1312 two large bells had been made for the church (Chapter 3.2), and this probably implies that a belfry tower had been built by then; but this might refer to the substantial crossing tower of the church, which was still the largest component of the priory visible from the south in the 16th century. It should be noted that Symonds and, therefore, this report, uses the term 'great tower' for the tower at the north-west of the church, and not for the crossing tower, which to Symonds was the Ivy chamber and the room beneath it.

A copy of the 1805 edition of Pennant's *Some account of London* (first published in 1790) in Sir John Soane's Museum contains interleaved illustrations which include, besides engravings, some pencil sketches and watercolours of London buildings and scenes by several artists, including Frederick Nash (1782–1856). One watercolour shows Duke's Place, that is, the Tudor mansion incorporated into the west range of the cloister (Fig 92). It seems probable that Nash meant the title 'Dukes Place' below his watercolour to refer to the range (centre rear), rather than the square in front of it (the monastic great court), which was called Broad Place by 1790. The drawing is not dated, but must be after 1790, and before the fall of the main range in 1822 which is covered next. It is here dated to *c* 1810.

The south part of the range has three and a half storeys, and is evidently covered in weatherboarding. Two bays of bay windows, each of two storeys, face west; these may be equated with the bay windows shown on the first floor by Symonds (Fig 15; Fig 16). This drawing, therefore, suggests that the Tudor mansion, whether built by Audley or Norfolk, had bay windows rising through both first and second floors (the Symonds plans are of the ground and first floors only). The large ground-floor doorway to the right (south) is probably the alley through the range, but there is no sign of the adjacent door up to the hall or the octagonal external stair shown by Symonds (the latter is shown by the subsequent drawings of Schnebbelie; Fig 93; Fig 94). The north part of the range has evidently been rebuilt; the building with rusticated arches is part of the Great Synagogue of James Spiller (1790), replacing the earlier synagogue which had already been enlarged by George Dance the elder in 1765–6 (Colvin 1995, 288; a view of the north-east corner of the court showing the west end of the Synagogue in the early 19th century is given in Roth 1950, pl 35).

In 1822 the central spine-wall of the range, with post-Dissolution buildings on both sides, partly collapsed by falling westwards. The site was inspected by R Schnebbelie (fl 1792–1849) on more than one occasion as it was cleared; some of his

Fig 92 Frederick Nash, *Duke's Place: the former great court, looking east, watercolour* c 1810 (*Sir John Soane's Museum, interleaved in Soane's copy of* Some account of London *by Thomas Pennant*, 4 edn (1805))

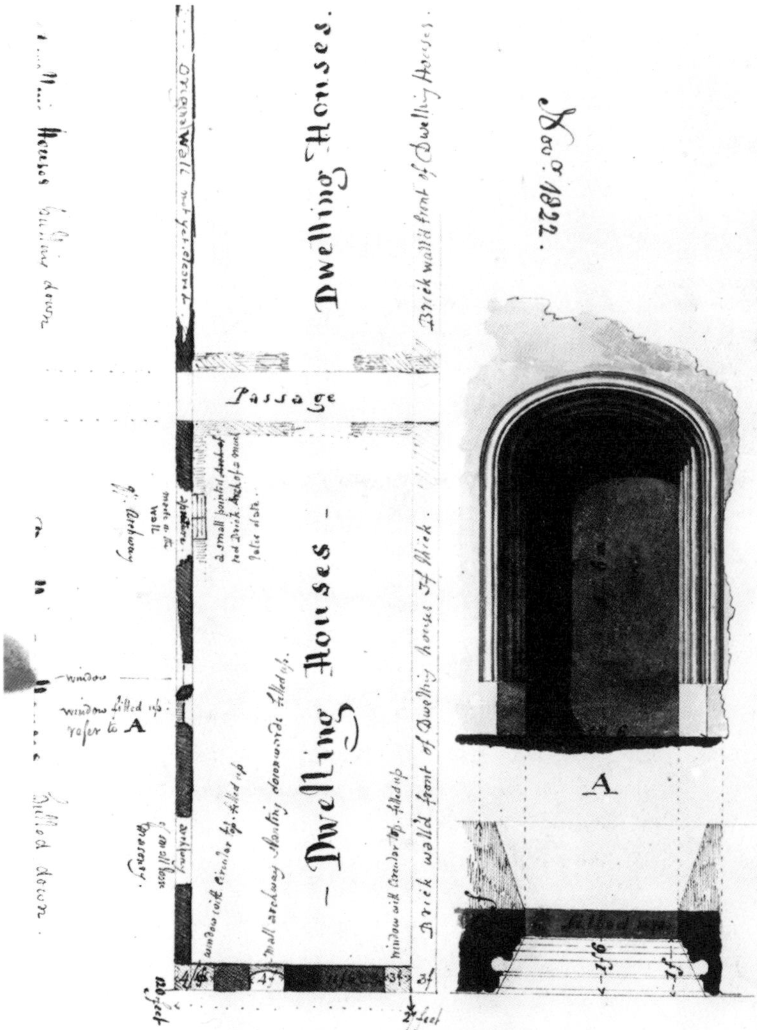

Fig 93 *R Schnebbelie, original drawings of west claustral range, 1815 (? or 1822): plan and 16th-century doorway (Museum of London)*

original sketches (Fig 93; Fig 94) were later engraved by W Taylor for Wilkinson's *Londina Illustrata* (1825). Schnebbelie's plan (below the engraved elevation, Fig 95) shows that the range was originally 120ft (36.6m) north–south and 27ft (8.2m) east–west externally. The view looks east, and provides a west elevation of the spine-wall of the range. The foundation of this wall, excavated in 1979 (below, site F) was of 12th-century date; interpretation of archaeological evidence and the Symonds plan suggests that this west elevation was originally the outer face of the 12th-century west range.

In the basement, an arch is seen through a hole in the masonry; in the original sketch (Fig 94) the back of a fireplace

Fig 94 R Schnebbelie, original drawings of west claustral range, 1815 (? or 1822): general view (Museum of London)

with a flue is seen going up the west side of the wall, but this is replaced by a second arch in the engraving (Fig 95). The fireplace is shown in the Symonds plan, in the basement of the range, and takes on a significance when the post-Dissolution uses of the west range, as hinted at by archaeological work on site, are considered (below, site F).

On the first floor, in both sketch and engraving, two openings with round heads, evidently doorways, are shown piercing the spine-wall, though the southern of the two is blocked up. Schnebbelie also drew this doorway and its mouldings (Fig 93); it is three-centred and incorporates scroll-mouldings, and therefore appears to be 16th-century in date. A door is shown in this position in the first-floor plan by Symonds (Fig 15; Fig 16).

The sketch and the engraving differ in details on the left-hand side, which must reflect two separate visits to the site by Schnebbelie as the building was demolished. In the sketch, but not in the engraving, are details of a later fireplace in the north wall of the visible range; this obscures a medieval archway which is shown in position in the engraving. In a further inset on the engraving Schnebbelie drew the top part of a pointed arch and its moulding profile: two hollow chamfers, a roll and a casement hollow of 14th- or 15th-century date. The position of this arch on his plan makes it highly likely that this was an arch at the top of the steps, giving entry from the main courtyard into the first-floor hall (compare Symonds's ground-floor and first-floor plans, Figs 13–16).

Finally, a low arch probably of stone at the right-hand side of both elevations may well be part of the east wall of the great tower, which continued the line of the spine-wall of the west range to the south, and perhaps part of a vault.

Excavations

West side of Mitre Square, 1979 (HTP79; site F)

In 1979 excavation took place after demolition of Victorian warehouse buildings on the west side of Mitre Square (Fig 2; Schofield 1985). Correlation of archaeological evidence and the Symonds plan after the excavation showed that the pedestrian passage which formed the north boundary of the archaeological site was that shown crossing the range by Symonds (Fig 13; Fig 14). Evidence for Roman occupation was divided into five groups (gpF1–F5, period I); it comprised quarry pits dug into the natural brickearth (the surface of which, where not cut into, lay between 11.38m OD and 11.53m OD) and the north-west corner of an undated but pre-medieval masonry building (gpF1). Surfaces to the north-west of this building, unconnected but of an internal character (gpF3), lay at about 11.50–11.60m OD. The late Saxon to early modern periods on the site were represented by groups F6–F19 (Table 2). A sequence diagram showing the relationships of the groups is given in Fig 96, and a plan showing the excavated masonry features is given as Fig 99. This can be compared with

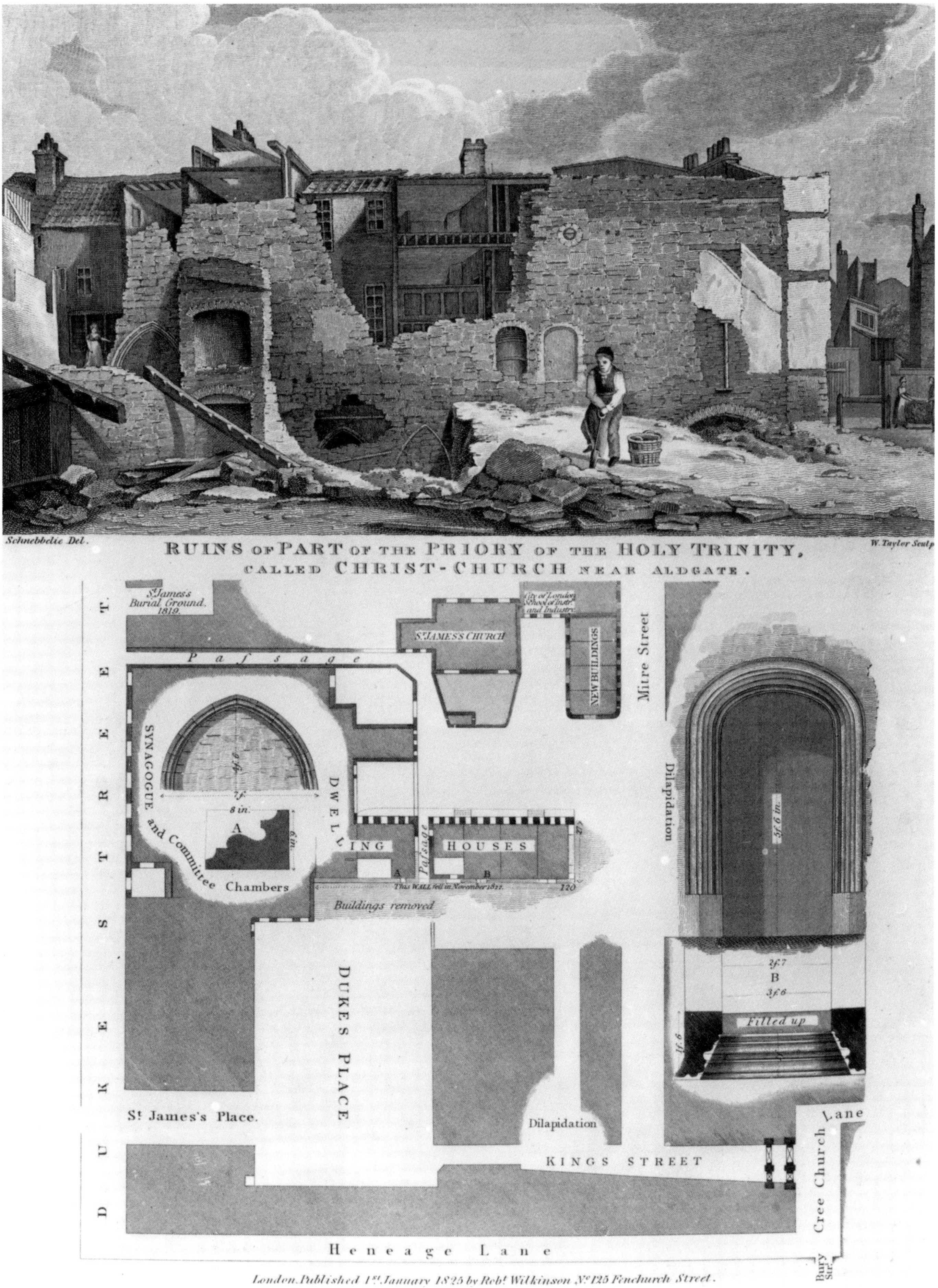

Fig 95 R Schnebbelie, the drawings as engraved in Wilkinson's Londina Illustrata (1825) (Museum of London)

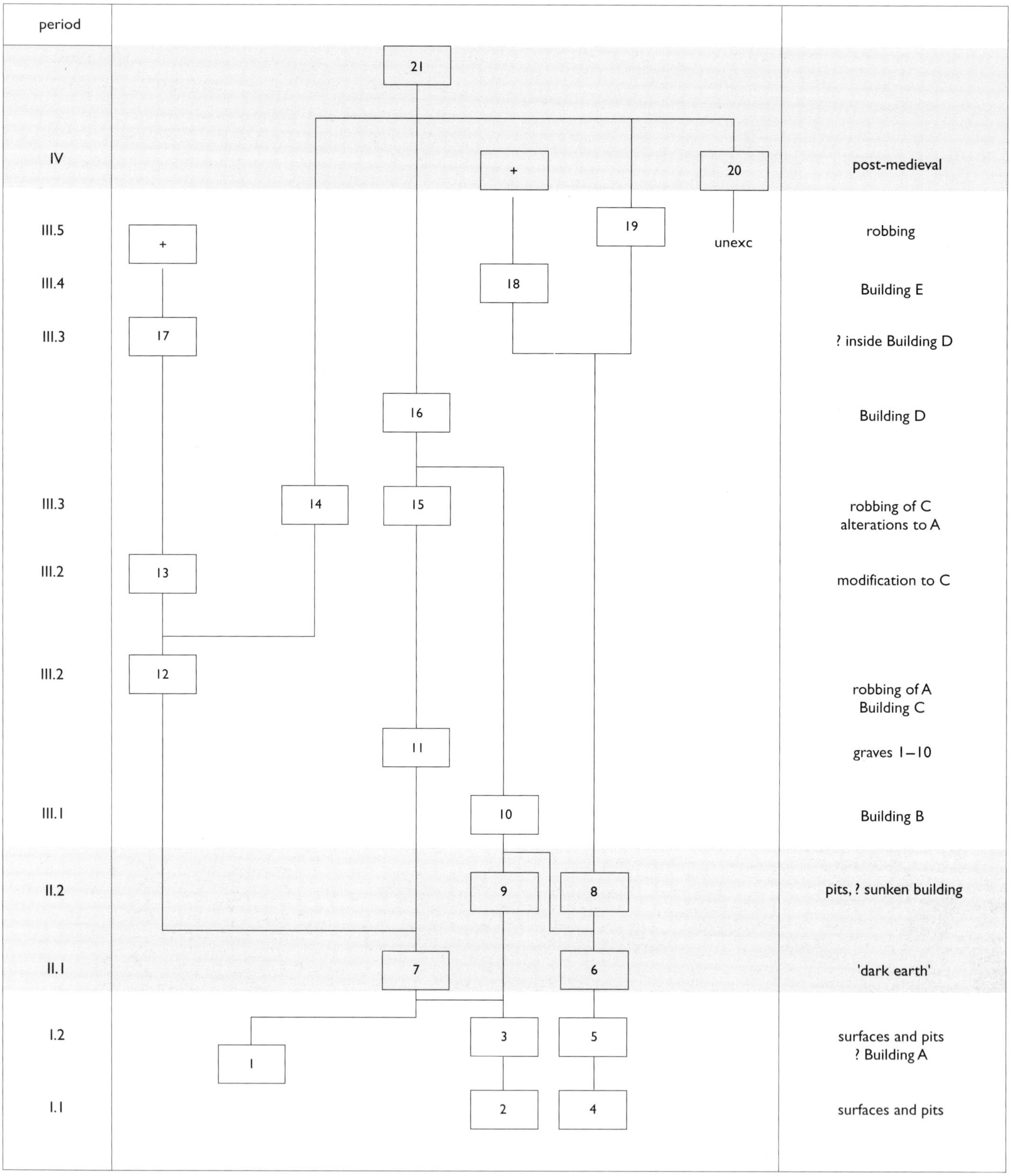

Fig 96 Site F: sequence diagram of stratigraphic groups, including Roman (gpF1–F5) and Saxon (gpF6–F9)

the overhead photographic view in Fig 98 (note that north is to the bottom of Fig 98 and towards the top of Fig 99).

PRE-PRIORY OCCUPATION (PERIOD II, gpF6–F9)

The north-west corner of a masonry building, summarily recorded at the south side of the excavation (period I, gpF1, Building A), was not dated by any artefacts and could be of Roman or late Saxon date (Fig 97). This building's significance for the present report is that it was robbed in period III (medieval) and may, therefore, have been showing above ground in the early 11th century, although this sighting, by itself, is unsatisfactory. The building probably extends

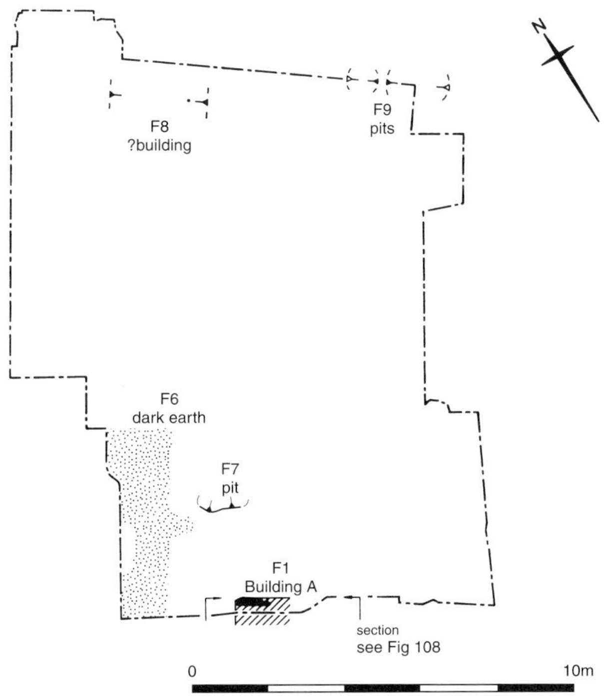

Fig 97 Plan of pre-priory, late Saxon occupation on site F (period II, gpF6–F8) (scale 1:200)

below Mitre Street.

Post-Roman 'dark earth' was recorded in two parts of the site (gpF6, gpF7), reaching 11.73m OD at its highest. Also allocated to group F7 was a single pit in the south-west area of the excavation, at least 1.1m across and cut from at least 11.73m OD. Most of the pottery is Roman (36 out of 40 original records), but three sherds of late Saxon shelly ware (LSS) from a large bowl (<P1>, Fig 199), were found in clay silt F[102] (gpF7), while seven sherds of early medieval sandy ware (EMS) and one of early medieval chalk-tempered ware (EMCH) were found in group F7 humic silt F[34] and F[133] (527g, 0.32 EVEs); as a group these can be dated to *c* 1050.

A dish-shaped cut, a surface and a single stakehole may represent a crude sunken-floored building in the north-west part of the site (gpF8). It contained only Roman residual finds. Two pits lay east of the structure, one of which contained only Roman pottery, while the other (F[184], gpF9) contained LSS dating to AD 900–1050. These fragmentary pieces of evidence, therefore, suggest that during the Saxon period 'dark earth' accumulated around and over Roman buildings, and that in the late Saxon period there was a small amount of activity on or near the site.

WEST CLAUSTRAL RANGE, BURIALS AND WEST END OF THE PRIORY CHURCH (PERIOD III, gpF10–F19)

No contemporary ground surface was recorded for the medieval and post-medieval periods, due to the truncation caused by the 19th-century basement from which excavation started. Because the foundations excavated (Fig 98) were of different dates, often with long gaps in time between them, it is necessary to discuss all the dating evidence for each individual

Fig 98 Overhead view of excavations in progress on site F, from the north; all the medieval and modern foundations, and several graves, have been exposed at the same time (1.0m scale)

group of strata together, before describing the next group. A substantial north–south foundation of chalk in sandy mortar was traced for 5.0m running south from the north edge of the excavation (period III.1, gpF10, Building B; Fig 99; Fig 100); it cut through 'dark earth'. Running east from it were two foundations of similar character, though damaged by later intrusions (gpF13, gpF15). The construction technique (Fig 101) suggests a 12th- or early 13th-century date (see discussion above, 4.2).

Correlation with the Symonds plan (Fig 13; Fig 14) suggests that this foundation lay below the wall running down the middle of the west range of the cloister. In its later, rebuilt, form it is therefore the wall which partly fell down in 1822, shown in ruins by Schnebbelie (Fig 94; Fig 95).

To the south-west of Building B were ten mortar- and stone-lined cists (gpF11; Fig 100), containing both male and female skeletons (Table 6). They were aligned with the priory church and hence probably date from after 1108 (period III.1–2). The mortar- and stone-lined cists (eg Fig 102) are of 11th/12th-century type with parallels in London (cf White

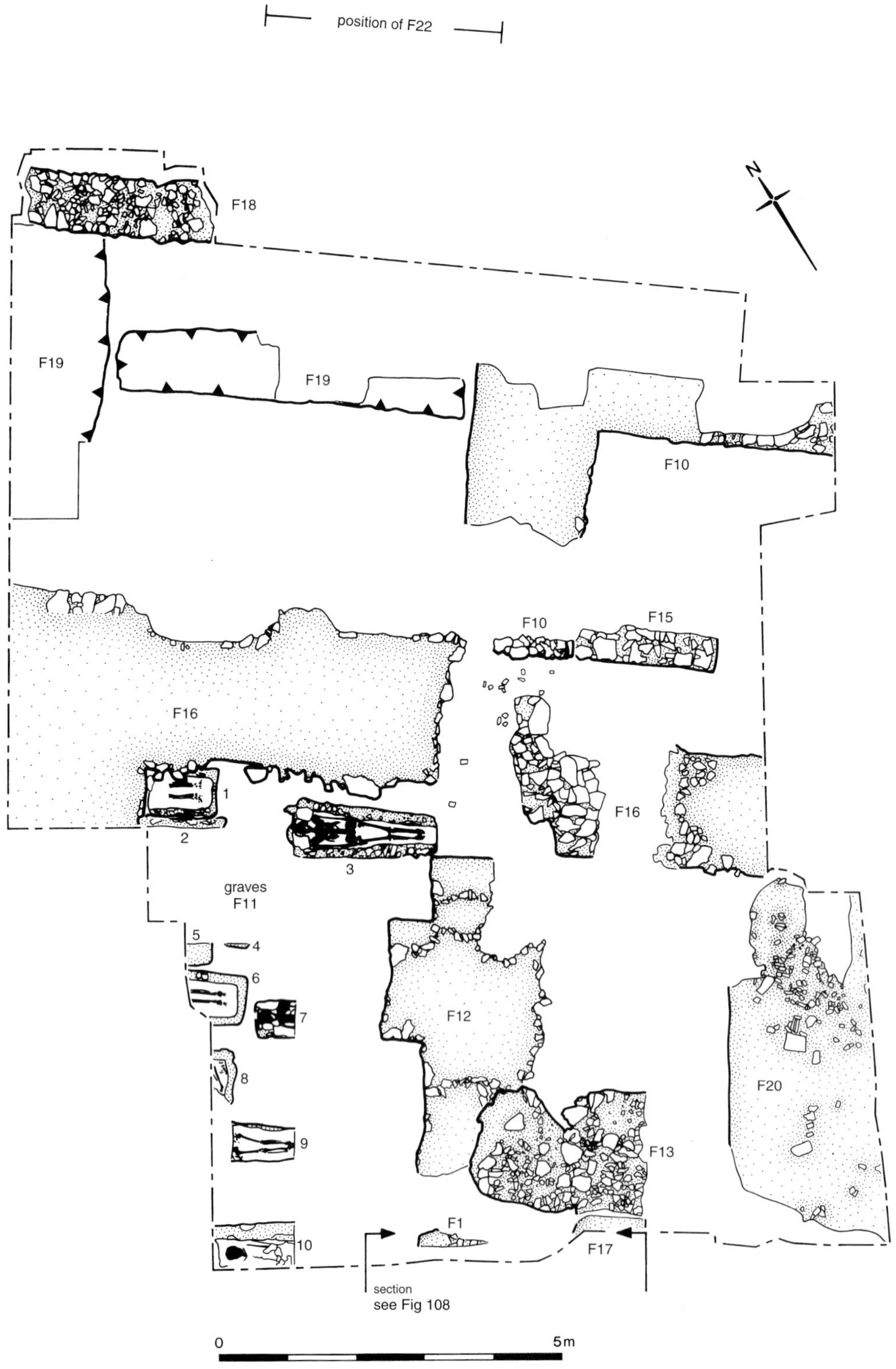

Fig 99 Plan of medieval and post-medieval features, to c 1650, on site F (stippling indicates surviving upper surface of mortar core) (scale 1:100)

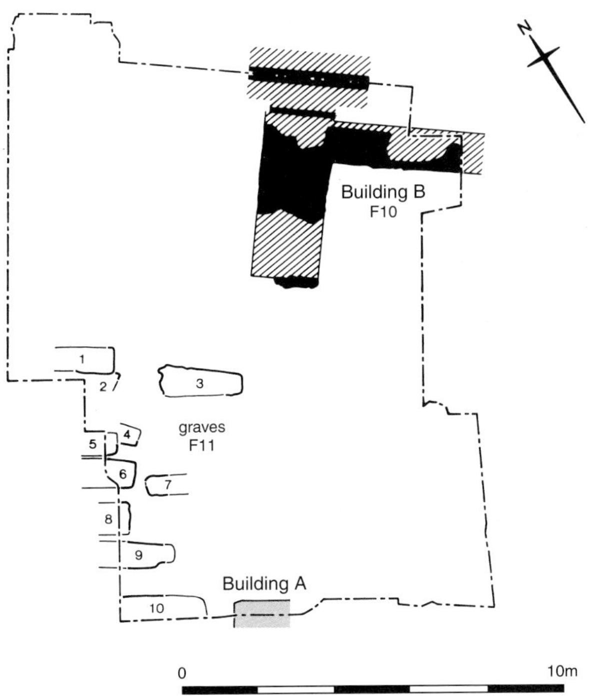

Fig 100 Plan of the west claustral range (Building B) and burials on site F (period III.1–2, gpF10–F11) (scale 1:200)

Fig 101 Section through foundation of the west claustral range (Building B) on site F, looking north (1.0m scale)

1988), and cut through 'dark earth'. One grave (grave 1) was cut by Building D in group F16.

The tight spatial grouping of the graves, and absence of further examples to the east, suggested at the time that the south-west corner of Building B formed the north-east corner of a delimited cemetery area which stretched beyond the area of excavation to the west (this was confirmed by the recording of burials five years later on site G, which lies adjacent) and south. The incorporation of many disturbed bones in the graves (eg Fig 103) suggests that previous burials, probably largely without cists, had been made in the area. No traces of coffins were observed. The pottery from the graveyard (gpF11) again comprises mainly Roman material (28 out of 32 records), but ten post-Roman sherds were found (76g), four in grave 3 (F[28], F[35]) and six in grave 9 (F[31]). Of these fabrics, LSS and EMS are probably residual, while early medieval sand- and shell-tempered ware (EMSS) and early Surrey ware (ESUR) date to *c* 1050–*c* 1150.

The masonry building (Building A) to the south of Building B was robbed by digging through 'dark earth', and a large masonry foundation of ragstone, flint and occasional tile in buff mortar constructed to form the north-west corner of a large building (Building C, period III.2, gpF12; Fig 104). Where the foundation intruded into underlying strata, the east edge was ragged, but the west side had a crisp edge and incorporated a protruding area 1.4m north–south by 0.6m east–west which resembled a buttress base on the west side immediately south of the corner. The end of the building was aligned due south of Building B, indicating a deliberate relationship. The burials of group F11, which may have been contemporary also with Building C, lay immediately to the west (Fig 100). It is suggested that Building C formed the west end of the Norman priory church. It was later robbed (gpF14) and replaced by

Table 6 Graves on site F, period III.1–2, group F11

Grave no.	Context no. of skeleton	Sex	Age (yrs)	Stature (m)	Comments
1	F[103]	f	adult	1.72	mortar- and stone-lined cist; cut by construction of Building D
2	-				no skeleton seen; mortar- and stone-lined cist (fragment only seen)
3	F[52]	m	25–35	1.78	mortar- and stone-lined cist (Fig 102)
	F[61]	m	adult	-	disturbed bones of two individuals at feet of F[52] (Fig 103)
	F[61]	-	4–5	-	
4	-				no skeleton seen; mortar- and stone-lined cist (fragment only seen)
5	-				no skeleton seen; mortar- and stone-lined cist (east end only seen)
6	F[134]	m	adult	1.72	mortar- and stone-lined cist
7	F[42]	f	18–20	-	mortar- and stone-lined cist
8	F[53]	f	adult	-	mortar- and stone-lined cist
9	F[41]	f	adult	1.57	mortar- and stone-lined cist
10	F[122]	m	28–40	1.80	mortar- and stone-lined cist

Fig 102 12th-century burial in mortar- and stone-lined cist (site F): grave 3, skeleton F[52], from the south (0.5m scale)

Fig 103 Detail of disturbed bones F[61] around feet of articulated skeleton F[52], in grave 3 (site F) (this picture was taken before Fig 102), from the south (0.1m scale)

Building D, the later west end (gpF16), which is why it does not appear on the Symonds plan. Although the strata at the south-east corner of site F were disturbed, it seemed likely that the distinctive mortar cists of the burials were intentionally bordered on the east by a line which in the 12th century would have been a southward extension from the stub foundation and probable wall of group F10 (Fig 99). Some of these burials, if not all, probably post-dated the foundation of the priory. If, as is normal on large church sites, the church was built from east to west, then it seems likely that this part of the cemetery was laid out respecting the intended future place of the west end of the church. In terms of the groups on Fig 99, the suggested sequence is, therefore, group F10–group F11–group F12.

The foundation recorded as group F12 is taken to be the west end of Building C. A further foundation was later added on the east (interior) side (gpF13); again only the bottom courses of mortared ragstone with occasional chalk and flint survived (Fig 104, right). The purpose of this modification is uncertain.

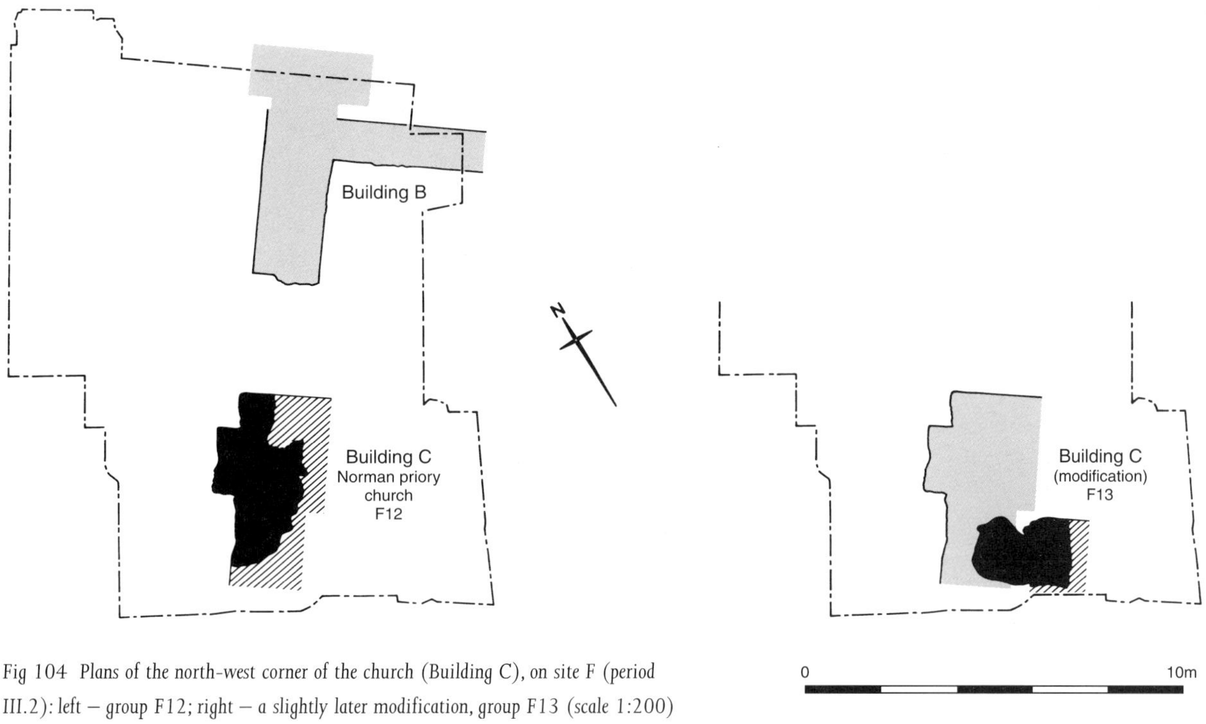

Fig 104 Plans of the north-west corner of the church (Building C), on site F (period III.2): left – group F12; right – a slightly later modification, group F13 (scale 1:200)

The pottery associated with the foundation of the west end of the priory church (gpF12) contains some Roman material, but a rather higher proportion of medieval pottery (18 sherds, 263g, 0.06 EVEs). Of these, two from F[126] are probably intrusive, as they date to *c* 1340–*c* 1450 (coarse Surrey-Hampshire border ware (CBW) and late medieval Hertfordshire glazed ware (LMHG), perhaps derived from gpF18 or gpF19). The sherds from F[108] mainly comprise early medieval sandy ware (EMS), which went out of use *c* 1050 and should be residual; the other wares are early medieval sand- and shell-tempered ware (EMSS) and one sherd of possible red-painted ware (REDP) from the Rhineland (undecorated), which could date to the 10th, 11th or 12th century. Taken together, these wares date to before *c* 1150, but they cannot provide a precise date for the construction of the church. The finds associated with the second foundation inside the church (gpF13) comprise one sherd of EMSS and one of early medieval shell-tempered ware (EMSH), the latter dating to *c* 1050–*c* 1150 (F[5]). The digging of the foundation group F13 is, therefore, datable only to this time-span or later.

In the next phase (period III.3) Building C was replaced by Building D, which extended to the north to join with Building B, and west over the burials of group F11, cutting several (Fig 105). First, the north-west corner of Building C was robbed (gpF14); a large robber trench on its west side was recorded in section, though not in plan, after initial clearance of the site (Fig 108). The layers of backfill contained only Roman pottery. Second, at the south end of Building B (gpF15) an undated foundation for another east–west wall was laid in mortared ragstone (shown in Fig 106, on the right), running east from the old 12th-century foundation of Building B which formed the west side of the main range. Third, a substantial foundation in mortared rough-hewn ragstone representing a new building

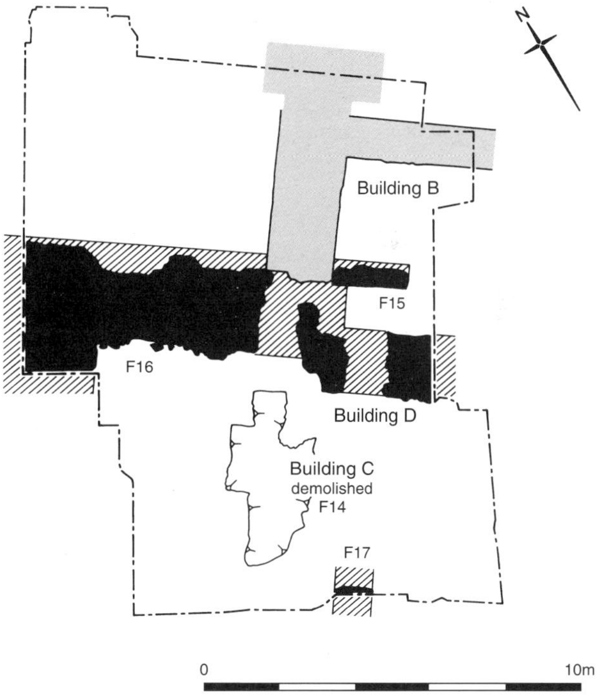

Fig 105 Plan of the rebuilt church (Building D) and the modification to the west claustral range (Building B) on site F, period III.3, groups F14–F17 (scale 1:200)

(Building D) ran both west beyond the limit of excavation and, probably reduced in width, to the east (gpF16; Fig 105; at the east side of the excavation, Fig 107). This group contained a single mortar-encrusted pottery strap handle in coarse London-type ware (LCOAR, 36g, possibly from an early baluster jug) datable to *c* 1150–*c* 1200. Fourth, an undated north–south foundation of rough-hewn ragstone blocks was recorded in the south baulk (gpF17; Fig 108); during initial clearance of the

Fig 106 View of the extension to the west claustral range (Building B) on site F, looking north-east, showing the two types of stone used: chalk for the earlier 12th-century foundation of Building B (bottom left), and ragstone for the later extension (right). The wall was badly damaged by the adjacent 19th-century east–west foundation (0.5m scale)

Fig 107 View of the north wall of the rebuilt church (Building D) on site F, looking east; the foundation (right) had a wide foundation trench, which was backfilled on the outer northern side (left) with mortar. The mortar has been partly removed but can be seen in section (0.5m scale)

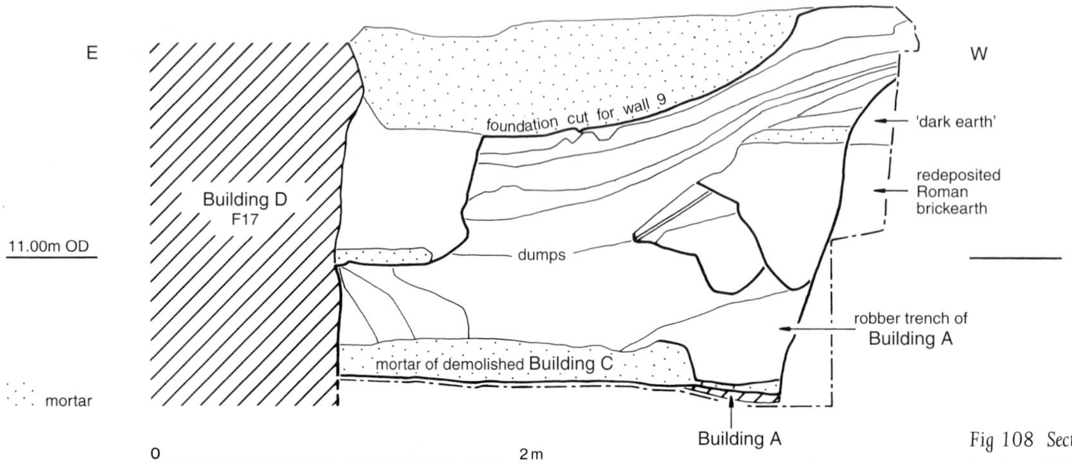

Fig 108 Section at south baulk on site F; for the location of this section see Fig 99 (scale 1:40)

site this foundation was seen to run north into the excavation for about 1.5m.

Though the evidence is sparse and fragmentary, these four building operations are taken together to imply considerable building works at the west end of the priory church: demolition of the north-west corner, at least, of the church; construction of a large and deeply-founded extension to the west, and new internal foundations at the point where the new work abutted the west range of the cloister; and a further internal foundation or wall within the new building.

Two further phases of activity were recorded in the north-west part of the excavation (Fig 109); their interrelationship is uncertain and they are put together as Building E (period III.4). A fragment of wall running east–west (gpF18) was of rough-hewn blocks of ragstone and chalk, and was not datable. Its slight depth of only 0.4m suggests that it was a minor wall or an internal partition. Nearby were two robber trenches for larger foundations; here they are reported in their proposed original phase, rather than that of their robbing, in order to make sense of them (gpF19). The north–south trench, of which only the east side was observed, was at least 1.4m wide and at least 4.1m north–south; with its bottom at between 12.05m OD and 12.65m OD, it was backfilled with silts, layers of mortar and fragments of tile, chalk, Reigate stone and slate. The east–west trench, 5.1m long and 1.0m wide, was dug to a depth of between 12.15m OD and 12.29m OD and was filled with brickearth, silts, and mixed chalk and ragstone rubble. The six sherds of medieval pottery from F[66] in one of the trenches date to the 11th and 12th centuries (EMS, EMSH, ESUR, LCOAR and London-type ware (LOND)), but those from F[65], F[82] and F[106] include several sherds of coarse Surrey-Hampshire border ware (CBW), which appears in a range of forms (cooking pots, jugs and a bowl), and single sherds of Mill Green ware (MG; F[106]) and Saintonge ware (SAIG; F[82]). These wares all date to after *c* 1270, and possibly to the 14th century. There was also a complete rectangular copper-alloy buckle F<31> (Chapter 8.6) and two floor tiles of 'Westminster' type (Chapter 8.3). Thus, though the original walls in these two groups may have been of pre-Dissolution construction, they were robbed later. This was probably after *c* 1585 since it is proposed that Building E is shown by Symonds (see below).

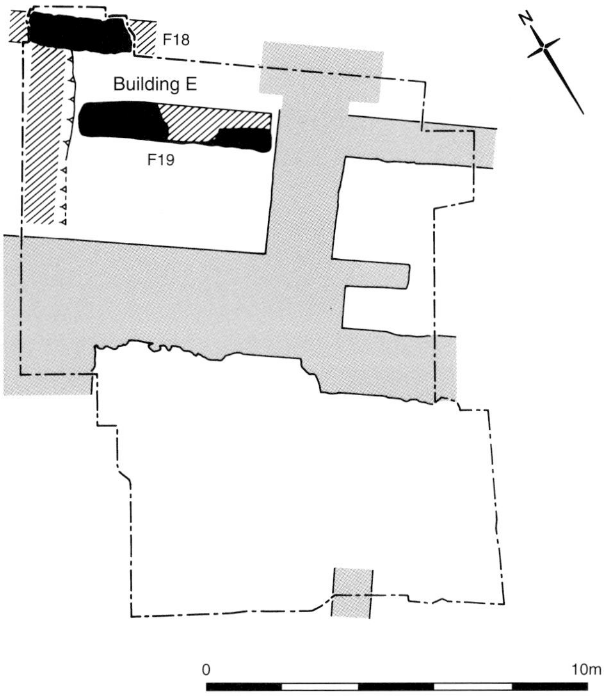

Fig 109 Plan of Building E on site F, period III.4, groups F18–F19 (scale 1:200)

CORRELATION WITH THE SYMONDS PLAN

The survey of *c* 1585 by Symonds (Figs 13–16) shows that at that time buildings B, D and E were all standing. The following sequence is suggested by correlation of the archaeological and plan evidence, with the addition of relevant documentary evidence (Fig 110).

Building B, of the 12th century (on archaeological and documentary grounds, probably of the first half of the century), originally stood by itself and formed the west range of the cloister. The Symonds plan shows two square pier bases within it, forming an undercroft 14m (46ft) by 7.6m (25ft) northwards to the passage across the range which is presumed to be original. The plan also shows three single-light splayed windows to the cloister on the east, divided by buttresses which may be later. To the south of this central undercroft is a small chamber, the west end of which was based on the stub foundation group F10; its east end to the cloister has a window of two lights.

Building C, the west end of a masonry building constructed in *c* 1150–*c* 1200 or later, is not shown by Symonds. The fragment excavated, it is proposed, is the north-west corner of the priory church, most logically the one which was laid out in the 1130s and 1140s and described previously (above, 4.3).

Correspondence with the Symonds plan for Building D is particularly close. It is highly probable that Building D is the building which includes the 'great tower', whose west side was probably reflected in the 19th-century boundary to the excavation site.

Building E, it is suggested, comprised the doubling in width of the west claustral range to the west some time after the 12th century and before *c* 1585. The north–south robber trench of group F19 probably shows the line of the west wall of the doubled claustral range (ie the wall fronting the great court).

Further evidence for the post-medieval history of Building E is given by some of the pictures and engravings. In about 1810 Nash's view of the great court of Duke's Place (Fig 92) shows the main range of the Tudor mansion, of three and a half storeys. The scene of its downfall in 1822 is shown by Schnebbelie (Fig 95). Wider reconstruction of the west claustral range in the medieval period is attempted later in this section.

12–14 Mitre Street, 1984 (MIR84; site G)

In May–June 1984 a watching brief was carried out on the site of 12–14 Mitre Street, on the north side of the street

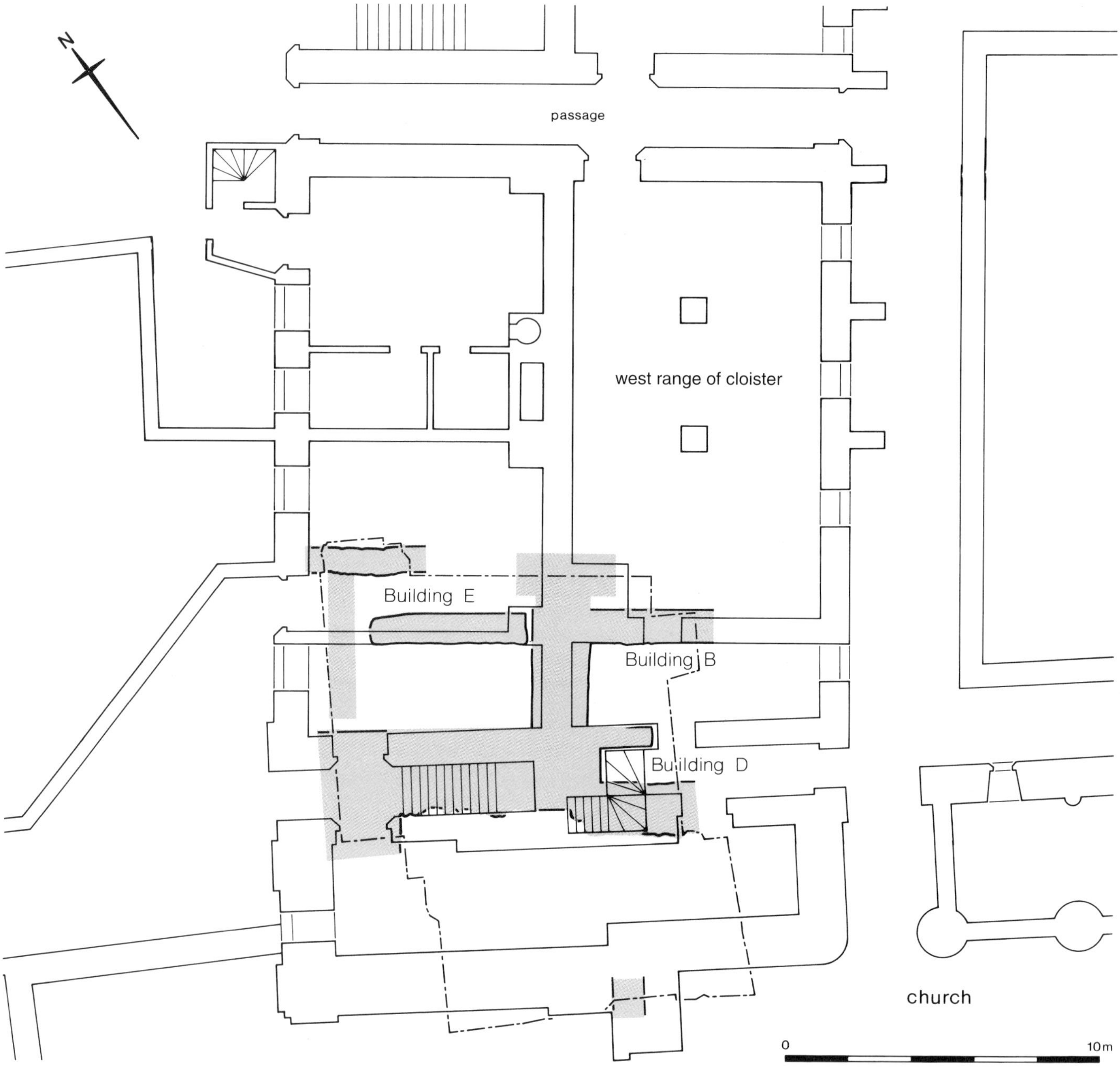

Fig 110 *Correlation of medieval foundations with the Symonds plan, for Buildings B, D and E, on site F (scale 1:200)*

immediately west of the Mitre Square (HTP79, site F) site (Fig 2); the archive report (Pye nd) used here is in note form and has not been improved for this study.

The earliest activity recorded comprised quarries dug into the natural brickearth and backfilled in the 2nd century AD. These were overlaid by dark grey-black organic silty clay, into which graves were cut. This graveyard soil produced pottery of *c* 1050–*c* 1200. No complete skeletons or articulated remains were recorded, but the soil had many disarticulated human bones in it. There were also three rubbish pits of similar date (gpG7.1); from one pit came pottery of the 10th or 11th century (G[125]). A medieval stone foundation observed in the north-east corner of the site was evidently the south-west corner of the great tower foundation recorded as Building D on the adjacent site F. No plans or sections are reproduced here.

The site is chiefly notable for a cesspit of early 18th-century date with important pottery in it (Chapter 8.5).

Reconstructing the west end of the nave, the great tower, and the west range of the cloister

The west end of the nave and the great tower

In the Mitre Square (site F) excavations, the north-west corner of a masonry structure was recorded as Building C. This lay in alignment southwards from the west side of the western claustral range, Building B, and it seems likely that Building C represents the west end of the priory church at the end of the 12th century. The single, disturbed foundation of Building C could not be accurately dated, except that it was after *c* 1150.

Building C was later demolished to make way for more substantial foundations (Building D) which include the western tower as shown by Symonds (Figs 13–16), extending westwards the line of the north aisle.

The great tower, Building D, which effectively formed the westernmost bay of the north aisle and, therefore, an imposing element of the west façade of the church up to the time of Symonds, is dated to the second half of the 12th century or later on the basis of a single sherd from its foundation on site F. This does, however, agree with the likely date for the clasping buttresses shown by Symonds.

Two contrasting functions can be suggested for Building D. It may have been a belfry; the making of a second bell in 1312 would suggest that one had been built by this date. The second bell weighed 2820lb, and the first, for which it was to be a companion, was greater in size. Such bells would have required a considerable structure to support their use; and a tower could have been part of the west end of the church structure (as at Augustinian Bridlington, Yorkshire East Riding, also in the 13th century) or free-standing to one side of the church. Alternatively, the tower may have principally functioned as an outer parlour, where members of the monastic community could meet the outside world. This would especially be required in this case as the prior, being alderman of Portsoken ward, had secular duties. Here parallels are supplied by the buildings at Cluniac Castle Acre Priory (Norfolk), where such an outer parlour of the mid 12th century partly survives (Coad and Coppack 1998, 36), and at Gloucester Cathedral, where Church House, in the same position relative to the west end of the (abbey) church, incorporates a stone building of the 12th century which functioned as part of the abbot's lodging. The ground floor of the tower may have functioned as an outer parlour, together with the first bay of the north aisle of the church which was partitioned off with stout walls and two narrow (probably medieval) windows into the church. On the analogy of Castle Acre the first-floor rooms might have contained a private chapel for the prior, but there is no direct evidence. The first-floor plan of Symonds bears no relation to the ground-floor plan, and there may be mistakes here (including the little chamber on the first-floor plan attached to the west wall of the church, which has nothing beneath it). The first floor may also have been rebuilt to a different plan by Audley or Norfolk in 1534–64.

West range of the cloister (? prior's lodging)

An outline history of the range can be constructed from a combination of archaeological and pictorial evidence, taken with the Symonds plan (Figs 13–16). The excavations on the west side of the cloister at site F suggest that the cloister was laid out in the 12th century, since Building B, from the character of its foundations, is of that date. The story of the Londoners processing round the cloister and looking into the refectory on an occasion before the fire of 1132 (Chapter 3.2) would imply that the cloister and refectory, and thus presumably the west range of the cloister and the chapter house and dormitory in the east range, were of the period between 1108 and 1132; the conventual buildings are said to have been damaged in the fire. But equally Building B (and the refectory, which is dealt with below) could both date from after 1132.

Schnebbelie's drawing of the range from the west in 1822, after the central spine-wall had partly fallen down (Fig 94; Fig 95), shows that the main portion to have fallen was the outer, west wall of the original range. The drawing also shows a 14th-century arch at the head of a stair into what was the main hall of the range on the Symonds plan. It therefore seems likely that the range was remodelled in the 14th century. Perhaps this was an addition when buttresses were added to the inner, cloister side of the west range, as shown by Symonds. The buttresses suggest that the upper floor of the range was either vaulted or that the trusses of an elaborate roof over the larger first-floor chamber, probably the hall and so called in *c* 1585, required lateral support. The buttresses may also help explain why the 12th-century spine-wall fell down to the west in 1822, bringing the western half of the building down with it, as shown by Schnebbelie. There were no buttresses on the west side of the spine-wall, since it ran down the middle of the doubled range. The stresses would have thrust to the west and eventually brought it down.

Though the position of the private apartments of the head of the monastery in Augustinian houses (as in other orders) was not fixed, they were usually located in the west range (whether the cloister lay to north or south of the church), between the church and the refectory (Dickinson 1968, 69–70). Examples are at Bradenstoke, Wiltshire (Brakspear 1922), and by the 13th century at St Bartholomew Smithfield, London (Webb 1921, ii, 131 and plan). Other sites included east of the cloister, near the infirmary, as at Kirkham, Yorkshire East Riding (Coppack et al 1995, 105), and in the later, early 16th-century prior's house at St Bartholomew Smithfield (moved to the east of its former position). A free-standing or even projecting set of rooms for the superior at Augustinian houses is the exception, probably because of the usual comparative poverty of the house (Robinson 1980, 155–62). A range called a prior's lodging by the excavators has been recorded at St Mary Spital, London, but there is no evidence for its date and very little for its function (Thomas et al 1997, 48).

It seems probable that the west range at Holy Trinity was, at least by the 14th century, the prior's lodging, and it may have been from the beginning. Evidence from many other monastic sites suggests that the prior probably had his own suite by the late 12th century; and given the wealth and status (in both local and national terms) of the early priors, we might even suggest that this was the function of Building B from the start.

The doubling in width of the range to the west could have occurred any time between the 12th and 16th centuries (the thick walls and mullioned windows shown on the ground floor of the range in the Symonds plan are not likely to be post-Dissolution work, though this cannot be ruled out). If the doubling of the range is significantly later than the 14th-century arch to the hall, then this first-floor entrance probably had a porch in front of it down to the court before the doubling of the range was constructed. The straight stair to the first floor shown by Symonds may be the remains of such a porch, which was a normal adjunct of a 14th-century hall of a magnate (Wood 1965, 150–2). A 15th-century example survives in the prebendal house of the abbot of Sherborne in Salisbury Cathedral close (RCHME 1993, 215–19) and such a porch is found on other monastic west ranges, as at the guest hall of Augustinian Bradenstoke Priory (Wiltshire), though here the first-floor part of the porch was of timber (Brakspear 1922, 231).

To further elucidate the medieval development of the range up to 1532, it is necessary to suggest some of the modifications of 1534–64 which can then be subtracted from the Symonds plans. Comparison of the ground- and first-floor plans of the range (Figs 13–16) shows that there were differences in construction between the southern and northern halves, at least by c 1585. Then the southern half had its spine-wall rising through both floors, whereas the northern half had it only on the ground floor. The west wall was of different character north and south of the stair to the hall on both floors. In the southern half, masonry rose vertically through two floors, whereas to the north, a range of five bay windows jettied out into the court (Fig 111). These windows and perhaps rebuilding of the first floor in this area may well be the work of Sir Thomas Audley or the Duke of Norfolk, as is suggested later (Chapter 6.2).

The ground-floor Symonds plan (Fig 13; Fig 14) shows that the west wall of the doubled range was in two parts, the southern slightly to the east of the northern. They also have different window arrangements: stone windows in the southern part and box windows of timber in the northern part. It therefore seems likely that these two parts were built at different times, and that the southern is earlier; but both may be medieval. Hence it is possible that the initial doubling of the range comprised only these three southern bays. A close parallel is provided by Castle Acre Priory (Norfolk), where the prior's lodging was also doubled in width, to the west, in the mid or later 14th century, thus enveloping the 12th-century porch to the original range, as here (Emery 2000, 74–5). A comparable range at the Cluniac Much Wenlock Priory (Shropshire) has the prior's bedchamber in a position above the parlour (Wood 1965, pl 16), and the new works of the 14th century at Holy Trinity would have allowed for similar extra chambers off the parlour, by means of the new stair shown by Symonds. If the doubling of the southern part of the range took this form, it would also have been broadly similar to a two-storeyed block built near the head of the hall of the town house in Southwark of the Bishop of Winchester in

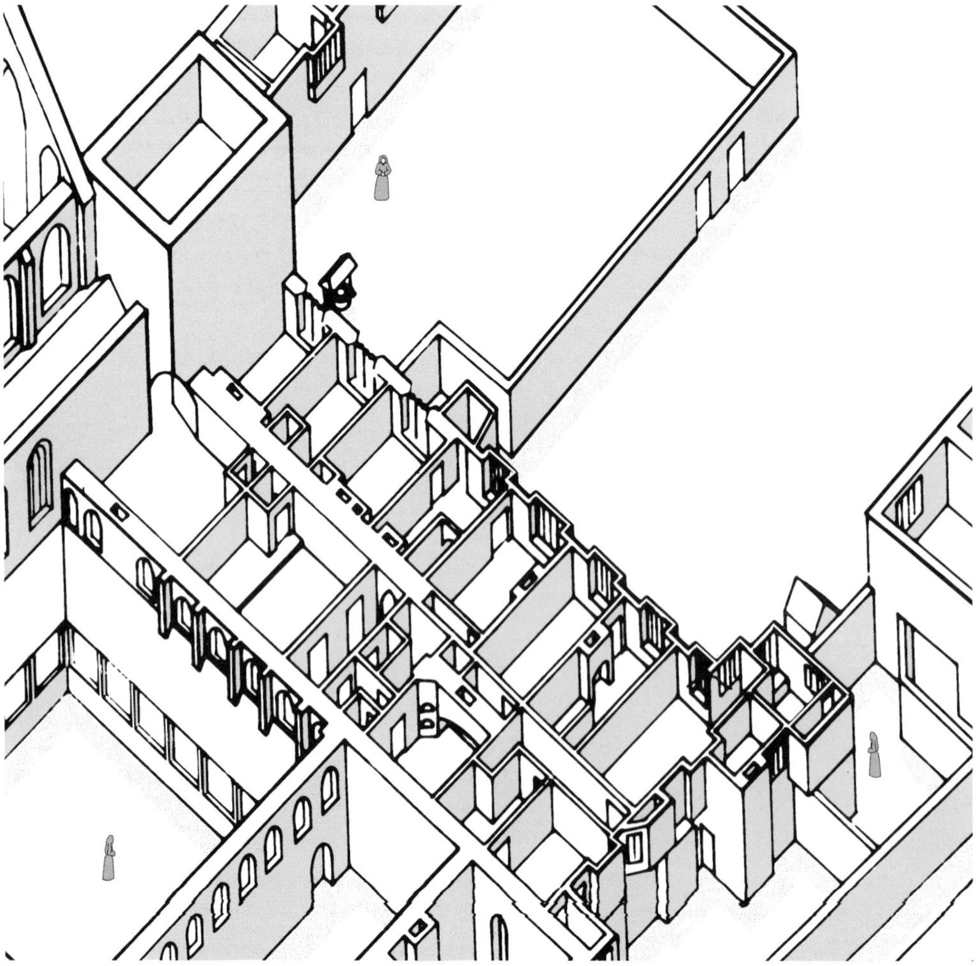

Fig 111 Reconstruction of the west range of the cloister from the Symonds plans of c 1585 (see Figs 13–16), from the north-east

1356–7 (Carlin 1985, 41).

Further details of the west range can be deduced from later drawings and engravings. Immediately south (ie right) of the fallen part of the spine-wall, Schnebbelie (Fig 94; Fig 95) shows a small circular window which would operate best in the gable of a building; but whether the room thus lit was to the east or west of the wall is not clear from the drawing. On the cloister side, buttresses are shown by Symonds alongside the first-floor hall, but not the parlour to the south (Fig 15; Fig 16); this would suggest that the parlour was roofed along its slightly longer axis (in the Symonds plan), east–west, at right angles to the hall, and this would fit with a gable at its west end with a circular window in it. However, it seems equally likely that in the 12th and 13th centuries there was one long chamber at first-floor level along most of the west claustral range, entered by the arched opening rebuilt in the 14th century. By the time of the Symonds plans, the first-floor space had been divided into hall and parlour, perhaps when the buttresses were also added to the hall part on the inner, claustral side.

To summarise, the structural sequence of the western range north of the tower admits of several different possibilities. The reasonably certain phasing is that the eastern half, of 12th-century date, was remodelled, possibly in the 14th century. The range was doubled in width to the west, perhaps (from the slight stagger in alignment of its west wall) in two separate operations. The first-floor windows shown by Symonds are likely to be of mid 16th-century date. The doubling to the west of the southern part of the range (Building E on site F) cannot be dated with precision. Given the building operations inferred from the admissions of debts as being under way in the priory during the middle decades of the 14th century, there is a strong possibility that the west range was remodelled, and at least the southern part of the doubling completed as a new suite of rooms for the prior, at the same time as the construction of the adjacent tower which may have functioned as a belfry, or outer parlour, or just possibly as both. In the phase plans presented at the end of this study, we suggest that the west range was doubled in width in two stages, the first before 1350, and the second in the later 14th century (Chapter 5.4; Fig 138; Fig 139).

4.6 Zone 3: the cloister, chapter house and east dormitory range, latrine block and adjacent city wall

Documentary and antiquarian evidence

The chapter house at Holy Trinity Priory was the setting for the granting by the *cnihtengild* of their lands to the priory in 1125 (*Cartulary*, no. 871); and in 1212, Henry FitzAilwin, traditionally regarded as the first mayor of the City of London, was buried in the entrance (Stow 1603, i, 141; ii, 315). FitzAilwin is mentioned a number of times in the priory cartulary. From about 1167–70 he was a regular witness to leases by the priory of land in the City (*Cartulary*, nos 41, 76, 206, 223, 228, 270, 273, 551, 663, 687, 824, 1012, 1015, 1022–4, 1051, 1061). He also donated rents to the priory: some time before 1193, Henry granted 5s of quitrent from lands in the parish of St Mary Bothaw (*Cartulary*, no. 426). A copy of the cartulary now in the Guildhall Library (GL, MS 122/2, fo 338r) adds in a marginal note next to this item 'Iste Henricus, Maior primus Lonon., obiit xiij Kal. Octobris [19 September] et sepultus est infra introitum capituli in medio sub lamina [the MS has 'lan'a', but Stow's editor Kingsford and others have taken this to be 'lamina'] marmorea' (Stow 1603, ii, 315, n): 'he was buried within the entrance of the chapter house, in the middle, under a marble slab'. The anonymous late 18th- or 19th-century translator of the copy of the cartulary in the Guildhall Library translates the last phrase as 'beneath the stone lantern' (GL, MS 122/2, fo 337v).

There are no drawings showing the exterior of the dormitory block which ran north from the chapter house towards the city wall. However, an engraving of 1797 by Bartholomew Howlett (1767–1827) shows the interior of a building somewhere near Aldgate which, it is proposed here, may be an interior view of the ground floor or basement storey of the dormitory, but about which some doubts must be expressed.

The engraving (Fig 112) is drawn from a viewpoint which appears to be in the corner of the lower floor of what had originally been a two-storey building, divided into four vaulted bays. The vaulting above the lower floor is shown intact in the end bay in which the viewer is situated. The vaulting in this lower floor, comprising two bays across the width of the building, consists of diagonal and transverse plain chamfered ribs supported on the walls by polygonal corbels and a free-standing octagonal pier with a moulded capital and base. Remains of diagonal ribs rising from the pier and the corbel against the further flanking wall indicate that the adjacent two bays were similarly vaulted. Arched wall ribs shown in the two flanking walls indicate that the whole of the lower floor was probably vaulted in this manner, that is eight bays, four by two, of quadripartite vaulting supported by three piers and corbel capitals.

The vaulting above the upper floor is unusual in medieval architecture, comprising transverse ribs supported by corbel capitals forming wide bays in which the vault is arched in both major axes, being neither barrel nor quadripartite. However, it does appear to be one build with the rest of the structure since it conforms to the apparent bay construction.

The far end wall is pierced by four openings: two doors one above the other, and a large round arched opening on the lower floor and a two-light pointed window in the upper floor with a quatrefoil piercing its head. The two-light window suggests a late 13th- or early 14th-century date, compatible with the vaulting of the lower floor.

The long flanking wall furthest from the viewer is pierced in the furthest bay by a tall round-headed opening which

Fig 112 Engraving by B Howlett, 1797, later marked 'Aldgate' (Guildhall Library, Noble Collection)

passes through the upper floor level. In the middle two bays of this wall are two arched recesses in which are set two lower arches. The perspective in the drawing is not wholly convincing and it is not clear whether the taller arches pass through the upper floor level or form the wall ribs for the vaulting of the lower floor.

Bartholomew Howlett engraved drawings of several old buildings in the London area: in 1806 he cooperated with Nash and Whichelo, whom we have already met, for Herbert and Brayley's *Lambeth Palace* (Adams 1983, 206–7); Howlett engraved a view of the interior of the chapel, and one of the Post Room in Lollards' Tower. His engravings were also used in books about London and its buildings in 1817–18 (ibid, 275, 298), and in 1819–27 he contributed 30 engravings to Wilkinson's *Londina Illustrata* (ibid, 307–23).

The exact location of the building shown in Fig 112 is not specified other than 'Aldgate'. However, since we know of no other large medieval structures in the Aldgate area which might have incorporated a two-storey masonry building of this date, it seems reasonable to assume that it did form part of the priory. As a two-storey building of at least four bays' length, divided into eight in its lower floor, it may have formed part of either range east or west of the cloister. The arrangement of openings in the far end wall, two doors one above the other, is perhaps best matched in the Symonds plans by the north wall of the east range. Although the door openings are shown as plain rectangles giving no indication of date, the off-centre position of the two-light window suggests that these doors were of medieval origin. This interpretation does not explain the passage leading off to the right of the engraving. If the identification with the dormitory is correct, the passage and its vaulting must be of post-Dissolution date, and presumably formed in brick.

But the attribution to the dormitory range, or to the priory at all, must remain doubtful, for two reasons. First, it seems rather unlikely that such a striking medieval survival would have escaped the attention of John Carter in 1790. Second, and more seriously, the plot of land where the dormitory range stood is shown empty of buildings, except for a small building at its north end, on a surveyor's map of shortly before 1790 (see Fig 168), the period when the drawing appears to have been made (the engraving is inscribed 'published' in 1797, though we cannot find out where). We include it here as a matter of record, but remain sceptical. This doubt, therefore, tinges the assessment of the unusual apparent occurrence of vaulting on two floors.

In 1622 the chapter house was demolished and its site occupied by a new parish church, St James Duke's Place. Illustrations of the exterior of the church (eg that of *c* 1810, Fig 164) do not show any pre-Dissolution details, and we must assume that demolition of the priory chapter house was complete; though a note on reused stonework observed in the church tower is included below (Chapter 6.4).

Excavations

Duke's Place, 1977 (DUK77; site H)

Between September 1977 and May 1978, excavations were carried out in advance of a pedestrian underpass in Duke's Place (DUK77). The long axis of the main trench lay north-east to south-west, perpendicular to the city wall and straddling it, immediately west of bastion 6. In the archive report (Tyler 1991), the extramural area was described as area A, and the smaller ($42m^2$) intramural area as area C (Fig 113). A third small area, area B, situated 40.5m to the south-east, was also extramural, and produced no evidence relevant to this report. The main features of the section across the wall are shown in a mural within the pedestrian passage which required the excavation, beneath Duke's Place.

Evidence for the nature of both the wall and the extramural ditches was recovered and has already been published, both for the Roman period (Maloney 1979, describing the circumstances of the excavation) and the medieval period (Maloney and Harding 1979). The wall and ditches will only be described here where they are relevant to the history of the priory buildings. The detailed description of the layers filling the medieval and later ditches (which may have had several recuttings in the four centuries after 1100) is not given here, though the study of the pottery includes items from the ditches.

In the archive report, archaeological contexts were divided into 40 groups (gpH1, gpH2 etc), further divided into subgroups (gpH1.1, gpH1.2 etc). Those relevant to the priory have been amalgamated into four periods (Table 2). For brevity, compass points used in this report refer to the site grid (which coincides nearly with the liturgical grid of the priory); site north–south was perpendicular to the city wall, and was close to true north-east/south-west.

The findings of the excavation, though concentrated in a single small trench, span several periods of the priory history, and the strata are first described and then interpreted, period by period.

PRIORY BUILDINGS, ? 12TH OR EARLY 13TH CENTURY (PERIOD I , gpH7, gpH14)

The Roman and medieval city wall (gpH7.1), described as 'Building 1' in the archive report, crossed the site from west to east. Situated 3.7m to the south and running parallel to it was a wall 1.15m wide (gpH14.1, Building 2; Fig 113). It was recorded in section at the east and west limits of the site, but had run the full width of the site, giving it a length of at least 7.3m. The highest point observed was at 13.39m OD, with the bottom not seen but below 10.95m OD. It appeared to be trench-built on the northern side, and to the south the chalk rubble core was faced with blocks of Reigate stone and ragstone. The bottom of this facing, at 11.11m OD, corresponded with the top of a 30mm thick, well-compacted surface of tan-coloured brickearth (gpH14.3), which extended at least 1.0m to the south of the wall.

Surmounting the wall, seen in a west-facing section, were four blocks of Reigate stone (gpH14.2) bonded on top of each other with a compact white mortar, with ashlar faces to the north (Fig 114). A vertical face to the east was visible in the section (ie behind the blocks shown in Fig 114), suggesting that these Reigate stone blocks formed the western jamb of an entrance through the wall, of unknown width but at least 0.81m high. Although the internal face of the jamb was not seen, it can be conjectured to some extent from its component stones, which were drawn *ex situ*. The northern edge of the jamb had a quarter-round chamfer, and one block had a projecting rebate on the face internal to the jamb, which would have

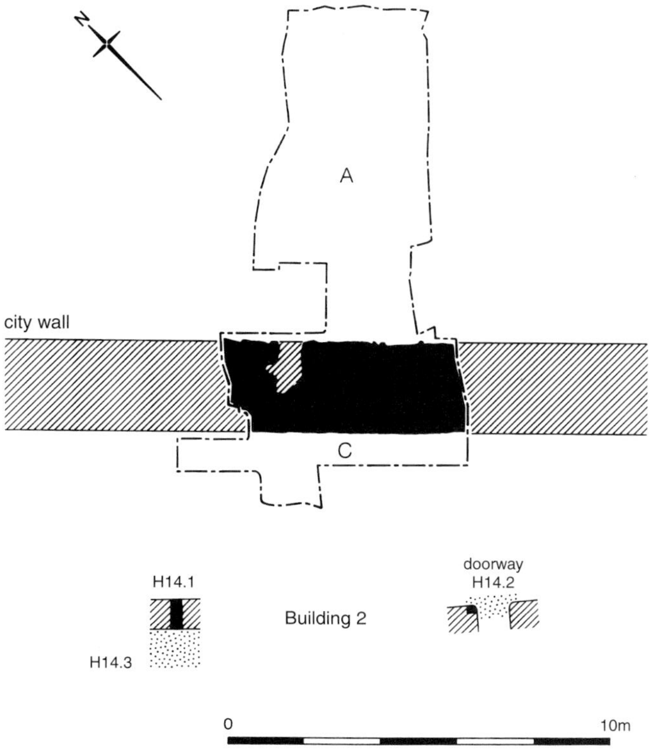

Fig 113 Plan of the city wall and north end of the dormitory (Building 2) on site H (period I) (scale 1:200)

Fig 114 Detail of the north wall of the dormitory (Building 2) on site H, looking south-east; the door jamb is in the vertical section (0.2m scale)

retained a door.

Continuing to the north of this jamb for at least 0.15m was a 5mm thick layer of crushed Reigate stone. It underlay the lowest stone of the jamb, which would suggest that it was working or construction debris from the Reigate stone jambs, although it may also have functioned as a surface (in which case its thinness suggests that it was highly compressed or eroded). Its top was at 13.45m OD.

The facing on the south side of the eastern fragment of the wall indicates that south was internal, while the Reigate stone surface to the north of the western fragment may have been external or internal; but here it is suggested that the two fragments formed the north wall of Building 2. The disparity of some 2.3m between the Reigate stone and brickearth surfaces shows clearly that the building was sunk into the ground to this depth at its northern end. The implication is that there must have been a set of stairs leading down from the group H14.2 entrance to the brickearth floor of the sunken room, but no evidence survived for their form.

No dating evidence was found for Building 2; however, stratigraphically it post-dated the bank (gpH8) laid against (and contemporary with) the internal face of the Roman city wall, which contained one sherd of early medieval sand- and shell-tempered ware (EMSS) of *c* 1000–*c* 1150 (gpH8.7). The level of the threshold, at 13.45m OD, is broadly comparable with the 12th-century construction level of 13.67m OD for chapel 1 at site A, 63m to the south-west.

Correspondence with the Symonds plan of *c* 1585 suggests that Building 2 was the north end of the dormitory range (see Fig 121) and therefore possibly of 12th- or early 13th-century date because of the building of the cloister to the south. It is likely that the doorway found in the excavation is the doorway shown on the ground-floor plan by Symonds, with stairs leading down into the undercroft of the dormitory. It is also possible that the view drawn by Howlett in 1797 (Fig 112) is of this building, but doubts have been expressed about the attribution. In Howlett's drawing the character of the ground-floor vaulting and the style of the two-light window in the north wall are late 13th- or 14th-century in date. The documented enclosure of the intramural lane by Prior Eustace (1264–80) in the decades after the Battle of Evesham (1265) provides a possible context for the rebuilding of at least the north end of the dormitory range, along with the enclosure of the lane up to the city wall and the new features which are described next.

A POSTERN GATE IN THE CITY WALL AND AN EXTRAMURAL BUILDING, POSSIBLY THE LATRINE BLOCK, LATE 13TH CENTURY (PERIOD II, gpH15–H16, gpH18–H19)

A rectangular cut (gpH15.1), up to 1.65m wide, was made into the internal south face of the city wall (Fig 115; Fig 116). The base of the cut was formed by a triple course of tile which ran through the wall at a level varying from 13.92m OD to 14.02m OD. Within the cut were two jambs (gpH15.2) made of four (west side) and five (east side) blocks of Reigate stone placed on top of each other without intervening mortar. The spaces

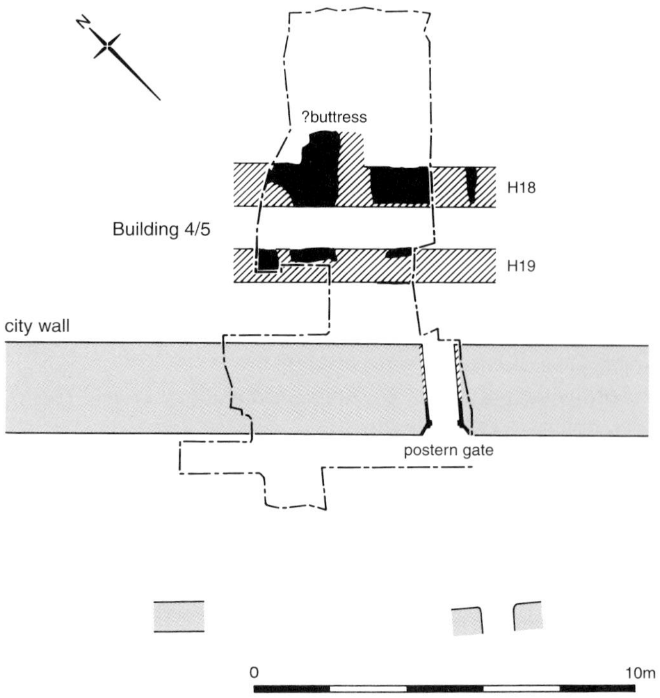

Fig 115 Plan of the postern through the city wall, and Building 4/5, on site H (period II) (scale 1:200)

Fig 116 View of the jambs of the postern in the city wall on site H, looking south-east along the inside of the wall; the brick arches which later blocked the postern have been cut away (top right) (0.5m scale)

between the edges of the cut and the Reigate stone blocks were backfilled with a rubble mixture of fragments of tile, Reigate stone, ragstone, slate and chalk, set in an orange sandy mortar. This rubble mix had been rendered with a cream mortar against which the jambs were set.

The jambs flanked an entrance 0.69m wide and at least 0.9m high, with a 45° splay on each side. On both jambs there was a vertical rebate behind the splay against which a door would have closed (for the stones see Chapter 8.2, <A8> and <A9>, Fig 190). The remains of the iron hinges on which the door would have hung were noted in the rebate on the south side of the stop of the western jamb, showing that the door opened to the south.

The floor of the entrance was formed by tiles originally within the primary wall construction, except at the southern, inner edge where they had been replaced with smaller fragments of medieval roof tile (Fig 116). The superstructure of the city wall had been heavily truncated on the north side, so that a width of only 0.8m survived, but it may be assumed that there was originally a passage through the entire 2.25m of the wall. The sides of this passage, which were rendered, were on an alignment not quite perpendicular to the city wall it pierced. The south face of the city wall had also been rendered on both sides of the entrance, with a similar mortar to that used to construct the jambs; the render was recorded down to 13.52m OD, at least 400mm below the level of the threshold. This level of 13.52m OD agrees closely with the top of the Reigate stone layer at 13.45m OD, 4.5m to the south outside Building 2. The alignment of the south, extant end of the wall passage (and probably all of it) was about 10° from a perpendicular angle with the line of the city wall, and pointed roughly towards the door in the end of Building 2. A sherd of 'Saintonge' pottery was reported as being embedded in the mortar of the doorway (Maloney and Harding 1979, 349) and it is likely that this is the same as a small rim, the edges of which are white with mortar, from a Mill Green ware (MG) jug found in the rubble H[454] (gpH16) which filled the doorway. This sherd dates the doorway to after 1270.

Two substantial masonry foundations were observed, north of and parallel to the city wall (Fig 115; Fig 117). In the archive report, because of their lack of stratigraphic connection, they were termed Buildings 4 and 5. In the present report it is proposed that they are the same building, and they are therefore termed Building 4/5. The northern foundation (gpH18, Building 4) was constructed of large blocks of ragstone set in a yellow mortar, and situated a minimum of 3.8m from the city wall. No return was observed, and truncation of the contemporary ground level meant that no associated surfaces survived. A depth of 0.45m was recorded, with a bottom at 10.95m OD, which low level, along with its construction of ragstone only, allows the possibility of a Roman date. But a piece of medieval roof tile in its fabric suggests a medieval date, and the construction practice using foundations of ragstone is found in other priory buildings, for example Building C at site

Fig 117 View of Building 4/5 on site H, from the north, with the foundation (gpH18) just behind the scale; the post-medieval wall of various phases at the rear is on the line of the Roman and medieval city wall (1.0m scale)

F, in the medieval period (above, 4.5).

Roughly halfway between this foundation and the city wall was a parallel foundation (gpH19, Building 5), truncated at 12.50m OD and surviving to a depth of 1.1m. The construction was entirely of chalk, suggesting an early medieval date; the absence of hard stone on either edge suggests an internal wall, and thus it is suggested that this was a wall parallel with and inside a structure formed by the ragstone wall to the north and the city wall to the south; the structure would have been 3.8m wide and at least 6.0m long. Only Roman pottery was found in association with this foundation.

Comparison with many other conventual sites would suggest that this was the latrine block of the priory, examples being the houses at Newark (Nottinghamshire), West Acre (Norfolk), Maxstoke (Warwickshire), Walsingham (Norfolk), Hastings (Sussex), Kenilworth (Warwickshire) and Kirkham (Yorkshire East Riding). At Norton Priory (Cheshire) the 12th-century dormitory ended in a smaller 13th-century range at right angles which housed the latrines (Greene 1989, 95), while at Butley Priory (Suffolk) the 13th-century latrine block (the precise character of which is uncertain) lay at the outer end of the dormitory, reached by a passage at right angles (Myres 1933, plan opposite 280). Both these houses were Augustinian. The proximity of the two walls is explained by these analogies and by others such as the 12th-century latrine blocks of St Michael's nunnery, Stamford, Lincolnshire (RCHME 1977, 31–2), Leominster Priory, Herefordshire (Brown and Wilson 1994), or Dundrennan Abbey, Kirkcudbright (Yeoman 1995, 19–20): a drain about 1.0m wide must have run east–west between the internal chalk wall and the north wall of the building. The protuberance on the latter's north side was presumably to support a buttress; perhaps, as at Stamford, there was arcading between buttresses. The inner wall would have supported the fronts of the seats, presumably at first-floor level, though there could have been seats at ground-floor level also.

The date of this building is not clear. Presumably there must have been some kind of latrine block from the early years of the priory, but neither archaeology nor documents throw any light on it. The door through the city wall and the foundations outside, which may have been of the latrine block, were of late 13th-century date, presumably of the 1270s during the priorate of Eustace. The documentary reference to his enclosure of the lane inside the city wall may have been to give access to the latrine block outside the wall; but equally the documented enclosure may refer only to the lane.

REINFORCEMENT OF THE CITY WALL AND BLOCKING OF THE POSTERN IN OR SHORTLY AFTER 1477 (PERIOD III, gpH15.3, gpH21, gpH25, gpH26)

In this period are placed two cesspits (or possibly two observations of one large cesspit), the blocking of the passage through the city wall, brick arches against the city wall and dump deposits; the chronological sequence of the cesspits and blocking – which of them came first – is not certain. They have all been placed on the period III plan (Fig 118). Though the cesspits may have functioned during the 14th century, an argument can be made that they functioned after 1477, when the city wall was blocked.

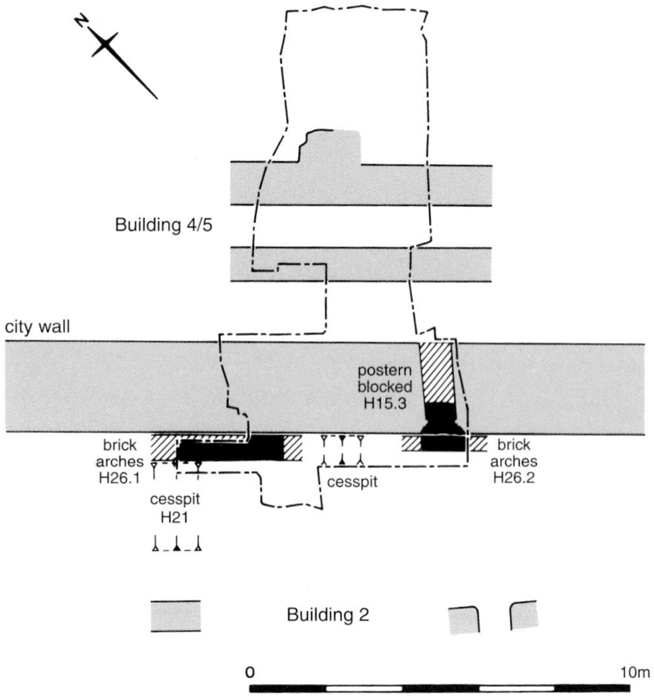

Fig 118 Plan of the postern blocked with brick arches, and cesspit(s) behind the city wall, on site H (period III) (scale 1:200)

Situated 1.0m to the south of the city wall (gpH7), between it and Building 2, was a timber-lined cesspit (gpH21). A 1.0m length was seen of a 100mm thick layer of heavily decayed wood, interpreted by the excavator as planks on edge, and forming the lining of the north side of a pit at least 1.25m deep. This timber lining was also seen in section to the east, giving a length of at least 1.8m for the north side of the pit. Its fills were green and brown peaty organic materials, with inclusions of mortar and charcoal. As seen in section, the timber lining survived to 13.50m OD, but the fill was recorded some 0.65m higher.

Recorded in the section at the western edge of the site was apparently a second pit (also gpH21) whose south edge contained a small fragment of timber lining, and whose north side aligned with that of the cesspit noted above. This was possibly another observation of the same cesspit, but this would give an east–west length of at least 4.0m. Alternatively, and less ambitiously, this second observation could be of a separate cesspit constructed next to the other one. Whatever the case, these two pits (or one large pit) are of importance because of their ceramic and artefactual contents. The pit(s) lay outside the north end of the dormitory (as shown by Symonds, at least) and appear to be the only trace of one phase of the latrine arrangements. They are designated pits 1 (the eastern) and 2 (the western); the pottery is illustrated in Fig 199 and discussed both here and more generally by ware in Chapter 8.5.

In pit 1 (Table 7; Table 8), the lowest fill (H[478]) contained Roman pottery and two sherds of Kingston-type ware (KING, 46g). One of these is of especial interest as it is

Table 7 Relative frequency of different medieval wares in pit 1 (gpH21, H[472], H[478], H[493], H[494]) by sherd count, estimated number of vessels (ENV), weight (in g) and estimated vessel equivalent (EVE) (for fabric codes see Table 18)

Fabric	Sherd count	Sherd count %	ENV	ENV %	Weight (g)	Weight %	EVEs	EVEs %
EARL	2	1.7	1	4.0	22	0.9	-	-
KING	85	71.4	12	48.0	1694	70.9	2.70	75.0
CBW	1	0.8	1	4.0	13	0.5	-	-
LMHG	1	0.8	1	4.0	4	0.2	-	-
LOND	24	20.2	7	28.0	589	24.6	0.56	15.6
MG	1	0.8	1	4.0	7	0.3	-	-
SHER	5	4.2	2	8.0	62	2.6	0.34	9.4
Total	**119**		**25**		**2391**		**3.60**	

Table 8 Relative frequency of vessel forms (all fabrics) in pit 1 (gpH21, H[472], H[478], H[493], H[494]) by sherd count, estimated number of vessels (ENV), weight (in g) and estimated vessel equivalent (EVE)

Fabric	Sherd count	Sherd count %	ENV	ENV %	Weight (g)	Weight %	EVEs	EVEs %
Jug	8	6.7	4	16.0	88	3.7	0.34	9.4
Baluster jug	1	0.8	1	4.0	17	0.7	-	-
Conical jug	1	0.8	1	4.0	14	0.6	-	-
Early rounded jug	1	0.8	1	4.0	13	0.5	-	-
Large rounded jug	1	0.8	1	4.0	30	1.3	-	-
Metal copy jug	1	0.8	1	4.0	15	0.6	0.15	4.2
Rounded jug	47	39.5	6	24.0	1186	49.6	0.57	15.8
Small rounded jug	43	36.1	6	24.0	704	29.4	2.16	60.0
Squat jug	7	5.9	2	8.0	78	3.3	-	-
Tulip-necked baluster jug	9	7.6	2	8.0	246	10.3	0.38	10.6
Total	**119**		**25**		**2391**		**3.60**	

from a small rounded jug with repoussé decoration of a lion passant (<P5>, Fig 199). The other is from a large rounded jug or storage jar which appears to have an applied strip (cf Pearce and Vince 1988, nos 143, 401). Above this, fill H[495] produced only Roman pottery, while H[494] contained Roman pottery as well as 67 sherds of medieval pottery from some 17 vessels (1069g, 3.06 EVEs), most of mid 14th-century date. South Hertfordshire-type greyware (SHER) is represented by four sherds from a jug or pitcher with rouletted decoration (<P4>, Fig 199). Fourteen sherds are of London-type ware (LOND), deriving from two rounded jugs with white slip decoration, and three baluster jugs, two of which are of tulip-necked form and date to *c* 1270–*c* 1350 (Pearce and Vince 1985, 135). The dominant fabric is KING, although 35 of the total 47 sherds are derived from the upper parts of two rounded jugs (<P6>, <P7>, Fig 199); the other sherds are from three small rounded jugs, a conical jug and a squat jug with pellet decoration (cf ibid, fig 70, nos 101–3); two of these vessels are also represented in H[501]. Single sherds of Mill Green ware (MG) and late medieval Hertfordshire glazed ware (LMHG) are also present in this group, the latter dating to after *c* 1340.

Context H[493] contained only seven sherds (84g). One of these is from <P4> (see above), while the others are from the thumbed base and lower body of an externally sooted squat jug in KING. The uppermost fill, H[472], contained Roman material and 44 medieval sherds. Of these, 32 are from a near-complete KING rounded jug (<P8>, Fig 199), while nine are from a LOND small rounded jug with paired thumbing at intervals around the angle of the base, which is slightly sooted; inside is a white residue. The other sherds derive from one or two similar jugs in LOND, a metal copy jug in KING and a residual sherd of coarse London-type ware (LCOAR). Pit 1 also contained one sherd of Frechen stoneware (FREC) which is assumed to be intrusive (H[494]).

The finds recovered from the section (H[501]) of pit 2 comprise a similar group (72 sherds, 1692g, 0.87 EVEs; Table 9; Table 10). Most sherds are from a rather worn London-type ware (LOND) small rounded jug with arcaded slip-decoration and spaced thumbing around the base angle, and a small perforation in the base (diameter 3mm), apparently intentional (<P9>, Fig 199). There is a very thick white deposit inside this jug; it is not a carbonate and cannot be derived from hard water, but the nature of the residue remains uncertain. In this context it is, however, of interest that three of the Kingston-type ware (KING) jugs (two small rounded jugs, one conical) have

Table 9 Relative frequency of different medieval wares in pit 2 (gpH21, H[501]) by sherd count, estimated number of vessels (ENV), weight (in g) and estimated vessel equivalent (EVE) (for fabric codes see Table 18)

Fabric	Sherd count	Sherd count %	ENV	ENV %	Weight (g)	Weight %	EVEs	EVEs %
CBW	1	1.4	1	11.1	5	0.3	-	-
KING	18	25.0	4	44.4	770	41.1	0.87	35.4
LMHG	18	25.0	2	22.2	462	24.7	-	-
LOND	35	48.6	2	22.2	635	33.9	1.59	64.6
Total	**72**		**9**		**1872**		**2.46**	

Table 10 Relative frequency of vessel forms in pit 2 (gpH21, H[501]) by sherd count, estimated nmber of vessels (ENV), weight (in g) and estimated vessel equivalent (EVE)

Fabric	Sherd count	Sherd count %	ENV	ENV %	Weight (g)	Weight %	EVEs	EVEs %
Drinking jug	2	2.8	1	11.1	387	20.7	0.81	32.9
Drinking jug/lantern	3	4.2	1	11.1	180	9.6	0.85	34.6
Jug	5	6.9	2	22.2	67	3.6	-	-
Conical jug	6	8.3	1	11.1	154	8.2	-	-
Rounded jug	46	63.9	2	22.2	855	45.7	0.74	30.1
Small rounded jug	10	13.9	2	22.2	229	12.2	0.06	2.4
Total	**72**		**9**		**1872**		**2.46**	

brown residues, and that a number of glass urinals were also found in the pit (Chapter 8.6). The most complete and unusual find is a small LOND drinking jug that had been adapted for use as a lantern (<P10>, Fig 199). The other pottery finds comprise a near-complete KING drinking jug (<P11>, Fig 199), a single sherd of coarse Surrey-Hampshire border ware (CBW) and 14 sherds from a large rounded jug in late medieval Hertfordshire glazed ware (LMHG), probably the same as that noted in H[494].

The combination of the different wares and forms suggests that both features were backfilled between the late 13th and mid 14th centuries. In pit 1, south Hertfordshire-type greyware (SHER) and Mill Green ware (MG) are represented by one vessel only (SHER is more common in the 13th century, while MG dates from *c* 1270); these wares are absent from pit 2. Coarse Surrey-Hampshire border ware (CBW), which started to reach London *c* 1270 and was the most common type from *c* 1350, is absent from pit 1, and is represented by only one sherd in pit 2. London-type ware (LOND) is present in both features, with late jug forms in pit 1. Kingston-type ware (KING) is the most abundant ware type, accounting for 71% of the pottery from pit 1 (48% of the ENV), and of this the most common form types are the rounded and small rounded jugs, the latter dated to *c* 1310–*c* 1400. Non-joining sherds of one such jug were found in both pits (upper body in pit 1, lower body in pit 2). The latest ware type present in both groups is late medieval Hertfordshire glazed ware (LMHG), which is represented by one sherd in pit 1 and 18 fragments from two vessels in pit 2. This ware is usually dated to after 1340, as this is the dendrochronological date for the waterfront (G7) in which it first occurs at Trig Lane (Jenner and Vince 1983, 152). This date, however, is a *terminus ante quem*, as the vessel was produced, marketed, used, broken and discarded before the construction of the waterfront; the ware may, therefore, have been reaching London a few years before 1340. In addition to a single sherd in an early 14th-century group at Ludgate Hill, scattered sherds of LMHG have also been found in groups of the same date at the London Millennium Bridge site south of Thames Street (Blackmore 2002), and so it is not out of place with the small rounded jugs from Kingston. The presence of this ware in the cesspit thus points to a date of *c* 1310–40 for the group as a whole. It may, therefore, be contemporary with the finds from the group F19 robber trenches on site F which were more broadly dated to the 14th century or later (above, 4.5). The pottery also suggests that either the two cesspits are one and the same, or that they were backfilled at the same time. Either way, <P4> and <P6>, which date to the late 12th or early 13th century, were thus of some age when discarded.

In this pit was a small but notable collection of non-ceramic artefacts illustrative of life in the priory (Chapters 5.6, 8.6): wooden tableware (Fig 209), an iron knife in a decorated leather scabbard (Fig 208), fragments of several glass urinals (Fig 210), and several richly decorated pieces of silk, possibly from monastic vestments (Fig 119; Fig 120).

At this time or later, the late 13th-century (period II) postern was blocked with masonry rubble consisting of fragments of Reigate stone, ragstone, chalk and tile in a loose sandy mortar (gpH15.3). Dating evidence was confined to two

Fig 119 Silk textile fragments H<133> and H<208> from cesspit, group H21 (scale 1:1)

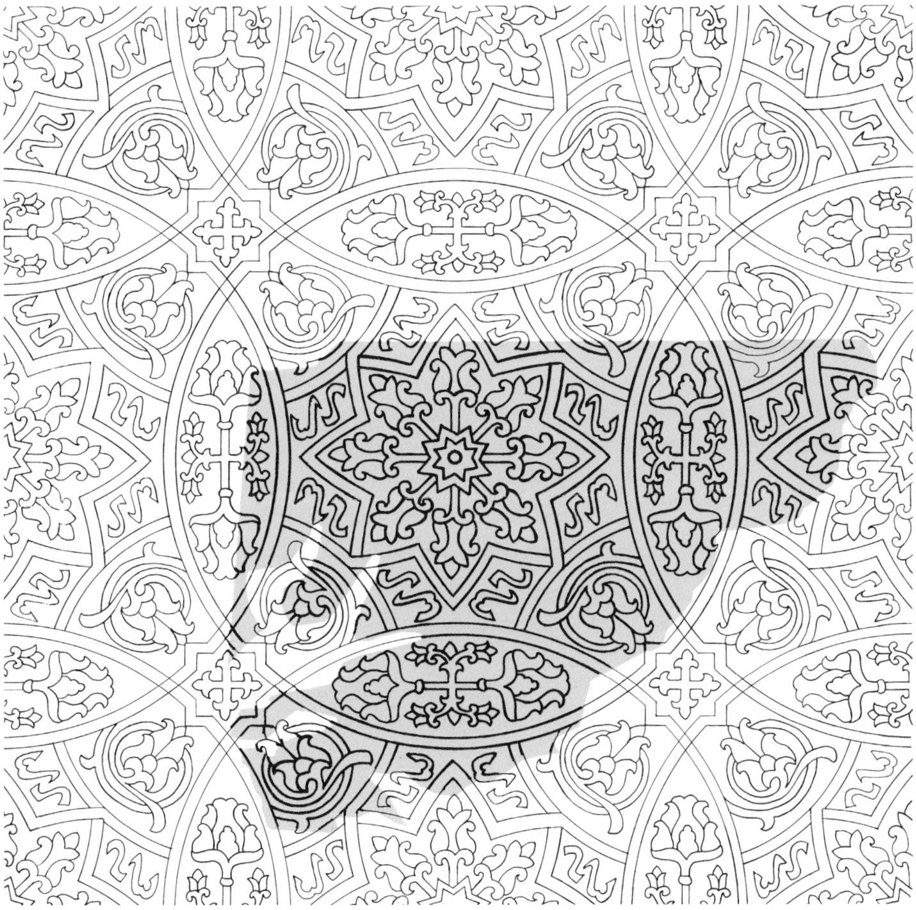

Fig 120 Reconstruction of pattern of silk textile H<133> from cesspit, group H21 (the shaded areas mark the extent of the fragments)

sherds later than *c* 1270 (see above).

Butted against the south (inner) face of the city wall was an arched brick foundation 0.4m wide (gpH26.1, gpH26.2), located within a construction trench cut into the Roman bank (Fig 118; shown on the right of Fig 116, in section). The brick arches survived to a height of 16.00m OD; they were two-centred, 0.65m high and 1.35m wide internally. The arches were formed by stretcher and header bricks radially orientated in elevation, with a wedge-shaped block of ragstone acting as keystone. Above and between the arches the bricks were laid in English bond; those sampled were 273–281mm in length, 120–131mm in breadth and 63mm in thickness. No provision was made in this brick structure for the group H15.2 postern gate, which therefore went out of use, and it seems likely that the blocking of the passage (gpH15.3) noted above is broadly contemporary with the group H26 brick wall. Pottery of 13th-century date (London-type ware (LOND) from gpH25.1) was recovered from one of the uppermost layers through which the brick foundations were cut.

Its position against the city wall suggests that this brick structure was a reinforcement. The form of construction, as well as its relationship to the wall and bank, are identical to a 61m long stretch of brick arches excavated by Professor W F Grimes between Aldermanbury and Coleman Street (Grimes 1968, 82–4). He interpreted the structure as the work of Mayor Jocelyn, who in 1477 carried out a major programme of repair to the city wall (Stow 1603, ii, 76). The arched brick foundation at Duke's Place was probably part of this project.

Between the city wall and Building 2 was a sequence of sandy silts (gpH25.1) including fragments of chalk, shell, tile, charcoal and daub. This material was recorded in section with a significant slope (up to 2 in 5) down to the south. The bottom level of 13.65m suggests that the lower deposits in the sequence may even have pre-dated the postern gate with its threshold above 13.92m OD. A layer of tiles at the topmost level of 14.80m OD may have been a surface. Recorded in section to the east of the group H25.1 material was another short sequence of dumps (gpH25.2), also sloping down to the south. These sealed the group H21 cesspit, and contained a higher proportion of mortar than the group H25.1 dumps. No dating evidence was recovered, so these dumps could be late medieval or post-Dissolution in date.

Features of this period, therefore, indicate three main phases of activity: 1) the digging of cesspits within the area between the city wall and Building 2, the dormitory (finds of the 14th century, though with a single 16th-century sherd); 2) the closure of the passage through the wall (undated); and 3) the construction of brick arches against the base of the wall during the 15th century, probably in or shortly after 1477. This would imply that Building 4/5, outside the wall, was denied access by the blocking and certainly by the construction of the brick arches, which might have been contemporary with the blocking. But the finds from the layers in cesspits dug into the intramural space were generally of the 14th century. Two possibilities are suggested by this evidence: 1) Building 4/5, suggested to be the latrine block, fell out of use in the 14th or 15th century, and that facilities were thereafter provided inside the city wall, against the end of the dormitory and in the formerly enclosed lane, with the effect of the building of the brick arches in 1477 being unknown; or 2) the closure of the passage and the building of the arches were both part of the refurbishment of the defences in 1477, and the cesspits are evidence of facilities in the period 1477–1532, in which case their finds are residual, and the piece of Frechen stoneware from one of the pits, if it is not intrusive, might indicate post-Dissolution use of the pit. If this is the case, then a building over the pit is not shown by Symonds around 1585. There does not seem to be any reason to prefer either of these proposed sequences, and the exceptional finds in the group H21 cesspit(s) can be taken to represent rejected priory objects from the period *c* 1300–*c* 1530.

The medieval city ditch, north of the wall and north of the latrine block, was recorded on sites H and K but is not reported in detail in this volume. Some pottery from the ditch is, however, of interest and is reported in Chapter 6.4 since the ditch contained mixed medieval and post-medieval material.

Reconstructing the cloister, chapter house, dormitory, latrine block and city wall (with a note on the infirmary)

The proposed correspondence between the excavated remains on site H and the Symonds plan (Fig 13) is shown on Fig 121, indicating that the doorway found in Building 2 may well be that shown by Symonds. A three-dimensional reconstruction of the dormitory, refectory and cloister is shown on Fig 122; this, like Fig 111, is based on the Symonds plans (Figs 13–16) and thus almost certainly includes some post-Dissolution features.

Cloister

At Holy Trinity Priory, a cloister was probably laid out in the earliest phase of construction, in the first half of the 12th century, if the inferences about the date of structures and burials on site F are correct (above, 4.5); but site F yields information only about the west side of the future cloister site. During the 12th century, buildings would have been erected on all four sides to delimit the cloister; thereafter, presumably, there would have been the building of the arcades and laying out of the garth itself, which might have included garden features. Unfortunately it has not yet been possible to investigate the area of the cloister garth or its walks, all of which lie under Mitre Square. The earliest cloister might have been of timber, only later rebuilt in stone. At Romsey Abbey (Hampshire) the stone cloister seems to have been constructed at the same time as completion of the adjacent nave, which though begun in the 12th was only finished in the middle of the 13th century, and decorated tiles of this date have been recorded in the cloister walk (Scott 1996, 59–68). At Holy Trinity Priory, we can suggest a similar sequence: the cloister walks (whether originally of stone or timber) would probably have been finished when all the surrounding major buildings were at least completed to eaves

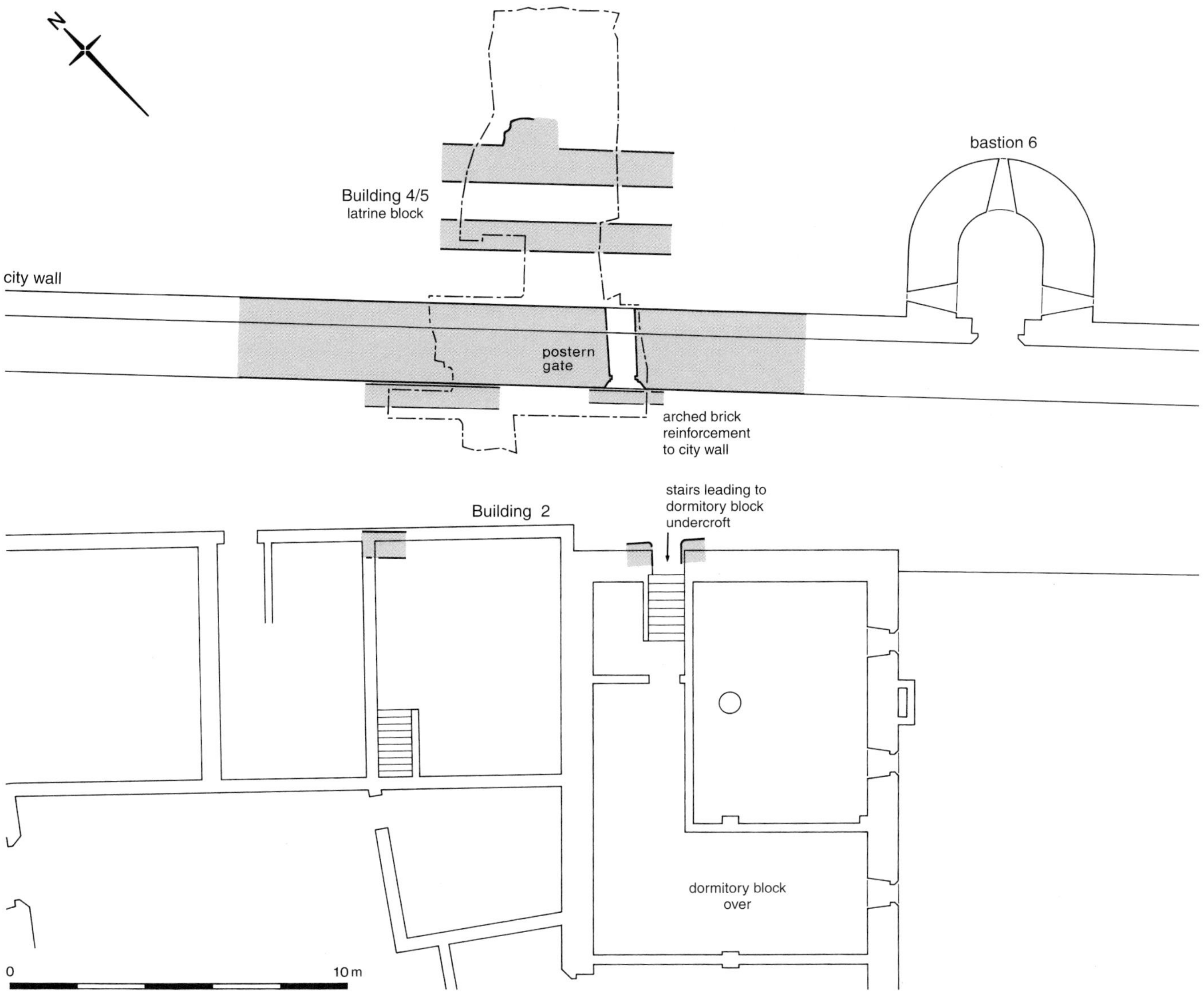

Fig 121 *Correlation of remains on site H with the Symonds plan (Fig 13) (in outline), together with the nearby interval tower on the wall, now known as bastion 6 (scale 1:200)*

level. The crucial building here would have been the great bulk of the nave to the south, and although the north wall of the nave has not been excavated, what is probably its north-west corner at site F (Fig 110) is dated here to the second half of the 12th century or later. The Symonds ground-floor plan (Fig 13; Fig 14) gives no indication of any substantial architecture along the cloister walks, but by then any stonework could easily have been dismantled. It seems reasonable to assume that there would have been a stone cloister for the great majority of the medieval period. Examples in stone at other London houses are known, or have recently been recorded: a 14th-century example at St Mary Spital (Thomas et al 1997, 55), part of the cloister of 1404–10 surviving at St Bartholomew Smithfield (Gormley 1996), and both loose and *in situ* fragments of another of 1502–26 at St Mary Clerkenwell (Sloane in prep).

From the earliest phase of construction of the church there would have been a prominent doorway from the north side of the nave to the cloister. At Romsey, this is the 'abbess's doorway', which has on its outside decoration constituting one parallel for that used in the south aisle of Holy Trinity Priory. Across the City of London at St Mary Overie, Southwark, a 12th-century doorway in this position survives, though in fragmentary condition. Illustrations of the 19th century (eg in Schofield 1999, fig 33) show its former fine state. The analogous but plainer doorway of *c* 1160 at St Bartholomew Smithfield also survives.

Chapter house

The chapter house was a standard component of the western European monastic plan by the middle of the 11th century, and one can therefore be expected from the initial foundation of Holy Trinity Priory. The form of the chapter house here is only known from the Symonds plans (Figs 13–16). It measured about 56ft by 30ft (17.1m x 9.15m). Originally it might have had a rounded east end, as at the Augustinian houses at Merton (Surrey) and at Cirencester (Gloucestershire), and as suggested for the late 11th-century Westminster (Gem 1986), but by

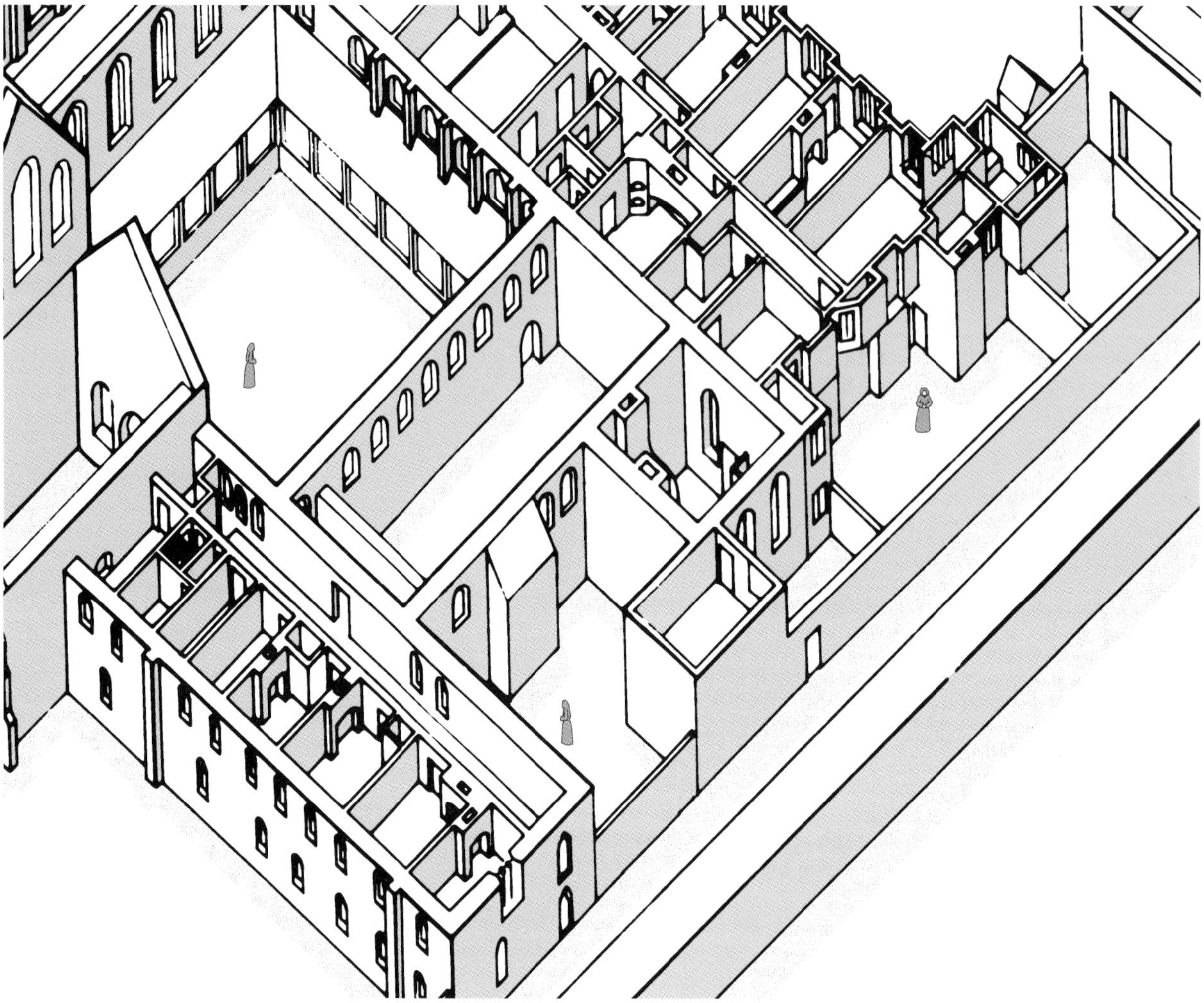

Fig 122 Reconstruction of the dormitory range, refectory and kitchen from the Symonds plans of c 1585 (see Figs 13–16), from the north-east

c 1585 it was rectangular. Wall responds can be seen on the ground-floor plan only. Responds suggest that a stone vault was intended, but there is no other evidence as to whether the chapter house was roofed in timber or stone. A chapter house of similar but smaller rectangular proportions was built in c 1150 at St Bartholomew Smithfield (Webb 1921, ii, 144–5, pl LXXI); and responds along the walls of a chapter house might signify a 12th-century date, as at Hastings, Sussex (Martin 1973). The chapter house at Holy Trinity would presumably have been an important building to erect in the 12th century (by 1132, according to the annals of the priory discussed in Chapter 3.2), and was in place by 1212 when Henry FitzAilwin was buried in its entrance, traditionally the most elaborately decorated part of the cloister. The buttresses at the north-east corner of the building, however, indicate rebuilding at a later date, perhaps in the 13th century, when a parallel is supplied by the chapter house at Norton Priory, Cheshire (Greene 1989, 95). The chapter house at St Bartholomew Smithfield was rebuilt at least twice, in the 13th century and around 1405, and the Symonds plan might well represent a cumulative picture.

Symonds shows that the chapter house rose through two storeys and that the dormitory range did not cross over it at first-floor level. Thus it appears that there was no night stair arrangement of the kind evident at St Augustine, Bristol (Paul 1912), where the stairs were contained within the thickness of the terminal wall of the transept. Instead, the stairs to the dormitory are shown to the north of the chapter house. Access from the dormitory to the church, therefore, appears to have been routed through the cloister and through the door into the north nave aisle. This arrangement survives at Castle Acre Priory (Norfolk), where the chapter house has a tunnel vault throughout its length and the stairs to the dormitory are relatively wide (Coad and Coppack 1998).

For the chapter house, Symonds notes 'this was the place for servis' on the ground-floor plan and 'this was the chapell' on the first-floor plan (though the chapter house remained a single chamber rising through both floors). In 1622 a new parish church, St James Duke's Place, was built on the site of the chapter house, but occupying a larger area (see Fig 164).

Dormitory range and the 'Dark Entry'

North of the chapter house was the dormitory range, about 110ft (33.5m) long. The excavation of the foundations of its north end on site H did not produce any clear dating evidence. The interior of the ground or basement storey of the dormitory, looking north, is possibly shown by Howlett in 1797 (Fig 112). Given the 13th- or early 14th-century character of the vaulting and windows shown by Howlett, it might be suggested that the dormitory was rebuilt or modified by Prior Eustace at the same time as (we propose) he consolidated the link across the lane with the latrine block building by inserting the postern door in the city wall. But Howlett's drawing cannot be guaranteed to be of the dormitory range at all.

Symonds (Figs 13–16) shows the ground-floor vault subdivided by walls, and partitions on the upper floor. The pattern of rectangular piers on the ground-floor plan, and their absence from the first-floor plan, indicates that the ground floor was vaulted and the upper floor was not. It is not possible to say whether any of the partitions in the first-floor dormitory are of pre-Dissolution date, though it is possible that it was divided into chambers for the canons. Partitions in the 13th century have been noted at Jervaulx, Yorkshire North Riding (Coppack 1990, 73), and at Castle Acre (Norfolk) in the 14th century (Coad and Coppack 1998, 31). Cubicles were an apparently regular feature of dormitories at Premonstratensian houses, such as Langley, Norfolk, and Leiston, Suffolk (Clapham 1923, 128), and at the Blackfriars convents at Gloucester and Bristol the dormitory was evidently divided into cells (Burton 1994, 145). Partition of dormitories was condemned by a General Chapter of the English Benedictines in the late 13th century, yet at Westminster the dormitory (which still largely survives) was divided with partitions formed by curtains by 1340, and probably before (Harvey 1993, 130).

At the south end of the dormitory range Symonds shows, on the ground floor, a small vice stair from the cloister going up to the dormitory on the first floor. Alongside the north wall of the chapter house, it looks as though a narrow bay has been filled with masonry or otherwise blocked by the building of the stair. The comparable bay above, in the first-floor dormitory, has an extra-wide window and a fireplace in the gable against the chapter house. It is possible that the space behind the vice stair on the ground-floor plan was a blocked-off chamber, perhaps a library; at Furness Abbey (Lancashire) there are two vaulted chambers either side of the chapter house like this, which are interpreted as libraries (Pevsner 1976, 92). On the other hand, a block of solid masonry supporting a stair to the cloister ran the width of the dormitory on the ground floor in exactly this way at Butley Priory, Suffolk (Myres 1933, plan opposite 280); so there may have been a reason for such pieces of masonry. This was also the position of the stair to the dormitory at St Bartholomew Smithfield, but the space seems to have been formed by two small chambers (or the stair itself and a chamber behind; Webb 1921, i, pls LXXII–LXXIII).

Symonds's plan of the first floor indicates that by the end of the 16th century other stairs within the dormitory rose at least one further storey higher. If the dormitory had an imposing roof, as is likely, then a second or attic floor might have been made in the roof-space after the Dissolution. Thus the first floor shown by Symonds and in our reconstruction (Fig 122) was probably overlaid by one further floor by *c* 1585.

Running along the western side of the dormitory range, and communicating between the intramural lane to the north and the cloister to the south, was a passage, later called Dark Passage by 1790, and then Church Passage, and which is still evident as St James's Passage but now much wider than in medieval times. In other religious houses, such as at Westminster and Norwich, this was called a 'Dark Entry' and was vaulted. Symonds shows that at the north-east corner of the cloister were two steps and an arch or doorway, but there is no evidence (such as the outlines of shafts or responds in the walls) that the passage was vaulted. The usual practice in monasteries was for each of the three sides of claustral buildings to have a passage through them, and all would be vaulted (Fernie 2000, 146).

Passage through the city wall and a building, possibly the latrine block

A postern doorway and passage were cut through the city wall. This was poorly dated to the late 13th or 14th centuries by two sherds of pottery. It was presumably the documented enclosure of the intramural lane created by Prior Eustace in the third quarter of the 13th century. This might also, therefore, be the date of Building 4/5 on the Duke's Place site, forming in all probability a single building aligned east–west immediately outside the city wall and entered through the passage. Parallels for this configuration are found in the better-preserved fragments of latrine blocks at many other priories.

Whatever form this building took, it must have been radically altered, if not demolished, by the alterations to the City's defences carried out by Mayor Jocelyn in 1477. The postern gate was stopped up and brick arches built along the back of the wall. This was probably also the time of destruction of the building outside the wall, which interfered with defensive considerations and to which access was now denied, at least at ground-floor level.

By the time of the Symonds plans in *c* 1585 (Figs 13–16), the intramural lane had been reopened. The north wall of the dormitory, as shown by Symonds – and by Howlett if his drawing (Fig 112) is of this building – contained evidently medieval features. It therefore would follow that if there was ever a building or construction connecting the north end of the dormitory range with the postern, it was an addition to the main building of the range, from which it was later removed.

This last point is relevant to the puzzle presented by one, or possibly two, cesspits dug into the space between the dormitory and the city wall (site H, gpH21.1). These cesspits contained wooden bowls, leather objects, glass urinals and fragments of 12th-century textiles (Chapter 8.6). The pottery was largely of 14th-century date, but included Frechen stoneware dating from the mid 16th century, which may be intrusive. It remains uncertain whether these pits date from the 14th century, that is during the lifetime of the latrine block building – in which case, what relation did they have to Building 4/5 outside the wall? – or, alternatively and perfectly possibly, whether all the material in the pit except the Frechen stoneware was residual, and the pits represent the later sanitary arrangements after the latrine block had been put out of use, that is in the period 1477–1532, with some immediately post-Dissolution use. Any structure above the pits would then have had to be demolished before the survey of *c* 1585, presumably during the reopening of the lane in the later 16th century.

The area east of the dormitory: the site of the infirmary

The function of the area east of the dormitory range and chapter house at Holy Trinity is largely unknown. In *c* 1585 Symonds shows the 'great garden of the priory' here (Fig 13; Fig 14), and the copperplate map (Fig 11) shows the garden laid out in beds, entered by a gate from the intramural lane.

It is probable that the area east of the chapter house contained the canons' cemetery, as at St Bartholomew Smithfield (Webb 1921, ii, 189) and other houses. No features or burials have been recorded. The other likelihood is that the area contained the priory infirmary.

The work of the canons for the sick in the infirmary of the priory is mentioned in 1270–1 and 1277–8 (*Cartulary*, nos 684, 1007). In 1349 Johanna Youn, widow, left her tenement in *Rethereslane* (Pudding Lane) to the priory, explicitly for the purpose of providing medicines, as well as for maintenance of two canons for a number of years (*Cal Husting Wills*, i, 580). The site of the infirmary is unknown, but parallels elsewhere would suggest that it lay east of the dormitory, in the area shown as a garden by Symonds. In this area a building or two connected buildings are shown by the copperplate map of *c* 1559 (Fig 11); it, or they, run at an angle to the dormitory range, and appear to have a circular tower at the east end. This area was redeveloped in 1908 as site B (Fig 67), but few features were recorded and none of this building.

The infirmary would conventionally be approached by a passage from the cloister through the ground floor of the dormitory range. Such a passage is known at St Bartholomew Smithfield; it passed through the dormitory range in the fourth bay from the outer end (Webb 1921, ii, 150, pl LXXII). There is no such passage shown on the Symonds plan for Holy Trinity (Fig 13; Fig 14), though an argument can be made for a passage or slype originally between the north transept and the chapter house (see above). The precise site of the infirmary, therefore, remains unknown. One model for its possible appearance is provided by the late 13th-century infirmary at the Augustinian Kirkham Priory (Yorkshire East Riding): this comprised an aisled hall of five bays with a porch, and had its own latrine block (Coppack et al 1995, 104–5).

4.7 Zone 4: the refectory and the kitchen in the north range

Documentary and antiquarian evidence

There are no individual drawings of the refectory and kitchen, only their representation on the Symonds plans (Figs 13–16). By the time of the map of Ogilby and Morgan (1676), the refectory had been demolished and its site had become two rows of small houses, with an alley or court between, probably to give access to the northern row (Fig 18). Presumably these dwellings incorporated parts of the walls of the medieval building, and they seem to have been built inside or at least to coincide in area with the footprint of the refectory.

Excavation

Duke's Place sewer, opposite 32–38, 1953 (GM53; site I)

In January 1953, while reinverting a sewer in Duke's Place (formerly Duke Street), Corporation of London workmen encountered a passage lying at right angles to the United Synagogue, which lay on the south side of Duke's Place. This was recorded for the Guildhall Museum by Ivor Noël Hume. The passage apparently proceeded in the direction of the city ditch, and presumably communicated through the city wall. The passage was found to form part of a sewer of chalk blocks, with walls 1ft 8in (0.5m) thick, an internal height of 4ft 6in (1.37m), a width of 2ft 8in (0.81m), and lying at a depth of 14ft 6in (4.42m) below street level. It was filled with 'dirt' reaching almost to the crown, from which was recovered pottery of the 16th and 17th centuries (Schofield 1998, 48). The pottery cannot now be traced. The approximate site of the chalk sewer is shown on Fig 2.

Reconstructing the refectory and the kitchen

Unfortunately, the precise alignment of the north range containing the refectory has to be guessed at since the construction of the 19th-century synagogue fronting onto Duke Street, as shown on the Goad Insurance map of the area in 1887 (see Fig 174), obliterated any earlier alignments in the area.

The refectory was evidently of early date. In *c* 1585 it had eight small and closely spaced windows at first-floor level on the southern, cloister side (Fig 15; Fig 16). The copperplate map of *c* 1559 (Fig 11) shows the south side of a notional four bays separated by pilasters or buttresses; but no buttresses are shown in the plan by Symonds (Fig 13; Fig 14) in comparison with, for instance, buttresses along the ?rebuilt cloister side of the west range, and so the projections on the refectory must have been shallow pilasters. It therefore seems likely that the refectory was of 12th-century date, and that it survived largely unaltered until the Dissolution. Symonds shows that it had a pulpit on the north side, as would be normal in such a building. The refectory was a ground-floor room rising through the equivalent of two storeys, as at the contemporary cathedrals of Norwich and Canterbury, and was not raised on an undercroft as at some other religious houses.

The door of the buttery of the priory is mentioned in *c* 1252–60 (*Cartulary*, no. 90). This was presumably 'the surfayng place' shown by Symonds at the junction of the refectory and prior's ranges, and adjacent to the kitchen (Fig 13; Fig 14); there is a similar space in this position in other houses, for example at Thetford (Norfolk). This room, at least in Tudor mansions, was for the 'surveying' of food by the steward before it was ceremoniously brought into the hall.

The large kitchen is shown by Symonds; it was refurbished by Audley around 1540 (Chapter 6.2) but there is no further indication of date. The priory kitchen occupied a similar position at St Bartholomew Smithfield, where it is undated (Webb 1921, ii, 154). Symonds shows that by *c* 1585 the Holy Trinity kitchen contained large fireplaces in the east and west walls, and an oven in the south-east corner. The drain discovered in Duke's Place in 1953 would have passed down its east side. There is no record of the direction of flow of the drain, but it is most likely that it ran from the cloister, communicating in some way with the kitchen, and then out through the city wall into the city ditch. Apart from the well in the great court shown on the panoramas (Fig 11; Fig 12) and by Symonds (Fig 13; Fig 14), this is the only record we have, to date, of the priory water system. Presumably it was as well organised as those at urban monasteries generally, especially those in London (Bond 1993). Researching it remains an archaeological objective for the future.

4.8 Zone 5: the great court and the main gate

Introduction

Following Symonds, the term 'great court' will be used for the open space west of the west range of the cloister. Originally this probably included the space west of the west end of the priory church, which had been partly filled in and obscured by the time of the Symonds plans (Figs 13–16). In other monasteries, this space would be an 'inner court'; the priory, being within the walls of the city, did not have an outer court, which, although present in some suburban London houses (St Mary Spital, St Mary Clerkenwell, St John Clerkenwell), was more a feature of monastic establishments in the countryside.

Documentary and antiquarian evidence

A drawing of the great court, looking east, of *c* 1810 by Frederick Nash has already been noted (Fig 92). Besides the western range of the cloister, this shows the east parts of the north and south sides of the court as existing in the early 19th century. The buildings forming the north side, on the left, are either weatherboarded or have slight jetties, and probably retain much of their structure as surveyed by Symonds. The south range, on the right, is of brick and is presumably originally the range of buildings put up by William Kerwin around the time of the Symonds plans; the foundations of this range are shown by Symonds. Presumably, also, the windows of these buildings had been replaced in the intervening centuries.

Two other artists' views show the character of the west side of the great court in the late 19th century; and elements of the 16th-century buildings as surveyed by Symonds are probably to be seen in these drawings. The first, a drawing by F Shepperd in 1874, looks south down Heneage Lane (Fig 123). The buildings on the left are on the western precinct boundary; they are essentially the range shown along the west side of the great court by Symonds, though presumably with alterations in the subsequent 300 years. By 1874 the houses had doors west to the Lane, and possibly faced that way; their ground floors may have incorporated the masonry of the precinct wall. Second, in 1884 John Crowther (?1837–?1902) made a series of careful watercolour drawings of old buildings in the northern part of the City of London, concentrating on the period before 1700; two of the watercolours were of the great court, one of which is reproduced here (Fig 124) and the other later (Chapter 6.4; Fig 173). Fig 124 shows the entrance to Sugar Baker's Yard on the right, and the narrow way into St James's Place (the former Court), looking north. Two buildings with slight jetties are shown, the larger one rising to four storeys. This is perhaps one of the buildings shown on the west side of the court by Symonds, though presumably much altered by 1884, when it was the Old Jewellery Mart public house.

The south or main gate to Creechurch Lane, comprising a large and a small entrance, is shown on the Symonds plans and was recorded by various artists between 1790 and 1825. The

Fig 123 F Shepperd, 'Heneage Lane', 1874, looking south (LMA, SC/PZ/CT/01/103)

Fig 124 John Crowther, buildings at entrance to St James's Place and Sugar Baker's Yard, watercolour 1884, looking north (Guildhall Library)

Fig 125 J T Smith, main gate to Duke's Place, engraving 1790, from the south-west (Wilkinson 1825)

Fig 126 Anon, 'Duke's Place', undated, from the south-west (Guildhall Library)

earliest was the topographer J T Smith (1766–1833). Viewing the gate from the south-west, this engraving (Fig 125) shows the mouldings of both entrances sharply delineated. The smaller two-centred entrance comprises two orders of single roll or bowtell moulding and a hood. The larger entrance with a two-centred segmental arch is similarly moulded although the inner order appears to be plain. A date in the 13th or 14th century would seem appropriate. A protruding stone at the point where one might expect to see a label stop on the west side of the larger entrance is probably associated with the diagonal timber strut supporting the jettied structure above. The proportioning of the smaller entrance suggests that the ground level had risen since its construction. This would imply that the larger entrance or gateway also originally stood higher out of the ground.

An undated and anonymous engraving (Fig 126) showing the gate from the south-west corresponds very closely with the view by J T Smith (Fig 125) although the representation of the mouldings and the handling of perspective is not as precise. A third engraving of 1793 by Nathaniel Smith (c 1740–1802) (Fig 127) shows the gateway as it appears in the J T Smith engraving although the mouldings of the larger entrance are less sharply defined. This view, however, also shows a timber post and curving braces supporting the back half of the building. A post or masonry pier is shown in this position on the Symonds plan.

Fig 127 *Nathaniel Smith, 'Duke's Place, the South and Principal Gate of the Ancient Monastery or Priory of the Holy Trinity', 1793, from the south (Guildhall Library)*

Fig 128 *The priory gateway by John Carter,* The ancient architecture of England, Vol 1 (1806), *pl LIV (1795, first published in 1802), from the south*

John Carter also drew the gate, in 1795, and first published his drawing in 1802 as plate LIV in his series *The ancient architecture of England* (Fig 128). The accompanying text describes the gate as 'The west gateway of the remains of the priory of Christchurch, Aldgate. The design gives the larger archway for horsemen and the lesser archway for foot passengers. These arches shew the regular pointed arch, and the segment of a pointed ditto, A2. Plan. B2 Architrave to the postern arch. C2 Ditto to the larger arch. The plinths are buried in the ground.' These drawings are scaled.

Next on the scene was Frederick Nash around 1810. The interleaved copy of the 1805 edition of Pennant's *Some account of London* (first published in 1790) in the Sir John Soane's Museum contains a watercolour of the gate (Fig 129). This view from the south-west corresponds with the view by J T Smith, especially in the representation of the mouldings. It also shows the timber post pictured by Nathaniel Smith but omits any detail relating to the superstructure.

Finally, the demolition of the gateway in 1822 was recorded by R Schnebbelie (fl 1792–1849) (Fig 130). This view from the south-east shows both archways intact but the superstructure has been demolished and the rear ground floor appears to be in the process of demolition. The larger arch is shown as four-centred and the corbel, shown by J T Smith as supporting a diagonal strut for the jettied building above, is shown as a carved label stop. Nor are the mouldings consistent with those shown in the earlier views. Because of these differences it seems likely that this is the least accurate representation of the gateway, possibly because the masonry itself was in the process of demolition when the drawing was made.

Fig 129 *Frederick Nash, watercolour of the outside of the main gate (undated, c 1810), from the south-west (Sir John Soane's Museum, Soane's copy of* Some account of London *by Thomas Pennant, 4 edn (1805), 226 interleaved)*

Fig 130 R Schnebbelie, '*Gateway of the Priory of the Holy Trinity called Christchurch, near Aldgate*' (1822), *from the south-east* (Wilkinson 1825)

Excavation

33 Creechurch Lane, 16a Bevis Marks, 1979 (CRE79; site J)

The only archaeological excavation of relevance to the great court is a watching brief carried out in 1979 at 33 Creechurch Lane, which occupied part of the range forming the west side of the court, backing onto Heneage Lane and the west boundary of the priory precinct (Fig 2; Egan 1981).

Cutting into natural brickearth was a ditch 4.0m long and aligned north-west to south-east which was infilled in or around the 4th century AD. Fragments of chalk and ragstone foundations seem to be of medieval buildings in the priory; several late medieval or post-medieval foundations of ragstone, chalk and brick were also observed. There were also six pits, probably all of medieval date. The evidence from this site has not been further processed for this study. The pottery has been scanned and notable are two sherds from a tin-glazed dish with foliage pattern dating to the late 16th century (<P42>, Fig 202).

Reconstructing the great court and the main gate

The outlines of the buildings on the north side of the great court shown by Symonds are recognisable on the Ordnance Survey maps of 1875 through to 1923, and on the Goad Insurance survey of 1887 (Fig 174). The kink in the alignment of Duke Street and Bevis Marks at the junction with Heneage Lane survived until the 1980s. The western perimeter of the precinct survives as the east side of Heneage Lane. The property divisions shown on this side of the lane in the Ordnance Survey map of 1875 seem to relate closely to those shown by Symonds. Partial reconstructions of two parts of the great court based on the Symonds plans (Figs 13–16) are given in Fig 131 and Fig 132. As before, these drawings probably include some post-Dissolution features, especially partitions, but these cannot be identified. It is likely that there were more new post-Dissolution buildings in the area of the court, where demolition and adaptation was more the rule, than elsewhere in the precinct.

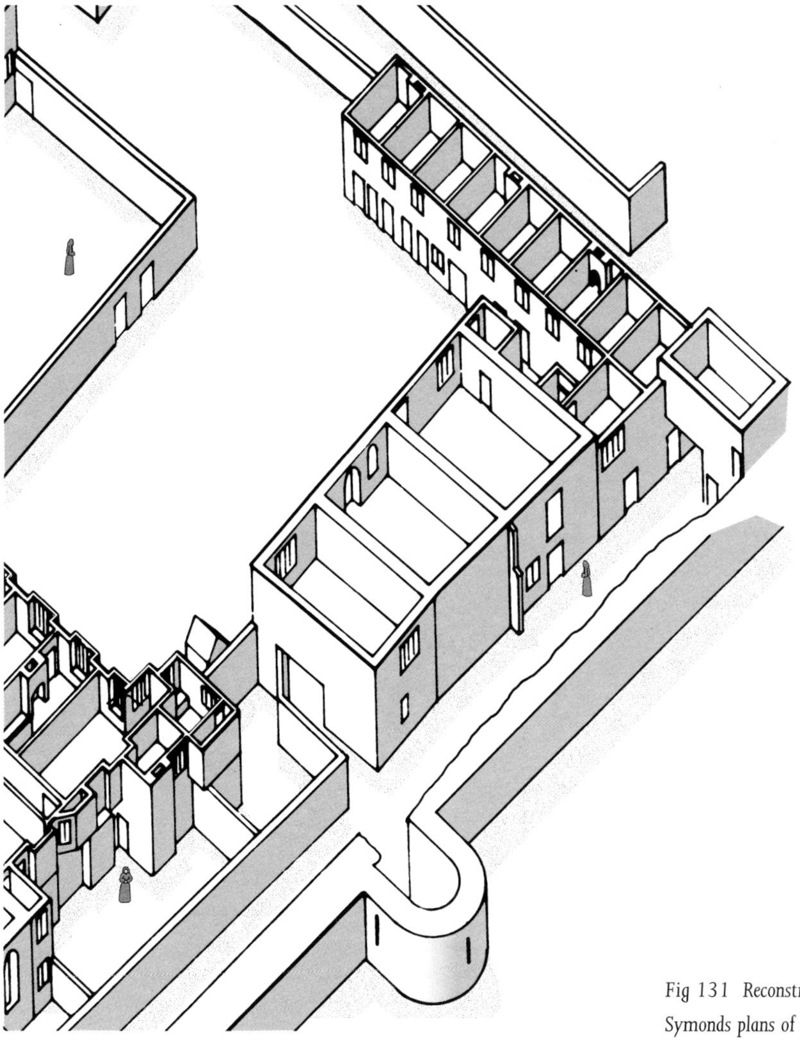

Fig 131 Reconstruction of the north-east part of the great court, from the Symonds plans of c 1585 (see Figs 13–16), from the north-west

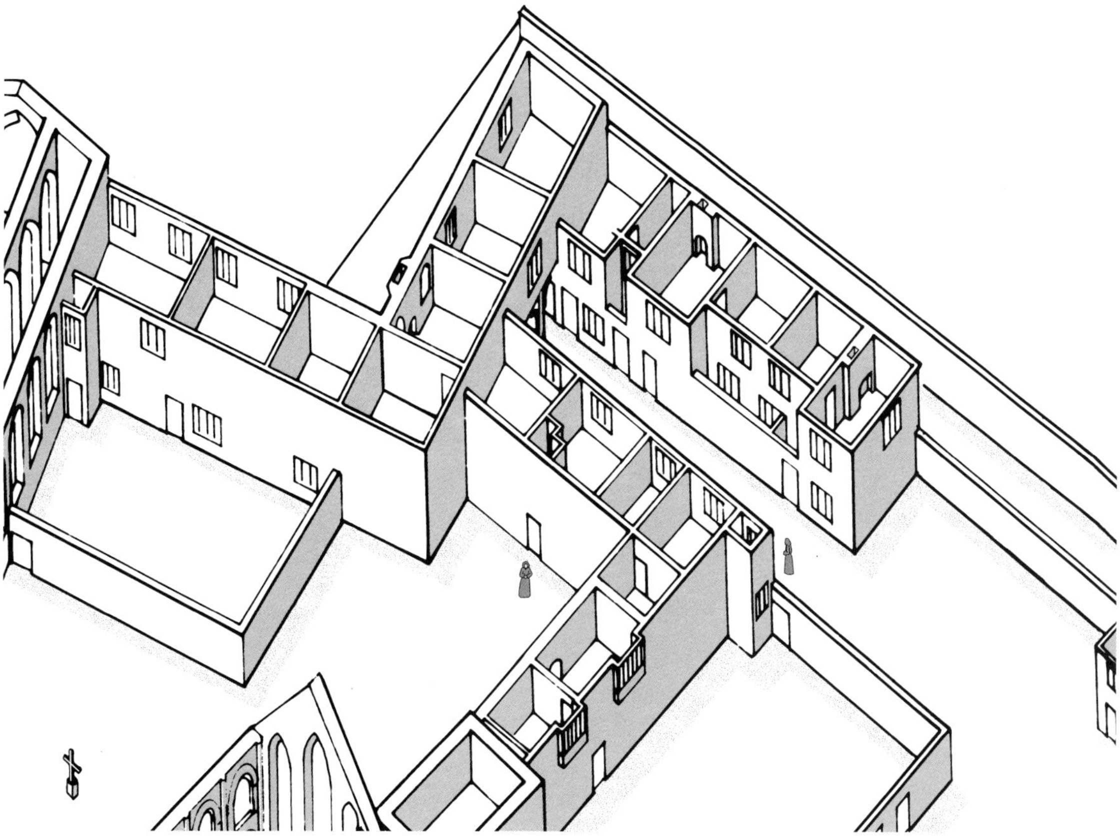

Fig 132 Reconstruction of the ranges near the main gate to the monastery, from the Symonds plans of c 1585 (see Figs 13–16), from the north-east

The majority of the buildings around the great court, in the Symonds plans, were timber-framed at both ground- and first-floor levels; little can be said about their likely date of construction. The watercolour of the court by Nash of *c* 1810 (Fig 92) shows the north range, one building having slight jetties suggesting construction in the first half of the 16th century; this could be either pre- or post-Dissolution. The range along the west side of the precinct is pictured twice: the outer western side by Shepperd in 1874 (Fig 123) and the east side near the site of the main gate to Creechurch Lane (by then demolished) by Crowther in 1884 (Fig 124). The watching brief at 33 Creechurch Lane (site J), towards the north end of this strip of buildings, did show that there were medieval pits here, later overlain by buildings which are probably those shown on the Symonds plans. Symonds also shows (Fig 13; Fig 14) a privy with three seats at the north end of the range, in the corner of the court, and this was presumably a public privy for the occupants of the buildings and for those using or working in the court. However, the correspondence of the Symonds plan with the present street-lines in Fig 2 shows that this building, which would have been an attractive archaeological objective, lies under the widened street on the north and outside site J.

At other monastic houses, the inner court – the equivalent of the great court here – generally contained the guest-house(s) (such as at Fountains Abbey, Yorkshire North Riding) and accommodation for corrodians, domestic workshops, granaries and stables (Burton 1994, 146–8). In the court at Holy Trinity and its approach from the south were two notable buildings with masonry components: the main gate and a building on two floors forming part of the north range of the court.

The main gate to the priory from Creechurch Lane, in *c* 1585, formed part of a range probably of masonry at least in its southern, exterior façade to the lane. The larger vehicular and smaller pedestrian arches survived to be drawn by Smith and others in the late 18th and early 19th centuries, before demolition in 1822. These arches have a 14th-century appearance. The back of the gatehouse is only hinted at in its post-medieval form, and was by then of timber.

A second stone building formed part of the north side of the great court; it is shown without distinction on the copperplate map and 'Agas' woodcut, but Symonds shows what is apparently a two-storeyed building of stone with a 'gatehouse' on its eastern side. At this time the lower rooms were being used as a bakehouse and stable, and there were school(s) in the upper room(s). The first-floor plan shows that this building may originally have been two adjacent structures, their party-wall reinforced by a buttress at its north end. The two openings to the court at ground level are probably of medieval date, and form a carriage entrance and associated door. The bakehouse may well have been of monastic date, and the associated building with the carriage entrance may have been a brewhouse, like a similar building at Christchurch, Canterbury (G Coppack, pers comm). The watercolour by Nash of the court in *c* 1810 (Fig 92) shows that these buildings were by then of three or four storeys.

On the southern side of the great court lay a garden, shown in the copperplate map of *c* 1559 (Fig 11) and labelled 'the gardin to the mansion house' on the Symonds plan (Fig 13; Fig 14). Here William Kerwin was laying out foundations for new buildings, later to be Sugar Baker's Yard (Fig 92 shows their appearance in *c* 1810, and the entrance to the Yard in 1884 is shown by Crowther in Fig 124). Possibly this garden had been the prior's garden before the Dissolution, but there is no direct evidence for that. It had a well, and there was a second well in the northern part of the great court. The latter, presumably one of the main wells of the priory, is shown with a well-head roof on the copperplate map (Fig 11).

In conclusion, the limited evidence for the great court of the priory suggests, as in the case of monastic conversions elsewhere, that the functions of buildings in the court were generally retained into the post-Dissolution period.

4.9 Zone 6: the medieval church of St Katherine Cree

The church of St Katherine Cree is not mentioned in the charter describing the boundaries of the soke of Aldgate given by Queen Matilda to the priory in *c* 1108 (*Cartulary*, no. 11); but by the time of Prior Richard in 1222–48 the parish of St Katherine was a distinct entity (ibid, nos 39, 50). Stow noted that the church was a very old building since, because of the number of raisings of street level during its lifetime, the visitor had to enter it by descending seven steps (Stow 1603, i, 142). However, only three steps are shown at the south door by Symonds (Fig 13; Fig 14), who conducted the survey at the same time as Stow was writing his text.

The church was rebuilt in 1628–31 (Chapter 6.4), and this retained the tower of 1504. The tower shown by Symonds in *c* 1585 must, therefore, be that standing today. The rebuilding retained a pillar at the south-west corner of the nave, still visible today, which appears as a 15th-century capital on a pillar about 3ft high. There are two differing accounts of the amount of this pillar which remains under the nave floor, below the exposed part. According to Strype (1720, i.ii, 65) this has a further length of 15ft (4.58m) below the ground, and shows the depth of the floor of the former church. If this is true, then the floor level in the medieval church was at about 14.00m OD. A hole dug next to the pillar in 1928 apparently showed that the bottom of the pillar is only 1.1m beneath the present floor level (GL, MS 9370, fos 147–8), that is at about 16.40m OD. These different accounts cannot at present be reconciled. A suggested plan has been published which shows the outline derived from the Symonds plan superimposed on the present plan of the church, which was rebuilt in 1628, and the location of the 15th-century pier (Schofield 1994, fig 76). The nave and two aisles shown by Symonds could well be a total rebuilding of the 15th century, after the church became an accredited parish church in 1414, of which the pier is the only remnant; but this would not explain Stow's account of it as 'very old'. Perhaps the pier was part of a partial rebuilding.

In 1422 the wardmote of Aldgate complained that the churchyard of St Katherine had not been enclosed for many years in prejudice of the rites of Holy Church, but it was now illicitly and unlawfully enclosed by the prior and his tenants (*Cal Plea and Mem R* 1413–37, 130). A churchyard with a cross is shown north of the church in the copperplate map of *c* 1559 (Fig 11) and the area is marked 'The church yard' by Symonds in *c* 1585. During the medieval period it seems likely that the parishioners of St Katherine's could be buried in the priory cemetery, a part of which was probably later cut off to form the post-Dissolution parish graveyard. As already discussed, it seems likely that there was also a parish area, perhaps an aisle, within the priory church, at least until the parish of St Katherine Cree was clearly established, and possibly thereafter. The Shearmen and later the Clothworkers still went to worship in the priory church on special occasions during their ceremonial year, even in the early decades of the 16th century.

5

Archaeological and architectural history of the priory to 1532

5.1 Introduction

This chapter is concerned with the ecclesiastical topography of the area in 1108, including the pre-priory church of Syredus and its graveyard; parallels for and influences on the design and functions of the medieval church and other conventual buildings; and the position and connections of the priory within its locality and within the City of London. A summary table of the development of the priory and its dissolution has already been given at the beginning of this report as Table 2, and the sequence proposed here is outlined below (5.3).

5.2 The site of the priory, Saxon occupation, and previous churches on the site and in the area (*c* AD 900–1108, period M1)

Introduction

The first questions to review are the nature of Saxon occupation in the area before the founding of the priory in 1108; what is known of the churches in the area in the 11th and 12th centuries, in part arguing back from the parish structure which is evident, as in the rest of the City of London, by *c* 1200; and any particular arguments for the location and alignment of the church of Syredus, which evidently preceded the priory, and which must have lain somewhere within the priory precinct.

Saxon occupation in the area

The gate at Aldgate, originally of Roman date, is probably that referred to in the *Anglo-Saxon Chronicle* for 1052 as the 'East Gate' (Garmonsway 1954, 181); but the location at London is only inferred from the context, and is not specifically mentioned. Observations on the south side of the gate site in 1907 (Merrifield 1965, 317) and on the north side in 1967 (Marsden 1969) suggest that there was a stone gate here in the late Roman period; one observation (Merrifield 1965, 317) suggested that some of its masonry resembled that of the Roman interval towers or bastions.

The Roman city wall, believed to have been built originally about AD 200, ran north-west from the gate; in the area of the later priory, two interval towers (now called bastions 6 and 7) were added, probably some time in the 4th century AD. These two towers are shown as surviving on the copperplate and 'Agas' panoramas of the 1550s and 1560s, each with a single storey projecting above the parapet of the wall (Fig 11; Fig 12), like other towers to the west and south-east. Both these bastions were still visible in the 18th century, and feature on City lease plans of properties in Houndsditch, the street running along the outer edge of the external ditch. They were both inspected by the antiquary William Maitland for his *History of London*, first published in 1739; he noted what is now called bastion 7 standing 26ft high, though sorely decayed; bastion 6, nearby, was 24ft high, 'perfectly round, and much more beautiful than the former; the bricks [Roman tiles] being found as if newly laid, while the stones in most parts are become a sacrifice to devouring Time' (Maitland 1765, i, 31). It is therefore likely that the wall and bastions were a formidable feature throughout the Saxon and medieval periods and constituted a natural boundary to the precinct.

Secular occupation within the gate along the main routes of Leadenhall Street (known in the medieval period as Aldgate Street) and Fenchurch Street may be presumed by the 11th century, but has not been certainly recorded in the vicinity. A single pit at site C in 1972, on the Aldgate frontage along the east side of the precinct, was dated to *c* 1050–*c* 1150. Several fine objects and a coin of Edward the Confessor were found on site D, on the Leadenhall Street frontage near St Katherine Cree (Figs 69–71; Chapter 8.6). At present, since the records of excavation on site D have not been fully analysed, the detailed contexts of these finds are not known; but they presumably reflect secular occupation along the north side of Leadenhall Street, matching the first reference to the nearby Aldgate in 1052.

There was little other evidence for pre-priory secular occupation on the study sites within the precinct itself. There were some late Saxon pits, one of which may have been the hollow below a small sunken-featured building (site F; Chapter 4.5); on site A (Chapter 4.2) there was a possible well within the graveyard sequence. Outside the precinct on its west side, at a site at 10–16 Bevis Marks in 1980, 11th- to 13th-century pits indicate occupation and perhaps property boundaries (site code BEV80; Schofield 1998, 163). In the 10th and 11th centuries, the area within the walls near Aldgate seems in general to have been a backwater; it is relatively bereft of finds of Saxon coins (Stott 1991, figs 4.5–4.6), though a coin of Edward the Confessor was found at site D, as just noted. Reconstruction of the development of the Saxon street pattern shows a relative lack of interest or development in this area during these centuries (Vince 1990, fig 65), though this picture might change as excavations and post-excavation analyses of sites in the area produce more finds and structures in the future.

By the early 12th century there was a church dedicated to St Botolph immediately outside the gate, as described in detail in the next section. This lay under what are now the steps of the present 18th-century church of St Botolph Aldgate. The cartulary of the priory shows that by the middle of the 12th century there were also a number of properties along the north side of the street outside the gate and east of the church, which were the nucleus of the medieval and later frontage (eg *Cartulary*, nos 890, 898). Secular occupation of the north side of the extramural street may have been fairly continuous for a distance to the east; the picture south of the street is less clear in these earlier years. Somewhere in the soke of the *cnihtengild*, coterminous with what is now the ward of Portsoken, was at least one principal tenement by 1125, since Osbert Trentmars rendered 7s 5d per annum to the knights of the *cnihtengild*, and they gave this rent to the canons when they granted the whole soke in that year (*Cartulary*, nos 935–7).

Churches and parishes in the area in the 11th and 12th centuries

Some further impression of life in the area in the 11th and 12th centuries is given by the local structure of parishes and their churches, a system which was itself evolving at this time. According to the opening narrative of the priory cartulary, Holy Trinity was founded on a site where a certain Syredus had established a church from which the dean and chapter of Waltham Holy Cross (itself founded in 1060) had received a rent of 30s per annum, but only for a few years before 1108 (*Cartulary*, no. 1; the full text is printed in ibid, appendix, 223–4). Stow (1603, i, 139) adds that the church of Syredus was dedicated not only to the Holy Cross but also to Mary Magdalen, and the first parish heading in the cartulary groups together the parishes of Holy Trinity, St Michael, Mary Magdalen and St Katherine (*Cartulary*, 5). It is probable that the medieval parish of St Katherine Cree comprised this amalgamation (Fig 133).

As context for the church of Syredus, the configuration of the three relevant parishes may be outlined as far as it is known. The parish of Holy Trinity is mentioned three times in the grants recorded in the cartulary: property there lay in Fenchurch Street (*Cartulary*, no. 80), and the parish was 'by Aldgate' (ibid, nos 993, 1020). The only part of St Katherine's parish which included Fenchurch Street was close to the latter's

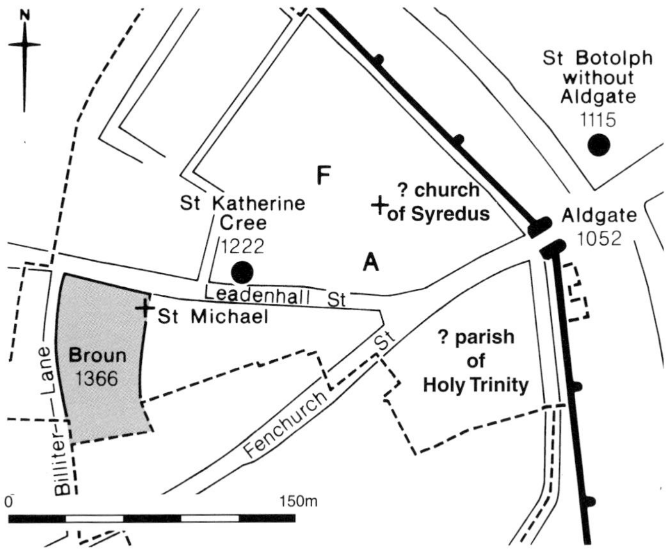

Fig 133 The parish of St Katherine Cree, with suggested location of the pre-priory church and of the chapel of St Michael; the locations of sites A and F are marked by their letters (scale 1:4000)

junction with Aldgate Street. This would suggest that Holy Trinity was in the south-east part of the later parish of St Katherine. By 1360 the garden called *Colemanhawe* south of Fenchurch Street, which was previously reckoned to be in Holy Trinity parish, was counted in the parish of St Katherine Coleman (ibid, no. 80).

The chapel of St Michael is mentioned in the description of the western boundary of the soke of Aldgate (ie the ward) given to the priory by Queen Matilda in 1108 (*Cartulary*, no. 11). In 1676, on Ogilby and Morgan's map, the western boundary of Aldgate ward north of Fenchurch Street bent westwards, west of Billiter Lane (later Street) to join Lime Street. In the cartulary this change in direction was 'by a small lane which is now blocked up because it was the scene of nocturnal thieves and so it goes by the small lane against St Michael's chapel to Lymstrete'. The meaning of 'against' here is 'opposite', and this can be taken to mean that the lane struck west from a point near the church. Thus, the parish of St Michael probably constituted the south-west part of the later parish of St Katherine, the bounds of which are also shown by Ogilby and Morgan in 1676 (Fig 18). There are three references in the cartulary to John, chaplain of St Michael, during the priorate of Stephen (1170–97) (*Cartulary*, nos 417, 700, 1058). In one case (ibid, no. 1058) the chaplain is joined as a witness to a deed by three other chaplains of the priory's city churches: St Olave Hart Street, St Clement Eastcheap, and St Edmund the King. These parish churches all lie in the eastern half of the City (Fig 8). The parish of St Michael was still being used as a term of locational reference in wills in the late 13th century (eg *Cal Husting Wills*, i, 51).

The location of the chapel or church of St Michael is indicated by a deed of 1314, in which the prior and convent of Holy Trinity Priory leased to John de la Marche land in the parish of St Katherine Cree. The land (Fig 134) was bordered on the north by the chapel of St Michael and its cemetery to the south-west of the chapel (*Cartulary*, no. 55; the reading

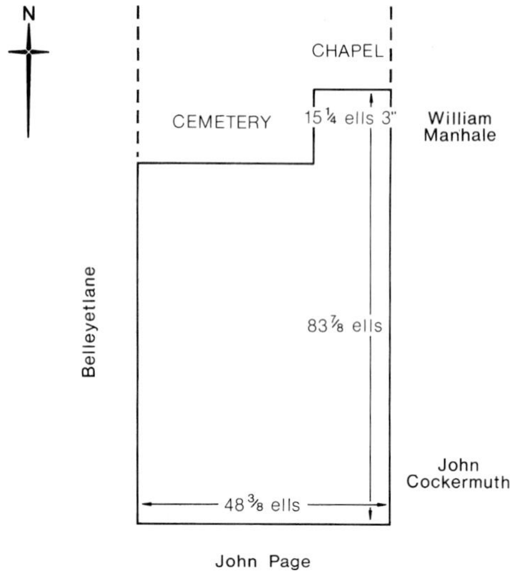

Fig 134 Sketch of de la Marche property in 1314, reconstructed from documentary evidence

cimiterium rather than ?*civitatis*, apparently read by the editor of the cartulary, is confirmed by CLRO, HR 46(67)). The rent was 53s 4d for this and one other tenement in the same parish (*Cartulary*, no. 55). Some subsequent occupants paying rent (presumably quitrent) are noted in the cartulary (ibid, nos 56–7) up to the abbot of Evesham in 1426. In 1366 Margery, widow of Thomas Broun, gave five messuages and 36 shops to Evesham Abbey (Honeybourne 1929, 355–60); the cartulary shows that this included the property in question (*Cartulary*, no. 56). In such grants the term 'shops' includes workshops, and only a few of them need have had street frontages. It should be noted (as it was by his editor) that Stow's quotation of a document relating to the foundation of the priory is a mistaken use of the deed of 1314 (Stow 1603, i, 140; ii, 292); and that the undercroft at the junction of Leadenhall and Fenchurch Streets, by Aldgate pump, which was often taken by antiquaries to be the crypt of St Michael's, was a notable part of a secular building (Schofield 2003a, 196, figs 231, a–b).

To establish a case for fragments found in 1973 being from St Michael's chapel, the history of the site has to be taken into the post-Dissolution years. In 1541 the Crown granted the property to Edward and Alice Cornwallis (*L and P Hen VIII*, 16, 107 (35)). In 1556, now called 'Principal Place', it was described as a large messuage with a large garden adjoining; at that time it formed the estate of Alice Cornwalleis (*sic*), along with 16 tenements or houses and three stables in Billiter Lane which were presumably attached and which may have formed the Billiter Lane frontage indicated in the priory lease (Fry 1896, 143). Alice's son Thomas sold the houses in 1562 to Sir Nicholas Throckmorton, who died in 1571 (Madge 1901, 143–4). Stow mentions the 'fair house with diverse tenements adjoining' and places it between Billiter Lane and Sugar Loaf Alley (Stow 1603, i, 138). The house is shown on Ogilby and Morgan's map of 1676 (Fig 18, marked C52), in the area outside that of the Fire, as Whitchurch House, which in 1678 was leased by the Royal African Company (Woods et al 1975). A tiny sketch of an imposing house of four gables is shown on the Aldgate ward map of 1739 by Jacob Ilive (Hyde 1999, 35, pl 2). Since the Great Fire of 1666 did not reach this locality, the sketch could depict the house of *c* 1600.

With an ell of 3ft, the distance of 83⅞ ells (or 251½ft) forming the east boundary of the site leased from the priory by John de la Marche in 1314 would fit between Leadenhall Street and Fenchurch Street at this point, and within the boundary of the later parish of St Katherine Cree. The chapel of St Michael and its cemetery, therefore, must have lain in the area between Billiter Lane to the west and the east boundary of the site of Principal Place, south of Leadenhall Street but north of the eventual site of Whitchurch House. The likely site of the chapel, in the east of this area, was occupied in 1676 by the narrow access court to the house with buildings on either side (Fig 18).

Excavations in 1973 on the site of Whitchurch House (the site was then known by its modern name of Africa House) produced two small sections of archaeological strata (Woods et al 1975, 252–66). At a spot coinciding with the north-east corner of the 17th-century house a 0.6m length of chalk and gravel foundations was recorded running east–west and overlying a pit backfilled in the second half of the 11th century. The building technique of chalk and gravel is of late Saxon to early medieval type, and two small sherds of the late 13th or early 14th century apparently coming from it (ibid, 260) may be contamination from later activity. We therefore suggest that this foundation may have originally formed part of the chapel buildings, perhaps even of the chapel itself.

To summarise the position within Aldgate, the church or chapel of St Michael probably lay in the south-west part of the later parish of St Katherine; and St Katherine's itself lay within the precinct, part of which became the parish churchyard by the 15th century. In the 11th century, the parish of St Michael presumably comprised a concentration of secular occupation on the Leadenhall Street and Lime Street frontages nearest to it, and the land to the north-east of St Michael's was perhaps comparatively unpopulated, presenting a suitable space in the ecclesiastical topography for Syredus' foundation (Fig 133).

The church of St Botolph Aldgate stands today immediately outside the site of the medieval gate, about 100m east of the priory church site. The church is first mentioned in 1125, when it was given to the priory with the land and soke of the *cnihtengild* (*Cartulary*, nos 871, 874–5; *Cal L Book* C, 220). At this date the church had a large garden attached to it, which also passed to the priory (*Cartulary*, no. 871). Lawsuits over burial rights from *c* 1130 to the 1160s indicate that the extent of the parish was unresolved, and this might be a sign of recent foundation (*Cartulary*, nos 964–9; Brooke 1975, 145). In 1157 Prior Ralph received confirmation that the parish belonged to the priory, and its bounds seem to have been coterminous with the ward of Portsoken (*Cartulary*, no. 964). The church is shown by Wyngaerde in *c* 1540 (Fig 10) and in the 'Agas' woodcut derived from the copperplate map of *c* 1559 (Fig 12; Fig 11). It was rebuilt in 1741–4 by George Dance the elder (Bradley and Pevsner 1997, 207–8).

In 1989–90 parts of the foundations of the north and west sides of the medieval church were recorded in a vault of the 18th-century church, below its main entrance steps. Together with a 1706 plan of the medieval church (GL, MS 3606/2), this discovery enables the position of the medieval St Botolph's to be established as beneath the forecourt of the 18th-century church, between Dance's south front and Aldgate High Street. What is interpreted as the junction between the first nave and a slightly narrower chancel (at least on the south side) was observed in the form of chalk and gravel foundations, but was not accurately datable. At least 17 burials were also excavated; some were in rough mortared cists of the type normally assigned to the 11th and 12th centuries (site code SAB87; Schofield 1994, 95–6, with the plan of 1706; Schofield 1998, 257–8).

The antiquity of St Botolph Aldgate is an unresolved question, since there are two possibilities (Brooke 1975, 146, n 2). On the one hand, it may be argued that since the church was already built and dedicated to St Botolph before the *cnihtengild* handed over the rights to the priory, it may have been there for some time; in which case it is coincidental that the dedication is shared with St Botolph's Priory, Colchester, the starting-point of the Augustinian transfer to London. Alternatively, the grant by the *cnihtengild* to the priory may have been of a church, perhaps of no great age, to which the name St Botolph was in the process of being assigned by the canons. The pre-1108 existence of St Botolph Aldgate is, therefore, by no means certain, and it can only be seen in its position outside the gate from 1125.

The 11th- and 12th-century cemetery on the priory site and inferences about the site, alignment and character of Syredus' church

The Leadenhall Street/Mitre Street excavations (site A; Chapter 4.2) found an extensive late Saxon, presumably 11th-century, graveyard overlain by the main priory church and by further burials aligned with the post-1108 church. To the south, burials excavated in 1990 at 78–79 Leadenhall Street (site D; Chapter 4.2), apparently extending southwards to Leadenhall Street itself, similarly comprised a majority of burials out of alignment with the priory church and a few in alignment with it, suggesting that this graveyard functioned both before and after the priory's foundation.

The types of burial on all the priory sites where graves were encountered are discussed below (5.4). This present section examines the question of whether we can make any inference about the church of Syredus, which evidently preceded the priory, from the burials on sites A and D. Since the site D group is reported here in outline only, the site A group may furnish more sensitive evidence of changes in the course of the 11th and 12th centuries.

The priory church of 'after 1108' lay on a north-west to south-east alignment of 125°, that is 35° to the south-east of west–east. The burials on site A, taken as a single group, shared a similar range of 35° in their alignments. It therefore seems possible that some, oriented conventionally east–west, reflected the alignment of the previous church, and that others reflected the alignment of the new priory church. But cemeteries of this period often display a range of alignments of burials to a single church building (eg the 12th-century chapel and cemetery within the inner bailey of Trowbridge Castle, Wiltshire: Graham and Davies 1993, fig 23). Consequently it is not safe to deduce the alignment of the church of Syredus from the variety of alignments of burials which may have been around it.

Although some of the burials were in roughly mortared cists, there were no features of distinction in the southern (sites A and D) or western (site F; Chapter 4.5) parts of the cemetery at Holy Trinity, with the sole exception of a male burial with a silver pectoral cross in the southern section at site A (grave 9).

There were no remains of stone grave covers, such as that of *c* 1050 with a carving of the Harrowing of Hell on it found beneath the floor of the chapter house of Bristol Abbey in 1832, and taken to be evidence of an underlying Saxon cemetery or a Saxon church, though how and why the cover came into the possession of the canons is 'a matter of conjecture' according to the most recent consideration (Dickinson 1976; Zarnecki et al 1984, 150; Walker 1998, xx). Similarly, there were no examples of stone coffins *in situ*, which would have been burials of status, as found for instance at St Paul's (Schofield in prep), Westminster Abbey (where a single stone coffin has been recorded north of the present church) and at the Old Minster in Winchester (Tweddle et al 1995, 231); although possible fragments of two stone coffins were among the moulded stones from the site, reused as rubble (Chapter 8.2; <A62> and <A63>, Fig 194).

It would, moreover, be in order for the canons' cemetery to be south-east of the choir of the monastic church, since the cloister lay on the north, thus mirroring the normal arrangement whereby canons' cemeteries lay to the north of a church which had the cloister on the south (as probably at St Bartholomew Smithfield: Webb 1921, ii, 188–9). The male buried in grave 9, with the pectoral cross, was presumably a canon. However, other graves in the vicinity were of women.

Late Saxon minsters elsewhere support a wide range of suggestions for the position of the church of Syredus in relation to the priory church which replaced it. A number of Norman foundations, including houses of the Augustinians, were founded on existing religious sites: for instance, at Reading, Much Wenlock and Lewes (Lyne 1997). At St Frideswide, Oxford, there was a minster by 1004, and excavation has found 9th- or 10th-century burials. The minster was refounded as an Augustinian house by canons from Holy Trinity itself either in *c* 1120, or even as early as 1111 (Postles 1993, 4–5). The pre-1120 church may have lain immediately north of the priory church (now the cathedral), which was built by *c* 1150 (Blair 1990, 236–8; 1996, 96). In other cases, the previous church lay to the north or north-west, as at Bury St Edmunds, Winchester Old Minster, Exeter and Rochester; but it could also be to the south (Peterborough, Durham and Haughmond, Shropshire). A further possibility is that the church of Syredus lay entirely beneath and aligned with the later church, as at Romsey, where the Saxon church is beneath the Norman nave (Taylor and Taylor 1965, 521–2; Scott 1996), or at Cirencester, where the pre-Conquest church also lay beneath the nave (Evans 1989; Wilkinson and McWhirr 1998). In this regard it is unfortunate that the scrap of masonry observed at the south end of site F as Building A, of unknown but probably pre-12th-century date, was only fleetingly observed and not photographed. We therefore do not know where the church of Syredus lay.

The architectural character of Syredus' church, presumably dating from the middle of the 11th century, also remains unknown, though links with Waltham Abbey (Essex) are likely. Waltham was founded as a college by Earl Harold Godwinson (the future Harold II) in 1060; the church of Syredus paid a rent to the dean and chapter of Waltham, and shared with Waltham a dedication to the Holy Cross. The establishment at Waltham was evidently on a lavish scale, and may have owed something to Harold's personal knowledge of canonical life in Lotharingia, the source of monastic influence which spread into Flanders and Normandy (Dickinson 1950, 95–6; Brooke 1969, 116–18). Some scholars have suggested that Harold's mid 11th-century church may have resembled another great pre-Conquest church, Edward the Confessor's Westminster Abbey (eg RCHME 1924, 18). From the middle of the 19th century, on the other hand, it has also been argued that the standing nave at Waltham dates from the early 1100s, and one recent discussion concludes that there is no evidence which can be confidently related to the pre-Conquest church (Fernie 1985, 48, 75). A description of work at the site claims that the third church on the site, that of Earl Harold of 1053–60, included a continuous transept with a tiny eastern apse (Huggins and Bascombe 1992).

The foundation within Aldgate was presumably intended to be a college of secular canons, though this is not known for certain. This would match the older foundation of St Martin le Grand, established in the middle of the 11th century north of St Paul's Cathedral, its main buildings lying in the area east of the present street of the same name. Further parallels between Holy Trinity and St Martin le Grand can be seen in their connections with patrons in the royal circle. Henry I's queen Matilda, founder of Holy Trinity, was the heiress of the Boulogne family which was one of the early patrons of St Martin's. Matilda endowed St Martin's with several churches in Essex, while Stephen granted it free warren privileges on other Essex lands. Henry of Blois was dean of St Martin's in Stephen's reign (*VCH* 1909, 555–66). Very little is known about the architecture or layout of the buildings of St Martin's: a crypt probably of 11th-century date with a vaulted extension to the east of at least two 13th-century bays long and two wide was recorded in 1825, but it is not known where this was other than somewhere west of Foster Lane (Kempe 1825, 6–8). The site has been redeveloped so many times that all remains have been removed, especially during wholesale development in 1913–14, when no medieval strata or structures were recorded (site code GM318; Merrifield 1965, gazetteer no. 35; Schofield 1998, 123, fig 21).

Such secular colleges were part of the organised religious provision in 11th-century towns (Blair 1988). Further, the acquisition by the Augustinian canons of a functioning religious institution at Aldgate is paralleled by what happened in Oxford at this time. Two secular colleges, of St George at the castle (Cooper 1976) and at St Frideswide's minster, were replaced by houses of Augustinian canons in the reign of Henry I; the college of St George was replaced by Oseney Abbey, located on a new site outside the walls (Postles 1993, 4–5). Nationally, as the Augustinians established houses in the period 1100–35, 43% of the known sites already had a religious community, which was then taken over by the

Augustinians (Robinson 1980, 35). So in this sense the establishment at Holy Trinity Priory was typical of the Augustinian approach.

In a paper of 1988 concerned with the possible existence of minster churches (in the meaning of major Saxon mother-churches which had a number of parish churches subordinate to them), Jeremy Haslam put forward a number of suggestions concerning the church of Syredus, St Botolph Aldgate, the wards of Aldgate and Portsoken, and St Peter ad Vincula, now within the Tower of London. Those which have a bearing on the present report were that 1) since 'it is likely' that the church of Syredus had spiritual jurisdiction over an area outside the gate of Aldgate, 'it can in turn be inferred that the *parochia* of this parish would have been more or less exactly coterminous with the ward of Aldgate'; 2) the church of Syredus was established as a minster by Alfred in the late 9th century AD; 3) a similar origin can be suggested for St Peter ad Vincula to the south; 4) a documented dispute (of 1157) between St Peter's and St Botolph Aldgate over the parish boundary between them (*Cartulary*, nos 964–5, 967–71) 'implies that the parish [of St Peter] comprised an extramural as well as intramural part' (St Peter's lies within the line of the Roman and early medieval city wall); 5) a parish with two parts like this must have been around a gate in the city wall for communication between the parts (Haslam 1988, 36–40).

All this is speculation, despite some of the assertions being later cited as 'evidence' (Haslam 1988, 40), and some of it is patently wrong. There is no evidence for proposition no. 1. The first paragraphs of the Holy Trinity cartulary explicitly say that the priory was founded 'in a place where Syredus had established a church' (*Cartulary*, no. 1) and, given that most authorities accept that Syredus dates to the 11th century, his church cannot be Alfredian. St Peter ad Vincula is first mentioned in the cartulary, in 1128–34 (*Cartulary*, nos 964, 966), so speculation about any earlier role or existence is hazardous. The parish boundary dispute of 1157 shows that both churches laid claim to the Portsoken area outside the walls, or part of it (Neininger 1999, 28, n), and nothing about any intramural part of the parish. There is no evidence at all for a gate in the city wall which might have been connecting two parts of the parish of St Peter.

5.3 Producing priory phase plans from the Symonds survey

It might be thought desirable that the Symonds plans (Figs 13–16) be redrawn to fit the excavated and map evidence with as little modification as possible. This task is not as easy as it might seem. The modification of the Symonds plans to fit the excavated, antiquarian and historic map evidence requires several processes: scaling, stretching the Symonds plans (which are themselves distorted) to fit the modern map evidence, and amendment of details.

As described in Chapter 3.3, providing a simple and accurate scale for the Symonds plans is not possible because they were not originally drawn to a consistent scale; they are dimensioned sketch-plans. For the majority of the buildings shown, because they are rectilinear, this results in the room proportions not necessarily being accurate. This problem makes the interpretation of the space behind the high altar particularly difficult.

The excavated and antiquarian evidence makes the amendment of details on the survey plans by Symonds inevitable. Symonds, not surprisingly, given the scale of his drawings, simplified the building details. These can be amended, but it depends upon where they are within the precinct. The survival of evidence from other sources across the site is very variable. The east end of the presbytery, for instance, is relatively well recorded, but some parts of the outer precinct are only recorded in maps. Thus we have been able to correct some of the details but not in a uniform way in every building of the precinct.

Furthermore, the Symonds plans have to be viewed within their historical context. They show the precinct as it appeared in *c* 1585. This has to be seen as a single phase in the development of the site. Some features which have been recorded in excavation, such as the apsidal interior of the south transept chapel, may have been altered or concealed by that time and accompanied by a rise in ground level. In summary, therefore, the Symonds plans have been redrawn throughout this study to represent the position in *c* 1585, amended where necessary by archaeological or cartographic evidence.

The next question is how to use the evidence in the Symonds plans to construct dated phase plans of the priory in the four and a half centuries before 1585. The most rational solution would seem to be to attempt the reconstruction of plans, based on all the available evidence, for each of the major phases in the development of the precinct through the medieval period and later (below, 5.4, 5.5). The suggested chronology of the development of the priory and its buildings is given in Figs 135–9.

Fig 135 is a reconstruction of the priory in *c* 1150. The church and principal claustral buildings are shown complete. The nave is on a slightly different alignment from the later plan (cf Fig 136). The foundation for the buttressed west end of the first nave was recorded at site F (Building C; Chapter 4.5). The layout of the buildings on the four sides of the cloister is approximately, but not exactly, square. The eastern arm is built with a rectangular ambulatory. The transept has apsidal chapels, which are square externally. It is suggested that there was a slype between the north transept and the chapter house, giving access to the eastern part of the precinct, though there is no direct evidence for this. The area east of the dormitory range probably contained the great garden, referred to by Symonds, and is the most likely location for the infirmary although nothing of this is recorded. The dormitory

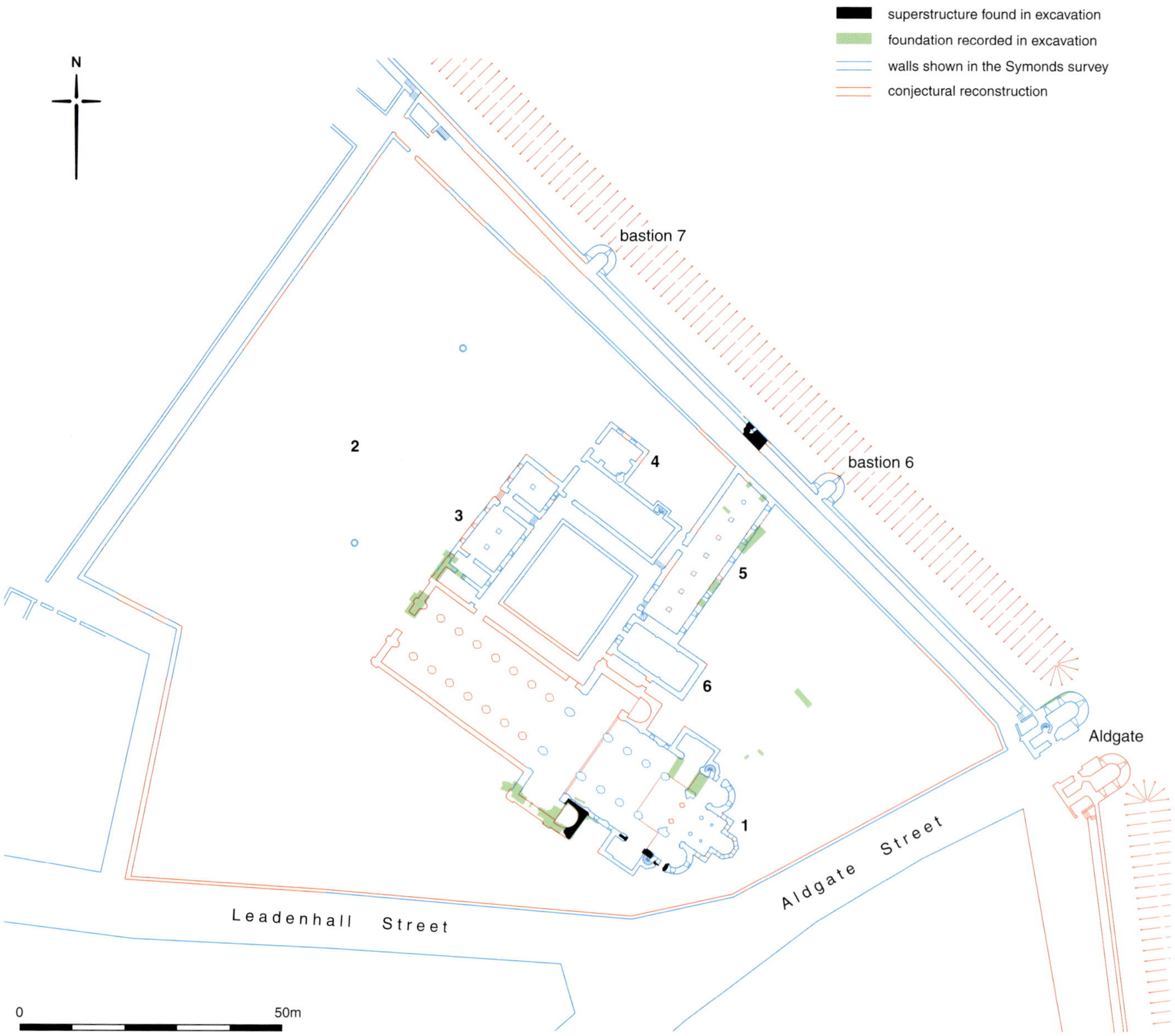

Fig 135 *A reconstruction of the priory in c 1150: 1 – church; 2 – great court; 3 – west range; 4 – refectory and kitchen; 5 – dormitory range; 6 – chapter house (scale 1:1250)*

range was probably built with a vault uninterrupted by cross-walls. The frater or refectory is entered from the cloister at the west end. There is a second door into the refectory in its west wall to allow food to be brought in from the kitchen. The kitchen has two large hearths, an oven and one entrance. The west range is subdivided at ground-floor level by a cross-passage from the cloister to the great court. The earlier cemetery to the south of the church continues to be used and is possibly attached to the church of Syredus which is perhaps located in the south-west corner of the site, the location of the later church of St Katherine Cree. The lane between the precinct and the wall has been enclosed.

Fig 136 shows the rebuilt nave as part of a reconstruction of the priory in *c* 1200. Most of the site remains intact but the nave is rebuilt on a new alignment, partly to allow for the construction of the 'great tower' abutting the west front and west range. The slype is absorbed into the north transept and the south transept extended southwards to match, with clasping buttresses at the corners and a door in the terminal wall. For this reconstruction we omit any use of the Howlett engraving (Fig 112).

Fig 137 shows a reconstruction of the priory in *c* 1280. The north transept chapel is extended eastwards, perhaps by Prior Peter in *c* 1220, as a Lady chapel. The side chapels (chapel 2 and its counterpart off the north aisle) are reworked with pointed chamfered arches into the aisles, buttresses at the corners, suggesting new vaulting, and enlarged windows. Buttresses are also added to the nave south aisle and the north-east corner of the chapter house. A latrine block is built on the city wall, or just outside it, with access from the east range at ground- and first-floor levels.

Fig 138 reconstructs the priory in *c* 1350. The west range has been expanded by the addition of a parallel range which, at its north end, stops short of the cross-passage

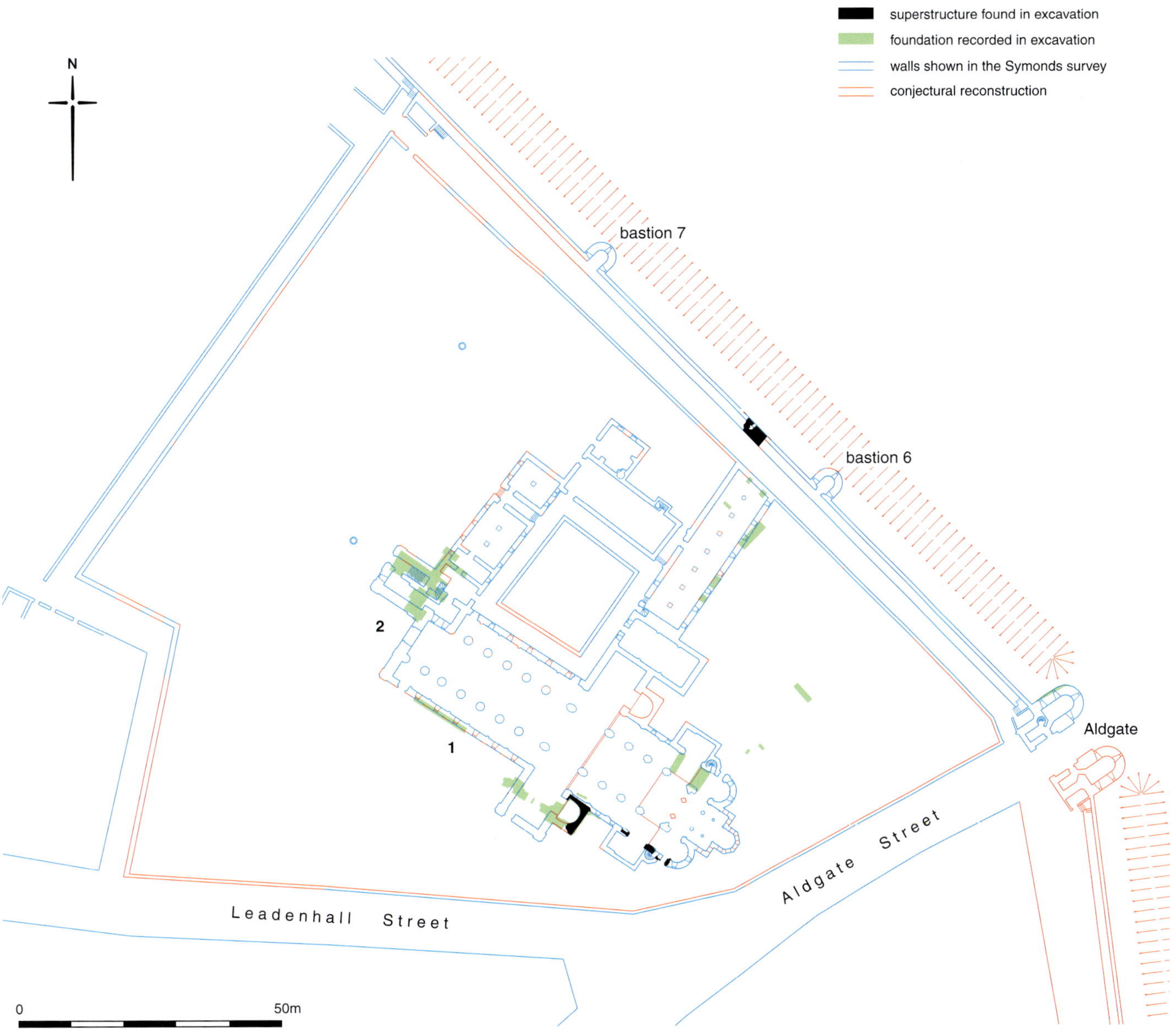

Fig 136 A reconstruction of the priory in c *1200: 1 – nave; 2 – west end (scale 1:1250)*

through the original range. The church of St Katherine Cree and the gate into Creechurch Lane have been built. A porch is added to the doorway at the west end of the nave south aisle. Buttresses are added to the east wall of the west range, and partition walls are probably introduced to subdivide the vault in the east range. Other masonry buildings, which appear on the Symonds plans around the perimeter of the site, may date from this period.

Probably by *c* 1500 (Fig 139), some tenement housing has been built within the precinct around the perimeter walls. The doubling up of the west range is extended northwards beyond the original west range; this extension is less substantial than either of the two previous phases. It is possible that the timber-framed first floor of this range shown by Symonds, jettying to the court, is of the period *c* 1500, but a post-Dissolution date is preferred. An overall reconstruction of the priory in *c* 1500 is given as Fig 140.

5.4 The development of the priory buildings in the early phases, and its context in London (1108–*c* 1350, period M2)

Factors in the alignment of the church and conventual buildings

The alignment of the priory church (Fig 135), 35° south of east, may have been influenced by the similar alignment of the nearby city wall at this point. It could be argued, however, that there would have been space for a more correctly aligned church of similar size if the cloister had been placed on the south side instead of on the north.

The alignment of the church and the cloister's position

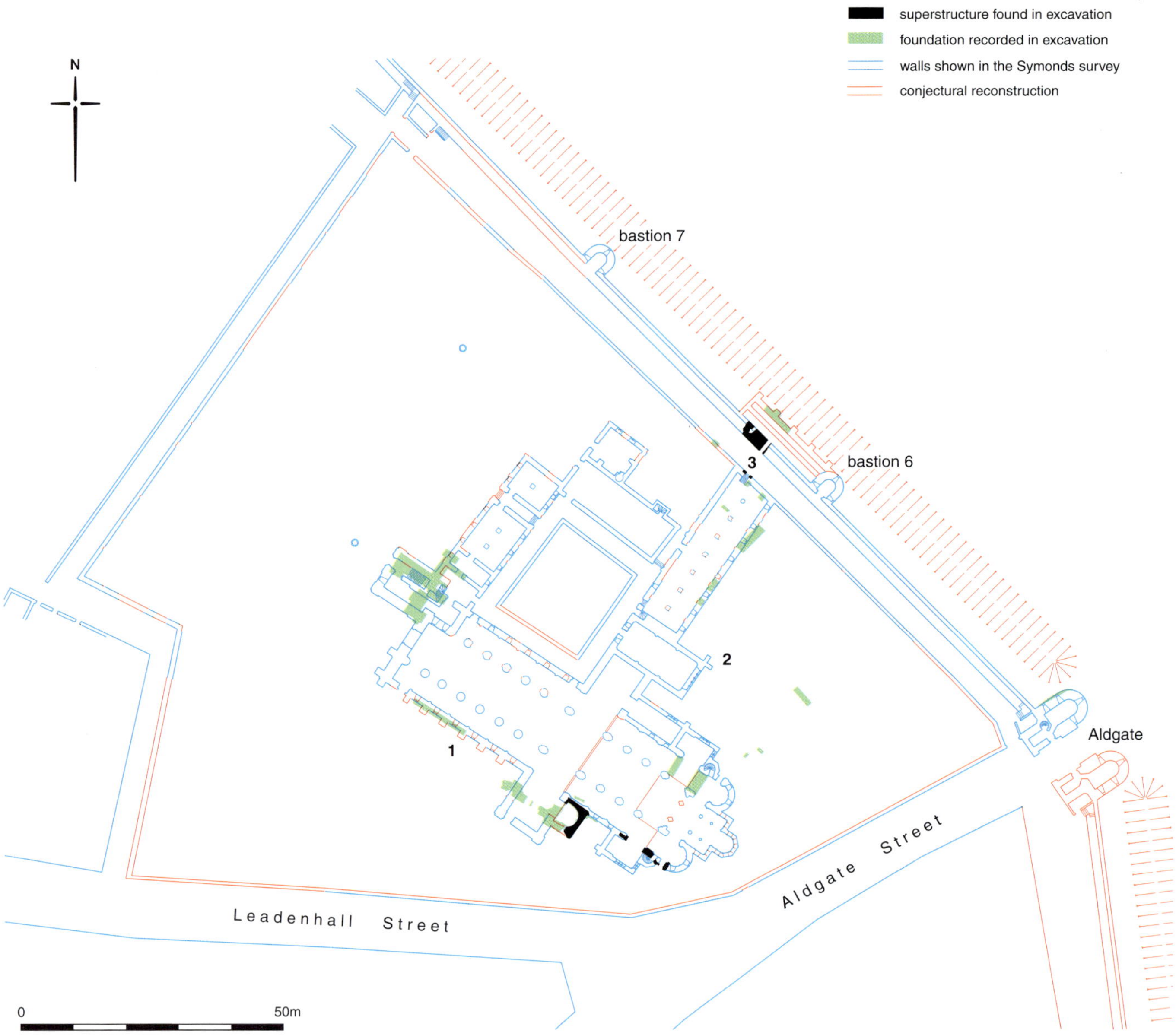

Fig 137 *A reconstruction of the priory in c 1280: 1 – buttresses to nave; 2 – chapter house; 3 – latrine block (scale 1:1250)*

on the north side of the church may have been related. One possibility is that the cloister was on the north side to be away from the bustle, or anticipated bustle, of the main street to the south (Leadenhall Street, then called Aldgate Street). This is the arrangement at other houses, such as Waltham, and both Christchurch and St Augustine's at Canterbury, where the Saxon cloisters were on the north side as well (in the case of St Augustine's, which is suburban, an important and no doubt noisy highway to Dover ran past the south side of the precinct, as it still does). A second possibility is that the adjacent city ditch was probably used as part of the monastic drainage system; the latrine block for the canons' dormitory, if correctly identified above with Building 4/5 on the Duke's Place site (Chapter 4.6), was positioned near or even over the city wall, thus requiring the cloister to be on the north side of the church. Drains for the kitchen and lavatorium, presumably on the north side of the cloister outside the refectory, would also be part of this system, as suggested for the observation of a drain at site I (Chapter 4.7). A similar consideration may be seen at work at Canterbury, where the 12th-century cloister is on the north side of the cathedral, and the famous waterworks plans show that the system at least partly drained into the town ditch nearby on the north. At Tintern Abbey (Monmouthshire) the cloister lay on the north in order to use the Wye in the drainage scheme, and the Tweed was similarly taken advantage of at Melrose (Roxburghshire). But at Holy Trinity we cannot say which was cause or effect; the handy use of the ditch may only have been a consequence of siting the cloister on the north. Additionally, there are many further examples of Augustinian houses with cloisters on the north side, such as Repton (Derbyshire), Worksop (Nottinghamshire), Weybourne (Norfolk) and Barnwell (Cambridgeshire) (D Robinson,

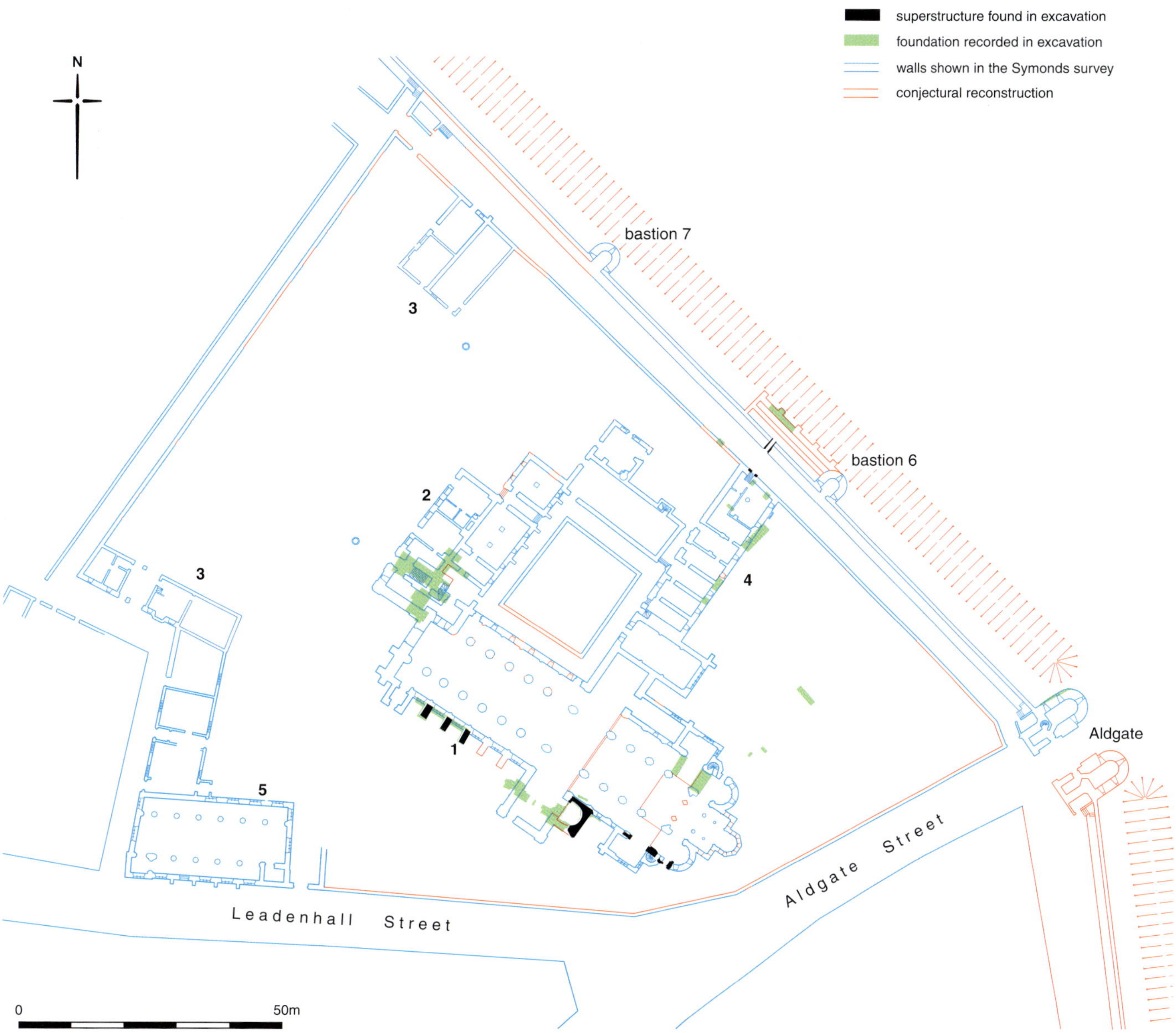

Fig 138 A reconstruction of the priory in c 1350: 1 – buttresses to nave and porch; 2 – doubling of west range; 3 – gate and courtyard buildings; 4 – ? modifications to dormitory range; 5 – St Katherine Cree (scale 1:1250)

pers comm).

Another influence on the arrangement of the priory buildings may have been the position of the church of Syredus; but, as just described, the location of this previous church remains unknown.

None of these factors, however, really explains the 35° deviation of the priory church building from a strict east–west alignment. The church is roughly parallel with the nearby city wall, and this may have been an overriding consideration. A similar consideration seems to have applied at Rochester, where because of its incorporation of the Roman city wall in its fabric (it forms the north side of the south range of the cloister) and the proximity of the High Street, the Norman church of the Benedictine cathedral priory deviates 27° south of an east–west line, while its Saxon predecessor church deviated 38° (St John Hope 1900, 3 and plan).

The design, architecture and development of the priory buildings, 1108–*c* 1350

Holy Trinity Priory, Aldgate, is potentially significant in the history of major monastic churches in London and Britain, in that it was the first Augustinian house to be built in London and its environs, and at the same time the first monastic house to be established in the city after the Conquest. In this discussion it is acknowledged that the Augustinian priory of St Mary Overie in Southwark has a foundation date of 1106, two years before Holy Trinity, but the accepted history is that building there did not take place until somewhat later in the 12th century. A map of the main religious houses in and around the City is given in Fig 141.

Fig 139 A reconstruction of the priory in c 1500: 1 – churchyard; 2 – extension; 3 – ? prior's garden; 4 – courtyard buildings; 5 – latrine block removed 1477; 6 – gate to Leadenhall Street (scale 1:1250)

The sequence of building, 1108–*c* 1350

A summary of the proposed building history, from the investigations and documentary evidence reported above, is as follows.

The priory of Holy Trinity Aldgate was founded in 1107 or 1108 just inside Aldgate. A church had recently been established on the site in the mid or late 11th century, but its location cannot be identified. A cemetery found on several sites probably functioned with it; the cemetery continued to be used after the construction of the new priory church. From the Symonds plans of c 1585 we can abstract many of the medieval parts of the church and other conventual buildings. The presbytery appears to have survived largely in its original form until the Dissolution; it had some form of giant order in the arcades, and lateral chapels on either side of the high altar. From the decoration of the piers and documentary evidence (the burials of the two children of King Stephen, shortly before 1147–8), the construction of the presbytery is placed c 1150 (Fig 135). The transepts, which may have been altered later, originally had single chapels (excavated in the case of the south transept, presumed in the case of the north). The transepts are broadly dated to the 12th century. The north transept chapel, it is suggested, was later extended, possibly in the early 13th century, to form the aisle or chapel shown by Symonds (Fig 137). A fragmentary foundation at the north-west of the church suggests that the church was completed during the second half of the 12th or the early 13th century.

The claustral buildings are known in detailed plan from Symonds, but their dates are imperfectly known. It is likely that all three claustral ranges were constructed during the 12th century. The canons probably had a latrine, of the middle or late

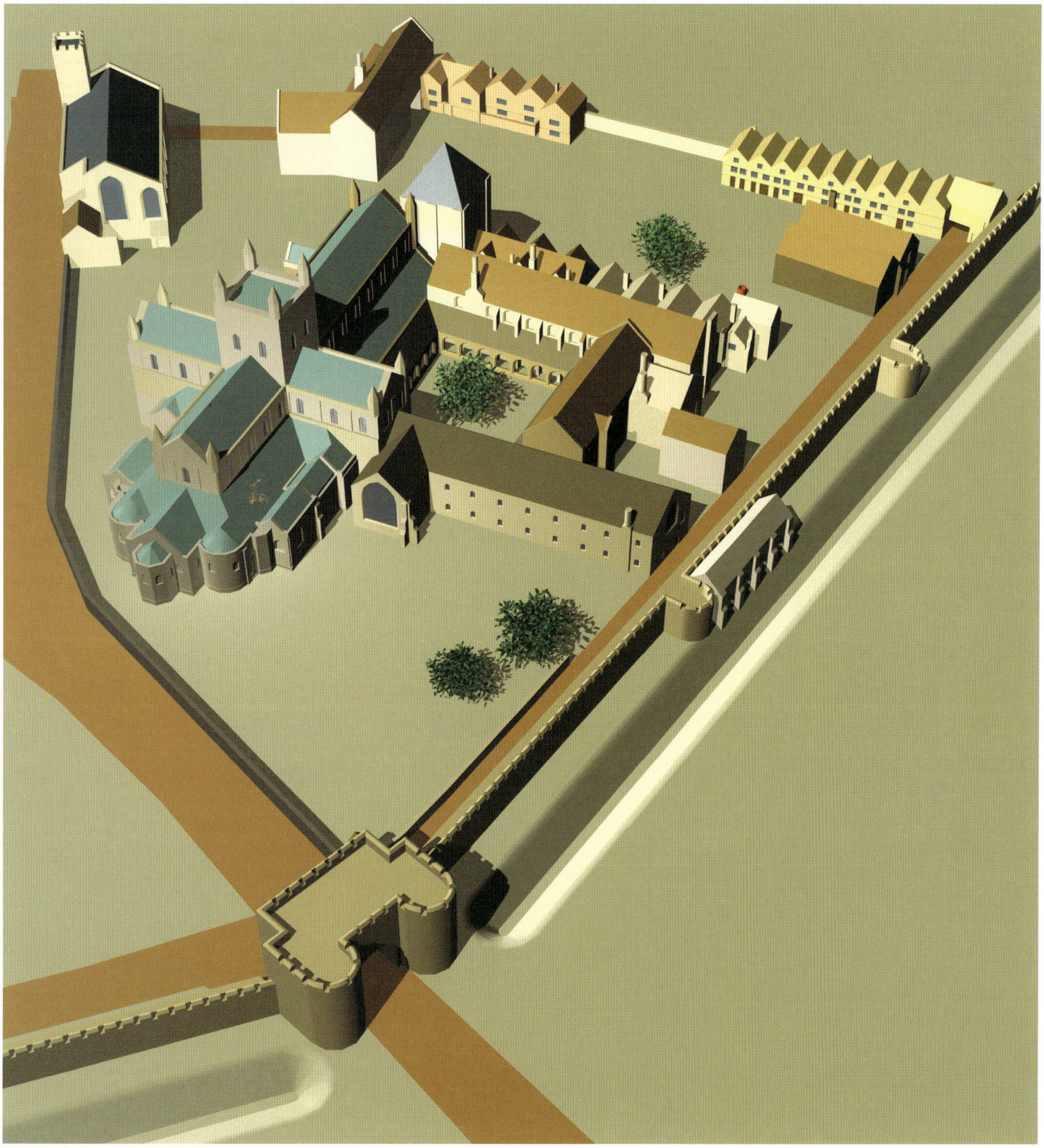

Fig 140 Reconstructed three-dimensional view of the priory at its fullest monastic extent in c 1500 (including the latrine block), from the north-east (Richard Lea)

13th century, over the city ditch on the north side of the precinct, and a doorway through the city wall (Fig 137).

The nave was rebuilt probably during the late 12th or 13th century, when buttresses were added to the south side. This resulted also in a rebuilt west end to the church, in a programme of building which included the great tower, which may have functioned as an outer parlour, at the north-west corner of the church (Fig 136). During the 13th century the Lady chapel was built, its site unknown but perhaps on the north side of the presbytery (Fig 137). By *c* 1350 (Fig 138) the west claustral range was doubled in width to the west, perhaps to provide extra accommodation for the prior.

General appearance and building materials

Details of the appearance of the priory buildings can be gleaned from the evidence for use of building materials. The 12th-century church of Holy Trinity Priory had an exterior in

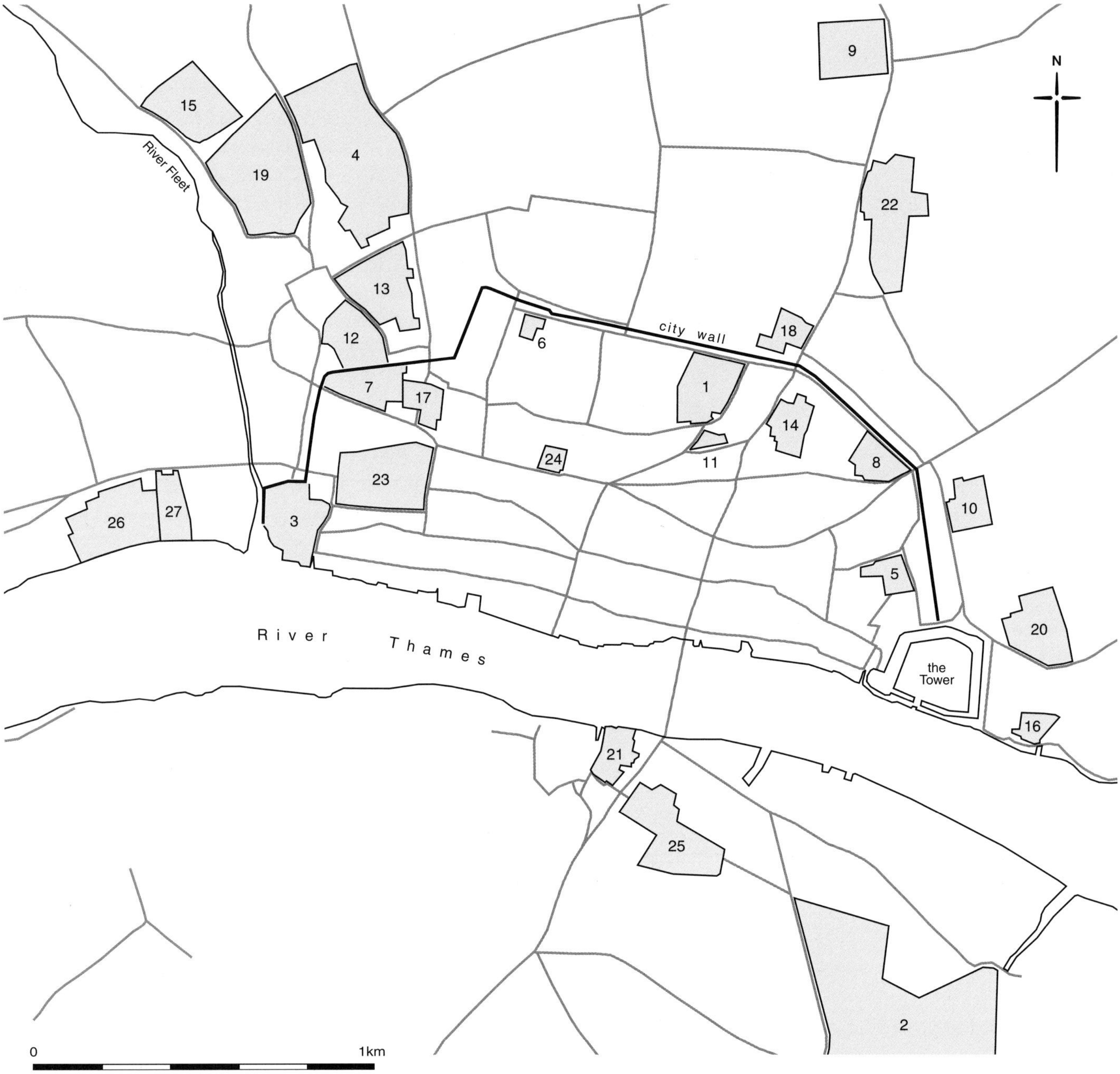

Fig 141 Map of medieval London, showing the main religious houses: 1) Austin Friars, 2) Bermondsey Abbey, 3) Blackfriars, 4) Charterhouse, 5) Crutched Friars, 6) Elsing Spital, 7) Greyfriars, 8) Holy Trinity Priory, 9) Holywell nunnery, 10) Minoresses, 11) St Anthony's Hospital, 12) St Bartholomew's Hospital, 13) St Bartholomew's Priory, 14) St Helen Bishopsgate, 15) St John Clerkenwell, 16) St Katharine's Hospital, 17) St Martin le Grand, 18) St Mary Bethlem, 19) St Mary Clerkenwell, 20) St Mary Graces, 21) St Mary Overie, 22) St Mary Spital, 23) St Paul's Cathedral, 24) St Thomas Acon, 25) St Thomas's Hospital, 26) Temple, 27) Whitefriars (scale 1:20,000)

uncoursed ragstone rubble rather than ashlar, using Caen stone for quoins (as on the south transept chapel), a characteristic shared with two other priory churches in the City at this date. Surviving fragments of 12th-century walling at St Mary Overie Southwark and St Bartholomew Smithfield are of uncoursed rubble. Thus there is no evidence as yet that any major Norman church in London had a true stone ashlar exterior (we are almost totally ignorant of the external character of St Paul's Cathedral at this time: Schofield in prep). The technique of walls in rubble with quoins of Caen stone was employed at the Tower of London (late 11th century, though now much restored), an example of a Norman High Romanesque style emanating both from the growth of the Caen stone industry and the stylistic centre of St-Etienne in Caen (Gem 1990, 47). A similar appearance of uncoursed masonry rather than ashlar on the exterior is shared by the small number of known secular stone buildings of the period in London (Schofield et al 1990, 167–9).

The outer face of the 14th-century main priory gate was built in squared stone (Fig 125). It is also possible that sections or parts of buildings were faced in ashlar, the rest being in rubble or roughly-coursed work, a feature seen at St Mary Spital in London. The doorway at the north end of the dormitory block at Holy Trinity was made of squared stone (Fig 114), and it is likely that such doorways were ubiquitous throughout the stone buildings in the priory.

A chamfered plinth was found on the best surviving length of 12th-century exterior masonry, the outside of the south transept chapel (Fig 46; Fig 47). Such a plinth was evidently a feature of church masonry at this time, and it is found on the north side of the transept at St Oswald's Priory, Gloucester, built in the first quarter of the 12th century (Heighway and Bryant 1999, 82). At the junction with the south wall of the presbytery, this plinth went one stone higher (Fig 49). Analogy with other major churches such as that at the Augustinian priory of Norton, Cheshire (Greene 1989, 83), would suggest that this plinth originally went round the whole exterior of the church except perhaps along the north wall of the nave, against the cloister, where its rain-deflecting properties were not required as there would be a roof over the cloister walk. Such a plinth was a design feature of large stone buildings; one went round the nave and chancel of the first church at St John Clerkenwell, of the 1140s (Sloane and Malcolm 2004, 29–32). In major buildings of the Blackfriars in London a century later, a chamfered plinth near ground level was given deliberate decorative emphasis by being composed of greenish-grey Reigate stone, to form a contrasting strip in the roughly-coursed wall (Spence and Grew 1989, 17).

Inside the church, the south wall of the presbytery at least was ashlar, of which 21 courses survived above a chamfered plinth. The use of ashlar on the interior of the north presbytery aisle is also indicated by the antiquarian drawings of that aisle. St Bartholomew Smithfield also demonstrates this contrast between the rubble exterior and the ashlar interior, again in the first half of the 12th century. Not all the interior was finished with ashlar, however; the south transept chapel was finished internally in rubble with ashlar dressings, and the rubble face covered with plaster.

The interior had painted decoration, but only tiny fragments survived. The eastern jamb of the entrance into the south side chapel (chapel 2), south of the altar, bore traces of parallel vertical lines in red paint. The interior of the chapel off the south transept (chapel 1) was rendered with three successive plaster faces. The first of these, light buff sandy mortar, also had traces of black, red and orange paint on it, but was thoroughly pecked for keying of the next layer. This was originally white plaster which had subsequently aged to an orange-beige, and it bore traces of orange, cream, and black paint.

It may be significant, however, that the light-coloured Caen stone pieces do not bear traces of paint, whereas pieces of Reigate stone were painted: for example, a vertical shaft with red and white paint (site A, <A17>, Fig 191), a four-light window with white mullion and cusps (site A, <A36>, Fig 193), and a casement hollow arch for a door or window, also painted white (site A, <A45>, Fig 193). These white-painted mouldings were late medieval, and the windows of the church may thus have stood out in white. On the other hand, the apparently unpainted surfaces of the Caen stones might also be because of their comparatively soft texture and the passage of time.

Twelfth- and 13th-century churches in London, both large and small, were enlivened with decoration in several colours. Romanesque decorated stones from St Paul's Cathedral, dug up in the 19th century and now held at the present cathedral, are painted in orange and red (Schofield in prep). At St Bartholomew Smithfield, the voussoirs of arches bordering the presbytery were picked out in succession in red, black and yellow (Webb 1921, ii, 17). At St John Clerkenwell, rebuilding of the church in the period 1185–*c* 1280 included arcade arches and capitals painted in vermilion and azure, and there was also gilding and ultramarine (Sloane and Malcolm 2004, 48–9, 283–4). Parish churches, such as St Nicholas Shambles, had architectural features picked out in black, blue and red (Schofield 1997).

No special study of tooling on the ashlar stones has been made, but diagonal tooling, which is normal in the 12th century, can be seen in a number of the photographs. This subject is discussed elsewhere (Alexander 1996), and the two surviving fragments of masonry, chapel 1 and the arch into chapel 2, remain on the site for examination.

The ceramic building material – roof and floor tiles – is summarised in detail in Chapter 8.3. In the early 12th to middle of the 13th century (period V) at site A (Chapter 4.2) shouldered peg tiles (normally going out of use by *c* 1200) and peg tiles (the predominant medieval form) were recovered in equal proportions. The Dissolution-period debris at site A produced both peg tiles and slates in quantity, indicating that part at least of the adjacent church had been roofed in slate. Several 'Westminster'-type decorated floor tiles of the 13th century, and others from the 14th-century manufactory in Penn (Buckinghamshire), were recovered from the sites, in both medieval and post-Dissolution contexts; a tiny number were found *in situ* at the entrance to the south transept chapel (chapel 1).

Specific influences on the architecture of the 12th-century church

Architectural precedents for Holy Trinity and influences on its design can be sought in a number of places. Firstly, the connections through the first prior, Norman, with Anselm, Archbishop of Canterbury, merit scrutiny. Queen Matilda founded Holy Trinity on the advice of Anselm, who had previously studied together with Norman in France (Dickinson 1950, 99). Anselm advised on the development of the community of canons at Colchester, which had been in existence since about 1093 (Robinson 1980, 13–14); he recommended the establishment of an Augustinian priory at Dunmow (Essex) in 1104, and possibly that at Llanthony (Monmouthshire) which was founded in 1108–18 (Anselm died in 1109). Thus it seems likely that the Augustinians were introduced and flourished under the encouragement of the archbishop, and it may have been he who suggested that the priests at Colchester should adopt the Rule of St Augustine

(Dickinson 1950, 124). A house to be established by the pious queen in England's largest town would probably have appealed to Anselm as suitable for pastoral work in an urban setting (Burton 1994, 46).

A further, probably more significant influence on the character of the early house must have been its place in royal favour. The priory was a royal foundation, and Norman became the queen's confessor; she wished to be buried there, but this desire was thwarted by a manoeuvre of the monks of Westminster who secured the queen's body after her death in 1118 (*Cartulary*, no. 13; Harvey 1977, 28, 373). Willis (1846, 21) says that she was buried at Winchester in the eastern crypt, after the translation of her bones there by Henry of Blois, under a marble stone with an epitaph, but this is repetition of a tradition only (J Crook, pers comm). Matilda spent part of her childhood at Romsey Abbey, and the architectural similarities to Romsey have already been explored. But Matilda was not the only patron of the day; the two decades after 1107 were notable for a number of religious foundations by other members of the royal court. Henry I founded five houses of canons, and assisted in the foundation of others, including St Bartholomew Smithfield (1123) and St Frideswide, Oxford. Many other houses, including Merton Priory (1114), were founded by royal officials. Together, Holy Trinity Aldgate and Merton Priory founded about ten daughter-houses, in every one of which the influence of a court figure can be seen. This was also the national picture, as 'the great mass of those who founded Augustinian houses in the time of Henry I were highly influential figures – curial officials, bishops, and well-established local potentates, nearly all of whom would have figured in the contemporary *Who's Who* had the twelfth century been considerate enough to publish such a work' (Dickinson 1950, 125–9, 141; cf Robinson 1980, 40–3). We might expect building of the priory church, especially at a royal foundation, to have begun within a few years of that foundation, that is shortly after 1108 for Holy Trinity Aldgate.

A problem with this line of thinking is that the remains recorded since 1790, principally of the eastern arm of the priory church and the south transept, are not demonstrably of the years immediately after 1108. Where datable, the mouldings of the presbytery seem to date from the 1130s and 1140s.

Two questions can be asked at this point: 1) where was the canons' church between 1108 and the 1130s?; and 2) were there any architectural or other consequences of the burial in the presbytery of two of the children of King Stephen in the years shortly before 1147?

Medieval chroniclers notoriously overstated the effect of fires, as at Canterbury in 1174 and possibly at Peterborough in 1116 (Reilly 1997, 5–6, 71–2). As noted previously, no trace of the fire of 1132 was found on the excavated sites (though they revealed only a small portion of the priory buildings) and evidence of documented fires on church or monastic sites is often not found. The change in architecture of one of the arches in the northern presbytery arcade of the church might be attributed to the fire, but really it can only have been due to a halt or change of mind of some kind. There seem to be three potential answers to the question of what the canons did for a church between 1108 and the 1130s:

1) they used the existing church of Syredus until the priory church was finished or sufficiently advanced;
2) they built a church in the period between 1108 and the 1130s, but this was elsewhere on the site, and no evidence has yet been recorded;
3) they built a church on the site of the known church, but it was burnt down in the fire of 1132.

At present this must remain a range of possibilities, which might be refined by future work.

The second question raised concerns the agreement in dates between the proposed construction of the presbytery and the reign (and perhaps some interest on the part) of King Stephen (1135–54). Two of his children who died in infancy, Baldwin and Matilda, were buried on either side of the altar before 1147. This may have been before 1135 rather than after, when Stephen may have been more inclined to have them buried in Westminster Abbey, especially as his son Geoffrey was appointed abbot there in 1138 (Judith Green, pers comm), though there was no tradition of Westminster being a mausoleum for family members of any royal clan until at least 1256 (Binski 1995, 93). Although Edward the Confessor was buried at Westminster, it did not become the burial place of further kings until the death of Henry III in 1272; he took the decision to be buried there in 1241, having previously elected for the Temple in London (ibid, 10). Norman kings had no traditional place of burial, and generally chose to be buried in one of the houses they had founded. Before Henry III's burial at Westminster, there was no notion of a traditional royal mausoleum in England (Biddle 1975, 134), and Stephen's actions should be viewed against this background.

Since the Londoners had supported Stephen's bid for the crown in 1135, the 1140s were a period of friendly relations between him and the city (Green 1992, 106–10). It seems remotely possible that he originally intended to be buried in Holy Trinity himself, probably immediately east of the altar, between two of his children. To be buried in front of the altar was the customary place for royalty, as in the cases of William the Conqueror at Caen, William II at Winchester and Henry I at Reading. On the other hand, this position was also reserved for the founder of the house (a tradition noted for instance by Giraldus in about 1200: Hill 1948, 79). Queen Matilda, the founder, had wished to be buried at Holy Trinity, as noted above, and perhaps a space had been reserved for her in anticipation of the event. She was actually buried at Westminster Abbey, by the high altar, on the south side (Harvey 1977, 373). As for Stephen, he founded the abbey of Faversham in 1147 and was buried there. A royal connection with Holy Trinity persisted, since Prior Ralph administered the last rites to both Stephen and his queen. Excavation at Faversham has revealed two deep vaults which had been dug out and destroyed in the 16th century; they lay next to each other in the central vessel of the immense eastern arm, about halfway between the crossing and the contemporary east end, and these are claimed to be 'royal vaults' (Philp 1968, fig 4). The vaults had been destroyed so thoroughly that no aspect of their architecture could be restored, with the exception of the survival of one corner respond-base fragment, perhaps from the upper part of a monument. There is no certainty that these two dug-out chambers were the royal tombs, but they provide the only potential information on Stephen's own burial.

A further connection of Holy Trinity in this period may have been with Stephen's brother, Henry of Blois. It has been pointed out above (Chapter 4.3) that the unusual decoration of 'discs' on the ribs above one bay in the south presbytery aisle of the church – the bay immediately south of the probable position of the altar – finds parallels, weak though they may be, with the great hall of Wolvesey Palace as rebuilt by Henry of Blois (Fig 85), as well as more generally on other British sites and abroad (for instance, at St-Etienne, Beauvais). He was clearly an influential figure in court circles, and on his elder brother. Henry was instrumental in Stephen's assumption of the crown in 1135, marshalling the support of the Church for his brother.

Henry's background was cosmopolitan. He had been brought up at Cluny, becoming a monk and a close friend of the abbot there, Peter the Venerable, and Henry remained at Cluny until summoned to become abbot of Glastonbury in 1126 (Poole 1955, 185–6). He was also interested in antiquity; at Rome in 1149–50 he bought some old statues and transported them back to Winchester, and his possessions included magnificent books, German vestments and an Islamic carpet (Brooke 1969, 148–9; Biddle 1976, 491, for his patronage of architecture at Winchester). At present, however, the evidence for any direct influence of Henry of Blois on the architecture of Holy Trinity Priory is weak.

There is no evidence that the priory's parochial functions had any effect upon the architectural development of the church, apart from the existence of the fairly large porch protruding from the westernmost bay of the south nave aisle, presumably of a date later than about 1300; but little is known about the nave, where the parish altar(s) would have stood. In contrast, one of the periods of expansion of the nunnery of St Mary Clerkenwell, over in the area north-west of the city, has been attributed to its acquisition in 1176 of parochial status. Thereafter the church there was expanded, and the inner courtyard of the nunnery consolidated in stone (Sloane in prep). So far, nothing like this can be identified at Holy Trinity Priory.

By the middle of the 12th century, the main outline of the church and claustral buildings was taking shape (Fig 135). Building work at many of the large Augustinian churches (as at those of other orders) proceeded slowly, particularly in the troubled middle years of the 12th century. At Cirencester (Evans 1991, 103), Merton Priory and other houses, the major buildings took several decades to complete, and sometimes longer.

The other parts of the monastery

By *c* 1350, it can be suggested that all the main elements at Holy Trinity Priory were in place: the large church with its Romanesque presbytery but 13th- or 14th-century nave (an arrangement similar to that at the sister-house of St Bartholomew Smithfield), the claustral buildings on the north side, the great tower, the main gate to Creechurch Lane, and probably some of the buildings around the great court as later surveyed by Symonds (Fig 138). This review can now pass from the church to the other monastic buildings.

As elsewhere in the country, the monastic gatehouse was often the longest-surviving fragment of the complex. The main gateway to Creechurch Lane, which survived until about 1820, was rebuilt in the 14th century. It is likely that there was a stone gatehouse in this position from the earliest decades of the priory's existence in the 12th century, as at Bristol and Cirencester. The gatehouse was an important point in the definition of a religious precinct within a town, and elsewhere is often early in the building history of the house, and profusely decorated (Fernie 2000, 207). Stone gateways at other London houses also survived into the 19th century, for instance two at Bermondsey Abbey; and one of 1504, at St John Clerkenwell, stands today north of the City, straddling a comparatively quiet street where traffic pressures have not required its removal (Sloane and Malcolm 2004, 169–73).

The excavations, together with the Symonds plans, have provided an outline history of the western claustral range and the house of the prior. A range of analogies for its character and position have been given in Chapter 4.5 where the remains were described in detail. The conclusion here is that rooms for the prior were probably part of the original scheme for the western range in the 12th century, especially as this prior had secular duties as the alderman of Portsoken, an extramural area but one growing in population. The building of the 'great tower' at the junction of the western range and the west end of the church, which may also have been within the last decades of the 12th century, is probably significant, especially if it contained an outer parlour for additional meetings with the secular world outside.

One omission from the present report, for lack of evidence, is discussion of the priory water-supply system. A drain seen in Duke's Place in 1953 (site I; Chapter 4.7) was almost certainly part of it, and the outer court had one or possibly two well-heads; but that is all we know. The latrine block, if correctly identified, used the city ditch as its drain (though it probably did not work properly, since there was no real flow of water in it). There is a similar lack of evidence for the water systems of other London religious houses, with the notable exception of Charterhouse (Barber and Thomas 2002); the water-supply systems at St Mary Clerkenwell (Sloane in prep), St John Clerkenwell (Sloane and Malcolm 2004, 211–12) and Bermondsey Abbey (Steele in prep) are or will be described in the publications on those houses. Elsewhere, Augustinian houses have been shown to have had systems as well-built and elaborate as those of any other order, for instance at Bristol (Boore 1989). Some 12th-century monastic drains were of great length and sophistication, like that at Paisley Abbey, near Glasgow (Yeoman 1995, 28–9).

Building at religious houses in London, *c* 1100–*c* 1350

The building history of Holy Trinity can be compared with what is known of other religious houses in the London area, both houses of Augustinian canons and generally.

There are no clear parallels in the surviving architecture of St Botolph's, Colchester itself, where the church dates from the 1160s (dedicated in 1177); only the nave, the north transept and a crypt under the south transept are known in detail (Colchester Archaeological Trust, pers comm; Peers 1917; *VCH* 1994, 304–6). In London, the two Augustinian priories of most direct relevance are St Mary Overie, Southwark, and St Bartholomew's Priory, Smithfield (founded in 1123), both of which had hospitals attached to them (St Mary Overie had St Thomas's Hospital, moved to a separate site by 1215, and St Bartholomew's Priory was a twin foundation with St Bartholomew's Hospital). St Mary Overie was founded in *c* 1106, thus preceding Holy Trinity in its foundation by two years, but there was probably not a community of regular canons there until some years later (Dickinson 1950, 119–20). Excavations of 1969–73 recorded foundations of the 12th-century chapter house and burials within it and to the west in the cloister. Architectural work of the 12th century on the church is largely confined to two doorways from the nave into the cloister on the north (perhaps of *c* 1160), a recess in the north wall of the nave, possibly the core of the transept walls, and the northern side of a curved chapel on the north transept (RCHME 1930, 58; Roffey 1998). Chalk walls of post-Roman date have also been noted beneath the 18th-century crypt under the west end of the presbytery (Hammerson 1978). Capitals and bases recovered from the cloister date from *c* 1190 (Webb 1956, 58), and the surviving blind arcade at the internal south-west corner of the nave could date from before 1212, when the church was badly damaged by fire. The subsequent (and surviving) east end is architecturally indebted to the Trinity chapel of Canterbury Cathedral (Wilson 1992, 176). The church was rebuilt by the end of the 13th century (the transepts probably by the middle of that century); in the 14th century were added a bishop's chapel, protruding from the east end, and flying buttresses to the presbytery.

The church at the priory of St Bartholomew Smithfield (since the Reformation, also known as St Bartholomew the Great) was less prone to disaster, but equally varied in appearance. From the foundation period of the 1120s to the 1160s survive the presbytery and ambulatory, with apsidal chapels originally to the north, south and east (only the southern one now remaining), and traces of one bay of the north arcade of the nave. In the 13th century the nave was rebuilt (the only surviving bay has a clerestory window with an early example of plate tracery dated stylistically to *c* 1230), and a Lady chapel added to the east end in *c* 1330. Excavation on the north side of the Lady chapel in 1988 recorded a number of burials and what was probably part of the foundation of the apsidal chapel which preceded the Lady chapel (site code SBG87); recording has also taken place in the portion of cloister which remains, that stretching from the processional door to the entrance to the former chapter house (Gormley 1996). Little is known about the buildings or artefactual archaeology of the medieval St Bartholomew's Hospital, though the documents are relatively profuse (Moore 1918; Kerling 1973; Thorn 1976).

There were a number of other Augustinian priories and hospitals founded around London in the 12th century, and it is possible that, with the aid of archaeological investigations which have taken place in some of them, architectural and other material connections between the various Augustinian houses might be established. The only one which has so far been the subject of a detailed archaeological and chronological study is the priory and hospital of St Mary Spital (founded in 1197), which has been reconstructed from excavations of the 20th century in the first monograph in this monastic series (Thomas et al 1997). Its function and constitution resulted in building forms which were unlike those of a normal priory, especially a great T-shaped infirmary and chapel building of 1235–80. But details, such as the normal walling in rubble with quoins in Reigate stone, are familiar. Other Augustinian houses of the 12th century were the hospital of St Katharine by the Tower, founded in *c* 1148 on land bought from Holy Trinity Priory, and placed in the custody of Holy Trinity (surrendered 1261: *VCH* 1909, 525); and the nunnery of Holywell, founded before 1158 (LCC Survey of London 1922, 153–87). At Holywell the nuns worshipped in their church which had a separate south aisle, which may have been partitioned off as at St Helen Bishopsgate (LCC Survey of London 1924, pl 83). A small amount of excavation in recent years has furnished details of burials in the church and the south-eastern cemetery, and walls of the 16th-century (and post-Dissolution) mansion of the Earl of Rutland (Thompson et al 1998, 62). But no architectural links with Holy Trinity Priory are known for either house. Further out from London, Augustinian Merton Priory was established in 1117, and publication of the extensive excavations of 1976–8 and 1986–90 can be expected to reveal any links with Holy Trinity Priory (Miller et al in prep).

The development of Holy Trinity Priory can also be placed within the more general history of the many religious houses in and around the City of London (Fig 141). Table 11 summarises the known major building works at London monasteries and hospitals from the late 11th century to *c* 1350 (for the purposes of Table 11, Table 12 and Table 16, the list is only of monasteries and hospitals in and around the City of London and in Southwark, together with Westminster Abbey).

Table 11 shows that a large number of monasteries and hospitals were founded in and around the City from the early 12th century onwards, with Holy Trinity Priory being among the earliest. Several were primarily hospitals, and it has recently been pointed out that the Normans may have introduced hospitals to England (Fernie 2000, 207). This wave of new building, which must in turn have stimulated the capital's economy, was a reflection of a general improvement in the national economy, the demise of Winchester and the concomitant rise of London as a royal centre (especially from the reign of Stephen, which is so significant for Holy Trinity)

Table 11 Main building works at some London monasteries and hospitals, 11th century to c 1350

Religious establishment	Main construction dates	References
11th century		
Bermondsey Priory/Abbey	founded 1089; E end of church and infirmary possibly of this date, or 12th century	Martin 1926; Grimes 1968, 210–17; Beard 1986; Steele in prep
Westminster Abbey	new church by Edward the Confessor, finished 1066; but lower parts of western towers suggested to be early 12th century; extensive monastic buildings and gardens	Micklethwaite 1876; RCHME 1924; Gem 1986; Tatton-Brown 1995
12th century		
St Paul's, new cathedral	started 1087, but much of fabric dates from after fire of 1136	*VCH* 1909, 409–33; Gem 1990; Schofield in prep
Holy Trinity Priory	founded 1108; presbytery and transepts about 1150; main claustral buildings probably in 12th century	
St Mary Overie, Southwark	founded 1106 but buildings later	*VCH* 1909, 480–4; RCHME 1930, 58–66; Dawson and Edwards 1974; Roffey 1998
St Bartholomew's Priory, Smithfield	founded 1123; presbytery and crossing, 1130s+	*VCH* 1909, 475–80; Webb 1921; RCHME 1929, 123–7; Bradley and Pevsner 1997, 196–203
St Bartholomew's Hospital, Smithfield	founded 1123	*VCH* 1909, 520–5; RCHME 1929, 123–9; Bradley and Pevsner 1997, 203–4
St Mary Clerkenwell	founded 1144, church soon after; buildings expanded after 1176, perhaps when nunnery obtained parochial rights	Sloane in prep
St John Clerkenwell	founded 1144; crypt and E end 1140s	Sloane and Malcolm 2004
St Katharine by the Tower	founded 1148; early buildings not known	Nichols 1825; *VCH* 1909, 525–30
St Martin le Grand	church rebuilt or repaired mid 12th century	Kempe 1825
Temple	founded 1128 in Holborn, transferred to Fleet Street; nave in use by 1161, consecrated 1185; rebuilt choir *c* 1240	*VCH* 1909, 485–91; Harben 1918, 568–70; Wilson 1992, 82; Bradley and Pevsner 1997, 266–70
Holywell Priory	founded before 1158; buildings unknown	LCC Survey of London 1922, 153–75
13th century		
St Mary Spital	founded 1197; refounded 1235; large complex by *c* 1320	Thomas et al 1997, 26–64
St Mary Overie	rebuilt after fire 1212; rebuilding in progress 1273	*VCH* 1909, 481; RCHME 1930, 58–66
St Helen Bishopsgate	nunnery founded 1216; dormitory range 13th century; most of double church (apart from chapels) also 13th century	Hugo 1863; *VCH* 1909, 457–61; RCHME 1929, 19–24; Bradley and Pevsner 1997, 221–3; LCC Survey of London 1924, 1–18, 31–6
St Mary Bethlem	founded 1247; buildings known in outline only	*VCH* 1909, 495–8; O'Donoghue 1914; Andrews et al 1997
St Thomas Acon	founded early 13th century	*VCH* 1909, 491–5
St Thomas's Hospital, Southwark	founded by 1215 (earlier within precinct of St Mary Overie)	*VCH* 1909, 538–42; Parsons 1932
Blackfriars	founded 1221, moved site 1275; church begun 1279, cloister in construction 1292, land bought for extension of friary 1312–13	*VCH* 1909, 498–502; Clapham 1912; Harben 1918, 78–9
Greyfriars	founded 1224, given site 1225; some buildings 1230s+; new larger church begun 1306, finished 1327; extensive 14th-century conventual buildings to north	Shepherd 1902; *VCH* 1909, 502–7; Harben 1918, 278–9; Johnson 1974
Whitefriars	founded 1241	*VCH* 1909, 507–10; Harben 1918, 624–5; Martin 1927
Austin Friars	founded 1253; church later	*VCH* 1909, 510–13; Cater 1912; Harben 1918, 325
Crutched Friars	before 1269	*VCH* 1909, 514–16; Harben 1918, 189
Westminster Abbey	Lady chapel added 1220+; main church rebuilt 1245+	Allen Brown et al 1971, 130–56; Pevsner 1973, 396–405; Wilson 1986; Wilson 1992, 178–83
St Paul's	tower 1221; 'New Work': choir rebuilt 1250s onwards, finished 1314	Harben 1918, 460–1; Longman 1873; Cook 1955; Morris 1990; Schofield in prep
St Martin le Grand	church rebuilt 1258–61	Carlin and Belcher 1989, 88
St Clare without Aldgate (Minoresses)	founded 1293 or 1294	*VCH* 1909, 516–19; Harben 1918, 150–1; Ellis 1985
St Bartholomew Smithfield	Romanesque nave taken down and rebuilt in 13th century	Webb 1921
Holy Trinity Priory	Lady chapel added; nave being (re-)built, great tower by early 14th century	
14th century to *c* 1350		
Bermondsey Abbey	much rebuilding *c* 1275–*c* 1350 indicated by moulded stones	Steele in prep
St Mary Spital	further expansion of infirmary *c* 1320–50	Thomas et al 1997, 65–7
Elsing Spital (Hospital of St Mary within Cripplegate)	founded 1329; crossing survives	*VCH* 1909, 535–7
St Paul's	east end finished by 1314; chapter house 1332	Morris 1990; Harvey 1978; Schofield in prep
St Bartholomew Smithfield	Lady chapel 1330s	Webb 1921; RCHME 1929, 123

and the growth of London as an international port (King 1996; Nightingale 1996). The high level of construction continued on religious sites, including the cathedral, throughout the 13th century and into the 1330s. During this period, the building campaigns at Holy Trinity, as far as they can be perceived, were part of a great surge of stone buildings, and complexes largely in stone, which changed whole areas of London's local topography for centuries until the Dissolution.

Further, as Table 11 also shows, London had at least 13 large religious institutions under construction, some probably largely complete, by *c* 1200. This does not include further outlying establishments such as the leper hospitals. No other city in Britain had so much religious building taking place in it at this date; and comparisons can only be made with the larger cities of Continental Europe, such as Cologne (Binding and Kahle 1983) and Rome, which had a 'new rebirth' of ecclesiastical architecture in the 12th century (Krautheimer 1980, 161–202). The intensity of building on monastic and hospital sites in the City and its environs (along with building at the cathedral) in the 12th and 13th centuries was, therefore, remarkable by European standards.

Burials, 1108–*c* 1350

Generally, until the 13th century, only founders and benefactors (including royalty) were thought worthy of burial within a monastic church (Burton 1994, 138); burials of the 13th century in the presbytery of a priory church are usually thought to be those of eminent canons, as for instance in the Gilbertine priory of St Andrew Fishergate, York (Kemp and Graves 1996, 158–9, fig 158). Burials for which there is sufficient concrete evidence (as opposed to traditions) at Westminster Abbey, in the 12th and 13th centuries, are of abbots, members of the royal family, or people with special connections to the monarchy or the abbey (Harvey 1977, 373–5). Within the mid 13th-century hospital at St Mary Spital, there were several burials in the chapel which formed one wing of the T-shaped building, and two of these may have been of the founders (Thomas et al 1997, 32–5). Within the priory church of Holy Trinity in the 12th century, in the presbytery, were the burials of two royal children and some of the early priors, as discussed above (Chapter 4.3). The exact positions of all these burials are unknown, but it is likely that some if not all were beneath the arcades of the presbytery, as in other cases of prestigious burials in major churches. As already discussed (Chapters 3.2, 4.3), Prior Peter, who died in 1221, was buried in a Lady chapel which he had himself built.

From the middle of the 13th century, according to the national pattern, burials of priests and notable secular people would also have been allowed in the church. Effigies of lay people (as opposed to clerics or knights and their wives) in or from monastic churches survive from *c* 1250 (Alexander and Binski 1987, 209). Slightly earlier, in 1227 x 1244, Master Alexander de Dorchester willed his body to be buried in the church of Holy Trinity; the prior was appointed one of his executors, and his bequests were numerous, including the repayment of a debt of £300 to the king (*Cartulary*, no. 529). In 1598 John Stow, either from personal observation or from collation of the documentary sources then at his disposal, listed over 30 monuments to knights and esquires in the church, and added 'and many other' (Stow 1603, i, 141). He does not give dates, apart from that of the tomb of Geoffrey de Mandeville (d 1215) – which would be a comparatively early case – though without saying where it was. It may have lain in the cloister. (The effigy of the earlier Geoffrey de Mandeville, who died in 1144, is in the Temple church: Bradley and Pevsner 1997, 270.) Burials in the priory church after 1350 (which it is assumed include most of those mentioned by Stow) are considered later in this chapter (below, 5.5).

There was clearly also a link between the priory and major figures of the City of London. Henry FitzAilwin was buried in the entrance to the chapter house in 1212. Just over a decade earlier, William, son of Isabel, a sheriff in the 1160s and in 1178–87, had also been buried in the priory, though where is not stated; he was important enough for his burial to be noted by the compiler of the priory cartulary (*Cartulary*, no. 1072). William, who died in 1197 or 1198, was probably a financier and dealer in houses and land, with Flemish connections; he has been called one of the two most notable figures in the administration of London in the mid 12th century (Keene 1990, 92; Brooke 1975, 221, 229, 234). Thus Holy Trinity Priory, in the late 12th and early 13th centuries, was the place of burial of two of London's civic leaders. It may be significant that such associations were not enjoyed by St Paul's Cathedral at this time; the first mayor to be buried at St Paul's was apparently Hamo Chikewell in 1308 (Stow 1603, i, 335), as the rebuilt and extended cathedral neared completion. At Holy Trinity, the custom lingered on into the later medieval period, with the wish of John Marcheant, Common Clerk of the City, to be buried in the priory church in his will of 1421 (*Cal Husting Wills*, ii, 431).

None of the excavated burials was clearly inside the church; this report is, therefore, concerned mainly with two areas of external cemetery. The first and larger lay on the south side of the priory church at site A, and, though not reported in detail here, at site D; the second comprised a smaller number of inhumations north of the north-west corner of the church, in the space later taken over for the great tower and the widening of the western claustral range to the west, on site F (Fig 2). No differentiation could be made between the groups on the basis of ceramic dating, and the whole cemetery is dated to a span beginning in the 11th or the 12th century, with some burials probably continuing until the early 13th century (those of group A29 outside the south transept).

From the presence of men, women and children in the graves on the two sites it is probable that both cemeteries, to the north-west of the church (on site F) and south of the church (on site A), included lay people. It is not possible to say whether the canons had their own exclusive cemetery at the priory; it might have lain in the area north-east of the church, but no burials have been located in the admittedly summary observations there. One mature man buried on the south side of the church (grave 9, site A) had a silver pectoral cross with him. It is not possible to say if his burial pre-dates or post-dates the foundation of the Augustinian priory.

A tentative typology of late Saxon and early medieval grave-types has already been established for London, from the evidence of the 11th- to 12th-century parish graveyard of St Nicholas Shambles (White 1988, 18–25). Six types have been identified: I, simple burial, perhaps in a coffin; II, with a stone pillow; III, grave with a floor only of chalk and mortar; IV, a cist of mortared stones, or simply lined with chalk and mortar; V, charcoal burial; VI, grave lined with dry-laid tile or stone. The burials on the priory site provide more examples of types I and IV.

Simple burials of type I, often demonstrably in wooden coffins (without nails, as far as could be ascertained), were found on site A, but the lined burials of type IV were in the majority south of the priory church and the only burial type in the smaller group of burials north-west of the church. Such lined or cist-burials are found at Saxo-Norman monastic sites and parish churches in the London area, such as Bermondsey Abbey (Grimes 1968, pl 101), St Bride Fleet Street (ibid, 185; Milne 1997, 92–3), and St Nicholas Shambles (White 1988, 22–4); and at many sites outside London, usually (though not exclusively) at churches of greater than parochial status, such as St John, Colchester (Crummy 1981, 45) and St Guthlac's minster, Hereford (Shoesmith 1980, 29). All these examples are dated to the 11th or 12th centuries. Although cists continued to be used in medieval cemeteries at major churches, they seem to have been most common in these two centuries.

No evidence for head- or footstones, or for grave covers (capstones), was found in the cemetery itself, as has been recorded in early medieval cemeteries at St Paul's (Schofield in prep), St Bride Fleet Street (Milne 1997, 84), Old Sarum (Clapham 1934, 159) or Lincoln (Stocker 1986). However, possible grave covers, perhaps from nearby graves disturbed in rebuilding the church, were reused in constructing the buttresses along the south nave wall in the 13th to 14th century (site E, period V; Chapter 8.3), and grave covers were probably present over some of the cist-burials (eg grave 6, site A).

We cannot be certain about which, if any, of the burials were made during the lifetime of the church of Syredus which preceded the priory. It is, moreover, clear that some cists were reused several times. At site F, grave 3 contained an adult male, and the disturbed bones of another man and an infant, piled at the feet of the new occupant (Fig 102; Fig 103); a number of other graves on site F also included disarticulated bone. If we assume that the disturbed bones were of previous occupants of the cists, rather than bones from earlier nearby burials shovelled in, then it is reasonable to assume that a cist might be used several times. Such reuse was not so evident in the cemetery south of the church, perhaps suggesting that the graveyard on site F, immediately outside the west end of the priory church, had a long-standing social significance during the 12th and early 13th centuries; reuse of graves in this zone was a deliberate policy, perhaps a result of requests by the dying or their relatives. At least one other cist (grave 56, site A) was empty, implying that it had been either prepared and not used, or had been cleared for reuse.

The length of use of the cemetery might be suggested by the number of generations of burial, that is a chronological sequence of graves which were physically connected by one cutting the next. At the parish church cemetery of St Mark's, Lincoln, it is suggested that burials were redug in the same spot about every 30 years (Gilmour and Stocker 1986, 91), and at the Old Minster, Winchester, every 20 years (Kjølybe-Biddle 1975, 106). If we use the figure of 20 years, and the longest sequence of 11 successive graves in site A group 25 (Chapter 4.2), then that part of the graveyard later overlain by the south-west corner of the south transept was in use for about 220 years. If the transept dates from the middle of the 12th century, this would place the first burial in the sequence around the middle of the 10th century. This reckoning is in our view too crude to affect the proposal followed in this report that the church of Syredus was the first religious establishment on the site for which there is (documentary) evidence, in the early or mid 11th century. Possibly, in this particular spot, the burial generations were much shorter than 20 years. Furthermore, this area lay west of the south transept, and the later burials in the 11-item sequence or chain could date from the 12th century after the priory had been established.

The details of the study of the human bones from the excavated sites, given in Chapter 8.8, can be summarised here. All the excavated burials lay outside the priory church; those from sites A and F have been reported in detail. It is important to stress that they were outside the church, since skeletons from burials inside major churches may be those of richer persons and exhibit different or particular conditions (for instance at St Mary Spital: Conheeney 1997).

The remains were generally poorly preserved due to truncation by later building work. Group A21 survived best of all the groups or samples, probably because of the physical protection afforded by the cists. Preservation of individual elements indicated that it was physical disturbance rather than poor excavation or soil processes that caused the poor preservation. With the exception of group A21, sites A and F were both characterised by this poor preservation.

Most groups were of mixed sex. Exceptions to this were site A, groups A22 and A23, where the adults were identified as exclusively male; it is possible that this is significant, if it might be thought that the two groups together formed some kind of spatially distinct entity. Site A and site F did vary in overall sex composition. Site A had a typical medieval priory composition with a ratio of 2.5 males to each female, whereas site F displayed a fairly even balance of males and females in both the burials and the disarticulated material. However, the site F burials were only a small group.

Ageing evidence suggests that, in keeping with other priory sites, very few immature individuals were buried here. Also, sites A and F appear to have a similar age composition amongst adults, although it was impossible to compare this with other sites as so many burials could only be placed in the general adult category rather than being assigned a precise age. Evidence of more severe dental disease and degenerative pathologies from site A suggested, however, that site A may well have held an older sample than site F.

Average stature at site A was 1.72m for males and 1.64m for females; amongst site F burials it was 1.77m for males and 1.65m for females. Both accord with the medieval range of heights and with modern British height. Overall, there was no difference in stature between site A and site F burials. In other aspects of physique, too, there was no difference between site A and site F burials (there was insufficient metrical data for site F disarticulated bones). Both groups were predominantly brachycranial or mesocranial, platymeric and eurycnemic, in common with the data from the majority of the comparative religious sites and the medieval period in general. In terms of stature, skull, humerus and femur dimensions, site A females were generally smaller than the males, but there was little differentiation and the sexes often overlapped. Site F could not be included in the analysis of sexual dimorphism because of lack of data.

People buried on site A had generally worse dental health than site F burials. Caries was more of a problem in group A21 than the other site A groups, and this higher rate was similar to that of the site F burials. This was the first similarity between these two groups that could be indicative of a shared higher status relative to all the other groups.

In addition to dental disease, degenerative conditions were the most frequent pathology present. This is a common observation amongst archaeological samples. Site A was worse affected in all categories of degenerative disease, suggesting that it contained more aged individuals than site F. In addition, the sample from site A included four cases of fracture which had healed, probably without treatment. Widespread Schmorl's nodes and enthesopathies (the skeletal outgrowth at the sites of muscle or ligament insertion caused probably by repetitive activity) suggest that all three samples were accustomed to heavy physical labour beginning at an early age, including group A21 and site F burials who, if indeed of high status, might be expected to have been spared this. There were very few instances of nutritional deficiency, three in all, and surprisingly these were amongst site F burials and group A21. Again, this would not be expected in higher-status burials, although it is possible that certain social behaviour could result in apparent nutritional hardship when there is not necessarily a straightforward cause for it. This evidence alone is not sufficient to hazard a reliable interpretation. There were six cases of periostitis and three cases of possible tuberculosis; if this is a correct diagnosis, it indicates a high frequency of tuberculosis.

The data were insufficient to allow for successful spatial analysis to identify genetic groupings. The only convincing relationship was between the occupants of two graves in group A21 who had septal apertures in common. The graves were separated by three other burials, which might suggest that the concept of a family plot did not exist unless the three burials in between were also related. Otherwise, little can be inferred.

In sum, therefore, the two cemetery sites displayed some internal differences of potential significance, but were generally similar: burials broadly of the 11th and 12th centuries, including some cist-burials, a combination known from other cemetery sites in London and elsewhere. The burials were of men and women, adults and children, and probably included religious personnel, most notably the man aged about 24 with a silver pectoral cross buried in grave 9 at site A. The skeletons, which would probably have been of high-status persons in order for them to be buried at the priory or its predecessor at all, displayed a variety of the expected osteological conditions.

Outside the precinct: the position of Holy Trinity Priory in London, its local context and its property management in the City

From the 10th century, major monastic establishments like the abbey of Cluny began to resemble small towns in their extent, facilities, organisation and architecture. This crystallisation of a building complex (or of several similar complexes, in a large town), most often with a high proportion of buildings in stone, must have been a potent element in the creation of a formal and organised townscape in the 11th and 12th centuries. In small British towns, a monastery was often the largest institution and the economic as well as cultural centre of the place; for instance, in differing ways and to differing extents, at Battle (Sussex), Beverley (Yorkshire East Riding), Bury St Edmunds (Suffolk), Chertsey (Surrey), Ely (Cambridgeshire), Glasgow (Lanarkshire), Ripon (Yorkshire West Riding), Southwell (Nottinghamshire), or St Andrews (Fife). At Cirencester (Gloucestershire), the Augustinian abbey 'dominates the archaeology of the medieval town, both physically and culturally' (Darvill and Gerrard 1994, 107); the precinct occupied nearly half the area of the town. The monastery did not only stand out by having buildings of stone or prestigious proportions above ground: the provision of a sophisticated water management system at such pre-urban nuclei must have been both locally exceptional and later influential on civic schemes. In this context Bond (1993) cites the examples of Benedictine houses such as Evesham and Pershore (both Worcestershire), and Abingdon (Oxfordshire); houses which subsequently became Augustinian, such as Waltham Abbey (Essex); and, for similar (and perhaps greater) effect within their towns, cathedrals such as Exeter (Devon), Lichfield (Staffordshire) and Wells (Somerset). In many towns in France, cathedrals were instrumental in forming areas of stone buildings, the churches and canonical residences, in the 12th and 13th centuries (Esquieu 1994); the similar effect of religious houses which were not cathedrals has been less studied.

The religious houses, both the earlier monasteries and the friaries, were all large private precincts which formed both obstacles and islands of apparent permanence in the urban topography. Their physical presence, always behind high walls and with controlled points of entry, would have been more noticeable in smaller towns. At Chester, for instance, an abbey, two other religious houses and three friaries occupied much of the small area of the medieval town, with three of the houses and the castle occupying between them a long continuous strip of land immediately inside the western defences; though there were streets between the precincts and a main street to the west gate, these reserved areas in total comprised four-fifths of the western third of the town. They formed a discrete district; and the siting of friaries in particular next to castles is a feature of other towns, such as Rhuddlan (Flintshire) and York. Though they may have been architecturally exclusive, the Chester friaries are also notable for developing a marginal area dotted with Roman ruins, and are thus also seen as beneficial to medieval urban development (Ward 1993, 113, 119).

How far was this true of the City of London? During the late 10th to 13th centuries, the topography of medieval London became fixed through the hardening of many divisions and structurings of space. By the 12th century the city contained perhaps 100 originally private churches, and these were taken over by the ecclesiastical authorities to form the medieval parish system. In the civil sphere, 24 wards were created; first listed in *c* 1127, they were fixed by the mid 13th century (Brooke 1975, 149–84). These two structurings would have bound together the settlement which even within the Roman walls was probably somewhat dispersed. The larger secular topographical units, some of them known as 'hagas', can be traced from documents (Schofield et al 1990). Within the city walls, all the religious houses (except the cathedral, which was already there) seem to have been established on property already occupied by other people, though the degree to which it was built up is unknown in every case. In certain cases, such as those of the friaries, it took generations to acquire all the properties necessary to lay out the full monastic plan of buildings; the friaries made an effort to obtain sites within the walls, and with the exception of the Whitefriars (Carmelites) they were successful. Outside the walls, religious foundations could be established in fields, or at least on less pressurised sites (as for instance at St Mary Clerkenwell and St John Clerkenwell in the 1140s, and later St Mary Graces and Charterhouse, though the latter order – the Cistercians – preferred rural or open sites). Thus the religious precincts in and around London are comparable to those of Chester or York or many other medieval towns in their effect on the local topography, but with the added nuance that in London the establishment of the precinct often brought about a change in land use, not from marsh or meadow, but often from streets of houses. In the case of Holy Trinity, the pre-priory land use is not clearly known; and there would have been a difference between pre-monastic land use in the early 12th century and that in the late 13th century, as experienced by the friaries. No late Saxon secular buildings have been found on the priory site, though there probably were some along the southern edge of the precinct on Leadenhall Street. At least one ruined Roman building was removed as part of the initial clearance (site A); this building was standing apparently to roof level, at least in part, since a portion of the cemented tiled roof was thrown into a pit (Chapter 4.2).

One significant feature of Holy Trinity's siting at Aldgate is that before 1108 the religious centre of the City of London lay around St Paul's on the western hill of the city; here were the three churches, St Paul's, St Martin le Grand and St Mary le Bow, which together also provided the three main schools of 12th-century London. So Holy Trinity was the first large religious establishment to be sited away from this western nucleus of traditional and ancient religious authority (Fig 142). Also, in

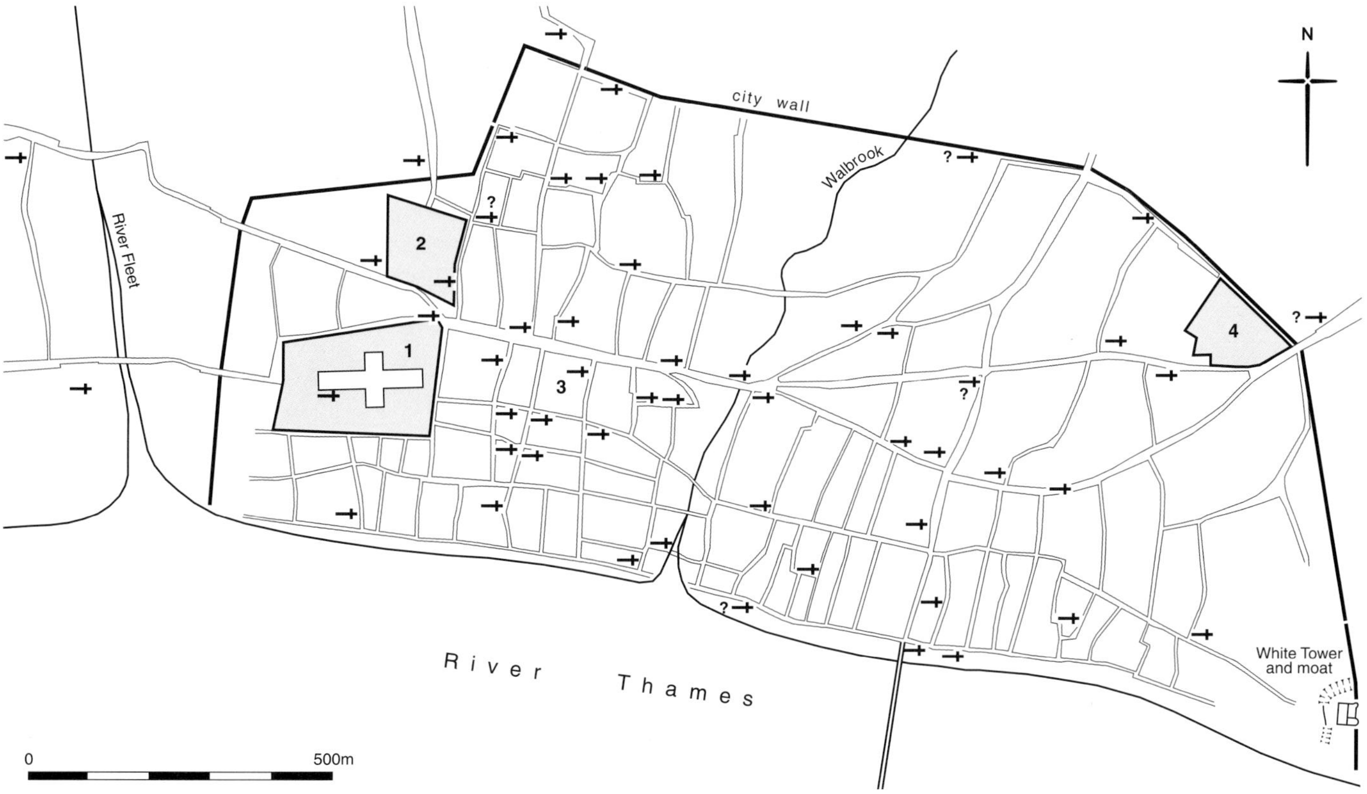

Fig 142 Map of London in the early 12th century: 1 – St Paul's Cathedral (its outline c 1300; the plan of the 12th-century building is not known); 2 – precinct of St Martin le Grand; 3 – St Mary le Bow; 4 – Holy Trinity Priory. Also shown are the sites of parish churches thought to exist by c 1120; some are only possible cases (scale 1:12,500)

1100 the site of the priory was on, if not beyond, the periphery of the built-up area of 11th-century London within its walls, as indicated by the locations of known parish churches and the density of streets. Further, though this has not yet been confirmed by archaeological work, the documentary evidence (especially the cartulary) suggests that the suburb of Aldgate, especially along the High Street outside the gate, began to flourish during the 12th century. The priory owned most of the land on either side of the street, as far as the city boundary, and must have had a hand in its development. Thus we can suggest that the foundation and early development of the priory and its urban holdings stimulated the eastern part of the City of London, and helped to broaden or extend the existing area of settlement both within the walls and outside them to the east.

From the middle of the 12th century, the priory of Holy Trinity and its buildings, largely of stone, must have dominated the area in both physical and architectural terms. Some of the effects of the priory and of its principal builders may be seen in the local topography (Fig 143). In addition, the cartulary provides evidence of deliberate policies of raising money for the priory, perhaps for building work, at various times in the two centuries under consideration. The cartulary also thereby hints at which areas of the City of London were commercially active at certain times. These two themes will now be explored.

In the immediate vicinity of the priory, Prior Norman rebuilt the gate of Aldgate, presumably then still a patched-up Roman structure (*Cartulary*, xiv, no. 4; RCHME 1928, 97); on the north-west (exterior) side, fragmentary traces of several successive rebuildings of the gate above the foundations of the Roman structure were recorded in 1967 (Marsden 1969, 20–6). The gate tower apparently standing during the 12th century was built of ragstone and was square in shape, and projected about 1.5m beyond the city wall. The steeply-sloping side of a ditch more than 2.5m deep, and perhaps V-shaped in section, lay just beyond the gate. The grey earth filling of the ditch contained pottery dating to the late 12th or early 13th

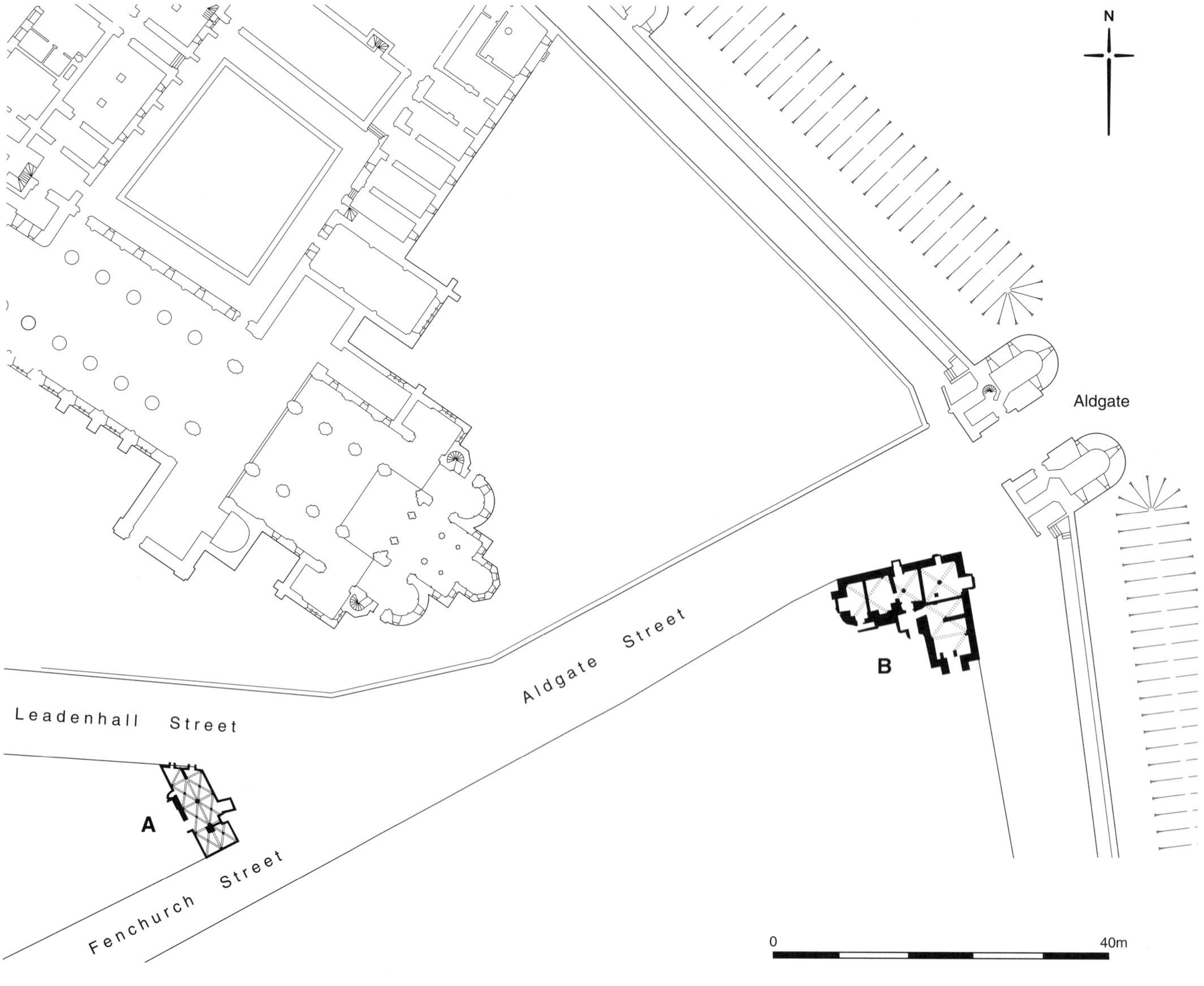

Fig 143 Medieval buildings in the Aldgate area; the form of Aldgate is conjectured from the Symonds plans; two known medieval undercrofts (A and B) are shown (they were recorded before destruction in the 19th century) (scale 1:800)

century.

The north edge of another gate tower was located, the robbed face of which suggested that it might have been D-shaped. It is possible that this was the gate rebuilt, according to Stow (1603, i, 9), in 1215. The tower projected at least 7.3m from the wall, and overlay the filled-in early medieval ditch which terminated immediately north-west of the gate, so that the roadway out of the gate was built on solid ground (Marsden 1969). This gate, presumably of the early 13th century, is shown with its rounded towers in Wyngaerde's panorama (Fig 10) and the western tower was surveyed by Symonds (Figs 13–16). Gates with rounded towers, often additions or extensions to Roman gates, were constructed at the East Gate in Rochester (Kenyon 1990, 192), and at the East Gate in Gloucester in the 13th century (Heighway 1983; Hurst 1986). In the Aldgate case, we can assume this meant that the area was developing, and it was felt that the gate, rebuilt a hundred years before, should be extended in plan and, therefore, made more imposing. It is not known if the priory had a hand in this second building of the gate, but as lord of the soke of Aldgate it may have had. By this time, 1215, the main priory buildings would have dominated the local landscape just inside the gate.

Links with recorded medieval structures of later decades can also be made. The priory owned a very large proportion of the secular property around the precinct, and on two sites on streets immediately to the south of the priory undercrofts, probably of 13th-century date, were recorded in the 18th and 19th centuries (Fig 143; Schofield 2003a, 75–6, 157, 196). Of these, that on the corner site of 15–18 Aldgate and 1 Jewry Street (B), recorded in the 1870s, was certainly on land owned by the priory (*Cartulary*, nos 36–7; Loftus-Brock 1880); the other, at the junction of Leadenhall and Fenchurch Streets by Aldgate pump (A), was part of a prominent tenement. It was taken to be part of the lost St Michael's church when recorded by antiquaries in 1790 and published in the *Gentleman's Magazine* for 1795. Presumably there were other stone buildings on the main street of Aldgate which ran past the east end of the priory church, and which together with the church, the highest building in the district until its demolition in the 1540s (see Fig 10), lent an impressive tone to the wide street immediately inside the gate.

There was frequently a link between the general level of wealth of an Augustinian house and the amount of income it received from urban rents. In 1288–91, about 60% of the income of Holy Trinity Priory derived from property within the City; in 1535, over 90% of the *Valor* of St Mary Overie, Southwark, comprised urban (London) rents (Postles 1993, 12). Augustinian houses in other towns often had substantial urban property: Oseney Abbey and Barnwell Priory became the largest landowners in Oxford and Cambridge respectively (Burton 1994, 243). Policies of property management may be perceived in the documentary records of other monastic houses, such as Oseney Abbey; depending upon the prior, this could include a lack of improvement to properties over a long period, perhaps to maximise income, but also investment in selds (specialised buildings for traders and craftsmen) in the parish of St Michael Northgate in Oxford (Postles 1993, 10–11). In Oxford and other towns, such as Leicester, there was an association between the Augustinian canons and suburban growth; and the effects of intrusion by the canons caused disputes over boundaries and other property matters in Dunstable and Cirencester (ibid, 13). Further north, the Augustinians founded the borough of Canongate between their extramural house at Holyrood and the boundary of the old town of Edinburgh; Canongate now forms the eastern half of the Royal Mile. The Holy Trinity cartulary shows that the priory maintained a lucrative interest in properties on both sides of Aldgate High Street, outside the gate; in the 15th century, when the cartulary was compiled, the quitrents from properties here were substantial. This is in contrast to the practice at Westminster Abbey, which had an estate of about 60,000 acres in south-east England and the Midlands by 1100; although there was much buying and selling of agricultural land, the monks of Westminster seem to have been 'markedly uninterested, or at least unsuccessful' in the property market in London itself (Harvey 1977, 168).

There might be links between the priory's periods of building or rebuilding within the precinct and its manipulation of its substantial urban rents. Besides its holdings of churches and lands in Middlesex, Hertfordshire and Essex (*VCH* 1909, 472–3), the priory owned land in 87 of the City's 108 parishes. The grants by the priory of land in the City which produced quitrents for the priory are listed in the cartulary. Some policies by the successive priors are suggested by the location and type of transactions described in the cartulary, at least up to the 1280s. An urban property market had developed in London and other towns by the early 12th century, and the policy of Holy Trinity has been described as 'dynamic' in disposing of much of its original endowment in an undeveloped part of the city, and acquiring rents in the busier, commercial districts (Keene 1996, 95, 103). Thus we can try to ascertain if the priory was deliberately trying to raise money from its extensive City holdings; urban rents made rebuilding and embellishment programmes possible. Such a connection has been made elsewhere: at the Benedictine abbey at Burton-on-Trent (Staffordshire), three of the known building periods at the abbey coincide with urban development activities in the town by the abbot (Slater 1996, 77–8). The story of the Holy Trinity cartulary is that though the priory sold properties and retained quitrents from the time of the earliest priors, the greatest period of creation of hard cash by manipulating property was 1222–68. From about 1270, the interest seems to come nearer home; in the two decades after 1270 all but three transactions recorded in the cartulary occurred in the eastern parishes. This is the period of construction of the two medieval undercrofts in the parish of St Katherine Cree which are shown in Fig 143. Thus there may have been a slight change in policy around 1270 in order to encourage, or at least be part of, economic growth in the immediate locality around the priory and within Aldgate.

The priory enjoyed bequests of money and lands in the City

from citizens, well into the later 14th century (*Cal Husting Wills*, i, 126, 238, 594; ii, 10, 39). Thus it might be suggested that the 13th- and early 14th-century construction programmes at the priory, probably including (possible rebuilding of) the dormitory range, possibly the chapter house, the great tower and the main gate, might have been partly funded by the policies of management of property on the lucrative City land market, supplemented by grants and acquisition of property on rural sites in the immediate environs of London. But equally, the money might have been intended for many other purposes, or just to improve the general finances of the house.

5.5 The priory and its buildings in the later Middle Ages (*c* 1350–1532, period M3)

The architectural development of the priory

There is a great contrast between the state of knowledge of the architectural development of Holy Trinity Priory for the period before *c* 1350 and that of the period between 1350 and 1532. Very little of this later period can be reconstructed from the archaeological or antiquarian record.

The new west end and the great tower, on all the available evidence, were constructed at this time. The latrine block had been extended over the city ditch, and a postern driven through a privatised section of the city wall. The great priory church as seen by Wyngaerde in 1540 (Fig 10) must have been fully in place. Some time during the 14th century (perhaps before 1350?) the west range of the cloister was doubled in width to the west, at least along part of its length, as the accommodation for the prior was extended. In the 15th century brick arches were built along the back of the city wall through the precinct, stopping-up the 13th-century postern and presumably destroying access at all levels to the building, probably a latrine block, which lay outside the wall and over the ditch (Fig 139). This is taken to be part of the documented programme of refurbishment of the city defences by Mayor Jocelyn in 1477, by analogy with other sites where the arches have been found. Late medieval moulded stones from the priory sites, none in *situ*, included window casements in several sizes and styles, fragments of octagonal shafts or responds, two fragments from screens or tombs, and two parts of fireplaces. The later medieval groups of pottery from Holy Trinity Priory are too small to permit valid comparisons with the much larger assemblages from other religious houses which have been recently studied, such as St Mary Clerkenwell, St John Clerkenwell, St Mary Spital and Bermondsey Abbey (Chapter 8.5).

Table 12 presents an outline of the development of the religious houses in London into which the few known facts and possible inferences concerning Holy Trinity Priory should be fitted.

One of the first buildings to display the Perpendicular style of architecture was St Paul's chapter house in the City of London, in 1332 (Harvey 1978; Wilson 1992). It is a notable feature revealed by Harvey's (1978) study that monasteries and priories throughout England figure in the history of the style. Presumably the master masons of the Perpendicular style were employed on London monastic houses; the mouldings of the west door of St Mary Overie (Fig 144) of *c* 1385 have been attributed to Henry Yevele (Harvey 1978, fig 32).

Nationally, during the 15th century, expenditure on the fabric of English cathedrals and monastic houses fell sharply; besides any effect of religious or cultural changes, this may have been a reflection of the long period of depression in the country's economy (Morris 1979, 180). Some monastic houses in London added or rebuilt parts of their complexes in the 15th and early 16th centuries, though in one case it was after building failure. At St Bartholomew Smithfield, the cloister was rebuilt in *c* 1409 and the tower rebuilt about the same time. At St Mary Overie, Southwark, the present crossing tower dates from the 15th century, and the (13th-century) nave fell down in 1469. It was replaced with a timber vault (some of the bosses survive in the present building) and a new west end largely of brick, though the lower part was of stone and must have been largely still 13th-century in origin, much of it possibly from before the fire of 1212 (Fig 144). Indeed, it is difficult to find a major religious building programme of the 15th century in London which used stone (cf the gatehouse of 1490 at Lambeth Palace, of brick with stone dressings). In brick and terracotta, there was some building of the early 16th century at St Mary Clerkenwell (Sloane in prep) and St John Clerkenwell (Sloane and Malcolm 2004, 174–7, 297–321), and, from engravings of the late 18th century, at the Minoresses outside Aldgate; so there was evidently construction at monastic houses in London going on up to the Dissolution. But, so far, there is little evidence of this from Holy Trinity; and the absence of any clearly post-1400 features either on the Symonds plans or in the excavations would suggest that very little building took place at the priory from 1350 to 1532. The only exception would be prominent tombs inside the church.

Burials, *c* 1350–1532

Although no burials of this period were excavated on the priory sites, fragments from screens or tombs were recovered as reused building rubble (<A57> and <A58>, Fig 194; Chapter 8.2). In 1348 Alan de Scarnynnge, clerk, declared in his will (not proved until 1361) that he should be buried in the conventual church at Holy Trinity (*Cal Husting Wills*, ii, 17); in 1361 John Malewyn wished to be buried in the church near Margery his late wife (ibid, 38). Other requests to be buried in the church occur throughout the period 1368–1488 (ibid, 118, 163, 267, 431, 591). Some testators mention specific places. In 1372 Simon de Hattefeld, potter, wished to be buried in front of the altar of St John the Baptist in the church; he left a tenement in the churchyard to the priory, in return for the celebration of an obit for his soul and that of his wife and others (ibid, 155–6). In 1375 John Hanekyn asked to be buried at the south door of the church (ibid, 184–5), and in 1376 John de Cantebrigge,

Fig 144 St Mary Overie, Southwark: west end, engraved from a drawing by F Nash, 1805 (Guildhall Library)

Table 12 Main building periods at London monasteries and hospitals, second half of the 14th to early 16th centuries

Religious establishment	Main construction dates	References
Second half of 14th century		
Austin Friars	church rebuilding begun 1354 (relation to previous church not known)	Hugo 1864; Cater 1912; 1915
Charterhouse	founded 1371; cells and frater	Knowles and Grimes 1954; Barber and Thomas 2002; Porter and Richardson in prep
Holy Trinity Priory	probably building work according to documentary sources (debts acknowledged 1369)	
St Helen Bishopsgate	transept chapels added 1370s	LCC Survey of London 1924, 31–6; RCHME 1929, 20–2
St Katharine by the Tower	church rebuilding started 1343, still in progress 1377	Nichols 1825; *VCH* 1909, 526–7; Jamieson 1972
St Martin le Grand	chancel rebuilt 1385–6 by Henry Yevele, at William Wykeham's expense	Harvey 1984, 363
St Mary Bethlem	new chapel *c* 1360–80	Andrews et al 1997, 41
St Mary Graces	founded 1350; cloisters in construction 1379	*VCH* 1909, 461–4; Mills 1985
St Mary Spital	infirmary extended probably early 14th century; subdivisions and domestic structures *c* 1350–*c* 1400	Thomas et al 1997
St Paul's	south transept: new door and window by Henry Yevele, 1387–8	Morris 1990; Harvey 1984, 363; Schofield in prep
St Thomas Acon	church rebuilt 1383+	*VCH* 1909, 493
Westminster Abbey	nave rebuilt 14th century; cloister rebuilt second half of 14th century; new infirmary 1364+	Pevsner 1973, 396–405; Wilson 1986; RCHME 1924; Harvey 1993, 89–90
Whitefriars	west end of church built over Crocker Lane, *c* 1350; body of church rebuilt by *c* 1420; small 14th-century undercroft (Britton's Court) probably part of Provincial's Lodging; land reclaimed from river 1396, perhaps for extension of precinct	Stow 1603, ii, 46; *VCH* 1909, 507–10; Clapham and Godfrey 1913, 263–7; Toy 1932
15th century		
St Bartholomew Smithfield	cloister rebuilt, early 15th century	*VCH* 1909, 477; Webb 1921
St Helen Bishopsgate	church rebuilt 1458+, 1470s by Crosby	*VCH* 1909, 459; RCHME 1929, 20–2; Bradley and Pevsner 1997, 221–3
St John Clerkenwell	new buildings, especially after 1480	Sloane and Malcolm 2004, 90–190
St Mary Clerkenwell	building works of late 15th century	Sloane in prep
St Mary Overie	tower rebuilt by 1424; nave fell down, rebuilt 1469	*VCH* 1909, 483; RCHME 1930
St Mary Spital	subdivisions and piecemeal additions, *c* 1350–*c* 1540; glazing of cloister walks early 15th century	Thomas et al 1997, 68–87, 96
Westminster Abbey	intermittent works on upper parts of nave and west towers; west window finished	Wilson 1986
16th century		
Crutched Friars	an extension to precinct for rebuilding of church and possibly other new buildings 1520–4	*VCH* 1909, 515
Holywell Priory	embellished with a chapel and probably other features by Sir Thomas Lovell, 1511–13	LCC Survey of London 1922, 153–87
St Clare without Aldgate (Minoresses)	priory buildings rebuilt after fire by *c* 1520	*VCH* 1909, 518–19
St John Clerkenwell	gatehouse of 1504; building(s), decorated with terracotta, early 16th century	Sloane and Malcolm 2004, 169–77
Westminster Abbey	second stage of western towers and west window 1513–34	Tatton-Brown 1995

fishmonger, elected for St Mary's chapel, where his son and two former wives were already buried (ibid, 197).

One burial or tomb noted by Stow was of Simon Kempe esquire (Stow 1603, i, 141). This seems to have included a brass to Simon Kamp (*sic*) and his wife Margaret, which was (along with many others, no doubt) sold at the Dissolution to be adapted and reused as the brass of Walter Curzon (d 1527; the brass laid down *c* 1533) in the church of the Austin Friars, Oxford; this was later removed to the parish church at Waterperry (Oxfordshire) where it remains. The top half of Margaret's effigy has been recorded (Page-Phillips 1980, 16, item 70L3). The original Latin inscription around the brass includes the lines 'Simon Kamp lies here in the flesh, buried under marble / His spirit is absent from here, suffused with light / Here Margaret his wife is buried together with him / I hope that heaven is ready for her' (S Freeth, pers comm; trans J Page-Phillips and Rev Fr Bertram).

The latest recorded request in the Husting Rolls, that of William Hobbys or Hobbes in 1488 (proved 1489), is specific about the inscription to be made on the marble stone to be set on his tomb. This was to read:

> *Hic jacet Willelmus Hobbes quondam medicus et Sirurgicus Illustrissimi domini ducis Eboracencis ac filiorum suorum regum Illustrissimorum Edwardi iiij et Ricardi tercii quorum anime et animabus propicietur Deus amen*
> Here lies William Hobbes once doctor and surgeon of the most illustrious lord Duke of York and of his sons the most illustrious kings Edward IV and Richard III (*Cal Husting Wills*, ii, 590–1).

This tomb, however, is not listed by John Stow in 1598. According to his editor's notes, Stow probably did not inspect the former church himself, but quoted from lists of monuments then in his possession (Stow 1603, ii, 291–2).

Others wished to be buried specifically in the churchyard, such as Thomas Rycher, chaplain, in 1360 (*Cal Husting Wills*, ii, 67, 229). In a will written in Norwich in 1377, Walter de Berneye expressed the wish to be buried either in the churchyard at Holy Trinity or in the cloister of Norwich Cathedral, depending on where he happened to die (ibid, 205).

In conclusion, it seems that though there was little if any large-scale construction in the priory precinct from 1350 to the Dissolution, there were a number of prestigious tombs in the church. The priory continued its early function as an attractive setting for the final resting places of knights and esquires, and those in royal and civic service.

5.6 Life in the priory 1108–*c* 1532 (periods M2 and M3)

Personnel and the *Liber Coquinae*

The priors of Holy Trinity were listed for the *Victoria County History* of London by Miss M Reddan (*VCH* 1909, 474) and up to the 18th prior in the cartulary (*Cartulary*, nos 14–30). Other officers mentioned in medieval documentary records are the subprior, sacristan and rent-gatherer (ibid, *passim*); and in 1222–48 and 1259 there are mentions of 'Hugh the Gate-keeper' and 'John the Gate-keeper [*janitore*]', who were presumably in charge of the monastery gate (ibid, nos 933, 945). The welfare of the choirboys of the priory was the subject of a bequest by Thomas de Algate, brother of the contemporary prior, in 1359 (ibid, no. 1032). Mention of one servant comes through the records of a scandal: on a visitation of the priory in 1493, the Bishop of London found that the prior, Thomas Percy, had begun an affair with a married woman, Joan Hodgis, and to facilitate this relationship had given her the office of embroiderer by letters patent to which he had forced the canons to affix the common seal. Percy was ejected as prior, and took his case to Rome, but without success (*VCH* 1909, 471).

A glimpse of daily life in the priory is provided by a document of the early 16th century (PRO, E36/108). This is a volume containing several items from the early years of Henry VIII's reign. The first is a cellarer's account, commencing:

> *Liber generalis omnium receptionum, tam in civitate, quam in patria, et omnium solutionum monasterii Sanctæ Trinitatis, Londinii, per me, Dominum Johannem Bradwell, priorem dicti monasterii, a festo Sancti Michaelis Archangeli, anno regni Regis Henrici octavi quinto, usque ad idem festum anno sexto. – Hayns, selerarius.*
> A general book of all receipts, in the city and in the countryside, and of all payments of the monastery of Holy Trinity, London, by me, Sir John Bradwell, prior of the said monastery, from the festival of St Michael Archangel, in the fifth year of king Henry VIII, to the same festival in the sixth year [1514–15]. – Hayns, cellarer.

This volume has been inspected for the present report, but the paragraphs which follow are transcribed from the comprehensive calendar in *L and P Hen VIII*, 2, I.38–40 (115), with some additional notes (including comments by Hazel Forsyth) inserted. The text in *L and P Hen VIII* includes commentary, summary and some suggestions for word-meanings. The suggestions or queries in the following paragraphs by the editor of the calendar are in round brackets, while the comments by Hazel Forsyth and the authors are in square brackets. The paragraph numbering in square brackets has been added here to continue the system used up to no. 3 in the original calendar.

1) Receipts in the city of London by Hugh Bartlett, 7th Oct. 5 Hen. VIII. to 22nd Dec. 6 Hen. VIII.

2) Receipts *in patria* from different tenants and others.

3) Reparations in the city; sc., carpenters, smiths, blacksmith's work, tiles, sand, carriage, and wages of laborers; chiefly to Dowgate and Katharine Cry Church. Labourers' wages, 5d. a day; a carpenter and his servant, 1s. For the garden, onion, parsley, thime, cole(?), nep [possibly an abbreviation for parsnip or turnip], borrige and hyssop seed, vines, leeks, beet and other herbs. Wages: gardeners, 4d a day; weeding, ditto. Preparations at Woodalaks. Wages to the subprior and others. Wine for the convent; on All Hallows' Day, 10d; Advent Sunday (a gallon of Rhenish), 10d; Conception of Our Lady, 8d; Christmas Day, 6d; a pair of shoes, 8d;

another, 9d. Pewter platters and dishes; a pair of hose, 17d; 2 shirts, 2s 4d. For the Christmas quarter: a gallon of Rhenish, 1s; a gallon of Malmsey, 8d; a gallon of Rhenish, 12d; 2 lbs of comfits, 16d; money, 15d. These four given at Kenyngton's dirge. Wine on Easter Even, 8d; the Annunciation of Our Lady, 8d; Easter Day, 10d; Ascension Day, 10d; Whitsunday, 10d. Summoner of the convent, 4s 2d a week. Almonry, including coats for the children of the chapel; eg, 3 pair of hose, 14d; a pair of shoes, 6d; soling ditto, 2d. Expenses of bread, wine and service at Michaelmas, including sweet wine, red wine, claret, Rhenish, Malmsey, bastard, ale, and wheat, chiefly for the entertainment of strangers, eg, the recorder, Mr More, Mr Draper, andc. The same for Christmas, the Annunciation and St John the Baptist's Day. Payments for rent to the Prioress of Holywell, the Bishop of London, the Master of St Katharine's (Hospital), the Abbot of Westminster and others. Payments of an ancient debt. Expenses for the church, including mending of books, singing bread, wax, mats for the choir, frankincense, white bread, gerdylls [?girdles], ink, paper, andc. For St Katharine Cry Church; sc, houselling bread, bastard, and Malmsey, bread, oil, singing wine, pricking of a mass, 12d; 7 vellum skins for the great book, 2s 8d; mending St Lawrence's relic, 1s; Mr Beell, for preaching the first Sunday of Lent, 3s 4d; covering a pontifical, 3s. At the Resurrection, 9 dozen of points for the 'harneschttes' men, 8d; the minstrels, 3s 4d; the waits, 3s 4d; to the keepers of Barkyng procession, for the hire of their pageant against Easter, 6s 8d; hire of harness for the Resurrection and for Trinity Sunday, 20s. A quart of ink, 4d; inkhorns, 2d; 2 penknives, 1s; parchment skin for the brevitor, 2½d. Holy cream and wine on Maundy Thursday, 14d. Fees to counsel, ie, Godson; Mores, of the Common Pleas; Green, common serjeant; Draper; Brooke, the recorder; Lovell; Martyn; Haws, attorney in the King's Bench; Copwood, of the Exchequer; Pecock, serjeant; Pygot, and Pollard. Expenses for tithes of Berden, Herts; and for the Charterhouse. Wages to servants in Michaelmas term; ie, steward, rent gatherer, cook, master of the children, laundress, carpenter, butler, bellringer, gardener, andc. The same for Christmas, the Annunciation, St John the Baptist's Day.

[4] Expenses for the prior's lodgings: 2 pair of shoes for my Lord, 20d; pair of hose for ditto, 6d; 6 'bocheskins' for my Lord's sleeves, 5s 6d; a yard of white kersey for the same, 2s 4d; a dozen of points, 1d; 2 burthen of rushes, 3d; 2 'penars' (or penner, a portable inkpot with separate compartments for quills, penknife, pounce box etc) and inkhorn, 4d; pair of spurs, 10d; 2½ oz black fringe for my Lord's riding hood, 2s 11d; 5 ells of holland, for shirts of my Lord, 4s 2d; ½ lb of psycards, 5d; mending a pair of cork shoes, 1d; 'byrchyne' hounds, 5d; grey hounds, 3d; 6 silk points, 1½d; pair of hose, 4s; an ell of sarcenet for covering my Lord's hat, 5s; 'binding of your black hat and the velvet', 1s; for medlars for my Lord on Mary Mawdelen's Day; 3 black silk buttons, 22d; andc. Spices for Ipocras [Hypocras], ie, 1 lb cinnamon bruised, 3s 4d; ½ lb ginger, 12d; 1 oz cloves, 5d; aniseed, ½d. For spice bread, 1½ oz of cloves and mace, 8d; ½ lb pepper, 8d; 1 oz saffron, 11d; 2 lb sugar, 10d; butter, 8d; eggs, 4d; strawberries for Trinity Sunday, 3s 4d. Wafers on Whitsunday and Trinity Sunday, 2s and 2s 8d. Purchases for my Lord's lodging: a load of savyn, 3s; smelts, 1d; 'cundetes' [conduit? – but why?] water on St John's even, 3s 3d; fustian for my Lord's sleeves, 9d; a quart of aqua vitæ, 4d; for making two pair of doublet foresleeves for my Lord, 5d; 2 rochetts [? or pockets] for ditto, 2s 8d; mending his girdle, 4d; tawny for servant's livery, £4; apothecary for pills for 'laske', 14d; medicine for my Lord, 20d; hats, when my Lord rode to his courts, 8s; for making his kirtle, 12d; ditto his riding hood, 8d; fishing net, 7s; 2 doz hoods, tawny for grooms' livery, 50s; ½ yd. velvet for my Lord's sleeves, 5s 8d; 2 yds white fustian for the same, 16d; mending my Lord's silver rings of his 'bage', 1s; pair of carving knives, 5s.

[5] Expenses for the mill: the miller and his wife.

[6] Expenses by way of rewards at dirges and christenings, and for presents, to various persons; sc., commissary, the Queen and the King's footmen, the mayor and the sheriff's yeomen, the King's waits, the Lord of Misrule of the King's house, and my Lord of Essex's minstrels, for a boar, a swan, a hen, venison, pears, andc; waits on Trinity Sunday; to Dr Taylor's servant, for bringing the Acts of Parliament. For mowing St Katharine Cry churchyard, 5d. Corrodies to Lady Bradbury and William Glazeare. To the porter 18d a week.

[7] Expenses of the stable: 2 bushel of oats, 7d; 2½ yds of broad black for a saddle cloth for my Lord at 2s 8d the yard; varnishing his stirrups, 4 silk points, and rewards for the saddler, 4d; a quarter of grains for the oxen, 11d (sometimes 12d); a bit, 16d; shoeing a horse, 1d; 2 loads of hay, 20s; a shovel, 4d; hire of 6 acres pasture, 21s 8d; pasture for 2 kine, 10s; 1 bushel of barley for the swans, 7d; chaff and oats, 20d; 2 grey ambling horses, £6 3s 4d; horse bread, 4d (sometimes 2d); a horseshoe, 2d; 1 load of straw, 4s; 3 ells 'hedlake' to amend horse collar, 6d.

'Liber Coquinæ.' – Victuals bought by William Heryff, steward of the convent, from Michaelmas 5 to Michaelmas 6 Hen. VIII, John Bradwell being the prior.

Saturday, 7th October, for the steward: salt fish, 8d; stock fish, 2d; haddocks, 9d; whitings, 6d; butter, 1d. Sunday: beef, in store; 2 geese, 12d; mutton, 14d; pigeons, 8d; eggs, ½d; butter, 1d. Monday: beef, in store; pork, 5d; mutton, 15d. Tuesday: beef, in store; pork, 4d; mutton, 14d; haddocks 4d; salt fish, 2d; eggs, 1d; shrimps, 1d. Thursday: beef, in store; mutton, 19½d; 3 rabbits, 6d. Friday: salt fish, 9d; herring(s), 9d; haddocks, 14d; butter, 1d; whitings, 6d; shrimps, 1d; flounders, 2d; oysters, 2d. Also: mustard, 2d; vinegar, 2d; onions, 1½d; malmsey, 2d; oatmeal, 1½d.

'Eadem septimana pro conventu.' – Saturday: salt fish, 7d; haddocks, 10d; stock fish, 1d; mussels, 4d; butter, 2d; bread, ½d. Sunday: beef, in store; 2 geese, 12d; mutton, 10d; chicken, 2d. Monday: beef, in store; pork, 8d; mutton, 10d; a cony, 2d. Tuesday: beef, in store; mutton, 18d. Wednesday: salt fish, 8d; stock fish, 6d; butter, 4d; flounders, 1d; shrimps, 4d;

haddocks, 10d; honey, 1½d. Thursday: beef, in store; mutton, 8½d; rabbits, 11d. Friday: salt fish, 7d; haddocks, 12d; herring(s), 7d; eels, 1d. Also: mustard, 2d; vinegar, 2d; onions, 1½d; salt, 1½d. (So on for every day in the year.)

In the provision for the convent, Saturday, Wednesday, and Friday were always fish days, sometimes with the addition of butter, eggs, or cheese; except when a feast day fell on Wednesday. The fish, besides that already mentioned, consisted of salmon, fresh cod, gudgeons, mackerell, soles, lampreys, red herrings, mullets, oysters, crabs, roaches, thornbacks, plaice, congers, sprats, gurnards, tenches, smelts, pikes and brills. The meat was beef, mutton, lamb, pork, and veal, fresh and in store, venison, rabbits, geese, pullets, teals, quails, cranes, capons, pigeons, larks and woodcocks. Other provisions were milk, cream, curds, butter, cheese, eggs, small raisins, oatmeal, peason, honey, onions, parsley roots, parsnips, pies, 'saucelgys' [sausages], almonds, figs, vinegar, mustard, salt, bay salt, white salt, pepper, 'stroke' (?) on Shrove Sunday, cloves and maces, currants, prunes, dates, ginger, cinnamon and saffron 'syvet' (civet). The provision for the convent is less plentiful and varied than that for the steward. In Advent nothing but fish was allowed in the convent; sometimes with a little mutton; never more than two pennyworth; sometimes milk. From 4 August 1514 to the end of the account, 'Dominus Grevys' is mentioned as being steward.

On Trinity Sunday, 17 June 1514, Mr Westby, Mr Deny, and Mr Blagge, of the Exchequer, Doctor Taylore, Mr Corbett, Mr Blondell, Mr Eylmer, Mr Chamley, Mr Oliver Turner, Mr Thuryston, Mr Ellis, draper, Mr Long, proctor, and Mr Exmew were entertained. The first course consisted of: 'brues to pottage', chickens and bacon, green geese, roast capon, pike, pheasant, custard. 'The second course': 'joly to pottage', pigeons, rabbits, 'heronzew' (heronshewes, a young heron), 'breame', 'quinces bak' tart [baked quince tart]. 'The first course for convent': 'brues (?broth) to pottage', chickens and bacon, green geese, capon, custard. 'The second course for the same': 'joly to pottage', pigeons, rabbits, 'quinces bake'.

On Thursday, 19 July 1514, the Bishop of London was entertained at breakfast by the steward.

This document, therefore, mentions further servants or officers of the priory: the butler, bellringer, carpenter, cellarer, cook, gardeners, saddler, laundress, lawyers ('counsel'), master of the children (and 'children of the chapel'), rent-gatherer, steward and summoner. At St Bartholomew Smithfield the complement included the prior, subprior, precentor, sacristan, cellarer, fraterer (*refectorarius*), kitchener (*coquinarius*), chamberlain, guest master, master of the infirmary, bailiff, auditor, steward (of the manorial estates), and chantry priests or chaplains (Webb 1921, i, 30–4). All these large religious establishments must have had a body of servants, as at Westminster Abbey (Harvey 1993, 146–78).

There were also corrodians from at least 1250, as mentioned in Chapter 3.2. They were perhaps accommodated somewhere in the precinct, though in general the term corrody covered a range of charitable arrangements, and the recipient was not necessarily required or expected to live in the precinct, as at Westminster Abbey (Harvey 1993, 179–209). The second earliest reference which has been traced to a corrody at Holy Trinity concerns a woman. In 1256 Avicia, widow and daughter of Ernold de Gotherunlane, gave property to the priory in exchange for a small loaf and a gallon of conventual beer daily for life, with an extra gallon on Sundays and Thursdays, and similar but smaller allowances for her maidservant, as well as a small allowance in money; to quote the original deeds, the canons had received her 'into the sisterhood of their house, to partake of all its benefits in life and death' (McMurray 1925, 169). The priory promptly leased out her property to others, but there is no certain evidence that Avicia and her maid took up residence in the priory itself.

In 1335 Edward III issued the priory with a charter relieving it of the obligation to maintain corrodians after the death of those to whom they owed an obligation (*Cartulary*, no. 1005; *Cal Pat R 1334–8*, 117). At St Mary Spital, there is evidence for a number of tenements being erected in the priory grounds or being adapted from existing buildings for private tenants by the early 15th century (Thomas et al 1997, 79), though it has not been possible to identify these buildings in the excavations there. At several religious houses, we may conclude, there would have been buildings of a secular character generally appearing in the areas of the monastery away from the religious foci of the place; though a tenement could be purposely situated next to the church, as at St Helen Bishopsgate, where in the west wall of the south transept, at first-floor level, there is a squint through the wall which would have given a view from a first-floor chamber, of a building now lost, into one of the late 14th-century chapels of the south transept. The cellarer's account for 1514–15 just quoted includes payments to two corrodians then at Holy Trinity, Lady Bradbury and William Glazeare.

Life in the priory, from the archaeological artefacts

Holy Trinity Priory was one of the richest foundations in London, but the artefacts from the different sites excavated to 1990 are poor in quantity when compared with other excavated religious houses in the London area. The silver pectoral cross and textile fragments (Fig 41; Fig 119; Fig 120) are exceptional items, but some common categories of religious artefact, such as bone styli, are absent, while the window glass is paltry (Chapter 8.6). The medieval pottery assemblages are small and there are no clear Dissolution horizons (Chapter 8.5). As at St Mary Spital, St Mary Clerkenwell and St John Clerkenwell, the pottery mainly comprises standard domestic wares, and the number of the imports is at all times limited, although a few unusual types are represented. There were few animal bones (Chapter 8.7), and no botanical samples were taken, although this could perhaps be remedied in future excavations within the precinct.

The comparative dearth of 'monastic' artefacts may of course also be remedied by future excavations within the precinct, but is largely due to the truncation to which the site has been exposed and to a lack of deeply cut features within the excavated areas. As a result there are only a few glimpses of what life in the priory may have been like at different times. The only evidence for the 12th century is a pit on site C, which contained a range of typical coarseware cooking pots and a decorated pitcher which is rather more special; these may have been among the first pottery vessels used in the priory, and may have been discarded at a time when improvements were made to the kitchen or refectory, as was the case at St Mary Clerkenwell (Sloane in prep). There are no useful later 12th- or 13th-century groups but a wood-lined pit or pair of pits on site H (gpH21.1) contained finds of the mid 14th century. This complex must have functioned as part of the latrine arrangements. The pit fills were not fully excavated but, taken together, they yielded a variety of medieval objects which range from the domestic and mundane to most exotic. A similar pit lay next to the masonry latrine of the infirmary at St Mary Spital, Bishopsgate, in *c* 1300 (Thomas et al 1997, 55–63, fig 32; period M4, pit C[1725]), and comparison between the two is instructive.

At Holy Trinity Priory the pottery from the site H pit(s) (gpH21.1) consists of sherds from up to 32 tablewares in seven fabrics; the forms comprise at least nine jug types, one with a very rare form of heraldic bossed decoration (<P5>, Fig 199), and one smaller drinking jug. Some of these have heavy internal residues, and the base of one has been perforated, suggesting that they had been reused as urinals or for some medicinal purpose. It is thus of interest that the primary fill of the second pit contained many fragments of green glass vessels, including enough rims and bases to permit their identification as urinals (Fig 210). These vessels were used to collect the first urine of the day, which was visually inspected for medical diagnosis. The form of the urinal seems to have remained constant throughout the medieval period, with a broad neck and wide lip. The body had to be thin, to give enough transparency for efficient examination of the contents, whereas the base was thicker and convex, requiring the vessels to be stored in a basket as they would not stand upright. The longevity of these vessels is likely to be low, and the site H examples are, therefore, unlikely to be significantly earlier than the mid 14th-century date indicated by the pottery.

Pit C[1725] at St Mary Spital contained pottery in six main fabrics and in six forms, mostly jugs; there was also a small amount of imported pottery such as Saintonge ware. No glass was present, but 18 wooden vessels, mostly shallow dishes, were found. Other finds comprise leather boots, and copious amounts of animal and fish bone, food and spice seeds, and box leaves perhaps from a nearby garden. At Holy Trinity, by contrast, only two fragments from a wooden bowl were found (Chapter 8.6). One is a rim fragment of a lipped dish (H<40>, Fig 209), and the other (H<41>) a flat piece, possibly from the same dish. These were recovered from the same fill of the pit (gpH21.1) as a knife with an iron blade and a handle of hawthorn wood in a leather sheath decorated with simple/pseudo armorial bearings (H<131> and H<181>, Fig 208). There were also two fragments of leather shoe upper (H<116>) and a ceramic lantern made from a London-type ware (LOND) drinking jug (<P10>, Fig 199). The most exotic find, from one of the main fills of the pit, comprises several fragments of patterned silk, deriving from two separate textiles which were probably made in Islamic Spain in the first half of the 12th century (H<133> and H<208>; Fig 119; Fig 120; Chapter 8.6). These items were therefore kept and used for 150 to 200 years before they were discarded, and this fits with the fact that the pottery from this feature, and also from group A38 on site A, includes a mix of contemporary wares and earlier types dating back to the 12th century.

The fills of pit C[1725] at St Mary Spital probably derived mainly from the food that the inmates of the hospital were eating, and included their faeces (Thomas et al 1997, 63); at Holy Trinity Priory this cannot be established, but the contents of the site H pit(s) (gp21.1) are markedly different. The former contained no outstandingly rich finds, and reveals far more about the day-to-day life of the occupants of the hospital, both staff (the lay sisters in this case) and the lay patients. There was also other evidence of day-to-day activities from other features at St Mary Spital, such as locks and keys, curtain rings, candle holders and sewing equipment. At Holy Trinity Priory, by contrast, the few objects illustrate one or two aspects of the canons' lives, but mainly emphasise the extraordinary foreign contacts which the priory enjoyed through its benefactors, and perhaps the founder herself; they also show the extent to which some objects were carefully curated for long periods of time.

The 15th century is not well represented in the finds, but one pit on site A (gpA40) contained a range of pottery which could have been discarded at the Dissolution. This includes part of an Italian altar vase (<P68>, Fig 205) which may have been used in the church or for more private devotion. It is also likely that another Italian vase of a rare type (<P67>, Fig 205) dates from this time, although it was found in a post-medieval context (A[268], gpA43).

6

The archaeological sequence: the post-medieval period, 1532–*c* 1900

6.1 Introduction

The post-medieval centuries have been divided into two periods (P1–P2). The first, P1, comprises the period of the Dissolution and its immediate aftermath (on this site, 1532–92), during which time the main range of a mansion was established on the west range of the cloister. The second period, P2, covers the years 1592–*c* 1900, summarising broadly the development of the area over three centuries to place the few recorded fragments in context.

6.2 The Dissolution and its immediate aftermath, 1532–92 (period P1)

In the account of this period, it has been thought most useful to bring the fragmentary archaeological evidence into as close a relationship as possible with the relevant documentary, cartographic and pictorial evidence. This means that the text is arranged to deal with several topics: 1) the destruction of the priory buildings and construction of the main post-Dissolution mansion in the west claustral range, a gallery which probably belonged to it going along the north aisle of the nave and a new building called the Ivy chamber in the crossing of the former priory church; 2) two tenancies of well-to-do people, one of which was sold off in 1590, which incorporated parts of the south transept and east end of the presbytery; 3) industrial uses and immigrants throughout the precinct, including evidence for tin-glazed pottery making. For each of these phases of activity, the documentary evidence is presented first, followed by the archaeological findings.

The destruction of the priory buildings and the creation of Duke's Place

Documentary evidence

In February 1532 Nicholas Hancock, the last prior, and 18 canons signed a deed giving the king their monastery and all its possessions (Jeffries Davies 1925, 9). As reasons they cited a much diminished income and overwhelming debts. Perhaps they hoped, or intended, that the king might restore it to prosperity. Henry considered a plan for a hospital endowed with lands of the priory, now generally referred to as 'Christchurch'; it was also rumoured that he intended to use the buildings for the accommodation of the Observant Friars from Greenwich, and transform their house, close by his palace, into a college. In the winter of 1532 Sir Thomas Audley asked Cromwell to persuade the king to give him a house belonging to Christchurch, somewhere outside London; this appears to be the first involvement in the priory's affairs of Audley, who obtained the priory precinct and much of its local property in stages in 1534 (ibid, 17–18; Marsden 1992; *L and P*

Hen VIII, 7, 419 (28), 587 (10); CLRO, Repertory 9, fos 262–3, 270). Audley was heading his letters 'Creechurch Place' by August 1535 (*L and P Hen VIII*, 9, 41). Ministers' Accounts for the period 1536–41 show that the former priory property adjoining the priory site in the parishes of St Katherine Cree and St Botolph Aldgate was granted exclusively to Audley by various letters patent (PRO, SC6/Hen VIII/2356 m 1; PRO, C66/666 m 45; 677 m 42; 682 m 20; 699 m 34).

Building accounts of 1541–2 for the former priory suggest overhauling of a kitchen, buttery and 'vaults', and the making of a new 'jakes' (ie privy) in the court; rooms being refurbished include the Comptroller's chamber, the 'great chamber next the hall', the 'great new chamber', the parlour, and 'Lord Bayne's chamber' (PRO, E101/674/24). The 'great chamber next the hall' and 'great new chamber' may well be the rooms at first-floor level on the west side of the prior's lodging (now the nucleus of the mansion), as depicted by Symonds (Fig 15; Fig 16) where box bay windows are shown. Nash's drawing of *c* 1810 (Fig 92) shows that by then there were rather similar bay windows rising through the first and second floors, but the window forms are understandably very different and the façade had probably been rebuilt at least once since 1500. The nearest analogies for the window arrangements shown by Symonds are a series of four rectangular bay windows at first-floor level forming part of a range built on the east side of New Palace Yard, Westminster, in the reign of Henry VIII (Colvin 1966, 30–1, pl 11). It is therefore suggested here that the building accounts of 1541–2 might refer to the modelling of the range with bay windows, although the windows have also been left in the reconstruction drawings as though they date to the early 16th century, the end of the monastic occupation. It is possible (and – from analogies supplied by numerous courtly houses of the mid 16th century – likely) that the bay windows also embellished a further, second floor of the range, but there is no direct evidence for this. However, since it is also possible that the range of windows to the court were built in the early 16th century, in the monastic period, they have also been included in the reconstruction drawings of the priory in *c* 1500 (Fig 139; Fig 140).

Stow's story of what happened to the priory buildings is vivid:

> Then was the priory church and steeple proferred to whomsoever would take it down ... but no man would undertake the offer, whereupon Sir Thomas Audley was fain to be at no more charges than could be made of the stones, timber, lead, iron, etc. For the workmen, with great labour, beginning at the top, loosed stone from stone and threw them down, whereby the most part of them were broken and few remained whole; and those were sold very cheap, for all the buildings then made about the city were of brick and timber. (Stow 1603, i, 142)

One question is, what does 'then' mean here? Jeffries Davies (1925, 20), quoting this passage, assumes that it referred to 1535, and conjures up a delightful image of Stow, the ten-year-old boy who lived nearby, gaping at this strange event. But Wyngaerde's panorama (Fig 10), conventionally dated to 1544, shows the priory church totally intact, with its roofs on. This problem cannot at present be resolved satisfactorily. Perhaps by 'then' Stow meant as late as 1544; or perhaps another look at the evidence for the dating of the Wyngaerde panorama will pull it back to *c* 1535. The present study puts the date of the Wyngaerde drawing at '*c* 1540' to get out of this difficulty, and this date does not disagree with the evidence of the drawing itself; some of the annotations on the drawing suggest a later date, but could have been added later.

Audley was in possession, and in residence, by 1535, and died in 1544. In 1558 Thomas Howard, 4th Duke of Norfolk, married Margaret, the elder of Audley's two daughters, and occupied the house; Queen Elizabeth visited it two days before her coronation in 1559 (Williams 1964, 48). She probably came a second time in 1561, when Sir William Cecil noted in his diary that she dined with him at Cecil House in the Strand, 'and she came by the fields from Christ Church' (Wheatley and Cunningham 1891, i, 343); in other words, she took the quick route by skirting the City on its north side. Thus there might have been two periods of noble rebuilding, under Audley and under Norfolk. In 1564, the duke bought the Charterhouse, across the City, and transferred his main business there (Knowles and Grimes 1954, 38). There are portraits both of the Duke of Norfolk and of Margaret Audley (Fig 145), dating to 1563 and 1562 respectively, which may have been painted to hang in Duke's Place at Aldgate (rather than at Charterhouse as suggested by Hearn (1995, 70–1, figs 27, 31)). There is no documentary evidence for building at Duke's Place under the duke in 1558–64, though it is possible that, in the spirit of

Fig 145 Portrait of Margaret Audley (1540–64) by Hans Eworth, painted in 1562 when the town house of the Duke of Norfolk was Duke's Place (English Heritage)

courtiers in the later Elizabethan years, he might have fitted it out for the queen's visit. The name Duke's Place, which must derive from Norfolk rather than Audley, suggests that Norfolk might have built the Ivy chamber and the gallery to it, presumably before 1564, to be surveyed in *c* 1585 by Symonds.

The household of the Duke of Norfolk would have been extensive and no doubt many retainers were housed in the buildings around the great court. One of Norfolk's entourage was his favourite boyhood tutor, John Foxe, the Protestant thinker and writer. Fox returned from exile during the Marian years, and at Norfolk's invitation lived at Duke's Place for 11 years from 1559 until he bought a house in Grub Street, near Cripplegate, in 1570. While Foxe lived at Duke's Place the first edition of his *Acts and Monuments* (1563) was published in London; and there too in 1568 his son Simeon was born (Mozley 1940, 62). Unfortunately Foxe's tenancy there cannot be more closely identified.

The duke's wife Margaret died in childbirth in 1564; by the end of that year, Howard was negotiating to buy Charterhouse and then moved there. He was executed in 1572, leaving his son Thomas aged 11; the estate went into wardship and the custody of Sir Thomas Bromley, Lord Chancellor (Marsden 1992, 19). In 1579 the City was disturbed about some building works undertaken by Bromley along the north side of the precinct, by the two interval towers or turrets (CLRO, Repertories, 19, fos 418, 476b, 518b; 20, fos 10, 13b). Thomas Howard came into his estate in 1582 and ten years later the City bought the precinct from him (CLRO, Repertories, 22, fo 417b; 23, fo 11).

The outline of the post-Dissolution mansion can be extracted from the Symonds plans (Fig 146). The name Duke's Place, later given to the whole precinct and even later to the street which still runs on the north side of the precinct, was originally the name of Norfolk's mansion forming the west range of the cloister. Presumably the entrance gate, the subsidiary buildings around the great court, and the monastic kitchen were simply taken over and kept in use, as at many other monastic sites. The roofs above the main vessels of the east arm and the nave have been removed and the Ivy chamber occupies the central crossing at first-floor level. A gallery leads from the main range of the

Fig 146 A reconstruction of the site recorded by Symonds in c 1585: 1 – church half demolished; 2 – Duke's Place (scale 1:1250)

mansion along the former north aisle of the nave to the Ivy chamber, and the nave has become a garden.

A glimpse of the interior of the main range much later is shown by Schnebbelie in 1822 (Fig 94; Fig 95). By 1822, the range on its eastern, inner claustral side and south of the passage had been divided into four houses of equal width (shown in Schnebbelie's inset plan, Fig 95). These do not seem to equate to the bays in the medieval range indicated by the buttresses shown by Symonds, and it therefore seems likely that the range had been rebuilt at least once (and perhaps more times) between 1585 and 1822. Even so, the masonry spine-wall of the range survived until 1822. Correspondence with the Symonds plan shows that the whole of site F lay beneath the west range of the cloister and, therefore, beneath the main range of the post-Dissolution Duke's Place mansion. There were, however, no deposits which could be assigned to the immediately post-Dissolution period, up to *c* 1580.

From the mansion and the main range, description can move to the former priory church, which Audley at least partly destroyed. The Symonds plans show that the junction of the main range of the house with the former west end of the priory church was still formed – for at least the two surveyed storeys – by the great tower, originally perhaps of late 12th-century date. From here a gallery led along the north side of the ruined church, supported on a wall which ran between the piers of the north aisle.

It seems likely that the noble mansion of Audley and of the Duke of Norfolk (Fig 147) included both the gallery and the Ivy chamber which had been built out of the crossing of the

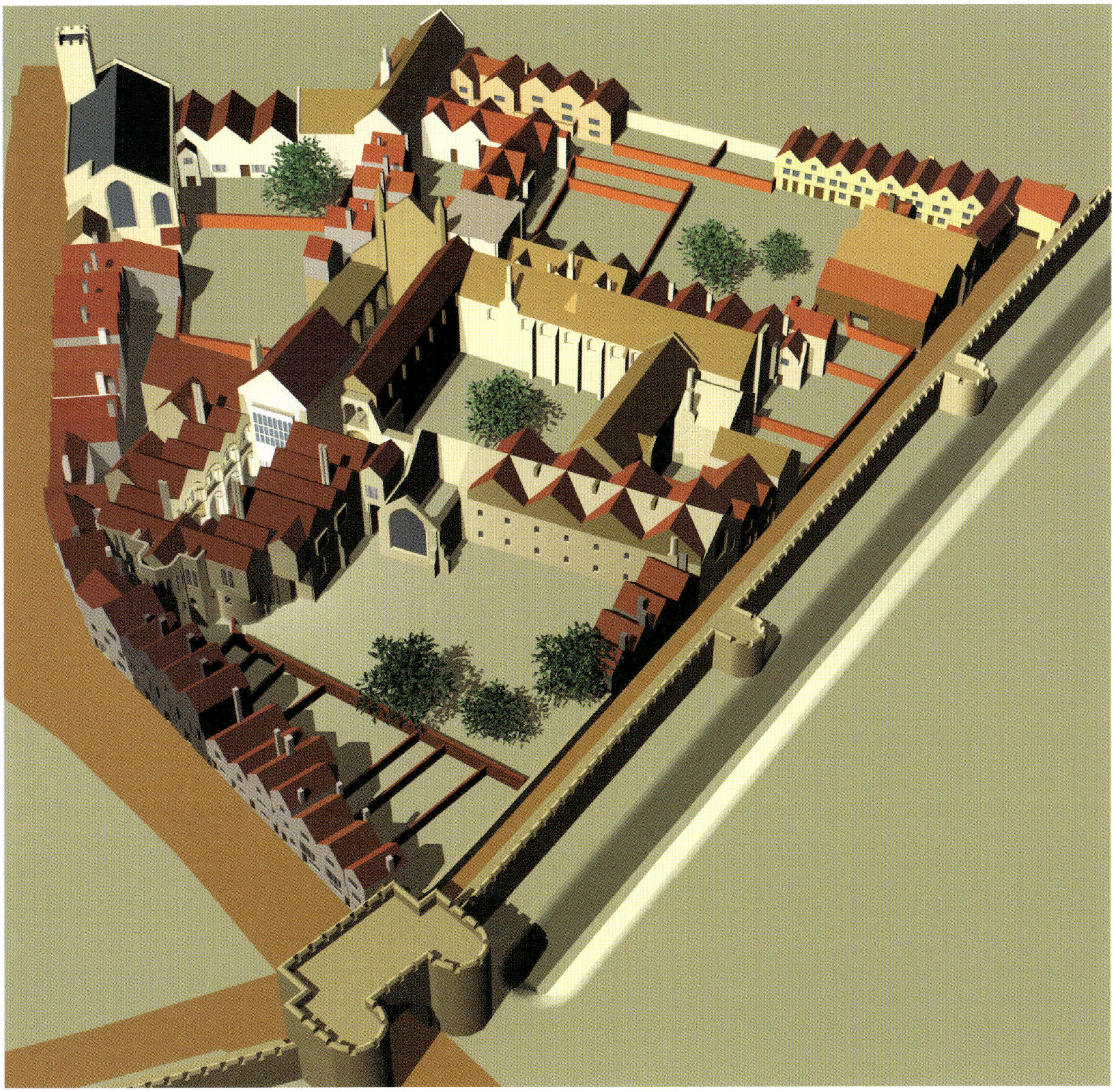

Fig 147 Reconstructed three-dimensional view of the former priory, c 1585 (Richard Lea)

priory church, as shown by Symonds; though the same first-floor plan (Fig 15; Fig 16) shows that by *c* 1585 the gallery had been interrupted by having a partition with a chimney built across it. The south aisle of the nave had been demolished at first-floor and higher levels.

A reconstruction of the east end of the former church in *c* 1585, including the Ivy chamber, is given in Fig 148. The conjunction of ancient fabric and new, no doubt partly in brick, may have looked somewhat like the surviving north nave wall at St Augustine's, Canterbury, which was rebuilt with brickwork of 1539 along its several bays and even reusing the nave responds to provide perched first-floor buttresses in brick.

Artefacts from the excavation sites which might be attributable to the Audley or Norfolk residences are almost totally lacking. The only item of relevance – and that not directly – is a piece of Continental stove tile on site F, to which other pieces found in the precinct in the past can be joined as a group (Chapter 8.4). It is proposed that some may derive from a single or a small number of identical stoves commissioned for the residence of the Duke of Norfolk in the 1560s.

There is, therefore, virtually no archaeological evidence to report for the immediately post-Dissolution structure of the main range of Duke's Place, or any post-Dissolution reuse of the great tower or construction of the gallery along the north aisle

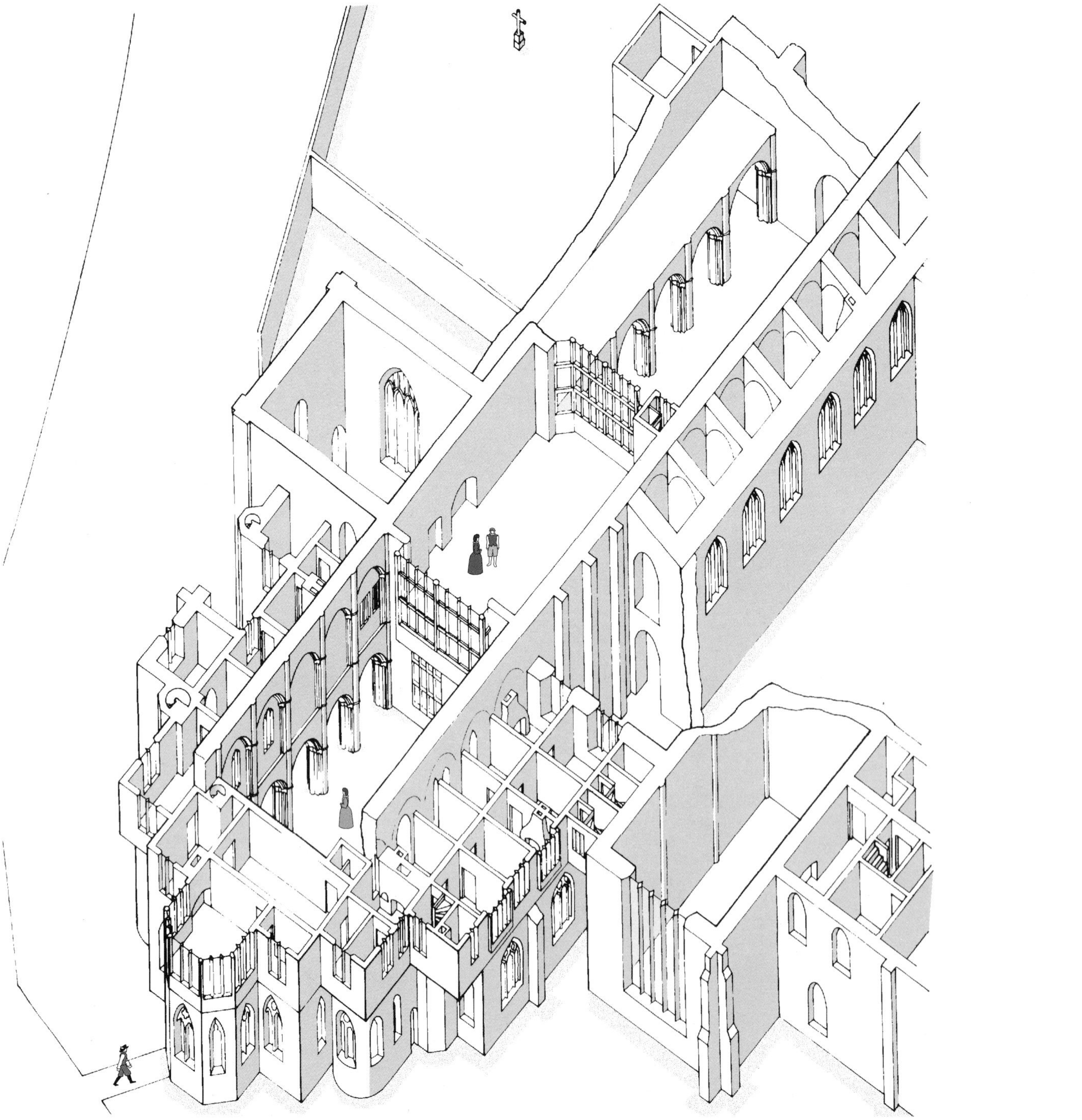

Fig 148 Axonometric reconstruction of the east end of the church and the Ivy chamber as surveyed by Symonds, c 1585 *(see Figs 13–16) (Richard Lea)*

of the former nave or of the Ivy chamber. Thus, the main range of Duke's Place remains known only from the watercolours, engravings and Symonds plans.

The Ivy chamber comprised an imposing space in the crossing of the former church, looking down on one side into the roofless presbytery with its 12th-century arcades, and on the other side into a garden made out of the nave of the church, in which the stumps of the nave piers could still be seen. On one side of the garden was the gallery, as in many Tudor mansions; on the other side, bordering the churchyard of St Katherine Cree, the south wall of the nave had been taken down to perhaps just above the tops of the aisle windows. This complex of gallery plus garden plus chamber, which was probably a combination of a banqueting house and viewing platform, is well known in rural houses of the period; an exactly contemporary example of the high banqueting house is the belvedere tower of Melbury House (Dorset) of *c* 1530–40 (Girouard 1978, 79). The gallery–garden–banqueting house combination was also present in other London mansions of any size occupied by prominent citizens or diplomats (Schofield 1999; 2003a, 89).

Mansions or lodgings of prominent people

By *c* 1585 there were two tenancies of notable people on the site of the priory church: a mansion bordering and including the south transept, which was sold to Henry Billingsley, a future Lord Mayor, in 1590; and the tenancy of Sir Francis Hinde, which was entirely at first-floor level around the east end of the former presbytery, looking down into the adjacent Leadenhall Street (or Aldgate Street, as the section immediately within the gate was known). Both tenancies were presumably originally part of the post-Dissolution mansion.

Documentary evidence

HENRY BILLINGSLEY

On the Symonds plans 'Darsey' occupied the south transept. The transept chapel (chapel 1) was part of Darsey's tenancy on the ground floor (Fig 13; Fig 14), but was entered from the adjacent Hinde tenancy on the first floor (Fig 15; Fig 16). The Darsey or Darcey tenancy was sold to Henry Billingsley by Lord Thomas Howard, the executed Duke of Norfolk's heir, in 1590 (GL, MS 7329/1). This comprised an 'edifice built with stones' on its east side, a garden to the west with a passage through the parish churchyard to Leadenhall Street, and a yard to the east, along with some other smaller units. In all it consisted of nine elements:

1) the great message, 83ft 5in (26.07m) north–south including a wall on its north side, 27ft 7in (8.42m) east–west;
2) a kitchen 12ft 11in (3.94m) east–west and 14ft 5in (4.42m) north–south 'next the yard and on the south side of the court or entry';
3) an 'edifice built with stones' on the east side of the main message, between it and the yard, on the north side of which were tenants of Auncell (who is named on the Symonds plan);
4) a garden to the west of the great message, between it and 'the churchyard' to the west, which was rhomboid in shape, 43ft 5in (13.24m) east–west along a brick wall on the north, 39ft 2in (11.96m) east–west along the south, 64ft 4in (19.62m) north–south along the west and 47ft 6in (14.49m) along the east; at the north-east corner, a stone foundation of the great message protruded into the garden;
5) a passage from the garden through the churchyard to the street;
6) the yard on the east side of the great message (which had a door into it), 42ft 6in (12.96m) east–west to a partition with the tenement of Marjorie Bradshaw, and 38ft 9in (11.82m) north–south from the brick wall forming the north side of the yard to the back of a tenement fronting (ie south) onto the street (ie Leadenhall Street);
7) a small message containing two shops and an entry from the Broad Way or Street (not identifiable) between those of William Melson on the west and Mrs Bradshaw to the east, the yard to the north and the High Street (Leadenhall Street perhaps) to the south;
8) a shed in the yard, now in the tenure of Walter Stopen;
9) a moiety (half) of a stable which, from its position adjacent both to London Wall and to the tenement in the tenure of Gregory Greene, 'used as a Schoole of Defence' (see Symonds ground-floor plan: Fig 13; Fig 14) lay in the north range of the priory great court.

It can be suggested that the great message included the south transept (shown in Darcey's tenure on the Symonds plan), and the building south of it which is partially shown by Symonds. The 'edifice built of stones' on the east of the message, on the north side of the yard, may have been chapel 1 (the brick walls noted below were only in the basement), though its upper part is shown to be in a different tenancy by Symonds, a few years before (see 'Sir Francis Hinde', below). On Ogilby and Morgan's map of the area in 1676 (Fig 18), these buildings can be tentatively identified; an alley runs from the likely site of the house through the churchyard to reach Leadenhall Street by going through the main gate of St Katherine Cree. But as argued above, chapel 1 had almost certainly disappeared by 1676. The garden and way to the gate are also shown on Symonds's ground-floor plan (Fig 13; Fig 14).

Thus we can reconstruct from documentary sources and Symonds, in part, the ground-plan of the house of Henry Billingsley, sheriff in 1584 and Lord Mayor for part of the year 1596. The 'great message' included both floors of the south transept, with the range extending south in unknown form (though presumably of post-Dissolution date) to Leadenhall Street, where there would have been a frontage of at least three storeys.

Billingsley, a member of the Haberdashers' Company, seems to have been living in the adjacent parish of St Katherine Coleman in 1582, when he was assessed for the subsidy roll, and was the highest-taxed householder in the parish, paying twice as much as the next highest payer; and twice as much as either Sir Francis Hinde or Sir Henry Darcey in St Katherine Cree parish (ie probably in their tenancies as described by Symonds in 1585)

(Lang 1993, nos 185, 189). He was President of St Thomas's Hospital from 1594 until his death in 1606 (Archer 1991, 141–2). Billingsley is also of note as the translator of *The Elements of Geometrie of Euclid*, published in 1570 with an introduction by John Dee which asserted the primacy of architecture over all the other mathematical arts and 'carefully explained the Renaissance idea of the architect', with supporting quotations from Vitruvius and Alberti (Airs 1995, 49; the title page of the translation is reproduced in Wittkower 1974, fig 121). Billingsley in his younger years was, in his own small way, one of the scholars involved in transmitting ancient knowledge to the present, part of the wider spirit of enquiry we call the Renaissance. His collaborator, John Dee (1527–1608), the famous Elizabethan mathematician and writer on alchemy, had lived in Mortlake, south-west of London, since 1570 (Smith 1909, 30), and so cannot be associated directly with this house.

By the time Thomas Hosmer Shepherd drew the buildings in this part of the street, in the mid 19th century (Fig 149; Fig 150),

Fig 149 Houses in Leadenhall Street, 1853, watercolour by T H Shepherd (LMA, SC/PZ/CT/01/108)

Fig 150 Houses in Leadenhall Street, 1853, pencil drawing by T H Shepherd (Guildhall Library)

the Billingsley property had been rebuilt at least once. The houses next door to the west, however, retained their bland timber-framed upper floors in Shepherd's drawings, and were probably built around Billingsley's time or a generation later.

SIR FRANCIS HINDE

In *c* 1585, according to the first-floor plan by Symonds, Sir Francis Hinde was tenant of a suite of rooms over the east end of the presbytery, with two rooms at the beginning of the north side (in line with the north presbytery aisle) and a similar pair of rooms along the south side of the presbytery, including the upper part of chapel 1 (Fig 15; Fig 16). Although the timber-framed ranges included many windows looking east over Aldgate, there were also two windows in the gallery arches of the presbytery. At this first-floor level, Symonds shows that the outer south wall of the presbytery between the two chapels had been replaced in timber, and also had windows. It seems likely, from the arrangement of the stairs, that further chambers lay above. The semi-octagonal bay window at the first floor of the east end of Hinde's tenancy was structurally based on the medieval masonry which still survived below; but the octagonal shape was also very modern, being a style common at country houses of the 1580s and 1590s. Hinde's tenancy, entirely on the first floor, was apparently entered by the spiral stair situated immediately east of the arch into chapel 2.

Symonds does not say who, if anyone, was tenant of the ground-floor part of the south presbytery aisle, through which entrance was gained to Hinde's stair. Symonds shows north and south aisles and the eastern chapel open, with no obstructions between the piers. It is not certain, from the combined evidence of archaeology and the plans, when the blocking of the arch into chapel 2 took place. It could have been at any time during the period 1532–1755, when it is shown on the lease plan of the latter year, with a doorway through it (Fig 20, in the south wall of the bay labelled A). Although the blocking is not shown by Symonds, there is again the suspicion that he omitted some details which conflicted with his desire to describe the detailed extent of the church.

Archaeological evidence

A sequence of immediately post-Dissolution features on site A is illustrated in plan (Fig 151; see also Table 2). Site A included much of the Darcey/Billingsley property. Because it is clear that by this time the development of the site of the former south transept and that of chapel 2, projecting from the south side of the choir to the east, were on separate secular properties, they are described separately.

THE SOUTH TRANSEPT AND CHAPEL 1

The fills of the large cut for emendation to the south-west corner of chapel 2 (gpA31, Fig 59) were sealed by an extensive sequence, up to 1.2m deep, comprising five layers of clayey and sandy silts, cut by two probable rubbish pits (gpA38; Fig 151). The layers included a significant amount of building material, amongst which roof slates and tiles were frequent, and which also included medieval window glass A<256> (gpA38; Chapter 8.6), a stone slate A<307> (Chapter 8.3) and worked stone. Most of the latter was ashlar, but one piece <A58> (Fig 194; Chapter 8.2,) possibly came from the crenellation of a screen or tomb. To the west there was a pronounced lip where the material had been deposited up against the external face of chapel 1. The considerable quantity of building material suggests that this was demolition debris.

The medieval wares assigned to group A38 (A[311], A[331], A[350], A[357]) comprise four fabric types that mainly date to *c* 1350 (93 sherds, 1267g, 0.30 EVEs). Sherds from the same vessels were noted in A[331] and A[350]. Most common is London-type ware (LOND), which includes sherds from up to four north French-style jugs, three highly decorated jugs, one baluster jug and one sherd from a cooking pot. Coarse Surrey-Hampshire border ware (CBW, 23 sherds) includes rounded and, possibly, conical jugs and 17 fragments from a single cistern dating to after 1340. The other wares comprise Mill Green ware (MG, 17 jug sherds), Kingston-type ware (KING, six jug sherds) and Cheam whiteware (CHEA, two sherds from a conical jug). Also present is a jetton A<34>, of 13th- or 14th-century date (Chapter 8.6). Overall, however, the

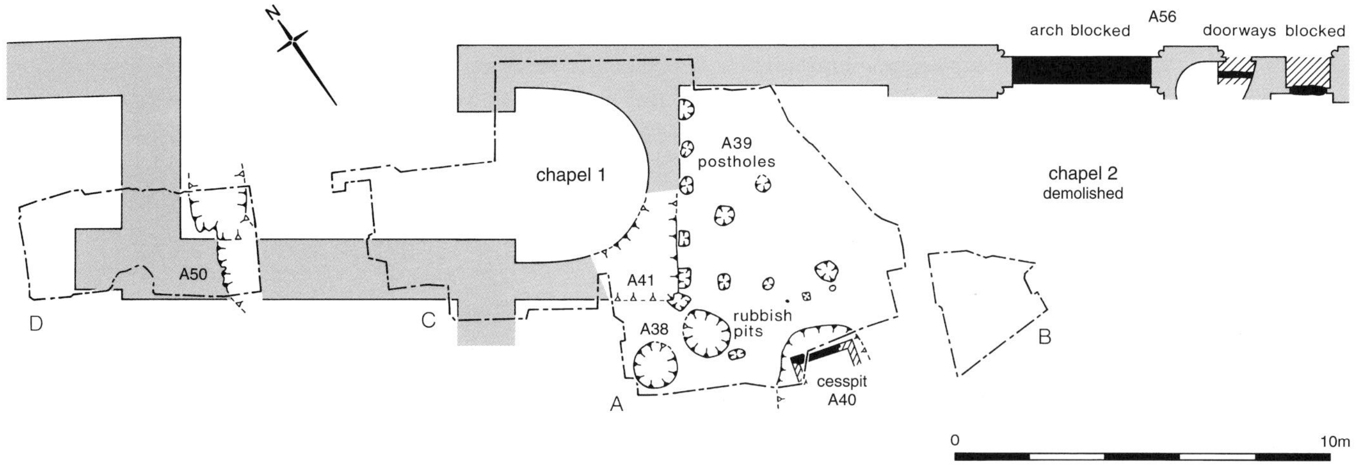

Fig 151 Plan of post-Dissolution period features on the site of the former south transept, including chapel 1 (site A, period VII, gpA38–A41, gpA50, gpA56) (scale 1:200)

group is taken to be of Dissolution date from the amount and variety of building material in it.

Group A39 consisted of 14 postholes and their fills which cut into group A38. Six of the larger postholes were placed directly against the external face of the east wall of chapel 1. This structure covered the western two thirds of area A in a grid-like pattern, filling an area 5.0m east–west by 5.4m north–south between chapels 1 and 2. The southern limit of the structure was aligned with the south sides of both chapels to east and west. There were no contemporary surfaces between the posts and no direct evidence as to their exact nature or function. Although they might represent a building of some kind on posts, another possible interpretation is that it was scaffolding erected against chapel 1, in order to effect its demolition or to gain access to the crossing tower and presbytery roof. Probably part of this process was a demolition cut (gpA41) observed in the masonry of the south-east corner of chapel 1.

The pottery from the group A39 postholes comprises three sherds (55g) of London-type ware (LOND), coarse London-type ware (LCOAR) and south Hertfordshire-type greyware (SHER) from A[232] and A[234], and seven of post-medieval date (86g). Of the latter, those from A[232] and A[285] comprise London-area early post-medieval redware (PMRE) and London-area post-medieval slipped redware (PMSR), which date to between *c* 1480 and *c* 1600; two sherds of green-glazed Surrey-Hampshire border ware (BORDG) and London-area post-medieval redware (PMR) from A[228] date to after *c* 1550 and *c* 1580 respectively, placing the removal of the posts in the second half of the 16th century.

To the south of the possible scaffolding was a brick-lined cesspit, the walls of which incorporated several pieces of reused ashlar. There were also four layers of clayey silts, which raised the ground level to 15.30m OD, and two pits with non-diagnostic fills (gpA40). The horizontal layers sloped downwards away from the level of the group A39 postholes, and might be demolition debris thrown from the scaffolding. The cesspit contained 25 sherds (523g, 0.39 EVEs). Fills A[310] and A[428] (gpA40) contained only medieval pottery dating to the mid 14th century (LOND, MG and CBW, including part of a cistern), but fill A[236] contained a single sherd of PMRE. Disregarding a PMR paint pot from A[278] as intrusive, the pottery from the fill of the cesspit might suggest that it was used in the late 15th century and that it was backfilled in the 16th century. The brick construction for a cesspit, however, suggests a date at least in the 16th century and possibly of the Dissolution period, since it included reused ashlar stones. Secondly, the backfill behind the brick lining of the cesspit (A[283], gpA40) contained a transitional group of pottery, with six sherds of 14th- or 15th-century date (CBW, late London-type ware (LLON), 'Tudor Green' ware (TUDG)), and ten of Tudor date. The latter comprise a range of redwares (early Surrey-Hampshire border redware (ERBOR), London-area early post-medieval redware (PMRE), and London-area post-medieval slip-decorated redware (PMSL)), a sherd of early Surrey-Hampshire border whiteware (EBORD), the base of a drinking jug in Raeren stoneware (RAER) and part of a central Italian tin-glazed ware (CITG) 'IHS' jug or vase with decoration in blue and white (<P68>, Fig 205). Thirdly, the cesspit was aligned with the adjacent Leadenhall Street rather than the priory church itself, suggesting that it lay at the rear of a property on the street. Taken together, this suggests a construction date between *c* 1530 and *c* 1550 for the cesspit.

In area D, two large cuts (gpA50) were probably associated with removal of a small length of the transept superstructure (though they were also on the site of a possible door in the medieval transept wall, for which there is no certain evidence), and were sealed by a mixed dump truncated at 13.52m OD.

The activity in this period is assigned to the Dissolution, here dated on documentary grounds from 1532 to *c* 1600. The amount of Roman residual pottery recovered from the backfill of two rubbish pits (gpA38) is noteworthy. Presumably the Dissolution destruction included some digging of the ground, perhaps to remove foundations, and this must have disturbed the underlying Roman stratification.

Further developments took place, also in the second half of the 16th century as suggested by a tight sequence of pottery dates. Immediately north of its mid point the east wall of chapel 1 was demolished and two phases of bricks added (gpA42.1, gpA42.2; Fig 152). The tops of these, at 14.86m OD and 15.07m OD, were close to the contemporary external ground level in area A, so they may have been roughly-made door sills. The north side of this possible door is shown in Fig 153. However, no jambs were observed, nor was there any marked compaction of the adjacent material in area A, such as would have occurred had there been any significant amount of traffic through it.

Truncating these small brick features, and surmounting the demolished wall of chapel 1 at 14.75m OD, was a 1.8m length of north–south orientated brick wall (gpA42.3), up to 0.8m high, the bricks laid in English bond (Fig 155). Parallel to it was a similar brick wall in English bond (gpA42.5), up to 2.91m in height and butted up against the former entrance from the church transept into chapel 1 (Fig 154). The two walls formed the east and west walls of a cellar, the digging of which had removed all the pre-Dissolution internal surfaces of chapel 1. Its north and part of its east walls made use of the chapel walls, and it was probably entered from the south (though there was only negative evidence for this). The east wall contained the lower part of a window opening (gpA42.3; Fig 155). The beaten earth floor (gpA42.4) of the cellar was at 13.10m OD, and in its centre stood a large block of yellow sandstone, presumably support for a timber post. No evidence survived for the roofing arrangements. Only six sherds (51g) of pottery were found in the group A42 demolition deposits (A[253], A[265], A[320]). Two are of medieval date (CBW, CHEA), while three, from A[253], are from different vessels in yellow-glazed Surrey-Hampshire border whiteware (BORDY, *c* 1550–*c* 1700). A further sherd from A[265] could be a Continental, German whiteware (GERW, *c* 1550–*c* 1630). The creation of the cellar is placed in the second half of the 16th century.

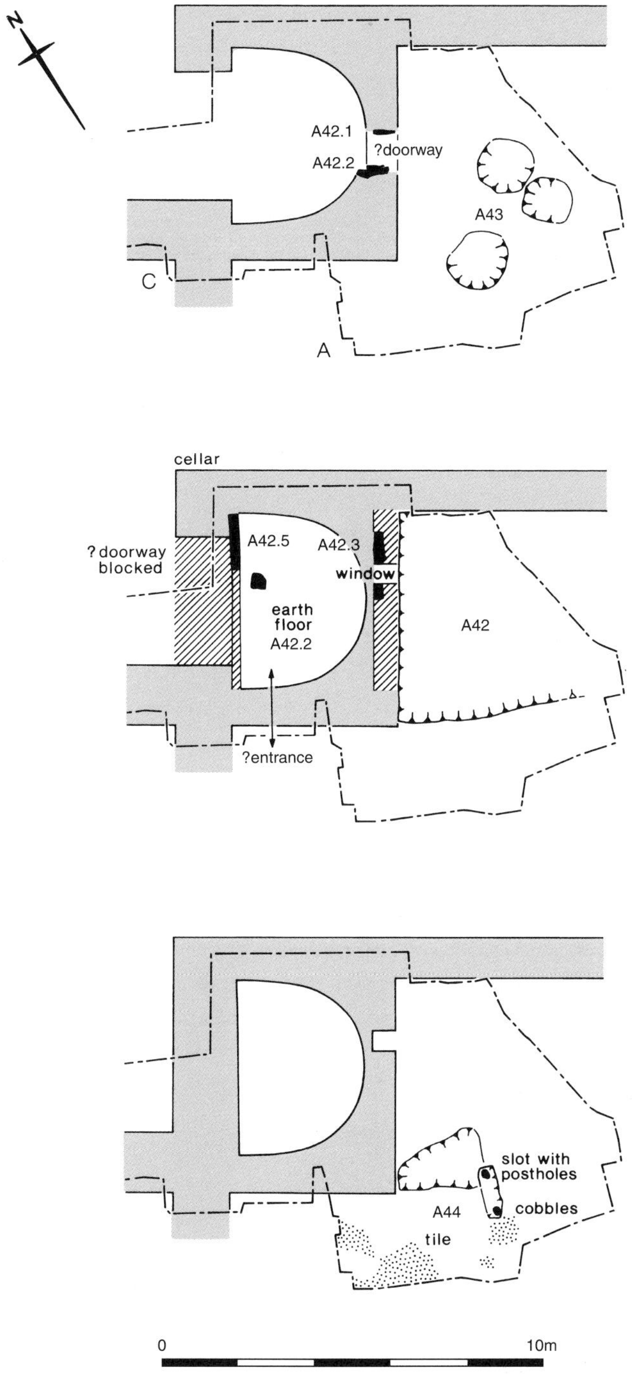

Fig 152 *Plans of successive stages of post-Dissolution period alterations to the south transept chapel 1 (site A, period VIII, gpA42–A44: top –VIIIa; middle –VIIIb; bottom –VIIIc) (scale 1:200)*

Fig 153 *Traces of a possible doorway through the east wall of chapel 1 in the post-Dissolution period (site A, gpA42.1–A42.2; cf Fig 152), with (towards the top) a line of bricks running across the line of the chapel wall; looking north (0.2m scale)*

In area A, the postholes and brick cesspit (period VII, gpA39, gpA40; Fig 151) were sealed by a sequence of four layers of clayey and sandy silts (gpA43), which raised the ground level to 15.60m OD. The uppermost of these incorporated a concentration of small stones which may have formed a surface. There were also four pits. The group A43 dumps contained 94 sherds of pottery (3002g, 2.03 EVEs), including ten residual medieval sherds which were scattered in every layer in this group (A[181], A[200], A[258], A[268] and A[308]). Layers A[258] and A[268] and pit fill A[308] probably date to the Dissolution. These contained a range of Tudor redwares (London-area post-medieval bichrome redware (PMBR), London-area early post-medieval redware (PMRE), London-area early post-medieval redware with metallic glaze (PMREM), London-area post-medieval slip-decorated redware (PMSL), including a skillet from A[268], with fragments of Martincamp-type ware (MART) and Raeren stoneware (RAER) from A[308], and a sherd from a tin-glazed Malling-type vase and part of a small central Italian tin-glazed (CITG) vase with floral decoration (<P67>, Fig 205) from A[268].

The larger dumps of pottery in group A43, A[181] and A[200] (64 sherds, 1583g, 1.56 EVEs), which sealed the earlier pits/layers are slightly later in date, as they contain sherds of Surrey-Hampshire border whiteware (BORD), single sherds of London-area post-medieval redware (PMR), Weser slipware (WESE) and a sherd of biscuit tin-glazed (BISC) albarello (<P45>, Fig 202) and another from the base of a plain blue-glazed jug or albarello, possibly a waster (A[200], <P46>, Fig 202). Context A[200] also contained part of a tin-glazed ring-handled vase. Redwares (PMRE, PMREM, PMR and PMSL) were most common in A[181], while Surrey-Hampshire border whitewares, although present in A[181], were more common in A[200]; both are represented by a wide range of forms, which include a flared handled bowl in green-glazed Surrey-Hampshire border whiteware (BORDG) from A[181] (cf Pearce 1992, 14–15, no. 101). A date of *c* 1580–*c* 1600 seems likely

Fig 154 *View of brick wall in the west side of the former south transept chapel 1 (site A, gpA42.5; cf Fig 152), looking west (0.5m scale)*

for these dumps, which may therefore be contemporary with the finds from group A39 (see above).

Group A44 was confined to the south part of area A, and comprised a multiplicity of small layers of sandy and clayey silts, some layers having significant proportions of powdered chalk or brickearth. In the central part of the area was a shallow north–south orientated slot, with a posthole at each end. This represented some flimsy or temporary structure. Just to the south of this was a small area of closely packed fragments of ragstone forming a cobbled surface at 16.07m OD. This was very well worn with no sharp corners, and sealed by three thin layers of trample. About 2.0m to the west were two slightly larger areas of horizontally-laid fragments of roof tile at a mean height of 15.50m OD. Whether these were part of the same horizon as the cobbled surface was not clear, but certainly there was considerable activity at this time in what was apparently still an external area. No edges of the surfaces survived to show whether the cobbled and tile surfaces were linear paths or yard areas.

A group of 56 sherds (1792g, 1.52 EVEs) was recovered from the cobbled surface and rubbish pit (gpA44, A[127], A[136], A[246], A[247], A[252], A[256]), of which only one is of medieval date. This was found in A[127], which also contained Raeren stoneware (RAER), Frechen stoneware (FREC), a sherd from a late Siegburg stoneware (SIEGL) jug with an armorial stamp, and a range of redwares and Surrey-Hampshire border whitewares; but the latter are absent from the other contexts in this group. A vase or small jar from A[246] with decoration of blue lines around the base is problematic but may be Italian or from the southern Netherlands; the profile is unlike that seen on the biscuit-fired

Fig 155 *View of brick used to rebuild the east wall of the former south transept chapel 1 (site A, gpA42.1–42.2; cf Fig 152), with a window opening (gpA42.3) in the middle, looking east-north-east (0.2m scale)*

wares from the pit group F22 (F[220]) (see below). Most wares would seem to date to *c* 1550–*c* 1600, and a single handle from a plain white tin-glazed chamber pot in A[247] (*c* 1630+) may be intrusive. The group also contained a copper-alloy Nuremberg jetton of the early 16th century (A<12>, A[127]; Chapter 8.6).

The evidence for the immediately post-Dissolution changes to the south transept and land south of it, which stretched off the excavation to the contemporary Leadenhall Street to the south, comprises the following (summarised in Table 13). During the second half of the 16th century, chapel 1 on the south transept had its lowest part converted into a cellar, at first with a doorway to the east but soon after blocked up. There may then have been an entrance through the terminal wall on the south side. Surfaces and a cesspit to the south suggest development of the property along Leadenhall Street at this point. The 'edifice built with stones' in Billingsley's purchase in 1590 may have been chapel 1, which had evidently been adapted for storage, perhaps as a warehouse. In effect the tenant of the Leadenhall Street property, by 1590 Sir Henry Darcey, had encroached onto the priory church site by taking tenancy of the south transept, as shown by Symonds, and the south transept was, therefore, sold with the property to Billingsley in that year.

THE BLOCKING OF THE ARCH OF CHAPEL 2 AND WORKS NEARBY

The arch into chapel 2 was at least partially blocked with rough coursed masonry faced with reused moulded Reigate stone A[25] (gpA56; Fig 156). The doorway at the top of the spiral stair was similarly blocked with rubble A[77] (gpA56; Fig 156). The stones used in the blocking A[25] included the largest group of moulded fragments recovered from the priory. They included, from the 12th century, a nook shaft, a large bowtell moulding, pieces of the chevron voussoir also found in group A53, an Attic base, two abaci, and possible vaulting fragments; from the 13th century, parts of three doorways (or two doorways and a cupboard or window), drip-mouldings, and a possible vault rib later recut perhaps for a door; from the later medieval period, pieces of at least two glazed windows in Reigate stone, a third glazed and traceried window, seven fragments of an arch, door or window, hood-moulds, ogee mouldings, octagonal shafts, a piece from a tomb, a piece possibly from a fireplace, coping stones, plain chamfers and rolls and other fragments, in a variety of stone types (Chapter 8.2).

The projecting part of the spiral staircase and the east, south and west walls of chapel 2 appear to have been demolished down to 15.80m OD. The door to the spiral staircase A[1453] was blocked (A[1454]) as was the door to the east (A[1455]) with blocking A[1456] (Fig 156). Brick and reused moulded stone and some timber were used to infill the upper part of the door to the staircase and form a north–south wall A[36], A[32] and A[83] with plastered faces A[85] and A[84]. The window opening was enlarged down to the new ground level to create a new large opening through the wall. The cut edges were finished with plaster A[87] and plaster and lath of an external character A[88]. The lower part of the new opening used the east jamb of the earlier door. The profile of the plastered surfaces at the bottom of the enlarged window, especially on the east side, suggests jettied buildings constructed against the surviving medieval masonry, and a slight jetty on each side of a passage leading to the new opening, with a first floor at the level of the medieval capitals.

The demolition of chapel 2 and its associated staircase, the reuse of much medieval stonework and the blocking of doors all clearly argue, however, that these are post-Dissolution alterations and presumably occurring after the Symonds survey of *c* 1585, since he shows the arch unblocked (Fig 13; Fig 14). The destruction of the spiral stair and blocking of its doorway stopped up the entry to Hinde's tenement above.

The blocking of the arch can only be dated to after the Symonds survey of *c* 1585, and could be of period P2 (after 1600, up to about 1730) as well as at the end of period P1. The plan of Smith and Cust's lease of 1755 which included the site of the chapel (Fig 20) shows that by that date the arch had been rebuilt as a brick wall, but that a doorway now went through it.

A BRICK WALL AND FURTHER BURIALS ON SITE E

On site E, immediately to the west of site A and comprising part of the south wall of the priory church nave (Fig 2; Fig 4),

Table 13 Summary of immediately post-Dissolution activity on the excavated part of site A (period P1)

Group	Date (approximate)	Interpretation
Period VII		
A38	medieval artefacts but post-Dissolution context	rubbish pits on property to south
A39	1550–1600	postholes, possibly scaffolding
A40	1550+	cesspit at rear of property on Leadenhall Street
A41	not dated, probably contemporary with group A39	
A50	not dated	removal of small part of transept wall or removal of masonry of monastic period doorway
Period VIII		
A42.1, A42.2	not dated	doorway forced into lower part of chapel 1 from east
A42.3–A42.5	1550–1600	cellar in lower part of chapel 1 (doorway out of use)
A43	1580–1600	dumps east of former transept
A44	1550–1600	surfaces of property to south

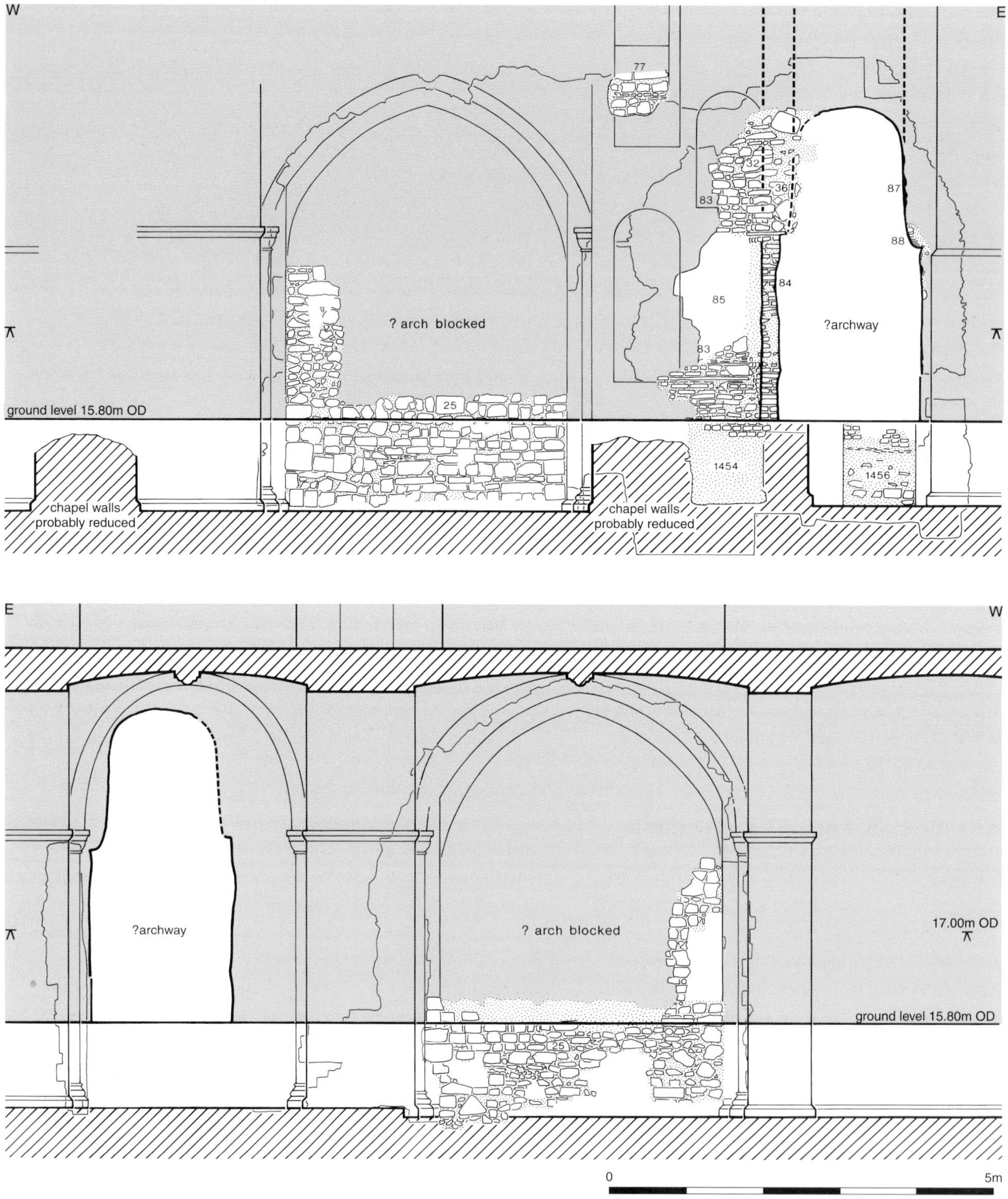

Fig 156 Elevations of the arch into former chapel 2, post-Dissolution contexts (site A, period VIII, gpA56) (original context numbers are shown, eg 84 = A[84]), drawing and interpretation: upper – south elevation; lower – north elevation (scale 1:80)

the period started with a sequence of dumps (gpE8, Table 2; not illustrated) containing building material which probably mark the destruction of the period IV nave wall, in as much as they physically sealed the demolished remains of one of the period V buttresses (Chapter 4.2; Fig 72), and it seems unlikely that the main wall would survive without its buttress. This activity is, therefore, equivalent to the demolition of chapel 1 (gpA39, A41) and the south transept (gpA50) during period VII of site A (Fig 151).

Four sherds of pottery were found in the dumped deposits assigned to group E8, of which one is residual medieval (E[22]). Those from E[58] comprise two sherds (from a green-glazed Surrey-Hampshire border whiteware (BORDG) cup and a London-area slip-decorated post-medieval redware (PMSL) dish) which could date to the later 16th century, and one from a north Italian marbled slipware (NIMS) bowl. The latter dates to after c 1600 and must be considered intrusive (a common problem with the excavation of graveyard soils, as here) because of the relationship of the destruction debris group E8 with an overlying wall that is shown by Symonds in *c* 1585 (Fig 13; Fig 14; for dating see Chapter 3.3).

Cutting into the destruction debris was a brick and stone wall running north–south (ecclesiastical alignment). It rested directly on, and was aligned with, the easternmost of the semi-demolished period V buttresses (shown in plan, Fig 72, bottom right, period VI; elevation, background of Fig 73), and there was a pronounced vertical crack caused by part of the wall not supported by the buttress having subsided into the soft graveyard soil.

The shallow foundation of the wall consisted of two courses of squared and moulded blocks of Reigate stone and yellow sandstone. The superstructure consisted of blocks of reused stone, mostly Reigate stone, capped with two courses of tile laid flat, and five courses of small hand-made bricks laid in alternate courses of headers and stretchers. There followed a course of Reigate stone and yellow sandstone, and three courses of bricks, with this pattern repeated again at the top of the wall. The superstructure stood to a height of 2.4m, but was not sufficiently robust to be load-bearing; it was probably a free-standing boundary wall rather than part of a building. This wall marked the eastern limit of the graveyard of the church of St Katherine Cree; it is shown on the Symonds plan (Fig 13; Fig 14), and must, therefore, date from before 1585. The fact that the wall rested on a buttress in a semi-demolished state suggests that the wall was built in the immediately post-Dissolution period.

Occupants and immigrants, 1532–92 (period P1)

The precinct of Holy Trinity has a second post-Dissolution history besides that of the noble house and properties of the well-to-do which occupied parts of it. During the 16th century, the precinct of St Katherine Cree, or Christchurch, became a socially independent entity with certain privileges and rules which set it apart from the outside City. This attracted immigrants, particularly foreigners who specialised in certain crafts; and it may later have influenced the decision by some well-placed London Jews to arrange, in the 1650s, for the first large influx of Jewish immigrants to London to settle in this area. The historical and archaeological development of the precinct in the 16th and 17th centuries is, therefore, of some significance.

Documentary evidence

In outline by 1541, and in detail by the 1570s, several industrial or trade-related uses can be detected in the priory buildings and its grounds. Some of the people involved were evidently London citizens, but others were immigrants. In the lay subsidy of 1541, 33 taxpayers are listed as 'strangers' living within the parish of St Katherine Cree (Lang 1993, no. 13). The term covered foreigners, either those who had been granted letters of denization or aliens (ibid, xx). Since the parish included a sizeable section of Aldgate and Fenchurch Street south of the precinct, it is not certain how many of these were actually occupants of the former priory. Their professions remain unknown, except that three are called 'Doctor' or 'Mr Doctor'. More certainly, by 1568 there were 159 'strangers' living in the precinct, of whom 145 were Dutch, 12 French and two Italian (Kirk and Kirk 1900–8, iii, 405–6). All these numbers refer to households, since it was the head of the household who was being taxed. The Dutch are traditionally thought to have come in part from Norwich, where by the early 17th century these 'strangers' accounted for approximately one third of the population of the city, and were a major force in its economic development at that time (Atkin 1993, 139). Thus, when Queen Elizabeth came to visit the Duke of Norfolk in 1559, the noble residence must already have been hemmed about with immigrant families.

More details are forthcoming in the lay subsidy of 1582. Here four households of Englishmen and 35 households of 'strangers' in the precinct are listed as being taxed (Lang 1993, nos 195–6). Presumably other English households were rated below the £3 threshold, and many other immigrants had less than £1 in moveable goods; these two groups would be exempt. The occupations of the 'strangers' are not given except in one case, that of Peter Busher, tailor, who was the highest-taxed one in the precinct.

Some of the tenants named by Symonds in *c* 1585 (Figs 13–16) ran businesses, possibly on the site; and those who are named as tenants all seem to have been English. Probably the most prominent, in that he occupied the largest area, was William Kerwin, mason. Kerwin had been appointed one of the four City Viewers in 1574 (CLRO, Repertory 18, fo 199) and was City Mason in the 1580s. It is possible that at the time of the Symonds survey of *c* 1585 he was using part of the priory as his place of work, perhaps as a builder's yard – and even as a quarry for building works such as the rebuilding in 1585–6 of Ludgate, for which he supplied at least some of the stone (Masters 1984, 38). He probably lived in Bishopsgate ward, since he is recorded as one of the petty collectors of the 1582 subsidy for that ward (Lang 1993, no. 210), and was buried in St Helen Bishopsgate church. His tomb (which survives) commemorates the death of his wife Magdalen in 1592 and his own death in 1594. The epitaph to Kerwin or Kirwin (transcribed and translated by Cox 1876, i, 59) reads:

> *Aedibus Attalicis, Londinum qui decoravi;*
> *Me duce surgebant aliis regalia tecta*
> *Exiguam tribuunt hanc mihi fata Domõ.*
> *Me duce conficitur, ossibus vinc meis.*
>
> The fates have afforded this narrow house to me, who have adorned London with noble buildings. By me, royal palaces were built for others. By me, this tomb is erected for my bones.

There are also inscriptions commemorating Magdalen and Benjamin Kirwin, son of William, who died in 1621. The tomb (which has been physically moved down and then up with the surrounding floor during major refurbishments in the 19th and 20th centuries) evidently originally stood over a vault, since Benjamin's inscription records that he had seven sons and five daughters, 'whereof five are buried in this vault'. The Latin *regalia tecta*, translated 'royal palaces' by Cox, is more literally 'royal roofs' or possibly 'royal buildings'. The identity of these buildings, and Kerwin's claimed connections with any royal building work, remain unknown, although he is recorded as building on several sites in the City for private owners and speculators from 1578 (IHR, London citizens MS, ii, 532–3).

There is also slight documentary evidence of two other commercial processes which would have required some installations: baking and the making or refining of sugar. The tenant of the former great kitchen in 1585 and in a lease of 1591 (LMA, Acc/2712/I/A/64 no. 1) was Brian Naylor, a baker. He is mentioned as living in the precinct in the lay subsidy of 1582 (Lang 1993, no. 195), when he was presumably occupying the kitchen.

In *c* 1585, as shown by Symonds, William Kerwin was laying out foundations on the site of the former prior's garden, in the great court. These must be the buildings shown on Ogilby and Morgan's map in 1676, where they are called Sugar Baker's Yard (Fig 18, marked h56). Their north side to the court in the early 19th century has already been shown (Fig 92); in 1884 John Crowther also drew the range, by then probably rebuilt piecemeal during the century (see Fig 173). It is not possible from the surviving evidence, all of it graphic, to make any suggestion that buildings were erected specially for industrial purposes by Kerwin. They may merely have been adapted for sugar production by 1676.

In the late 15th century, sugar was imported from Spain or Portugal (Cobb 1990, nos 12, 47–8, 107, 116). By the time of Ogilby and Morgan's map in 1676, however, there were 14 alleys in the City called Sugar Baker's Yard or Sugar Loaf Alley/Court. Some were outside the walls, but others were in the middle of the City, off Distaff Lane and Garlick Hill. They were part of a booming industry in the importation and refining of raw sugar from the Caribbean islands such as Jamaica and Barbados (Dunn 1972; Davis 1973, 132–3, 251–60; Brooks 1983). Refining works may have been established in London by the early 17th century, as they had been in Antwerp and Amsterdam. No installation manufacturing sugar has been excavated in the City, so the form of such works remains unknown.

The third industry which is to be expected on the former priory site was the making of tin-glazed pottery and tiles. A workshop was established near Aldgate in *c* 1570 by Jacob Jansen and Jasper Andries, and ceramics found previously in the area have been attributed to this workshop (Noël Hume 1977). Important further evidence of this pottery was found on site F in the present project, and the detailed documentary evidence for Jansen and his colleagues is drawn together in the specialist pottery appendix (Chapter 8.5).

Archaeological evidence

The plan for site F (Fig 157) shows for convenience the three groups (gpF19, gpF20, gpF22) which are assigned to periods P1 and P2 (see Table 2). Medieval walls on the west side of site F were robbed, probably at the Dissolution or soon after; they have been reported in the medieval period sequence (Chapter 4.5; Fig 109) to indicate their original functions (gpF19), but the robber trenches are noted here (with the same group number, gpF19). Of the other two groups shown on Fig 157 only one is of period P1: a pit seen in the watching brief (gpF22). Its contents are of great significance.

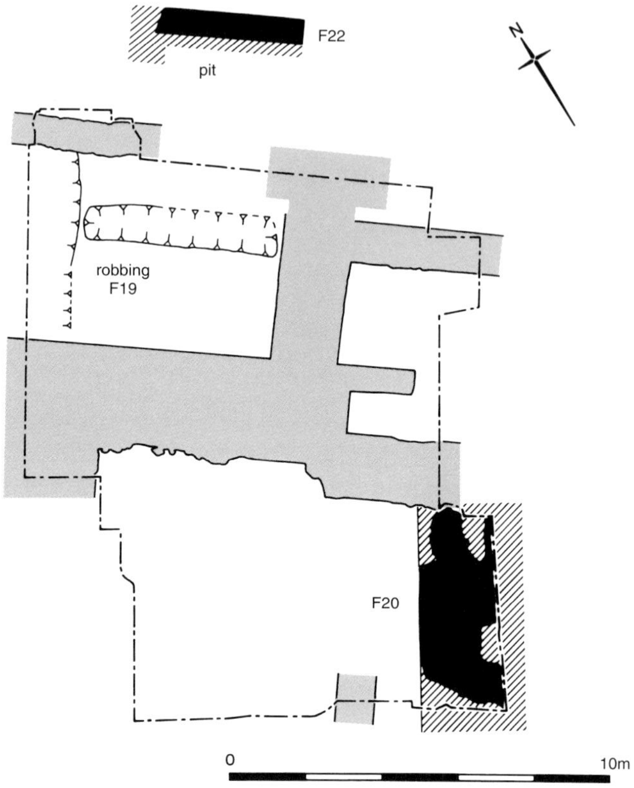

Fig 157 Plan of post-Dissolution (periods P1 and P2) activity on the site of the former west claustral range (site F, period IV, gpF19, gpF20, gpF22) (scale 1:200)

During construction works and when the concrete slab previously covering the northern part of the site (shown towards the bottom of Fig 98) had been removed, a pit at least 0.65m deep and at least 0.85m across was found in the north-west part of the site (gpF22; Fig 157). Two layers were recorded, of which the lower F[221] was composed of grey-green sandy silt with many flecks of charcoal, up to 0.35m deep, while the upper F[220] comprised bands of brown sandy clay with many inclusions of eggshell and oyster fragments alternating with bands of charcoal, and was up to 0.3m deep.

This feature contained the largest and most important single group of pottery from this site (441 sherds, 12,180g, 11.04 EVEs), furnishing evidence for both foreigners and pottery production in the area. The following paragraphs describe the contents of the pit as a group, summarised by fabric and function in Table 14 and Table 15, and selected sherds are illustrated (Fig 200; Figs 202–4). The wares, forms and other evidence for this Aldgate pottery manufactory are discussed more fully in Chapter 8.5.

The bulk of the pottery comprises ordinary domestic

Table 14 Relative frequency of different wares in a pit, group F22 (fills F[220] and F[221]) by sherd count, estimated number of vessels (ENV), weight (in g) and estimated vessel equivalent (EVE) (for fabric codes see Table 19)

Fabric	Sherd count	Sherd count %	ENV	ENV %	Weight (g)	Weight %	EVEs	EVEs %
ANDAL	1	0.2	1	0.8	19	0.2	0.02	0.2
BISC	109	24.7	29	22.3	3343	27.4	2.83	25.6
BORD	1	0.2	1	0.8	4	<0.1	-	-
BORDG	10	2.3	6	4.6	228	1.9	0.81	7.3
BORDO	9	2.0	1	0.8	82	0.7	-	-
BORDY	9	2.0	5	3.8	121	1.0	0.31	2.8
DUTR	14	3.2	10	7.7	490	4.0	0.42	3.8
DUTSL	22	5.0	2	1.5	305	2.5	0.75	6.8
FREC	5	1.1	2	1.5	473	3.9	0.25	2.3
PMBL	1	0.2	1	0.8	5	<0.1	-	-
PMR	8	1.8	2	1.5	438	3.6	0.32	2.9
PMRE	193	43.8	44	33.8	4478	36.8	3.67	33.2
PMREC	2	0.5	1	0.8	83	0.7	-	-
PMSRY	7	1.6	4	3.1	395	3.2	0.10	0.9
RAER	6	1.4	4	3.1	652	5.4	0.08	0.7
RBOR	23	5.2	1	0.8	520	4.3	0.50	4.5
TGW	14	3.2	12	9.2	314	2.6	0.75	6.8
TGW A	7	1.6	4	3.1	230	1.9	0.23	2.1
Total	**441**		**130**		**12180**		**11.04**	

Table 15 Relative frequency of the pottery in a pit, group F22 (fills F[220] and F[221]), according to functional category by sherd count, estimated number of vessels (ENV), weight (in g) and estimated vessel equivalent (EVE)

Fabric	Sherd count	Sherd count %	ENV	ENV %	Weight (g)	Weight %	EVEs	EVEs %
Display	2	0.5	1	0.8	160	1.3	-	-
Serving drinks	11	2.5	5	3.8	819	6.7	-	-
Drinking	4	0.9	4	3.1	397	3.3	0.25	2.3
Food (consumption)	2	0.5	2	1.5	22	0.2	0.18	1.6
Food (serving)	1	0.2	1	0.8	34	0.3	0.39	3.5
Hygiene	1	0.2	1	0.8	9	0.1	0.08	0.7
Kitchen/serving	125	28.3	40	30.8	3363	27.6	3.90	35.3
Kitchen	218	49.4	55	42.3	5150	42.3	4.31	39.0
Pharmaceutical	73	16.6	20	15.4	2202	18.1	1.93	17.5
Unidentified	4	0.9	1	0.8	24	0.2	-	-
Total	**441**		**130**		**12180**		**11.04**	

kitchen wares, typical of the late 16th century; other forms, such as drinking and storage vessels, or displayable items, are much rarer, but include part of a tankard in post-medieval black-glazed ware (PMBL) dating to after *c* 1580. Cooking vessels of all fabric types amount to *c* 42% of the group by weight, and *c* 49% by sherd count, while other kitchen/serving wares comprise a further *c* 28%. The most frequent forms are cauldrons (eg <P12>, Fig 200), pipkins (including <P13>, Fig 200) and sherds from one or other type (<P14>, Fig 200). Also present are a skillet (<P15>, Fig 200), dishes and bowls (eg <P16>, Fig 200), while a colander is in London-area post-medieval slipped redware with clear (yellow) glaze (PMSRY). Most of the pottery in the pit comprises redwares produced within the general region (*c* 48% by sherd count, *c* 44% by weight), by far the most common fabric being London-area early post-medieval redware (PMRE, *c* 44% by sherd count and *c* 37% by weight). The latest pieces are part of a frying-pan and a flanged dish in London-area post-medieval redware (PMR; <P17>, <P18>, Fig 200), and a flanged dish in Surrey-Hampshire border redware (RBOR; <P21>, Fig 200), which date to after *c* 1580; there are, however, no examples of the contemporary local post-medieval fine redware (PMFR).

Whitewares from the Surrey-Hampshire borders (BORD, BORDG/O/Y) and dating to after *c* 1550 form the third most common local/regional ware (6.5% by sherd count, *c* 3.6% by weight). These include sherds from three tripod pipkins, a skillet (<P19>, Fig 200), two dishes, two flanged dishes similar to <P21>, one with zigzag decoration on the rim (cf Pearce

1992, fig 19, no. 18), one cup, one or two porringers and part of a condiment dish (<P20>, Fig 200; ibid, fig 43, no. 391).

The most significant finds in the pit are the English tin-glazed tablewares (TGW) and a range of biscuit ware (BISC) vessels which, although not visibly flawed, were for some reason discarded before they had been tin-glazed and refired; the latter account for some 25% of the assemblage (Fig 158). The tablewares include five dishes (eg <P22>–<P25>, Fig 202), a deep bowl (<P26>, Fig 202), a possible butter dish with a central spike (<P27>, Fig 202), a lid or corrugated cup (<P28>, Fig 202) and two handled bowls or cups (<P29>, <P30>, Fig 202). Also present are up to 14 dry drug jars or albarelli (eg <P31>–<P39>, Fig 202) and two wet drug jars (<P40>, <P41>, Fig 202). When the composition of the group is considered by form type, the biscuit ware pharmaceutical vessels comprise *c* 17% of the pit group (*c* 18% by weight).

The tin-glazed wares are very similar in form to the biscuit wares, and are chemically different from those made in the Low Countries and Antwerp (Hughes and Gaimster 1999, 65). Nine samples were analysed (Chapter 8.5), and it was found that although their composition is not identical to that of the biscuit wares, they are consistent with a source in London; and, given their findspot, it is safe to assume that they were made at Aldgate. Most sherds are from dishes (<P47>–<P54>, Fig 203), but two bowls and a small ointment pot (possibly a waster) are also present (<P55>–<P57>, Fig 203).

Imported tin-glazed wares comprise a small ointment jar from Italy (<P58>, quantified as TGW, but subsequently identified as central Italian tin-glazed ware (CITG)) and a large late Andalusian tin-glazed ware (ANDAL) dish with simple geometric decoration in blue, possibly once lustred (<P64>, Fig 204). Also present are three stoneware jugs, including a large jug from Raeren (RAER; <P61>, Fig 204), a small Frechen drinking jug (FREC; <P62>, Fig 204) and an everted rim in RAER possibly from a chamber pot (<P63>, Fig 204). A number of Dutch redware vessels are also present, including a handled slipped bowl (DUTSL; <P59>, Fig 204) and a remarkably small strainer (DUTR; <P60>, Fig 204).

The pit also contained fragments of tin-glazed tile and a fragment of an imported Cologne-type ceramic stove tile, part of a decoration showing the head of Logic, one of the Seven Liberal Arts (F<89>, F[220]; Fig 197, no. 5; Fig 198, no. 1). The fact that this has green glaze over a broken edge may indicate that the piece was used in a kiln, but the precise reason is not clear.

The combination of the different fabrics and form types suggests that the backfilling of the pit probably took place between *c* 1580 and *c* 1600, and so the debris from the making of tin-glazed pottery and tiles may be from the establishment of Jacob Jansen or one of his associates in the later 16th century. Compared to the volume of other pottery types, and to assemblages from tin-glazed pottery production sites in Southwark

Fig 158 Biscuit wares from a pit, group F22 (fills F[220], F[221]): from left to right, back row – dish <P22>, wet drug jar <P40> and spiked dish <P27>; middle row – albarelli bases <P57>, <P34> and <P31>, and wet drug jar <P41>; foreground – handled bowl <P30>, albarelli rims <P38> and <P39>, and base <P33>

and Lambeth (eg Britton 1987), the amount of tin-glazed and biscuit wares in this group is relatively small; and this, together with the proportion of ordinary domestic pottery sherds, suggests that this feature was not primarily intended as a waster pit, and/or that it was on the periphery of the industrial area. This group of sherds is a significant contribution to the study of Jansen's working practices and his range of forms, subjects discussed further in Chapter 8.5. A tin-glazed plate in the Museum of London's collection (Fig 159) has also been attributed to this workshop; the history of this plate is unknown before it was loaned to the London Museum in 1913 and donated two years later.

In sum, archaeological evidence for immediately post-Dissolution uses on the site of the west range comprised only a pit containing tin-glazed pottery and tile wasters which lay in a room within the ground floor of the range. On the Symonds plan this room, part of the overall tenancy of Kerwin, is shown with, in one corner, a large oven of domestic character (Fig 13; Fig 14). The outline of the flue of this oven is shown by Schnebbelie in his original drawing (Fig 94; note the changed shape in the engraving, Fig 95). It seems on present evidence unlikely that this was a kiln; the main objection, besides its comparatively small size, is that it lay in the middle of a building complex, and that the flue went up the side of what had been the duke's hall.

Although it is unlikely that this (probably) domestic oven was involved in pottery production, evidence is growing for the manufacture of tin-glazed wares within the precinct from the 1570s. The documentary evidence for Jacob Jansen and other Dutch immigrant potters has been outlined by Noël Hume (1977) and Britton (1987), and is further detailed in Chapter 8.5. Pottery production by aliens thus formed a second industry within the fringes of the Elizabethan city, to be compared with the glassworks of Jacob Verzelini, established in the hall of the Crutched Friars by 1575, when it burned down; subsequently it was re-established on the site, to the trepidation of the neighbours (Sutton and Sewell 1980). Like the glassworks, the workshops of the potters at Duke's Place may have been situated within the stone buildings of the priory. After the execution of the Duke of Norfolk in 1572, there can have been little wish to have noble gatherings in the ducal part of the former priory.

There is the prospect of further information on these post-Dissolution changes being obtained during any future redevelopment of the priory site. As this study went to press, an archaeological evaluation included a test pit within Sugar Baker's Yard (now Court) which produced more imported German stove tile fragments of the same series as that from Holy Trinity Priory and possibly from the same stove (Drummond-Murray 2004). The pit lay immediately west of the main range and a few metres south-west of the finds in 1979 reported here. It also produced further tin-glazed wasters, probably from Jansen's works, and raises the possibility that the sugar baking works implied by the alley name in 1676 may have been a successor to Jansen's pottery and tile manufactory.

Fig 159 Tin-glazed plate in the Museum of London, attributed to the Aldgate workshop, dated 1600 or 1602 and inscribed THE.ROSE.IS.RED.THE.LEAVES.ARE. GRENE.GOD.SAVE. ELIZABETH.OVR.QUEENE (diameter 257mm; MoL C84)

6.3 The character of post-Dissolution building in London precincts and elsewhere: some parallels and discussion

It has been argued that the dissolution of Holy Trinity Priory, Aldgate, was significant in that it was the first in England where the monastery was completely secularised (Jeffries Davies 1925). Medieval kings had transferred assets from one house to another, or suppressed houses in favour of others or in favour of their own charitable foundations; but Cardinal Wolsey was the first to make a house extinct and appropriate its property and buildings solely for royal use. While this interpretation of events may not be universally accepted by historians writing more recently (Rosenfield 1970), it points to the fact that the dissolution of Holy Trinity was chronologically in advance of that of the main Dissolution of religious houses in England, and thus would have been uncharted territory and to some degree experimental.

The rapid change in the character of the Holy Trinity precinct during the second half of the 16th century, from noble mansion to something with elements of both an industrial zone and a district favoured by foreign immigrants, is in significant contrast to the fortunes of other former religious precincts elsewhere in the City of London, and especially those on the west side towards Westminster. The fate of Holy Trinity can also be compared with those of other Augustinian houses throughout England (Dickinson 1968). A brief survey of what happened to 19 religious houses in London and its immediate environs, up to c 1600, is given in Table 16, and shows the variety of new uses.

At the Dissolution, conventual churches at three London monastic houses (St Bartholomew's Priory, Smithfield; St Helen's nunnery, Bishopsgate; St Clare's nunnery, Minories) and at three friaries (the Austin Friars, Blackfriars and Greyfriars) were at least partly retained as parish churches; but by the end of the reign of Henry VIII, the majority of the religious precincts had been transferred to courtiers or officials of the Court of Augmentations, a process which was taking place throughout England. Some general uses for the London houses, for instance for the King's Revels or as armour or munitions stores, are noted in Table 16; but this study concentrates on those precincts which in the immediately post-Dissolution years became either single or multiple polite residences. Austin Friars, for instance, passed to Sir William Paulet, Lord Treasurer; St Bartholomew's Priory, one of the other Augustinian houses, to Sir Richard Rich, Lord Chancellor; and to the south-east of the city, Bermondsey Abbey passed to Sir Thomas Pope, Treasurer of the Court of Augmentations. Only one of these houses can be seen today: the Charterhouse, north-west of the City. Here the roof timbers of buildings in Wash House Court, the Library and the Great Chamber have been dated by dendrochronology to their expected date ranges of c 1530 for the court (ie pre-Dissolution) and the 1540s for the other buildings (Howard et al 1997, 124, 126). These mansions are all of a group, being the product of a short phase from 1534 to c 1570; and this constitutes one distinct fate for several of the London precincts in the immediate post-Dissolution years. They are matched by other, perhaps better-known cases outside London, such as the building of the mansion of Audley End on the site of a Benedictine abbey near Saffron Walden (Essex) in the 1540s by the same Thomas Audley who acquired Holy Trinity Priory.

Something of contemporary wishes in the design of buildings and gardens, and in decoration, may be drawn from what is known of these houses, though the character of the monastic buildings often inhibited new building on a substantial scale. At St Bartholomew's Priory, Sir Richard Rich moved into the prior's lodging when he took up occupancy of the house in 1540 (Webb 1921, ii, xx), just as Audley had done a few years

Table 16 Post-Dissolution uses of some London monasteries and hospitals

Religious establishment	Main construction dates	References
Austin Friars	mansion given to Sir Richard Rich 1539; other parts to William Paulet 1539; west half of church to Dutch congregation 1550	Stow 1603, i, 176–7; Harben 1918, 35
Bermondsey Abbey	granted in 1541 to Sir Robert Southwell who sold it to Sir Thomas Pope in the same year; Pope died 1559, other noble owners to end of 17th century; large mansion still visible in the early 19th century	Wheatley and Cunningham 1891, i, 168; Steele in prep
Blackfriars	granted in several portions; part to Thomas Cawardine, Keeper of the Royal Tents and Master of the Revels, for a house; another part became the Blackfriars theatre 1596	Harben 1918, 78–9; Chambers 1923, ii, 475–515
Charterhouse	granted to Sir Edward North; sold to Duke of Norfolk 1565; bought by Thomas Sutton 1611, became Charterhouse School	RCHME 1925, 21–30; Knowles and Grimes 1954; Howard et al 1997, 126 (dendrochronology)
Crutched Friars	granted to Sir Thomas Wyatt; part became a glass house which burned down 1575; part became Lumley House, possibly built by Wyatt, later converted into the Navy Office	Stow 1603, i, 148; Harben 1918, 182; Sutton and Sewell 1980
Greyfriars	all site granted to City 1547; church became a parish church; Christ's Hospital founded in conventual buildings 1552	Stow i, 319; Harben 1918, 278–9
Holy Trinity Priory	granted to Thomas Audley 1534; to Duke of Norfolk 1558; sold by Lord Thomas Howard to City 1592	
St Bartholomew Smithfield (priory)	site granted to Sir Richard Rich 1544; church partially demolished, presbytery became parish church	Stow 1603, ii, 28; Webb 1921, ii, *passim*
St Bartholomew's Hospital	granted to City 1547	Stow 1603, ii, 24; Harben 1918, 49
St Clare without Aldgate nunnery (Minories)	part granted to bishops of Bath for their town house, rented out to others; nuns' chapel made into Holy Trinity, a parish church, in 1566; part an armour store and workshop	Stow 1603, i, 126; Harben 1918, 150; Ellis 1985
St Helen Bishopsgate	retained its parish status; conventual buildings sold in parts, eg the dormitory range and chapter house to Thomas Kendall to become Leathersellers' Hall	Harben 1918, 297; Schofield 2003a, 188, figs 55–6
St John Clerkenwell	dissolved 1540; nave demolished by Somerset 1549; used by Clerk of Revels and for storage of tents; split into at least 10 noble houses by 1619	Sloane and Malcolm 2004
St Mary Bethlem	granted to City 1547; hospital transferred to new site in Moorfields after 1666	Harben 1918, 447; Andrews et al 1997
St Mary Clerkenwell	cloister became house of Duke of Newcastle	Sloane in prep
St Mary Graces	site granted to Sir Arthur Darcy 1542; became the Victualling House (Navy) 1560s	Stow 1603, i, 125; Harben 1918, 394; Mills 1985
St Mary Overie	delftware kilns in 17th–18th century	Dawson 1971a; 1971b
St Mary Spital	1538 hospital closed and site granted mainly to Stephen Vaughan, court official; other occupants in 1540s	Thomas et al 1997, 131–76
St Thomas Acon	majority of site granted to Mercers' Company 1542; incorporated into existing Mercers' Hall complex	*VCH* 1909, 494
Whitefriars	granted to several individuals, church converted into town houses by time of Stow in 1598	Stow 1603, ii, 47; Harben 1918, 625

previously. It was natural, and most common, for the church to be left a ruin, the new house occupying the prior's range and other domestic ranges, as at Bermondsey Abbey (Steele in prep), south-east of London, or further afield at Newstead Abbey (Nottinghamshire) or Lacock Abbey (Wiltshire). Occasionally, but less often, there was more widespread demolition and the main range of the new house might be placed on the outline of the church, as at Little Leighs (Essex), another mansion of the 1st Lord Rich (RCHME 1921, 158–61).

In the London cases, it is so far difficult to identify suites of rooms, such as the combination of great chamber, withdrawing chamber, bedchamber and closet, and long gallery, which are a feature of large houses of this period; and which, in fact, had been present in several pre-Dissolution monastic houses elsewhere, such as Rievaulx, Fountains and Castle Acre (G Coppack, pers comm). If the Audley mansion originally extended to and included the Ivy chamber in the crossing of the priory church, then the high end of the hall would have led via a gallery to a kind of prospect house, the Ivy chamber which looked down on one side into the nave and on the other into the presbytery, both roofless. The arrangement of hall – gallery along the garden – prospect house first appears in London in the plan of Bridewell Palace, where the prospect house was represented by the range along the Thames, built in 1520–3. The prospect house could also take the form of a banqueting house on the roof or forming the top chamber of a tower, as at Melbury House (Dorset) and Lacock (Girouard 1978, 79, 106). These banqueting chambers were a feature of country houses from the 1540s (Girouard 1983), and the Ivy chamber at Holy Trinity must have been an early and imposing example.

The copperplate engraving of London of c 1559 supplies some details of the garden of Winchester Place, built by Paulet in the years around 1550 on the site of the Austin friary. Here is shown a formal garden, a fountain, and a blocked-up gatehouse in the garden wall which marked the north end of a path through the friary, now enclosed and no longer available for public access (Stow 1603, i, 176; Schofield 1993, 37, fig 4.7; Schofield 2003b). Gardens were clearly of importance in the post-Dissolution layout at St Mary Spital, where the main house, composed of the former prior's lodging but invading the north aisle of the hospital choir (the rest of the great structure being demolished), was given a gallery to overlook the new open spaces to the south (Thomas et al 1997, 131–2).

Some of the precincts contained several prestigious lodgings or mansions, St Bartholomew Smithfield being the best example. Here, as shown by a rental of 1616, the stone buildings in the middle of the priory still contained five mansions: Sir Percival Hart held the Lady chapel and gallery alongside the church, Arthur Jarvis had the prior's lodging, Sir Henry Carey had the 'farmery' (infirmary), Sir Edward Barrett the house of the master of the farmery, and Lord Abergavenny was tenant above the chapter house and dormitory (Webb 1921, ii, 77–9, 144, 151, 171–6). Hart and Jarvis were able to enjoy the former monastic water supply, brought from north of the city, as their private privilege (ibid, 161).

The character of these mansions is shown most elaborately by watercolours painted by J C Buckler in the first two decades of the 19th century of Bermondsey Abbey, the house of Sir Thomas Pope, though it is not possible to locate the internal views precisely within the house. In this case the new house was built around the cloister (Fig 160), and the whole vast church became open space. At the same time, judging from Buckler's drawings, large timbers were freely employed to frame new upper floors (Fig 161) and rooms and galleries were constructed (Fig 162).

Fig 160 Sir Thomas Pope's mansion at Bermondsey Abbey: the 'principal front' in 1808, watercolour by J C Buckler (Guildhall Library)

Fig 161 Sir Thomas Pope's mansion at Bermondsey Abbey: view in the 'west wing' in 1807, watercolour by J C Buckler (Guildhall Library)

Fig 162 Sir Thomas Pope's mansion at Bermondsey Abbey: room 'on the north side' in 1816, watercolour by J C Buckler (Guildhall Library)

It is not clear whether these timbers were new or had been taken from the several large buildings, especially the church, which would have been granted with the site. A large house called Priory House constructed on the shell of some of the outbuildings of St Oswald's Priory, Gloucester, in the 16th or 17th century furnishes a possibly significant parallel (Heighway and Bryant 1999, 98–9). Antiquarian drawings of the Gloucester buildings, including one by the same J C Buckler in 1819, show that just as at Bermondsey a ground floor of masonry and brick – some kind of adaptation of the medieval buildings – was overlaid by a first floor of timber-framing, with large panels and imposingly large timbers. It may be, as suggested by these records of Bermondsey and Gloucester, that the large timbers were taken from the priory buildings. From this we might further suggest that the availability of such large timbers in quantity, in the 1530s and 1540s especially, contributed to the new architecture of the arriviste owners, and to a sort of architectural style in timber born of this availability.

The Tudor mansion of Bermondsey survived into the first decade of the 19th century to be recorded, probably both because of its peripheral situation relative to the City, and to its distance from Westminster. In the City, any exclusivity was not to last; or perhaps, in certain cases, it was illusory from the start in the 1530s. At Holy Trinity Priory, Audley had tenants in the 1540s, which may have included those on the outer fringes to the main streets, but also probably included tenants within the close. At St Bartholomew Smithfield, the prestigious enclave was also soon bordered by new buildings of different character. The 3rd Lord Rich, who came into possession of the former St Bartholomew's Priory in 1581, began to redevelop the fairground to the north of the priory church and laid out several streets which survive today as Cloth Fair, Middle Street and Newbury Street. Several buildings from this private housing venture remained until the early 20th century. Houses of three or four storeys with garrets encroached onto the site of the demolished nave of the priory church (the presbytery being kept for parochial use, ensuring its survival to the present day), and others were built against the presbytery and Lady chapel to the east (Webb 1921, ii, 293). The houses put up by Rich in the 1580s and 1590s (Leech 1996) were of substantial character and seem to have been at least respectable, as their situation next to the nucleus of superior residences would suggest.

Thus a second phase of building, that of dwellings which were smaller and let out to tenants, can be seen in the two precincts after about 1570; the era of the noble or courtier town house based in the shell of the monastic buildings was quickly over. This was the period of development of the Strand, west of the City, as a suburb of mansions for those attending Court at Westminster. At St Bartholomew's Priory, on the western side of the City, the proximity of the Court probably encouraged the continuance of the courtly enclave. At Holy Trinity Priory on the eastern side, the majority of the precinct was by 1592 in City ownership. Its tenants included a knight, Sir Francis Hinde, and an alderman, Henry Billingsley, but otherwise the priory site was occupied by (among others) the City Mason William Kerwin, a baker, and Dutch immigrants. Pottery and tiles were almost certainly made in the former precinct, and by 1676 it is likely that sugar was baked or refined here also, though in both cases the industrial premises may have been small.

In a paper of 1968, J C Dickinson drew together information

on the variable survival of Augustinian houses in England as monuments above ground or as marks now perceptible only by aerial photography. He attributed the partial preservation on some sites to several factors: 1) the preservation of a complete house because it was a cathedral, at Carlisle; 2) the use of some houses as new cathedrals, to meet a perceived need for more; this eventually involved six new cathedrals, of which two were Augustinian houses, at Oxford and Bristol; 3) the occasional purchase of the whole church for parish use; and 4) the more frequent purchase or allocation of part of the conventual church for parish use; this and the previous practice ensured the survival of at least part of 33 Augustinian churches in England. The rest, over 170 in number, were transferred into secular hands and exposed to a greater degree of attrition. Holy Trinity falls into this large group. Like many other instances, the substantial gatehouse (or the ground floor at least) survived to become the last substantial vestige above ground to be removed, in the 1820s. Other aspects of the Tudor mansion carved out of the priory resembled other mansions, including those in the present countryside where more has survived. Monastic buildings in towns were valuable and convenient sources of lead and stone, though in the Holy Trinity Aldgate case Audley does not seem to have managed that very well, by Stow's account (above, 6.2). In *c* 1585, mason William Kerwin occupied much of the church site and was laying out buildings in the former great court. It is tempting to suggest that he was using the priory buildings, or at least those in his tenancy, as a quarry for his building works.

6.4 The period 1592–*c* 1900 (period P2)

Introduction

This second period of post-Dissolution activities is a long one, and only a summary is given here. The archaeological remains of this period were scant on all sites, and to some extent were only summarily recorded. This period is notable for the building of St James Duke's Place in 1622 and the influx into the area of Jewish immigrants from the mid 17th century. The area, based on two synagogues of the two main congregations within the Jewish faith, became London's first and main Jewish area after the Resettlement of 1657 and especially after the rebuilding of the Ashkenazi synagogue in 1722. The reporting on this period highlights the main topographical developments, and provides some momentary snapshots of the buildings and their archaeology in the period 1592–*c* 1900.

Documentary evidence

The rebuilding of Aldgate

The gate of Aldgate was still one of the principal entrances to the medieval city, and its rebuilding in 1606–9 was a statement of civic pride in an ancient past. The gate described by Stow (and shown by Wyngaerde in Fig 10) was taken down, and a box-like structure embellished with classical ornaments erected. The figures of two Roman soldiers stood on the outer battlements, with stone balls in their hands, ready to defend London; beneath, in a square panel, was a statue of King James I. On the inside was a figure of Fortune, and gilded figures of Peace and Charity copied from Roman coins which had been discovered when digging the foundations of the gate. An inscription stated 'Senatus Populus Que Londinensis Fecit 1609, Humfrey Weld, Maior' (Wheatley and Cunningham 1891, i, 27).

A bird's-eye view of the gate is given by Wenceslaus Hollar in 1667 (Fig 163). Hollar shows Aldgate as rebuilt in the early 17th century and a general view of Duke's Place, correct in its general layout but not reliable for any individual building. He shows the 16th-century and later development of housing over the city ditch along Houndsditch, but not bastions 6 and 7, which are known from 18th-century leases to have survived largely intact. Outside Aldgate lies the medieval church of St Botolph Aldgate with its churchyard, before the rebuilding by Dance. Engravings, watercolours and early photographs show that the street of Aldgate within the gate, and Aldgate High Street outside the gate, was full of large and fine timber-framed houses dating from the first half of the 17th century (eg Schofield 2003a, 149, fig 180).

St James Duke's Place

In the immediately post-Dissolution decades the precinct had its own place of worship in the former chapter house; this is indicated by Symonds (Fig 13; Fig 14). On the direction of King James a new church was built on the site of the chapter house at the City's expense by the mayor and aldermen, in the place where there had been a church 'fifty years since' called Trinity or Duke's Place church (*Cal S P Dom*, 12, 648–9). It was consecrated in 1623 (ibid, 10, 479), so the chapter house must have been used as a neighbourhood church since *c* 1570. In the reign of Charles I this church was judged a parish church and not a precinct of St Katherine Cree (Strype 1720, i.ii, 61). One of the very few views of its exterior is by J Coney (1786–1833), shortly before 1812 (Fig 164). The plan of St James Duke's Place is given a decade later by Schnebbelie (Fig 95).

The nave was rebuilt in 1727 (Seymour 1734, i, 313). The Tuscan arches of the tower shown in the Coney view recall Nicholas Stone's work at St John's, Great Stanmore (Middlesex), of the early 1630s; the traceried openings, if of the 1620s, are another instance of the Gothic survival as manifested nearby at St Katherine Cree. The 1727 nave rebuilding may have reused the arched doorcase shown in the view; otherwise, its triple hipped roof and three arched windows are quite conventional (R Bowdler, pers comm). The reredos from St James's, transposed to St Katherine Cree when St James's was demolished in 1874, is said to be perhaps of 1728 (Pevsner 1973, 161; Bradley and Pevsner 1997, 229, where the

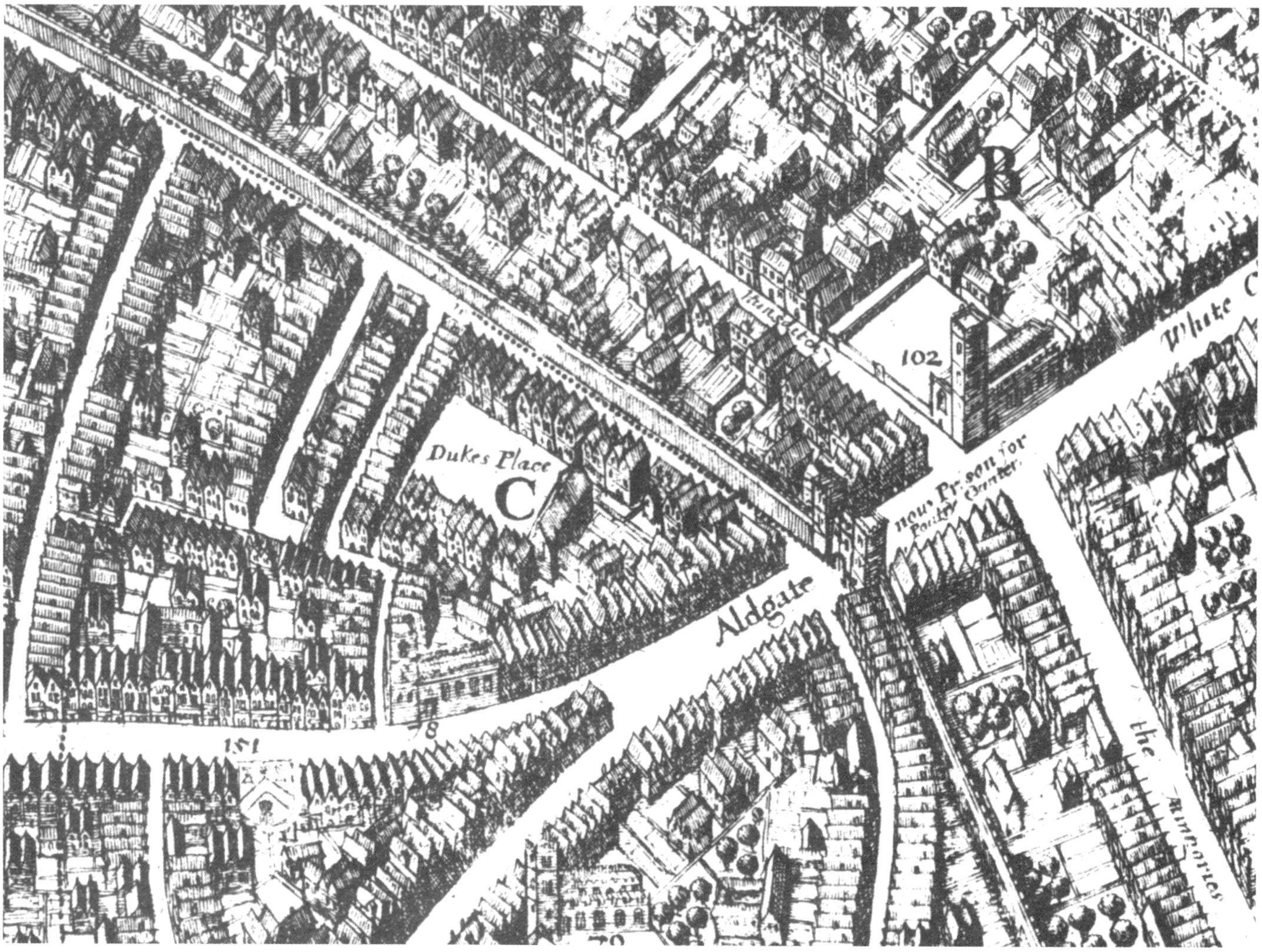

Fig 163 *Duke's Place and its surroundings as shown by Wenceslaus Hollar, 1667* (Guildhall Library)

Fig 164 St James Duke's Place with, on the left, the range built probably in the 17th century on the site of the priory refectory; watercolour by J Coney (engraved 1812) (Guildhall Library)

attribution to St James's is omitted). At least one piece of stained glass from St James's was also transposed to St Katherine's, and this might even have come from the priory (RCHME 1929, 10); it shows a mailed arm and fist holding a bundle of arrows.

St James's aquired notoriety because marriages could be celebrated there without a licence, and so it became the venue for a local and handy version of the practice associated with Gretna Green in Scotland. This privilege was eventually rescinded by an Act of Parliament in 1753 (Wheatley and Cunningham 1891, i, 532). As a church in the City, it figured in the survey by Godwin and Britton (1839, ii; each church with separate pagination). The authors state that 'this church is in a very dilapidated and dirty state ... the present church [as rebuilt in 1727] is a plain warehouse-like erection of brick, quite unworthy of description'. In the east window were the arms of Sir Edward Barkham, Lord Mayor in 1621–2. The Godfrey and Britton text (page 3) also notes that 'the tower displays in the various external openings, pointed-headed window frames of stone, each in two lights, with trefoil heads. These probably once formed part, not merely of the church erected in 1622, but some of the priory buildings previously.' These presumably medieval windows are not shown in any of the few views of the church.

The rebuilding of St Katherine Cree and the character of Leadenhall Street in the 17th century

The parish church of St Katherine Cree was rebuilt in 1628–31, and survives (RCHME 1929, 8–10; Bradley and Pevsner 1997, 228–9). The church is of importance as an example of Laudian work, in its mixture of Gothic and Renaissance details; the 'traditional' attribution to Inigo Jones reported by the Royal Commission has now been discarded in favour of Edward Kinsman (Colvin 1995, 588), although there is no direct evidence of his involvement. The building retained the tower of 1504, though the details were changed either in this building or later. The church of 1631 is shown by Hollar in his bird's-eye view of the City after the Great Fire (Fig 163), but he shows the south door going into the nave, and not into the tower as it must have been and is now.

Also in 1631, a fine gateway from Leadenhall Street to the parish churchyard (Fig 165) was added at the east end of the church by the gift of William Arenen, goldsmith, who died in that year (Strype 1720, i.ii, 65). This gateway survives, transposed to the north side of the present churchyard. Immediately inside the gate, on the right, was the Aldgate ward Watch House in the 18th century.

As a postscript to the detailed treatment of Billingsley's house of 1590 (above, 6.2) we can add here two photographs of the buildings which replaced his frontage to Leadenhall Street, one taken in the 19th century (Fig 166) and the other in the 1950s (Fig 167). Both show a brick house of the late 17th century, which is also shown in 1853 by Thomas Hosmer Shepherd (Fig 149). This plain building (72 Leadenhall Street) did not last through the 1960s.

The development of the former priory site after 1600

All the printed sources concerning Duke's Place state that the mansion of the dukes of Norfolk was sold with the rest of the precinct to the City in 1592. This remains likely, and cannot be contested; but no detailed documentary evidence has been found in City or other records (such as the surviving papers of the Howards (catalogued in HMC 1996, 60–3) to show what became of the house. In particular, it is strange that there are many 18th- and 19th-century lease plans of properties forming small units within the precinct, some of which have been used in this study, but no such plans of the main mansion in the west range of the former cloister. Similarly, no evidence has been found in City records of the names of tenants of the mansion. Thus the 17th to early 19th centuries are, for the mansion, a blank. An 1819 plan of the range and buildings to the west shows that by that date the west half of the range had been sold, since it formed part of a private estate (see Fig 169), leaving the east half in the Corporation's possession; and the spine-wall which divided the range, no doubt largely of

Fig 165 *Aldgate ward Watch House in 1830, watercolour by an unknown artist (Guildhall Library)*

Fig 166 Leadenhall Street looking west, photographed in the late 19th century (Guildhall Library); compare the street as shown on the Goad Insurance map of 1887 (Fig 174)

Fig 167 Nos 72 and 73 Leadenhall Street (right), with the Billingsley property (left), photographed in the 1950s (Guildhall Library)

medieval date, partly fell down in 1822. For the 16th and 17th centuries, however, there is very little at present from this mansion to compare with the evidence for the 17th-century mansions constructed at other former monastic sites in and around London, such as at St Mary Clerkenwell (Sloane in prep) or St John Clerkenwell (Sloane and Malcolm 2004, 246–52).

The priory area is shown in Ogilby and Morgan's map of the City in 1676 (Fig 18). The name Duke's Place is given both to the large house in the west claustral range, with Duke's Place Court to its west (the former great court of the priory), and to the street which ran along the inside of the city wall from Aldgate to Bevis Marks, the ancestor of the present Duke's Place (street). The body of the priory church is not recognisable as an outline, though with knowledge of the Symonds and later plans we can see that a predecessor of the 18th-century Mitre Court ran between buildings fronting onto Aldgate to open into a court. This must represent the presbytery of the church; beyond to the west, the nave of the church is divided into buildings on its north side and gardens on the south. Numerous small alleys and tenements fill out most of the precinct; what is identifiable from Symonds as the refectory has been rebuilt as two rows of small houses with an alley between; perhaps the refectory walls formed the houses' outer margins. The passage linking the squares called Duke's Place Court and Duke's Place by Ogilby and Morgan in 1676 is shown by our study to have evolved from the passage through the west claustral range of the priory, as shown by Symonds (Fig 13; Fig 14); this passage, widened, still exists today.

The Jewish community

In 1657, shortly after the Jews were readmitted to England by Oliver Cromwell, the first synagogue of the Resettlement was set up in Creechurch Lane (Samuel 1924). In 1663 Samuel Pepys and his wife went there, out of curiosity, to watch a festival of the Rejoicing of the Law (Latham and Matthews 1971, 334–5). The Jews came from two Sephardim communities, in Holland and Portugal (Samuel 1961). In 1673 the synagogue was enlarged to more than double its size, to seat 174 men and 84 women (ibid, 35–6). It was replaced by a new building on a separate site, in Bevis Marks, in 1701; this building still stands today (RCHME 1929, 10–12; Bradley and Pevsner 1997, 272–3). Meanwhile, Ashkenazi or German Jews established their own synagogue north of the priory refectory, next to the kitchen, in 1690 (Roth 1950, 15–16); it was extended to the west in 1722. The building of 1722 has been described as 'for so many years ... the heart of the London Ghetto' (Roth 1950, 14). This rebuilding must have incorporated the site of the conventual kitchen; a rectangular building is marked 'Jews' Synagogue' on the Aldgate ward map of 1739 (Hyde 1999, 35, pl 2). It was enlarged again in 1766, and now with the title Great Synagogue was rebuilt to the designs of James Spiller in 1790 (ibid, 167–8; see Fig 92).

Already by 1695 there were 264 adult Jews in the parish of St James Duke's Place, forming 26% of the parish; from at least 1748 Jews helped to run the precinct by being part of the Vestry of the parish (Rubens 1966, 182–3). From 1722, as a result of the Resettlement, London began to be looked upon as a place of refuge for persecuted Jews from Continental Europe (George 1979, 132). In 1734 Seymour reported that there were 300 houses in the adjacent parish of St Katherine Cree, of which 60 were those of Jews (Seymour 1734, i, 317). He gives no equivalent figure for the parish of St James Duke's Place, presumably due to an oversight.

Human figures in Jewish attire are shown in several of the engravings of priory buildings in the late 18th century (eg Fig 125; Fig 126). Horwood's map of 1799 (Margary 1985) shows the two main synagogues (that of the Portuguese and Spanish Jews in Bevis Marks, and the Great Synagogue of the German Jews in Duke's Place) and a third building, also marked 'Synagogue', forming much of the south side of the former cloister area (then called Little Duke's Place), that is a new building on the site of the former north nave aisle. Wyld's map of 1840 shows the two main synagogues, and a 'New Synagogue' south of Leadenhall Street; the building in Little Duke's Place has gone. By 1900, enlarged by further immigration of Jews in the later 19th century, the Jewish East End lay almost totally outside Aldgate in Whitechapel, particularly in the southern part of Spitalfields, Mile End, and south of Whitechapel High Street to the line of the Blackwall railway viaduct which went, as it does today, into Fenchurch Street Station (Lipman 1961, endpaper).

Development in the 18th and 19th centuries: the Sir John Cass Foundation

Mitre Court, the ancestor of the present Mitre Street which runs west from Aldgate, is first named on Rocque's map of 1747; it then still had the restricted entrance shown by Ogilby and Morgan in 1676 (Fig 18). Another snapshot of the post-Dissolution development of the precinct is given in 1755, when Sir William Smith having died, the Corporation leased his tenancy to his son Edmund, as outlined in Chapter 4.2 and shown in the lease plan (Fig 20). Both were members of the Clothworkers' Company. William Smith was apprenticed in 1685 and became free of the Company in 1696; his son Edmund was free by patrimony in 1729, elected to the livery in 1734, elected First (Upper) Warden for 1761, elected Master in 1767 but excused service, and had died by December 1779 (D Wickham, Clothworkers' Company, pers comm).

William Smith had been leased the property by the City a year before his death, in 1754. It comprised the remains of the Ivy chamber block in the former crossing of the priory church, now an alehouse; a long property at the north-east corner of the court which was the former presbytery, incorporating some of the piers to be recorded by Carter in 1790 and revealed further by the fire of 1800; and, on the south side of the former presbytery, a range shown by Whichelo in 1803 (Fig 32).

The precinct as a whole is shown on a plan or map now in the City of London Record Office, and presumably drawn up by the City surveyor; it dates to shortly before 1790, since the Great Synagogue is shown before Spiller enlarged it to include the front of the former monastic great court (Fig 168). With our knowledge of the earlier maps, it is clear that Mitre Court is on the site of the monastic presbytery, and the way through to the site of the former north transept is clearly shown. A court called New Court has been built to the west, in the space between the west end of the priory church and the way leading southwards to the priory gate. The plan also shows that St James Duke's Place (the lower of the two black rectangles) had two churchyards, one encroaching into the former cloister area, the other on the north-east side of the church. Further to the north-east, Shoemakers' Row is the relict of the intramural way, and the city wall with what modern archaeologists call bastions 6 and 7, the Roman and medieval interval towers, which could still be made out by the surveyors. Beyond the wall, the city ditch has been wholly built over by houses and their gardens along Houndsditch.

The area resisted the inexorable change to its topography demanded by London's commercial needs during the 19th century. This is fortunate for the student of the medieval and post-medieval priory, and is illustrated by drawings and by maps. In the Guildhall Library Print Room collection is a plan of property of John Dueffell, Mrs Mary Maze and Mrs Ann Prichard, surveyed in May 1819 (Fig 169). This plan comprises two blocks at right angles. The left-hand, southern, block is that originally laid out by Kerwin on the south side of the former great court of the priory, in 1819 situated between the remaining space of the court (called, perhaps in error, 'DUKES PLACE' on the plan) and 'Sugar Baker's Yard' to the south. The buildings on the right of the plan are on the site of the west claustral range, on both sides of a covered passage, which is the location of the excavation on site F and buildings to the north; in other words, this is the main range of Duke's Place three years before the spine-wall of the west range of the cloister (shown dividing the pink from the grey properties on the right of the plan) fell down in 1822. Also visible in Fig 169 is the west end of 'THE NEW STREET' – the present Mitre Street – still in formation to the south. One of the buildings on the south side of Duke's Place is labelled 'Polish synagogue'. Nothing else is known about this third synagogue in the former precinct; it was presumably a place of worship for Jews from Eastern Europe before the massive immigration of the 1880s.

Several artists drew buildings in and on the periphery of the precinct during the 19th century. In 1830, Thomas Hosmer Shepherd (1793–1864) drew a view down Aldgate Street

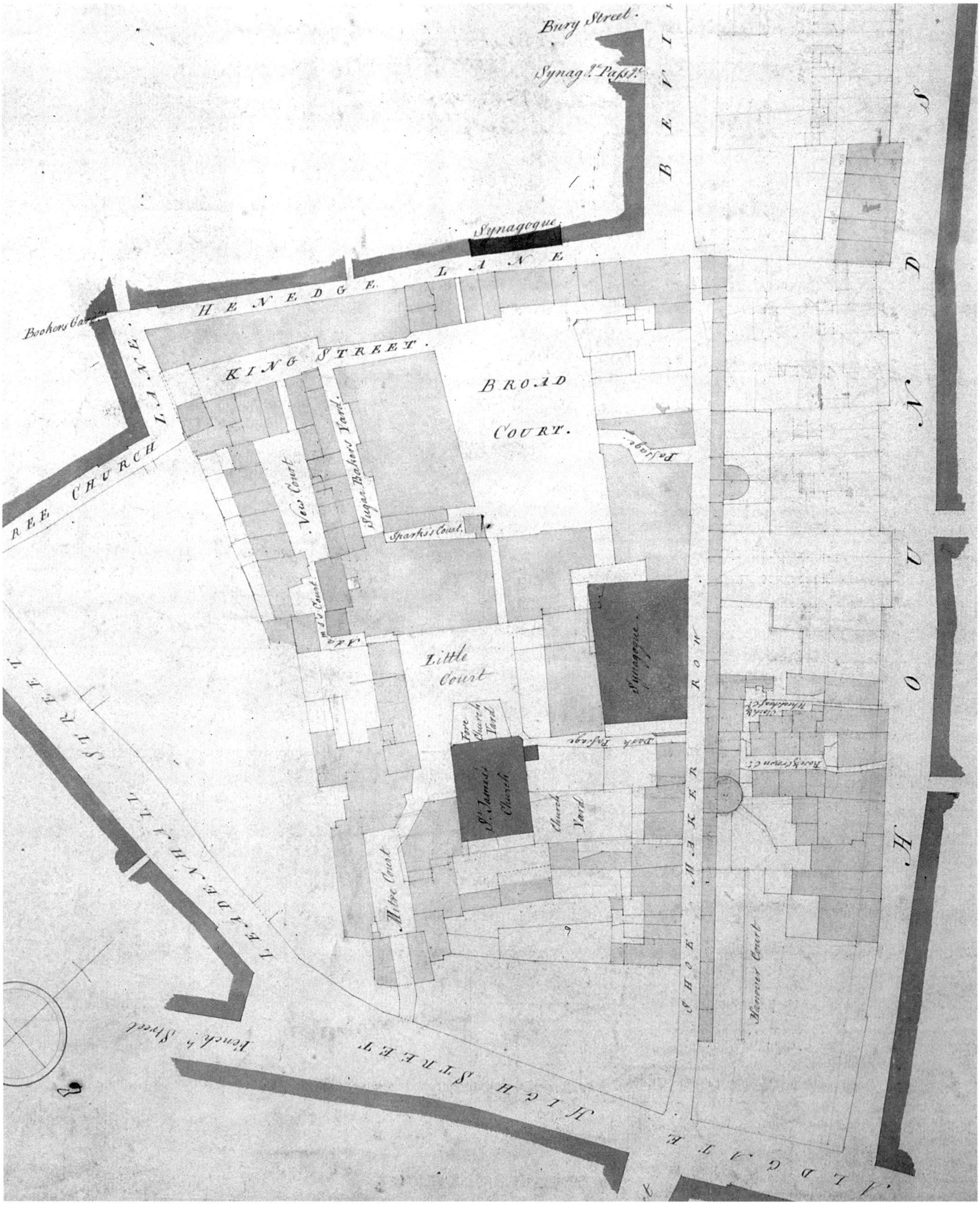

Fig 168 Map of Duke's Place precinct, shortly before 1790 (CLRO, Surveyor's City Lands Plans Portfolio I, 38)

looking south-west, which shows the nature of buildings on both sides of the street and of the apex of the corner between Leadenhall Street and Fenchurch Street (Fig 170). On the right-hand side this drawing shows an impressive block of four-storey timber-framed buildings, in this form probably of 17th-century date (though the lower parts might be earlier). There is a narrow alley between this block and the nearer brick building on the extreme right. The alley does not, however, appear on

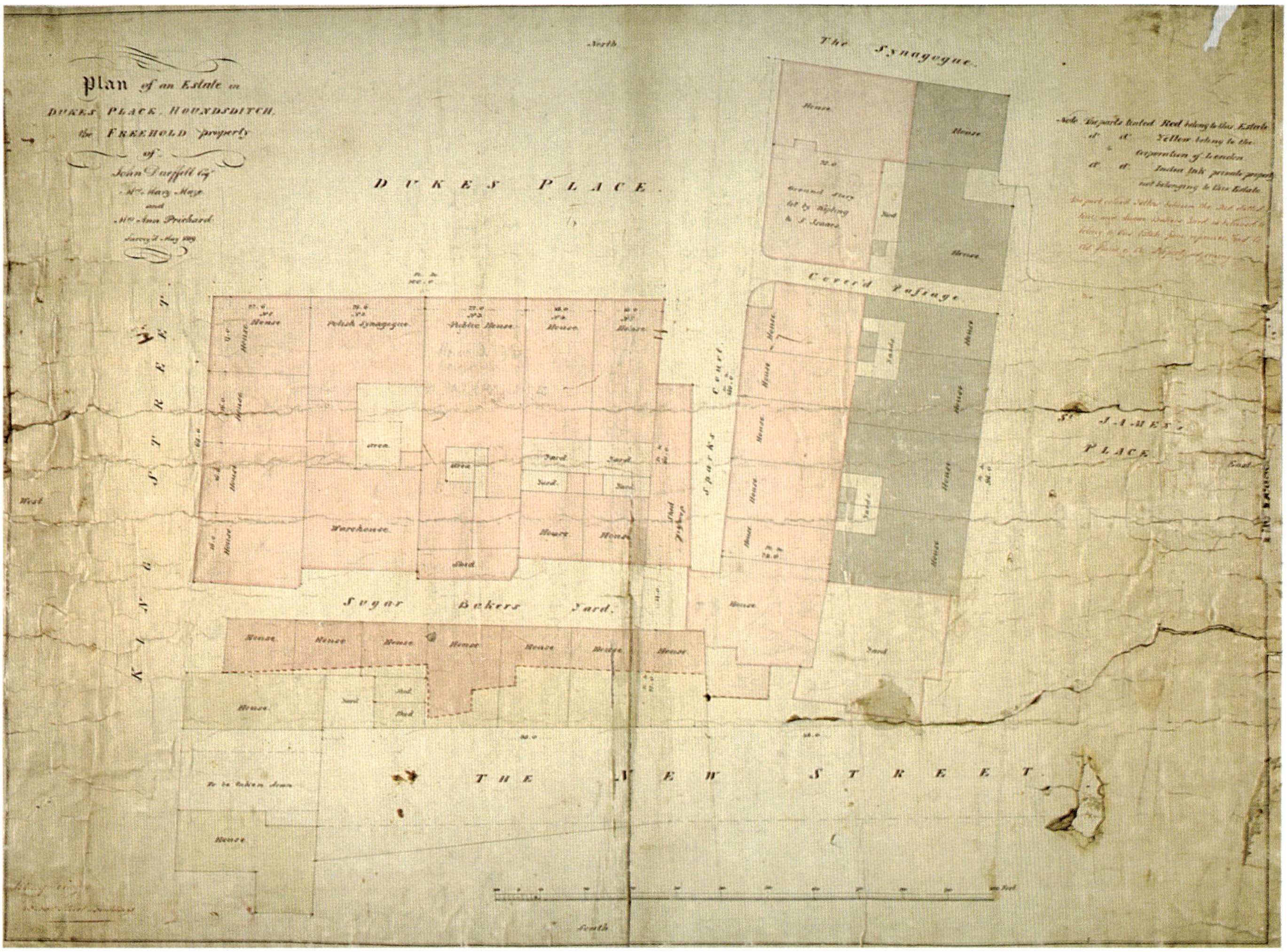

Fig 169 Plan of property belonging to John Dueffell and others (1819), showing (left) the range on the south side of the great court ('DUKES PLACE') and (right) much of the west claustral range, as it was in rebuilt form in 1819 (Guildhall Library). The key (upper right corner) explains that the parts shaded 'red' (the two versions of pink) belong to the estate; those shaded yellow belong to the Corporation of London; and those shaded in 'Indian ink', that is grey, do not belong to the estate. The note adds that the part coloured yellow between the red dotted line and 'Sugar Baker's Yard' is believed to belong to this estate from reference made to old plans of the property adjoining

contemporary maps. The length of the combined frontage suggests that this drawing shows the Aldgate frontage between Duke's Place (then Duke Street) and Mitre Street, that is, the site excavated as site C.

In 1844, Shepherd also recorded a market in the great court (Fig 171); here, two decades after the fall of the main range recorded by Schnebbelie, the site of Norfolk's mansion is still in ruins. Behind is the tower of St James's church. Spiller's synagogue is seen on the left, and the court has brick ranges on its north and south sides. The market was where the Jews could be found as petty traders; in 1818, for instance, it was noted that both fishermen and poachers swept the Thames night and day for whitefish (mostly roach, dace and bleak, a small river fish), but only for their scales, which were sold in the Duke's Place market to Jews for the manufacture of beads, in imitation of pearls (Faulkner 1839, 31).

In the 1870s, F Shepperd and an anonymous observer sketched the humble houses along the west side of the precinct. Three Herring Court (Fig 172), immediately north of St Katherine Cree, can be seen on Ogilby and Morgan's map of

Fig 170 View down Aldgate Street looking south-west in 1830, engraving by T H Shepherd (Guildhall Library)

Fig 171 Duke's Place (the great court) in 1844, pencil drawing by T H Shepherd (Guildhall Library)

1676 (Fig 18) as a small court; the drawing accurately agrees with the map, so perhaps it shows houses of the mid 17th century, though this is not certain. Shepperd's drawing of Heneage Lane looking south in 1874 (Fig 123) shows buildings based on the precinct wall, which presumably still formed the frontage in their basements or beneath their front walls. In 1884, John Crowther composed his careful watercolours of the entrance to what was then St James's Place, showing the timber-framed buildings on the west side of the entrance to the great court (Fig 124) and of the range then on the south side of the great court, on the site of Kerwin's new buildings in *c* 1585, but by 1884 a collection of interesting buildings of later date, rebuilt piecemeal (Fig 173).

The Goad Insurance map of 1887 (Fig 174) shows the area and can be compared with the sites of all the excavations in this project detailed on Fig 2, Fig 4 and Fig 5. This section of the map shows the Great Synagogue on Duke Street (now Duke's Place, widened); St James's Place is the former great court of the priory, and Mitre Square is the site of the cloister. The parish church of St James Duke's Place, on the site of the monastic chapter house, has been demolished and replaced by Horner and Sons Chemical Warehouse. Behind it to the east lies the Aldgate Ward School (not the same as the Sir John Cass Primary School, which was the ward school for Portsoken). Between Duke Street and Houndsditch lies the site of the city ditch, covered over by houses from the late 16th century. In 1888 Mitre Square achieved notoriety as the site of the second murder associated with Jack the Ripper, that of Catherine Eddowes (Rumbelow 1987, 61–87).

On the site of the north aisle of the presbytery and the Mitre Tavern in Mitre Court there is now the City's only primary school, which has a long history itself. The first Cass school was built in 1709–10 near St Botolph Aldgate church, funded by Sir John Cass, alderman, as a re-establishment of an existing parish charity school, but now to serve the ward of Portsoken. In 1718 Sir John Cass died, having not executed his second will which endowed the school. By a suit in Chancery this second will was made effective and the school reopened, after a period of being closed, in 1748 (Harben 1918, 533; Glynn 1998). The statue of Sir John Cass, carved by L F Roubiliac in 1751 (based on memories of Sir John by colleagues, since he had died 32 years earlier), is now in the Guildhall Art Gallery.

The building shown in Schnebbelie's watercolour of 1812 (Fig 175) is not the original school of 1710, and was probably

Fig 172 Anonymous pencil drawing of Three Herring Court, dated 1877 (LMA, SC/PZ/CT/01/102)

Fig 173 The south side of St James's Place (the former monastic great court) in 1884, watercolour by John Crowther (Guildhall Library)

Fig 174 The priory area on the Goad Insurance map of 1887 (Guildhall Library)

Fig 175 The Sir John Cass Foundation School in Aldgate; watercolour by R Schnebbelie, 1812 (Guildhall Library)

built in the first half of the 18th century. It had been a Quaker boarding school and the Bell Tavern before being leased from Christ's Hospital by Sir John Cass School in 1762, and it incorporated the Portsoken ward Watch House. The elementary part of the school, after a short time in Jewry Street, was established on the present site in 1908 (Glynn 1998). The construction of the primary school building was the occasion of the archaeological observations reported here as site B. The Sir John Cass Foundation celebrated its 250th anniversary in 1998, and the primary school still functions today.

Archaeological evidence

Site A

On site A (Fig 2; Fig 4; Fig 5), cutting into the group A43 dumps (Fig 152) in the northern part of area A was the south-west corner of a brick-lined structure (gpA46) which might have been a large (at least 2.0m north–south) cesspit or a cellar (Fig 176); a lens of coal and charcoal on the floor suggests a storage function. The pottery (A[124], A[186], A[187]) amounts to 11 sherds (220g, 0.19 EVEs). The group is dated to the mid 17th century by a tin-glazed dish with floral decoration (A[124]). The other wares comprise both green- and yellow-glazed Surrey-Hampshire border whiteware (BORDG/Y), post-medieval black-glazed ware (PMBL), London-area post-medieval redware (PMR), London-area post-medieval slipped redware with yellow glaze (PMSRY), and part of a mug with incised decoration in post-medieval fine redware (PMFR; A[187]). The brick structure probably functioned beneath the large building that is shown on this part of the site by Ogilby and Morgan in 1676 (Fig 18); by 1753 this was a warehouse (Fig 20).

Nearby, group A45 comprised a rectangular cut or pit 2.44m long and 1.2m wide aligned north-west to south-east, and at least 1.4m deep (not fully excavated), which cut into the top of the south-east corner of the transept masonry (Fig 176). Its six layers of fill were very mixed and the pit was evidently part of a modern sewer trench which was traced, with fragments of sewer pipe, elsewhere on the site.

Group A47 in area C (Fig 176) comprised: 1) a refacing in brick of part of the curved inner wall of chapel 1, now forming the side of a cellar; 2) an east–west arched brick vault (Fig 177)

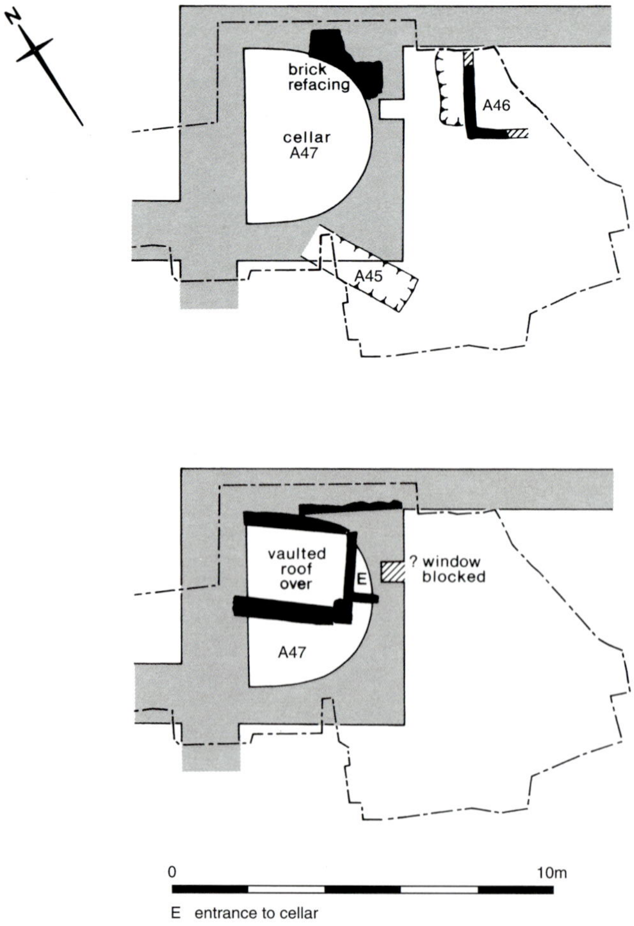

Fig 176 Plans of 1592–c 1900 (period P2) features on the site of south transept chapel 1 (site A, periods VIIId and VIIIe, gpA45–A47) (scale 1:200)

Fig 177 *View of vaulted brick cellar, fitting within the masonry of the former chapel 1 (site A, gpA47), looking west (0.5m scale)*

fitting within the body of the chapel masonry; and 3) further refacing of the inner wall of the chapel at its north end, possibly to straighten up some of the curve. Finds include several pieces of ashlar, and cut or moulded stones from the church: two fragments of a plain chamfered plinth in Caen stone (see Chapter 8.2, in the same group as <A11>) and two fragments possibly from a window, also of Caen stone (Chapter 8.2, note after <A77>). The group (A[102], A[130], A[131]) is dated to the 18th century by English stoneware (ENGS), white salt-glazed stoneware (SWSG) and late tin-glazed wares, including a substantially complete Lambeth polychrome tin-glazed plate (TGW G; A[130]). The 98 sherds (2703g, 4.85 EVEs) also include Surrey-Hampshire border redware (RBOR), combed slipware (STSL), London-area post-medieval redware (PMR) and a biscuit albarello base fragment (<P44>, Fig 202); imports comprise small amounts of Dutch redware (DUTR), Chinese porcelain (CHPO) and Westerwald stoneware (WEST).

Group A48 (not illustrated) was observed in section at the southern limit of area C, and consisted of a brick cellar with a heavily scorched floor. The north wall of chapel 1 was rebuilt with two parallel walls (gpA49, not illustrated in plan) constructed from a variety of building materials including stones apparently robbed from the facing of the chapel wall. These rebuilds seemed to form the south wall of another cellar. A total of 21 sherds of pottery (570g) was recovered from group A49 (A[103]). This mainly comprises redwares, with a number of whitewares, a tin-glazed bowl and a tin-glazed chamber pot. The latter suggest a late 17th-century date for this group. Covering the whole of areas A and C was a large area of rectangular granite setts with well-rounded tops (also placed in gpA49), and with a central east–west keyline of larger setts laid end-to-end (Fig 178;

Fig 178 *Courtyard (perhaps 17th-century in origin, but laid with granite setts of the 19th century) at the beginning of excavation on site A, from the east; the walls of chapel 1 were to be discovered beneath it*

shown in 1979 in Fig 35). To the south were large (up to 1.35m long), horizontally laid granite slabs. To the west the granite setts lay up against the lowest parts of 19th-century and modern brick walls. Finds from this group include a piece of later medieval coping stone (<A64>, Fig 194), ashlar blocks, and a copper coin, possibly an 1860 penny (A<3>).

Group A53 (not illustrated) cut into groups A37 (Fig 45) and A52 in area E, and may represent either poorly-built foundations or merely reburied moulded stones from the site, probably in the 19th century. These comprised ashlar and worked fragments, including more of the aforementioned chamfered plinth, a piece of vaulting rib (<A25>), a half-round shaft (<A16>), and a voussoir moulded with a roll and chevrons (<A18>), all in Caen stone (Fig 191).

At the surviving medieval arch, a brick wall was constructed to run north, at right angles to the arch immediately to its west A[10] (Fig 179). The bricks were hand-made, maroon in colour, and laid generally in alternating courses of headers and

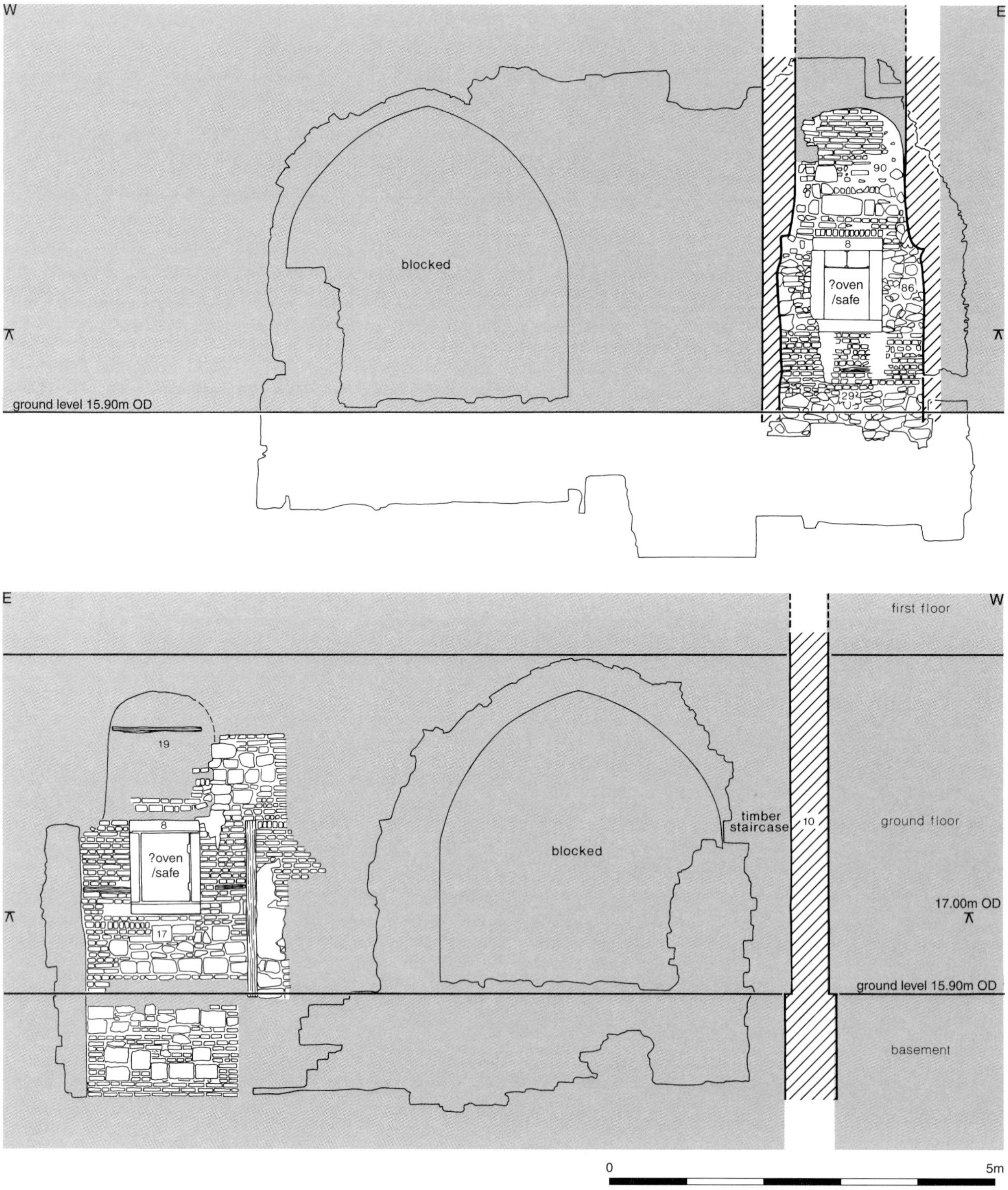

Fig 179 Elevations of the arch on site A, 1592–c 1900 (period P2) contexts, drawing and interpretation: upper – south elevation; lower – north elevation (original context numbers are shown, eg 8 = A[8]) (scale 1:80)

stretchers (English bond). Bonding timbers were built into the east side of the wall. Marks and impressions on both sides of the wall at its south end indicate panelling with a timber staircase on its east side. A basement and two floors above were indicated by these features and associated plaster surfaces with a ground-floor level at 15.90m OD.

The large opening through the wall in the area of the medieval window and door was blocked with brick, reused stone, timber A[17], A[29], A[86] and A[90], and an oven or safe constructed from Portland stone and iron A[8].

The alterations are consistent with brick-built domestic accommodation on the north side of the wall. They must post-date 1753 since the north–south wall A[10] does not appear on the lease plan of that year (Fig 20) and the oven blocks the opening through the wall shown in the same drawing. Furthermore, the reduction in the thickness of the medieval wall on its north side, the removal of the vaulting, shaft and capital, and the rebuilding in brick, must post-date 1790 when John Carter made his records of the site. They probably occurred during the rebuilding which followed the fire of 1800.

The arch was rediscovered after the 'recent destruction' reported by Norman (1897–8). On the north side of the wall a yellow stock brick chimney-stack with fireplaces at ground-floor (16.20m OD) and first-floor (19.60m OD) levels was constructed against the medieval wall A[64]. This probably followed the 'recent destruction' of the 1890s. The latest work followed the demolition activity of 1967–8 when the monument was consolidated, with brickwork and coping stones, to protect it from weathering (Marsden 1969).

Site C

On site C four post-medieval brick-lined pits were recorded, one of which was circular and may have been a well, containing material of the 17th century (in three cases) and the 19th century (in the fourth case). These pits would also have been part of building complexes along the Aldgate frontage.

Site E

On site E, cutting into the destruction debris of the monastic church buttress (but seen in section only) was a large cut 4.3m long and 1.8m deep. It contained seven wooden coffins, with their skeletal occupants, stacked on top of and beside each other. The coffins were rectangular in shape, and the wood survived partly in fibrous form, partly only as a stain. Their length varied from 1.4m to 1.9m; they had been held together with iron tacks and corner brackets, and one bore an iron handle near each end. The skeletons were badly disturbed by machining, but all appeared to have been articulated and extended, head to the west. A backfill of one of the coffins in the burial pit produced three pottery fabric types of *c* 1600–*c* 1750, giving a date of the 17th century or later.

Post-dating the wall and burial pit was a further deep dump (gpE9) of graveyard soil which raised the ground level to 17.80m OD. This contained many burials, but was cleared very quickly by the machine, and so details were not recorded. Several wooden coffins were observed and eight of lead, which were at least 1.8m long and unornamented. The graveyard soil (gpE9, E[2]) contained four sherds. Of these, the neck of a Frechen stoneware (FREC) globular jug, a butterpot in Midlands purple ware (MPUR) and a London-area post-medieval slip-decorated redware (PMSL) dish could date to *c* 1580–*c* 1650; the latest piece is a sherd of refined white earthenware (REFW) dating to the 18th century. The burial ground continued in use until 1851. Sealing the whole sequence was a loamy soil (gpE10) with indications of tree roots, interpreted as topsoil.

Site F

On site F, a north–south foundation, 3.6m long and at least 2.0m wide, of post-medieval brick rubble with ragstone rubble and incorporating two pieces of a large stone window mullion, was recorded in the south-east part of the excavated area (gpF20). The mullion fragments are catalogued as <A10> (Fig 190). Six sherds of pottery (101g, 0.11 EVEs) were found in the foundation; these comprise post-medieval redware (PMR; F[57]), a sherd from a small dish in yellow-glazed Surrey-Hampshire border whiteware (BORDY; F[63]) and a sherd of Chinese export porcelain (F[75]); together these confirm a date of after *c* 1680 for this construction, which may have been built in the 18th century. This indicates that two probably conjoining pieces of a large window mullion from a priory building, perhaps the church, were possibly still standing together somewhere nearby at this late period. The robbing of the west wall of Building E reported above as group F19 must also have happened in the post-Symonds period, perhaps even as late as the clearing-up and rebuilding after the falling-down of the range in 1822.

Site G

Significant pottery came from three post-medieval contexts: modern rubble G[8] (gpG10.1), and the fills of cesspits G[65] (gpG8.2) and G[100] (gpG6.1]. One sherd was found in G[8], while G[65] contained 71 sherds from up to 11 vessels dated to the mid 17th century. These include a complete tin-glazed ointment jar and most of a squat tin-glazed jar that probably had a blue and white design; the glaze on these vessels has decayed, but they do not appear to be wasters. Also present were substantial parts of two chamber pots in post-medieval redware (PMR) and in plain white tin-glazed ware; other forms include a drinking jug, pipkin and small flanged dish in Surrey-Hampshire border whiteware (BORD), and part of a Portuguese tin-glazed ware (POTG) dish with a Chinese landscape design (<P70>, Fig 205). The unstratified sherds include part of a large biscuit-fired tin-glazed ware (BISC) albarello (<P43>, Fig 202) and a Dutch slipped redware (DUTSL) bowl or pipkin (<P65>, Fig 205).

A brick-lined cesspit (G[100], gpG6.1) contained a large group of pottery, tile, glass, bone and clay tobacco pipe, dated by the pottery to *c* 1740–5. It comprised 165 sherds from a total of 43 vessels. Many are reconstructable, if not complete. The following summary is derived from the full report on this group by Pearce (1998).

The bulk of the pottery comprises coarsewares for kitchen or sanitary use; several vessels are sooted and eight have burnt residues. Most of these are in post-medieval redware (PMR: 34%, 17 vessels, nine with a reconstructable profile), and Surrey-Hampshire border redware (RBOR: 15%, four vessels, two reconstructable). The forms in PMR include five large, deep bowls that had one or two handles, a smaller bowl and three almost complete wide dishes. Also present are four pipkins with long, curved, ladle-type strap handles, one with a tripod base, another discarded complete (apart from its handle) inside a slightly larger iron vessel (Pearce 1998, 98) and four chamber pots (three nearly complete) with everted, flanged rims and clear glaze internally. Forms in RBOR comprise sherds from two paint pots and two substantially complete flanged dishes. In addition there are two probable Dutch redware (DUTR) vessels: a near-complete large skillet and a carinated bowl, both of which may have been antique when discarded. Surrey-Hampshire border whitewares (BORD) comprise only 3.6% of the group, probably because they were going out of production during the early 18th century and are relatively rare in London by *c* 1750. The three vessels comprise an unusual pipkin, a chamber pot and a sherd from a green-glazed whiteware (BORDG) flanged dish (ibid, no. 3), a form made from *c* 1550 until at least the early 18th century.

Tablewares and other finewares are less abundant; nearly all were used for serving and display. They include sherds from a plain saucer in white salt-glazed stoneware (SWSG), a teabowl in Chinese blue-and-white export porcelain (Pearce 1998, fig 3, no. 1) and 15 vessels in tin-glazed ware (TGW, 40% of the assemblage by sherd count), of which nine are substantially complete or can be reconstructed in profile. These wares were probably made in Lambeth; with the exception of a mid to late 17th-century polychrome bowl fragment, all date to between the late 17th century and the second quarter of the 18th century. The decorated pieces comprise a dish, two bowls (ibid, fig 3, no. 3; fig 4, no. 4), two teabowls (ibid, fig 4, no. 5), two coffee cups (ibid, fig 4, nos 6–7) and four plates (ibid, fig 4, no. 8). The latter include the most remarkable find from the Mitre Street pit, an almost complete plate painted in dark and pale blue with the word *chalav* ('milk') in Hebrew characters (Fig 180; ibid, fig 5, pl 1;) which at present has no archaeological parallels from London. Four vessels have a plain white glaze: a chamber pot, a plate and two porringers (ibid, fig 3, no. 2).

Taken together, the different fabrics and the number of vessels which must have been near-complete when discarded indicate that the group was deposited over a short period of time, probably as a single event such as a household clearance. The range of fabrics, and absence of ceramic types which can be dated to later than *c* 1740 (eg creamware), places the date of the group at *c* 1720–50, and most probably *c* 1740–5 (Pearce 1998, 98–100, 104).

Fig 180 *A tin-glazed plate with the word 'milk' in Hebrew characters (diameter 200mm, G[100], gpG6.1)*

Correspondence between modern and 18th-century maps is tricky in this area, but it seems likely that the house over this cesspit was in New Court, which was entered from King Street on the west, and which was eventually opened up to form the west half of Mitre Street. The house would, therefore, have stood in a court a few yards directly west of the third synagogue building shown on Horwood's map in 1799. There is clearly some potential for research into Jewish households in the precinct and around Aldgate during the 18th and 19th centuries.

Site H

The late medieval city ditch was examined in section as part of the excavation of site H and some other fragmentary layers and features attributed to this period were recorded on this site. The records have not been examined in detail for this report but the descriptions are in the archive. The pottery from two groups of layers was, however, examined because of its potential relevance to the post-medieval pottery of other priory sites. The pottery is in two groups: from the ditch fill immediately north of the wall on site H and from the excavation in and around bastion 6, a few metres to the east, in 1971 (site K).

The pottery from the fills of the medieval city ditch on site H (gpH12) comprises medieval and later material. The earliest finds were from cut feature H[86] (gpH12.1), which contained a total of 54 very small sherds derived from fills H[43], H[44] and a mix of the two. The six sherds from the upper fill H[43] are all medieval, comprising Kingston-type ware (KING), Cheam whiteware (CHEA) and coarse Surrey-Hampshire border ware (CBW), but those from H[44] and the combined layers include both medieval and later material, with sherds from jugs in CBW, a barrel jug in CHEA and part of a lobed cup in 'Tudor Green' ware (TUDG), a drinking jug in Raeren stoneware (RAER), jars and pipkins in London-area early post-medieval redware (PMRE), and a pitcher or cistern with white slip decoration, possibly in Cheam redware (CHEAR). Taken together these suggest a date of *c* 1480–*c* 1500 for these fills, assuming that the one sherd of refined white earthenware (REFW) is intrusive. The uppermost level was truncated in this part of the ditch, but was excavated elsewhere (gpH12.3, H[23], H[24], H[27], H[34] and H[40], 24 sherds; gpH12.4, H[73], six sherds). The pottery mainly comprises utilitarian redwares and whitewares dating to the late 16th and 17th centuries but also includes sherds of biscuit ware jar/albarello in H[34], part of a green-glazed white earthenware tankard from Germany (GERW, H[24]) and the base of a Dutch redware (DUTR) bowl (H[27]). Similar material was found in H[6] (gpH12.6), which contained the greater part of a GERW pipkin (<P66>, Fig 205) and much of a tripod pipkin with a ladle handle in slipped post-medieval redware (PMSR). The latest material is from dumped layers (gpH12.5, H[3], H[17], H[18] and H[30]). This comprises 30 sherds of 17th-century pottery, mainly Surrey-Hampshire border whitewares and redwares. Part of a tin-glazed porringer was found in H[3], while H[18] contained a fragment of Chinese porcelain; both probably date to after 1680. Residual medieval sherds were found in H[24] (LCOAR) and in H[6] and H[30] (CBW).

Layers H[4], H[21] and H[22], a brick surface which sealed the ditch (gpH30.1), contained pottery very similar to that described above, with the bases of two biscuit-fired jars (one complete small example), larger tin-glazed jars and a range of redwares dating to *c* 1630–*c* 1700. This feature appears to be contemporary with some of the pits by bastion 6 (ER1352–4; see below).

The largest single group from the site comprises 332 sherds, of which only two are medieval, from H[213], assumed to be the backfill of the city ditch in area B. The various post-medieval forms and fabrics (14,019g, 14.06 EVEs) suggest that the feature was filled in *c* 1640–50. The bulk of the assemblage consists of redwares, which amount to *c* 40% by both sherd count and weight. These would have been used in the kitchen or for storage. Most sherds are from cauldrons, pipkins and skillets; the majority are plain, but one tripod pipkin has bichrome glazing (PMBR), while two cauldrons and a large skillet with socketed handle are in slipped redwares. Of interest is a cluster of small Surrey-Hampshire border redware (RBOR) skillets with ladle handles, of which eight are present (one complete). Tablewares are limited to a tyg in post-medieval black-glazed ware (PMBL) and a dish in metropolitan slipware (METS). Whitewares are more common here than in the pit, group F22, amounting to 38% by sherd count and 32% by weight. These include up to ten tripod pipkins, one virtually complete and others substantially so. Also present are part of a chamber pot, a porringer, a straight-sided jar with milled cordon, five bowls, four flanged dishes and part of a drinking jug.

Other fabrics present in the ditch include a range of tin-glazed ware dishes and bowls, some possibly of Dutch origin; others, including a large mid 17th-century dish with Wan-li style border, are more likely to be local. Also present are part of a polychrome jar with a large kiln scar and 15 biscuit-fired sherds that are possibly derived from a nearby pottery, although perhaps later in form than those from the pit group F22. Imports comprise sherds from a cauldron and a colander in DUTR, two sherds from a GERW pipkin and part of a Spanish olive jar (OLIV). Residual imports include the base of a large RAER stoneware storage jar with deep basal thumbing, two Frechen stoneware (FREC) bellarmine bottles with portrait medallions on them and sherds from a type II Martincamp stoneware flask (MART 2).

A group of six whole pots dated to the late 16th or 17th century and a sherd from a FREC bellarmine with a medallion bearing the date of 1591 were found in a pit cutting a ditch (Maloney and Harding 1979, 352, fig 7). A large group of 138 sherds (4890g, 5.45 EVEs), was found in a rubbish pit (gpH23.2, not illustrated), most of which is from the general fill (H[1], 66% by sherd count, 73% by weight). The bulk of the group comprises redwares, with a smaller amount of tin-glazed ware. The lack of Surrey-Hampshire border whitewares and the presence of English stonewares (London stoneware (LONS), white salt-glazed stoneware (SWSG) and Nottingham stoneware (NOTS)) points to a date of after 1720 for the group, but probably before 1740. The most interesting features of the group are a near-complete Portuguese dish (<P69>, Fig 205) found in the lowest fill H[212] and a later fill H[72], and the complete base of a biscuit-fired tin-glazed ware (BISC) chamber pot. The former dates to the first half of the 17th century and was thus some hundred years old when discarded. The latter is much later than wares from the Duke's Place (Aldgate) production site (above, 6.2), and must derive from Wapping or another factory.

The pottery from site H at this period comes, therefore, from three related activities just outside and north of the city wall: the backfilling of the city ditch in the 17th century to *c* 1680 (gpH12.1–12.5); a brick surface sealing the ditch, *c* 1630–*c* 1700 (gpH30.1); and pits of *c* 1720–40 (gpH23.1–23.2) which are likely to be at the ends of properties which had by then formed along the south side of Houndsditch. These properties and their buildings, which were probably established by *c* 1600 in their first, largely unknown form, are shown on the City lease plans and surveyors' maps of the 18th century (eg Fig 168).

Pottery and other finds from bastion 6 (site K)

In 1971 P Marsden of the Guildhall Museum excavated a small site outside the city wall in Duke's Place (site K; Schofield 1998, 49). This site lay a few metres east of the excavation of site H, six years later (Fig 2; Fig 4; Fig 5). Marsden recorded the base of the late Roman bastion 6, which formed the base of the medieval interval tower shown by Symonds. The position of bastion 6 is shown on Fig 131. A broad medieval ditch was recorded beside the wall, and in the berm a 'medieval cesspit'. This may be part of the extramural latrine block, but the records for this site have not been examined for the present volume. Also found on site was pottery and kiln material, which have been discussed by Noël Hume (1977, 111–14). This is relevant to the findings of wasters within the priory nearby on site F on the western side of Mitre Square, about 60m to the south-west. The finds are in the Museum of London's archaeological archive, with their GM (Guildhall Museum) context numbers in the ER (Excavation Register) series.

Two groups, ER1352 (56 sherds, 1570g, 1.58 EVEs) and ER1355 (11 sherds, 91g, 0.08 EVEs) contain mainly 16th- or 17th-century material, with a few tin-glazed sherds which are clearly later, probably of late 17th- or 18th-century date. These comprise two dishes from ER1355, and up to nine sherds from ER1352, including part of a strainer which probably dates to after 1750. The other nine sherds from ER1355 comprise biscuit ware with tin-glazed sherds dating to the late 16th century: a small sherd from an Italian flower vase, and part of an altar vase which could be from Italy or the Netherlands (Noël Hume 1977, no. 16), as well as three sherds from two polychrome dishes and one with blue and white decoration which dates to the late 16th or early 17th century. ER1352 contains plain white tin-glazed ware (TGW C) and metropolitan slipware (METS), and thus dates to after 1630. Also present are a range of red- and whitewares, including part of a Surrey-Hampshire border whiteware (BORD) lid (cf Pearce 1992, fig 45, no. 439) and a large flared bowl, possibly originally handled, with a slightly hooked flanged rim (cf ibid, fig 25, no. 99). The few imports comprise Frechen stoneware (FREC), a sherd of Weser slipware (WESE), a small whiteware dish with a rich green glaze, possibly Dutch, and a Dutch slipware (DUTSL) bowl which, unusually, has a manganese-speckled glaze.

The date of the biscuit wares from these different features is problematic. From the ceramic dating evidence, the fragments of albarello from ER1348 (five shoulder fragments, 17g) and ER1349 (base and body sherd, 16g) and a possible bowl sherd ER1351 (9g, with a bubbled slip or glaze inside) could be contemporary with those from site F, but some or all of the others could be later. Most are from ER1353, which contained 18 biscuit-fired sherds (369g), two from dishes (Noël Hume 1977, no. 12) including one with unfired glaze, 15 from jars/albarelli (ibid, nos 1–3, 8–10), and a cup (ibid, no. 15), with two saggars (ibid, no. 17) and a tile fragment, possibly part of a kiln structure. Three fragments of biscuit ware were found in ER1354, while a trivet (ibid, no. 18) was present in ER1352. Since their study by Noël Hume, it has generally been assumed that they relate to the Aldgate pottery (above, 6.2, 'Occupants and immigrants, 1532–92 (period P1)'. However, while the finds from ER1353 certainly appear to be very similar to those from site F, the possibility remains that they were made by successors of Jacob Jansen, perhaps in 1600–20.

Conclusions for the period 1592–*c* 1900 (period P2)

This long and varied period, of over three centuries, has been reported summarily here because of the fragmentary nature of the archaeological remains. But it gives an impression of several significant changes to the physical and social topography of the area.

We do not know how long the Jansen pottery was in business within the precinct, but it does not seem to have lasted much into the 17th century. Although there was probably at least one establishment for baking sugar within the complex, there is no evidence of other industries that would have required the stone buildings to be adapted. William Kerwin, possibly, was removing stone for his building works, the 'palaces' of which we know nothing. The significant 17th-century development is the arrival of the Jews in 1657, though their archaeology has only been touched upon here.

By the middle of the 18th century, as shown in the lease plans in Chapter 4.2, the priory buildings had either been destroyed or were hidden away behind brick, timber and plaster façades. Although the major buildings such as the claustral ranges determined the main lines of buildings on the ground until the 20th century, the built environment above ground level was thoroughly contemporary: houses developing along Leadenhall Street, with predominantly small houses and shops in the warren of streets and small squares (inherited from the monastic plan) behind, shown most vividly on the Goad Insurance map of 1887 (Fig 174). Partly because of the Jewish connection, this area within Aldgate was part of the East End of London, the large multi-ethnic neighbourhood mostly outside Aldgate to the east.

7

Conclusions

7.1 Introduction

In his study *The origins of the Austin canons*, published in 1950, J C Dickinson laid out what was known of the origins and early development of the Augustinians in Britain, and of the part played by Holy Trinity Priory, Aldgate, in that development. Although his study was not architectural or archaeological, Dickinson implicitly set much of the agenda for further investigation of Augustinian houses. He argued that out of 43 houses of English regular canons which were probably founded in the time of Henry I, at least 33 were established or substantially aided by members of the royal entourage. Further, in the early decades of the 12th century the Augustinians enjoyed something approaching a monopoly of monastic patronage by royalty and other leaders of society. In this spectacular development, Dickinson thought that Holy Trinity Priory would have played a crucial role as the hub in the spread of Augustinian settlement throughout England. Further, once Holy Trinity and Merton Priory (which may have been a daughter-house of Holy Trinity) were established, they together colonised about ten further daughter-houses (Dickinson 1950, 128–9, 161).

By 1215, when enthusiasm for new foundations was definitely on the wane, at least 173 houses of the canons had been established in Britain. For the most part they were small, and would remain so for their entire existence. Thus a large house like Holy Trinity Priory was never typical. Its size and initial wealth, however, did perhaps give it the chance to embody in its architecture and decoration some of the implicit or even explicit principles and philosophies, if they existed as discrete entities, in the Augustinian mind-set. These ideas or fashions had as much if not more chance of being expressed at Holy Trinity than elsewhere.

Thirty years after Dickinson, in his study of the geography of the Augustinian settlement in England and Wales, David Robinson noted that despite Dickinson's scholarship, 'very little has appeared in subsequent years which examines the Augustinians' (Robinson 1980, 2). The canons had been ignored, even though they were the most numerous religious order in England and Wales. For Robinson, one secret of the Augustinians' swift expansion and appeal was the brevity and vagueness of the monastic rule they followed, that of St Augustine of Hippo. This meant it was flexible; and this brevity and vagueness 'not only encouraged new foundations and its adoption by communities of regular canons, but also the transfer of allegiance by older groups of differing background and origin' (ibid, 9). There remained an obscurity not only about the rule and how it was observed, but a difficulty 'in tracing the emergence of groups of regular canons which were eventually to become those communities adopting St Augustine as their patron' (ibid, 6). In these obscure times, the foundation of Holy Trinity Aldgate by Queen Matilda, on the advice of Archbishop Anselm, 'focussed national attention on the Rule of St Augustine' (ibid, 14).

The following paragraphs take stock of these and other questions at the end of this investigation, which has chronicled antiquarian and modern archaeological work from around 1790 to about 1990. These conclusions end with a view forwards to the possibility that the unanswered questions, of which there are many, may be addressed in the future.

7.2 The establishment and development of Holy Trinity Priory, Aldgate

A combination of archaeological work on different sites in 1908, 1953 and 1977–89, the Symonds plans of *c* 1585 (which have been studied in detail here for the first time, and a date proposed for them) and antiquarian observations of 1790–1803, have begun to reconstruct the history of the priory, its major buildings and its influence on the topography of this part of the City of London.

We know most about the presbytery and the south transept. Substantial parts of the south side of the presbytery, south transept and south side of the nave have been excavated; an arch leading from the south aisle of the presbytery into a side-chapel survives in one of the buildings on the site of the priory, Swiss Re House, and part of the south transept, with an apsidal chapel, is preserved elsewhere in the basement of the same building, having been moved during construction (Chapter 8.1). Excavations have also taken place on part of the west claustral range, the north end of the dormitory range and a possible latrine block building outside the city wall (built in the 13th century, and probably removed in 1477), and at other small sites in the precinct. By scrutinising the Symonds plans, and stretching them on the modern map, we can reconstruct all the main buildings of the priory, though they are only broadly datable when there is no archaeological evidence for them.

The present study has shown that we can assemble some information about the presbytery and transepts of the priory church in the 1130s or 1140s, including some probable connections with King Stephen and his family, and give a broad outline of the development of the buildings in later centuries. Although the building of the church at Holy Trinity Priory, and no doubt other aspects of its artistic and intellectual life, were part of the '12th-century Renaissance' identified in England and on the Continent by scholars of architecture, sculpture, manuscripts and objects in ivory, bone and metal (Zarnecki et al 1984), there is as yet little evidence of that renaissance to be reported from the site of this priory. But this report has aimed to establish the topographical and archaeological framework which might be filled out by future work in the area.

The Symonds plans, being of the buildings at two levels (ground-floor and an approximation of first-floor) provide the best detailed survey of an Augustinian priory in Britain. They must also rate as one of the best contemporary surveys (even allowing for 50 years of post-Dissolution building) of any medieval monastic house in Britain. This study has been able to elucidate only part of the complex: we can roughly date various parts (though not all) of the priory church, and the west claustral range in its various periods. The rest of the precinct – the eastern and northern claustral ranges, all sides of the great court – are known in outline only, and certain elements such as the infirmary, school and library, or facilities for corrodians, remain totally obscure. But if we compare the outline of the priory buildings perceptible on the Symonds plans with what we know of other Augustinian houses, or even of other monasteries in Britain, we find that Holy Trinity Priory is comparatively well documented. Though many religious houses are now imposing ruins in guardianship, they are in the majority of cases partial in terms of extent above ground. The Symonds plans, aided by the survival of antiquarian drawings of many details of the priory buildings from the late 18th and early 19th centuries, make Holy Trinity Priory one of the best-recorded Augustinian priory complexes by comparison with those which have perhaps survived physically to a greater extent, but as ruins. Thus comparison of the complete Holy Trinity plan with the more fragmentary plans of surviving Augustinian houses could be fruitful.

A particular feature of this report has been the reconstruction, principally from the Symonds plans, of the post-Dissolution house of Sir Thomas Audley and then of the Duke of Norfolk. It was one of several slightly bizarre urban palaces hacked out of monastic building complexes in London and elsewhere. Already by 1560, and certainly by 1600, the precinct, like many others in and around London, was fragmenting into smaller housing and industrial premises, the latter often in the hands of immigrants including the Dutch. At Holy Trinity Priory we may be seeing one of the earliest manifestations of the tin-glazed pottery and tile industry of the late 16th and early 17th centuries in London.

7.3 Future research questions for Holy Trinity Priory, Aldgate

Future research directions can be suggested, either based on the present study or complementing it by taking different approaches, including conducting the type of analyses which were not undertaken in this study for various reasons. For example, there has been little evidence to address in this study concerning the priory water system, an important feature of many religious houses elsewhere (Bond 2001a).

Because of the nature of the investigations since 1790 and the character of their data, certain categories of find have been either omitted from this report or dealt with in a summary fashion. There has been no analysis of the animal bone from the priory sites apart from one note, because very little was recovered; so at this point in the study of the priory there can be no investigation of the distribution of faunal remains which has proved so fruitful for other sites (O'Connor 1993; Thomas et al 1997; Sloane and Malcolm 2004; Sloane in prep). Neither has there been any analysis of pollen spectra or plant remains (as was undertaken at Reading: Hawkes and Fasham 1997, 74–94). There has, therefore, been no study of the provision and consumption of food or drink at the monastery, as studied at other sites (Bond 2001b), with the exception of the brief illustration provided by the *Liber Coquinae* of 1514–15. Detailed study of the distribution of pottery (and other classes of artefacts such as glass) within the precinct has not been attempted, though it has been useful elsewhere (Moorhouse 1993). These analyses might take place in the future, when more information of the right kind has been obtained from other sites to be excavated in the precinct.

The present study has, however, hopefully put the future study of Holy Trinity Priory on a secure footing. Architecturally, we would like to know more about the character of the upper part of the presbytery, about the nave (which is probably of at least two periods of building) and its relation to the great tower; and about the cloister with its north and east ranges. It is likely that the ranges around the cloister, including the chapter house, are badly damaged, but since the site of the chapter house is now covered by the playground of Sir John Cass Primary School it is possible that low levels survive; there will also, perhaps, be details of the church of St James Duke's Place to be found here, below the damage caused by 19th-century basements. Much of the nave, including the central part of the west end, lies beneath Mitre Street, and most of the monastic cloister lies probably intact beneath Mitre Square. From these two zones, in particular, details of the architecture will be forthcoming not only from foundations, but no doubt also from a further collection of moulded stones. Above all, this study has demonstrated that a combination of archaeological excavation, documentary research and antiquarian surveys can produce a rich and significant history of that part of the City of London which lay outside the area damaged by the Great Fire of 1666. Bringing together and comparing these different types of evidence has made possible a reconstruction of Holy Trinity Priory and its fate at the Dissolution.

8

Specialist appendices

8.1 The incorporation of south transept chapel 1 and the standing arch of south presbytery chapel 2 into Swiss Re House, Leadenhall Street

Richard Lea

Chapel 1

The discovery of the remains of chapel 1 beneath the setts of the 19th-century courtyard on site A in 1984 was unexpected (Chapter 4.2). Although its importance was clear, the masonry posed a problem for the intended development, in that it lay on the site of the future lift-shaft in the new building.

After discussion with the Corporation of London and with English Heritage, the developer Speyhawk took the decision to incorporate the chapel in its building, but not in exactly the same position. Accordingly, in 1985 when all archaeological excavation had finished, the chapel was temporarily moved about 20m to one corner of the site at ground level (Fig 181). After the foundations for the lift-shaft had been made, the chapel was swung back into position, but somewhat lower. It is now within a basement chamber inside the new building, though not normally accessible to the public (Fig 182).

Chapel 2

The arch was listed Grade I after its rediscovery in 1967 as the sole surviving above-ground fragment of the church of Holy Trinity Priory. At that time little more was known about it other than its '15th-century' appearance and that some 12th-century work was also in evidence. The rest was obscured by later brickwork (Fig 61).

In April 1984, anticipating the site's redevelopment, the GLC Historic Buildings Division, soon to become part of English Heritage London Division, commissioned the Museum of London's Department of Urban Archaeology (DUA) to conduct a preliminary archaeological survey of the arch. In this outline report the main phases of construction present in its fabric were successfully identified. A photogrammetric record was also made by the City of London Polytechnic to record the arch before any further work took place, and an assessment of the archaeological survival across the rest of the site was also made by the Museum of London. Basements extending across the greater part of the site had reduced the probability of good survival of medieval remains. The yard surface too did not look promising, since such surfaces typically conceal relatively modern pipe trenches and services.

The proposed office development by Speyhawk (architects, GMW Partnership) was to be designed around the arch so that it would stand in the foyer area. It was also their intention to carry out conservation works to its fabric to improve its presentation.

The Museum agreed to carry out necessary recording work on the arch, to analyse and interpret the archaeological

a

b

Fig 181 Moving chapel 1, 1985: a – preparations; the masonry is undercut in small sections, viewed from the south-west; b – the voids beneath the masonry become the site of a single concrete beam, to which hawsers are attached, viewed from the east; c – the chapel is moved about 20m to one corner of the site

c

evidence and to advise on its eventual conservation and presentation. While the site was excavated during 1984, Victorian and modern brickwork encasing the earlier work was unpicked and removed to expose its medieval core. Archaeological recording took place simultaneously. However, the removal of the brick tended to destabilise the structure, so scaffolding (which had been erected for access) had to be modified to give lateral support to the arch.

The architects and developers were keen to reveal as much as possible of the priory structure by stripping away the post-medieval brickwork which enclosed it. The medieval fabric was, however, shown to survive largely as rubble corework without its original ashlar facing. The fragility of the core presented special problems for conservation yet it did preserve valuable evidence for the original form of the 12th-century church. Contained within it was evidence for the course heights of the original ashlar facing, impressions of the backs of important stones, including the diagonal vault ribs for the bay to the north and a relieving arch linking the south aisle to the chapel. The corework, therefore, had to be preserved as found but its fragmentary condition dictated additional support. It was also felt that its appearance would have been unintelligible to any but the most inquisitive of observers. Given the good quality of

Fig 182 View of chapel 1 in its restored setting within the basement of Swiss Re House, June 1990, from the south-west

the archaeological and antiquarian evidence it was therefore proposed that the conservation work should take the form of partial restoration. Ashlar, and where appropriate, moulded stone was to be used to express the original medieval form of the structure and provide support as required. The new work was to conceal as little as possible of the 12th-century structure except where the rubble core could not be stabilised or adequately supported in any other way. It was also agreed that the floor levels immediately around the arch should match the medieval levels as far as possible.

So that ground works and piling could take place on the main site contract without causing damage to the arch through vibration, it was encased in polystyrene foam, sheet plywood and a steel cage supported by diagonal stays. As the surrounding ground level was reduced, no medieval floors were encountered but the lower parts of the arch, still faced with later brickwork, were revealed.

The architects needed to determine the exact level of the finished floor around the arch, so the level of the medieval floor had to be ascertained. At this stage, access was severely restricted by scaffolding and steels, but with some further unpicking of brickwork around the bases of the jambs it became clear that the ashlar on the north face of the east jamb did not continue below the level of 14.52m OD. This indicated the medieval floor level immediately west of the jamb.

While the main contract continued on the site, the arch was left in its protective casing. When fitting-out work commenced on the new development, the supporting steel, plywood and polystyrene was removed and new scaffolding erected around the arch to allow access. Further recording and unpicking, including removal of the post-Dissolution blocking of the arch (A[25]; Fig 156) and later brickwork, took place around the lower parts of the arch and the new evidence was integrated into the interpretation of the structure. From the Museum's elevation drawings, it was clear that the 12th-century ashlar and core were all of one build and that the course heights either side of the arch were uniform. The plinth profile was taken from a sample recovered from the main excavation. The shaft profile was taken from samples incorporated into the blocking of the arch, that is context A[25]. They may well have been removed from the monument when the arch was blocked. The capital and abacus were taken from the drawing of the architectural details of the bay immediately north of the arch by John Carter in 1797 (Fig 23; Fig 25). The course heights were taken from the surviving evidence in the rubble core. The geometry of the staircase was derived from the surviving archaeological evidence (Fig 62; Fig 156). This, although tentative because of the very fragmentary nature of the evidence, was confirmed by analogy with a staircase at St Mary le Bow (Schofield 1994, fig 19). There, the staircase in the north-west corner of the crypt, exposed in 1955, was of very similar construction. The side walls and vault are of ragstone, the step height is *c* 200mm and the steps are set at 22.5° intervals. The stair at St Mary le Bow is probably of late 11th-century date.

The architects put the restoration work out to tender in January 1987 and London Stone were appointed as contractors. The choice of Totternhoe stone, a form of clunch, was then made for the new stonework to blend in with the original Caen stone. London Stone were to remove all loose facing stones and other material and consolidate the core before reconstruction work took place. The Museum made a photographic record of the arch before any reconstruction took place, and recorded the process of conservation and repair (the photographs are in the archive for site A).

The ceiling height in the foyer and the means of access to the lower floor level required the removal from the top of the structure, throughout its length, of *c* 100mm of brick facing and medieval rubble core, and a further 500mm of the same material at its west end. Between the jambs of the arch itself, the brick facings were removed and the lower part of the masonry blocking, A[25] (Fig 156), was recorded in elevation before it too was removed. Within the masonry blocking were large quantities of moulded stone which were set on one side for detailed recording. The blocking was removed to a level about 500mm below the level of the medieval floor to allow for the construction of the new floor. Evidence for a step in the floor of the south aisle immediately north of the east jamb of the arch was also recorded.

On the south side of the arch, the ashlar blocks forming the doorway at the east end of the structure and the facing of the flat respond on the north face, east of the arch, were removed in order to consolidate the core behind them. Each block was numbered and recorded so that it could be replaced in exactly the same position. The corework behind the ashlar was also recorded.

The wall construction was consolidated by drilling holes, 0.5–1.0m deep, at 45° to the horizontal, for the insertion of 20mm diameter stainless steel rods, cemented in place to bind the elements of the wall together. The rods were inserted at regular intervals from both sides. Some of the rods were inserted through the ashlar facing.

Reconstruction then commenced with the replacement of the removed ashlar. Next, areas robbed of facing, necessary for the stability of the arch, were rebuilt using ashlar and mouldings adhering to the course heights visible either in the ashlar or in the core. At this stage there was still no detailed evidence for the nook shaft bases, as none had survived *in situ* and none had been recovered by excavation. The course heights, the form of the plinth and the nook shaft itself indicated its general form but no record or trace of their moulding profiles survived. It was, however, felt that anything other than a fully finished base would not be in keeping with the restoration, and consequently a profile for an attic base, derived from contemporary examples at Canterbury, was drawn up to fit within the necessary parameters. These were duly dressed and installed (Fig 183; Fig 184). Restoration of the capitals and ribs took place in April 1987. The arch itself was supported and decayed stones replaced, their mouldings based on the surviving dimensions and forms of the other arch stones.

The floor finishes were chosen to evoke the monastic interior and exterior surfaces, gravel for the exterior and tile for the interior. For reasons of practicality, however, in the confined space to the north of the arch, a single floor level was chosen for the area inside the south aisle instead of the two levels implied by the archaeological evidence.

The arch with its surrounding masonry is now a notable feature of the foyer of Swiss Re House (Fig 3).

Fig 183 *View of the restored east jamb of the arch into chapel 2, looking east; new ashlar is in Totternhoe stone and the column base is based on general patterns at Canterbury in the 12th century*

Fig 184 *View of the base of a nook shaft in the north-east corner of chapel 2 during restoration, looking north-east; the scale rests on one of the original stones which indicates the position of the nook shafts for the corner shaft, which would have stood on the reconstructed base (0.2m scale)*

8.2 The architectural fragments

Richard Lea

Introduction

Medieval moulded stones were recorded at the Sir John Cass Primary School site (site B) in 1908 and at the sites excavated by the Museum of London in 1977–86. These have been analysed by groups on the basis of moulding profiles and petrology. Mouldings sharing a common moulding profile and petrology are related to a designated typestone within each group and wherever possible connnections with other groups are discussed.

A small proportion dates from the 12th century, and in this group the use of Caen stone is predominant. There appear to be very few mouldings dating from the 13th century. The bulk of the moulded stonework appears to date from the 14th century onwards and is mostly cut from Reigate stone.

The 12th-century mouldings include a carved capital, chevron arch mouldings, base mouldings, shafts, jambs and plinth stones. The larger group of later medieval fragments includes door jambs, several windows, some tracery, hood-moulds possibly related to the windows, fragments from internal work such as a screen, piscina or monumental tombwork, possible fireplaces, a possible vault rib, coffins and coffin slabs, coping stones, various ogee mouldings and casement hollows, hollow chamfers and plain chamfers, and a range of miscellaneous stones.

Illustrated stones are catalogued with an architectural fragment number in angled brackets, <A1>–<A92>, on the first line of the entry. For the sites excavated in 1977–86 the catalogue also includes, for each reported stone, its accessioned finds number (within the finds register for each site) in angled brackets, followed by the number of the context in which it was found, in square brackets. The group number of the context is given after the context number. The [+] symbol (eg A[+]) indicates an unstratified item, generally found during initial clearance of the site. Apart from those from site B, the stones are identified by their accessioned finds numbers in the archive. The sites are presented in chronological order of excavation: Sir John Cass Primary School (site B; Figs 185–9), Duke's Place (site H; Fig 190), Mitre Square (site F; Fig 190), Leadenhall Street/Mitre Street (site A; Figs 191–5) and the south side of Mitre Street (site E; Fig 196). The assistance of Mark Samuel in accessioning the stones is acknowledged and appreciated.

The geological types have been confirmed by Joan Blows, a geologist, with the following comments. Samples were examined in hand specimen. The Caen stone samples consist of a cream, finely textured limestone. Caen limestone from archaeological excavations has previously been examined under a high-powered petrological microscope and identified as a bioclastic limestone (ie one containing broken shell fragments). The stone comes from Caen (Calvados) in Normandy, and forms part of the Lower Bathonian Stage of the Middle Jurassic. The samples identified as Reigate stone comprise essentially a friable greenish-grey glauconitic, micaceous, calcareous siltstone. Some of the samples appear to be less calcareous than others. Reigate stone comes from the Upper Greensand Formation of the Lower Cretaceous Strata. This stone was, however, quarried not only in the Reigate area of Surrey but also from other areas in the formation, notably around Merstham and Godstone. It has been recognised that once the stone has been extracted and removed from its source, its precise origin cannot readily be identified (Sowan 1975). As the examination of the stone samples from the priory proceeded, it became clear that the two types of stone, Caen and Reigate, could be differentiated in three ways: visual differences; a difference in the manner of break with a geological hammer, the Caen stone being somewhat stronger than the Reigate stone; and third, the Caen samples were considered to have a higher bulk density than the Reigate samples, so that they were heavier in weight.

Sir John Cass Primary School site, 1908 (site B)

The moulded stones were photographed on site by A E Henderson in 1908 and some were drawn for the unpublished site plan (omitted from Fig 67, because redrawn here); their present location is unknown, and they may not have been retained (Fig 185–8). It is a tribute to the archaeological recorders on this site in 1908 that we can discuss the stones in this report from their records. Five different mouldings are represented; they are catalogued here as <A1>–<A5>, and four are redrawn from the photographs (Fig 189).

Fig 185 The plain vault boss for the rib <A1> from site B (photographed by A E Henderson in 1908)

Fig 186 Profiles of (left) the arch moulding or vault rib <A2> (c 355 x 160mm) and (right) an example of the vault rib <A1> from site B (photographed by A E Henderson in 1908)

Fig 187 Two stacks of moulded stones from site B: upper left – two examples of the arch moulding or vault rib <A2> (c 355 x 160mm); lower left – a casement hollow <A5>; upper right – three examples of the vault rib <A1>; lower right – the springer <A3> (photographed by A E Henderson in 1908)

Fig 188 Scalloped capital <A4> from site B; its dimensions were not accurately recorded (photographed by A E Henderson in 1908)

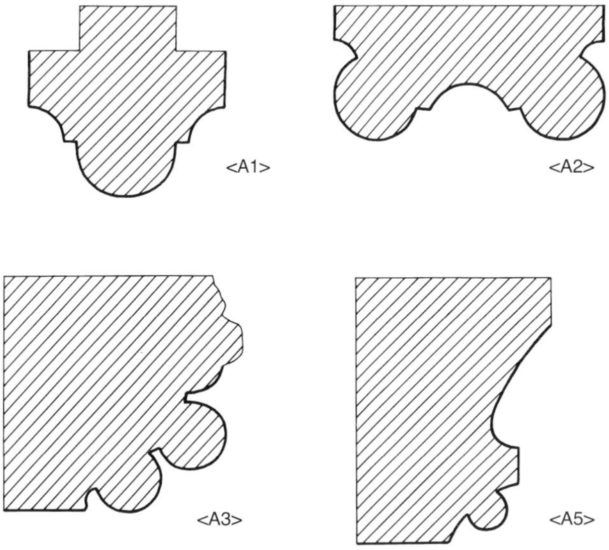

Fig 189 Moulded stones <A1>–<A3> and <A5> from site B (scale 1:10)

Twelfth-century work

Examples of the unornamented vault rib of the type shown in some of the drawings of *c* 1800, together with a matching undecorated boss, and various other moulded fragments, including a scalloped capital, were recorded.

<A1> Vault ribs and boss
(Figs 185–7; Fig 189)
site B
Vault ribs labelled 'arch stones', moulded with a large central soffit roll between two hollow chamfers, are dimensioned in the 1908 site plan drawing as 10in x 10in (c 255 x 255mm), including the tail, although by scaling from the photograph (Fig 186) a width of about 240mm looks more reasonable. Since the Sir John Cass Primary School now includes the site of the three presbytery bays B–D, it seems reasonable to assume that these vault ribs are of the same type as the ribs recorded in *c* 1800 by Carter (Fig 23), Powell (Fig 29) and Whichelo (Fig 31). The photograph of the matching vault boss (Fig 185) shows that the boss was undecorated but had been drilled through its centre, presumably for the suspension of some form of lighting. Similar ribs occur extensively in the aisles of Romsey Abbey, Peterborough Cathedral, Ely Cathedral, and in the transepts of Durham Cathedral; they appear to have been used throughout the 12th century.

<A2> Arch mouldings or vault ribs (Fig 186; Fig 187; Fig 189)
site B
A second group of 'arch stones' is moulded with two rolls with a sunken hollow between. These mouldings measure 14in x 7in (c 355 x 180mm). The breadth of this moulding suggests a substantial arch. A possible location within the east end of the church would be between bays B and C. A similar design was used for the transverse ribs in the nave aisles of Peterborough Cathedral, probably of 1177–93.

<A3> Springer (Fig 187; Fig 189)
site B
A springer measuring 13in x 9in x 12in (330 x 230 x 305mm), and moulded with heavy rolls, would appear to be a springer for a diagonal vault rib moulded with three large rolls, rising between two wall ribs moulded with similar rolls. This stone may relate to 12th-century vaulting fragment <A25> from site A, although only one roll survived on that stone.

<A4> Capital (Fig 188)
site B
A scalloped capital was photographed (Fig 188) but not drawn or measured. The large flat pilaster responds with scalloped capitals either side of the arch to the right in the Malcolm engraving (Fig 34) match well with the small sketch elevation of a capital superimposed on the Powell finished drawing (Fig 29) of the capitals, respond and vault rib, and with the scalloped capital photographed here by Henderson.

Later medieval work

<A5> Moulded stone (Fig 187; Fig 189)
site B
A casement hollow-moulded stone measuring 10in x 15in x 13½in (255 x 380 x 345mm). The form of the roll set in a hollow closely matches the window fragments <A82> from site E, although the casement hollows do not fit exactly.

Duke's Place (DUK77; site H)

All of the moulded stones in this group were found *in situ* (Fig 190). The stones were found in area 3 of the excavation, in two separate contexts which relate to two different medieval doors. The stones in context H[507] (gpH14.2) formed the south-east jamb of a door in a wall running parallel to and about 7.0m south-west of the outer face of the city wall. The stones found in context H[453] (gpH15) formed the two jambs of a door through the city wall. Since both doors are medieval and are located within the precinct they are presumed to be monastic. The stones were accessioned with numbers of the type <205/1>, <205/2>, and so on. In this report and in the moulded stone and typestone files this form has been simplified to <2051>, <2052>, and so forth.

The doorway south-west of the city wall (gpH14.2)

The outer face of the doorway H[507] was *c* 7.0m south-west of the outer face of the city wall and *c* 4.8m south-west of the inner face of the city wall. It was set in a wall running approximately parallel to the line of the city wall. The doorway H[507] and the wall were observed in section only. The section formed the south-east limit of the site, area 3, and the outer face and the tails of the stones forming the north-west jamb of the doorway were visible. The doorway formed part of Building 2, broadly of 12th- or 13th-century date on archaeological grounds.

<A6> Door jamb (Fig 190)
H<2053>, H[507], group H14.2; 12th or early 13th century
Moulded with a quarter-round chamfer and a chamfer stop.

<A7> Door jamb fragments (Fig 190)
H<2054>, H[507], group H14.2; 12th or early 13th century
Three fragments, moulded with a quarter-round chamfer. The jamb is datable only broadly to the medieval period on stylistic grounds.

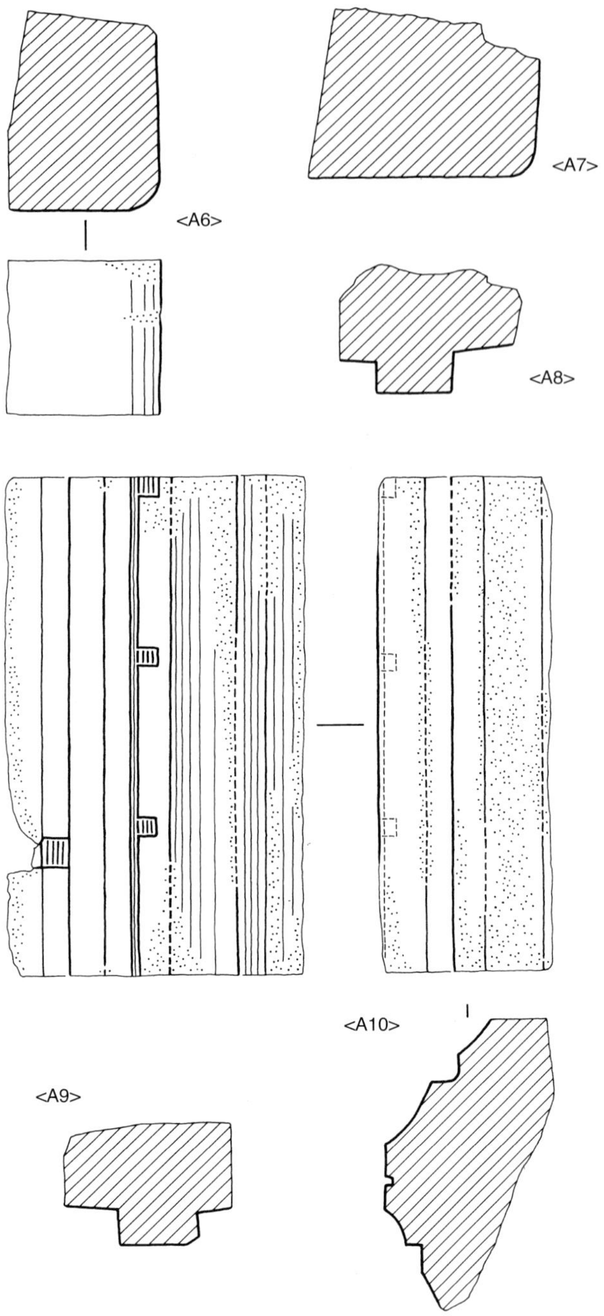

Fig 190 Moulded stones <A6>–<A9> from site H and <A10> from site F (scale 1:10)

The doorway through the city wall (gpH15)

The two typestones are very similar, the only difference being in the small chamfer on the internal arris of the jamb. The exact location of each stone within the group is not recorded but it would appear from the site photographs that the south-east jamb was dressed with the small chamfer, type <A9>, while the north-west jamb was left square, type <A8>. The small chamfer may well have been cut after the stones had been set. The iron hinge-post fragment was found set in the square type, <A8>, and must have been set in the north-west jamb. The door was thus hinged in the rebate of the south-west face of the north-west jamb. Documentary evidence (Chapter 4.6) suggests that a likely date would be *c* 1265–80.

<A8> Door jamb fragments (Fig 190)
H<2041>, H[453], group H15; *c* 1265–80

Four fragments, moulded with a rebate and a splay. The typestone also had the tail of an iron hinge-post set in its upper face.

<A9> Door jamb fragments (Fig 190)
H<2047>, H[453], group H15; c 1265–80
Three fragments of a rebated door jamb, moulded with a splay and a small plain chamfer.

Mitre Square (HTP79; site F)

<A10> Window jamb fragments (Fig 190)
F<99>, F[63], group F20; after 1680
Two fragments of a glazed window jamb, moulded externally, with two orders of hollow chamfers, internally with a hollow chamfer, a rebate and a splay. An iron hinge in the rebate probably served for an internal shutter; this might suggest that this mullion, though large, did not come from the priory church. The external, exposed faces are weathered, whereas the internal exposed faces are in good condition. Probably 14th- or 15th-century in date, but found used as rubble in a post-Dissolution foundation (gpF20).

71–77 Leadenhall Street, 32–40 Mitre Street (LEA84; site A)

A total of 190 fragments of worked stone were recovered from site A. Of these, 102 fragments were analysed according to their moulding profiles and petrology. Some types are represented by several fragments, while others were found to be unique. A series of 68 typestones was established to represent the group overall.

One fragment, A<368> (A[242]), appears to be Roman (not illustrated). Only 14 of the typestones appear to date from the 12th century, and the bulk of the material appears to date from the 14th century onwards. There appear to be very few mouldings dating from the 13th century. Most of the moulded stone was recovered either from the post-Dissolution blocking of the arch (gpA56; Fig 156) or from unstratified contexts.

Twelfth-century work

Mouldings recovered from the excavation and apparently dating from the 12th century include chamfered plinth stones, nook shafts, a large bowtell, an attached shaft, a group of chevron arch voussoirs, an Attic base, two abaci and some possible vault fragments (Fig 191).

PLAIN CHAMFERED PLINTHS

Some chamfered plinth stones were found *in situ*, forming part of the south transept apsidal chapel. Concave chamfered plinth stones were used inside the apse.

<A11> Caen stone plinth (Fig 191)
A<218>, A[+]
A plain chamfered plinth. Five other examples were recovered from the excavation, A<189> (A[130] recovered from the post-Dissolution gpA47), A<213> (A[1311], gpA53, 19th-century), A<220> (A[113], gpA47), A<224> (A[+]), and A<231> (A[130], gpA47) (not illustrated).

<A12> Caen stone plinth (Fig 191)
A<219>, A[+]
A plain chamfered plinth for a concave length of wall.

NOOK AND ATTACHED SHAFTS

<A13> Caen stone nook shaft (Fig 191)
A<234>, A[+]
Diam 135mm. Vertical tooling marks on the shaft and diagonal marks on the ashlar faces.

<A14> Reigate stone nook shaft (Fig 191)
A<479>, A[25], group A56; between 1585 and 1730
Weathered; Diam 140mm. Appears to be identical to the nook shaft <A13>, except in petrology.

<A15> Reigate stone nook shaft (Fig 191)
A<485>, A[+]
Diam 134mm. The stone is quite micaceous.

<A16> Caen stone shaft (Fig 191)
A<251>, A[1311], group A53; 19th century
A half-round shaft, Diam 204mm. Presumably for an attached shaft or part of a composite pier.

BOWTELL AND CHEVRON MOULDINGS

<A17> Reigate stone bowtell moulding (Fig 191)
A<431>, A[25], group A56; between 1585 and 1730
Large, Diam c 115mm, decorated with white and red paint. The vertical edge in the survival of the paint on one of the faces suggests usage as an order in a composite pier or as a shaft framing a recess.

<A18> Caen stone voussoir (Fig 191)
A<267>, A[1311], group A53; 19th century
Moulded with a roll, forming two chevrons. The converging planes of the voussoir and the curving outer face indicate a round arch span of c 4.0m. This is possibly the same as the arch moulding recorded by Carter above the arch of bay C of the north presbytery aisle (Fig 24).

<A19> Reigate stone voussoir (Fig 191)
A<459>, A[25], group A56; between 1585 and 1730
A chevron-moulded voussoir, moulded with a sunken hollow. The converging planes indicate a round arch span of c 1.7m.

<A20> Reigate stone voussoir (Fig 191)
A<392>, A[25], group A56; between 1585 and 1730
Later recut as a pier moulding for a pier with Diam c 850mm.

<A21> Voussoir (stone unidentified) (Fig 191)
A<486>, A[+]
Later recut as a pier moulding for a pier with Diam c 850mm.

ATTIC BASE

<A22> Caen stone Attic base (Fig 191)
A<430>, A[25], group A56; between 1585 and 1730
Moulded with a roll and a hollow chamfer. The straight section presumably implies use for a pilaster or composite pier rather than a round pier.

ABACI

This pair of abaci fragments, with similar but not matching mouldings, resemble the abaci shown by Carter in his drawing of the pier capital between the bays C and D (Fig 22; Fig 24).

<A23> Caen stone abacus fragment (Fig 191)
A<418>, A[25], group A56; between 1585 and 1730
Moulded with a hollow chamfer and a small roll.

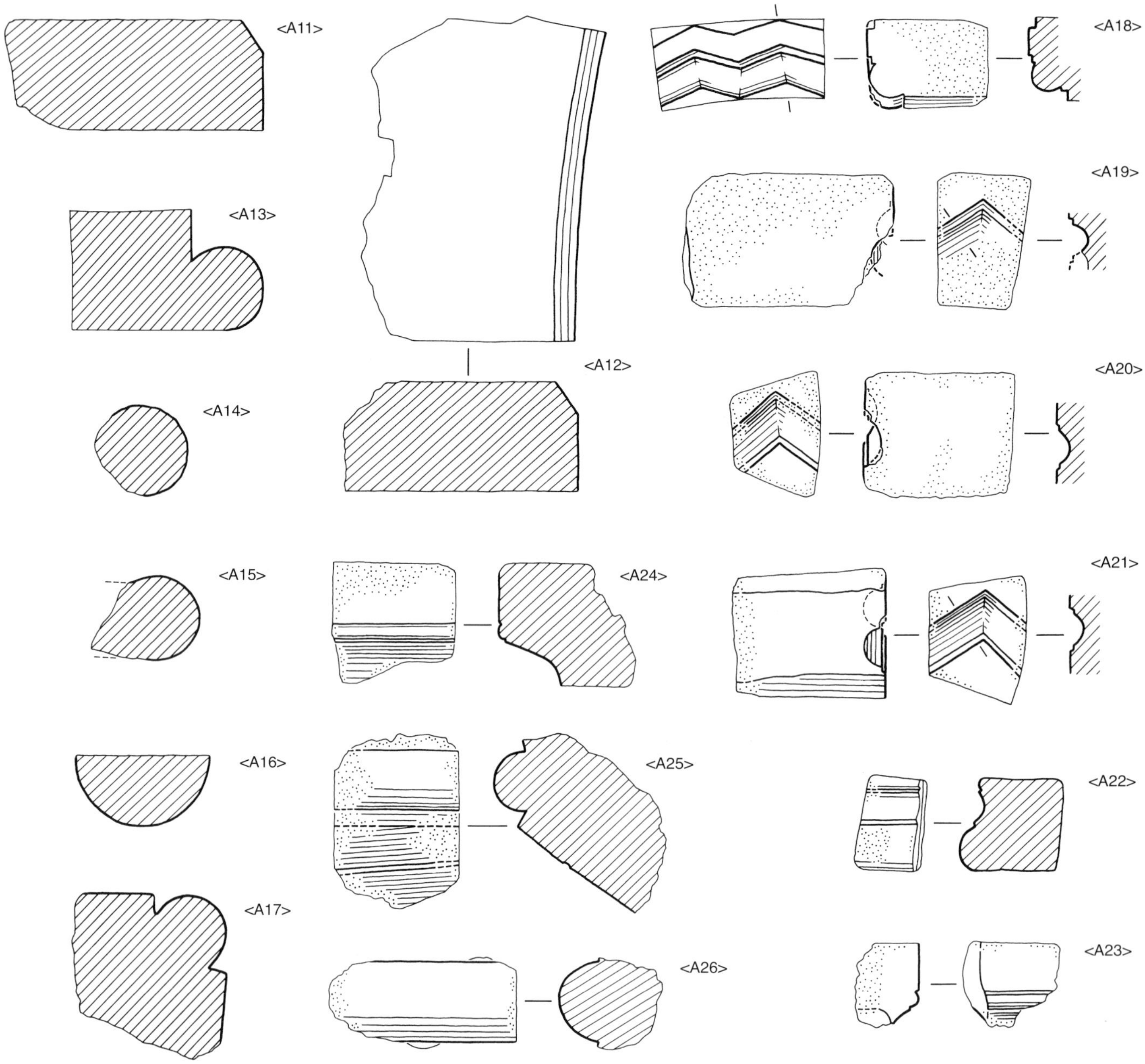

Fig 191 12th-century mouldings <A11>–<A26> from site A (scale 1:10)

<A24> Caen stone abacus fragment (Fig 191)
A<420>, A[25], group A56; between 1585 and 1730
Moulded with a hollow chamfer and a small roll.

POSSIBLE VAULTING FRAGMENTS

<A25> Caen stone possible vaulting fragment (Fig 191)
A<223>, A[1311], group A53; 19th century
Moulded with a large roll and traces of two further rolls. This fragment broadly resembles the vault fragment <A3> recovered from site B.

<A26> Reigate stone possible vaulting fragment (Fig 191)
A<436>, A[25], group A56; between 1585 and 1730
An attached half roll, possibly related to the moulding <A25>.

Possible 13th-century mouldings

The mouldings in this group, comprising three plain chamfer-moulded doors, a group of drip-mouldings and a possible vault fragment, can only be assigned broadly to the 13th century (Fig 192).

ROUND-HEADED OR TWO-CENTRED PLAIN CHAMFER DOOR

<A27> Reigate stone door fragment (Fig 192)
A<428>, A[25], group A56; between 1585 and 1730
A fragment from the springing of the head of a door, possibly round-headed or two-centred, moulded with a plain chamfer and a rebate for the door leaf. The rebate behind the door leaf rises vertically, presumably to allow the door to open within the thickness of the wall.

PLAIN CHAMFER STOP FOR A DOOR

<A28> Caen stone door stop (Fig 192)
A<419>, A[25], group A56; between 1585 and 1730
A plain chamfer stop moulded with a bar.

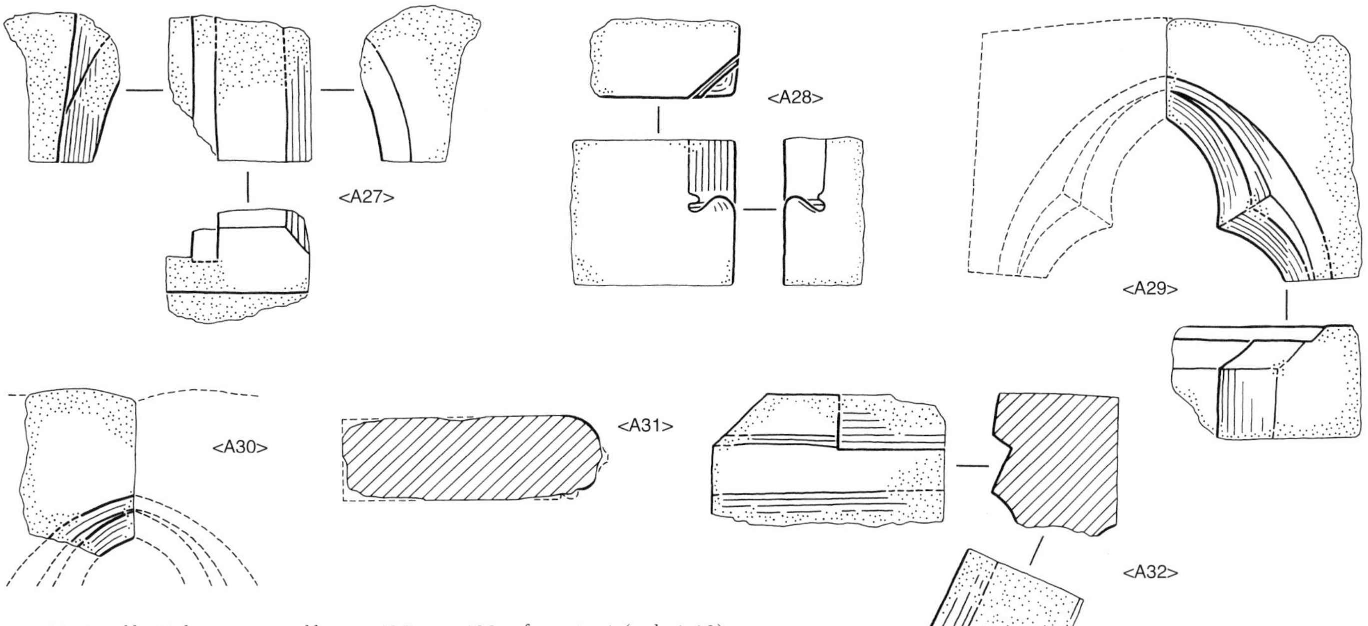

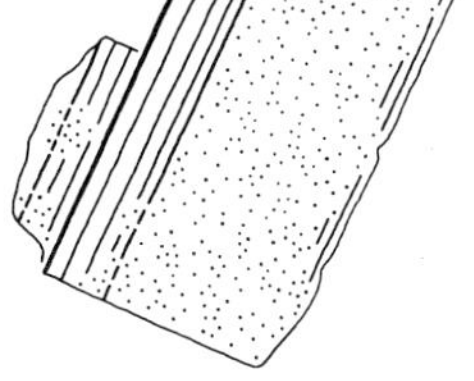

Fig 192 Possible 13th-century mouldings <A27>–<A32> from site A (scale 1:10)

TREFOIL HEAD FOR A PLAIN CHAMFER-MOULDED CUPBOARD DOOR OR UNGLAZED LANCET WINDOW

<A29> Reigate stone trefoil head (Fig 192)
A<407>, A[25], group A56; between 1585 and 1730
A cusped fragment from the head of a two-centred arch moulded with a plain chamfer, the stone highly glauconitic. The opening would have measured 320mm across.

<A30> Reigate stone trefoil head (Fig 192)
A<441>, A[25], group A56; between 1585 and 1730
Moulding similar to <A29> but taller overall.

DRIP-MOULD

<A31> Reigate stone drip-mould (Fig 192)
A<417>, A[25], group A56; between 1585 and 1730
A very heavily weathered fragment. Seven additional examples of this type were recovered from A[25]. All were in Reigate stone and very heavily weathered: A<412>, A<432> (Reigate stone, but no distinct glauconite observed), A<438>, A<460>, A<464>, A<472> and A<477> (not illustrated).

POSSIBLE VAULT FRAGMENT

<A32> Possible vault fragment (stone unidentified) (Fig 192)
A<429>, A[25], group A56; between 1585 and 1730
A fragment moulded with two hollow chamfers which may have functioned as a hollow chamfer vault rib. The moulding is extended beyond the side of the rib, which suggests a junction with another element such as a wall rib. However, it may also have functioned as a window jamb, moulded with hollow chamfers and an angled splay. The stone was later recut with a plain chamfer and a rebate, possibly for a door.

Later medieval mouldings

OGEE- AND HOLLOW CHAMFER-MOULDED GLAZED WINDOW, WITH A THREE-QUARTER HOLLOW-MOULDED CASEMENT

This group represents a glazed window in Reigate and Caen stone with an ogee- and hollow chamfer-moulded mullion and a three-quarter hollow-moulded casement (Fig 193). Examples of the jamb <A35> and <A36>, mullion <A34>, a tracery fragment A<457> (Reigate stone) and a cusp fragment <A39>, were recovered from the post-Dissolution blocking of the arch (A[25], gpA56; Fig 156).

<A33> Clunch stone window fragment (Fig 193)
A<421>, A[25], group A56; between 1585 and 1730
A fragment moulded with a fillet fitting that on the jamb <A35>, in clunch stone (ie hard chalk).

<A34> Reigate stone mullion (Fig 193)
A<442>, A[25], group A56; between 1585 and 1730
Moulded with a glazing slot, an ogee and a hollow chamfer.

<A35> Reigate stone jamb (Fig 193)
A<468>, A[25], group A56; between 1585 and 1730
Moulded with a hollow chamfer on the splay, a three-quarter hollow, and an ogee which fits the mullion <A34>. A socket for an iron glazing bar was cut into the reveal.

<A36> Caen stone jamb (Fig 193)
A<473>, A[25], group A56; between 1585 and 1730
Moulded with a glazing slot, hollow chamfer, ogee, and three-quarter casement hollow, fitting the jamb <A35> and mullion <A34>. A socket for an iron glazing bar was cut into the reveal next to the glazing slot. White paint survives on the moulded surfaces on the opposite side of the glazing slot. This implies that the moulded surfaces were internal and that glazing bar external. The small rebate adjacent to the hollow suggests that the window may have had internal timber shutters.

GLAZED AND TRACERIED WINDOW WITH MAJOR AND MINOR MULLIONS

The presence of a system of major and minor mullions indicates a window of at least four lights. Fragments of a minor mullion <A37>, a tracery fragment A<457> (see <A39>) moulded with

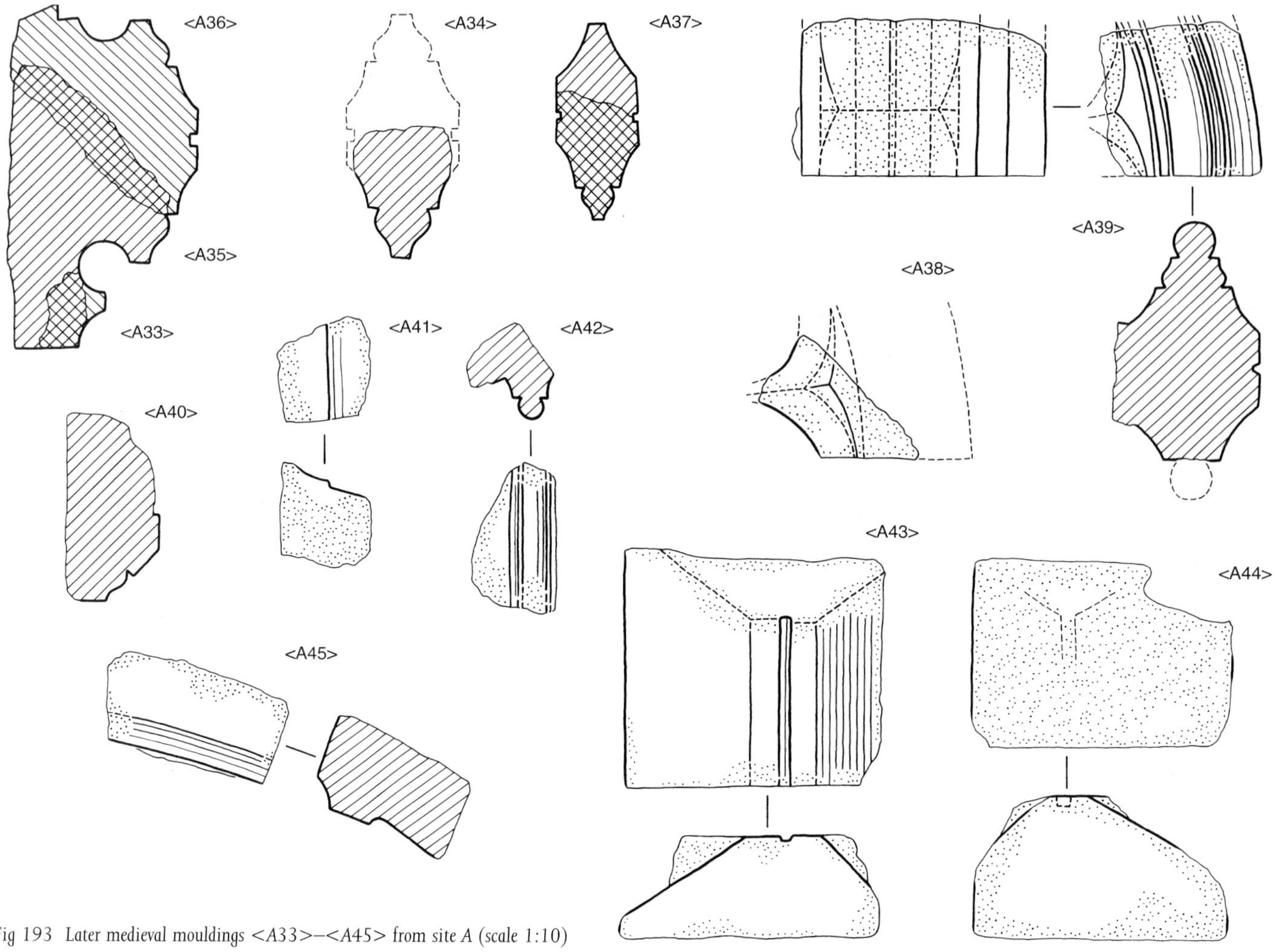

Fig 193 Later medieval mouldings <A33>–<A45> from site A (scale 1:10)

major mullion form, and a cusp fragment <A38> were found.

<A37> Reigate stone mullion (Fig 193)
A<427>, A[25], group A56; between 1585 and 1730
A minor mullion, moulded with a glazing slot; on one side of the slot, a hollow chamfer and an ogee, and on the other a large hollow chamfer. A further example, A<448> (A[25]) (not illustrated), bore traces of white paint.

<A38> Reigate stone cusp fragment (Fig 193)
A<437>, A[25], group A56; between 1585 and 1730
A cusp fragment which matches the tracery fragment A<457> (see <A39>). It bore traces of white paint.

<A39> Reigate stone cusp fragment (Fig 193)
A<456>, A[25], group A56; between 1585 and 1730
Moulded with hollow chamfers and a glazing slot and matching the profile of the mullion <A37>. Originally part of A<457> (A[25]) (not illustrated), a tracery fragment moulded with a glazing slot, hollow chamfers and an ogee fitting the mullion <A37>, and an additional roll. The combined moulding profiles imply a system of major and minor mullions which indicate a window of at least four lights. The relatively large cusp and large radius of curvature in the arcing of the main element also suggests a relatively large window. The fragment marks the junction between two large elements, possibly between the major mullion and the jamb or between two major mullions.

PLAIN CHAMFER- AND OGEE-MOULDED GLAZED WINDOW

<A40> Reigate stone jamb fragment (Fig 193)
A<490>, A[25], group A56; between 1585 and 1730
Moulded with a plain chamfer and ogee and a glazing slot.
A further example, A<478> (A[25]) (not illustrated), was also recovered. Both fragments were heavily weathered on one side of the glazing slot. This suggests that the weathering ocurred while the stone was *in situ* and that the ogee moulding was internal. The weathering had obliterated all traces of what would have formed the external moulding.

POSSIBLE WINDOW JAMB

<A41> Reigate stone possible window jamb (Fig 193)
A<484>, A[25], group A56; between 1585 and 1730
A fragment moulded with a hollow chamfer and an angled splay, possibly from the junction between the jamb and an internal splay.

TRACERIED WINDOW

<A42> Reigate stone tracery fragment (Fig 193)
A<425>, A[25], group A56; between 1585 and 1730
Moulded with a roll and hollow chamfers, and bearing traces of white paint.

SILL FROM A GLAZED WINDOW, RELATED TO <A81>

<A43> Reigate stone window-sill fragment (Fig 193)
A<405>, A[25], group A56; between 1585 and 1730
Moulded with plain chamfers and a glazing slot, and cut to receive an iron glazing bar. The sill incorporates the junction with a jamb but the profile is too badly eroded to allow identification.

Both chamfers are weathered, but that on the same side of the glazing slot as the socket for the glazing bar is more weathered than the other. A plain chamfered window-sill A<404> (A[25], not illustrated) matches <A43>, but was cut from Caen stone.

SILL FOR A GLAZED WINDOW

<A44> Reigate stone window-sill (Fig 193)
A<466>, A[25], group A56; between 1585 and 1730
A plain chamfered sill moulded with a glazing slot and a return for a jamb. The mouldings are heavily obliterated by the weathering, preventing identification of the jamb moulding profile. There are traces of a glazing slot but the even weathering on all the exposed surfaces suggests that this occurred when the window had lost its glazing. Further examples are A<471> and A<476> (both from A[25], not illustrated).

CASEMENT HOLLOW ARCH MOULDING, FOR AN ARCH, DOOR OR WINDOW

Seven fragments of this arch moulding were recovered, totalling c 1.5m in length. The estimated radius of the arch is c 1.15m.

<A45> Reigate stone arch moulding (Fig 193)
A<443>, A[25], group A56; between 1585 and 1730
Fragment of a casement hollow-moulded arch moulding, painted white, the Reigate stone greenish-grey with no discrete glauconite observed. It has a skewback and may, therefore, be from the apex of an arch. Further fragments are A<435>, A<454>, A<455>, A<461>, A<463> (all from A[25]) and A<487> (A[+]) (not illustrated). One fragment within this group (A<487>) is moulded on its non-exposed faces, suggesting possible reuse when the moulding <A45> was cut. It was not possible to determine whether the recutting took place before or after the stone was cut to match the profile of <A45>.

HOOD-MOULDS

<A46> Reigate stone drip-mould (Fig 194)
A<408>, A[25], group A56; between 1585 and 1730
Moulded with ogees and a fillet.

<A47> Caen stone hood-mould (Fig 194)
A<409>, A[25], group A56; between 1585 and 1730
A chamfered hood-mould with a small roll and a hollow drip-mould. Further examples are A<410> and A<474> (both from A[25], not illustrated).

OGEE MOULDINGS

<A48> Reigate stone arch moulding (Fig 194)
A<444>, A[25], group A56; between 1585 and 1730
A roll- and ogee-moulded arch moulding. The fragment has a skewback and therefore probably formed the apex of an arch.

<A49> Reigate stone possible arch moulding (Fig 194)
A<445>, A[25], group A56;

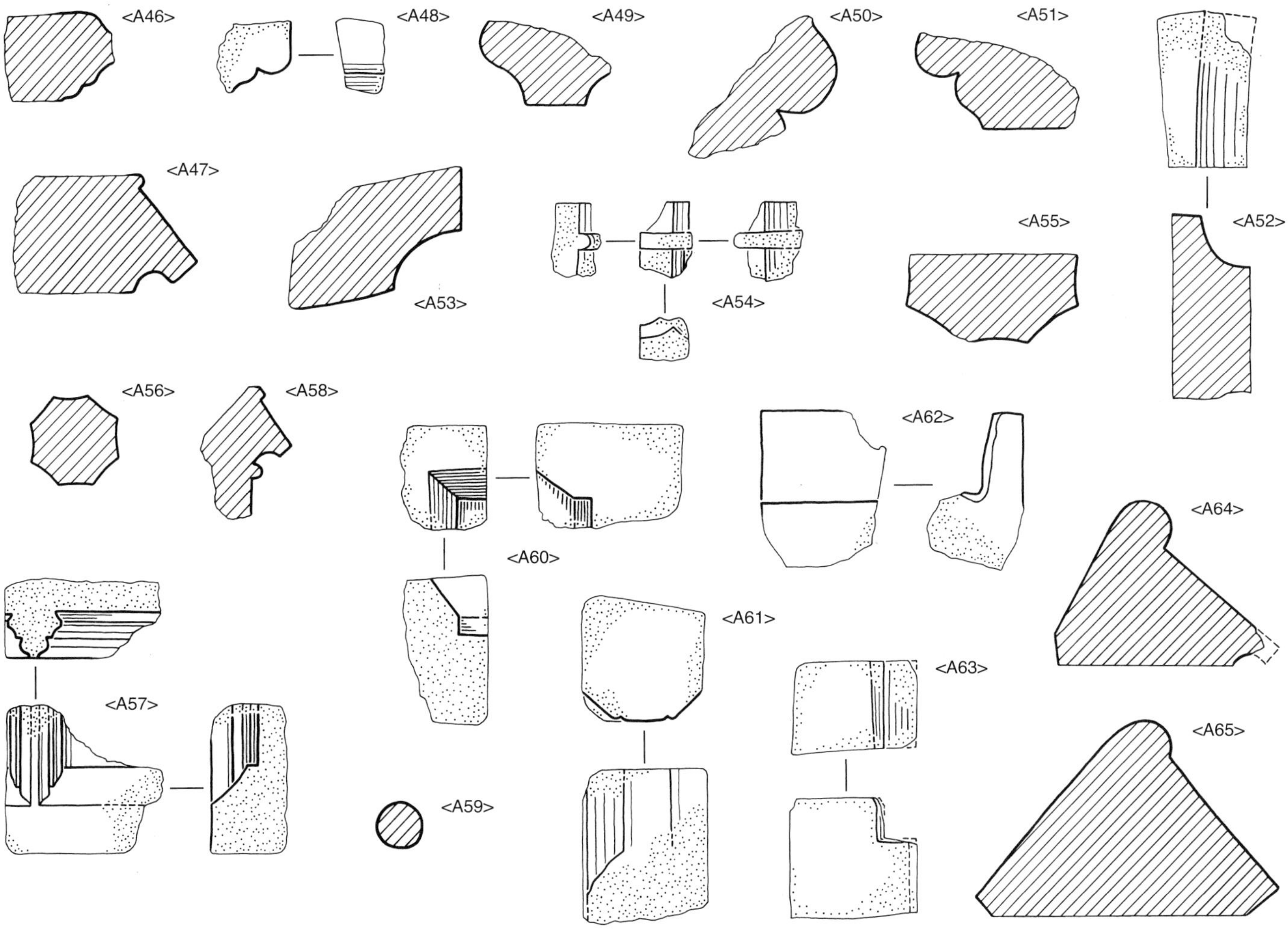

Fig 194 Hood-moulds, ogee mouldings and miscellaneous fragments <A46>–<A65> from site A (scale 1:10)

between 1585 and 1730
A fragment moulded with ogees either side of a broad fillet. The symmetry of the moulding suggests uses as an arch or jamb moulding. It was not possible to determine whether the moulding was arched or not because of its short length.

<A50> Reigate stone moulding fragment (Fig 194)
A<447>, A[25], group A56; between 1585 and 1730
A fragment moulded with a large roll and ogee with traces of white paint. The ogee moulding suggests the beginnings of a casement hollow.

<A51> Reigate stone moulding fragment (Fig 194)
A<458>, A[25], group A56; between 1585 and 1730
A fragment moulded with a large roll and ogee, a broad fillet, a hollow chamfer and a small plain chamfer. The asymmetry and the hollow chamfer suggest a casement hollow. A further example is A<469> (A[25]) (not illustrated).

SECOND ORDER HOLLOW-CHAMFER ARCH MOULDING

<A52> Reigate stone arch moulding (Fig 194)
A<221>, A[+]
An arch moulding with a casement hollow. Some of the moulded surfaces are burnt pink. An edge in this coloration indicates the position of the inner order arch moulding.

LARGE CASEMENT HOLLOWS

<A53> Reigate stone moulded fragment (Fig 194)
A<470>, A[25], group A56; between 1585 and 1730
A fragment moulded with a casement-type hollow. A further example is A<434> (A[25]) (not illustrated).

CONCAVE OCTAGONAL SHAFT MOULDINGS

A small group of fragments all moulded with a concave octagonal section. Two shafts were moulded in different sizes: the larger shaft <A56> was clearly free-standing, while the smaller <A55> was probably a respond. The fragment <A54>, moulded with a small annular roll, may have fitted the larger shaft <A56>. All three were probably used internally as parts of a tomb or a screen.

<A54> Shaft (stone unidentified) (Fig 194)
A<230>, A[+]
A concave octagonal shaft or respond moulded with a small annular roll. Possibly fits the shaft or respond <A55>.

<A55> Caen stone shaft (Fig 194)
A<393>, A[+]
A concave octagonal shaft, Diam *c* 250mm. The octagonal section is not complete, only five sides being represented. The 'sixth' side appears to be original since it respects the arrises of the section. It therefore seems more likely that this was a respond rather than a free-standing shaft which was subsequently recut.

<A56> Reigate stone shaft (Fig 194)
A<433>, A[25], group A56; between 1585 and 1730
A free-standing concave octagonal shaft, Diam *c* 135mm. A further example is A<413> (A[25]) (not illustrated).

FRAGMENTS POSSIBLY FROM SCREENS OR TOMBS

<A57> Caen stone panelling fragment (Fig 194)
A<423>, A[25], group A56; between 1585 and 1730
A fragment of panelling from the junction of a mullion with a sill. The mullion is moulded with a hollow chamfer and an ogee moulding. The scale of the moulding suggests use as part of a screen or tomb.

<A58> Caen stone hood-mould (Fig 194)
A<187>, A[331], group A38; probably post-Dissolution
Small, with a roll and hollow drip-moulding. The moulding of the top of the stone resembles a coping stone. The size of the moulding suggests use within an internal structure such as a screen or tomb, possibly as part of a crenellation.

SMALL-DIAMETER SHAFT

<A59> Shaft (stone unidentified) (Fig 194)
A<341>, A[+]
A shaft, Diam *c* 62mm, of dense grey stone.

POSSIBLE HEARTH FRAGMENT

<A60> Possible hearth stone, Reigate stone (Fig 194)
A<480>, A[+]
A fragment moulded with a plain chamfer and a rebate both of which return. This suggests use as the corner of a hearth stone recessed into the floor.

POSSIBLE JAMB FROM A FIREPLACE SURROUND

<A61> Reigate stone possible jamb (Fig 194)
A<491>, A[25], group A56; between 1585 and 1730
A fragment moulded with plain chamfers, quirks and a chamfer stop. The symmetry of the moulding and the axis of the return implied by the chamfer stop suggest use as the base of a jamb for a fireplace surround.

POSSIBLE COFFIN FRAGMENTS

<A62> Reigate stone possible coffin fragment (Fig 194)
A<195>, A[+]
A rebated fragment, possibly from a stone coffin.

<A63> Reigate stone possible coffin fragment (Fig 194)
A<451>, A[25], group A56; between 1585 and 1730
A fragment cut with a rebate and a small chamfer, possibly from the head of a stone coffin.

COPING STONES

<A64> Reigate coping stone (Fig 194)
A<235>, A[103], group A49; probably 19th century
Moulded with a roll and a hollow drip-mould.

<A65> Kentish rag coping stone (Fig 194)
A<411>, A[25], group A56; between 1585 and 1730
Moulded with a roll and plain chamfer drip-moulds.

PLAIN CHAMFER MOULDINGS

<A66> ?Caen stone chamfer moulding (Fig 195)
A<394>, A[+]
Plain, with exposed surfaces drilled to receive pegs or nails.

<A67> Caen stone chamfer moulding (Fig 195)
A<422>, A[25], group A56; between 1585 and 1730
A fragment, plain, chamfer-moulded with a heavily painted, curved surface. Possibly from the rear arch of a window.

<A68> Chamfer moulding (stone unidentified) (Fig 195)
A<488>, A[+]
A radiussed plain chamfer moulding, of medium-grain laminated sandstone.

MISCELLANEOUS

<A69> Reigate stone arch moulding (Fig 195)
A<191>, A[473], groupA31; rebuilding of chapel 2, after *c* 1270

A hollow chamfer and roll arch moulding, later recut as a plain chamfer. It is possible that originally this stone was cut as a vault rib similar to the vault rib <A2> with two rolls separated by a hollow. Perhaps these ribs were originally used in the vault of chapel 2 and the vault was altered when the surviving arch was inserted between chapel 2 and the south aisle.

<A70> Caen stone rebate (Fig 195)
A<233>, A[+]
Probably for a door.

<A71> Reigate stone roll fragment (Fig 195)
A<252>, A[+]
A fragment of a roll.

<A72> Caen stone chamfer string (Fig 195)
A<253>, A[+]
Plain. Unusual in that the string is not treated as a separate course.

<A73> Caen stone possible drain (Fig 195)
A<261>, A[+]
A drain or water spout, the Caen stone slightly greyer than the other examples.

<A74> Kentish rag moulding fragment (Fig 195)
A<449>, A[+]
A half-round moulded fragment.

<A75> Caen stone moulding (Fig 195)
A<453>, A[25], group A56; between 1585 and 1730
A quarter-round moulding.

<A76> Reigate stone chamfer moulding (Fig 195)
A<462>, A[25], group A56; between 1585 and 1730
A plain chamfer moulding with a hollow drip-mould, presumably for an overhanging section of wall. A further example is A<440> (A[25]) (not illustrated).

<A77> Reigate stone voussoir (Fig 195)
A<481>, A[+]
Plain, undecorated.

Two additional architectural fragments were recovered on site A. Piece A<254> (A[130], gpA47) is a splay fragment of Caen stone with a socket for an iron bar (not illustrated). Piece A<204> (A[130], gpA47) is a fragment of Caen stone, possibly ashlar or a window element, with sockets for iron, possibly connected with A<254> (not illustrated).

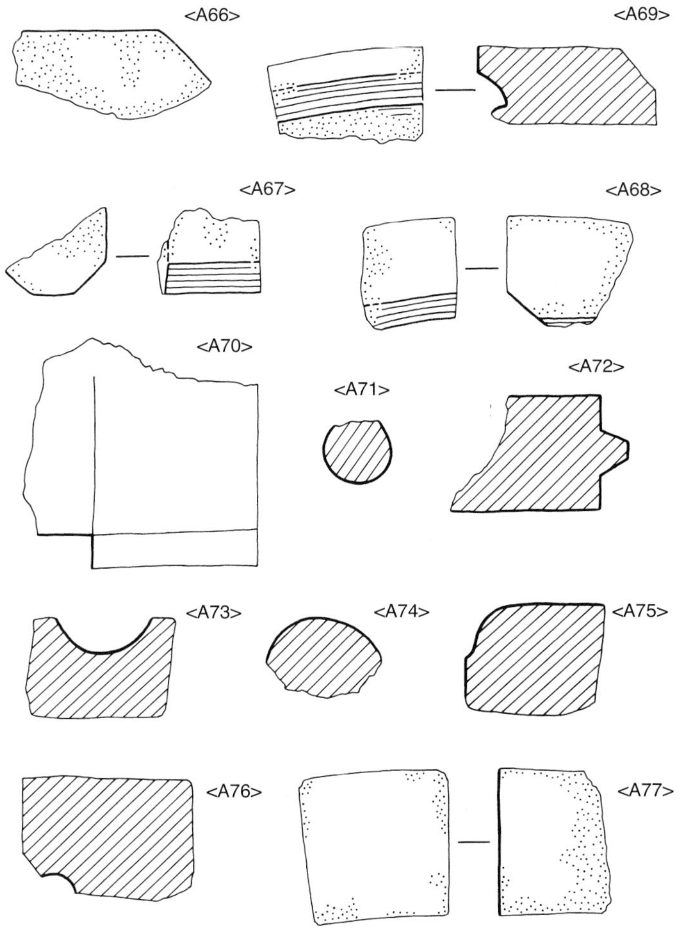

Fig 195 Chamfer mouldings and miscellaneous fragments <A66>–<A77> from site A (scale 1:10)

32–34 Mitre Street (MIT86; site E)

A total of 15 fragments of moulded stone were recovered from this site, some of which relate to mouldings found on the neighbouring site A. The group includes a fragment of a fine 12th-century carved capital, a group of fragments from a later medieval glazed window, the head of a small blind traceried arch, possibly part of a piscina and various miscellaneous fragments (Fig 196).

Twelfth-century work

<A78> Reigate stone capital fragment (Fig 75; Fig 196)
E<8>, E[8], group E8; probably second half of 16th century
A fragment of a carved capital, decorated with acanthus leaves and beads.

<A79> Reigate stone bowtell moulding (Fig 196)
E<5>, E[8], group E8; probably second half of 16th century
Probably from a window splay, in Reigate stone with very fine glauconite.

Later medieval work

GLAZED WINDOW MOULDED WITH PLAIN CHAMFERS, ROLLS AND A CASEMENT HOLLOW

This group is linked to the site A group by the window-sill <A43> which fits the jamb <A80>.

<A80> Reigate stone window jamb (Fig 196)
E<2>, E[8], group E8; probably second half of 16th century
Moulded with a plain chamfer and a casement hollow which matches the mullion <A81>.

<A81> Reigate stone window mullion (Fig 196)
E<6>, E[8], group E8; probably second half of 16th century
A glazed window mullion, moulded with plain chamfers and rolls both internally and externally.

<A82> Reigate stone casement hollow (Fig 196)
E<9>, E[8], group E8; probably second half of 16th century
A splay moulded with a casement hollow and a roll set in a hollow. This stone is linked to the jamb fragment <A80> by the moulding of the casement hollow and by its tooling.

SMALL GLAZED WINDOW WITH A POINTED HEAD SET WITHIN A RECTANGULAR FRAME

<A83> Caen stone window fragment (Fig 196)
E<11>, E[8], group E8; probably second half of 16th century
A fragment from the head of a window, moulded with two ogees and a hollow chamfer. The hollow chamfer dies into a flat panel. The outer mouldings are straight and meet at right angles, implying a rectangular frame. The mouldings fit with the jamb fragment <A84>.

<A84> Caen stone jamb fragment (Fig 196)
E<15>, E[8], group E8; probably second half of 16th century
A fragment from a small glazed window, moulded with hollow chamfers and two ogees. The mouldings fit those in the head <A83>.

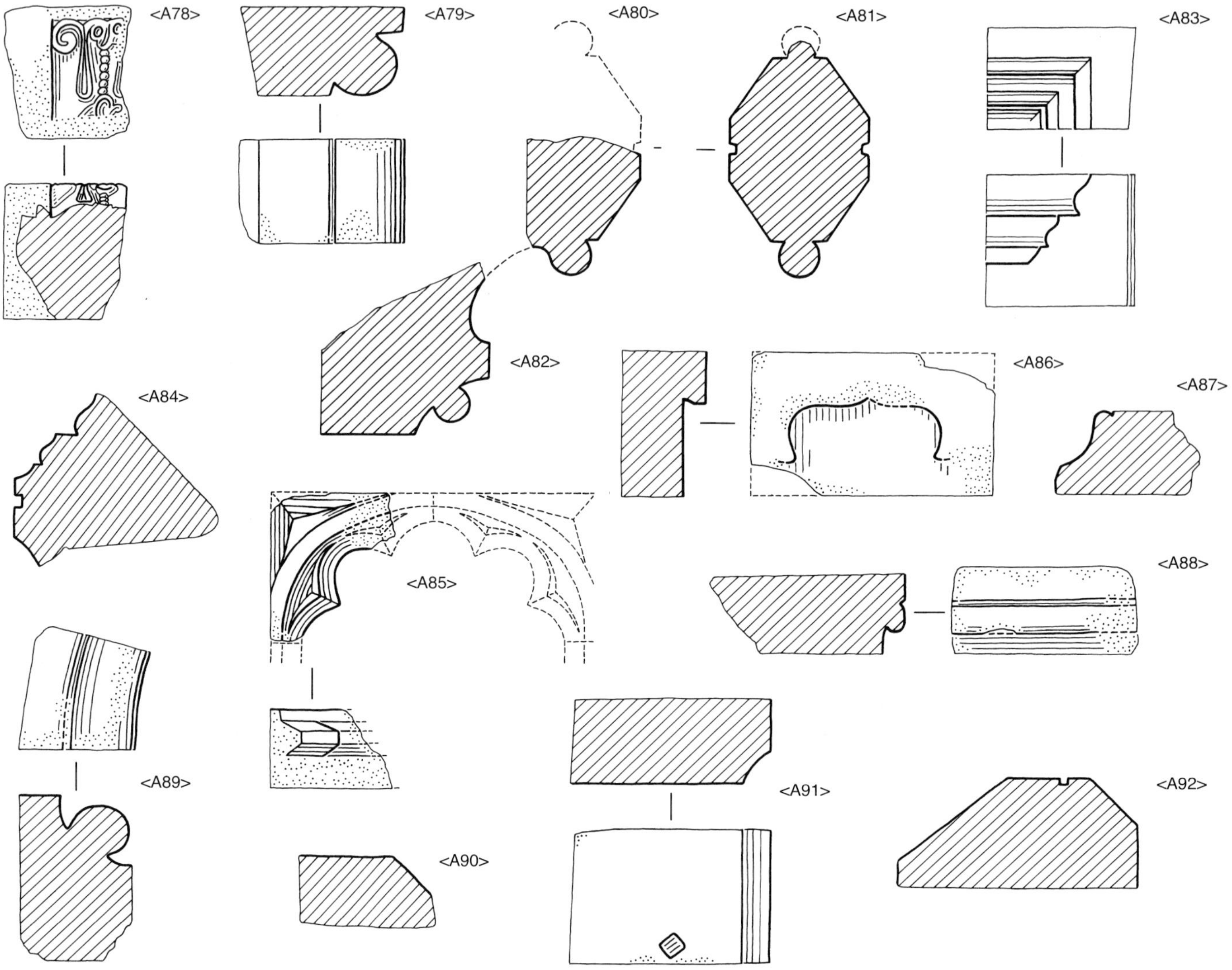

Fig 196 Moulded stone fragments <A78>–<A92> from site E (scale 1:10)

HEADS OF TWO SMALL ARCHED RECESSES

Both stones resemble the fragment <A57> from site A in size, quality of moulding, and in the use of Caen stone, but none of the mouldings match.

<A85> Caen stone arched recess (Fig 196)
E<3>, E[8], group E8; probably second half of 16th century
The head of a small arched recess moulded with cusping, probably cinquefoil under a four-centred head. The jamb profile is moulded with a hollow chamfer.

<A86> Caen stone arched recess (Fig 196)
E<7>, E[8], group E8; probably second half of 16th century
The head of a small cusped arched recess with an ogee head. The face of the stone appears to have been cut back. The size of the moulding suggests a piscina.

Miscellaneous fragments

<A87> Caen stone moulded slab (Fig 196)
E<1>, E[16], group E6; late 12th century or later
An ogee-moulded slab. The moulding profile broadly resembles the 12th-century abaci from site A (<A23> and <A24>) but a 12th-century date seems unlikely with an ogee moulding.

Several blocks with this moulding formed a plinth for one of the nave buttresses on site E (Fig 74), but the presence of a quirk in the upper face of the stones suggests a prior use before serving as an offset on the buttress, since it would be water-holding. The short length of each of the moulded stones suggests that they were not parts of a coffin slab, but formed an offset plinth for an internal structure or a string or cornice. They would have been reused as the buttress offset in the 14th century.

<A88> Reigate stone moulding fragment (Fig 196)
E<4>, E[8], group E8; probably second half of 16th century
A fragment moulded with a roll and probably a spandrel.

<A89> Reigate stone arch moulding (Fig 196)
E<10>, E[8], group E8; probably second half of 16th century
An arch moulding with a roll set in a hollow; arch radius *c* 600mm.

<A90> Reigate stone chamfer moulding (Fig 196)
E<12>, E[8], group E8; probably second half of 16th century
Plain.

<A91> Caen stone jamb (Fig 196)
E<13>, E[8], group E8; probably second half of 16th century
A hollow chamfer-moulded jamb for an unglazed window, cut to receive a square-sectioned iron bar.

<A92> Caen stone window-sill (Fig 196)
E<14>, E[8], group E8; probably second half of 16th century
Plain, chamfered, from a glazed window.

8.3 The building materials

Ian M Betts

Building stone

with contributions by Mark Samuel

The foundations of both the south transept and chapel 1 of the priory church were constructed largely of chalk, although the bottom courses had been constructed of tightly-packed fragments of ragstone, to give extra support. (In this report the term 'ragstone' usually means Kentish ragstone, a sandy limestone.) The chalk foundations were constructed in courses, with a layer of silt in between. The excavator interpreted this silt as trample, but site photographs show it as deeper than trample layers might be expected to have been, and it could be that this silt was deliberately laid between courses to act as a bedding layer. Other stones found in the south transept footings were Purbeck marble, a red laminated sandstone, a worked piece of oolitic limestone, a pink sandstone, Reigate stone and tufa. Most of these could have been reused Roman material.

On the west side of the cloister, at site F, the foundations of Building B were of chalk, whereas Building C had foundations of ragstone and flint, and Building D of rag or Reigate stone. The foundations of Building B had no mortar, whereas those of Buildings C and D were mortared. The use of alternate layers of chalk and silt/gravel is a 12th-century foundation technique (Schofield et al 1990, 164–5), the bedding layer helping to minimise potentially destabilising voids which would occur if irregular chalk blocks were merely thrown into the trench.

The main masonry components of Holy Trinity Priory to be investigated were chapel 1, which opened off the east side of the south transept of the church, and an arch which opened into chapel 2 off the south presbytery aisle. The superstructure of chapel 1 employed ragstone, with occasional fragments of reused Roman tile, in both facing and core. The exception was the plinth which ran right through the apsidal wall and consisted of well-dressed blocks of Caen stone.

The 12th-century wall of the south presbytery aisle, as recorded around the standing arch leading into chapel 2, had a rubble core of unworked or roughly-shaped fragments of Reigate stone, ragstone, flint, chalk and pebbles of all sizes. The yellow-ochre coarse sandy mortar bonding them contained frequent fragments of cockle shell, possibly left over from the burning of shell to produce the lime in the mortar.

The ashlar blocks forming the jambs of both the late 13th- or 14th-century arch (gpA55), and its undated predecessor with the broken-off nook shafts, were made of Reigate stone, except for four blocks of Caen stone and three unworked blocks of chalk in the earlier phase. The ashlar work in the internal elevation was also of Reigate stone, with the facing being otherwise accomplished with small blocks of ragstone. Tile (up to 30mm thick and presumably Roman) was also used to level up stone courses.

At site E to the west three external buttresses against the south aisle of the church nave were recorded. As well as ragstone (the predominant material) and chalk, the materials used for these included reused moulded fragments of Reigate stone, and fragments of flint, 'granite' (probably a misidentification), yellow sandstone and slate. The last-named was manifest as large (up to 1.2m long) flat pieces which may have been reused grave covers. The stone described as granite in the site record may have been Purbeck marble.

Chalk, ragstone and Reigate stone were also the main building materials in evidence at the Duke's Place site (site H), near the north perimeter of the monastic precinct. Reigate stone was used for the jambs of the entrance at the north end of Building 2 (site H, period I), and this material, along with ragstone, was also used for the internal facing of the undercroft below the dormitory into which this entrance led. Behind this facing the wall had a core of chalk rubble. Reigate stone was again used for the jambs of the postern gate, with slate, chalk, flint and rag rubble backfilling the cut into the city wall.

The moulded stones recovered from the priory site were of several stone types: notably Caen stone (for plinths, arches, vault ribs, capitals, nook shafts, window-sills, and parts of a tomb), Reigate stone (for door jambs and heads, drip-moulds, window jambs, mullions, sills and tracery, rolls, voussoirs and cushion capitals), and clunch (ie hard chalk) for windows.

A small number of surfaces were excavated. These included brickearth, used for the internal floor of the undercroft of Building 2 at site H, and which probably derives from natural strata disturbed by the digging of the undercroft; and crushed Reigate stone (possibly waste from the dressing of the jambs) which formed the surface between this door and the postern gate (site H, period II) in the city wall.

As well as forming the large slabs in the buttresses at site E (see above), slate was used for roofing. Slates were found in the cesspit at site H (gpH21), which contained material from the 14th century, though some of it at least was possibly deposited later. Slate has been recorded from mid to late 14th-century deposits at the Billingsgate Lorry Park (BIG82) site in Thames Street (Betts 1991; Schofield and Dyson in prep). The presence of a considerable number of slates in the robber trench on site F (gpF19) confirms that some part at least of the western range was covered in slate, at least at the Dissolution.

At site A, slate also appeared in Dissolution-period layers (gpA38), where it is interpreted as demolition debris. There were many fragments of roofing slate, suggesting that at least one of the chapels was roofed with that material (but see below). One complete slate A<307> was recovered, measuring 280 x 105mm in plan and 5mm thick. It was shaped to a point at one end, and 60mm from the point was a rectangular nail hole measuring 11 x 9mm. However, another roofing slate had no less than six nail holes. Slates also occurred in the later 16th-century activity comprising groups A42 and A43.

Ceramic building material

All ceramic building material is classified by fabric types (described below). All fabric types are various shades of red, brown or orange, some with grey cores, unless stated otherwise. The numbers refer to samples held in the Museum of London fabric reference collection.

Roof tiles

FABRIC TYPES

2271: occasional quartz (up to 0.7mm), red iron oxide and calcium carbonate (up to 1mm)

2273: sandy fabric, frequent large quartz (up to 1mm), with varying amounts of calcium carbonate (up to 2mm), occasional gastropod shells

2275: fairly common quartz (up to 0.5mm) and black and dark red iron oxide inclusions (up to 2mm), a scatter of calcium carbonate in certain tiles

2276: as fabric 2271, but with fine moulding sand (most up to 0.1mm)

2586: common quartz (up to 0.5mm), a more sandy version of fabric 2271

2587: very fine sandy fabric with frequent quartz and black iron oxide (most up to 0.2mm), scatter of red iron oxide (up to 1mm), frequent lighter clay bands and rounded inclusions giving a lumpy texture

2816: fine sandy fabric with frequent quartz (up to 0.3mm), silty streaks and occasional iron oxide (up to 2mm)

3097: frequent silty lenses in a white speckled clay matrix, moderate quartz and red iron oxide (up to 1mm)

CURVED AND SHOULDERED PEG TILES

Fabric type: 2273

The earliest ceramic roofing tiles used at the priory comprise shouldered peg tiles and curved tiles. The latter may have been employed as ridge tiles along the crest of the roof. Both these early roof tile types were first introduced into London around the mid 12th century. They seem to have fallen out of use when thinner, lighter and probably cheaper peg tiles became increasingly common in the late 12th and early 13th centuries (Betts 1990, 221–3).

Shouldered peg tile as wasters were found associated with the very truncated remains of a tile kiln at Niblett Hall near Fleet Street, where the last firing was dated by archaeomagnetic study to some time during the period *c* 1210–80 (Geoquest 1993, 3).

RIDGE AND PEG TILES

Fabric types: 2271, 2276, 2586, 2587, 2816, 3097

These were the principal types of ceramic roofing tile used in London until pantiles were introduced in the mid 17th century. There seems little doubt that the priory tiles would have been made in tileworks situated close to London. Tilemaking is recorded in Stepney from 1366 (McDonnell 1978, 114), and in the later 14th and 15th centuries Woolwich was supplying both London and Westminster (Cherry 1991, 194). There is also evidence for the production of roofing tile at the nunnery of St Mary Clerkenwell by the 14th or 15th century (Betts 1995; Betts in prep b).

At site A shouldered peg tiles and peg tiles were recovered in roughly equal proportions in the 12th- to 13th-century (period V) dumps (gpA30), representing an external area, whereas in later dumps peg tiles greatly predominate. The Dissolution-period (period VII) demolition debris (gpA38–A40) produced considerable quantities of peg and ridge tile, as well as slate, suggesting that both materials were in use for roofing in this part of the church. The peg tiles, none of which are complete, measure on average ? x 161 x 12mm (fabric 2271) and ? x 142 x 11mm (fabric 2276). Both round and square nail hole types are present, the latter being a feature of certain peg tiles of late medieval and post-medieval date. One of the peg tiles bore an animal print and a possible batch mark. Peg tiles continued to be found in the post-Dissolution period (period VIII), being laid as a surface during the group A44 activity.

A number of later peg tiles (A[471], gpA30) have surviving length and breadth measurements. Tiles in fabric 2276 measure, on average, 267 x 160 x 13mm and have two nail holes 13mm square. A peg tile in unusual silty fabric type 3097 has an almost identical size of 268 x 160 x 12mm and two approximately round nail holes 14mm in diameter, and may have come from a tilemaking centre outside the London area.

At site H, there were a few fragments of peg tile in the early to mid 14th-century fill of the cesspit (gpH21), and further fragments were recovered in the construction backfill of the suggested mid 13th-century postern gate (gpH15.2).

PANTILES

Fabric type: 2275

Pantiles were first introduced in the London area around the mid 17th century, but only became common after the Great Fire of 1666. The earliest pantiles were imported from Holland, and the first London-made pantiles seem to have been those produced at Tilbury from *c* 1695 (T P Smith, pers comm).

Relatively few pantiles were recovered. One pantile (fabric 2275) from an extramural rubbish pit at site H (gpH23.2, *c* 1720–40) is unusual in having a blackened top surface. This appears to be paint rather than the black glaze which is occasionally found on pantiles used in the London area.

Medieval floor tiles

FABRIC TYPES

1678: common small quartz and calcium carbonate (up to 0.2mm), occasional iron oxide (up to 0.8mm)

1810: sandy fabric, frequent large quartz (up to 0.5mm), occasional iron oxide (up to 2mm)

1977: common quartz (up to 0.6mm), frequent red iron oxide and clay inclusions (up to 2mm) and silty bands and lenses

2194: sandy fabric, frequent quartz (up to 1mm)

2199: little visible quartz, scatter of muscovite and black iron oxide (up to 0.01mm), and red iron oxide (up to 1mm)

2316: fine sandy fabric, common quartz (up to 0.3mm), occasional iron oxide (up to 1mm)

2317: moderate very small quartz (up to 0.1mm), occasional

black iron oxide (up to 0.05mm)
2320: fine sandy fabric, common quartz (up to 0.3mm), occasional black iron oxide (up to 1mm), calcium carbonate and rock fragments (up to 2mm)
2323: moderately sandy fabric with quartz (up to 1.3mm) and calcium carbonate (up to 1.5mm), plus occasional black iron oxide (up to 0.6mm) and red iron oxide and clay inclusions (up to 5mm)
2324: fine sandy fabric, common quartz (up to 0.2mm) with frequent red iron oxide (up to 2mm), and occasional silty bands and inclusions (up to 1mm)
2497: abundant small quartz and calcium carbonate (up to 0.2mm), and occasional iron oxide (up to 1mm)
2504: as fabric 2497 but with slightly less quartz and calcium carbonate
2505: very fine sandy fabric, common quartz (most up to 0.1mm) and black iron oxide (up to 0.01mm), and frequent red iron oxide (up to 2mm)
2850: common quartz (up to 0.5mm), frequent red iron oxide and clay inclusions (up to 2mm) and common silty bands and lenses
2892: sandy fabric, common quartz (up to 0.6mm) and red iron oxide (up to 2mm), scatter of calcium carbonate with occasional flint
2894: varying amounts of well-sorted quartz (up to 0.8mm), and occasional iron oxide (up to 1mm); a less sandy version of fabric 1810

DECORATED AND PLAIN ENGLISH FLOOR TILES

Fabric types: 2199, 2892, and probably 2505 ('Westminster'); 1810, 2894 (Penn)

Both plain and decorated English floor tiles were recovered. The decorated tiles are of two types, 'Westminster' (Betts 2002) and Penn (Fig 197, no. 1); Table 17 records the designs according to Eames's British Museum classification (Eames 1980; 'E' nos) and Betts's 'Westminster' catalogue (Betts 2002; 'W' nos). 'Westminster' and Penn tiles are by far the two most common types of decorated floor tile found in London, having been found associated with a number of parish churches as well as various monastic sites (ibid).

The name 'Westminster' derives from Westminster Abbey muniment room where tiles of this type were first recognised, and their date range, although problematic, seems to run from the mid to the late 13th century. Both decorated and plain tiles were manufactured. The distribution of known examples from southern England suggests production in the London area. Some were made at a floor tile kiln excavated in the 19th century near Farringdon Road, Clerkenwell (Price 1870; Betts 2002).

The only floor tile found *in situ* at the priory is of probable 'Westminster' type (fabric 2505). This plain green-glazed tile

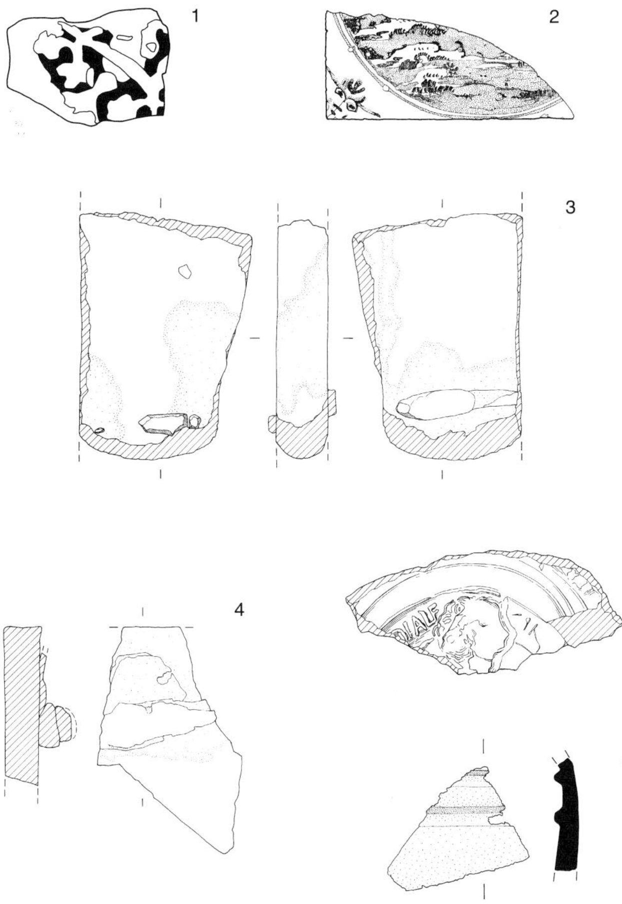

Fig 197 Medieval and later tile: 1) decorated Penn floor tile H<37> (scale 1:3); 2) tin-glazed wall tile A<313>; 3) floor tile with setters attached on both sides F<90>; 4) roof tile with setter attached on one side F<91>; 5), 6) stove tile fragments F<89> and H<198> (scale 1:3)

Table 17 Decorated floor tiles of 'Westminster' and Penn types from the priory

Site and accession no.	Period and group	Type	Eames 1980 design no.	Betts 2002 design no., fig no.
A<24>	gpA17, intrusive in period I (Roman)	'Westminster'	E2185	W95, fig 43
A<25>	gpA56, infilling of arch into chapel 2	'Westminster'	E2016	W47, fig 40
F<77>	III, gpF19	'Westminster'	E2048	W52, fig 40
F<102>	III, gpF19	'Westminster'	-	W57, fig 40
British Museum collection	-	'Westminster'	E2111	W60, fig 40
British Museum collection	-	'Westminster'	E2458	W109, fig 44
H<37>	III, gpH21	Penn	E2426	-
British Museum collection	-	Penn	E2027	

came from the uppermost of the period V (gpA32) mortar surfaces leading into chapel 1 from the south transept of the church at site A (shown in Fig 54, lower right). A plain brown-glazed triangular tile, in a definite 'Westminster' fabric type, was recovered from the period VI dumps (gpA31).

The two 13th-century decorated 'Westminster' tiles from site F (W57 and E2048/W52) were recovered from robbing backfill (gpF19), along with a number of plain glazed examples from the same source. One of these has a brown glaze and is triangular in shape. Neither of the decorated tiles from site A came from securely dated contexts: the tile with design E2016/W47 is from infilling of the arch into chapel 2 (gpA56), while the tile with design E2185/W95 is recorded as being from a Roman layer in period I and is therefore contamination of that layer.

Measurement of 'Westminster' tiles has revealed two distinct size groups which vary in thickness from 24mm to 27mm. The smaller tile (from gpF19, 104mm square) has a green glaze while the larger tiles (three examples, 131–133mm square, two plain and one decorated (A<25>, E2016/W47)) have a yellow glaze. The majority of 'Westminster' tiles found in London measure 100–120mm, which corresponds to the smaller size group. Larger-sized 'Westminster' tiles have been found at a number of other London sites, and it is not certain at present whether these large tiles are contemporary in date with the more numerous smaller examples (Betts 2002, 21–2).

Two further 'Westminster' tiles from the priory are in the British Museum: designs E2111 and E2458 are described respectively as a possible 'Westminster' design and a possible Wessex design (Eames 1980, 307). Examination of the British Museum tiles, together with other tiles of the same designs found elsewhere in London, has confirmed that both are definitely of 'Westminster' type (Betts 2002, 2, table 1, W60 and W109).

Penn tiles take their name from the tilemaking centre in Buckinghamshire where they were made. The first period of Penn floor tile production pre-dates the Black Death, although tiles with designs from this period are extremely rare in London. The site H tile probably belongs to the second or third periods of Penn production, when large numbers of such tiles were arriving in the city from c 1350 to the late 1380s (Eames 1980, 221–6).

The single 14th-century decorated Penn tile (Fig 197, no. 1) came from the cesspit, group H21. It is extremely unusual in showing wear on its bottom surface. This can only have occurred if at some stage the tile had been set into the floor upside down, presumably because the top surface was now too worn. Exactly the same wear pattern occurs on the bottom surface of 'Westminster' tile A<25> with design E2016/W47, and may indicate that both were reused in the same tile floor.

Two tiles from post-Dissolution deposits (period VIII, gpA42, gpA46) at site A can be identified as Penn by their fabric type. Unfortunately, both are so worn that it is impossible to determine whether they were originally plain or decorated – although the vast majority of Penn tiles brought into London were of decorated type. One of the worn Penn tiles, from A[253] (gpA42), measures 110 x 106 x 20mm. This is similar to the majority of Penn tiles found in London, which are c 105–115mm square. Another Penn tile from the priory is in the British Museum (Eames 1980, 295, design E2027).

OTHER ?ENGLISH GLAZED FLOOR TILES

Fabric types: 2194, 2320, 2317, 2324

The origin of a number of medieval tiles from site A cannot be determined. None are in diagnostic fabric types, although most are probably English. Most are badly worn; two fragments from post-Dissolution contexts are glazed, one plain yellow (period VIII, gpA42), the other mottled green and yellow (period VII, gpA38).

PLAIN GLAZED FLEMISH FLOOR TILES

Fabric types: 1678, 2323, 2497, 2504 (calcium carbonate type); 1977, 2850 (silty type); 2320, 2316 (no diagnostic inclusions)

Flemish tiles can normally be identified by nail holes in their upper surface, although these may be absent from fragments or covered by slip on yellow-glazed examples. In this case a Flemish origin can often be suggested based on fabric type. Flemish tiles imported into London are normally made from either a silty clay or a clay characterised by frequent calcium carbonate in the clay matrix. Occasionally the clay contains no diagnostic inclusions, which is the case with three of the priory floor tiles (fabrics 2320, 2316).

All the Flemish tiles used at the priory are plain with either a green, yellow or brown glaze. Two floor tiles are slightly unusual in having a white slip covered by a green glaze; although the fabric (2320) is not diagnostic, this is normally a feature associated with Flemish manufacture. One of these tiles is unstratified from site F, while the other is from a post-Dissolution context at site A (period VIII, gpA44) and has a line scored with a knife through the wet clay to facilitate a post-firing division which never took place.

The dating of Flemish plain glazed floor tiles remains very problematic. It is still uncertain when they first arrived in London, although it would seem highly unlikely to have been before the 13th century when plain glazed 'Westminster' tiles appear to have been readily available. On sites in London the majority of earlier Flemish tiles are made from calcium carbonate-rich clays. These tiles were superseded, at least in part, around the late 15th century by floor tiles made from silty clays. The latter are also normally larger in size, although there in no significant difference in size between the two types found on the site of the priory.

Two Flemish tiles were found in post-Dissolution demolition debris at site A (period VII, gpA38, gpA39); one, with a dark green glaze, has a round nail hole 1mm in diameter near the single surviving corner. Another tile from site A (period VII, gpA52) has four nail holes, again 1mm in diameter, one near each corner. This tile, which bears the remains of dark green glaze, measures 128 x 127 x 33mm. Both these floor tiles are in calcium carbonate-rich fabric types.

There is only one Flemish tile in a silty fabric with a nail hole (site A, period VIII, gpA44). The hole is irregular in shape due to the nail board being removed from the clay at an angle. However, part of the outline suggests that the nail may have been roughly square, a characteristic feature of many later Flemish floor tiles. The tile has a plain brown glaze. A number of partly complete silty floor tiles (fabric 1977) were recovered from post-Dissolution contexts at site A (period VIII, gpA42, gpA47). None have nail holes, but all are so worn that all trace of such holes may have been removed by wear. The tiles are 119–122mm square, and were presumably plain-glazed, although only their edges have traces of glaze surviving.

Post-medieval floor and wall tiles

FABRIC TYPES

1819: fairly sandy fabric with common quartz (up to 0.2mm), moderate red and black iron oxide (up to 0.3mm), common red clay lenses and rounded cream silty inclusions (up to 4mm) in pink clay matrix, occasional calcium carbonate
2196: fairly sandy fabric, common quartz (up to 0.2mm), moderate red and black iron oxide (mainly up to 1.2mm), occasional red clay bands in white matrix
2197: fairly sandy fabric with common quartz (up to 0.2mm), moderate amounts of red and black iron oxide (up to 0.5mm), occasional pink and red clay bands in cream or pink clay matrix
3064: sandy fabric, common quartz (up to 0.4mm) with scatter of light red iron oxide (up to 0.8mm) in white clay matrix

BISCUIT-FIRED AND TIN-GLAZED FLOOR TILES AND A WALL TILE

Fabric types: 2196, 2197 (floor tile); 3064 (wall tile)
A decorated tin-glazed floor tile (fabric 2196) was recovered from an extramural rubbish pit at site H (gpH23). This may have derived from the post-Dissolution Duke's Place mansion. The tile, which is very worn, is coloured yellowish-green and light blue. Tin-glazed floor tiles were first manufactured in London during the late 16th century and production continued until they fell out of fashion around the mid 17th century (Horne 1989, 13).

It is probable that the tile was manufactured in the London area as there is evidence of tin-glazed floor tile production from both site A and site F. A biscuit-fired floor tile blank (fabric 2196) came from a post-Dissolution context at site A (period VIII, gpA42) dated to 1600 or later. This tile has a roughly square nail hole 1 x 1mm in size. From site F (unstratified context) came a biscuit-fired tin-glazed floor tile blank (fabric 2197) with green glaze covering the underside, edge and part of the top. There are the remains of 'setters' – small pieces of clay added to the tile surface to separate individual tiles during the firing process – attached to the upper and lower surfaces. Further biscuit-fired tin-glazed floor tiles were found in a pit at site F (discussed below, 'Evidence for tin-glazed tile manufacture at site F').

Site A produced a fragment of decorated tin-glazed wall tile (A<313>, fabric 3064) from an unstratified context. Presumably of 18th-century date, the tile shows the bottom of a landscape in purple on a white background (Fig 197, no. 2).

Post-medieval stove tiles

FABRIC TYPES

3098: common quartz (up to 0.5mm) with occasional red and black iron oxide (up to 1mm)
3099: as fabric 3098 but with only occasional quartz

PANEL AND HALF-CYLINDER STOVE TILES

Fabric types: 3098, 3099
The two fragments of stove tile found, panel tile F<89> (Fig 197, no. 5; Fig 198, no. 1) and half-cylinder tile H<198> (Fig 197, no. 6) are discussed in detail, together with a number of related finds from the vicinity, by D Gaimster (below, 8.4).

Medieval and post-medieval brick

FABRIC TYPE

3033: varying amounts of large quartz (up to 0.8mm), with common iron oxide and occasional calcium carbonate and small rounded pebbles

BRICKS

Site H produced a number of brick features, of which only two are reported here. The arched brick foundation (gpH26) is interpreted as part of the late 15th-century reinforcement of the city wall. Four bricks were sampled: three are 273–281mm in length, 120–131mm in breadth and 63mm in thickness; the other is only 253mm in length, but had been warped and distorted during firing. Excluding the latter, this gives an average brick size of 277 x 124 x 63mm, making these bricks, red in colour, of an unusually large size. Significantly, they fall within the range (275–280 x 115–130 x 60–65mm) of those measured within the surviving late 15th-century city wall reinforcement, built by Mayor Ralph Jocelyn, at the present St Alphage Garden off Wood Street.

A complete brick was recovered from a 17th/18th-century well (gpH22). This measures 217 x 105 x 60mm, which is considerably shorter and slightly narrower than the late 15th-century examples discussed above. Bricks of this size, sometimes referred to as 'Tudor bricks', were first made in the London area in the mid to late 15th century and continued in use until at least the mid 17th century.

Evidence for tin-glazed tile manufacture at site F

Fabric types: 1819, 2276, 2324, 3099
A pit in the west claustral range at site F (gpF22) contained an assemblage of building material which is connected with the manufacture of tin-glazed floor tiles. In addition, there is also evidence, including from this pit, for the manufacture of tin-glazed pottery (below, 8.5). The layers filling this pit have been dated on pottery evidence to the period *c* 1580–*c* 1600. The following types of tile were present.
1) Two biscuit-fired tin-glazed floor tiles (fabric 1819), one

of which has a circular nail hole 2mm in diameter near one corner.

2) Floor tile (F<90>, fabric 2324) with a white slip which is only partly covered with a yellow glaze. This could be a fragment of medieval tile reused as kiln furniture. There is glaze on the broken edge which suggests that the lead-glaze may have melted when the tile was refired. Setters are attached to both the top and bottom tile surfaces; the bottom surface setter has an impression showing how the tiles were stacked in the kiln (Fig 197, no. 3). This would have consisted of a row of tiles set vertically, followed by a line of tiles set horizontally.

3) A single fragment of roof tile (F<91>, fabric 2276), almost certainly peg tile, with a setter attached to the bottom surface (Fig 197, no. 4). Brown glaze covers most of the setter and part of the lower surface and edge. Covering part of the setter is a lump of clay which was removed from the tile to which it was formerly attached. This clay is not the type used for roofing tile but is very similar to that used for the manufacture of certain tin-glazed floor tiles. This would suggest that the roof tile was used as a kiln support to aid the stacking of the floor tiles. There is evidence for the use of roofing tiles as kiln furniture at both the Pickleherring and Platform Wharf tin-glazed floor tile and pottery factories (Betts 1994; 1996; Betts in prep a).

The most likely source of the biscuit-fired tin-glazed floor tiles and other kiln material is the 'Aldgate pottery' situated within post-Dissolution Duke's Place. There would have been little difficulty in producing both tin-glazed pottery and floor tiles as both were usually fired in the same kiln (Britton 1987, 12).

A fragment of imported Cologne-type decorated stove panel tile F<89> (Fig 197, no. 5; Fig 198, no. 1) with a representation of Logic, in the Seven Liberal Arts series dated to 1561–2, pre-dates the establishment of the Aldgate pottery by some nine or ten years. This tile (fabric 3099), also from the pit at site F, somewhat unusually has green glaze covering both the top and part of the broken edge. Gaimster believes that this may have been the result of the refiring of the broken fragment in the tin-glazed kiln of the Aldgate pottery (below, 8.4).

8.4 Evidence for Continental tile-stoves at Holy Trinity Priory and Duke's Place

David Gaimster

Introduction

Excavations on the site of Holy Trinity Priory produced a small number of earthenware stove tile fragments which relate both to the late medieval monastic occupation and subsequent aristocratic residence of Duke's Place. Previous archaeological research has identified a significant import trade in luxury ceramic stoves into London during the 15th and 16th centuries (Gaimster 1988a; Gaimster et al 1990). According to chemical analysis (NAA), most British stove tile finds of this period were imported from the Rhineland, followed by northern Germany and the south Netherlands (Cowell 1990). During the early 16th century the success of this luxury import trade stimulated earthenware potters working on the Surrey-Hampshire border to enter into competition by producing a series of armorial tiles for the native market. These tiles moulded with the royal arms and cyphers of Tudor and early Stuart monarchs continued to be produced until the second quarter of the 17th century (Gaimster 1988b; Cowell and Gaimster 1995).

The smokeless ceramic stove represents a dramatic transformation of the English interior of the late Middle Ages and early modern period (Gaimster 1994; 2000; 2001). The archaeological distribution of these finds forms not only an index of material comfort in the home but also a physical measure of Continental cultural and technological influence across the Channel (Gaimster 1993). In contrast to the restricted social distribution of the 15th century, following the Dissolution imported tile-stoves were commissioned for the homes of the aristocracy and country gentry, many of them former monastic houses, and for wealthy merchants' houses in which there was a growing accent on conspicuous consumption (Gaimster and Nenk 1997, 181). Finds of late elaborate Gothic-style tile-stoves at Fountains Abbey (Yorkshire North Riding) and the abbey of St Mary Graces, near the Tower of London, are representative of the ecclesiastical setting of such imports prior to the Reformation. Stove tiles moulded with similar designs from the 1507 Pottergate fire deposit in Norwich and from sites in the City of London and Southwark reflect the increasingly secular context for stove use during the early years of the 16th century (ibid, 179–81). In terms of their dating, the Holy Trinity stove tiles straddle both sides of the Dissolution period and reflect the growing emphasis on material comfort in the metropolitan home of the period.

In addition to the two finds made during recent excavations on the site of Holy Trinity Priory, this report also considers a further group of imported stove tiles found in the vicinity over the years, and now housed in the Museum of London collections, which relate closely both in terms of date and relief design. All but one fragment among the two groups share the same form and architectural scheme, and may even derive from a single or a small number of identical stoves bought or ordered for the London residence of the Duke of Norfolk which had been established in the midst of the monastic complex by 1554. Only one tile can be attributed on the basis of its form and moulded relief design to the final years of monastic occupation.

The finds

Panel-tile fragment (Fig 197, no. 5; Fig 198, no. 1)
F<89>, F[220], group F22
Fragment from the centre of a rectangular panel tile moulded with the head of a full-length allegorical figure (Gaimster 1988a, fig 26). L 111mm. The head is superimposed over a scroll identifying the personification concerned: 'DIALECTICA' (Logic). Orange to buff earthenware body covered with a thick layer of

Fig 198 *Stove tile fragments:* 1) *panel tile F<89>, with the figure of Logic; three crest tiles,* 2) *palmette (MoL A4595),* 3) *leaf-mask (MoL A4600), and* 4) *classical portrait (MoL A4589); three separator-tiles,* 5) *Atlas (MoL A4593),* 6) *Atlas, complete example (MoL A4598) and* 7) *caryatid (MoL A4594) (scale c 1:2)*

dark green copper-rich lead glaze which has run over the broken edge of the fragment. The position of the glaze may be a product of accidental refiring. The fragment could have been used as packing in the kiln used by the tin-glazed earthenware business established by Jacob Jansen in the former precinct of Holy Trinity Priory by 1571 (Edwards 1999; below, 8.5).

The stove tile represented by this fragment takes the form of a rectangular panel tile moulded with the female allegorical figure of Logic, one of the Seven Liberal Arts. The figures set within a Renaissance arch supported by herms are based directly on a series of woodcut engravings by Hans Holbein published between 1535 and 1543 (Unger 1988, 119–28). This tile series was produced in Cologne during the 1560s to 1570s. Several of the Cologne Liberal Arts figures are moulded with tablets containing the date 1561, the original production date of the mould (eg ibid, 121–4).

Stove tile fragment (Fig 197, no. 6)
H<198>, H [33], group H12.3; fill of city ditch (*tpq c* 1600)
Fragment of flange from a half-cylinder stove tile. L 55mm. Buff to off-white earthenware body with bright green copper-rich

lead glaze over a thin surface layer of white slip. The decorative front panel is moulded with parallel vertical bars forming part of the box-frame.

The mouldings recall the flange decoration on the display surface of half-cylinder tiles made in Cologne in the Rhineland during the first quarter of the 16th century (Unger 1988, nos 61–5, 69).

The off-white body fabric clearly derives from a whiteware production source, such as Cologne, the origin of many imported stove tiles found in the London area (Gaimster 1988a). Such tiles, their front panels moulded with elaborate late Gothic-style foliate designs, almost certainly belong to the immediate pre-Dissolution phase of the priory buildings.

Related finds from Duke's Place (MoL Hilton Price collection, 1913)

Note: MoL A4590, A4592, A4596, A4599, A4601: not traced/sold 1920.

CREST TILES

MoL A4589 (Fig 198, no. 4)
Crest tile in the form of a trapezium-shaped gable moulded in the centre with a male portrait in classical dress and hairstyle within an egg-and-dart frame. L 147mm. The trapezium supports a fanlight pediment above. Off-white to buff earthenware body covered with a green copper-rich lead glaze.

The whiteware fabric suggests a Cologne origin, where such gabled portrait crest tiles are well known. Portraits of classical personages are common, particularly Antique heroes in full armour. One example, which shares many details of design with the Duke's Place tile, belongs to a stove constructed of tiles moulded with biblical scenes and heroes dating to 1572–3 (Unger 1988, 148–78, no.153). Renaissance-style gabled portrait tiles with fanlight ornament are known from excavations across northern Europe, particularly in north Germany and the south Baltic Sea region. Minor variations on this combination of designs are known from the production and consumer sites in the Werra region of north Germany (Stephan 1991, figs 123–5) and from Copenhagen, Lund and Malmö.

MoL A4595 (Fig 198, no. 2)
Crest tile moulded in the form of a stylised palmette, possibly an acanthus, perched on top of a fluted column base. H 142mm. Concave vertical profile. Red earthenware body with green copper-rich lead glaze over a white slip. The distinctive redware body suggests an origin just outside the Cologne area, somewhere in the lower or middle Rhineland, in the 1560s to 1570s.

MoL A4600 (Fig 198, no. 3)
Crest tile moulded with a grotesque leaf-mask supporting a further mask between two crouching putti. H 127mm. Concave vertical profile. Red earthenware body with green copper-rich glaze (no trace of white slip). The redware body suggests a lower or middle Rhineland origin, also in the 1560s to 1570s. Tiles made using the same mould have also been found in Fleet Street, London (now in the Royal Ontario Museum, Toronto, inv 928.17.14A–14B).

SEPARATOR-TILES

MoL A4593 (Fig 198, no. 5), A4597, A4598 (Fig 198, no. 6)
Vertical separator-tiles. Complete tile (A4598) H 280mm. T-section moulded with the figure of Atlas, arms folded, supporting an Ionic capital, and standing on a fluted column base. Off-white earthenware body with a green copper-rich lead glaze. Probably made in Cologne, *c* 1570–80. A whiteware Atlas separator-tile made from the same mould can be seen in Unger 1988, no. 199. The Atlas figures would have covered the vertical seams between rectangular panel tiles moulded with allegorical figures in the same style as can be seen in the case of a reconstructed stove of the Nine Muses in the Cologne Museum of Applied Art (Strauss 1972, pl 130; Unger 1988, 201 (fig)). Other London finds of mould-identical tiles are known from Fleet Street, London (now in the Royal Ontario Museum, Toronto, inv 928.17.17).

MoL A4594 (Fig 198, no. 7)
Part of vertical separator-tile. Surviving H 160mm. T-section moulded with the figure of a female caryatid in classical dress (Gaimster 1988a, fig 25). The figure holds her arms up to support the capital above. Off-white earthenware body with polychrome-glazed surfaces. Although discoloured, it is possible to make out green on the drapery, manganese purple on the lower legs, yellow on the collar, headdress and tunic, and a white tin-glaze on the body of the figure. Probably made in Cologne, *c* 1570–80. A whiteware caryatid figure made from the same mould can be seen in Unger 1988, no. 207. Caryatids would have been used to cover the seams between rectangular panel tiles as in the case of the Atlas figures discussed above.

Discussion: Cologne-type stove tiles in London

Renaissance-style whiteware stove tiles from Cologne and redware equivalents made from the same moulds in neighbouring parts of the Rhineland form the largest group of imported 16th-century stove tiles found in the London area (Gaimster 1988a). The largest assemblage of Cologne stove tiles was found off Fleet Street, probably close to the Inns of Court, during the final decades of the 19th century, probably all on one site (MoL 84.158/1–11 and 7124, 7125, 17034–41 etc). The best-preserved were listed in the catalogue of the Guildhall Museum (1908, 251, nos 337–46). The Fleet Street tiles share the same design repertoire as the Holy Trinity Priory finds. Allegorical figures from the Seven Liberal Arts and Cardinal Virtues series, including Logic and Hope, along with Atlas and caryatid separator-tiles, account for most of the surviving dozen or so fragments (Gaimster 1988a, figs 18–22). The rectangular panel tiles with the figure of Logic found at Holy Trinity Priory and Fleet Street must derive from the same mould (MoL 7124; Gaimster 1988a, fig 18). Leaf-mask crest tiles and an Atlas separator-tile identical to the Duke's Place finds from the same Fleet Street source, and probably from the same stove(s), were sold by the collector G F Lawrence to the Royal Ontario Museum, Toronto (inv 928.17.14a–c). Lawrence was a well-known figure on City of London building sites between the two World Wars.

South of Fleet Street, Professor W F Grimes's post-war excavations at St Bride's church produced a fragment of a redware stove tile moulded with the figure of 'GRAMMATICA' and the dated tablet 1561 in the same allegorical series (Milne 1997, 116). Further finds of mid 16th-century Renaissance-style stove tiles of Cologne type have been found in London's historical inner suburbs, notably to the east of the City in Wapping (Guildhall Museum 1908, nos 135–6; Gaimster 1988a, fig 24 for Atlas separator-tiles) and on the south bank of the Thames at Norfolk House, Lambeth, another London residence of the Duke of Norfolk, where the foundations of a tile-stove were preserved *in situ*, including a rectangular panel tile moulded with the figure of Music in the Seven Liberal Arts series (Webber 1991, fig 3).

Finally, it is precisely this type of Cologne-type stove tiles, doubtless available on the London pottery market, which Sir Martin Frobisher bought in bulk for use on his 1578 *Meta Incognita* expedition to the North American Arctic in 1578. They were transported originally for the purpose of heating the colony Frobisher had planned to establish. Recent excavations by Canadian and US institutions on the site of Frobisher's base-camp on Kodlunarn (Qallunaat) Island in Frobisher Bay have produced over 25,000 fragments of Cologne-type stove tile moulded with the figures of Logic, Hope and others in the Liberal Arts and Cardinal Virtues series, several moulded with the dated tablet of 1561 (Auger et al in prep; Gaimster et al in prep).

The 1578 time capsule from Kodlunarn Island, Canada, provides a dated horizon for the circulation of these tiles in London, particularly for tiles made with the same moulds found in the Aldgate area of the City of London. The secure date is particularly relevant to the question of who ordered the installation of a single or a series of Cologne-type tile-stoves at Duke's Place during the 1560s or 1570s. Unfortunately, it is not possible to match the archaeological contexts with the occupation span of the Duke of Norfolk, tightly dated to the decade 1554–64 (Chapters 3.3, 6.2). The aristocratic character of Duke's Place, however, serves to place these products in the appropriate social milieu for the time and place.

8.5 The pottery

Lyn Blackmore

Introduction

The dating evidence provided by the pottery for the stratification on most of the sites has been included in the sections above dealing with the individual sites. At two appropriate points (pits on sites F and H), this included detailed analysis of a group of ceramics (Chapter 4.6; Tables 7–10; and Chapter 6.2; Table 14; Table 15). This appendix comprises an introduction, by period, to the fabrics and forms of the local, regional and imported wares present in the assemblages from sites A, E, F, G, H, J and K, with notes on the illustrated pieces, and a general discussion of the collection, which, excluding the finds from sites C and D and a few sherds that could not be located, amounts to 2844 sherds (including unstratified material); the bulk of the collection is of post-medieval date. Some assemblages had been initially spot-dated, and selectively quantified as part of specific ware studies (see below), by members of the then Department of Urban Archaeology (DUA) of the Museum of London, but the pottery had never been studied as groups that could be related to a specific site. For this reason the bulk of the collection was fully quantified by the present author, using the standard fabric codes employed by the Museum of London (Table 18; Table 19). Excluding all of site K (which was not analysed to the same level) and the 18th-century pit group G[100], which was counted but not weighed (Pearce 1998), the fully quantified material amounts to 59,402g, 56.36 EVEs (Table 22; Table 23). Unless otherwise stated, percentages quoted below are based on Table 24 and Table 25. Selected pottery profiles, numbered <P1> onwards, are illustrated in Fig 199, Fig 200 and Figs 202–5 (for context details see Table 20 and Table 21).

Table 18 Codes for medieval pottery fabrics in this assemblage (date ranges refer to their occurrence in London)

Fabric	Expansion	Date range (approximate)
ANDE	Andenne-type ware	1050–1200
BADO	Badorf ware	900–1200
CBW	coarse Surrey-Hampshire border ware	1270–1500
CHEA	Cheam whiteware	1350–1500
DUTR	Dutch red earthenware	1300–1650
EARL	Earlswood-type ware	1200–1400
EMCH	early medieval chalk-tempered ware	1050–1150
EMFL	early medieval flint-tempered ware	970–1100
EMGR	early medieval grog-tempered ware	1050–1150
EMS	early medieval sandy ware	970–1100
EMIS	early medieval Surrey iron-rich sandy ware	1050–1150
EMSH	early medieval shell-tempered ware	1050–1150
EMSS	early medieval sand- and shell-tempered ware	1000–1150
ESUR	early Surrey ware	1050–1150
KING	Kingston-type ware	1230–1400
KINGSL	Kingston-type slipware	1250–1400
LANG	Langerwehe stoneware	1350–1550
LCALC	calcareous London-type ware	1080–1200
LCOAR	coarse London-type ware	1080–1200
LCOAR SHEL	coarse London-type ware with shell inclusions	1080–1200
LLON	late London-type ware	1400–1500
LMHG	late medieval Hertfordshire glazed ware	1340–1450
LOGR	London-area greyware	1080–1150
LOND	London-type ware	1080–1350
LSS	late Saxon shelly ware	900–1050
MG	Mill Green ware	1270–1350
MG COAR	Mill Green coarseware	1270–1500
NEOT	St Neots ware	970–1100
NFM	north French monochrome ware	1170–1300
NFRY	north French yellow-glazed ware	900–1200
REDP	red-painted ware	900–1250
SAIG	Saintonge ware with even green glaze	1280–1350
SAIU	unglazed Saintonge ware	1250–1650
SHER	south Hertfordshire-type greyware	1140–1300
SIEG	Siegburg stoneware	1300–1500
SSW	shelly-sandy ware	1140–1220
STAM	Stamford-type ware	1050–1150
THET	Ipswich-/Thetford-type ware	900–1100
TUDG	'Tudor Green' ware	1350–1500

Table 19 Codes for post-medieval pottery fabrics in this assemblage (date ranges refer to their occurrence in London)

Fabric	Expansion	Date range (approximate)
ANDAL	late Andalusian tin-glazed ware	1480–1550
BISC	biscuit-fired tin-glazed ware	1570–1800
BORD	Surrey-Hampshire border whiteware	1550–1700
BORDB	Surrey-Hampshire border whiteware with brown glaze	1550–1700
BORDG	Surrey-Hampshire border whiteware with green glaze	1550–1700
BORDO	Surrey-Hampshire border whiteware with olive glaze	1550–1700
BORDY	Surrey-Hampshire border whiteware with clear glaze (yellow)	1550–1700
CHEAR	Cheam redware	1480–1550
CHPO	Chinese porcelain	1580–1900
CHPO VERTE	Chinese porcelain with famille verte decoration	1690–1730
CITG	central Italian tin-glazed ware	1480–1550
CREA	creamware	1740–1880
DTGW	Dutch tin-glazed ware	1600–1800
DUTR	Dutch red earthenware	1300–1650
DUTSL	Dutch slipped red earthenware	1500–1650
EBORD	early Surrey-Hampshire border whiteware	1480–1550
ENGS	English stoneware	1700–1900
ERBOR	early Surrey-Hampshire border redware	1480–1550
FREC	Frechen stoneware	1550–1700
GERW	German whiteware	1550–1630
ITGW	Italian tin-glazed ware	1480–1800
LCWW	Low Countries whiteware	1480–1650
LONS	London stoneware	1670–1900
MART	Martincamp-type ware	1480–1550
METS	metropolitan slipware	1630–1700
MPUR	Midlands purple ware	1580–1700
NIMS	north Italian marbled slipware	1550–1700
NOTS	Nottingham stoneware	1700–1800
OLIV	Spanish olive jar	1550–1750
PMBR	London-area post-medieval bichrome redware	1580–1700
PMBL	post-medieval black-glazed ware	1580–1700
PMFR	post-medieval fine redware	1580–1650
PMR	London-area post-medieval redware	1580–1900
PMRE	London-area early post-medieval redware	1480–1600
PMREC	early post-medieval calcareous redware	1480–1600
PMREM	London-area early post-medieval redware with metallic glaze	1480–1600
PMSL	London-area post-medieval slip-decorated redware	1480–1600
PMSR	London-area post-medieval slipped redware	1480–1600
PMSRG	London-area post-medieval slipped redware with green glaze	1480–1650
PMSRY	London-area post-medieval slipped redware with clear (yellow glaze)	1480–1650
POTG	Portuguese tin-glazed ware	1600–1700
RAER	Raeren stoneware	1480–1610
RBOR	Surrey-Hampshire border redware	1580–1800
RBORB	Surrey-Hampshire border redware with brown glaze	1580–1800
REFW	refined white earthenware	1800–1900
SIEGL	late Siegburg stoneware	1500–1600
SNTG	south Netherlands maiolica	1480–1575
STSL	combed slipware	1650–1800
SWSG	white salt-glazed stoneware	1720–1780
TGW	unsourced English tin-glazed ware	1570–1800
TGW A	tin-glazed ware with Orton type A decoration	1612–1650
TGW C	tin-glazed ware with Orton type C decoration	1630–1800
TGW F	tin-glazed ware with Orton type F decoration	1670–1690
TGW G	tin-glazed ware with Orton type G decoration	1701–1711
WESE	Weser slipware	1580–1630
WEST	Westerwald stoneware	1590–1800

Table 20 Catalogue of the illustrated pottery

Catalogue no.	Context	Fabric	Form	Site	Period	Group	Fig no.
<P1>	F[102]	LSS	dish	F	II	F7	199
<P2>	A[437]	EMSS	bowl	A	V	A30	199
<P3>	C[pit 4]	EMCH	spouted pitcher	C	-	-	199
<P4>	H[494]	SHER	jug, rouletted	H	III	H21	199
<P5>	H[478]	KING	jug with lion stamp	H	III	H21	199
<P6>	H[494]	KING	rounded jug	H	III	H21	199
<P7>	H[494] H[501]	KING	rounded jug	H	III	H21	199
<P8>	H[472]	KING	rounded jug	H	III	H21	199
<P9>	H[501]	LOND	squat/rounded slip decorated jug	H	III	H21	199
<P10>	H[501]	LOND	drinking jug reused as lantern	H	III	H21	199
<P11>	H[501]	KING	drinking jug	H	III	H21	199
<P12>	F[220]	PMRE	cauldron	F	IV	F22	200
<P13>	F[220]	PMRE	pipkin	F	IV	F22	200
<P14>	F[220]	PMRE	cauldron/pipkin	F	IV	F22	200
<P15>	F[220]	PMRE	skillet	F	IV	F22	200
<P16>	F[220]	PMRE	handled bowl	F	IV	F22	200
<P17>	F[220]	PMR	frying-pan	F	IV	F22	200
<P18>	F[220]	PMR	dish	F	IV	F22	200
<P19>	F[220]	BORDG	skillet	F	IV	F22	200
<P20>	F[220]	BORDG	condiment dish	F	IV	F22	200
<P21>	F[220]	RBOR	flanged dish	F	IV	F22	200
<P22>	F[220]	BISC	dish	F	IV	F22	202
<P23>	F[220], F[221]	BISC	dish	F	IV	F22	202
<P24>	F[221]	BISC	dish	F	IV	F22	202
<P25>	F[220]	BISC	dish, unfired glaze	F	IV	F22	202
<P26>	F[220]	BISC	bowl	F	IV	F22	202
<P27>	F[220]	BISC	tazza/butter dish	F	IV	F22	202
<P28>	F[220]	BISC	lid ?or corrugated cup	F	IV	F22	202
<P29>	F[220], F[221]	BISC	handled bowl/cup	F	IV	F22	202
<P30>	F[220]	BISC	handled bowl	F	IV	F22	202
<P31>	F[220]	BISC	jar/albarello	F	IV	F22	202
<P32>	F[220]	BISC	jar/albarello	F	IV	F22	202
<P33>	F[220]	BISC	jar/albarello	F	IV	F22	202
<P34>	F[220]	BISC	jar/albarello	F	IV	F22	202
<P35>	F[220]	BISC	jar/albarello	F	IV	F22	202
<P36>	F[220]	BISC	jar/albarello	F	IV	F22	202
<P37>	F[220], F[221]	BISC	jar/albarello	F	IV	F22	202
<P38>	F[220]	BISC	jar/albarello	F	IV	F22	202
<P39>	F[220]	BISC	jar/albarello	F	IV	F22	202
<P40>	F[220]	BISC	wet drug jar	F	IV	F22	202
<P41>	F[220]	BISC	wet drug jar	F	IV	F22	202
<P42>	J[+]	TGW	dish, floral	J	-	-	202
<P43>	G[+]	BISC	jar/albarello	G	-	-	202
<P44>	A[130]	BISC	jar/albarello	A	VIII	A47	202
<P45>	A[200]	BISC	jar/albarello,	A	VIII	A43	202
<P46>	A[200]	TGW	jar/albarello, allover blue glaze	A	VIII	A43	202
<P47>	F[220]	TGW	dish, fruit and flowers	F	IV	F22	203
<P48>	F[220], F[221]	TGW	dish, floral/rosette	F	IV	F22	203
<P49>	F[220]	TGW	dish, fruit and flowers/ overlapping arcs	F	IV	F22	203
<P50>	F[220]	TGW	dish, rosette, floral, sgraffito	F	IV	F22	203

Table 20 (cont)

Catalogue no.	Context	Fabric	Form	Site	Period	Group	Fig no.
<P51>	F[220]	TGW	dish, overlapping arcs and zigzag	F	IV	F22	203
<P52>	F[220]	TGW	dish, lattice	F	IV	F22	203
<P53>	F[220]	TGW	dish, overlapping arcs and zigzag	F	IV	F22	203
<P54>	F[220]	TGW	dish, acanthus panel	F	IV	F22	203
<P55>	F[220]	TGW	bowl, floral	F	IV	F22	203
<P56>	F[220]	TGW	bowl, lattice	F	IV	F22	203
<P57>	F[220]	TGW	ointment jar	F	IV	F22	203
<P58>	F[220]	TGW/ CITG	ointment jar	F	IV	F22	203
<P59>	F[220]	DUTSL	handled bowl	F	IV	F22	204
<P60>	F[220]	DUTR	strainer	F	IV	F22	204
<P61>	F[220]	RAER	large globular jug	F	IV	F22	204
<P62>	F[220]	FREC	small globular jug	F	IV	F22	204
<P63>	F[220]	?RAER	?chamber pot	F	IV	F22	204
<P64>	F[220]	ANDAL	bowl	F	IV	F22	204
<P65>	G[100]	DUTR	jar	G	-	-	205
<P66>	H[6]	GERW	pipkin	H	IV	H12.6	205
<P67>	A[268]	CITG	vase	A	VIII	A43	205
<P68>	A[283]	CITG	altar vase	A	VII	A40	205
<P69>	H[72], H[212]	POTG	dish	H	IV	H23	205
<P70>	G[65]	POTG	Chinese-style dish	G	-	-	205

This work resulted in the readjustment of some of the original pottery identifications and dating, and has given a better impression of the ceramic trends on the site of Holy Trinity Priory. The total assemblage is small by comparison with other monastic sites in London, such as St Mary Spital (Stephenson 1997), St Mary Clerkenwell (Blackmore in prep a) or St John Clerkenwell (Blackmore 2004b); this partly reflects the location and size of the different trenches, but it would seem from other excavations in the Aldgate area (Marsden 1969; Chapman and Johnson 1973; Orton and Pearce 1984; Blackmore in prep b) that medieval pottery is not particularly abundant in this part of the City. Although post-medieval pottery is more common, most excavated material comes from cesspits and deeply-cut features such as the ditches outside the city wall.

The following comments concentrate on the larger, fully quantified assemblages, although other finds are noted where relevant. For ease of reference, context numbers are prefixed by the site letter code (eg H[494]), but where periods are quoted it should be remembered that each site has its own sequence. Unless otherwise stated, percentages quoted are of the medieval or post-medieval sherd counts from sites A, F and H (see Table 24; Table 25); the term ENV is used for the estimated number of vessels.

Possible Saxon pottery

An intriguing find from C[140] (ER1332; for ER, ie Excavation Register, see Chapter 1.3) comprises sherds from a jar or

Table 21 Correlation of context to group references for the pottery from sites A and E–H

Context	Group	Group deposition date (approximate)
Site A		
A[102]	A47	18th century
A[103]	A49	19th century
A[115]	A27	1080–1150
A[122]	A51	1230–1350
A[124]	A46	mid 17th century
A[127]	A44	1550–1600
A[130]	A47	18th century
A[131]	A47	18th century
A[133]	A51	1230–1350
A[136]	A44	1550–1600
A[145]	A27	1080–1150
A[181]	A43	1580–1600
A[186]	A46	mid 17th century
A[187]	A46	mid 17th century
A[200]	A43	1580–1600
A[232]	A39	1550–1600
A[234]	A39	1550–1600
A[246]	A44	1550–1600
A[247]	A44	1550–1600
A[252]	A44	1550–1600
A[253]	A42	1550–1600
A[256]	A44	1550–1600
A[258]	A43	1580–1600
A[265]	A42	1550–1600
A[268]	A43	1580–1600
A[278]	A40	1530–50
A[283]	A40	1530–50
A[285]	A39	1550–1600
A[308]	A43	1580–1600
A[310]	A40	1530–50
A[311]	A38	1530–50
A[316]	A40	1530–50
A[320]	A42	1550–1600
A[331]	A38	1530–50
A[350]	A38	1530–50
A[357]	A38	1530–50
A[428]	A40	1530–50
A[429]	A31	14th century
A[434]	A31	14th century
A[437]	A30	12th century
A[438]	A31	14th century
A[484]	A29	end of 12th/early 13th century
A[488]	A29	end of 12th/early 13th century
A[489]	A31	14th century
A[513]	A28	12th century
A[526]	A23	1050–1150
A[535]	A22	1050–1150 but contaminated
A[550]	A22	1050–1150
A[595]	A23	1050–1150, possibly after 1080
A[624]	A21	1050–1150
A[629]	A29	end of 12th/early 13th century
A[630]	A21	1050–1150
A[635]	A23	1050–1150
A[649]	A23	1050–1150
A[697]	A21	1050–1150
A[851]	A20	1080–1150
A[908]	A23	1050–1150
A[1046]	A22	1050–1150
Site E		
E[2]	E9	18th century
E[22]	E8	1550–1600
E[58]	E8	1550–1600

Table 21 (cont)

Context	Group	Group deposition date (approximate)
Site F		
F[5]	F13	12th century
F[28]	F11	1050–1150
F[57]	F20	18th century
F[63]	F20	18th century
F[65]	F19	?14th century
F[66]	F19	?14th century
F[82]	F19	?14th century
F[102]	F7	1050
F[106]	F19	?14th century
F[108]	F12	1050–1150
F[114]	F7	1050
F[126]	F12	late medieval wares, intrusive
F[184]	F9	900–1050
F[220]	F22	1580–1600
F[221]	F22	1580–1600
Site G		
G[8]	G10.1	20th century
G[65]	G8.2	mid 17th century
G[100]	G6.1	1740–5
G[125]	G7.1	10th or 11th century
Site H		
H[1]	H23.2	1720–40
H[3]	H12.5	after 1680
H[4]	H30.1	1630–1700
H[6]	H12.6	1550–1630
H[17]	H12.5	after 1680
H[18]	H12.5	after 1680
H[21]	H30.1	1630–1700
H[22]	H30.1	1630–1700
H[24]	H12.3	late 16th or 17th century
H[30]	H12.5	after 1680
H[43]	H12.1	1480–1500
H[44]	H12.1	1480–1500
H[72]	H23.2	1720–40
H[74]	H23.2	1720–40
H[212]	H23.2	1720–40
H[213]	not grouped in archive report	1640–50
H[308]	not grouped in archive report	11th or 12th century
H[316]	not grouped in archive report	14th century
H[454]	H16	after 1270
H[472]	H21	14th century
H[478]	H21	14th century
H[493]	H21	14th century
H[494]	H21	14th century, sherd of Frechen stoneware intrusive
H[501]	H21	14th century

pitcher in a reduced sandy ware with slightly burnished outer surface. The fabric could be Roman, but the distinctive rim form, which is externally bevelled and triangular in section, is quite unusual for the Roman period. It is more in keeping with the imported north French black wares found to the west of the former Roman city in the middle Saxon trading settlement of Lundenwic (fabrics NFBW, NFGW: cf Blackmore 1988, 89–91, fig 22, nos 30, 36). Two probable Saxon burials have been found in the eastern part of the City at Rangoon Street (Schofield 1998, 187), but so far there is no evidence for early or middle Saxon settlement in the area.

Table 22 The broad distribution of the quantified medieval pottery, including unstratified material

Site	Sherd count	ENV	Weight (g)	EVEs
A	189	120	2865	1.74
E	2	2	18	-
F	62	47	1147	0.52
H	351	166	5759	7.11
G	19	19	231	0.18
J	10	6	341	-
K	127	-	1082	0.86
Total	760	362	11443	10.41

Table 23 The broad distribution of the quantified post-medieval pottery, including unstratified material (note: weight for site G excludes pit group G[100])

Site	Sherd count	ENV	Weight (g)	EVEs
A	298	212	7743	8.72
E	10	10	189	1.07
F	450	137	12354	11.15
H	668	263	24368	24.47
G	246	60	3266	0.54
J	3	2	39	-
K	409	-	7524	6.24
Total	2084	654	55483	52.19

Medieval wares

As shown in Table 22, most of the 760 sherds of medieval pottery were found on site H, while the second largest group was from site A. Only 62 sherds were recovered from the excavations on site F. A total of 127 sherds was found on site K, but the stratigraphy is less reliable; virtually no medieval pottery was found on sites E and G. Each assemblage varies slightly in character and in the distribution of the wares; the best single group is from the cesspit(s) on site H (gpH21). Most of the collection comprises small sherds of fairly local origin, and the number of imports is disappointingly low.

Early medieval fabrics

Early medieval wares, mainly derived from cooking pots, account for *c* 17% of the medieval pottery from sites A, F and H (by sherd count and weight). Most of these are from site F (41 fragments, 844g); only five sherds from site H date to before *c* 1150. Fabric descriptions for the different wares and forms represented (EMCH, EMFL, EMGR, EMS, EMSH, EMIS, EMSS, ESUR, LSS, NEOT, STAM, THET) have been published elsewhere (Vince and Jenner 1991), and are not repeated here.

The most common fabric by sherd count is early medieval sandy ware (EMS, 21 sherds; Table 24) which amounts to a surprising 29% of the medieval pottery from site F, but

Table 24 Overall quantification of the medieval pottery from sites A, F and H, by sherd count, estimated number of vessels (ENV), weight (in g) and estimated vessel equivalent (EVE) (for fabric codes see Table 18)

Fabric	Sherd count	Sherd count %	ENV	ENV %	Weight (g)	Weight %	EVEs	EVEs %
ANDE	1	0.2	1	0.3	6	0.1	-	-
CBW	111	18.4	82	24.6	1423	14.6	0.92	9.8
CHEA	31	5.1	19	5.7	353	3.6	0.55	5.9
DUTR	2	0.3	2	0.6	22	0.2	-	-
EARL	3	0.5	2	0.6	25	0.3	-	-
EMCH	3	0.5	3	0.9	24	0.2	0.04	0.4
EMFL	1	0.2	1	0.3	7	0.1	-	-
EMGR	1	0.2	1	0.3	5	0.1	-	-
EMS	21	3.5	15	4.5	335	3.4	0.12	1.3
EMSH	6	1.0	6	1.8	81	0.8	-	-
EMSS	34	5.6	25	7.5	425	4.3	0.22	2.3
ESUR	12	2.0	11	3.3	173	1.8	0.30	3.2
KING	126	20.9	36	10.8	2582	26.4	3.62	38.6
KINGSL	2	0.3	1	0.3	9	0.1	-	-
LANG	1	0.2	1	0.3	9	0.1	-	-
LCOAR	13	2.2	13	3.9	173	1.8	-	-
LCOAR SHEL	4	0.7	3	0.9	50	0.5	0.05	0.5
LLON	3	0.5	3	0.9	99	1.0	0.27	2.9
LMHG	26	4.3	10	3.0	544	5.6	-	-
LOGR	2	0.3	2	0.6	14	0.1	-	-
LOND	122	20.3	38	11.4	2267	23.2	2.30	24.5
LSS	17	2.8	14	4.2	575	5.9	0.43	4.6
MG	28	4.6	19	5.7	253	2.6	0.10	1.1
MG COAR	2	0.3	2	0.6	7	0.1	-	-
NEOT	1	0.2	1	0.3	14	0.1	-	-
NFM	1	0.2	1	0.3	1	<0.1	-	-
REDP	2	0.3	2	0.6	10	0.1	-	-
SAIG	1	0.2	1	0.3	1	<0.1	-	-
SHER	15	2.5	9	2.7	195	2.0	0.45	4.8
SIEG	1	0.2	1	0.3	16	0.2	-	-
SSW	2	0.3	2	0.6	26	0.3	-	-
STAM	3	0.5	2	0.6	20	0.2	-	-
THET	1	0.2	1	0.3	17	0.2	-	-
TUDG	3	0.5	3	0.9	10	0.1	-	-
Total	**602**		**333**		**9771**		**9.37**	

late Saxon shelly ware (LSS) is more common by weight. One of the earliest stratified finds is part of a large LSS dish (<P1>, Fig 199); at 410mm in diameter this is rather larger than the closest parallels illustrated by Vince and Jenner (1991, fig 2.24, nos 18–19) and also differs in the form of the rim which, although flat-topped, is not flanged but has a rounded edge more like that of the bowls (ibid, nos 13, 14). Other finds include part of an early medieval sand- and shell-tempered ware (EMSS) bowl (<P2>, Fig 199) residual in A[437] (gpA30), and sherds from Ipswich-/Thetford-type ware (THET) jars or pitchers with applied thumbed strips (A[635], gpA22; G[125]; cf ibid, 89, fig 90.205), perhaps similar to a vessel found at St Bride's (Blackmore 1997, 97, fig 67). Fingertipping was noted on rim sherds of early Surrey ware (ESUR; A[526] and A[630]), and was also present on four rims from a pit on site C (Clark 1973, 40–1, fig 19, nos 2, 6–8), which also contained part of a pitcher with combed decoration in early medieval chalky ware (EMCH) (<P3>, Fig 199; ibid, fig 19, no. 4; Vince and Jenner 1991, 70, fig 2.54, no. 137). Various sherds of the same early fabrics also came from site K (ER1341–3, ER1347, ER1349).

Local greywares

London-area greyware (LOGR) is very rare on the Holy Trinity sites, with only two sherds from site H. South Hertfordshire-type greyware (SHER; for dating see Blackmore in prep a) is also surprisingly scarce on the site, with only two sherds from site A and 13 from site H. The latter include a jug or pitcher with slightly flaring collared rim and rouletted or punched decoration found in the group H21 pit (<P4>, Fig 199). This vessel may date to the late 12th rather than the 13th century; similar rim forms are known in LOGR (Vince and Jenner 1991, fig 2.64, no. 171) and coarse London-type ware (LCOAR; cf ibid, fig 2.74, no. 194) as well as in London-type ware (LOND; Pearce et al 1985, fig 21, no. 40). Rouletted decoration is found on spouted pitchers made in LOGR (cf Vince and Jenner 1991, fig 264, no. 177; fig 265), and occasionally on jugs in SHER (Blackmore 1989, 103), but spouted pitchers were not made in the latter ware (Pearce in prep).

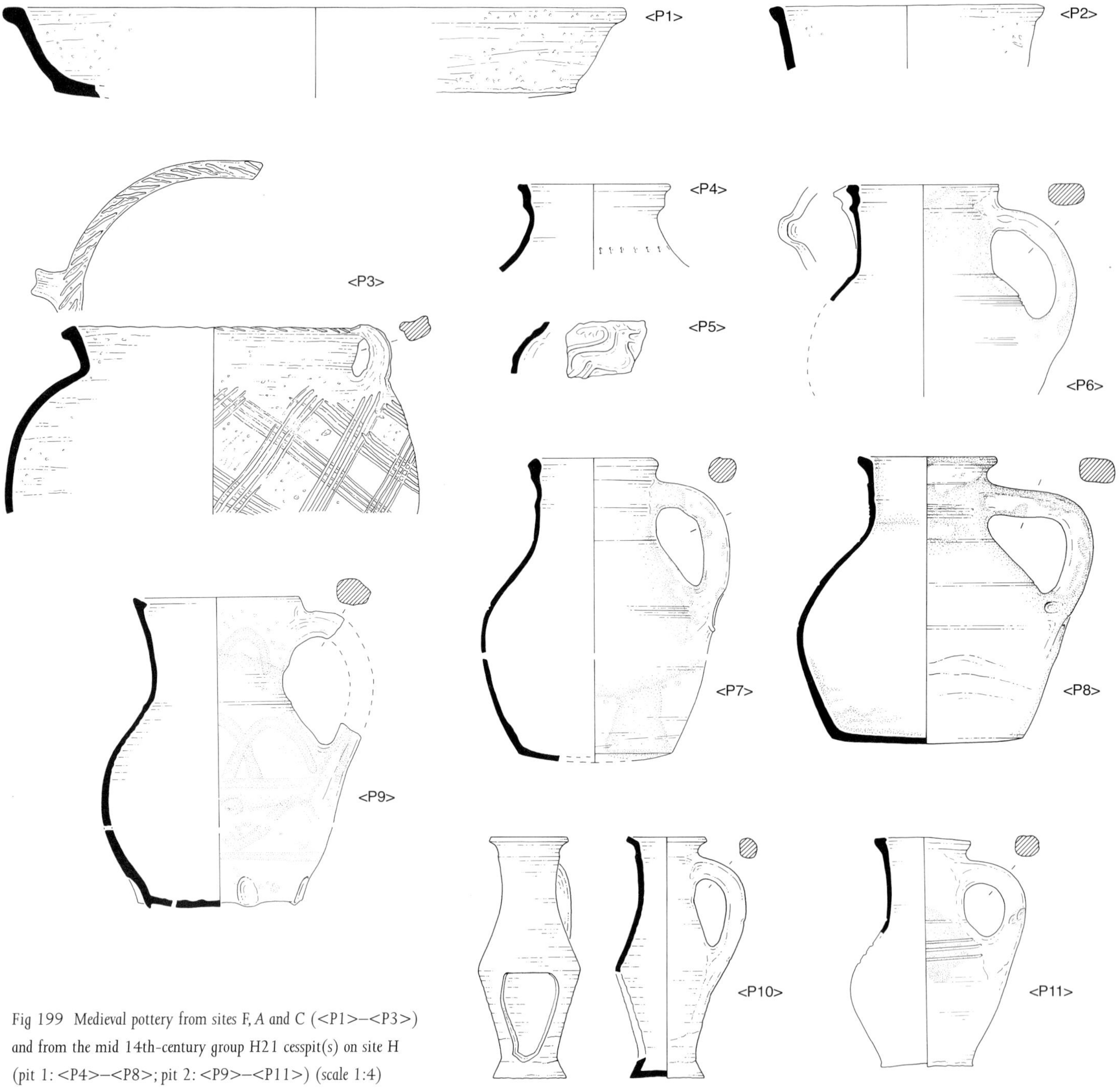

Fig 199 *Medieval pottery from sites F, A and C (<P1>–<P3>) and from the mid 14th-century group H21 cesspit(s) on site H (pit 1: <P4>–<P8>; pit 2: <P9>–<P11>) (scale 1:4)*

London-type wares and shelly-sandy ware

London-type wares have been discussed by Pearce et al (1985) and Blackmore and Vince (1994). Taken together, the various London-type wares from sites A, F and H (LCOAR, LCOAR SHEL, LOND, LLON, SSW) account for 24% of the medieval assemblage by sherd count (27% by weight; 59 ENV). The most common of these is LOND; shelly-sandy ware (SSW) is represented by only two sherds, while the 12th-century coarse ware LCOAR and its variants are limited to 17 sherds. Three of the latter are from early rounded jugs, the remainder from cooking pots, two with rims typical of the late 11th century (A[513] and A[488]).

Cooking pots in LOND are limited to three sherds from two vessels, and all other sherds are from jugs; most are from site A, where LOND accounts for 25% of the medieval pottery (13% by weight). Only two sherds are in the early style and most date to after *c* 1180; the latter include sherds from two Rouen-style, three north French style, and two squat/rounded jugs from the cesspit(s) on site H (gpH21) which are typical of the late 12th or early 13th century. One has paired thumbing at intervals around the base angle (H[472]; cf Pearce et al 1985, fig 48, no. 163), while the other has spaced single thumbing (<P9>, Fig 199). The long flaring neck of the latter is similar to those of two jugs in the Museum of London collections (cf ibid, 24, 31, fig 48, nos 161–2), but the form is also clearly related to a small tripod pitcher (cf ibid, 39, fig 23, no. 47a). A small hole (diameter *c* 3mm) in the base of <P9> appears to be intentional, but a second hole is adjacent to a large flint pebble in the fabric of the pot which has caused a weakness at this point. The thick white deposit inside this jug is not a carbonate and remains to be identified, but it is not impossible that the jug was used as a urinal. The most unusual find from the cesspit(s) on site H is a small baluster-shaped drinking jug (<P10>, Fig 199) which has a shield-shaped opening in the lower body. The fact that this is not opposed to the handle but slightly off-centre, and that the inside of the pot is soot-blackened, suggests that the jug was damaged and so adapted for use as a lantern. Such vessels are extremely rare but similar reuse is seen on a pear-shaped jug from Ludgate Hill which has circular cut-outs in the wall (ibid, 47, fig 53, no. 195).

Three highly decorated jugs, one with applied ring-and-dot motifs and pellets (A[331], gpA38) date to the 13th century, while two tulip-necked baluster jugs from site H (gpH21) date to the 14th century. Late London-type ware (LLON) is limited to three sherds, from a pipkin with everted rim (A[268]), a dripping dish (A[283]) and a lid (H[323]).

Kingston-type and Earlswood-type wares

Kingston-type ware (KING) and a slipped variant (KINGSL) are conventionally dated from *c* 1230 in London (Pearce and Vince 1988), although they may start a little earlier. In this assemblage KING appears to be common (21% of the medieval wares from sites A, F and H, *c* 27% by weight, 37 ENV). However, none was found on site F and the totals are artificially inflated by three rounded jugs from the cesspit(s) on site H (gpH21). The first of these, in an extremely fine fabric, is a lipped jug with a collared rim and oval handle (<P6>, Fig 199), while the second has a plain round rim with a very slight cordon and a rod handle (<P7>, Fig 199; cf ibid, fig 75, no. 132, strap-handled). The third is of more carinated form (<P8>, Fig 199). The same group includes a sherd with unusual repoussé decoration in the heraldic style showing a lion passant (<P5>, Fig 199), a small rounded drinking jug with rilled shoulder (<P11>, Fig 199), and the lower part of a conical jug. The latter has a brown residue inside and a kiln scar in red clay on the underside of the base. Other jug sherds include a large rounded example with an applied strip (H[478]; cf ibid, no. 143), one with applied pellets (A[133]) and a metal copy jug (H[472]). Only one sherd of KING was recorded as being from a cooking pot (H[316]). Earlswood-type ware (EARL), which dates to *c* 1200–*c* 1400 (Turner 1974), is limited to two small jug sherds.

Mill Green ware

This Essex ware dates from *c* 1270 to *c* 1350 (Pearce et al 1982; Meddens 1992) and usually ranks among the five most common fabrics found on sites in London. At Holy Trinity Priory most of the sherds are very small and the ware amounts to only 5% of the main assemblages (3% by weight), although it is the third most common type on site A. Most sherds are from jugs in the standard fine ware (MG), but a few Mill Green coarsewares (MG COAR) are also present.

Coarse Surrey-Hampshire border ware, Cheam whiteware and 'Tudor Green' ware

Coarse Surrey-Hampshire border ware (CBW) probably started to reach London from *c* 1270, and was the dominant ware from *c* 1350 to *c* 1500 (Pearce and Vince 1988, 52–68, 84–5, 91). It accounts for 18% of the main medieval assemblages (15% by weight), but this reflects the generally small size of the sherds. Up to 54 of the 82 ENV are from site H, where CBW is the most frequent fabric in terms of vessel numbers; by weight, however, it is more common on site A (21%). No new forms are present, and most sherds are from utilitarian vessels such as cooking pots and cisterns, with a cluster of the latter on site A (A[283], A[310], A[311], A[316]). A few bowls are also represented; one has a flat-topped rim (A[200]), while another has a flanged rim (A[181]). A bowl (F[65]) has a bevelled flanged rim which is slightly upturned at the edge (cf ibid, fig 118, no. 502). Only one dish is present (A[181]). Jugs include two sherds from a conical jug (F[323]) and a barrel jug (A[127]); the latter form is usually associated with CHEA, and is rare in this fabric. Sherds from two probable cisterns are present among the finds from site K (ER1341).

Cheam whiteware (CHEA; Pearce and Vince 1988, 68–77, 85–8, 91; Orton 1982) is comparatively rare on the priory sites (5%) and 25 of the 31 sherds are from site H (Table 24). With the exception of a dish (A[300]), all finds are from jugs; of note is part of a possible conical jug, a form more usually associated with CBW (A[311], gpA38); the sherds found have an unusually even and glossy green glaze. The three sherds of 'Tudor Green' (TUDG) derive from lobed cups (A[308], H[44] and H[43/44]).

Late medieval Hertfordshire glazed ware

This ware (LMHG) has been discussed by Jenner and Vince (1983), Vince (1985) and Turner-Rugg (1995). Although totalling 4% of the medieval assemblage (6% by weight), all but one of the 26 sherds are from site H, and 15 of these are from a large mid 14th-century rounded jug found in the cesspit(s) (gpH21).

Medieval imported wares

These are very rare on all parts of the Holy Trinity Priory site. Wares dating to the 11th or 12th centuries comprise sherds from a pitcher in Andenne-type ware (ANDE; A[697], period 3), two sherds of probable red-painted ware (REDP; F[108], H[308]) and ?Badorf-type ware (BADO; G[8]), while a sherd of north French monochrome ware (NFM; H[323]) dates to the late 12th or 13th century. Of 14th-century date are a sherd of green-glazed Saintonge ware (SAIG; F[82]), the neck of a Siegburg stoneware (SIEG) *Jakobakanne* (H[316]) and a residual fragment from a Langerwehe stoneware (LANG) cup (A[181]; cf Hurst et al 1986, fig 92, no. 288). Three sherds of unglazed Saintonge ware (SAIU) pitcher were found on site K (ER1347, ER1350). A Dutch redware (DUTR) pipkin and a lid from site K (ER1344) could date to the late 14th or 15th century.

Post-medieval wares

Large groups of post-medieval pottery were found on sites A, E, F, H and K (Table 14; Table 23; Table 25). The largest amount is from site H, where most finds derive from the mid 17th-century deposit H[213] (330 sherds). In second place is site F (441 sherds, of which 86 are from the late 16th- to early 17th-century pit, gpF22). In third place is site K, where most finds derive from ditches outside the city wall. Smaller groups were recovered from sites A and G, notably from contexts A[103], A[130] and A[131] and the 18th-century cesspit G[100], which contained 165 sherds. Other finds of later English pottery, which include a range of Staffordshire wares and English stonewares, are not considered here.

Redwares

Redwares are by far the most common class of post-medieval pottery on each site, the most frequent fabrics being London-area early post-medieval redware (PMRE) and London-area

Table 25 Overall quantification of the post-medieval pottery from sites A, F and H, by sherd count, estimated number of vessels (ENV), weight (in g) and estimated vessel equivalent (EVE) (for fabric codes see Table 19)

Fabric	Sherd count	Sherd count %	ENV	ENV %	Weight (g)	Weight %	EVEs	EVEs %
ANDAL	1	0.1	1	0.2	19	<0.1	0.02	<0.1
BISC	144	10.2	46	7.5	4340	9.8	3.41	7.7
BORD/B/G/O/Y	216	15.3	92	15.0	5858	13.2	7.15	16.1
CHEAR	4	0.3	4	0.7	149	0.3	-	-
CHPO/CHPO VERTE	7	0.5	6	1.0	31	0.1	0.28	0.6
CITG	3	0.2	2	0.3	79	0.2	-	-
CREA	1	0.1	1	0.2	7	<0.1	0.20	0.5
DTGW	1	0.1	1	0.2	5	<0.1	0.07	0.2
DUTR	18	1.3	14	2.3	1589	3.6	0.50	1.1
DUTSL	23	1.6	3	0.5	317	0.7	0.75	1.7
EBORD	3	0.2	3	0.5	31	0.1	-	-
ENGS	4	0.3	2	0.3	85	0.2	0.15	0.3
ERBOR	2	0.1	1	0.2	27	0.1	-	-
FREC	32	2.3	12	2.0	1214	2.7	1.00	2.3
GERW	16	1.1	4	0.7	387	0.9	0.50	1.1
ITGW	1	0.1	1	0.2	5	<0.1	-	-
LCWW	1	0.1	1	0.2	12	<0.1	-	-
LONS	1	0.1	1	0.2	3	<0.1	-	-
MART	3	0.2	2	0.3	40	0.1	-	-
METS	3	0.2	1	0.2	342	0.8	0.08	0.2
MPUR	2	0.1	2	0.3	131	0.3	-	-
NOTS	1	0.1	1	0.2	4	<0.1	-	-
OLIV	2	0.1	2	0.3	306	0.7	0.52	1.2
PMBL	6	0.4	5	0.8	229	0.5	0.15	0.3
PMBR	3	0.2	3	0.5	42	0.1	0.20	0.5
PMFR	66	4.7	24	3.9	2018	4.5	1.61	3.6
PMR	138	9.7	71	11.6	5175	11.6	5.55	12.5
PMRE	302	21.3	130	21.2	8913	20.0	6.43	14.5
PMREC	2	0.1	1	0.2	83	0.2	-	-
PMREM	2	0.1	2	0.3	22	<0.1	0.08	0.2
PMSL	2	0.1	2	0.3	16	<0.1	-	-
PMSRG/Y	74	5.2	45	7.4	3327	7.5	1.13	2.5
POTG	13	0.9	2	0.3	353	0.8	0.87	2.0
RAER	21	1.5	19	3.1	1431	3.2	0.32	0.7
RBOR	126	8.9	25	4.1	4013	9.0	7.75	17.5
REFW	2	0.1	2	0.3	7	<0.1	-	-
SIEGL	1	0.1	1	0.2	14	<0.1	-	-
STSL	3	0.2	2	0.3	49	0.1	-	-
SWSG	13	0.9	6	1.0	220	0.5	0.85	1.9
TGW	67	4.7	46	7.5	1953	4.4	2.32	5.2
TGW A	11	0.8	7	1.1	450	1.0	0.64	1.4
TGW C	64	4.5	11	1.8	968	2.2	1.56	3.5
TGW F	6	0.4	1	0.2	159	0.4	0.10	0.2
TGW G	1	0.1	1	0.2	4	<0.1	-	-
WESE	1	0.1	1	0.2	16	<0.1	-	-
WEST	3	0.2	2	0.3	22	<0.1	0.15	0.3
Total	**1416**		**612**		**44465**		**44.34**	

post-medieval redware (PMR). Excluding site K, the largest amount is from site A, where the different redware fabrics listed below amount to 60% of the total post-medieval pottery by sherd count and 62% by weight. On sites F and H they amount to 48% and 54% by sherd count and weight respectively, while on site G they comprise *c* 50% of pit group G[100]. Most sherds in all fabrics derive from kitchen wares, mainly cauldrons, pipkins and dishes; very few non-domestic vessels were identified. Detailed descriptions of the different fabrics and forms are not included here, as these will be discussed more fully in surveys of the redwares used in London (Pearce and Nenk in prep), for which seven samples from group F22 were studied using neutron activation analysis (NAA) (M J Hughes, pers comm, who kindly permitted the inclusion of some of the results of this work in advance of publication).

LONDON-AREA EARLY POST-MEDIEVAL REDWARE

The dominant 16th-century redware in London is PMRE (partially glazed), which appears in the archaeological record from *c* 1480. This ware dominates on site F (43%; 36% by weight), and accounts for *c* 21% of the sherds from site A (29% by weight), but is very much in the minority on site H. Three sherds (sample 136, <P16>, Fig 200; sample 138, <P14>, Fig 200; sample 139, <P13>, Fig 200) were shown by NAA analysis to come from Harlow (cf Cunningham 1985). One skillet similar to <P15> (Fig 200) (sample 134) may be from Rayleigh or Stock (both Essex), while one vessel matches the composition of Woolwich wares (sample 135, <P12>, Fig 200), and must relate to the first phase of that industry (Blockley 1978, 43–52, 83–4). Sherds assigned the code PMREM are in fabric PMRE but have a dark green/black glaze with a metallic sheen.

The best single group is from F[220], where a number of different forms were represented which typify the range of late 16th-century types from the site as a whole. A substantially complete cauldron with everted rim has a rilled shoulder (<P12>, Fig 200), while a small cauldron has a lid-seated collared rim (<P14>, Fig 200). One cauldron and three pipkins or cauldrons have everted lid-seated rims with a characteristic internal bevel, while the tripod pipkins include three examples with lid-seated rims, one with a ladle handle (<P13>, Fig 200). Other forms in this group include two flared tripod skillets with folded collared rims (<P15>, Fig 200), and a large bowl with rounded profile and horizontal handles (<P16>, Fig 200). The finds from the city ditch (H[213]) include the complete profile of a tripod pipkin with lid-seated everted rim and a straight-sided bowl. Other forms include a carinated bowl (H[305]), jars with thumbing around the neck (A[102]), and a lid (A[283]).

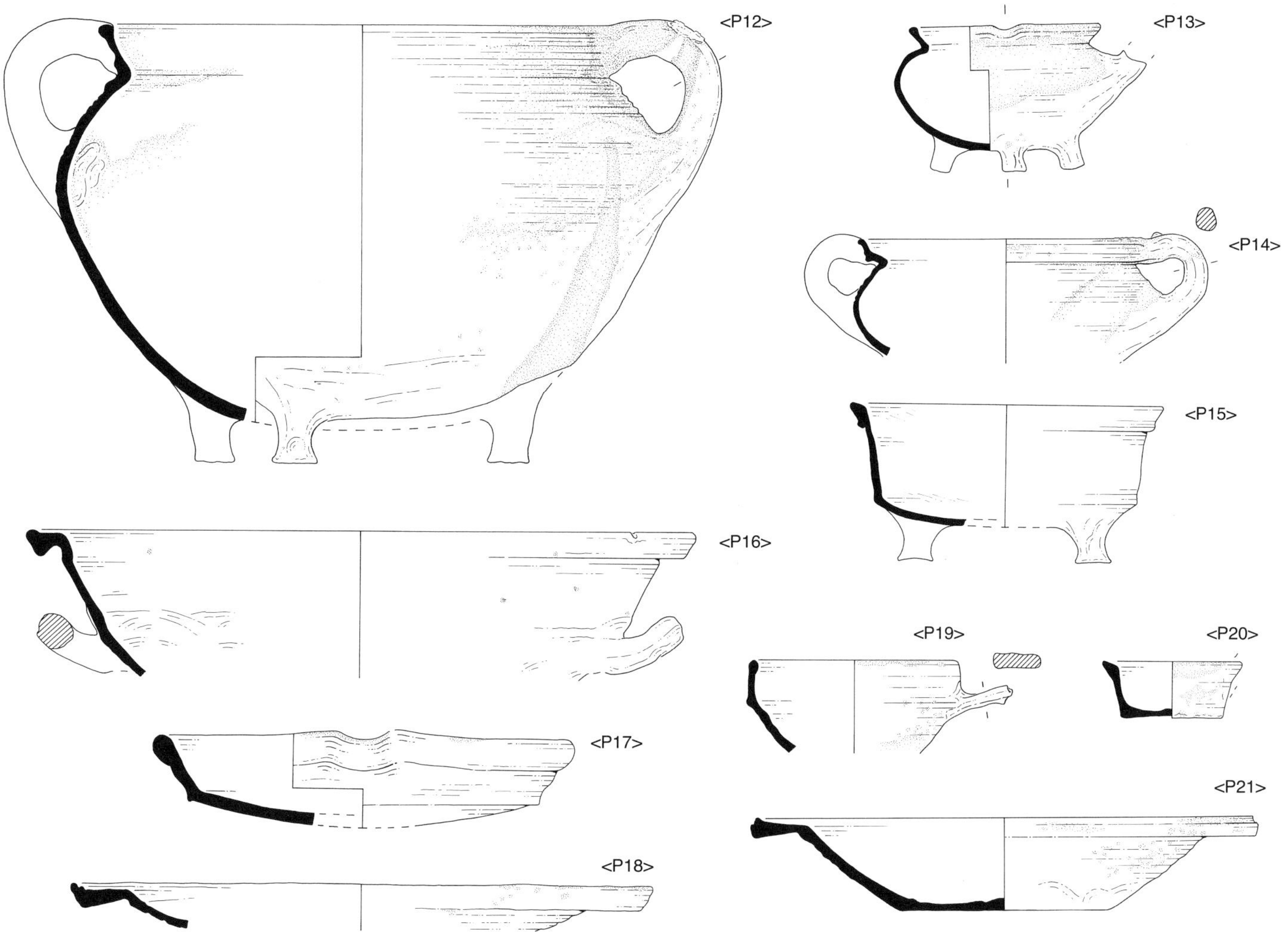

Fig 200 *Post-medieval redwares (<P12>–<P18>) and whitewares (<P19>–<P21>) from a pit, group F22 (F[220]) (scale 1:4)*

CHEAM REDWARE, BICHROME REDWARE, CALCAREOUS REDWARES
These wares, which are usually found in contexts dating to *c* 1480–*c* 1550, are very rare on all the excavated parts of the priory. Early post-medieval calcareous redware (PMREC; two ?jug sherds from site F) contains fine calcareous inclusions and may be from Essex; it is rare in London and seems to be most common in the eastern part of the City (eg at the Tower Postern and St Mary Graces).

LONDON-AREA POST-MEDIEVAL SLIPPED REDWARE
Formerly known as 'Guy's ware' (Dawson 1979), this class of pottery has a slip-coated surface under a clear or green glaze (PMSRY, PMSRG); it comprises *c* 12% of the post-medieval wares from site A, and *c* 5% of the assemblage from site H. Finds from group F22 include four vessels with horizontal loop handles: part of a colander, a large carinated dish and one or two large flared bowls (now missing). Later finds include cauldrons and a possible skillet with large socketed handle from H[213], and a squat tripod pipkin in PMSRG with everted flat-topped and lid-seated rim, carinated profile, ladle handle and short legs (H[6]). Sherds from a large jug were found by bastion 6 (ER1348, ER1349).

LONDON-AREA POST-MEDIEVAL REDWARE
This ware (PMR), which developed from the PMRE industry, was introduced *c* 1580, and was the most common redware during the 17th to 19th centuries. It accounts for *c* 13% of the post-medieval assemblages from sites A and H, but only 3% on site F, where the few finds include a frying-pan probably made at Rayleigh or Stock (<P17>, Fig 200; NAA sample 137), a cauldron with biconical profile and folded rim (now missing) and a rather crudely made flanged dish (<P18>, Fig 200). Of interest are sherds from two bird pots found by bastion 6 (ER1351), as these tend to occur in areas where Dutch communities settled. A cluster is known from the area of St John Clerkenwell (Stephenson 1991; Blackmore 2004a). Also from site K is a large 17th-century cauldron with rich brown glaze (ER1354).

The mid 17th-century finds from the city ditch are probably from Woolwich (Pryor and Blockley 1978); they comprise a range of bowls, pipkins, tripod pipkins, cauldrons/pipkins, a cauldron with collared rim, jars, a storage jar with thumbed neck and a chamber pot. These forms are also found in other contexts on the site. Other finds include the greater part of a heavily sooted porringer (H[72]) which has a horizontal loop handle, and jars with thumbed necks and horizontal handles, in one case with thumbing on the handles (A[130]). A sherd from the base of a paint pot (A[278]) is unusual as this form is usually associated with Surrey-Hampshire border redware (RBOR).

The finds from the 18th-century cesspit G[100] have been discussed by Pearce (1998, 97–8) and noted above (Chapter 6.4, site G); they include a number of forms which were made in fabric E2 at the Woolwich Ferry kilns in the late 17th century (Pryor and Blockley 1978), some of which continued in use well into the 18th century. These include large deep bowls with lid-seated or squared, rolled rims and single or paired horizontal loop handles, wide dishes with thickened or rolled rims, tripod pipkins with ladle-type strap handles and redware chamber pots. Similar forms have been found in a context of *c* 1700–20 at a site south of Aldgate High Street, outside the wall (Orton and Pearce 1984), a clearance group of *c* 1740 at Burlington Road (Blackmore 1984, 103, fig 5) and a deposit dated *c* 1770 at Crosswall, near Fenchurch Street station (Vince 1981).

POST-MEDIEVAL FINE REDWARE AND BLACK-GLAZED WARE
These wares (PMFR, PMBL) appeared at about the same time as PMR. Both are rare in all the priory assemblages, although PMFR accounts for 17% of the pottery from H[213] (13% by weight). Most sherds of this ware derive from pipkins or tripod pipkins with internally lid-seated rims, with a substantially complete example from site K (ER1354). Other forms include a dish (NAA sample 132, missing) which is probably from Stock or Rayleigh, Essex (Newton et al 1960), a jug and a mug from H[213], two deep bowls (H[21], H[4]), a colander (H[4]) and part of a mug or tankard (A[187]). The latter is of note as it is cordoned and has incised diagonal grooves, a style more usually associated with RBOR (cf Pearce 1992, figs 35–6). One of the PMFR sherds from site K may be from a bird pot (ER1353).

SURREY-HAMPSHIRE BORDER REDWARE
This ware (RBOR) was produced alongside the whitewares discussed below from *c* 1580. It amounts to *c* 5% of the post-medieval pottery from sites A and F, where the three flanged dishes in F[220] (<P21>, Fig 200, and two now missing) must be relatively early examples of the type. Most are from site H (*c* 13%), where the total EVE is inflated by a number of small flat-based skillets with ladle handles and pouring lips from H[213], one of which is complete (cf Pearce 1992, 20–1, fig 30, no. 175). Among the latest pieces are two flanged dishes and two paint pots from the 18th-century cesspit fill G[100] (Pearce 1998, 98).

Whitewares

Early Surrey-Hampshire border whiteware (EBORD) dates from *c* 1480, while the developed wares (BORD, BORDG, BORDO, BORDY) date from *c* 1550 and remained popular until the early 18th century (Pearce 1992; 1998, 97). Taken together these wares represent 15% of the post-medieval pottery from sites A, F and H (13% by weight). Most sherds are from sites A (21%) and H (15%), and the largest single group is from H[213]; almost all the 31 sherds from site F are from group F22.

The kitchen wares are dominated by tripod pipkins, but include a skillet with straight handle (<P19>, Fig 200) and a small skillet with ladle handle (cf Pearce 1992, fig 30, no. 175) which is exactly the same size as the more common equivalents in RBOR (see above). A small lipped skillet was found on site K (ER1348; cf ibid, fig 30, no. 183). The bowls include examples similar in profile to others from the City (ibid, fig 23, no. 74; fig 24, nos 85, 87 for rim). Another bowl is of flaring form, with an everted rim and loop handle (A[181]).

Open forms include a number of dishes and flanged dishes; some of the latter have incised decoration (F[220] and H[213]), and one example has stamped decoration (site K, ER1353). A small dish with narrow flanged rim is oxidised so that the yellow glaze looks amber in colour (F[63] and F[114]). Other tablewares comprise porringers, including a large fragment from site K (ER1349; cf Pearce 1992, fig 26, no. 112), cups and rounded drinking jugs, including a substantially complete example from G[65] (cf ibid, fig 32, nos 208, 216).

Rarer types comprise part of a simple straight-sided condiment dish from F[220] (<P20>, Fig 200; Pearce 1992, 38, fig 43, no. 391), a sherd which may be from a fuming pot (A[181]), and another from a cylindrical jar (H[3], BORDY; cf ibid, fig 45, no. 426). A straight-sided jar with slightly tapering profile and a milled cordon may have been used as a butterpot (H[213], BORDY). The greater part of a moneybox was found on site K (ER1349). Two vessels from the 18th-century cesspit G[100] are of note (Pearce 1998, 97): a complete chamber pot with Pearce type 2 rim and mottled brown glaze (cf Pearce 1992, 32, fig 41, nos 332–6) and the first recorded example of a whiteware 'paint pot'; the latter is a typical 18th-century Surrey-Hampshire border redware form (cf Vince 1981, fig 3, no. 9).

Tin-glazed and biscuit wares

Tin-glazed wares are fired twice, first to 'biscuit' stage (BISC; Fig 158), and then again following the application of glaze and decoration (TGW). Altogether tin-glazed wares amount to 11% of the post-medieval sherds from sites A, F and H; the greatest amount is from site H (16.4%, 14.2% by weight), followed by site A (11%, 8% by weight). The finds from site F amount to only 5% of the post-medieval pottery from that site, but include the group from the pit (gpF22), which contained 21 of the 23 glazed sherds, and 109 out of the total 144 biscuit sherds from sites A, F and H; some of the latter have a coating of unfired tin glaze. These comprise the most important element of the post-medieval pottery assemblage, as they indicate that pottery was produced in the vicinity of the site (see below). A few fragments of biscuit tile were also found in this pit (above, 8.3).

Ten sherds of biscuit ware (all from site F), and 12 glazed sherds (ten from site F and two from site A) were submitted for neutron activation analysis (NAA) at the British Museum as part of a wider research project to differentiate between English and Continental tin-glazed wares (sample numbers are listed in Hughes and Gaimster 1999, 57, 64–5, and table 1, and will also be published in Edwards in prep). The biscuit wares were found to cluster neatly, with only one outlier on the plot; it would seem that all sampled pieces were made from a single batch of clay, and it is not impossible that they were from a single firing (Hughes and Gaimster 1999, 64–5). Three of the glazed sherds were found to be probable Italian imports (see below), while the others were more disparate than the biscuit wares. Although most are chemically compatible with a London provenance, the fabric alone can neither prove or disprove that they were made at Aldgate (ibid, 65). However, cluster analysis of these data and those from other NAA samples has confirmed that a jug in the Museum of London collections (A4670, Fig 201; Garner 1948, pl 3a; Britton 1987, no. 7) and the earliest dated tin-glazed plate from London (MoL C84, Fig 159; ibid, no. 25), the source of which has been debated (Tait 1992), fall within, or close to, the biscuit ware group (Hughes and Gaimster 1999, 65). Aspects of the fabrics, typology and methods of manufacture and decoration of these wares have been or will be discussed elsewhere (Hughes and Gaimster 1999; Edwards 1999; Edwards in prep), but it is appropriate here to describe the stylistic affinities of the finds from group F22, and the post-Dissolution Aldgate pottery is also considered below within this section.

SIXTEENTH- TO EARLY 17TH-CENTURY BISCUIT WARES FROM A PIT, GROUP F22

The biscuit wares vary considerably in colour, with some pieces buff throughout, others almost terracotta in colour; several have a salmon-coloured body with buff outer and/or inner margin (Fig 158). The same applies to kiln assemblages from Antwerp; it could result from mixed clay or firing conditions, but it has been noted that the redder sherds turn white after the second firing (Veeckman 1999, 116).

Dishes and bowls

Five biscuit ware dishes are represented in the pit (gpF22). The three rims, with diameters of 200–300mm, are of Britton type A (Britton 1987, 29, appendix 1), with a smooth back and

Fig 201 Tin-glazed jug, possibly from the Aldgate pottery, found in Whitecross Street, London; the polychrome decoration comprises gadroons around the neck and base and a floral vine around the body (height 161mm; MoL A4670)

upturned, inwardly bevelled edge which stands proud of the upper surface, giving a 'hooked' profile (<P22>–<P24>, Fig 202). This form has been found at the kiln site of c 1550–75 at Steenhowersvest and elsewhere in Antwerp (J Veeckman, pers comm; cf Dumortier and Veeckman 1994, nos 1, 15), as well as in Utrecht and Rotterdam (Britton 1987, 29; Edwards in prep). A related profile has also been found at Middelburg (Hurst et al 1986, 122, no. 169). A base sherd (<P25>, Fig 202), which has an unfired glaze inside, may be from a dish similar to <P22>–<P24>. The bases, which are rather thicker and cruder than those of the glazed wares, are closely paralleled at Shoytestraat, Antwerp (Oost 1992, fig 3). Two have a splayed profile (<P22>, <P23>), while <P24> and <P25> have a straighter edge; the former are perforated, and the others were probably so. An unusual form is a dish with an integral spike inside the bowl (<P27>, Fig 202) and an ornate pedestal base (incomplete), which may have been intended as a butter dish. There are parallels for this form in the Netherlands, some with an iron spike (Korf 1981, 150, no. 394) while later finds from London include a tin-glazed example from Spitalfields (site

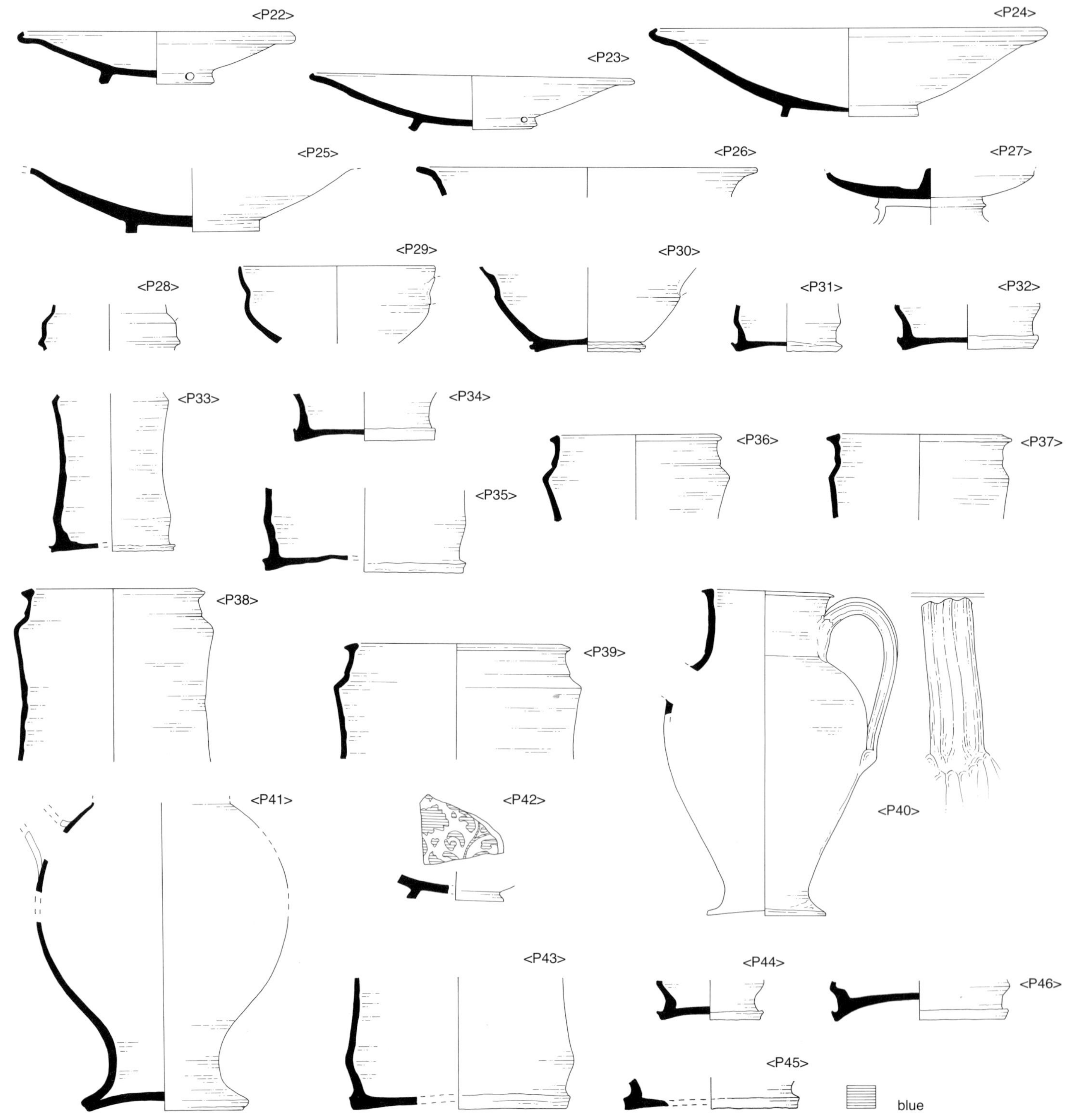

Fig 202 Biscuit tin-glazed wares from a pit, group F22 (<P22>–<P41>), and from sites J, G and A (<P42>–<P46>) (scale 1:4)

code SRP98, [609]; N Jeffries, pers comm). Ring-footed examples with lids have been published by Britton (1987, fig 12, cat no. 121). Another very thin-walled sherd (<P28>, Fig 202) resembles the base of <P27>, but has the vestige of a handle scar and so may be from a corrugated cup.

Two small bowls would originally have had two horizontal handles; one is represented by the rim (<P29>, Fig 202), while the other (<P30>, Fig 202) has a concave base with a rather uneven 'pseudo' footring. Only one tin-glazed parallel for this form is known from London (Edwards 1999, 17), although the type has been found in Norwich (Jennings 1981, 200), Antwerp (Veeckman 1999, fig 6.14) and Middelburg (Hurst et al 1986, 124, no. 170).

Dry drug jars

Production of tall waisted jars (albarelli) first developed in the East, but the tradition spread to Spain in the 13th century and thence to Italy, where jars bearing the name of the contents were first produced in the mid 15th century (Drey 1978). The 15 biscuit examples range from medium to large in size. The bases, which include two complete examples (<P31>, <P34>, Fig 202), range from 70mm to 150mm in diameter, with three of 100mm. As in Antwerp (Veeckman 1999, 116) all were thrown on a slightly convex wheel and have a distinctive expanded form that is usually bevelled in to the base angle (<P31>–<P33>, Fig 202), although more straight-sided examples are also present (<P34>, <P35>, Fig 202). This form is not typical of Spain, but is seen on some late 15th- and 16th-century jars from central Italy (Drey 1978, pl 4C). The five rims range between 120mm and 160mm in diameter (<P36>–<P39>, Fig 202), and are less similar to the Antwerp forms, which tend to have concave necks and rims which are not internally beaded (Dumortier and Veeckman 1994, 140, nos 34–9).

Syrup/wet drug jars

Two spouted jars were found in the pit. The more complete (<P40>, Fig 202) has a shouldered body which tapers to the base, a relatively long neck, plain flat-topped rim with slight external bead, and a broad strap handle with central ridge (height 230mm, rim diameter 87mm); the spout is missing. The other is taller and more baluster-shaped (<P41>, Fig 202); part of the spout is present, but the rim and handle are missing. It is thus uncertain whether the neck was similar to that of <P40> or shorter, like those of contemporary south Netherlandish imports found in Devon and Colchester (Allan 1999, fig 12.3.83; Cotter 1999, fig 13.1.2), although the latter have a different base form.

The antecedents of the Aldgate forms include the rather more rounded jars from Manises and Faenza (Drey 1978, pl 3A, pl 16B–C) made in the mid and late 15th century respectively, and the baluster-shaped jars made at Deruta (ibid, pl 12C, dated *c* 1525), although these have slightly more rounded rims. Similar forms, although often more elaborate, were made at Montelupo around 1570. The closest contemporary parallels for the profile of <P40> are to be found in Antwerp (ibid, pl 60B, dated 1546) and at Castel Durante (ibid, pl 23D, dated 1569; pl 24D, dated 1579). The former, however, has a shorter, slightly inverted neck and a more splayed base, while the latter have plain strap handles. A similar form, dated 1579, has been found at Vlissingen (Hurst et al 1986, 125). On all these jars the spouts are plain, suggesting that those of the Holy Trinity finds would have been the same.

SIXTEENTH- TO EARLY 17TH-CENTURY TIN-GLAZED WARES FROM A PIT, GROUP F22

As a rule, the term 'maiolica' is used for early Continental wares (from Spain, Italy and the Netherlands) which had a tin-rich glaze over the front and a lead glaze on the back, a tradition followed by later Netherlandish and English potters; these wares were fired on kiln stands. Pottery with a tin-glaze on both surfaces, which was usually fired in saggars, is conventionally known as faience or delftware (Hurst et al 1986, 120). The finds from site F (Fig 203) are intriguing as they have a thin tin-glaze on the back, and the finds from site K (below) suggest that some of the later finds (at least) were fired in saggars.

Dishes

Sherds from 11 glazed dishes were found in the pit; the three bases all have neat, straight-sided footrings. Two rim types are present, of which the first, Britton type A (see above) is represented by three examples (<P50>–<P52>, Fig 203). Only two other glazed examples of this rim form are known in London, both lacking a secure provenance. One is in the Museum of London (acc no. Z3354; Britton 1987, no. 15); the other, in the Burnett Collection, was probably found in Southwark (Noël Hume 1977, 78, fig X, no. 1). The second rim type (<P53>, Fig 203) is more rounded, both on the upper face and on the underside, and is similar to Britton type B. Neither form is paralleled in the Netherlandish series presented by Korf (1981, 42). The dishes are decorated with a variety of stylistically related designs, typically outlined in blue and deriving from Italian wares of the late 15th to mid 16th century; the glaze on the back appears to be a mix of lead and tin.

The most common motif is the rosette, which originated in the East, and was copied in Spain, in Italy (Drey 1978, 116, pl 59A), and finally in the Netherlands (ibid, pl 59B). The most figurative interpretation is on a thick-walled dish which has an allover floral pattern showing a large orange/yellow double-rosette flower with a latticed centre and a fruit (?pomegranate) in purple/yellow, set against foliage in green (<P47>, Fig 203). This design has antecedents in Venice (cf Mariaux 1995, 82, no. 34; Lightbown and Caiger-Smith 1980, 115; Wilson 1987, 166; Edwards 1999, 138). No exact northern parallels have been found, but related designs are seen on imported albarelli from Colchester (Cotter 1999, fig 13.1.4), and plates dated to much the same period, such as an example dated 1583 from Haarlem (Wilson 1987, 166, no. 259). They are also found on Dutch wall tiles (cf de Jong 1971, fig 16a; Korf 1981, no. 208). Leaves painted in the same style also occur on the Museum of London jug noted above (Fig 201) and on two other dishes from the pit. Of these, <P48> (Fig 203) has a rosette at the centre and is

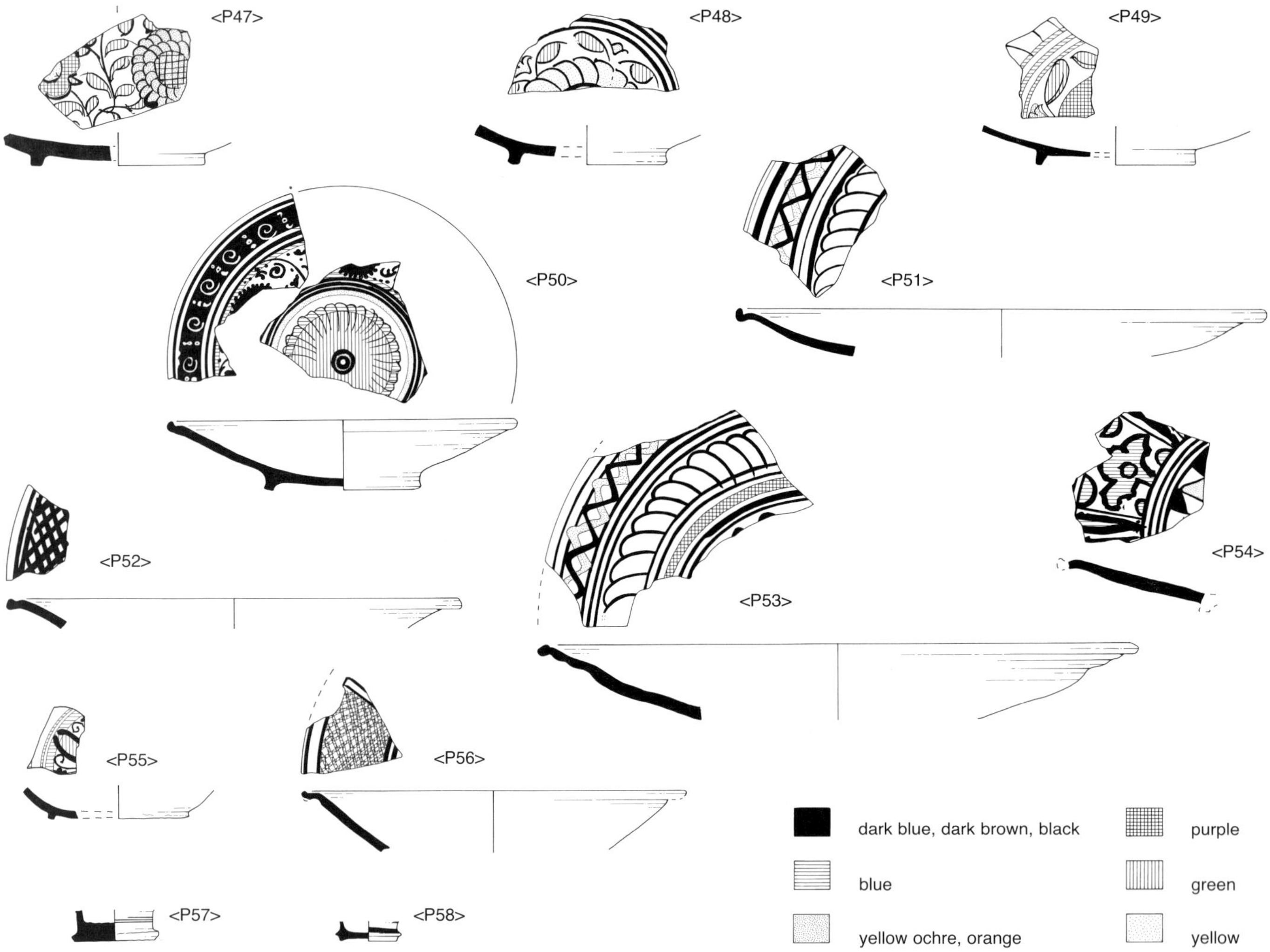

Fig 203 *Tin-glazed tablewares and an albarello (<P47>–<P57>), with the base of a possible Italian albarello (<P58>) from a pit, group F22 (scale 1:4)*

similar to a late 16th-century dish from Haarlem (ibid, 107, no. 207); the back is covered in a pale blue glaze. In the case of <P49> (Fig 203) the central motif is largely missing, but the purple zone is probably part of a fruit; the leaves are banded by concentric rings and (probably) overlapping arcs in blue, as seen on <P51> and <P53> (Fig 203).

The finest piece (<P50>, Fig 203) is neatly painted with a central rosette in blue, ochre and green, banded by concentric rings in orange and blue, and a zone of closely spaced daisy-like flowers with dotted petals around the edge and stylised leaves. This recalls both the bryony patterns found on Spanish lustreware, which were taken up in Italy in the late 15th and early 16th centuries (cf Wilson 1987, 36–8, nos 31, 33, 34), and the *alla porcellana* style of decoration popular in 16th-century Italy, traditions that were copied and reinterpreted on dishes (Dumortier and Veeckman 1994, 148; cf Korf 1981, 121–5) and tiles (Caiger-Smith 1973, no. 78) made in the Low Countries. The flanged rim has *sgraffito* decoration of alternating coils and three radial dots, which appear white against the dark blue ground. This again is an Italian tradition of the earlier 16th century which was copied at Antwerp (Veeckman 1999, 115) and elsewhere in the Netherlands (cf Drey 1978, colour pl B, pl 6A; Korf 1981, fig 106), although the three radial dots are not known at Antwerp (J Veeckman, pers comm). Similar schemes with central rosettes may be seen on dishes from Groningen and Nijmegen (Korf 1981, nos 239, 268), but the closest parallel found for the flowers on <P50> is on an armorial dish with *sgraffito* rim which is dated 1572 (Baart 1999, 128, fig 7.31). A small rim sherd from a similar dish with *sgraffito* decoration and a blue glaze on the back was found on site G (G[8]).

Two other dishes have different rim forms but very similar schematic decoration in blue and manganese which includes bands of overlapping arcs (derived from the rosette motif) and overlapping zigzag lines making a lattice border on the flange (<P51>, <P53>, Fig 203). The centres are missing but probably contained rosettes, or perhaps fruits (cf Dumortier and Veeckman 1994, 174, no. 17). This design is placed at 1560–1600 by Korf (1981, fig 105, 95), with a peak of *c* 1570–80. Still more geometric is the diamond lattice border panel in blue on <P52> (Fig 203), a typical late 16th-century Low Countries design (ibid, 226–9) which recalls the hatching seen on Italian 'Archaic' maiolica.

All the above are proficiently painted and cannot be considered wasters, but one piece (<P54>, Fig 203) stands out as it has a rather crudely executed panel border containing a devolved acanthus leaf (Edwards in prep). This resembles the foliate elements of certain contemporary wall tiles (cf de Jong 1971, figs 6a, 7, 23c, 23e) including a find from Antwerp (Dumortier and Oost 1992, no. 11). The surviving part of the bowl suggests that this had a geometric design based on marquetry (cf Korf 1981, nos 243–5). In addition there are three small sherds from other dishes, and two poorly-glazed pieces.

Deep dishes and other forms

One deep dish or bowl is unusual as it has a trapezoidal lattice panel in manganese banded by blue lines (<P56>, Fig 203). Such panels are more commonly of triangular form (cf Korf 1981, nos 226–9); other shapes include schematic petals (cf ibid, nos 233–4). The latter style is not unknown in Antwerp (Dumortier and Veeckman 1994, 152, fig 23), but so far none have been found in manganese (J Veeckman, pers comm). Another base sherd (<P55>, Fig 203) has a floral design in green, dark blue and light blue which is paralleled at Antwerp (Korf 1981, no. 171); this has only a slight footring and a rather unevenly finished tin glaze on the back. Lastly, there is the complete base of a small glazed jar (albarello) with wheel marks on the underside of the flat base (diameter 49mm), and decoration of blue bands under a poor tin glaze (<P57>, Fig 203). Unlike the biscuit forms, this jar is completely straight-sided up to the point where it has broken.

OTHER 16TH- TO EARLY 17TH-CENTURY GLAZED AND BISCUIT WARES

Other late 16th-century tin-glazed tablewares which could be either imports or local products include a dish sherd with *calligraphico a volute* style decoration from site K (ER1353; Noël Hume 1977, 114, fig XIX, no. 14); an unstratified dish fragment from site J (<P42>, Fig 202) with allover *alla porcellana* foliate decoration in blue similar to that on <P50> (cf Korf 1981, no. 280; Dumortier and Veeckman 1994, 163, no. 5); and a bowl from site K (ER1353) with a chequer design. The latter was a popular tradition in the Netherlands from *c* 1550 onwards (Korf 1981, 127–9; Dumortier and Veeckman 1994, 152) and, on the evidence of a plate found in Aldgate Street (Britton 1987, no. 15), was possibly copied at Aldgate. Finally there is a base (<P46>, Fig 202) with a pale blue glaze which may be from a plain Malling-style jar/albarello (Hurst et al 1986, 126–7), a type now known to have been produced in Antwerp (Hughes and Gaimster 1999, 61–2; Dumortier and Veeckman 1994, 140, fig 4).

The finds from the ditch H[213] would seem to date to the earlier 17th century, and include a polychrome albarello with large kiln scar which has a more glossy glaze and brighter colours than the finds from group F22. The tablewares (all from H[213]) comprise a rim sherd from a polychrome dish with yellow dashes around the rim edge and part of a possible pomegranate motif on the border; a small bowl with a geometric centre; and a bowl or porringer decorated with a chequer design. This has blue dashes around the rim like the Continental examples, but the bowl/porringer noted above has concentric bands around the rim, perhaps reflecting the date or source of the piece.

Sherds of biscuit ware were also found elsewhere within the former priory precinct, including the bases of two jars from site A, two small (<P44>, <P45>, Fig 202) and a larger example (unstratified) from site G (<P43>, Fig 202). Most finds, however, are from outside the city wall, with 33 sherds (14 ENV) from site H and a further 29 sherds (24 ENV) from site K (ER1348, ER1349, ER1351–3; Noël Hume 1977). On both sites jars/albarelli are the most common type; one example from H[213] has unfired glaze. Other forms from site K comprise two wet drug jar bases, two dishes, a bowl and a cup handle (ibid, fig XIX, nos 10–12, 15). Of special note are a trivet and two saggars (ER1355; ibid, fig XIX, no. 18). Trivets were used in Italy in the 16th century and so this find could be contemporary with the first Aldgate pottery. Saggars appear to be a later tradition in London, but since production at Aldgate is said to have ceased by *c* 1620, these finds must date to the early 17th century. Given that forms and techniques are likely to have changed little in the lifetime of the Aldgate pottery, and the fact that the finds from H[213] and ER1352–5 occur with pottery types dating to after *c* 1630, it is not easy to date the biscuit sherds more closely than *c* 1570–*c* 1620. The jars/albarelli are certainly similar to those from site F, but some are considerably larger in size (one base, not illustrated by Noël Hume, is a surprising 190mm in diameter); the one dish rim (ibid, fig XIX, no. 12) is of Britton type E, and very similar in form to that of the 'Rose is red' plate (Fig 159), the earliest dated piece of English delftware (Britton 1987, 105, appendix V). It is likely, therefore, that these finds were made by successors of Jacob Jansen between 1592 and 1615. The finds from H[213] appear to be of 17th- rather than 16th-century date; the three dish rims are of Britton types C and E (ibid, appendix V), while the six jars/albarelli have neatly finished bases, one with clear wire marks on the underside. The chamber pots from H[1] and H[74] are probably of later 17th-century date and their source is unknown.

MID 17TH- TO 18TH-CENTURY TIN-GLAZED WARES

Polychrome wares

These include part of a charger with central rosette and geometric border (TGW A, H[131]); similar decoration was used on wares produced in the mid 17th century at Platform Wharf, Rotherhithe (R Stephenson, pers comm) and in the Low Countries (cf Korf 1981, no. 263). Polychrome plates went out of fashion in the mid 17th century, and until the 18th century most vessels were either plain white, or blue and white. Of early 18th-century date is a near-complete Lambeth polychrome plate with floral decoration (TGW G, A[130] and A[131]), while a 'punch bowl' from the cesspit G[100] has floral decoration painted using a square-ended brush, and is typical of the period *c* 1715–40 at both Lambeth and Bristol (Garner and Archer 1972, 38; Pearce 1998, 98, fig 4, no. 4).

Plain white wares

This group (TGW C) comprises sherds from ointment pots, plates and chamber pots. A complete small drug jar was found in E[65], while a near-complete porringer with beaded rim was found in A[131]; the latter is very like another with handle form of Orton's type C, dating to *c* 1680–*c* 1710, found in G[100] (Orton 1988, 311; Pearce 1998, 98, fig 3, no. 2). A rim from a polygonal plate was found on site K (ER1352).

Blue and white wares

A fragmented but near-complete large dry drug jar found in E[65] probably dates to *c* 1612–50 (cf Orton 1988, fig 138, no. 1256). Most finds are from H[213]; they include fragments from a dish with Wan-li-style border (cf ibid, fig 137, no. 1368). The decorated wares from the mid 18th-century cesspit G[100] have been discussed by Pearce (1998). In addition to a mid to late 17th-century bowl, tea bowls and a coffee cup (ibid, fig 3, no. 3; fig 4, nos 5–6), they include five plates, one almost complete and bearing the word *chalav* ('milk') painted in Hebrew characters (Fig 180). The most unusual find from the site, this has a simple border design and a shallow profile typical of the early 18th century (Britton 1987, 194, profile J), suggesting that it was made in Lambeth (see below). One of the few known parallels for this piece is a deep delftware plate or soup dish in the Jewish Museum in Camden Town, London (acc no. 1982-10-19), which has the Hebrew word *basar* ('meat') at the centre. It is likely that both were part of sets made as a special commission, either from an individual or a retailer supplying the Jewish community, using templates for the inscriptions (see also below).

The latest find from the site comprises three small sherds from a strainer or colander, found on site K (ER1352), which was possibly made in London. The form, which dates to the second half of the 18th century, is closely paralleled at Williamsburg, USA (Austin 1994, 198–9, figs 399–400).

Post-medieval imported wares

FRENCH WARES

These are limited to a few fragments from early Martincamp stoneware (MART) costrels found in A[308] and in the city ditch (H[213]). Beauvais *sgraffito* wares often figure in Dissolution groups, but are absent here.

LOW COUNTRIES REDWARES AND SLIP-COATED WARES

These fabrics (DUTR, DUTSL) mainly occur in London in contexts dating to the 15th to 17th centuries, and are rare after *c* 1650, although it is not impossible that they continued to be bought in by, and used in, households which had connections with the Low Countries (see below, 'Discussion'). Most finds are from group F22, and from site H (mainly from the city ditch), but a few pieces were found on site K (ER1351–2).

One of the most common forms is the ring-footed bowl; the most complete example is a slip-coated, clear-glazed bowl with collared rim and horizontal loop handle from F[220] (<P59>, Fig 204; NAA sample 133). A near-complete ring-footed jar with everted neck, possibly originally handled (<P65>, Fig 205), was found in cesspit G[100] and may have been of some age when discarded. Vessels of similar form have been found in the area of St John Clerkenwell, where there may also have been a Dutch community in the late 16th/early 17th century (Blackmore 2004b, 347, fig 173, <P76>). The most unusual find, from site K (ER1352), has a manganese-speckled glaze inside, the first example from London seen by the present writer. No slip-decorated bowls have been found on any of these sites.

Other forms found in F[220] comprise three cauldrons and cauldron/pipkins, a frying-pan, and a small colander with horizontal handles (<P60>, Fig 204); the base of a larger one with tripod feet was found in the city ditch (H[213]). A large tripod skillet from G[100] has a carinated profile, a straight, oval-sectioned handle (incomplete) and a pouring lip (Pearce 1998, 98).

LOW COUNTRIES/GERMAN WHITEWARES AND SLIP-DECORATED WARES

German slipwares of Weser type (WESE) are not uncommon in 17th-century contexts in the City, but plain Dutch/German whitewares are rare (although this may be because they were, in the past, confused with Surrey-Hampshire border whitewares). In this case, little WESE was found (A[181] and site K (ER1352)), but six whiteware vessels are represented (GERW, LCWW). The most complete is a small tripod pipkin

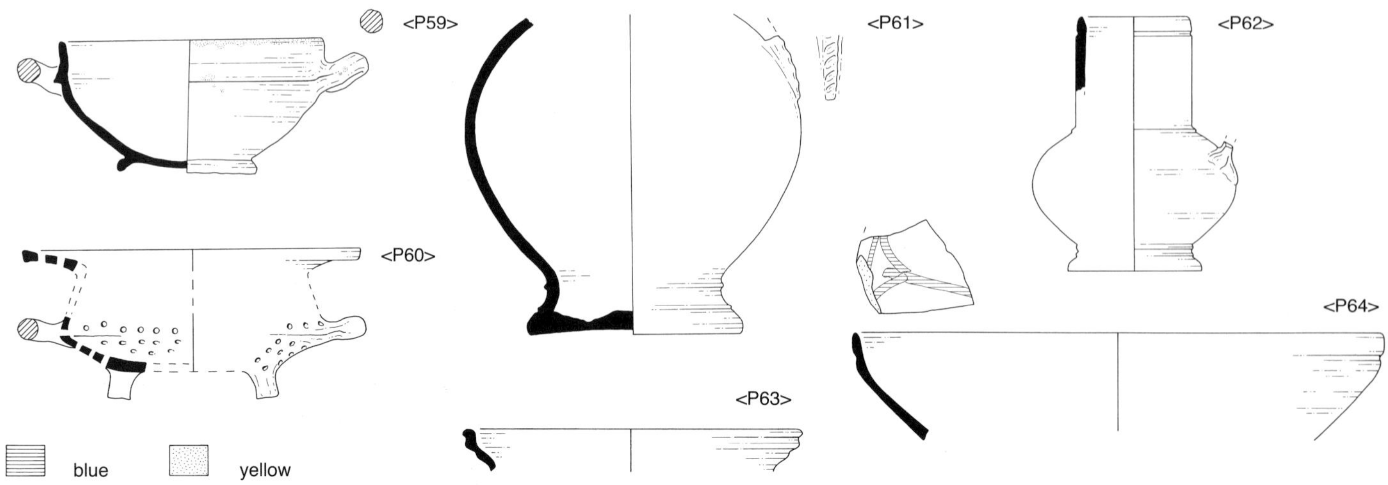

Fig 204 Dutch redwares (<P59>, <P60>), German stonewares (<P61>–<P63>) and a Spanish dish (<P64>) from a pit, group F22 (scale 1:4)

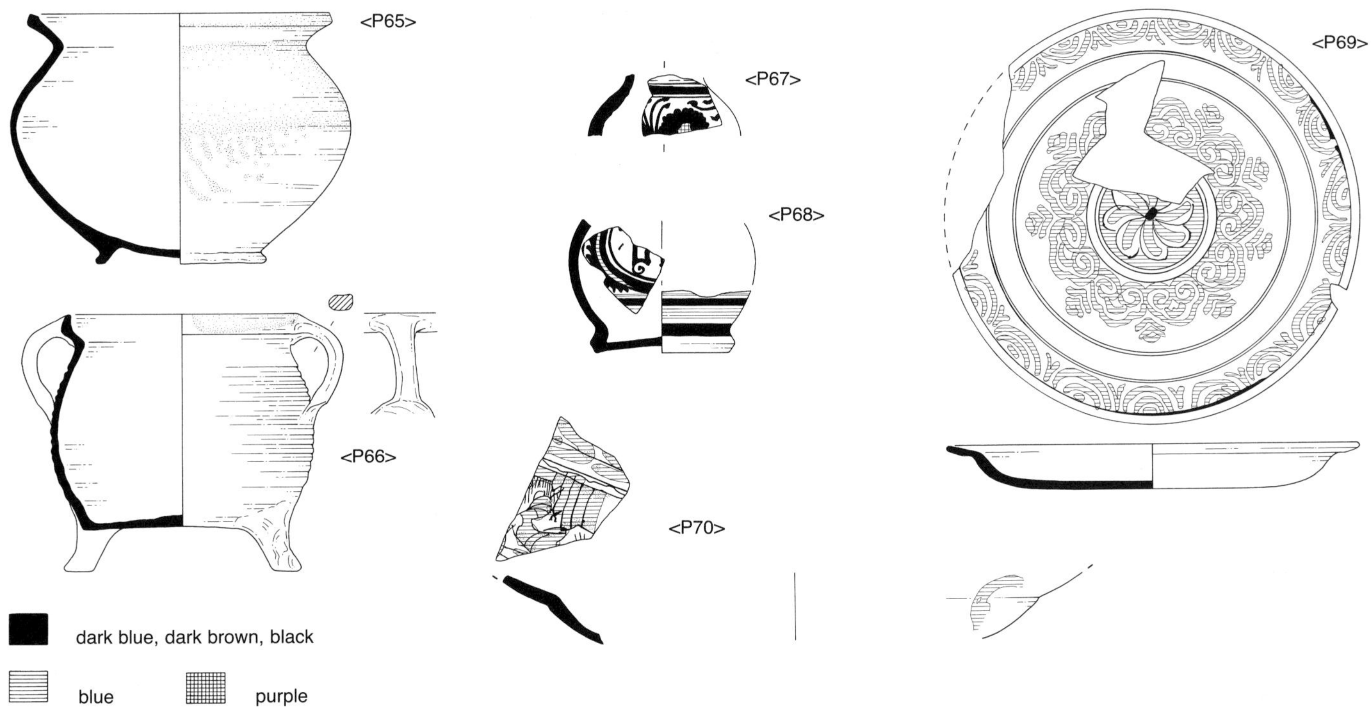

Fig 205 Dutch redware (<P65>), German stoneware (<P66>), Italian tin-glazed ware (<P67>, <P68>) and Portuguese dishes (<P69>, <P70>) from sites A, G and H (scale 1:4)

from H[6] (<P66>, Fig 205), the profile of which is more typical of Rhenish whitewares than the Dutch forms (eg Duisburg: Gaimster 1988c, 159). Both <P66> and a body sherd from A[265] have an internal yellow glaze streaked with brown. The other sherds derive from a pipkin found in the ditch (H[213]), a mug (H[24]), a green-glazed bowl or dish with a thumbed footring from site A[200], recorded as being from Holland, but possibly from Germany, and a small dish rim from site K (ER1352).

STONEWARE

Raeren stoneware (RAER) is the most common on sites A and F, but rare on site H. Of note are a drinking jug with rouletted decoration found in A[200] and a base sherd from a large jar found in the city ditch (H[213]); the upper surface of the footring is frilled in the usual way, but the underside has deep finger impressions at intervals of *c* 15mm. Later forms include the complete base and body section of a large rounded jug with cabled rat-tail handle (<P61>, Fig 204) which was found in the pit on site F (gpF22, F[220]); the base form is typical of the period 1550–1600 (Hurst et al 1986, no. 309). Another sherd from this context is from a large jug with incised horizontal lines around the girth (cf Gaimster 1997, no. 91), while a third piece, possibly from Langerwehe (LANG), is an everted cordoned rim which may be from a jar or a chamber pot (<P63>, Fig 204).

Frechen stoneware (FREC) is rare on sites A and F, but a near-complete drinking jug (<P62>, Fig 204) dated to *c* 1575–*c* 1625 was found in the pit, group F22; this is similar to an example illustrated by Hurst et al (1986, no. 333) but has a slightly squatter body. The ware is more common on sites H and K (ER1352–4); finds of note comprise sherds from two bellarmines with fine portrait medallions in foliate borders (both H[213]), a portrait medallion, bearing the date 1591 (Maloney and Harding 1979, fig 7; now missing), and a 'Bellarmine' witch-bottle (DUK77 [2] <1>; Maloney 1980, 157–9).

Other stonewares comprise a sherd from a late Siegburg (SIEGL) jug or bottle with an armorial stamp (A[127]; for probable profile cf Hurst et al 1986, 184, pl 34) and three sherds of Westerwald stoneware (WEST), one a tankard fragment from an 18th-century context on site A (A[130]).

PORTUGUESE, SPANISH, ITALIAN, AND DUTCH TIN-GLAZED WARES

Portuguese

A near-complete plate (<P69>, Fig 205) found in H[212] and H[72] is decorated in blue with a simple design around a central rosette which is outlined in dark green/black (POTG); the different fields are defined by fine concentric bands in dark green/black, while the back is plain. This piece can be dated to *c* 1600–25 by similar finds from Amsterdam (Baart 1987, no. 1). A slightly later piece, dating to *c* 1650, is a large flanged dish in the Chinese style with blue circles at intervals around the back (<P70>, Fig 205). This piece is unusual in that panel design is not in the Wan-li style, which usually comprises floral and symbolic motifs, but shows a figure bending over a stack of sacks; the adjacent panel contains tulip-like flowers. Portuguese wares are rare in London, and, as is often the case in Holland (ibid, 19–20), they seem to occur in areas where there may have been Dutch or Jewish residents (see below, 'Discussion'). The most notable example is a near-complete plate dating to the mid 17th century found on the site of St John Clerkenwell (Blackmore 2004b, 346–7).

Spanish

A single sherd from a Spanish tin-glazed bowl (<P64>, Fig 204) was found in the pit, group F22. This vessel is in a calcareous fabric with sparse schist-like inclusions suggestive of a source in Andalusia, although the simple geometric decoration in pale blue is similar to that produced at Paterna; there is no trace of any lustre, if this ever existed, while the back is plain. The closest parallel found for the upstanding rim and internal decoration is a rather smaller and deeper 'Nasrid' bowl from Granada dated to the 14th to 15th century, although this is also decorated on the back (Flores Escobosa and del Mar Muñoz Martín 1995, fig 19.8.3); upstanding rims also occur on a range of other Andalusian bowls and dishes of the 13th to 15th centuries (ibid, figs 19.6–8), although none of the illustrated pieces have exactly the same profile. This piece is the first of its kind from London, and no other parallels have so far been found elsewhere in England, so that dating is uncertain. The sherd was classified as late Andalusian tin-glazed ware (ANDAL), but could be earlier; it is not impossible that it was used in the priory, but more likely that it came from the same source as the other material in the same pit. The only other Spanish wares are two sherds of amphora found in H[213].

Italian

These comprise five tin-glazed sherds (ITGW) and one of north Italian marbled slipware (NIMS) from site J. Two of the former, both from vases dating to *c* 1480–*c* 1550 which were probably lost at the Dissolution, were submitted for neutron activation analysis. The first (BMRL 32155X) comprises a base and a body sherd, probably from a two-handled altar vase of the period *c* 1450–*c* 1550 (<P68>, Fig 205), found in the backfill behind the brick lining of a cesspit A[283]. The decoration comprises a glossy white glaze externally, with blue bands around the base and most of the 'Y' of the Bernardine sacred monogram within a circular band flanked by narrower lines and palm-like sprays in the spandrels (Blake 1999, 44, fig 2.4, no. 11); there is a matt tin glaze internally. The style of this vase was formerly associated with Faenza, in Romagna (ibid, 25–6). Chemical analysis, however, has shown that this vase is central Italian tin-glazed ware (CITGW) from Tuscany, probably from the lower to mid Arno valley, and possibly from Montelupo or Pisa (ibid, 23–4; Hughes and Gaimster 1999), and that it belongs to the same chemical group as a small jug from Askett, Buckinghamshire (Blake 1999, fig 2.2, no. 2) and larger jugs from Gateway House (Noël Hume 1977, pl 3, centre; Blake 1999, fig 2.1, no. 7) and Southampton (Platt and Coleman Smith 1975, fig 209, no. 1348). Jugs and vases of this sort are known from several sites in London, and a sherd from a similar vase decorated in blue and ochre, found in the city ditch on site K, probably belongs to this Italian group (not published in Noël Hume 1977; Blake 1999, 36, n 159). Other findspots in the eastern part of the City include the Tower Postern (site code TOL79), the Royal Mint (MIN86) and various dumped deposits just outside the city wall in the Moorfields area.

The other sherd (BMRL 32149Y) is from a small handle-less baluster-shaped vase found in a post-Dissolution dump (<P67>, Fig 205). This has floral decoration of blue tendrils and a daisy-like flower, the centre of which is painted in manganese; the external glaze is dull and slightly crazed, while that inside is matt (Blake 1999, 23–4, fig 2.4.11). This vase probably had a continous vegetal frieze like that on a more complete vase from Southampton (Platt and Coleman Smith 1975, fig 196, no. 1175, identified as Netherlandish; Gutierrez and Brown 1999, 147, fig 10.1.3). It may, however, have combined a foliate design with the royal arms of England, as seen on three vases from Askett (Buckinghamshire), the Tower of London, and 'the City of London' (Rackham 1939, 285–6, pls 55–7; Gaimster and Nenk 1997, fig 13.2; Blake 1999, 23–7, nos 5, 14; Gaimster 1999a). NAA analysis has shown that <P67> is in the same chemical group as the latter three vases, and that they are from the same general area of Italy as <P68>, but from a different source (Blake 1999, 42–4; Hughes and Gaimster 1999, 66). This high-status form, which is shown in contemporary manuscripts (Gaimster 1999b, 1; Hurst 1999, 95) is closely related to a class of 15th-century Valencian lustreware vase like that found near Cannon Street and others from the City (Gaimster and Nenk 1991, fig 6; Vince 1982, fig 15, nos 11, 12). The form is not exactly paralleled in Italy (Blake 1999, 25), but this may be because, like the ring-handled vases, it was produced for export, and it is significant that several of the 11 known English finds (Hurst 1999, 94–5) are from religious or high-status sites (Gaimster 1999a, 142), and/or from ports such as Southampton and Exeter (Allan 1999, fig 12.2, no. 52).

In addition to the above, the composition of one of the glazed ointment pots from F[220] (<P58>, Fig 203; quantified as TGW) was also found to be most closely related to pottery fabrics from northern Italy, especially Liguria and Piedmont (sample BMRL 32163R: Hughes and Gaimster 1999, 65–6). The fabric is visually identical to the biscuit wares, but the base form differs in that it has a collared profile.

Low Countries

Anglo-Netherlandish wares have been discussed above. South Netherlands maiolica (SNTG), which dates to after 1480, often occurs in Dissolution groups, but the only finds from the priory are from later contexts. They comprise a sherd from a Malling-type ring-handled vase, probably from Antwerp (Oost 1992, 102; Hughes and Gaimster 1999, 61–2), found in A[268] (and recorded as TGW), and the base of an 'altar vase' or jug found on site K (ER1355; Noël Hume 1977, 118, fig XIX, no. 16); Blake (1999, n 159) suggests that the latter may be Italian, but the fabric and glazing are more typical of the Netherlands. These pieces could have been discarded before 1540, but dating is difficult as production of both types in Antwerp continued into the late 16th or early 17th century (Hurst 1999, 96–7; J Veeckman, pers comm), and the bastion 6 sherd was found in a group dating to after 1630. A sherd from a ring-handled vase is said to have been found in A[200], but is currently missing.

CHINESE PORCELAIN

This is limited to seven sherds (CHPO); one of the more complete pieces is a late 17th- or early 18th-century tea bowl found in the 18th-century cesspit G[100] which also produced the plate with Hebrew inscription (Pearce 1998, 98, fig 3, no. 1).

Discussion

The medieval assemblages

The priory was founded in 1108, and so it is likely that most of the 'early medieval' pottery from the site dates to the late 11th or earlier 12th century. While it is not impossible that some graves pre-date the priory, it is likely that the few late Saxon sherds found reached the site with rubbish brought out of the main area of occupation towards the river. The published finds from site C date to *c* 1050–*c* 1150 (Chapman and Johnson 1973, 3, 12; Clark 1973). They could, therefore, pre-date the foundation of the priory, but it seems more likely that they are contemporary with a similar range of wares from a ditch at 1–2 Aldgate (Marsden 1969). The latter were first dated to the early 13th century, but can now be placed at *c* 1140–50; the fact that they include some fairly large fragments suggests that occupation was beginning to develop in the area to the south of the priory and by the Aldgate in the mid 12th century. Elsewhere in the area, however, medieval pottery is sparse (for example at Lloyd's Register of Shipping: Blackmore in prep b).

Pottery dating to the 12th and 15th centuries is scarce on all excavated parts of this priory; there are very few pit groups, and those of any significance date to the mid 14th century. The asemblage is thus of limited use in interpreting changes in land use or lifestyle, but it nonetheless informs on the archaeology of the site. This was one of the richest foundations in London; the paucity of medieval material cannot reflect the standard of living in the priory, but must result from other factors such as the degree of truncation noted on site C (Chapman and Johnson 1973, 3) and on the nearby site of Navigation House, Aldgate (NAV87: Schofield 1998, 254), and/or the location of the areas investigated which were largely beneath buildings (Fig 2). It is to be expected that, as found at St Mary Spital (Thomas et al 1997, 56–9), larger and more varied pottery assemblages were discarded elsewhere within the precinct, perhaps in the area of the great court or, as at St Mary Clerkenwell, in nearby pits and quarries (Blackmore in prep a). It is also possible that waste was discarded outside the precinct and north of the city wall. Although this is not borne out by the finds from the excavated section of ditch on site H or near bastion 6, some interesting 13th- to 15th-century material, possibly from a site of some status, was discarded across the road on the site of 1–2 Aldgate.

The finds from the cesspit(s) on site H (gpH21), at the north end of the dormitory range, are thus important for several reasons, not least because they offer a tantalising glimpse of what may still be found on other parts of the site. Most of the finds date to the late 13th or earlier 14th century (up to *c* 1340), but the south Hertfordshire-type greyware jug <P4> (Fig 199) and London ware jugs (eg <P9>, Fig 199) could be up to 200 years older, and would have been antiques if they were used and discarded together with the later pieces. An intriguing feature of the group is that it includes several jugs with residues (both brown and white), as well as several glass urinals. It is possible that the jugs were used to store urine and other substances for reuse, for example in medical remedies, as a solvent or in cloth production; indeed, documentary evidence suggests that there was a special demand for monkish urine (Moorhouse 1993, 129, 143). The virtual absence of coarse Surrey-Hampshire border ware (CBW) from this group is of interest, given that the rarer late medieval Hertfordshire glazed ware (LMHG) is present. The latter must have been a fairly new acquisition when it was discarded, suggesting that although there was a degree of conservatism and careful curation of pottery vessels there was at the same time an awareness of new fashions, and the occasional accident in the priory; the same has been noted in other assemblages from religious houses (Blackmore 2004b; Blackmore in prep a). Most of the pottery from a pit on site A (gpA38) is of a similar date, but is considered to be residual, or at least discarded at the Dissolution.

The groups from Holy Trinity Priory are too small to permit valid comparisons with the much larger pre-Dissolution assemblages from other religious houses which have recently been studied, notably St Mary Clerkenwell (Blackmore in prep a), St John Clerkenwell (Blackmore 2004b) and St Mary Spital (Stephenson 1997). These different excavations suggest that Surrey whitewares came into use slightly later on sites outside the city than within it (Thomas et al 1997, 56–9; Stephenson 1997, 184–5) and that Kingston-type wares (KING) are less abundant than CBW (Blackmore in prep a). The quantities at Holy Trinity Priory are extremely small, but it may be noted that in the broad quantification of the medieval wares, KING is outnumbered by CBW on site A, but the reverse is the case on site H; on site F, KING is absent altogether, while CBW amounts to only nine sherds. On the evidence available, therefore, it appears that although vessels in CBW may have been used on the site before *c* 1350, they were rarely being discarded until the later 14th century, at least in the excavated areas. This is the same as at St Mary Clerkenwell, where the ware does not appear in any quantity until after *c* 1350 and is most common in the 15th century (Blackmore in prep a). Imports are rare on all these religious sites until the 15th century, and most finds occur in Dissolution-period groups; Holy Trinity is no exception, and the number of stratified medieval imports is probably in proportion to that on other monastic sites.

The 16th- to early 17th-century assemblages

The post-medieval groups from the priory are characterised by the absence of some types as much as by the presence of others. Fabrics typical of the period 1480–1550, such as Cheam redware (CHEAR), bichrome redware (PMBR), south Netherlands maiolica (SNTG) and Raeren stoneware (RAER) are very rare, while others such as Cistercian ware are absent altogether. This reflects the fact that, although a Tudor group was found on site A (gpA40), Dissolution-period dumps are lacking here; it is thus likely that most sherds of London-area early post-medieval redware (PMRE) and post-medieval slipped redware (PMSRG and PMSRY), which have a broad date range of *c* 1480–*c* 1650, date to after *c* 1550. The main late 16th-century groups are associated with the construction of a cesspit, from the infill of a pit on site A (gpA43, gpA44) and from a pit on site F (gpF22) which contained a number of biscuit wares. These groups are dominated by local wares, but include imported earthenwares, mainly redwares but also a few whitewares, which support the documentary evidence for the changing nature and population of the area as tenements were created in the former precinct. Some at least became the home of immigrants from the Low Countries, and according to the 18th-century historian John Strype, there were 44 Dutch residents in one house alone, probably Duke's Place, as early as 1568 (Britton 1987, 28; see below).

Tin-glazed pottery production

Undoubtedly the most important aspect of the post-medieval pottery is the evidence that one of the earliest tin-glazed pottery production sites in London, if not the first, was located nearby, a production which had its origins in late 15th-century Italy (Caiger-Smith 1973, 163–4). As summarised by Britton (1987, 18–19), the movement of Italian artists and scholars to Antwerp, the new cultural centre in the north, began around 1508. Among these migrants was the potter Guido di Luca Savini of Casteldurante, who became known as Guido Andries and who, with other Italian potters in Antwerp, developed the art of tin-glazed pottery production there. Some of his children became potters, and in 1564 Joris Andries started a factory in Middelburg. During the 1560s rapidly escalating religious persecution led to a mass exodus of Protestants from the Low Countries, and in 1567 Jasper Andries and Jacob Jansen moved to Norwich, possibly with Joris Andries, and began to work as potters there. In 1570, possibly tempted by a more lucrative market in the capital, Jasper Andries and Jacob Jansen (also known as Janssen, Janson and Johnson) petitioned Queen Elizabeth for permission to settle in London and for a patent to produce, for a period of 20 years, 'Galley pavinge tyles and vessels for potycaries' on a site near the waterside, as they had been doing in Norwich (Garner 1948, 1–2, 4; Edwards 1974, 77–8; Noël Hume 1977, 1, 3, 107–11; Britton 1987, 27–9; Dumortier 1999, 108; Edwards 1999; Wilson 1999, 9).

The fact that the pottery was established in Aldgate and not by the river may reflect a number of factors. As other potters were also granted a patent in 1570 (Edwards 1974, 8, 78), it would appear that Andries and Jansen were unsuccessful in their request for sole rights (Britton 1987, 20), and the subsequent movements of Andries are unclear; it is possible that he either did not move to London or did not work as a potter (ibid, 21–2; Noël Hume 1977, 107). Jansen, however, married a widow who had a shop at the sign of the Rose in Duke's Place, and it was doubtless practical to market his wares through her business. In 1571 Jansen, then known as Johnson 'pott maker', and his wife were listed in the aliens' returns as living in the precinct of Crychurch (St Katherine Creechurch) (Kirk and Kirk 1900–8); six other Flemish potters were also living in Duke's Place at this time, although the name then applied to the whole of the former priory precinct. Documentary sources suggest that production of tin-glazed wares continued unchallenged in this area for some 40 years. Jacob Jansen lived at Duke's Place until his death in 1593, while between 1571 and 1615 no fewer than 13 Flemish potters were resident there. These included Lucas Andries, brother of Jasper, who died in Aldgate in 1572 (Dumortier 1999, 108). Potters were still living in Duke's Place in 1617 and 1621 (Edwards 1974, 8; Noël Hume 1977, 109–11; Britton 1987, 27–8).

The first material evidence for pottery production found in the Aldgate area comprises a trivet, two saggars and sherds which were recovered from site K (see above, 'Other 16th- to 17th-century glazed and biscuit wares'). Of these, 23 sherds from four contexts were published by Noël Hume (1977, 111–12), but in fact there are 33 sherds from seven contexts. At the time these could not be more closely dated than *c* 1525–*c* 1650; indeed, the lowest deposit contained glazed wares which were dated to as late as *c* 1640–85, and the source and dating of the biscuit sherds was thus left open (ibid). Biscuit wares (a cup and a bowl) were also found during excavations in 1974 at a site south of Aldgate High Street, outside the wall, but these were associated with tin-glazed pottery and other wares which probably date to the later 17th century (Orton and Pearce 1984, 41). Until the excavations of 1979, therefore, there was no archaeological evidence to prove that a pottery had actually operated in the area, and certainly not as early as the 1570s. The finds from the pit on site F, however, could well derive from the pottery founded by Jansen. Of particular interest are the wet and dry drug jars, since it was part of the original petition by Andries and Jansen to produce such vessels (Noël Hume 1977, 107).

Dating the finds from the pit (gpF22) is problematic. It is tempting to try and place it in the 1570s, but a slightly later date is perhaps more appropriate. As described above, the decoration on the tablewares, which may be either blue-and-white or polychrome, is typical of the late 16th to early 17th century. Both the forms and decoration of the glazed pieces are closely comparable with finds from Antwerp (Britton 1987, 28–9), where potteries operated by Guido Andries and his associates at Sint-Jansvliet and other workshops at Schoytestraat and in the Steen have now been excavated (Oost 1992, 106; Dumortier 1992). The unglazed wares from group F22 are also of very similar manufacture, and although there are some slight differences in rim and base profiles, the same forms are also found in Antwerp (Britton 1987, 29). Comparison of the biscuit forms from Norwich with those finds from site K showed that the former are rather thicker and cruder than those from London (Noël Hume 1977, 108), but the latter compare well with the finds from group F22. This feature also contains some local wares that are currently dated to after 1580, while the biscuit ware butter dish is a form usually dated to after *c* 1600 in Holland (Ruempol and van Dongen 1991, 178–9).

Scientific analysis has shown that the glazed and biscuit sherds from Holy Trinity Priory can be clearly differentiated from the imported wares, and that two other pieces are chemically very like the biscuit wares and can be attributed to the same production. These comprise the 'Rose is red' plate, dated 1600 or 1602 (Fig 159) (Britton 1987, no. 25; Tait 1992; Hughes and Gaimster 1999, 65) and a drinking jug with rose-leaf decoration (Fig 201) (Britton 1987, no. 7) similar to that on one of the dishes from F[220]; a jug of very similar form now in the Fitzwilliam Museum, Cambridge (Noël Hume 1977, 113, pl 58) almost certainly belongs to the same group. Given that the wares from site K probably date to the 17th century, and their similarity to the finds from site F, it is possible that group F22 dates to between *c* 1580 and 1610, and possibly to 1590–1600, although perhaps including some earlier glazed pieces. If so, it may represent a clear-out after the death of Jansen in 1593, or work by one of his successors. If the wasters from site K are from the same factory, which is said to have ceased production *c* 1620, they might date *c* 1600–20, although several must be redeposited as they occur with material dating to after 1630.

To summarise, despite the fact that the original petition by Jansen and Andries referred only to paving tiles and apothecary jars (Wilson 1999, 9), the small size of the sample and the uncertainties noted above, there is sufficient evidence to show that by *c* 1600 – and possibly in the 1570s – the first Aldgate pottery was producing drug jars in a range of sizes and a number of other forms. The jars and dishes, both strongly influenced by their Italo-Flemish antecedents, were intended primarily for display, the former in apothecary shops, the latter in private houses. Possible examples of the output include two late 16th- or early 17th-century dishes in the Antwerp style from a cesspit at the site of Lloyd's Register of Shipping, Fenchurch Street (FCC95 [3067]), although these could be genuine imports (Blackmore in prep b). Rather less is known of the character of the later pottery industry in the area, although it has been suggested that there was a link between the Aldgate pottery and one established at Wapping in the 1660s (Noël Hume 1977, 5; Britton 1987, 31–2).

The mid 17th- to 18th-century assemblages

The main pottery assemblages of this later period are from the ditches on sites H (gpH12.6) and K, and a cesspit on site G (G[100], gpG6.11). The first two comprise useful assemblages, but cannot be related to specific households. The third, by contrast, is of importance as a closely datable collection of the 1740s. The group has been described in detail (Pearce 1998) but it may be noted here that it represents part of a clearance; this may have been prompted by death, illness, or a removal, but the fact that most domestic groups appear to date to the mid 18th century suggests a wider trend, perhaps related to changes in fashion and lifestyle. On the whole the contents are typical for a middle-class household of the period in London (ibid, 103). However, the presence of the tin-glazed plate with Hebrew inscription (also originally part of a set) makes this the first group that can be attributed to a Jewish household in post-medieval London.

Between 1290 and 1656 no Jews lived in England, but with the Resettlement a community grew up in the Aldgate area. Most of the original Sephardi settlers came directly from the Iberian Peninsula, or else via Holland. It is possible that the two Portuguese plates found on sites G and H are connected with the Sephardi population in the area, which by 1753 numbered around two thousand. A further plate, dated *c* 1625–50 but found in a late 17th- or early 18th-century cesspit on the site of Lloyd's Register of Shipping, close to the former Hambro synagogue, may also have come from a Sephardic household (Blackmore in prep b).

A community of Yiddish-speaking Ashkenazi Jews, who came mostly from Germany and were reputedly more strictly observant than the Sephardi Jews and used the Hebrew script, also settled in the area. By 1753 the Ashkenazi community numbered about four thousand. The lettering on the Mitre Street plate is of Ashkenazi style; the primary function of the inscription would have been to help those who prepared and served the food to avoid mixing milk and meat products, but its prominence also implies a didactic function. Artefacts which can be related to Jewish life are extremely rare in archaeological contexts in London; and it is of interest that most known finds are related to meat products, while items associated with dairy products seem to be much rarer (Pearce 1998, 106–7).

In the 1690s most of the wealthier Jewish households were Sephardim, and this seems to have remained the case in the 1740s, despite the fact that the community was considerably smaller than that of the Ashkenazi Jews, which in the 1690s included all recorded Jewish servants. While it is not impossible that the plate was used in an Ashkenazi household, documentary evidence suggests that it was used by Ashkenazi servants in a Sephardic household (Pearce 1998, 95–6, 105–6). Either way, this find is of importance in adding to the picture already presented by the pottery for the increasing social diversity of the Aldgate area and the changes which were taking place there between the 16th and 18th centuries.

8.6 The non-ceramic finds

Geoff Egan

Introduction

Many of the non-ceramic finds from the medieval and later periods of the sites included in this publication are tiny, unidentifiable scraps and are, therefore, not listed. Preservation factors were not kind to some of the metalwork, and all the medieval window glass is decayed. On the other hand, bone/antler and post-medieval glass have survived fairly well, and pits yielded limited leather, textile and wooden items in good condition.

Abbreviations used in the catalogue are explained in Chapter 1.3. Bone/antler identifications are by Alan Pipe and wood genus identifications by Rowena Gale, unless indicated otherwise.

Pre-priory finds

The small assemblage of pre-institutional medieval finds includes two Saxon combs (one with its case), evidence for weaving, and a single coin dating from just before the Conquest. Those from site D came from features along or near the Leadenhall Street frontage, and thus might reflect secular properties there. Site D contexts were not studied in detail for this report; hence neither group nor period are given for them.

Combs

Antler comb fragment
D<222>, D[183] (not grouped, from pits pre-dating the cemetery)
Fragment of connecting strip, surviving L *c* 49mm, W *c* 15mm, antler with iron rivet.

Antler and bone comb (Fig 69 closed, Fig 206 open)
D<42>, D[1842] (not grouped, from pits pre-dating the cemetery)
Single-sided comb (90mm x 28mm) in case (121mm x 30mm); antler, with the exception of one or perhaps more of the strips, which is bone. The comb consists of ?four panels with teeth (graded at the ends) and two connecting strips, held together by four rivets of iron and one of copper alloy (the last probably a repair). The case consists of two pairs of strips connecting two sub-triangular end panels (one incomplete) by means of a pair of iron rivets at each end; the strips are each decorated with four dot-and-two-circle motifs flanked by oblique hatching longitudinally and defined at the ends by two or three transverse parallel grooves. A discrepancy of *c* 5mm between the length of the comb and the case may indicate that this was not an original pairing. Date: 10th or 11th century.

Textile manufacturing equipment

Ceramic loom weight
F<71>, F[87], group F16; ?late 12th century
Fragment, surviving L 86mm, about one quarter of doughnut shape (noted in Pritchard 1984, 66).

Bone ?bodkin
D<100>, D[557] (not grouped)
Fragment, surviving L *c* 44mm; eye and point both broken off.

Bone ?needle
D<105>, D[1930] (not grouped)
This could be a needle, but is too fragmentary to be certain (I Riddler, pers comm).

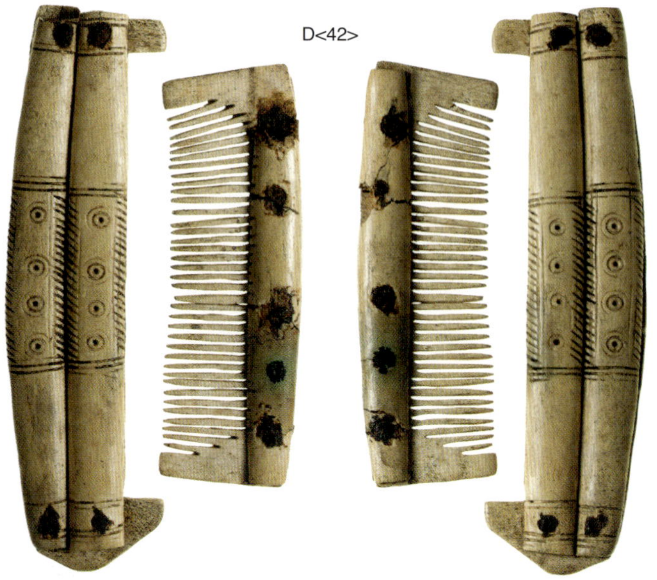

Fig 206 Saxon comb and case D<42>, open, showing both sides (case 121mm long, comb 90mm long)

Coin

Silver coin (Fig 70)
D<52>, D[2030] (not grouped, from pits pre-dating the cemetery)
Edward the Confessor small-flan penny or halfpenny of London (1042–66), short-cross issue, moneyer +LIFINC ON LVNDE; little sign of wear.

Priory period finds

There is just about enough in the bead, the fragments of glass and lead from institutional windows and the notable textiles, as well as sundry burial goods, to indicate a specific religious focus for the medieval assemblage. However, some categories commonly encountered at sites of religious houses are completely absent, as for example bone styli, which are otherwise almost a diagnostic category for such sites (Egan 1997, 109, table 14: category H). Only three of the 21 categories defined by Egan (ibid) have been recognised here: a rosary bead (category B), an item of grave goods (category D), which in this instance is – most unusually – of precious metal, and seven jettons of appropriate date (category R). Rich, exotic textiles here arguably take the place in the assemblage of ornate metalwork (category A). This is, overall, a low degree of correspondence compared with the pattern usually evident from the sites of such institutions. The window glass, comprising less than half a dozen fragments, is paltry compared with that in the assemblages from several other London religious houses. A sizeable 14th-century pit group (gpH21, H[501]) comprises parts of one or more leather shoes, a notable scabbard with a much smaller knife, two wooden vessels and at least 11 urinals. The last are commonly found in groups at locations where religious houses formerly stood. The small knife, unremarkable in itself, was found concealed in the lining of an armorial scabbard for a much larger tool or weapon, and is for this reason a most unusual survival. The numismatic finds assigned to this period comprise one silver penny and a lead token, as well as seven copper-alloy jettons used for accounting. A couple of pieces of mould are probably residual from bell-casting for the institution, a bone skate suggests a degree of indulgence in recreation (though it may be from a secular context along Leadenhall Street), and a horseshoe evokes travel, presumably beyond the city.

Structural items

Lead cames
D<108>, D[409] (not grouped)
L *c* 40mm. An archive record drawing shows no reeding (an absence which would be expected of medieval cames).

Window glass, ?rectangular quarry
F<106>, F[220], group F22; post-Dissolution, *c* 1580–*c* 1600
Incomplete and superficially corroded; 71+mm x 47mm; originally pale green (retains three grozed edges).

Window glass, painted
A<256>, A[350], group A38; Dissolution period
Three superficially corroded, green pieces with undiagnostic surviving areas of paint.

Decayed, undiagnostic opaque window glass fragments were found as follows: seven pieces (A<51>, A[484], group A29; fill of grave 64, early 12th to mid 13th century); one green piece (D<257>, D[212] (not grouped)); two pieces (D<333>, D[592] (not grouped)).

Items pertaining to religious observance

Jet bead
H<114>, H[311] (not grouped in archive report)
Plain oval, L 16mm, Diam 14mm. Presumably from a rosary (the mineral is likely to have come from Whitby in Yorkshire; cf Egan and Pritchard 1991, 309).

Silver cross pendant (Fig 41)
A<60>, A[609], group A21, grave 9, at shoulder of male burial; *c* 1040–*c* 1100 or possibly later
Incomplete, 23mm x (estimated) 17mm, Wt 0.48gm; slender equal arms with upper loop, terminal knops and central square engraved on both sides with a saltire cross.

The saltire motif frequently appears on lead/tin accessories and other items of Norman date (Egan 2000, 108) as well as precious metal ones like finger rings. Despite its small size (the bullion value of the complete object would originally have corresponded to decidedly less than that of half a contemporary penny) the present find was a prestigious object in the context of a burial; the rare instances of medieval Christian grave goods of this date are presumably indicative of important personages.

This tiny pendant has some fairly close parallels in form also of Norman date; the most notable, though, is slightly later but also from a grave, that of Bishop Peder Elafsen (d 1246) at Øm Abbey in Denmark (Glob 1980, no. 7). In this country, a copper-alloy item from Norwich described as a shroud pin is a more substantial but comparable cruciform grave find (Norfolk Archaeological Unit 1999, 38). Nearer to home are a number of other broadly comparable, but probably later and, therefore, less immediately relevant, cross accessories with arms terminating in lobes, for example a pendant of gilded copper alloy (probably for a horse harness) from the site of Bermondsey Abbey in Southwark (Egan in prep b, no. 420), from a deposit assigned to the late 14th/early 15th century).

Textiles

Fragments of two exotic patterned silks found in a pit are among the most notable London textile finds from the Middle Ages. They have been fully published by Frances Pritchard (in Crowfoot et al 1992) and her account furnishes the following comments.

Textile fragments (Fig 119; Fig 120)
H<133>, H[494], group H21; 14th century
Previously published as Crowfoot et al 1992, 106–21, figs 79–81, no. 459.
Nine tattered fragments in lampas weave, finely-woven pattern of intersecting circles, plant ornament and Kufic writing, in a warp-faced tabby on a weft-faced 1.2 twill ground; it is a non-reversible, double-weave (the reverse has the appearance of an unpatterned 1.2 twill, neither the main warp nor the pattern weft being visible); a hem 4–5mm wide runs along the edge of six of the fragments; assignable from parallels among Continental episcopal burial garments to the 12th century; probably from a leading workshop in Spain or the Middle East (for the latter possibility see von Wilckens 1992, 41–2, nos 61–2; Muthesius 1997, 90, n 2, pl 70A, no. M1090B).

Silk textile fragments (Fig 119)
H<208>, H[494], group H21; 14th century
Previously published as Crowfoot et al 1992, 97–9, figs 70–1, no. 458.
Two fragments of lightweight silk with torn edges (*c* 146mm x 55mm and 50mm x 45mm): self-patterned weave on tabby ground; small-scale pattern of saltire cross infilled with tiny lozenges (repeat 20mm x 20mm); threads Z-twisted and unspun; yarn is not of a consistent high quality, with occasional slubs in the ground weft; traces of red dye; comparable with textiles produced in Spain. Possibly part of a facing or lining.

Dress and dress accessories

In addition to the ?shoe fragments, which are fairly uncommon finds from religious institutions because of poor preservation in most soils away from the River Thames, these comprise relatively common forms of copper-alloy accessories, the most notable of which is H<73>, from the top end of the mass-produced range. The silk surviving from the strap of H<72> implies some spending power but is not necessarily indicative of great wealth (which is attested by the preceding textiles).

Leather ?shoe fragments
H<116>, H[501], group H21; 14th century
?Shoe upper(s); two fragments, the largest 100mm x 72mm.

Copper-alloy buckle (Fig 207)
H<72>, H[305] (not grouped in archive report)
Sub-oval frame, *c* 16mm x 23mm, with folded sheet plate *c* 25mm x 15mm, having slot for pin and two holes for rivets; ? unthrown silk survives within plate, from strap (identified by F Pritchard).

Copper-alloy buckle (Fig 207)
H<73>, H[305] (not grouped in archive report)
Oval frame, 22mm x 33mm, with lip for missing pin, and integral forked spacer, *c* 24mm x 36mm, having double-stepped central void; two fragments from associated sheet plate(s) survive.

Cf Egan and Pritchard 1991, 80–1, no. 325 (assigned to the late 14th century and with the remains of a worsted strap) for another with a spacer similarly stepped internally.

Copper-alloy strap loop
F<31>, F[66], group F19, robber trench of Building E; pottery of 11th–14th centuries
Corroded, sliding loop, 24mm x 20mm (strap aperture 17mm); knop at centre of top is voided (possibly but not necessarily for the insertion of a stone; glass is far more likely than an actual mineral to go in base metal).

Cf Egan and Pritchard 1991, no. 1254, fig 149, dated to the late 12th century.

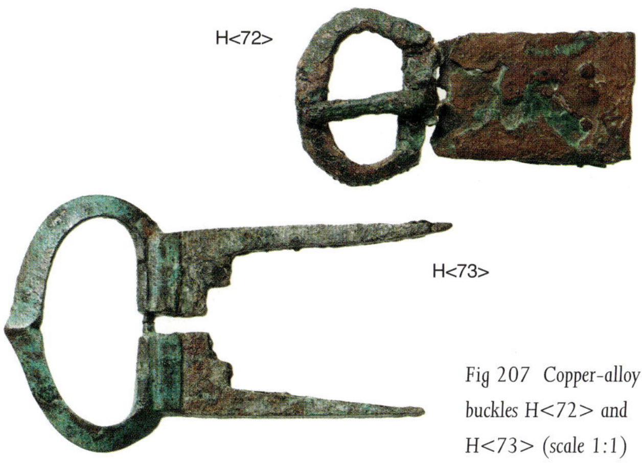

Fig 207 Copper-alloy buckles H<72> and H<73> (scale 1:1)

Household items

Knife and scabbard (Fig 208)
H<131> and scabbard H<181>, H[501], group H21; 14th century
Previously published as Cowgill et al 1987, knife no. 96 and scabbard no. 457 (ibid, 88; 154; 37, pl 7; 90, fig 61; 153, fig 97). References in site records to a maker's mark on the blade seem to be inaccurate.
Small, whittle-tang knife with convexo-plain blade, L 42mm, W 11mm, Th 2mm (tang L 23mm, set just below back); plain, rectangular-sectioned handle, of wood from one of the Pomoideae family; found wholly inside square-sectioned, relatively blunt-ended scabbard, between its outer layer and lining (in four pieces), all of calf leather with the grain facing inwards (identification by G Edwards, Ancient Monuments Laboratory, English Heritage); the lining protrudes at the top; the outer leather has a side seam with edge/grain stitches, and impressed decoration of four vertical panels (two on each face), three with four and one with five shields of different arms, within rectangular linear border; four crescentic cuts for missing, suspensory thong; there may originally have been a cap for the scabbard.

At just over half the length of the scabbard it was found in, the knife was probaby secreted inside as an expedient (rather than being specifically intended as what was later known as a by-knife: a secondary, much smaller fighting blade to accompany a sword in the same scabbard).

The heraldry is in all likelihood purely decorative. T Wilmott (in Cowgill et al 1987, 45–50) notes that the shield with a bend company between two cotises on the present scabbard does not appear among surviving contemporary rolls but may correspond to the arms of the Hertfordshire family of Leventhorpe in the late 1300s; this potential correspondence on one or perhaps two of the 17 blazons featured on the leather, not backed up by evidence of appropriate tinctures, does not seem particularly compelling for identification.

?Scabbard
H<115>, H[501], group H21; 14th century
One side of an incomplete, flat-ended ?scabbard, *c* 25mm x surviving 80+mm, with roughly impressed grid marking out two areas with traces of accomplished tooled decoration, one possibly with a human figure (?saint). The abraded decoration here hints at an object of very high quality.

Stone hone
A<55>, A[102], group A47; 18th century
Micaceous schist, subrectangular section, L 100mm.

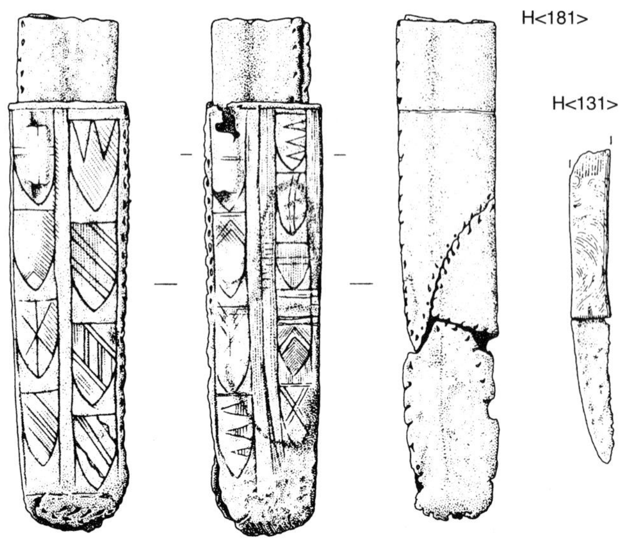

Fig 208 Knife H<131> and scabbard H<181> (scale 1:2)

Ash wood dish (Fig 209)
H<40>, H[501], group H21; 14th century
Edge fragment from (now very flat) dish, Diam 230mm with rim W 30mm; *Fraxinus* sp (ash).

Ash wood bowl
H<41>, H[501], group H21; 14th century
Fragments from plain edge and angle to base of bowl, Diam *c* 180mm; *Fraxinus* sp (ash).

Urinals

These thin-walled, translucent glass vessels (Fig 210) are often found at the sites of religious houses and other institutions or in affluent milieux, where they were used to help diagnose the state of health of individual inhabitants from the colour and other qualities of the urine (cf L Keys in Egan 1998, 252–4). The state of preservation of the items from the site H cesspit (H[501], gpH21), which retain in their entirety the original surface, colour and translucency, is most unusual among excavated potassium glass (green 'forest' glass) of medieval date.

Urinal fragments
H<187>, H[501], group H21; 14th century
Five wall fragments, presumably from the following urinals.

Urinal fragments (Fig 210, no. 1)
H<191>, H[501], group H21; 14th century
Flaring rim fragments, Diam 46mm.

Urinal fragments (Fig 210, nos 2, 3, 5)
H<192>, H<193>, H<195>, H[501], group H21; 14th century
Fragments of flaring rims, respective Diam 47mm, 44mm and 49mm; bases with pontil marks (the latter with wall fragments).

Urinal fragments (Fig 210, no. 4)
H<194>, H[501], group H21; 14th century
Fragments of base, wall and flared rim, the latter Diam 55mm.

Urinal fragments (Fig 210, no. 6)
H<196>, H[501], group H21; 14th century
Fragments of flared rim, Diam 51mm, and base.

Urinal fragments
H<197>, H[501], group H21; 14th century
Fragments of flared rim.

Urinal fragments
H<243>, H<4>, H[501], group H21; 14th century
Angled rim fragments (from different vessels).

Urinal fragment
H<245>, H[501], group H21; 14th century
Angled rim fragment.

Urinal fragments
H<246>, H[501], group H21; 14th century
Fragment of flared rim, and two wall fragments.

Urinal fragments
H<247>, H[501], group H21; 14th century
One flared rim and one wall fragment.

Urinal fragments
H<248>, H[501], group H21; 14th century
Flared rim, Diam 104mm, and base fragment with pontil mark.

?Urinal fragment
H<199>, H[478], group H21; 14th century
Corroded base, probably of urinal.

Numismatica

The numismatic items comprise a penny from a northern mint, a lead token that has been pierced repeatedly and four jettons from three different series but all of fairly common varieties.

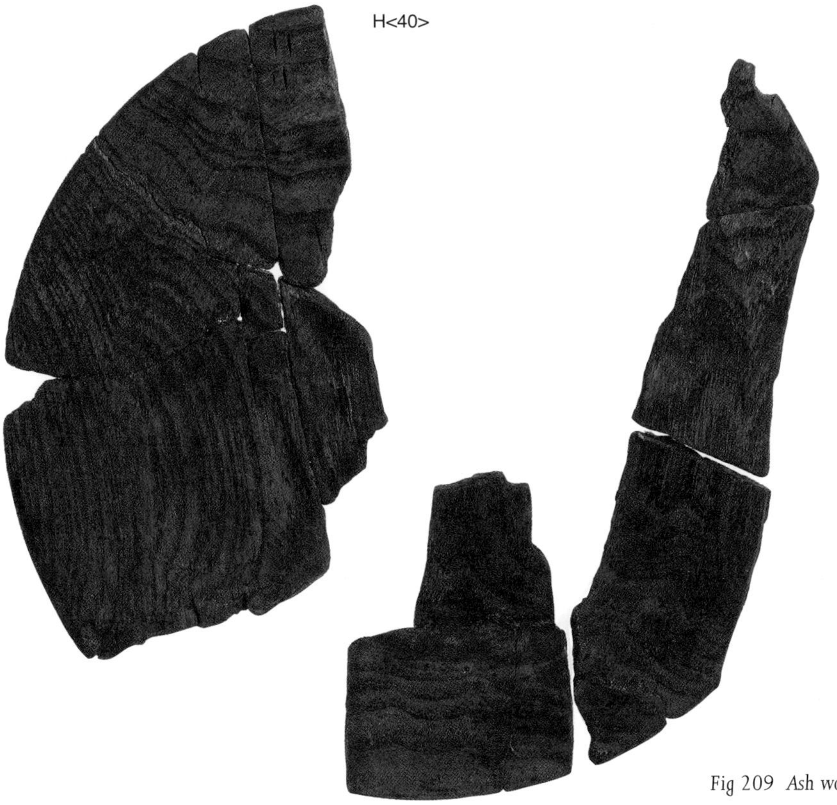

Fig 209 *Ash wood dish* H<40> *(diameter* c *230mm)*

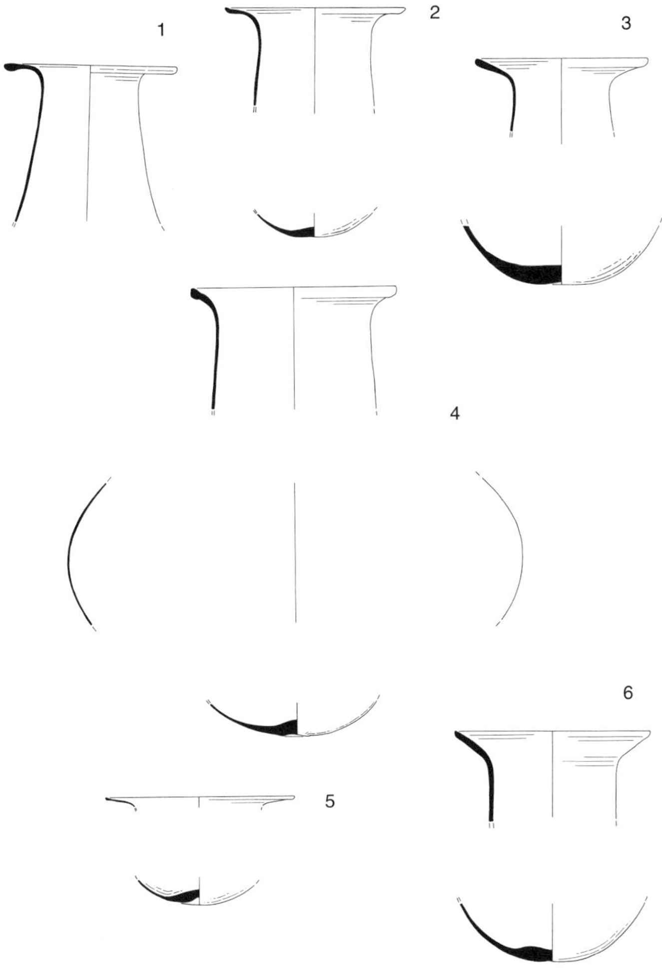

Fig 210 *Urinals from site H:* 1) H<191>, 2) H<192>, 3) H<193>, 4) H<194>, 5) H<195>, 6) H<196> *(scale 1:4)*

COIN

Silver coin
H<218>, H[305/323] (not grouped in archive report)
Edward I penny; 1299–1301, Chester class 1b (identification by J Clark and P Stott).

TOKEN

Lead token
F<4>, F[66], group F19, robber trench of Building E; pottery of 11th–14th centuries
Diam 16mm; lombardic letter A (cross-hatched) // shield with ?cross-hatched saltire cross; pierced three times along one side. Late 13th/14th-century (dating by P Stott and J Clark).

JETTONS

Jettons were used for accounting. The current dating scheme for these items (Mitchiner 1988) is open to question in several details; archaeological fixed points are still needed to confirm suggested time spans for the use of most issues. (F<22> and F<23> from the same post-Dissolution deposit were, according to the current conventions, issued respectively before and after *c* 1550; this is by no means impossible if the former was some years or decades old when discarded.)

English

Copper-alloy jetton
A<34>, A[331], group A38; Dissolution period
Incomplete; Diam 17mm; cross moline // cross moline. (Identified by P Stott as late 13th/early 14th-century.)

Cf Mitchiner 1988, 116–17, nos. 239–41 or 252 for the type indicated by the description, assigned to *c* 1310–55.

French

Copper-alloy jetton
H<104>, H[306] (not grouped in archive report)
Diam 24mm; cross fleurdelisée in

ornate quatrefoil, A V E G in outer angles // arms of France modern, AVE MARIA GRATIA PLE around (lombardic letters). ?Late 14th/early 15th-century.
Cf Mitchiner 1988, 175ff, nos 440ff, assigned to 1385–c 1415 (rather than 224–31, nos 665–711, assigned to the 15th century as a whole) for the type indicated by the dating given.

Nuremberg
These are both stock issues.

Copper-alloy jetton
A<12>, A[127], group A44;
c 1550–c 1600
Crumpled; Diam 24mm; ship on a sea, VOLGVE (LA) GALEE:DE:FR around // lozenge with four fleurs-de-lis, crown VIVE:LE: BON:ROY:DE:FRAN around (lombardic letters). Early 16th-century.

Copper-alloy jetton (Fig 211)
A<21>, A[+]
Diam 25mm; five-petalled rose with crowns and fleurs-de-lis, BOE... around // orb etc, (?crown)OD..NE... around (lombardic letters). Early 16th-century; nonsense legend (?1520s–30s, P Stott).

Furnishing

Bone panel
D<225>, D[1788] (not grouped)
Triangular, c 26mm x 17mm, with circle-and-dot motif. Probably from a casket or box; such mounts are usually of Norman date or earlier.

Horse equipment

Iron horseshoe
A<117>, A[592], group A23;
c 1050–c 1150
Incomplete horseshoe branch with three nail holes (corrosion too advanced to identify further details).

Production

Bell mould
H<200>, H[307] (not grouped in archive report)
Two undiagnostic ceramic bell mould fragments in a post-Dissolution deposit.
Ceramic mould fragments from casting copper-alloy items like bells and domestic vessels are sometimes found in considerable quantities close to the sites of casting pits. The sparsity of the present finds of this category suggests that the location of the pits from which they derive was not in the immediate vicinity of the excavation area.

Leisure

Bone skate (Fig 71)
D<14>, D[949] (not grouped in archive report)
Incomplete skate, made from cattle metatarsal (identified by I Riddler); L 179mm; one side broken off modified distal end; at proximal end worn through to central cavity from use.
Although bone skates are not uncommon in London (Egan 1998, 294–5), this one is a notable find in that it was recovered some distance from the River Thames, and so may have been used on one of the city's other frozen waterways. As it is from site D, the find may not be from the priory, but from secular occupation along Leadenhall Street.

Selected post-Dissolution items

The objects included here comprise two common dress accessories from the post-Dissolution period, a couple of decorative glass items of tableware, two jettons (one a generation or more old when discarded), a piece of decorative chain mail, a thimble, a piece of waste crystal glass which is significant in that it probably derives from the earliest known factory for this material in London, located nearby (the other pieces of glass need not necessarily be factory waste), a printing block for a 19th-century firm (presumably local) and coffin furniture from the post-medieval cemetery.

Dress accessories

Copper-alloy buckle (Fig 212)
H<2>, H[213] (not grouped in archive report); ceramic date c 1640–50
Corroded; incomplete, double-oval frame, surviving 32mm x 34mm, with fleur-de-lis type motif on outside edge; loop of pin survives. Late 16th century.

Copper-alloy dress clasp (Fig 212)
A<49>, A[+]
Hooked dress clasp, corroded; cast, 23mm x 12mm; double-voluted main motif (as Ionic capital). A characteristic category of accessory of the early 16th century, but in this case one of the very few with an overtly classical reference.
Cf Egan in prep a, nos 151–5, for other cast, one-piece clasps from London (the precise method of wearing them remains obscure).

Copper-alloy wire loop
A<20>, A[250], group A44;
c 1550–c 1600
Twisted wire loop, corroded; Diam 11mm.
A characteristic accessory of the early 16th century, these may, sewn densely onto purses, have

Fig 211 Copper-alloy jetton A<21>, obverse (left) and reverse (right) (scale c 2:1)

Fig 212 Copper-alloy buckle H<2> and dress clasp A<49> (scale 1:1)

acted as protective armour against street thieves trying to cut them open (cf Egan in prep a, nos 271–83).

Pins

See below ('Superstition', H<1>), for pins used for a purpose other than dress.

Tableware

Glass ?cup fragments
H<219>, H[6], group H12.6;
c 1550–*c* 1630
Folded foot (15 fragments).

Glass vessel fragment
G<4>, G[100], group G6.1;
c 1740–5
Fragment of base, Diam *c* 52mm, with pushed-in centre and pontil mark; multiple horizontal trails on flaring body, and looped trail from vertically applied ?handle on one side. From an ? ornate drinking vessel.

Domestic work

Copper-alloy thimble
A<26>, A[247], group A44;
c 1550–*c* 1600
H 19.5mm; single ring at base, where Diam is *c* 15mm; pits appear to be irregularly angled strokes.

Production

Glass rod (Fig 213)
F<88>, F[220], group F22;
c 1580–*c* 1600
Rod, Diam 8mm, of colourless ('crystal') glass, with running opaque-white cylinder set concentrically; broken off at both ends, surviving L *c* 64mm; slightly bent towards one end. Drawing waste for crystal latticinio cane.

There has been some speculation, backed up by analytical work, that canes with white glass to be used on crystal vessels made in the early factories in London were imports, either from Antwerp or Venice. The dating suggests that this rod derives from Carré's or Verzelini's Crutched Friars glasshouse; if so, it is potentially one of the earliest pieces of glass production waste from London, and possibly is the sole piece so far recognised from either of these earliest historically attested crystal-glass manufacturers, who were respectively active from *c* 1567–74 and from the 1570s to the 1590s (Godfrey 1975, 16–33).

Stone lithographic block
A<145>, A[+]
'Daniel de Pass and Co.' (a 19th-century shipping company).

Fig 213 Rod of colourless glass F<88> (scale 1:1)

Jettons

Copper-alloy jetton (Fig 214)
F<22>, F[220], group F22;
c 1580–*c* 1600
Diam 22mm; five-petalled rose with crowns and fleurs-de-lis, fleur-de-lis NEBVN fleur-de-lis EDV... around // large orb etc, EBV... rose DNVED rose NVBN rose ... around (lombardic letters). Early 16th-century; nonsense legends.

Copper-alloy jetton
F<23>, F[220], group F22;
c 1580–*c* 1600
Diam 23mm; (weakly registered) (rose) with crowns and fleurs-de-lis // orb etc, HA..SA....ES... around (roman letters). Late 16th/early 17th-century.

Military

Copper-alloy chain mail
H <120>, H[318] (not grouped in archive report)
Eleven oval-sectioned links, Diam 9–10mm, each connected to four others (where there is survival); overall surviving area *c* 30mm x 25mm.

Superstition

Group of copper-alloy pins (? and other items)
H<1>, H[2] (not grouped in archive report; from the backfill of the city ditch)
Tapered ?wire (inventoried as

Fig 214 Copper-alloy jetton F<22>, obverse (left) and reverse (right) (scale c 2:1)

'pin') found in a stoneware witch-jar (Maloney 1980) with same accession number along with 'two to three dozen pins' (a drawing on the record card suggests that the item referred to is a different category of object, possibly a waste sheet strip or a lace chape). The contents of the witch-jar featured in an identification competition in the *London Archaeologist* in 1981 (issue 4, 51); the photograph shows that the pins were of the wound-wire head form.

See Merrifield 1987, 163–75, on the use of buried vessels, usually stoneware *bartmann* jars like the present one, containing pins and the like as sympathetic-magic protection by the superstitious against perceived or possible supernatural attack.

Items probably from the graveyard of St Katherine Cree

Iron coffin handles
E<22/1>–<22/5>, E[59/60], group E8; probably second half of 16th century
Five, corroded; single-arched, ? with horizontal pivots; two sizes appear to be represented: E<22/1> appears to comprise a handle, L c 110mm and a ?nail, L 110mm; E<22/4 and E<22/5>, L c 95mm; E<22/2> and E<22/3>, L c 110mm.

Copper-alloy studs
E<17>, E[2], group E9; ?17th century or later
Two; plain, domed heads, Diam 14mm.

These too may well be coffin accessories; hundreds were used to make up patterns and hold textile wrappers on coffins in place from at least the 17th century.

8.7 The animal bones from a 12th-century deposit at site A

Alan Pipe

Introduction

This appendix describes and interprets the animal bone assemblage recovered by hand collection from a 12th-century context A[649] (gpA23) at site A, one of the layers in a pit or well (Chapter 4.2). It considers the assemblage as a whole and then discusses in more detail the partially complete, articulated dog skeleton which comprised the bulk of the material in terms of bone weight and fragment count. A fuller version of this report is held in the archive at the Museum of London (Pipe 2000).

Methodology

The animal bone was washed, air-dried at room temperature and then bagged and labelled as a context group. Each bone fragment was then weighed to the nearest 0.1g using an electronic balance and described in terms of species, skeletal element, handedness, fragmentation, epiphysial fusion, tooth eruption and wear, and pathological change. Identifications of species, skeletal element, and handedness were made using the MoLSS Environmental Archaeology Section reference collection in conjunction with Cohen and Serjeantson (1996) and Schmid (1972). Fragmentation was described using the numerical zone method of Rackham (1986). Estimates of age from epiphysial fusion and dental eruption and wear were taken from Schmid (1972). All data were entered directly onto the MoLAS/MoLSS Oracle 7 animal bone post-assessment database. Although all fragments were identified to species level whenever possible, a few heavily fragmented and/or eroded bones were assigned to the approximate taxonomic and skeletal element categories 'cattle-sized mammal', 'sheep-sized mammal', 'unidentified mammal', 'long bone fragment' and 'unidentifiable fragment' as required.

Results

A total of 268 fragments (0.34kg) of animal bone was recovered from context A[649]. These derived from frog or toad (probably common frog *Rana temporaria* or common toad *Bufo bufo*), chicken (*Gallus gallus*), ox (*Bos taurus*), pig (*Sus scrofa*), a nearly complete articulated skeleton of a dog (*Canis familiaris*) and part of the skull of a cat (*Felis catus*). The lack of complete, fully adult bones prevented accurate measurement of any bone, and it was therefore impossible to justify speculation on, or calculate stature and 'build' of, any species. No evidence of burning or gnawing was seen on any bone.

The remains of the dog provided the bulk of the assemblage (253 fragments, 304g). All this material derived from one partially complete, articulated skeleton. The dog was lying extended and flat on its right side; the remains included the complete skull and both complete mandibles, all areas of the vertebral column, the sternebrae, and proximal ('upper') elements of the fore-limbs, the scapula and humerus ('shoulder blade and upper fore-limb') and the caput ('ball') of the proximal femur ('thigh bone') of one hind-leg. No butchery marks were recorded. The skeleton had been severely truncated, resulting in complete removal of the lower fore-limbs and pelvis, and almost the whole of the hind-limbs.

The skull and mandibles showed good dental preservation and recovery. All permanent cheek teeth between, and inclusive of, the second premolar and the second molar were fully erupted but unworn, although the third molar was completely unerupted, with only the initial crypt perforation visible. This indicates an age at death of between 5 and 6 months. The canine teeth had erupted but had only attained approximately half the full crown height, indicating a maximum age of 4.75 months at death.

The evidence from epiphysial fusion also strongly indicates that the animal was subadult. The proximal and distal epiphyses of the humerus were both completely unfused, indicating a maximum age at death of 6–8 months. The distal epiphysis of the scapula was fused, indicating a minimum age of 6–8 months. Overall, therefore, the dental and fusion evidence points to a young animal certainly in the first year, and quite probably in the first half-year, of life. All estimates of minimum and maximum age at death are taken from Schmid (1972) with the exception of that for the scapula, which is cited by Amorosi (1989).

There was no evidence for dental pathology or, indeed, any pathological change associated with the skull or mandibles. Definite pathological changes were, however, recorded from a rib fragment and the neural spine of a thoracic vertebra. In each case, there was an indication of an incompletely healed simple fracture possibly resulting from physical trauma such as that from a kick or blow (Baker and Brothwell 1980, 85). Both injuries were still healing when the animal died and there is no evidence for infection at the wound sites.

With the exception of the distal scapula epiphyses, none of the recovered axial or appendicular bones were fused. This precluded any worthwhile measurement, as the animal was very much a subadult at death and was still growing. Comparison of the mandibles with the MoLSS reference collection indicates that the animal was very similar in general facial size to a large adult fox (*Vulpes vulpes*) although the mandibular and facial 'build' was somewhat broader, shorter and more sturdy. Although it is impossible to comment definitely on its probable stature, the animal was by no means a lap-dog and might well have fulfilled a working role had it not died while still skeletally immature.

Discussion

This deposit provided a small but interesting mixture of archaeological animal bone. The faunal species composition within the deposit represesents a mixture of deliberate dumping of waste from consumption of beef and pork (ox and pig), chance casualties due to the action of the open feature as a 'pit-fall' trap (frog/toad and possibly chicken, cat and dog), and deliberate disposal of non-dietary remains (human, and possibly cat and dog). The recovery of single, comparatively fragile bones from chicken and human, rather than other more robust limb-bones, implies that recovery from the pit or well was incomplete and, for some species at least, may suggest redeposition. It is therefore not possible to comment on carcass-part representation in detail, or to speculate at greater length on the significance of the faunal composition of the deposit.

8.8 The human skeletal remains

Janice Conheeney

Introduction

Human remains were recovered for analysis from two areas (sites A and F) of Holy Trinity Priory during separate periods of excavation (Fig 2); they were also recovered from site D but have not been analysed, while the human bone from site E was not retrieved for examination. Site F (HTP79; Table 6) was reported on in 1979 by Deborah Downs and site A (LEA84; Table 4) by Barbara West in 1986 (Downs 1979; West 1986). All remains in the 1986 report were analysed as one group and the 1979 sample was regarded as a separate, potentially later group. The following account is a reworking of the data collected by those two authors. Completion of the stratigraphic part of the analysis has meant that the 1986 osteological data can be split into groups for the first time. This has allowed various questions to be addressed (see below, 'Aims of the analysis') including examination of the archaeological hypothesis that the 1979 group may be contemporaneous with the latest of the 1986 groups (ie from the excavation of 1984). The original osteological reports are available in the archive. The data used in this report are entirely the work of Downs and West, but any interpretation of those data is the responsibility of the present author.

Limitations and composition of the sample

There were a number of factors that limited the scope of this analysis. These were partly a product of the nature of the sample, and partly reflected the problems associated with re-analysing data recorded by two independent observers.

The skeletal remains from site A and site F have been dated to roughly the same period, Saxo-Norman, that is the 11th to 12th centuries. However, there is no demonstrable archaeological link between the two areas and so the two samples have been treated separately in the analysis.

The number of individuals from site A is given in Table 4 and from site F in Table 6. The site F material was divided by Downs into nine cist-burials and a disparate assemblage of disarticulated bones from 11 later contexts, comprising bones from about 19 persons (Downs 1979). This group of 'disarticulated' bones, almost certainly from the cemetery excavated on site F or nearby, was examined to see if it contained any differences or special pathological cases. As Table 6 shows, the nine cist-burials comprise seven individuals laid out in cists and the remains of two further persons, an adult and a child of 4–5 years, whose remains had been pushed to the east end of the cist in burial 3. At the time of excavation these disturbed bones were not recognised as being from two individuals, and they are designated F[61].

The cemetery is believed to have extended to the west and south beyond the excavated area of site F, so the total extent of the cemetery is not known. The proportion of the whole cemetery that the recorded graves represent cannot, therefore, be estimated and the remains cannot be regarded as reliably representative of all those individuals buried in the cemetery. In all the areas there was heavy truncation and disturbance of earlier burials by later ones.

Aims of the analysis

The archaeology of the site suggested several questions that the osteological analysis could hope to clarify.

1) How do site F and site A compare, as there is no demonstrable archaeological link from which to decide if these are two separate groups of people?

2) Are there any similarities between site F cist-burials and site A, group A21 burials, as both are of cist-type and could represent higher-status burials?
3) Can any of the specific groups likely to be buried here, such as brethren, parochial congregation or wealthy lay benefactors, be identified?

Methodology

The data

On the whole, Downs's and West's methods are comparable for the quantitative aspects of the recording. Any differences in recording are described below. It is more difficult to assess if there is variation in those aspects requiring subjective assessment – hence the caution. The methods employed are described in some detail in order that the reader can make their own assessment of the validity of the results obtained.

Preservation of remains

Downs and West catalogued the surviving parts of each skeleton on a checklist and on a proforma diagram. From these, the present author was able to abstract the data required for the analysis of the state of preservation, including estimates of the percentage of each skeleton present, and for calculation of prevalence figures in the pathology section. The data were used to test for differences in preservation between the samples and to examine the relative preservation of different parts of individual skeletons (following Mays 1991b) in order to comment on factors which may have influenced the survival of the bone.

The dentitions of both groups were recorded on the standard chart by Brothwell (1981, 53). The chart records tooth and alveolar bone presence and absence, and the health status of each tooth and associated section of alveolus.

Sex and age estimation

West employed a wide selection of accepted methods of assessing dimorphic characteristics of the pelvis and skull to determine sex (Brothwell 1981; Genoves 1969; Anderson 1962; Gray 1977; Ferembach et al 1980; Black 1978; Phenice 1969). Downs relied on the descriptions of these features in Brothwell (1972, the earlier edition of Brothwell 1981). Downs states that, where no other indicator survived, she used general robustness of the bones to distinguish males from females.

West combined estimates derived from a number of ageing methods to produce a 'best' estimate for adult skeletons. The methods included dental attrition (Brothwell 1981, 72), fusion of cranial sutures (Meindl and Lovejoy 1985) and changes in the pubic symphysis (McKern and Stewart 1957; Gilbert and McKern 1973; Brooks 1955; Meindl et al 1985). She assessed the age of immature individuals from the stage of fusion of epiphyses and dental eruption along with comparison with growth standards produced by Maresh (1943), Hoffman (1979), Gindhart (1973) and Sundick (1978).

Downs relied on dental attrition for age estimation of adults (Brothwell 1972) and fusion and the sequence of dental eruption (Schour and Massler 1944) for immature individuals.

Metrical data

West recorded 34 cranial and 36 postcranial measurements from each site A skeleton when the relevant skeletal elements were in sufficiently good condition. Downs states that the majority of burials from site F were severely truncated and few measurements were possible. Both West and Downs followed the conventions set out in Brothwell (1972; 1981, 82–7) in recording these measurements.

Stature was calculated from long bone length using the regression formulae of Trotter and Glesser (1952; 1958). It was necessary to use whichever long bones survived for these calculations, given the fragmentary nature of both samples, despite the fact that it would have been more desirable, in terms of comparability and reliability, to standardise the bone used throughout the stature analysis.

Non-metric data

Non-pathological variability of specific traits was recorded in order to test for a genetic component to the distribution of burials and to compare these samples with those from other sites. Occurrences of the traits were plotted onto plans of the burials and particular attention was paid to those individuals presenting more than one trait in common. The data were also examined for patterns of recurring traits, following the study by Saunders (1989) on occupationally related skeletal modification.

Dental pathology

Caries prevalence was recorded by tooth and location on the tooth. For each tooth type it was calculated as the number of that tooth with caries as a percentage of the number of that type of tooth present. Total caries prevalence for each area was also calculated as the total number of teeth with caries as a percentage of all teeth present.

Abscess prevalence was calculated as the number of individuals suffering from abscesses as a percentage of all the individuals with dentitions present. Frequency of ante-mortem tooth loss was calculated in the same way.

Drawing comparisons between site F and site A was considered reasonable for quantitatively recorded aspects of the dental pathology such as caries, abscess and ante-mortem loss. With the subjectively assessed aspects such as level of severity of calculus, periodontal disease and hypoplasia, the possibility of inter-observer variability made such comparisons less reliable.

No distinction was made between periodontal disease and alveolar recession in the analysis, as these related features were not recorded separately in the first instance.

Skeletal pathology

The frequency of degenerative diseases of the spine, such as osteoarthritis, osteophytic development, intervertebral disc disease and ossification of the ligamentum flavum, were calculated as the number of individuals suffering from each condition as a percentage of the total number of individuals in that sample or group who had surviving vertebrae. The most common locations of each of these conditions were also noted.

The frequency of nutritional deficiencies was calculated as the number of individuals with a specific complaint as a percentage of all the individuals in that sample or group with the relevant body part surviving.

Location and stage of healing of any traumatic pathology were noted, as were the occurrence and location of infectious disease and metabolic disorders.

Comparative material

Holy Trinity Priory is of particular interest amongst monastic houses as it was the earliest established Augustinian house in the London area and the richest of any London house. Documentary evidence suggests that the burials would probably include those of members of the priory, members of the parochial congregation attached to the church and wealthy lay benefactors who had requested burial there. One of the aims of the analysis was to examine any osteological evidence that could contribute to this reconstruction.

The major characteristics of the Holy Trinity individuals were compared to those from a number of sites of roughly contemporary date (Table 26).

Preservation of remains

The remains were generally poorly preserved due to truncation by later building work. Group A21 survived best of all the groups or samples, probably because of the physical protection afforded by the cists. Preservation of individual elements, and of the two infant skeletons at site A, indicated that it was physical disturbance rather than poor excavation or soil processes that caused the poor preservation; the survival of skeletal elements as a percentage of the maximum number of elements possible was markedly uneven and usually below 60%, even on site A, with the exception on site A of the main arm and leg bones (Table 27; Conheeney 1999).

Demography

Twenty-eight adults and two juveniles from site A, where juvenile is defined as 6–15 years, had surviving recording sheets. Of these, West assessed 20 as male or possibly male and eight as female. A total of 27 adults and one infant were recovered from site F. Downs assessed four of the cist-burials as male and four as female or possibly female, and one as infant, defined as 0–5 years. The disarticulated bone consisted of seven males or possible males, five females or possible females and seven skeletons of indeterminate sex. The subsample size became very small when any of the three samples was broken down by age or sex. Therefore only general observations were possible and nothing could be statistically demonstrated. This should be borne in mind when judging the veracity of the proffered conclusions.

Sex composition

Sites A and F had burials of both sexes, with a male to female ratio of 2.4:1 at site A, south of the priory church, and of 1:1 in the cist-burials on site F, but the sample sizes are too small to make anything of this (Table 28). Most groups were of mixed sex (Table 29). Exceptions to this were site A, groups A22 and

Table 26 Comparative cemetery sites

Site (MoL site code)	Reference	Period	Site type
Outside London			
Chelmsford Priory	Bayley 1975	medieval	Dominican house (male and female burials)
Chester Greyfriars	West 1990	medieval	Dominican house (male and female burials)
Chichester, St James and St Mary Magdalene	Lee and Magilton 1989	1118–c 1700	leper hospital (male and female burials)
Guildford friary	Henderson 1984	1274–1538	very small Dominican house (male and female burials)
High Wycombe (Bucks), St Margaret	Farley and Manchester 1989	medieval	hospice for ageing clergy (male and female burials)
Ipswich Blackfriars	Mays 1991b	1263–1538	benefactors and friars (male and female burials)
Ipswich Whitefriars	Mays 1991a	1278–1538	probably lay benefactors and priors (male and female burials)
Oxford Greyfriars	Lambrick 1990	medieval	Dominican house (male and female burials)
York, St Helen-on-the-Walls	Dawes and Magilton 1980	medieval	parish church cemetery
London medieval			
Blackfriars, Carter Lane (PIC87)	Keily 1989	medieval	Dominican house (male and female burials)
Royal Mint site, Black Death burials (MIN86)	Waldron 1993	14th century	effectively parish church cemetery
St John Clerkenwell (JON89)	Conheeney 2004	medieval	headquarters of Order of St John of Jerusalem (male and female burials)
St Mary Graces (Royal Mint site) (MIN86)	Waldron 1993	15th–16th centuries	Cistercian house (male and female burials)
St Mary Spital (NRF88)	Conheeney 1997	12th–16th centuries	priory hospital
St Nicholas Shambles (GPO75)	White 1988	11th–12th centuries	parish church cemetery

Table 27 The relative survival rates of various skeletal elements at Holy Trinity Priory compared to St Mary Spital

Skeletal element	No. of elements in site A sample	No. of elements in site F cist-burial sample	No. of elements insite F disarticulated sample	Site A sample as % of number expected	Site F cist-burial sample as % of number expected	Site F disarticulated sample as % of number expected	No. of skeletal elements at St Mary Spital as % of number expected
Skull	12	6	9	40.0	66.7	47.0	72.8
Mandible	13	2	5	43.3	22.2	26.0	71.2
Sternum	7	2	-	23.3	22.2	-	60.0
Scapula	27	7	1	45.0	38.9	2.6	71.6
Clavicle	29	6	2	48.3	33.3	5.5	68.4
Sacrum	51	5	-	34.0	9.0	-	61.6
Humerus	33	9	1	55.0	50.0	2.6	76.0
Radius	46	7	4	76.7	38.9	10.5	72.8
Ulna	45	3	1	75.0	16.7	2.6	73.2
Femur	55	11	5	91.7	61.1	13.2	77.2
Patella	33	6	2	55.0	33.3	5.3	43.2
Tibia	50	10	3	83.3	55.6	7.9	73.6
Fibula	49	10	3	81.7	55.6	7.9	75.2

Table 28 The sex composition at Holy Trinity Priory (sites A and F) and at comparative sites

Site	Males	Females	Indeterminate	Male:female ratio
Outside London				
Chelsmford Priory	68	44	12	1.5:1
Chester Greyfriars	25	10	3	2.5:1
Chichester, St James and St Mary Magdalene	50	14	12	3.6:1
Guildford friary	69	11	33	6.3:1
High Wycombe, St Margaret	4	2	6	2.0:1
Ipswich Whitefriars	11	3	1	3.7:1
Ipswich Blackfriars	151	64	14	2.4:1
Oxford Greyfriars	47	1	1	47:1
York, St Helen-on-the-Walls	338	394	45	1:1.2
London medieval				
Blackfriars, Carter Lane	14	5	29	2.8:1
Holy Trinity Priory, site A	19	8	3	2.4:1
Holy Trinity Priory, site F cist-burials	4	4	1	1:1
Royal Mint site, Black Death burials	210	167	46	1.3:1
St John Clerkenwell	7	2	0	3.5:1
St Mary Graces (Royal Mint site)	110	61	65	1.8:1
St Mary Spital	52	26	11	2:1
St Nicholas Shambles	90	71	19	1.3:1

A23, which were exclusively male, but these were small groups and do not by themselves indicate a special area for the canons.

Age composition

Ageing evidence suggests that, in common with other monastic sites, very few immature individuals were buried here (Table 30; Table 31). Also, site A and site F appear to have a similar age composition among the adults, although it was impossible to compare this to other sites as so many could only be placed in the general adult category rather than being assigned a precise age. However, evidence of more severe dental disease and degenerative pathologies at site A suggests that it may well have held an older sample than site F.

Physique

The metrical data for this section are available in the archive (there was insufficient metrical data for site F disarticulated bone).

Average stature at site A was 1.72m for males and 1.64m for females; among site F *in situ* cist-burials it was 1.77m for males and 1.65m for females. Both were consistent with the medieval range of heights (Table 32). Neither the site F *in situ* cist-burials nor site A, group A21 fell at the top of the range of statures for Holy Trinity which, in combination with other indicators, could have supported the archaeological hypothesis that these two groups were of relatively high status.

Table 29 The sex composition of the groups

Group	Male	?Male	Indeterminate	Female	?Female	Juvenile	Infant	Total
Site A								
A21	5	-	-	2	-	-	-	7
A22	4	1	-	-	-	1	-	6
A23	2	-	-	-	-	-	-	2
A24	3	-	-	2	-	-	-	5
A25	4	-	-	2	-	-	-	6
?A21	-	-	-	1	-	-	-	1
A29	1	-	-	1	-	-	-	2
A35	-	-	-	-	-	1	-	1
Total	**19**	**1**	-	**8**	-	**2**	-	**30**
Site F								
Cist-burials	4	-	-	3	1	-	1	9
Disarticulated	6	1	7	2	3	-	-	19
Total	**10**	**1**	**7**	**5**	**4**		**1**	**28**

Table 30 The age composition of the three samples

Age group	Site F cist-burials (%)	Site F disarticulated (%)	Site A (%)
0–5 years	11.1	-	-
6–15 years	-	-	6.7
16–25 years	11.1	15.8	23.3
26–35 years	22.2	-	23.3
36–45 years	-	-	6.7
46–55 years	-	5.3	10.0
>55 years	-	-	3.3
Adult	44.4	78.9	26.7
Elderly	11.1	-	-

Table 31 The age composition at Holy Trinity Priory (sites A and F) and at comparative sites

Site	% surviving >45 years	% immature individuals
Outside London		
Chelmsford Priory (males only)	17.2	10.1
Guildford friary (males only)	30.0	11.5
Ipswich Blackfriars (males only)	32.3	9.6
Oxford Greyfriars	20.4	4.9
York, St Helen-on-the-Walls	23.0	-
London medieval		
Blackfriars, Carter Lane	>4.2	17.0
Holy Trinity Priory, site A	>13.3	6.7
Holy Trinity Priory, site F cist-burials	>11.1	11.1
Holy Trinity Priory, site F disarticulated	>5.3	-
Royal Mint site, Black Death burials	>12.0	29.5
St John Clerkenwell	-	24.9
St Mary Graces (Royal Mint site)	>17.8	23.3
St Mary Spital	>8.7	29.4
St Nicholas Shambles	6.4	-

Table 32 Average statures of males and females at Holy Trinity Priory (sites A and F) and at comparative sites

Site	Average male stature (m)	Average female stature (m)
Outside London		
Chester Greyfriars	1.69	1.61
Chichester, St James and St Mary Magdalene	1.70	1.64
Guildford friary	1.73	1.61
Ipswich Blackfriars	1.73	1.61
York, St Helen-on-the-Walls	1.69	1.57
London medieval		
Blackfriars, Carter Lane	1.73	1.56
Holy Trinity Priory, site A	1.72	1.64
Holy Trinity Priory, site F *in situ* cist-burials	1.77	1.65
Royal Mint site, Black Death burials	1.67	1.58
St John Clerkenwell	1.73	1.60
St Mary Graces (Royal Mint site)	1.68	1.60
St Mary Spital	1.70	1.60
St Nicholas Shambles	1.73	1.58

Dental pathology

Deciduous or mixed dentitions were excluded from the following calculations of prevalence. The site F disarticulated group was excluded as their disarticulated nature precluded the calculation of accurate prevalence rates. Wear data have not been included in this analysis but are available in the archive. The sample showed evidence of wear at a rate which was roughly in accordance with that set out by Brothwell (1981, 72) in his table for ageing by tooth wear, although some individuals presented severe wear relative to their skeletal age. There were no congenital complaints. Site A had generally worse dental health than the site F cist-grave group.

Acquired pathology

CARIES

Apart from a carious lesion in a deciduous canine in a site F cist-burial, the caries pattern conformed to the usual modern pattern with teeth posterior to the premolars affected in both the mandible and maxilla.

When the wider caries incidence rates were compared to those of the priory sites, site A burials had lower rates than all five sites for which the prevalence rate was calculated in the same way (Table 33).

Table 33 Incidence rates of caries at Holy Trinity Priory (site A) and at comparative sites

Site	Caries incidence rate as % of teeth present
Outside London	
Chester Greyfriars	9
Ipswich Whitefriars	15
Ipswich Blackfriars	10
London medieval	
Holy Trinity Priory, site A	2
St John Clerkenwell	14
St Nicholas Shambles	6

ABSCESSES

Abscess prevalence could be expected to follow the caries prevalence, since the major cause of abscess is pulp exposure due to caries or heavy wear. However, this was not the case at Holy Trinity Priory. Site A individuals and site F cist-burials had very different prevalence of abscesses at 3.3% and 11.1% respectively, whereas their caries prevalence had been similar.

At first sight, site F cist-burials had much more of a problem with abscesses than site A individuals. This would appear improbable, given that the caries prevalence of the two areas was similar and the age structure is considered similar, so that neither had more time than the other to develop the problem. An explanation could be that this is a reflection of the greater ante-mortem tooth loss among site A individuals compared to those from site F.

DENTAL CALCULUS

Given the subjective nature of recording calculus, periodontal disease and hypoplasia severity, comparisons cannot be drawn between site F and site A in this and the next two sections.

Calculus was a moderate to severe problem among site A individuals, that is, 84.5% of the sample had moderate or greater deposits of calculus. This suggests that the diet was probably fairly stodgy rather than fibrous, allowing the deposition of plaque, and that dental hygiene was not of a high standard if the plaque could remain in place and calcify to calculus.

Among site F cist-burials 33.3% had no calculus, 50% had only slight deposits, and there were no severe cases. Whereas it was impossible to compare those with gradable amounts of calculus between site F and site A, the difference in those with no calculus (and, therefore, an objective observation) could be compared. This suggests that calculus was a worse problem in site A individuals than in site F cist-burials, particularly so since both are thought to be of a similar age structure and neither, therefore, would have suffered more from the cumulative nature of this age-related complaint.

PERIODONTAL DISEASE

There were 84.7% of site A individuals with some degree of periodontal disease. It was mainly a slight to moderate problem, with only 15.4% having severe levels. Only 33.3% of site F cist-burials suffered from periodontal disease and all of these were slight cases. Both of these patterns fit very well with the moderate to severe pattern of calculus for site A and the slight to moderate levels for site F. The presence of calculus is thought to be one possible factor in the onset of periodontal disease. Therefore, periodontal disease could be expected to lag slightly behind the level of calculus in severity.

HYPOPLASIA

Hypoplasia is an interruption of the normal development of the tooth enamel usually attributed to bouts of severe childhood illness or stress of some sort (Hillson 1986; Johnston and Zimmer 1989). At site A 15.4% of individuals presented signs of hypoplasia, indicative of the proportion who may have suffered from severe childhood stress. This was very low compared to a 50.9% incidence at the Franciscan friary at Chester, but in the same order as some areas of the cemetery at St Mary Spital, London, at around 16.7–20%. These areas at St Mary Spital are thought to have held fairly poor people who had been cared for in the priory hospital (Conheeney 1997, 226).

Site F cist-burials had an extremely high prevalence at 83.4%, but this was based on only six individuals and could therefore be a product of such a small sample size.

OTHER PATHOLOGY

Burial A[504] at site A (gpA29, grave 64) had very large mental foramina 'with signs of infection' around them (West 1986). West suggested that this might indicate that the blood supply into the alveolae was infected. She also recorded resorption and deposition of new bone over the entire surface of the palate with signs of infection penetrating through into the sinuses. This individual had severe dental disease and very heavy and uneven attrition. Perhaps the infection and dental disease were triggered by heavy attrition that had resulted in pulp exposure.

Skeletal pathology

Congenital pathology

There was only one case of congenital pathology among all three samples: a sacralised fifth lumbar vertebra in skeleton

A[1065] at site A (gpA22, grave 14). This defect is common (Ortner and Putschar 1981, 355) and would not have affected the life of the individual.

Acquired pathology

DEGENERATIVE DEFECTS

Degenerative changes and dental disease were the most frequent type of pathologies present. Osteoarthritis is normally a complaint associated with ageing, so it is interesting to note that the total site A incidence rate is 36.7% compared to the site F cist-grave group rate of 11.1%, when the ageing data had suggested that the two samples are of a similar age structure. The parts of the body most frequently affected by these changes were the ankles, wrists and hands, the cervical and thoracic vertebrae, the sterno-clavicular joint and the hip. This predominance of involvement of the small joints is not uncommon in archaeological samples (a similar distribution is present in the Ipswich Blackfriars: Mays 1991b), but in modern populations the large joints such as the knee and the hip are most frequently affected (Ortner and Putschar 1981, 419).

The majority of a modern population show vertebral osteophytes by 50 years of age (Bass 1987, 19) and there is much debate as to the influence of stress-related occupational factors on this age-related phenomenon. Again, site A as a group was much more affected than the site F cist-burial group, who were apparently unaffected, perhaps supporting the suggestion that site A was composed of relatively older people. Thoracic vertebrae were most affected, then lumbar and, least of all, cervical. Sufferers can be unaware of the condition in life.

Males and females in the site A sample were almost evenly affected by intervertebral disc disease at 25% and 26% respectively. None of the site F cist-burial group were recorded as affected. The most obvious indication of this defect is erosion and deposition of bone on the end plates of the vertebral body as a result of degeneration of the disc. The sufferer may have felt some stiffening of the joints involved but it is difficult to estimate the pain experienced, as one individual can be unaware of a bony change that would trouble another. Mostly cervical and some thoracic vertebrae were affected.

Other bony exostoses occurred most frequently on rib facets in site A individuals and site F disarticulated bone, and in one group of metatarsals in the latter sample. The changes to rib facets are a common ageing phenomenon, and the case involving metatarsals was probably due to trauma.

TRAUMA

The healed fractures noted were varied and did not conform to any pattern. It was therefore impossible to infer a common cause such as a widespread activity. Four people at site A had fractures, two of which were among the six burials from group A22. Skeleton A[1065] (grave 14), a male of about 25–35 years, had a depression on the right frontal bone of about 6mm diameter. It was partially healed but still pitted at the base of the hollow, which was about 2–3mm deep at the deepest point. West (1986) believed it was most likely to be a depressed fracture. Another adult male, skeleton A[655] (grave 19), had a possible healed greenstick fracture to the left femur. The shaft was bowed, and there was some swelling and some periosteal bone. The right fibula shaft was thickened and West surmised that this may have been in response to the femur injury. In group A24, a 16–18-year-old male, A[617] (grave 27), had the right laminae of two lumbar vertebrae twisted and deformed downwards as if from a healed break. One spinous process protruded into the neural canal, which must have caused pain, and one must wonder whether there was loss of feeling to the legs; West does not report any changes to the leg bones. Finally, another adult male, A[500] (gpA25, grave 57), had a right third metacarpal with a crushed head that had healed successfully but with some resorption of bone and shortening of the shaft. Although not a fracture, a fifth male had a badly compressed lumbar vertebral body, deformed to such an extent that an angle of slope was produced in the articular facets. This may well have produced considerable discomfort if the sciatic nerves were pinched.

The condition of the fractures suggests that no treatment was given to the injured person. The pitting on the depressed fracture and the periosteal bone on the greenstick fracture suggest that these wounds may have become infected and that the infection was still present when the person died. This could imply that wounds were not tended and kept clean. The distortion of the femur shaft and the shortening of the metacarpal would suggest that fractures had not been reduced.

The site F sample did not include any fractures. A male aged about 25–35, F[52] (gpF11, grave 3), had a very curved right fifth metacarpal which Downs (1979) queried as a possible greenstick fracture. This is more usually attributed to the wearing of tight footwear (White 1988, 45). A second adult male F[134] (gpF11, grave 6) had a possible bunion on the left foot.

A specific type of trauma, Schmorl's nodes, occurred in individuals from both the site A and site F cist-burial groups. These lesions are interpreted as the result of herniation of the intervertebral disc into the end plates of the vertebral body, sometimes attributed to overlifting in a young person. Males and females were affected in both samples, and the thoracic vertebrae were most affected, followed by the lumbar. This is the usual distribution of the nodes. Their presence suggests that both sexes from both samples were undertaking heavy physical work from an early age. Interestingly, site F cist-burials and site A, group A21 were both heavily affected. There were 57% of group A21 and 60% of site F cist-burials with nodes present. These were the putative higher-status burials, and thus of people who might have been expected to be excluded from such heavy physical labour.

The presence of enthesopathies was recorded for both samples, but there is no pattern to their distribution.

NUTRITIONAL DEFICIENCIES

Changes possibly indicative of nutritional stress were present. Cribra orbitalia is generally accepted as indicative of iron deficiency anaemia during childhood either because of illness or nutritional compromise (Stuart-Macadam 1989). Two individuals were affected, one of the site F *in situ* cist-burials (F[52]) and one at site A (gpA21, A[782]), both adult males. None of the other site A groups were affected.

CIRCULATORY DISORDERS

Four cases of possible osteochondritis dissecans were present: three at site A and one in a site F *in situ* cist-burial. This condition usually occurs on the articular surfaces of the long bones when a small piece of bone atrophies and ultimately detaches itself from the remainder because of poor blood supply (Manchester 1983, 69–70). A small pit is left in the bone though this may eventually heal. The condition is fairly commonly reported in archaeological samples and modern populations, so the 10% prevalence at site A (and 11.1% in the smaller site F cist-burial group) is not unusual.

The location of the lesion varied between the four cases but all were common places for the complaint to occur. All three site A cases were from group A21. Skeleton A[833] (grave 3) was affected on the left femoral condyle, A[685] (grave 8) on the base of two proximal phalanges, and A[674] (grave 11) on the base of a proximal foot phalange. The site F individual, skeleton F[42] (grave 7), had a pit on the left glenoid fossa. Again, site A, group A21 and site F cist-burials were the only two groups affected. This could suggest a link between the two groups, although there is no obvious indication what this might be, and it could just be a quirk of the data. The defect would have had no direct effect on the person but could have contributed to the onset of osteoarthritis of the joint in later life, and the pain and loss of mobility associated with it.

INFECTIOUS DISEASE

West (1986) reported two cases of possible tuberculosis in site A individuals. Skeleton A[481] (gpA24, grave 31) had lesions resembling the early onset of tuberculosis in one lumbar and two cervical vertebrae. Skeleton A[492] (gpA29, grave 63) had considerable resorption on the fifth lumbar vertebral body inferior margin and two corresponding patches on the first sacral body. In the site F disarticulated remains, skeleton F[35] had three cervical vertebrae with collapsed bodies, which were fused together with eburnation 'on the most anterior point'. This could be describing tuberculosis. The sample has a rather high frequency of the condition if all are genuine cases, with 11.1% of all skeletons recovered from Holy Trinity affected.

OTHER PATHOLOGY

Periostitis was fairly common, with four individuals from site A affected (skeletons A[609] (gpA21, grave 9), A[766] (gpA22, grave 16), A[611] (gpA23, grave 26) and A[539] (gpA24, grave 29)) and one from each of site F cist-burials and site F disarticulated bone (F[134] and F[88]). The bony changes were restricted to the leg bones, particularly the tibia and fibula. These bony changes are the result of inflammation of the periosteal lining of the lower leg bones due to what can be minor trauma such as frequent everyday knocks. Much higher frequencies of periostitis have been found elsewhere for the medieval period (Mays 1991b) and it has been suggested that periostitis of the lower limb was common, particularly among the lower social classes.

A female, skeleton F[53] (gpF11, grave 8) from among the site F cist-burials, showed signs of hyperostosis frontalis interna. This condition is almost always found to occur in postmenopausal women.

Spatial analysis

The data were too weak to allow for successful spatial analysis to identify possible genetic groupings. The only potentially convincing relationship was between the occupants of two graves in group A21 with septal apertures in common, but even these lacked additional shared non-metric traits or physical characteristics which would have strengthened the inference. The graves were separated by three other burials, which could suggest that the idea of a family plot did not exist unless the three burials in between were also related.

Conclusion

Thirty individuals from site A, nine from the cist-burials of site F, and 19 from the disarticulated, probable cleared earlier burials from site F have been included in this analysis. Site A and site F cist-burials are thought to belong to the same period, that is the 11th to 12th centuries.

Bearing in mind the limitations of the data, the questions posed by the archaeological evidence listed above in 'Aims of the analysis' may be answered as follows. It might be suggested that the burials on site A, south of the priory church and possibly associated with its predecessor, were predominantly male, whereas the small number of burials on site F, north-west of the west end of the church, were of both sexes in a more equal proportion. But the numbers are too small to be confident. Both sites contained cist-burials which were probably of high-status individuals. No distinct group of canons or lay patrons could be identified by skeletal analysis alone.

FRENCH AND GERMAN SUMMARIES

Résumé

Le prieuré de la Sainte-Trinité, fondé en 1107 ou 1108, est situé juste à l'intérieur d'Aldgate, dans la partie orientale de la Cité de Londres, au nord de Leadenhall Street. Cette publication, la première à restituer l'évolution du prieuré augustinien et de ses bâtiments, est fondée sur des sources diverses : principalement des observations et des fouilles archéologiques effectuées en 1908, 1953 et de 1977 à 1990, mais aussi deux plans de toutes les constructions principales relevées au rez-de-chaussée et au premier étage, vers 1585, par John Symonds ; enfin des observations effectuées par des érudits entre 1790 et 1825 au cours du dégagement et de la démolition progressive de certaines parties de l'établissement.

Une église existait à la fin du XIe siècle et un cimetière mis au jour dans plusieurs secteurs de la zone d'étude a pu lui être associé ou bien fonctionner avec la nouvelle église prieurale édifiée dans la première moitié du XIIe siècle. Pour cette époque, l'élévation de la partie orientale de l'église peut être largement restituée ainsi qu'une part des bâtiments conventuels. Deux des enfants du roi Etienne furent enterrés près de l'autel majeur peu avant 1147 ; un lien semble avoir existé avec la famille royale et peut-être avec Henri de Blois, frère du roi. Une chapelle mariale fut érigée entre 1197 et 1221 et une reconstruction programmée est attestée entre la fin du XIIe siècle et les environs de 1350, par des données textuelles comme archéologiques. Le cloître s'étendait au nord de l'église et les chanoines disposaient probablement de latrines, datant de la fin du XIIIe siècle, installées au-dessus du fossé de la ville, sur le côté nord de l'enclos, et d'une porte privée dans l'enceinte de la ville. Ces deux éléments furent détruits, probablement quand le mur fut renforcé par des arcs en briques, à l'initiative de la Cité, en 1477. Le mobilier provenant du prieuré est peu abondant mais comporte des fragments de soie appartenant à des vêtements liturgiques (du tissu fabriqué en Espagne musulmane), de la céramique, des urinoirs en verre ainsi que des objets en métal, en cuir et en bois. En outre, les fragments architecturaux découverts ont aidé à la restitution des bâtiments prieuraux.

Deux zones du cimetière extérieur ont été fouillées. La plus grande était au sud de l'église, l'autre, qui a livré un moindre nombre d'individus, au nord de l'angle nord-ouest du lieu du culte, dans un secteur utilisé plus tard pour la construction de la grande tour et l'agrandissement vers l'ouest de l'aile occidentale du cloître. Aucune différence chronologique entre les groupes de sépultures ne pouvait être faite sur la base de la céramique, de sorte que le commencement du cimetière est attribué au XIe ou XIIe siècle, les tombes les plus tardives appartenant peut-être au début du XIIIe siècle. La présence d'hommes, de femmes et d'enfants dans les deux zones suggèrent l'inhumation de laïques. On ne peut affirmer l'existence d'un cimetière réservé aux chanoines, mais cela est probable ; dans ce cas, il aurait pu s'étendre au nord-est de l'église, bien qu'aucune tombe n'ait été reconnue lors des observations limitées conduites dans ce secteur. Un adulte de sexe masculin, enterré au sud de l'église, portait une croix pectorale en argent sur l'épaule. L'état sanitaire des squelettes correspondait au statut probablement élevé des individus inhumés.

Le prieuré de la Sainte-Trinité fut dissout en 1532, trois ans avant la Dissolution générale. Le site passa aux mains de Thomas Audley, qui construisit une résidence en adaptant les vastes bâtiments prieuraux avant sa mort en 1544. Le domaine passa ensuite, via sa fille, au duc de Norfolk, qui y reçut la reine Elizabeth. La résidence, avec l'ancienne église transformée en galerie, la grande salle de réception et les jardins, peut être partiellement reconstituée à partir des plans de Symonds des environs de 1585. L'enclos fut vendu à la Cité en 1592 mais dès les années 1560 la demeure principale avait été cernée de petites maisons et d'établissements industriels. Parmi ces derniers, sont identifiées en 1571 les installations de Jacob Jansen, un hollandais auquel on doit le début de la fabrication de céramique de Delft à Londres, et rapidement la zone attira d'autres potiers. Si les ateliers n'ont pas été mis au jour, plusieurs zones autour du prieuré ont livré des ratés de cuisson, dont une fosse contenant des déchets de céramiques et de tuiles, peut-être des années 1570 : creusée, selon les plans de Symonds, à travers le sol du soubassement de l'aile occidentale du cloître, cette fosse fut découverte sous l'ancienne grande salle de Thomas Audley et du duc de Norfolk.

En 1657, les Juifs furent officiellement autorisés à revenir en Angleterre et, grâce aux efforts de quelques familles déjà installées, ils s'établirent dans l'enclos et la paroisse voisine de Sainte-Catherine de Cree. L'une des synagogues fut construite à l'emplacement de la cuisine du prieuré, à côté de la maison de maître qui semble avoir progressivement glissé vers l'abandon jusqu'à son écroulement en 1822. Les quelques traces archéologiques de la communauté juive sont donc examinées de manière succincte.

La reconstitution des bâtiments, fondée sur les données architecturales et textuelles, constitue un élément majeur de cette publication. L'analyse de la céramique fait le lien entre les différentes phases d'occupation du site et fait apparaître la part respective des productions locales, extérieures et importées entre le Xe et le XVIIIe siècle. Est aussi discutée en détail l'origine, à Londres, de la fabrication de céramique glaçurée à l'étain.

Toutes les données rassemblées permettent donc d'établir la place du prieuré de la Sainte-Trinité dans le mouvement augustinien, dans l'histoire des maisons conventuelles de Londres et, autant que faire se peut en l'état actuel des connaissances, dans l'évolution de l'architecture romane en Grande-Bretagne. Cet ouvrage comble aussi un vide important dans la compréhension des changements sociaux et technologiques qui eurent lieu à Londres du XVIe au XVIIIe siècle.

Zusammenfassung

Das Priorat der Dreifaltigkeit, Aldgate (gegründet 1107 oder 1108) lag gerade noch innerhalb von Aldgate im östlichen Teil der City of London, nördlich Leadenhall Street. Der vorliegende Bericht, der erste Versuch, die Entwicklung des Augustinerpriorats und seiner Gebäude zu rekonstruieren, basiert auf verschiedenen Quellen: in der Hauptsache sind es archäologische Beobachtungen und Ausgrabungen von 1908, 1953 und 1977-90, zusätzlich aber auch zwei Lagepläne der wesentlichen Prioratsgebäude, Erdgeschoß und erster Stock, die um 1585 von John Symonds gezeichnet wurden, und schließlich auf antiquarischen Beobachtungen von 1790-1825, als Teile des Priorats abgedeckt und nach und nach zerstört wurden.

Im späten 11. Jh. stand schon eine Kirche, und der Friedhof, der an mehreren Stellen des Untersuchungsgebiets gefunden wurde, gehörte entweder zu ihr oder zu der neuen Prioratskirche, die in der ersten Hälfte des 12. Jhs gebaut wurde. Ein Großteil der Architektur des östlichen Flügels dieser Kirche kann rekonstruiert werden, wie auch etwas von den anderen Prioratsgebäuden jener Zeit. Zwei Kinder des Königs Stephan wurden nahe dem Hochaltar in den Jahren kurz vor 1147 begraben; es scheint, daß es eine Verbindung zur königlichen Familie gab und möglicherweise auch zu Heinrich von Blois, des Königs Bruder. 1197-1221 wurde eine Marienkapelle erstellt. Hinweise auf koordinierten Wiederaufbau-Arbeiten vom späten 12. Jh. bis ungefähr 1350 stammen aus einer Kombination urkundlicher und archäologischer Nachweise. Der Kreuzgang lag nördlich der Kirche und vom späten 13. Jh. an hatten die Chorherren wahrscheinlich eine Latrine über dem Stadtgraben auf der Nordseite des Klostergeländes und ein Tor durch die Stadtmauer. Beide Elemente wurden entfernt, wahrscheinlich im Zuge der Verstärkung der Mauer durch Ziegelbögen im Auftrag der City im Jahre 1477. Das Vorkommen von Artefakten im Priorat war schwach, schloß aber Seidenstücke von Meßgewändern (hergestellt im islamischen Spanien), Töpferware, gläserne Urinflaschen, Metallarbeiten, sowie Gegenstände aus Leder und Holz ein. Auch architektonische Fragmente wurden gefunden, die dazu beigetragen haben, die Prioratsgebäude zu rekonstruieren.

Es wurden weiterhin zwei Teile eines Aussenfriedhofs ausgegraben. Der größere Teil lag auf der Südseite der Prioratskirche, der andere umfaßte eine kleinere Anzahl Bestattungen nördlich der Nordwestecke der Kirche, auf dem Raum, auf welchem später der große Turm stand und die Ausweitung des Klaustrumwestflügels stattfand. Es konnte keine auf Keramik basierende Differenzierung zwischen den einzelnen Grabgruppen gemacht werden. Der gesamte Friedhof ist aber auf einem Zeitraum beginnend im 11. oder 12. Jh. zu datieren, wobei einige Gräber noch aus dem frühen 13. Jh. stammen könnten. Das Vorhandensein von Männern, Frauen und Kindern in den Gräbern der beiden Friedhofsteile machen es wahrscheinlich, daß es sich um Laien handelte. Man kann nicht genau feststellen, ob die Chorherren ihren eigenen, exklusiven Bezirk des Friedhofs belegten, obwohl man dies für wahrscheinlich hält. Dieser Sonderfriedhof mag nordöstlich der Kirche gelegen haben, obwohl während die dortigen zugegebenermaßen begrenzten Untersuchungen keine Gräber geortet werden konnten. Ein erwachsener Mann, der auf der Südseite der Kirche begraben wurde, hatte ein silbernes Brustkreuz auf seiner Schulter. Die Skelette zeigten verschiedene

Knochenkonditionen im Einklang mit dem wahrscheinlich hohen Status der Toten.

Das Dreifaltigkeitspriorat wurde 1532, drei Jahre vor der allgemeinen Dissolution, aufgelöst. Das Gelände ging an Thomas Audley über, der dort unter Ausnutzung weiter Teile der Prioratsgebäude vor seinem Tod 1544 ein Haus errichtete. Das Eigentum ging dann über seine Tochter an den Herzog von Norfolk, der hier auch Königin Elisabeth bewirtete. Das Haus unter Einbeziehung umgebauten Teile des grossen Kirchengebäudes als Empore, Festhalle und Garten kann teilweise durch die Symonds-Plänen von ungefähr 1585 rekonstruiert werden. Der Besitz wurde 1592 an die City verkauft. Um 1560 jedoch war das große Haus schon von einer Anzahl kleinerer Häuser und Industriegebäude innerhalb des ehemaligen Klosterbezirks umgeben. Urkundlich belegt gehört zu letzteren die Töpferei des Jacob Jansen im Jahre 1571, eines aus Holland eingewanderten Töpfers, dem zugeschrieben wird, daß er die Herstellung von Delfter Keramik in London einführte. Bald zog die Gegend auch andere Töpfer an. Obwohl keine Werkstätten gefunden wurden, gab es Funde von Ausschußwaren an mehreren Plätzen um das ehemalige Priorat herum. Eine Grube, möglicherweise aus den 70er Jahren des 16. Jhs, die Töpfer- und Fliesenabfall enthielt, würde nach den Symonds-Plänen in den Fußboden eines unterirdischen Gewölbes im Klaustrumwestflügel gegraben worden sein und befand sich unter der früheren Halle Audleys und Norfolks.

1657 wurde es den Juden offiziell erlaubt, wieder nach England zurückzukommen. Auf Grund der Bemühungen einer kleinen Zahl von Juden, die schon hier lebten, ließen sie sich auf dem Prioratsgelände und in der benachbarten Gemeinde St Katherine Cree nieder. Eine ihrer Synagogen wurde über der Küche des Priors, angrenzend an das große Haus, das allmählich in Verfall geriet, errichtet. Tatsächlich fiel es 1822 zusammen. Die Archäologie der jüdischen Gemeinde wird kurz betrachtet.

Die Rekonstruktion der Gebäude, auf der Basis einer kombinierten Untersuchung aus Architekturresten und urkundlichen Nachweisen, bildet einen wesentlichen Bestandteil dieser Publikation. Die Analyse der Töpferware verbindet verschiedene Phasen der Grabungsstelle und faßt mehrere örtliche, nicht lokale und importierte Ware zusammen, die nach Datierung vom 10. bis ins 18. Jh. reichen. Der Nachweis der frühesten zinnglasierten Töpferwarenherstellung in London wird im einzelnen behandelt.

All diese Zeugnisse zusammen ergeben ein Bild des Dreifaltigkeitspriorat im Rahmen der Geschichte der Augustinischen Bewegung und der Geschichte der Londoner Klöster, und soweit aufgrund der bisherigen Nachweise möglich, die Entwicklung der romanischen Architektur in Großbritannien. Auch füllt es eine bedeutende Lücke in unserem Verständnis der sozialen und technologischen Veränderungen, wie sie vom 16. bis ins 18. Jh. in London stattfanden.

BIBLIOGRAPHY

Manuscript sources

Bodleian Library, Oxford, Department of Western Manuscripts (Bodleian)

MS Top. Gen. E. 1 19 notebook of J C Brooke

British Library (BL)

Add MS 24433 drawing by J C Buckler (Bermondsey Abbey)
Add MS 29926, fo 242 drawing by J Carter

Conway Library, Courtauld Institute of Art, University of London

Photograph of Wolvesey Palace, Winchester

Corporation of London Record Office (CLRO)

CCPR Card Calendar to Property References in the Journals and Repertories

City Lands Journal vol 92 (pp 171–2, 217, 234) fire damage in Mitre Court inspected by City Lands Committee, 14 Nov 1800, and record of subsequent arrangements

Court of Husting Rolls (HR) 46, 72, 75

Letter Book AB

PLANS

City Lands (Bridge House) Properties Plan Book, ii, 23v, 26, 33, 44 (44) lease plan of Mitre Tavern, 1743

Comptroller's City Lands Deeds Box 11, 20 plan of property leased to Edmund Smith and Peregrine Cust, 1755

Comptroller's City Lands Plan 24B, 120, 540A (540A) plan of the fire damage in Mitre Court, 1800

Surveyor's Plans Portfolio I, 38 plan of Duke's Place precinct, shortly before 1790

REPERTORIES OF THE COURT OF ALDERMEN, VOLS 9, 18–19, 21–23

Repertory 9, fos 262–3, 270 part of the record of Sir Thomas Audley's staged acquisition of the former priory precinct in 1534

Repertory 18, fo 199 William Kerwin, mason, appointed as one of the four City Viewers in 1574

Repertory 19, fos 418, 476b, 518b City complaint about building work undertaken by Sir Thomas Bromley, Lord Chancellor, along the north side of the former priory precinct in 1579

Repertory 21, fo 422b; 22, fo 379 discussions in 1586 between City representatives and Lord Thomas Howard leading to the purchase from him of the former priory (1592)

Repertory 22, fos 414b–417b Lord Thomas Howard applies to the Crown for licence to alienate his property in the former priory

Repertory 23, fo 11 Lord Thomas Howard sells the precinct to the City in 1592

English Heritage, London Region photographic collection, London

'Holy Trinity Aldgate, City, pre-1946' photograph of plan of c 1790 probably by J Carter; photograph of drawing (1803)

of Mitre Court by C J M Whichelo

Glasgow University Library (GUL)
Hunter MS U.2.6 priory cartulary compiled 1425–7

Guildhall Library, City of London (GL)
MANUSCRIPTS DEPARTMENT
MS 122/2 transcript of Holy Trinity Priory cartulary
MS 3606/2 plan of church of St Botolph Aldgate in 1706
MS 3776, fos 2–3 drawings by David Powell, c 1800
MS 4318 William Kerwin as Master of the Masons' Company in 1579
MS 7329/1 Lord Thomas Howard sells part of the former priory to Henry Billingsley, alderman, in 1590
MS 9370, fos 147–8 record of hole dug next to pillar in south-west corner of nave of St Katherine Cree church in 1928

PRINTS AND DRAWINGS DEPARTMENT
Watercolours, drawings and engravings by Anon, J C Buckler, J Coney, J Crowther, W Hollar, F Nash, A C Pugin, R Schnebbelie, T H Shepherd, N Smith
Plan of property belonging to John Dueffell and others in 1819
Goad Insurance map, 1887
Noble Collection, engraving by B Howlett
Photographs of Leadenhall Street in the late 19th century and the 1950s

Hatfield House (Herts), library of the Marquis of Salisbury (HH)
CPM I/10, I/19 John Symonds's plans of the former Holy Trinity Priory, c 1585

Institute of Historical Research, University of London (IHR)
London citizens MS Benbow, R M, 1993 Notes to index of London citizens involved in City government 1558–1603 (2 vols), unpub MS

London Metropolitan Archives (formerly Greater London Record Office) (LMA)
MANUSCRIPTS
Acc/2172/I/A/64 no. 1 Brian Naylor, baker, as tenant of the great kitchen of the former priory by 1591

WATERCOLOURS AND DRAWINGS
BC15010 watercolour by Anon
SC/PZ/CT/01/102 drawing by Anon
SC/PZ/CT/01/103 drawing by F Shepperd
SC/PZ/CT/01/108 watercolour by T H Shepperd

Museum of London, Department of Paintings, Prints and Drawings
Drawings by R Schnebbelie

Public Record Office, London (PRO) (now part of The National Archives)
E36/108 the *Liber Coquinae*, 1514–15
E40/4913 charter of Thomas Becket, Archbishop of Canterbury, donating the church of St Mary, Bixley (Kent) to the priory, 1162 x 1170
E101/674/24 building accounts of 1541–2

MINISTERS' ACCOUNTS
SC6/Hen VIII/2356 m 1 concerning grant of former priory property to Sir Thomas Audley, 1536–41

LETTERS PATENT
C66/666 m 45, C66/677 m 42, C66/682 m 20, C66/699 m 34 granting former priory property to Sir Thomas Audley, 1536–41

Royal Commission on Historical Monuments (England) (RCHME)
LCC/GLC Collection, 96/05800 HB/10779/0008 plan of excavations beneath Sir John Cass Primary School in 1908

Sir John Soane's Museum, London
Sketch-plan by J Thorpe of the east end of the priory church (vol 101/145)
Watercolours by F Nash and drawings by C J M Whichelo interleaved in Soane's copy of Thomas Pennant's *Some account of London*, 4 edn (1805)

Printed works

Adams, B, 1983 *London illustrated 1604–1851: a survey and index of topographical books and their plates*, London
Airs, M, 1995 *The Tudor and Jacobean country house: a building history*, Stroud
Alexander, J S, 1996 Masons' marks and stone bonding, in Tatton-Brown and Munby, 219–36
Alexander, J, and Binski, P (eds), 1987 *Age of chivalry: art in Plantagenet England 1200–1400*, Roy Acad Arts exhibition catalogue, London
Allan, J, 1999 South Netherlands maiolica in south-west England, in Gaimster 1999b, 157–66
Allen Brown, R, Colvin, H M, and Taylor, A J, 1971 (1963) *The history of the King's Works: Vols 1–2, The Middle Ages*, repr, London
Amorosi, T, 1989 *A postcranial guide to domestic neonatal and juvenile mammals: the identification and ageing of Old World species*, BAR Int Ser 533, Oxford
Anderson, J E, 1962 *The human skeleton*, Ottawa
Andrews, J, Briggs, A, Porter, R, Tucker, P, and Waddington, K, 1997 *The history of Bethlem*, London
Archer, I, 1991 *The Haberdashers' Company*, London
Armstrong, P, Tomlinson, D, and Evans, D H, 1991 *Excavations at Lurk Lane, Beverley, 1979–82*, Sheffield Excav Rep 1, Sheffield
Atkin, M, 1993 The Norwich Survey 1971–1985: a retrospective view, in *Flatlands and wetlands: current themes in East Anglian archaeology* (ed J Gardiner), E Anglian Archaeol Rep 50, 127–43, Norwich
Auger, R, Bouchard, P, and Gaimster, D R M, in prep Cologne-

type stove-tiles recovered from Sir Martin Frobisher's base-camp established on Kodlunarn Island, 1578, in Stenton in prep

Austin, J C, 1994 *British delft at Williamsburg*, Williamsburg

Baart, J, 1987 Portugese faience uit Amsterdamse bodem, in *Portugese faience 1600–1660*, Amsterdams Historisch Museum exhibition catalogue, 19–27, Amsterdam and Lisbon

Baart, J, 1999 North Netherlands maiolica of the 16th century, in Gaimster 1999b, 125–36

Baker, J R, and Brothwell, D R, 1980 *Animal diseases in archaeology*, London

Barber, B, and Bowsher, D, 2000 *The eastern cemetery of Roman London: excavations 1983–90*, MoLAS Monogr Ser 4, London

Barber, B, and Thomas, C, 2002 *The London Charterhouse*, MoLAS Monogr Ser 10, London

Barber, B, Chew, S, and White, W, 2004 *The Cistercian abbey of St Mary Stratford Langthorne, Essex: archaeological excavations for the London Underground Limited Jubilee Line Extension Project*, MoLAS Monogr Ser 18, London

Barral I Altet, X, 1998 *The Romanesque: towns, cathedrals and monasteries*, Cologne

Bass, W M, 1987 *Human osteology: a laboratory and field manual of the human skeleton*, 3 edn, Missouri Archaeol Ass Spec Pub, Columbia

Bayley, J, 1975 Chelmsford Dominican priory: human bone report, unpub Engl Heritage Ancient Monuments Lab rep 17/75

Beard, D, 1986 The infirmary of Bermondsey Priory, *London Archaeol* 5(7), 187–91

Betts, I M, 1990 Building materials, in Schofield et al, 220–9

Betts, I M, 1991 Building materials: Billingsgate Fish Market car park (BIG82), unpub MoL rep

Betts, I M, 1994 A 17th-century delftware factory, Platform Wharf, Rotherhithe, unpub MoL rep

Betts, I M, 1995 Building materials: St Mary Clerkenwell nunnery, unpub MoL rep

Betts, I M, 1996 Building materials: Fastolf Place, Southwark, unpub MoL rep

Betts, I M, 2002 *Medieval 'Westminster' floor tiles*, MoLAS Monogr Ser 11, London

Betts, I M, in prep a The building materials, in Bluer and Blatherwick in prep

Betts, I M, in prep b The building materials, in Sloane in prep

Biddle, M, 1975 *Felix urbs Wintonia*: Winchester in the age of monastic reform, in *Tenth-century studies* (ed D Parsons), 123–40, London

Biddle, M (ed), 1976 *Winchester in the early Middle Ages*, Winchester Stud 1, Oxford

Billings, R W, 1838 *Architectural illustrations and account of the Temple church, London*, London

Bilson, J, 1922 Durham Cathedral: the chronology of its vaults, *Archaeol J* 79, 101–60

Binding, G, and Kahle, B, 1983 *2000 Jahre Baukunst in Köln*, Cologne

Binski, P, 1995 *Westminster Abbey and the Plantagenets: kingship and the representation of power 1200–1400*, New Haven and London

Black, T K, 1978 A new method for assessing the sex of fragmentary skeletal remains: femoral shaft circumference, *American J Phys Anthropol* 48, 227–32

Blackmore, L, 1984 The medieval and post-medieval pottery, in P S Mills, Excavations at Burlington Road, *Trans London Middlesex Archaeol Soc* 35, 101–9

Blackmore, L, 1988 The pottery, in R Cowie and R L Whytehead with L Blackmore, Two Middle Saxon occupation sites: excavations at Jubilee Hall and 21–22 Maiden Lane, *Trans London Middlesex Archaeol Soc* 39, 81–110

Blackmore, L, 1989 National Gallery extension: the stratigraphic distribution of the pottery, in R L Whytehead and R Cowie with L Blackmore, Excavations at the Peabody site, Chandos Place and the National Gallery building, *Trans London Middlesex Archaeol Soc* 40, 101–4

Blackmore, L, 1997 Stratified pottery, 5th to 17th century, in Milne, 54–7

Blackmore, L, 2002 Further discussion of the pottery, in J Ayre and R Wroe-Brown, *The London Millennium Bridge: excavation of the medieval and later waterfronts at Peter's Hill, City of London, and Bankside, Southwark*, MoLAS Archaeol Stud Ser 6, 90–1, London

Blackmore, L, 2004a Bird pots, in Sloane and Malcolm, 276–7

Blackmore, L, 2004b The pottery, in Sloane and Malcolm, 331–55

Blackmore, L, in prep a The post-Roman pottery, in Sloane in prep

Blackmore, L, in prep b The post-Roman pottery, in R Bluer and T Brigham with R Nielsen in prep, *Excavations at Lloyd's Register of Shipping, London, 1996–7*, MoLAS Monogr Ser

Blackmore, L, and Vince, A, 1994 Medieval pottery from south-east England found in the Bryggen excavations 1955–68, in *The Bryggen Papers Suppl Ser* 5 (ed A E Herteig), 9–160, Bergen

Blair, J (ed), 1988 *Minsters and parish churches: the local church in transition 950–1200*, Oxford Univ Comm Archaeol Monogr 17, Oxford

Blair, J (ed), 1990 *Saint Frideswide's monastery at Oxford: archaeological and architectural studies* (repr of articles originally published in *Oxoniensia* 53, 1988), Gloucester

Blair, J, 1996 The archaeology of Oxford Cathedral, in Tatton-Brown and Munby, 95–102

Blair, J, and Ramsay, N (eds), 1991 *English medieval industries: craftsmen, techniques, products*, London

Blake, H, 1999 *De Nomine Jhesu*: an Italian export ware and the origin of Renaissance maiolica pottery making in the Netherlands, in Gaimster 1999b, 23–56

Blockley, K, 1978 The pottery report, in Pryor and Blockley, 43–85

Blockley, K, Sparks, M, and Tatton-Brown, T, 1997 *Canterbury Cathedral nave: archaeology, history and architecture*, The Archaeology of Canterbury ns 1, Canterbury

Bluer, R, and Blatherwick, S, in prep *Medieval moated houses of Southwark: the Rosary, Rotherhithe and Fastolf Place*, MoLAS Monogr Ser

Bond, J, 1993 Water management in the urban monastery, in Gilchrist and Mytum, 43–78

Bond, J, 2001a Monastic water management in Britain: a

review, in Keevill et al, 88–136

Bond, J, 2001b Production and consumption of food and drink in the medieval monastery, in Keevill et al, 54–87

Bony, J, 1939 La Technique normande du mur epais à l'époque romane, *Bulletin Monumental* 98, 153–88

Boore, E J, 1989 The Lesser Cloister and a medieval drain at St Augustine's Abbey, Bristol, *Trans Bristol Gloucestershire Archaeol Soc* 107, 217–22

Bradley, S, and Pevsner, N, 1997 *The buildings of England: London 1, The City of London*, London

Brakspear, H, 1922 Excavations at some Wiltshire monasteries, *Archaeologia* 73, 225–52

Britnell, R, and Hatcher, J (eds), 1996 *Progress and problems in medieval England: essays in honour of Edward Miller*, Cambridge

Britton, F, 1987 *London delftware*, London

Britton, J, 1828 *The history and antiquities of Peterborough Cathedral*, repr 1997, Glossop

Brooke, C, 1969 *The 12th-century renaissance*, London

Brooke, C, 1993 Bishop Walkelin and his inheritance, in Crook 1993a, 1–12

Brooke, C N L, assisted by Keir, G, 1975 *London, 800–1216: the shaping of a city*, London

Brooks, C M, 1983 Aspects of the sugar-refining industry from the 16th to the 19th century, *Post-Medieval Archaeol* 17, 1–14

Brooks, S T, 1955 Skeletal age at death: the reliability of cranial and pubic age indicators, *American J Phys Anthropol* 13, 567–97

Brothwell, D R, 1972 *Digging up bones: the excavation, treatment and study of human skeletal remains*, 2 edn, London

Brothwell, D R, 1981 *Digging up bones: the excavation, treatment and study of human skeletal remains*, 3 edn, London

Brown, D L, and Wilson, D, 1994 Leominster Old Priory: recording of standing buildings and excavations 1979–80, *Archaeol J* 151, 307–68

Burton, J, 1994 *Monastic and religious orders in Britain 1000–1300*, Cambridge

Butler, L, 1987 Medieval urban religious houses, in *Urban archaeology in Britain* (eds R Leech and J Schofield), CBA Res Rep 61, 167–76, London

Butler, L, 1993 The archaeology of urban monasteries in Britain, in Gilchrist and Mytum, 79–86

Caiger-Smith, A, 1973 *Tin glaze pottery in Europe and the Islamic world*, London

Cal Husting Wills *Calendar of wills proven and enrolled in the Court of Husting, London, 1258–1688* (ed R R Sharpe), 1889–90, London

Cal L Book C *Calendar of the letter books of the City of London: letter book C, AD 1291–1309* (ed R R Sharpe), 1901, London

Cal Pap Reg *Calendar of papal registers: papal letters Vol 6, AD 1404–15* (ed J A Twemlow), 1904, London

Cal Pat R *Calendar of the patent rolls*, 1894–1974, London

Cal Plea and Mem R *Calendar of plea and memoranda rolls preserved among the archives of the Corporation of the City of London, 1323–1437* (ed A H Thomas, 4 vols, 1926–43); 1437–82 (ed P E Jones, 2 vols, 1953–61), London

Cal S P Dom *Calendar of state papers, domestic: Edward VI, Mary, Elizabeth I and James I* (ed M Everett Green), 12 vols, 1856–72, London

Cambridge, E, and Williams, A J T, 1995 Hexham Abbey: a review of recent work and its implications, *Archaeol Aeliana* 5 ser 23, 51–138

Carlin, M, 1985 The reconstruction of Winchester House, Southwark, *London Topogr Rec* 25, 33–58

Carlin, M, and Belcher, V, 1989 Gazetteer, in *The City of London from prehistoric times to c 1520* (ed M Lobel), British Atlas of Historic Towns 3, 63–99, Oxford

Carter, J, 1806 *The ancient architecture of England: Vol 1*, London

Cartulary *The cartulary of Holy Trinity Priory, Aldgate* (ed G A J Hodgett), London Rec Soc Pub 7, 1971, London

Cater, W A, 1912 The priory of Austin Friars, London, 1253–1538, *J Brit Archaeol Ass* 2 ser 18, 25–44

Chambers, E K, 1923 *The Elizabethan stage* (4 vols), Oxford

Chapman, H, and Johnson, T, 1973 Excavations at Aldgate and Bush Lane House in the City of London, 1972, *Trans London Middlesex Archaeol Soc* 24, 1–73

Cherry, B, 1978 Romanesque architecture in eastern England, *J Brit Archaeol Ass* 3 ser 131, 1–29

Cherry, B, and Pevsner, N, 1998 *The buildings of England: London 4, North*, Harmondsworth

Cherry, J, 1991 Pottery and tile, in Blair and Ramsay, 189–209

Clapham, A W, 1912 On the topography of the Dominican friary of London, *Archaeologia* 63, 57–84

Clapham, A W, 1915 *Lesnes Abbey in the parish of Erith, Kent*, London

Clapham, A W, 1923 The architecture of the Premonstratensians, with special reference to their buildings in England, *Archaeologia* 23, 117–46

Clapham, A W, 1934 *English Romanesque architecture: after the Conquest*, Oxford

Clapham, A W, and Godfrey, W H, 1913 *Some famous buildings and their story*, London

Clark, J, 1973 Early medieval pottery from pit P4, in Chapman and Johnson, 40–1

Coad, J, and Coppack, G, 1998 *Castle Acre castle and priory, Norfolk*, English Heritage Guide, London

Cobb, H S (ed), 1990 *The overseas trade of London: exchequer customs accounts 1480–1*, London Rec Soc Pub 27, London

Cocke, T, and Kidson, P, 1993 *Salisbury Cathedral: perspectives on the architectural history*, London

Cohen, A, and Serjeantson, D, 1996 *A manual for the identification of bird bones from archaeological sites*, rev edn, London

Colvin, H M, 1966 Views of the Old Palace of Westminster, *Architect Hist* 9, 23–184

Colvin, H M, 1995 *A biographical dictionary of British architects, 1600–1840*, 3 edn, New Haven and London

Colvin, H, and Foister, S, 1996 *The panorama of London c 1544 by Anthonis van den Wyngaerde*, London Topogr Soc Pub 151, London

Colvin, H M, Ransome, D R, and Summerson, J, 1975 *The history of the King's Works: Vol 3, 1485–1660 (part 1)*, London

Colvin, H M, Summerson, J, Biddle, M, et al, 1982 *The history of the King's Works: Vol 4, 1485–1660 (part 2)*, London

Conheeney, J, 1997 The human bone, in Thomas et al, 218–30

Conheeney, J, 1999 Reconstructing the demography of medieval London from studies on human skeletal material: problems and potential, *Trans London Middlesex Archaeol Soc* 50, 78–86

Conheeney, J, 2004 The human bone, in Sloane and Malcolm,

394–405

Cook, G H, 1955 *Old St Paul's Cathedral: a lost glory of medieval London*, London

Cooper, J, 1976 The church of St George's in the castle, *Oxoniensia* 41, 306–8

Coppack, G, 1990 *English Heritage book of abbeys and priories*, London

Coppack, G, Harrison, S, and Hayfield, C, 1995 Kirkham Priory: the architecture and archaeology of an Augustinian house, *J Brit Archaeol Ass* 3 ser 148, 55–135

Cotter, J, 1999 Imported apothecary jars from Colchester, Essex, in Gaimster 1999b, 167–9

Cowell, M R, 1990 Report on nine early post-medieval stove-tile fragments from St Mary Graces, in Gaimster et al, 40–4

Cowell, M R, and Gaimster, D R M, 1995 Post-medieval ceramic stove-tiles bearing the royal arms of England: further scientific investigations into their manufacture and source in southern England, in *Trade and discovery: the scientific study of artefacts from post-medieval Europe and beyond* (eds D R Hook and D R M Gaimster), Brit Mus Occas Pap 109, 105–16

Cowgill, J, de Neergaard, M, and Griffiths, N, 1987 *Knives and scabbards*, HMSO Medieval Finds from Excavations in London Ser 1, London

Cowie, R, 2000 *Londinium* to *Lundenwic*: Early and Middle Saxon archaeology in the London region, in *London under ground: the archaeology of a city* (eds I Haynes, H Sheldon, and L Hannigan), 175–205, Oxford

Cox, J E, 1876 *The annals of St Helen's Bishopsgate* (2 vols), London

Crook, J, 1989 The Romanesque east arm and crypt of Winchester Cathedral, *J Brit Archaeol Ass* 3 ser 142, 1–36

Crook, J, 1993a Bishop Walkelin's cathedral, in Crook 1993b, 21–36

Crook, J (ed), 1993b *Winchester Cathedral: nine hundred years*, Chichester

Crook, J, 1996 Recent archaeology in Winchester Cathedral, in Tatton-Brown and Munby, 135–52

Crook, J, 1999 The Rufus tomb in Winchester Cathedral, *Antiq J* 79, 187–212

Crouch, D, 1986 *The Beaumont twins: the roots and branches of power in the 12th century*, Cambridge

Crowfoot, E, Pritchard, F, and Staniland, K, 1992 *Textiles and clothing*, HMSO Medieval Finds from Excavations in London Ser 4, London

Crummy, P, 1981 *Aspects of Anglo-Saxon and Norman Colchester*, CBA Res Rep 39, London

Cunningham, C M, 1985 The Stock pottery, in C M Cunningham and P J Drury, *Post-medieval sites and their pottery: Moulsham Street, Chelmsford*, CBA Res Rep 54, 83–8, London

Darvill, T, and Gerrard, C, 1994 *Cirencester: town and landscape, an urban archaeological assessment*, Cirencester

Davenport, P, 1996 The cathedral priory church at Bath, in Tatton-Brown and Munby, 19–30

Davis, R, 1973 *The rise of the Atlantic economies*, London

Davis, R H C, 1967 *King Stephen, 1135–1154*, London

Dawes, J D, and Magilton, J R, 1980 *The cemetery of St Helen-on-the-Walls, Aldwark*, The Archaeology of York 12/1, London

Dawson, G, 1971a Two delftware kilns at Montague Close, Southwark: Part 1, *London Archaeol* 1(10), 228–31

Dawson, G, 1971b Montague Close: Part 2, *London Archaeol* 1(11), 250–1

Dawson, G, 1979 Excavations at Guy's Hospital, 1967, in *Research volume of the Surrey Archaeological Society*, Surrey Archaeol Soc Res Vol 7, 27–65, Guildford

Dawson, G, and Edwards, R, 1974 The Montague Close delftware factory prior to 1969, in *Research volume of the Surrey Archaeological Society*, Surrey Archaeol Soc Res Vol 1, 47–63, Guildford

Desrosiers, S, 1999 Draps d'areste (II): extension de la classification, comparaisons et lieux de fabrication, *Soieries médiévales: technique et culture* 34, 89–119

Dickinson, J C, 1950 *The origins of the Austin canons and their introduction into England*, London

Dickinson, J C, 1968 The buildings of the English Austin canons after the Dissolution of the monasteries, *J Brit Archaeol Ass* 3 ser 31, 60–75

Dickinson, J C, 1976 The origins of St Augustine's, Bristol, *Trans Bristol Gloucestershire Archaeol Soc* 100, 109–26

Douglas, D C, and Greenaway, G W (eds), 1953 *English historical documents: Vol 2, 1042–1189*, London

Downs, D, 1979 Human skeletal remains: Holy Trinity Priory 1979, unpub MoL rep

Drey, R A, 1978 *Apothecary jars*, London

Drummond-Murray, J, 2004 Mitre Square, London, EC3: a report on the evaluation, unpub MoL rep

Dumortier, C, 1992 De geleyerspotbackers in de Schoytestraat te Antwerpen, in Veeckman, 109–11

Dumortier, C, 1999 Maiolica production in Antwerp: the documentary evidence, in Gaimster 1999b, 107–11

Dumortier, C, and Oost, T, 1992 Antwerpse majolicategels uit het voormalig refugiehuis van de abdij van Hemiksen, in Veeckman, 23–9

Dumortier, C, and Veeckman, J, 1994 Un Four de majoliques en activité à Anvers vers 1560, *Bulletin des Musées Royaux d'Art et d'Histoire* 65, 163–217

Dunn, R S, 1972 *Sugar and slaves*, London

Dyer, C, 1989 *Standards of living in the later Middle Ages: social change in England c 1200–1520*, Cambridge

Dyer, C, 2002 *Making a living in the Middle Ages: the people of Britain 850–1520*, New Haven and London

Eames, E S, 1980 *Catalogue of medieval lead-glazed earthenware tiles in the Department of Medieval and Later Antiquities, British Museum* (2 vols), London

Edwards, J, 1999 A group of biscuit and glazed wares from Holy Trinity Priory, City of London, in Gaimster 1999b, 137–41

Edwards, J, in prep *Post-medieval pottery in London 1500–1700: Vol 2, Tin-glazed wares*

Edwards, R, 1974 *London potters circa 1570–1710*, J Ceram Hist 6, Stafford

Egan, G, 1981 Excavations at Creechurch Lane, unpub MoL rep

Egan, G, 1998 *The medieval household: daily living c 1150–c 1450*, HMSO Medieval Finds from Excavations in London Ser 6, London

Egan, G, 2000 Butcher, baker, spoon and candlestick maker?, in Kicken et al, 102–14

Egan, G, in prep a *Material culture in London in an age of transition: Tudor and Stuart period finds c 1450–c 1700 from excavations at riverside sites in Southwark*, MoLAS Monogr Ser 19

Egan, G, in prep b The non-ceramic finds, in Steele in prep

Egan, G, and Pritchard, F, 1991 *Dress accessories c 1150–c 1450*, HMSO Medieval Finds from Excavations in London Ser 3, London

Eliassen, F-E, and Ersland, G A (eds), 1996 *Power, profit and land: landownership in medieval and early modern northern European towns*, Aldershot

Ellis, R, 1985 Excavations at 9 St Clare Street, *London Archaeol* 5(5), 115–21

Emery, A, 2000 *Greater medieval houses of England and Wales: Vol 2, East Anglia, Central England and Wales*, Cambridge

Esquieu, Y, 1994 *Quartier cathédrale: une cité dans la ville*, Paris

Evans, A K B, 1989 Cirencester's early church, *Trans Bristol Gloucestershire Archaeol Soc* 107, 107–22

Evans, A K B, 1991 Cirencester Abbey: the first hundred years, *Trans Bristol Gloucestershire Archaeol Soc* 109, 99–116

Farley, M, and Manchester, K, 1989 The cemetery of the leper hospital of St Margaret, High Wycombe, Buckinghamshire, *Medieval Archaeol* 33, 82–9

Faulkner, T, 1839 *The history and antiquities of the parish of Hammersmith*, London

Fawcett, R, 1990 *Jedburgh Abbey*, Edinburgh

Ferembach, D, Schwidetzky, I, and Stloukal, M, 1980 Recommendations for age and sex diagnoses of skeletons, *J Human Evol* 9, 517–49

Ferguson, S, 1986 The Romanesque cathedral of Ely: an archaeological evaluation of its construction, unpub PhD thesis, Univ Columbia

Fernie, E C, 1979 Observations on the Norman plan of Ely Cathedral, in *Medieval art and architecture at Ely Cathedral* (eds N Coldstream and P Draper), Brit Archaeol Ass Conf Trans 2, 1–7, London

Fernie, E C, 1983 *The architecture of the Anglo-Saxons*, London

Fernie, E C, 1985 The Romanesque church of Waltham Abbey, *J Brit Archaeol Ass* 3 ser 138, 48–78

Fernie, E C, 1993a *An architectural history of Norwich Cathedral*, Oxford

Fernie, E C, 1993b Design principles of early medieval architecture as exemplified at Durham Cathedral, in Jackson, 146–56

Fernie, E C, 1998 The Romanesque church of Bury St Edmunds Abbey, in *Bury St Edmunds: medieval art, architecture, archaeology and economy* (ed A Gransden), Brit Archaeol Ass Conf Trans 20, 1–15, London

Fernie, E C, 2000 *The architecture of Norman England*, Oxford

Flores Escobosa, I, and del Mar Muñoz Martín, M, 1995 Cerámica nazarí (Almería, Granada y Málaga) siglos XIII–XV (Nasrid pottery from Almeria, Granada and Malaga: 13th to 15th centuries), in *Spanish medieval ceramics in Spain and the British Isles* (eds C M Gerrard, A Guttiérrez, and A G Vince), BAR Int Ser 610, 245–77, Oxford

Foreman, M, 1996 *Further excavations at the Dominican priory, Beverley, 1986–9*, Sheffield Excav Rep 4, Sheffield

Fry, G S (ed), 1896 *Abstracts of inquisitions post mortem relating to the City of London returned into the Court of Chancery: Part 1, 1485–1561*, London Middlesex Archaeol Soc, London

Fry G S (ed), 1906 *Abstracts of inquisitions post mortem relating to the City of London returned into the Court of Chancery: Part 3, 1577–1603*, London Middlesex Archaeol Soc, London

Gaimster, D, 1988a A survey of Cologne-type stove-tiles found in Britain, in Unger, 44–54

Gaimster, D, 1988b Post-medieval ceramic stove-tiles bearing the royal arms: evidence for their manufacture and use in southern Britain, *Archaeol J* 145, 314–43

Gaimster, D, 1988c Pottery production in the Lower Rhineland: the Duisburg sequence *ca* 1400–1800, in *Zur Keramik des Mittelalters und der beginnnenden Neuzeit im Rheinland – Medieval and later pottery from the Rhineland and its markets* (eds D Gaimster, M Redknap, and H-H Wegner), BAR Int Ser 440, 151–72, Oxford

Gaimster, D, 1993 Cross-Channel ceramic trade in the late Middle Ages: archaeological evidence for the spread of Hanseatic culture to Britain, in *Archäologie des Mittelalters und Bauforschung im Hanseraum: eine Festschrift für Günther Fehring* (ed M Gläser), Schriften des Kulturhistorischen Museums in Rostock, 251–60, Rostock

Gaimster, D, 1994 The archaeology of post-medieval society, c 1450–1750: material culture studies in Britain since the war, in *Building on the past: papers celebrating 150 years of the Royal Archaeological Institute* (ed B Vyner), 283–312, London

Gaimster, D, 1997 *German stoneware 1200–1900: archaeology and cultural history*, London

Gaimster, D, 1999a Imported maiolica vases bearing the royal arms of England: a reconsideration, in Gaimster 1999b, 141–3

Gaimster, D (ed), 1999b *Maiolica in the north: the archaeology of tin-glazed earthenware in north-west Europe c 1500–1600*, Brit Mus Occas Pap 122, London

Gaimster, D, 2000 Saints and sinners: the changing iconography of imported ceramic stove-tiles in Reformation England, in Kicken et al, 142–51

Gaimster, D, 2001 The archaeology of the tile-stove in late medieval and early modern England: an interdisciplinary research programme, in *Recherches archéométriques* (ed M Fortin), Cahiers Archéologiques CELAT, 78–82, Quebec

Gaimster, D, and Nenk, B, 1991 A late medieval Hispano-Moresque vase from the City of London, *Medieval Archaeol* 35, 118–21

Gaimster, D, and Nenk, B, 1997 English households in transition c 1450–1550: the ceramic evidence, in *The age of transition: the archaeology of English culture 1400–1600* (eds D Gaimster and P Stamper), Soc Medieval Archaeol Monogr 15 (Oxbow Monogr Ser 98), 171–95, Oxford

Gaimster, D, Goffin, R, and Blackmore, L, 1990 The Continental stove-tile fragments from St Mary Graces, London, in their British and European context, *Post-Medieval Archaeol* 24, 1–49

Gaimster, D, Auger, R, and Bouchard, P, in prep Chemical analysis of 16th-century stove-tiles recovered from Qallunaat

Island, Ca, in Stenton in prep
Garmonsway, G N (trans/ed), 1954 *The Anglo-Saxon Chronicle*, London
Garner, F H, 1948 *English delftware*, London
Garner, F H, and Archer, M, 1972 *English delftware*, rev edn, London
Gem, R, 1982 The significance of the 11th-century rebuilding of Christ Church and St Augustine's, Canterbury in the development of Romanesque architecture, in *Medieval art and architecture at Canterbury before 1220* (eds N Coldstream and P Draper), Brit Archaeol Ass Conf Trans 5, 1–19, London
Gem, R, 1986 The origins of the Abbey, in Wilson et al, 6–21
Gem, R, 1990 The Romanesque architecture of Old St Paul's cathedral and its late 11th-century context, in Grant, 47–63
Genoves, S, 1969 Estimation of age and mortality, in *Science in archaeology: a survey of progress and research* (eds D Brothwell and E Higgs), 429–39, London
Geoquest, 1993 Archaeomagnetic study of a tile kiln at Niblett Hall, City of London, unpub MoL rep
George, M D, 1979 (1925) *London life in the 18th century*, repr, London
Gilbert, B M, and McKern, T W, 1973 A method for ageing the female os pubis, *American J Phys Anthropol* 38, 31–8
Gilchrist, R, 1994 *Gender and material culture: the archaeology of religious women*, London
Gilchrist, R, and Mytum, H (eds), 1993 *Advances in monastic archaeology*, BAR Brit Ser 227, Oxford
Gilmour, B J J, and Stocker, D A, 1986 *St Mark's church and cemetery*, The Archaeology of Lincoln 13/1, Lincoln
Gindhart, P S, 1973 Growth standards for the tibia and radius in children aged one month through 18 years, *American J Phys Anthropol* 39, 41–8
Girouard, M, 1978 *Life in the English country house*, New Haven and London
Girouard, M, 1983 *Robert Smythson and the Elizabethan country house*, New Haven and London
Glob, P V (ed), 1980, *Danefæ*, Copenhagen
Glynn, S, 1998 *Sir John Cass and The Cass Foundation*, London
Godfrey, E S, 1975 *The development of English glassmaking 1560–1640*, London
Godwin, G, and Britton, J, 1838–9 *The churches of London: a history and description of the ecclesiastical edifices of the metropolis* (2 vols), London
Goode, C, and Jones, S, 1990 Excavations at 78–79 Leadenhall Street (LHN89), unpub MoL rep
Gormley, M, 1996 St Bartholomew-the-Great: archaeology in the cloisters, *London Archaeol* 8(1), 18–24
Graham, A H, and Davies, S, 1993 *Excavations in the town centre of Trowbridge, Wiltshire, 1977 and 1986–88*, Wessex Archaeol Rep 2, Salisbury
Grainger, I, and Phillpotts, C, in prep *The abbey of St Mary Graces, East Smithfield, London*, MoLAS Monog Ser
Grant, L (ed), 1990 *Medieval art, architecture and archaeology in London*, Brit Archaeol Ass Conf Trans 10, London
Gray, H, 1977 *Gray's anatomy*, New York
Green, J, 1992 Financing Stephen's war, in *Anglo-Norman Studies 14 (Proceedings of the Battle Conference, 1991)*, 91–114, Woodbridge
Greene, J P, 1992 *Medieval monasteries*, Leicester
Greene, P, 1989 *Norton Priory: the archaeology of a medieval religious house*, Cambridge
Grimes, W F, 1968 *The excavation of Roman and medieval London*, London
Guildhall Museum, 1908 *Catalogue of the collection of London antiquities in the Guildhall Museum*, 2 edn, London
Gutiérrez, A, and Brown, D, 1999 Italo-Netherlandish maiolica from Southampton, in Gaimster 1999b, 147–50
Halsey, R, 1982 Dunstable Priory, *Archaeol J* 139, 46–7
Halsey, R, 1985 Tewkesbury Abbey: some recent observations, in Heslop and Sekules, 16–35
Halsey, R, 1990 The 12th-century church of St Frideswide's Priory, in Blair, 115–68
Hammerson, M, 1978 Excavations under Southwark Cathedral, *London Archaeol* 3(8), 206–12
Harben, H A, 1918 *A dictionary of the City of London*, London
Harvey, B, 1977 *Westminster Abbey and its estates in the Middle Ages*, Oxford
Harvey, B, 1993 *Living and dying in England, 1100–1540: the monastic experience*, Oxford
Harvey, J H, 1978 *The Perpendicular style, 1330–1485*, London
Harvey, J H, 1984 *English medieval architects: a biographical dictionary down to 1550*, London
Haslam, J, 1988 Parishes, churches, wards and gates in eastern London, in Blair, 35–44
Hawkes, J W, and Fasham, P J, 1997 *Excavations on Reading waterfront sites 1979–88*, Wessex Archaeol Rep 5, Salisbury
Hearn, K, 1995 *Dynasties: painting in Tudor and Jacobean England 1530–1630*, Tate Gallery exhibition catalogue, London
Hearn, M F, 1971 The rectangular ambulatory in English medieval architecture, *J Soc Architect Historians* 30, 187–208
Hearn, M F, 1975 Romsey Abbey, a progenitor of the English national tradition in architecture, *Gesta* 14, 27–40
Heighway, C, 1983 *The East and North gates of Gloucester and associated sites: excavations 1974–81*, Western Archaeol Trust Excav Monogr 4, Bristol
Heighway, C, and Bryant, R, 1999 *The golden minster: the Anglo-Saxon minster and later medieval priory of St Oswald at Gloucester*, CBA Res Rep 117, London
Henderson, J, 1984 The human remains, in R Poulton and H Woods, *Excavations on the site of the Dominican friary at Guildford in 1974 and 1978*, Surrey Archaeol Soc Res Vol 9, 58–67, Guildford
Henwood-Reverdot, A, 1982 *L'Eglise Saint-Etienne de Beauvais*, Beauvais
Heslop, T A, and Sekules, V (eds), 1985 *Medieval art and architecture at Gloucester and Tewkesbury*, Brit Archaeol Ass Conf Trans 7, London
Hill, F, 1948 *Medieval Lincoln*, repr 1990, Stamford
Hillson, S, 1986 *Teeth*, Cambridge
HMC, 1883 Roy Comm Hist Manuscripts, *Ninth report: Part 1, Report and appendix*, London
HMC, 1996 Roy Comm Hist Manuscripts, *Principal family and estate collections: family names A–K*, Guides to Sources for British

History 10, London

Hoey, L, 1989a The design of Romanesque clerestories with wall passages in Normandy and England, *Gesta* 28, 78–101

Hoey, L, 1989b Pier form and vertical wall articulation in English Romanesque architecture, *J Soc Architect Historians* 48, 258–83

Hoffman, J M, 1979 Age estimation from diaphyseal length: two months to 12 years, *J Forensic Sci* 24, 461–9

Honeybourne, M A, 1929 The extent and value of the property in London and Southwark occupied by the religious houses before the Dissolution of the monasteries, unpub MA thesis, Univ London

Horne, J, 1989 *English tin-glazed tiles*, London

Howard, R E, Laxton, R R, and Litton, C D, 1997 List 75: Nottingham University Tree-Ring Dating Laboratory results, general list, *Vernacular Architect* 28, 124–7

Huggins, P J, and Bascombe, K, 1992 Excavations at Waltham Abbey, Essex, 1985–91: three pre-Conquest churches and Norman evidence, *Archaeol J* 148, 282–343

Hughes, M, and Gaimster, D, 1999 Neutron activation analysis of maiolica from London, Norwich, the Low Countries and Italy, in Gaimster 1999b, 57–91

Hugo, T, 1863 The last ten years of the priory of St Helen's Bishopsgate, with the topography of the house, *Trans London Middlesex Archaeol Soc* os 2, 169–203

Hugo, T, 1864 Austin Friars, *Trans London Middlesex Archaeol Soc* os 2, 1–24

Hurley, M F, and Sheehan, C M, 1995 *Excavations at the Dominican priory, St Mary's of the Isle, Crosse's Green, Cork*, Cork

Hurst, H R, 1986 *Gloucester: the Roman and later defences*, Gloucester Archaeol Rep 2, Stroud

Hurst, J G, 1999 Sixteenth-century south Netherlands maiolica imported into Britain and Ireland, in Gaimster 1999b, 91–106

Hurst, J G, Neal, D S, and van Beuningen, H J E, 1986 *Pottery produced and traded in north-west Europe 1350–1650*, Rotterdam Pap 6, Rotterdam

Hyde, R, 1999 *Ward maps of the City of London*, London Topogr Soc Pub 154, London

Iscan, M Y, and Kennedy, K A R (eds), 1989 *Reconstruction of life from the skeleton*, New York

Jackson, M J (ed), 1993 *Engineering a cathedral*, London

Jamieson, C, 1972 *The history of the Royal Hospital of St Katharine by the Tower of London*, Oxford

Jarrett, M G, and Mason, H, 1995 'Greater and more splendid': some aspects of Romanesque Durham Cathedral, *Antiq J* 75, 189–234

Jeffries Davies, E, 1925 The beginning of the Dissolution: Christchurch Aldgate, 1532, *Trans Roy Hist Soc* 4 ser 8, 127–50

Jenner, A, and Vince, A, 1983 A dated type series of London medieval pottery: Part 3, A late medieval Hertfordshire glazed ware, *Trans London Middlesex Archaeol Soc* 34, 151–70

Jennings, S, 1981 *Eighteen centuries of pottery from Norwich*, E Anglian Archaeol Rep 13, Norwich

Johnson, T, 1974 Excavations at Christ Church, Newgate Street, 1973, *Trans London Middlesex Archaeol Soc* 25, 220–34

Johnston, F E, and Zimmer, L O, 1989 Assessment of growth and age in the immature skeleton, in Iscan and Kennedy, 11–21

Jones, P E, and Reddaway, T F (eds), 1962–6 *The survey of building sites in the City of London after the Great Fire of 1666 by Peter Mills and John Oliver*, London Topogr Soc Pub 97–99, London

Jonge, C H de, 1971 *Nederlandse tegels*, Amsterdam

Kahn, D, 1991 *Canterbury Cathedral and its Romanesque sculpture*, London

Keene, D, 1990 Well Court documentary evidence, in Schofield et al, 89–113

Keene, D, 1996 Landlords, the property market and urban development in medieval England, in Eliassen and Ersland, 93–119

Keene, D, and Harding, V, 1985 *A survey of documentary sources for property holding in London before the Great Fire*, London Rec Soc Pub 22, London

Keevill, G, Aston, M, and Hall, T (eds), 2001 *Monastic archaeology: papers on the study of medieval monasteries*, Oxford

Keily, F, 1989 Skeleton report for Carter Lane (PIC87), unpub MoL rep

Kemp, R, 1904 *Some notes on the ward of Aldgate*, London

Kemp, R L, and Graves, C P, 1996 *The church and Gilbertine priory of St Andrew, Fishergate*, The Archaeology of York 11/2, London

Kempe, A J, 1825 *Historical notes of the collegiate church or Royal Free Chapel and sanctuary of St Martin-le-Grand, London*, London

Kenyon, J, 1990 *Medieval fortifications*, London

Kerling, N, 1973 *Cartulary of St Bartholomew's Hospital, founded 1123: a calendar*, London

Kicken, D, Koldeweij, A M, and ter Molen, J R, 2000 *Lost and found: essays on medieval archaeology for H J E van Beuningen*, Rotterdam Pap 11, Rotterdam

Kidson, P, 1996 The Mariakerk at Utrecht, Speyer and Italy, in *Utrecht, Britain and the Continent: archaeology, art and architecture* (ed E de Bièvre), Brit Archaeol Ass Conf Trans 18, 123–36, London

King, E, 1996 Economic development in the early 12th century, in Britnell and Hatcher, 1–22

Kirk, R, and Kirk, F (eds), 1900–8 *Returns of aliens dwelling in the City and suburbs of London* (4 vols), London

Kjølbye-Biddle, B, 1975 A cathedral cemetery: problems in interpretation, *World Archaeol* 7(1), 87–107

Knowles, D, 1966 *The monastic order in England*, Cambridge

Knowles, D, and Grimes, W F, 1954 *Charterhouse*, London

Korf, D, 1981 *Nederlandse maiolica*, Haarlem

Krautheimer, R, 1980 *Rome: profile of a city, 312–1308*, Princeton, NJ

Kubach, H E, 1978 *Romanesque architecture*, London

Lambrick, G, 1990 Further excavations at the second site of the Dominican priory, Oxford, *Oxoniensa* 50, 131–208

L and P Hen VIII *Letters and papers, foreign and domestic, of the reign of Henry VIII* (eds J S Brewer, J Gairdner, and R H Brodie), 22 vols in 35, 1864–1932, London

Lang, R G, 1993 *Two Tudor subsidy assessment rolls for the City of London: 1541 and 1582*, London Rec Soc Pub 29, London

Latham, R, and Matthews, W (eds), 1971 *The diary of Samuel Pepys: a new and complete transcription: Vol 4, 1663*, London

LCC Survey of London, 1922 *The parish of St Leonard Shoreditch* (eds J Bird and P Norman), Survey of London 8, London

LCC Survey of London, 1924 *The parish of St Helen Bishopsgate: Part 1* (eds M Reddan and A W Clapham), Survey of London 9, London

Lee, F, and Magilton, J, 1989 The cemetery of the hospital of St James and St Mary Magdalene, Chichester: a case study, *World Archaeol* 21(2), 273–82

Leech, R, 1996 The prospect from Rugman's Row: the row house in late 16th- and 17th-century London, *Archaeol J* 153, 201–42

Lees, B A, 1935 *Records of the Templars in England in the 12th century: the inquest of 1185 with illustrative charters and documents*, Brit Acad Rec Soc Econ Hist os 9, London

Lethaby, W R, 1900 The priory of Holy Trinity, Aldgate, *Home Counties Mag* 2, 45–53

Lightbown, R, and Caiger-Smith, A (eds), 1980 *C Piccolpasso, I tre libri dell'arte del vasiao (The three books of the potter's art)* (2 vols), London

Ling, R, 1993 A relief from Duke Street, Aldgate, now in the Museum of London, *Britannia* 24, 7–12

Lipman, V D (ed), 1961 *Three centuries of Anglo-Jewish history*, London

Loftus-Brock, E P, 1880 Description of an ancient crypt at Aldgate, recently demolished, *J Brit Archaeol Ass* 1 ser 36, 159–64

Longman, W, 1873 *A history of the three cathedrals dedicated to St Paul in London*, London

Lundgren, K, and Thurlby, M, 1999 The Romanesque church of St Nicholas, Studland (Dorset), *Dorset Natur Hist Archaeol Soc Proc* 121, 1–16

Lyne, M, 1997 *Lewes Priory: excavations by Richard Lewis, 1969–82*, Lewes

McAleer, J P, 1999 *Rochester Cathedral 604–1540: an architectural history*, Toronto

McDonnell, K, 1978 *Medieval London suburbs*, London

McHardy, A K, 1977 *The Church in London 1375–92*, London Rec Soc Pub 13, London

McKern, T W, and Stewart, T D, 1957 *Skeletal age changes in young American males*, Natwick

McMurray, W, 1925 *The records of two City parishes*, London

Maddison, J, 2000 *Ely Cathedral: design and meaning*, Ely

Madge, S J (ed), 1901 *Abstracts of inquisitions post mortem relating to the City of London returned into the Court of Chancery: Part 2, 1561–77*, London Middlesex Archaeol Soc, London

Maitland, W, 1765 (1739) *History of London*, rev edn, London

Malcolm, J P, 1803–7 *Londinium Redivivum* (4 vols), London

Maloney, C, 1980 A witch-bottle from Duke's Place, Aldgate, *Trans London Middlesex Archaeol Soc* 31, 157–8

Maloney, J, 1979 Excavations at Dukes Place: the Roman defences, *London Archaeol* 3(11), 292–7

Maloney, J, and Harding, C J, 1979 Dukes Place and Houndsditch: the medieval defences, *London Archaeol* 3(13), 347–54

Manchester, K, 1983 *The archaeology of disease*, Bradford

Maresh, M M, 1943 Growth of major long bones in healthy children, *American J Diseases in Children* 66, 227–54

Margary, H, 1979 *The A–Z of Elizabethan London*, Margary in assoc Guildhall Library, Kent

Margary, H, 1985 *The A–Z of Regency London*, Margary in assoc Guildhall Library, Kent

Mariaux, P-A, 1995 *La Majolique: la faïence italienne et son décor dans les collections suisses, XVe-XVIIIe siècles*, Geneva

Marks, R C, 1970 The sculpture of Dunstable Priory c 1130–1222, unpub MA thesis, Univ London (Courtauld)

Marsden, P, 1969 Archaeological finds in the City of London, 1966–8, *Trans London Middlesex Archaeol Soc* 22(2), 1–26

Marsden, P, 1980 *Roman London*, London

Marsden, P, 1992 Precinct, power and people: the jurisdiction and inhabitants of the precinct of Holy Trinity Aldgate after the Dissolution of 1532, unpub MA thesis, Univ London (Birkbeck)

Martin, A R, 1926 On the topography of the Cluniac abbey of St Saviour at Bermondsey, *J Brit Archaeol Ass* 2 ser 32, 192–228

Martin, D, 1973 *Hastings Augustinian priory: an excavation report*, Hastings Area Archaeol Pap 2, Robertsbridge

Martin, W, 1927 Excavations at Whitefriars, Fleet Street, 1927–8, *J Brit Archaeol Ass* 2 ser 33, 293–320

Masters, B, 1984 *Chamber accounts of the 16th century*, London Record Soc Pub 20, London

Mays, S A, 1991a The burials from the Whitefriars friary site, Buttermarket, Ipswich, Suffolk (excavated 1986–88), unpub Engl Heritage Ancient Monuments Lab rep 17/91

Mays, S A, 1991b The medieval Blackfriars from the Blackfriars friary, Ipswich, Suffolk (excavated 1983–85), unpub Engl Heritage Ancient Monuments Lab rep 16/91

Meddens, F, 1992 A group of kiln waste from Harding's Farm, Mill Green, Essex, *Medieval Ceram* 16, 11–43

Meindl, R S, and Lovejoy, C O, 1985 Ectocranial suture closure: a revised method for the determination of skeletal age at death based on the lateral anterior sutures, *American J Phys Anthropol* 68, 57–66

Meindl, R S, Lovejoy, C O, Mensforth, R P, and Walker, R A, 1985 A revised method of age determination using the os pubis, with a review and tests of accuracy of other current methods of pubic symphyseal ageing, *American J Phys Anthropol* 68, 29–46

Mellor, J E, and Pearce, T, 1981 *The Austin Friars, Leicester*, CBA Res Rep 35, London

Merrifield, R, 1965 *The Roman city of London*, London

Merrifield, R, 1987 *The archaeology of ritual and magic*, London

Micklethwaite, J T, 1876 Notes on the abbey buildings of Westminster, *Archaeol J* 33, 15–48

Miller, P, Saxby, D, and Conheeney, J, in prep *Excavations at the priory of St Mary Merton, Surrey*, MoLAS Monogr Ser

Mills, P, 1985 The Royal Mint: first results, *London Archaeol* 5(3), 69–77

Milne, G, 1997 *St Bride's church, London: archaeological research 1952–60 and 1992–5*, Engl Heritage Archaeol Rep 11, London

Mitchiner, M, 1988 *Jettons, medalets and tokens: Vol 1, The medieval period and Nuremberg*, London

Monnas, L, 2001 Textiles for the coronation of Edward III, *Textile*

Hist 32, 2–35

Moore, N, 1918 *The history of St Bartholomew's Hospital* (2 vols), London

Moorhouse, S, 1993 Pottery and glass in the medieval monastery, in Gilchrist and Mytum, 127–48

Morey, A, and Brooke, C N L (eds), 1967 *The letters and charters of Gilbert Foliot*, London

Morris, R, 1979 *Cathedrals and abbeys of England and Wales: the building church, 600–1540*, London

Morris, R K, 1990 The New Work at Old St Paul's Cathedral and its place in English 13th-century architecture, in Grant, 74–100

Mozley, J F, 1940 *John Foxe and his book*, London

Muthesius, A, 1997 *Byzantine silk weaving AD 400 to AD 1200*, Vienna

Myres, J N L, 1933 Butley Priory, Suffolk, *Archaeol J* 90, 177–281

Neininger, F (ed), 1999 *English episcopal acta: Vol 15, London 1076–1187*, Oxford

Newton, E F, Bebbings, E, and Fisher, J L, 1960 Seventeenth-century pottery sites at Harlow, Essex, *Trans Essex Archaeol Soc* 25, 358–77

Nichols, J B, 1825 *Account of the Royal Hospital and collegiate church of Saint Katharine, near the Tower of London*, London

Nightingale, P, 1996 The growth of London in the medieval English economy, in Britnell and Hatcher, 89–106

Noël Hume, I, 1977 *Early English delftware from London and Virginia*, Colonial Williamsburg Occas Pap 2, Williamsburg

Norfolk Archaeological Unit, 1999 *Norfolk Archaeological Unit annual review 1998–9*, Norwich

Norman, P, 1897–8 Notes on a recent discovery of part of the priory of Christ Church, Aldgate, *Proc Soc Antiq London* 2 ser 17, 110–17

Norman, P, and Reader, F W, 1912 Further discoveries relating to Roman London, 1906–12, *Archaeologia* 63, 257–344

O'Connor, T P, 1993 Bone assemblages from monastic sites: many questions but few data, in Gilchrist and Mytum, 107–12

O'Donoghue, E G, 1914 *The story of Bethlem Hospital from its foundation in 1247*, London

OED, 1967 *The shorter Oxford English dictionary*, 3 edn (ed C T Onions), Oxford

Ogilby, J, and Morgan, W, 1676 'Large and Accurate Map of the City of London', reproduced in Margary, H, 1976, *Large and Accurate Map of the City of London by John Ogilby and William Morgan, 1676*, Margary in assoc Guildhall Library, Kent

Oost, T, 1992 Halfprodukten, steunstukken en misbaels: afval van een majolicawerklaats, in Veeckman, 99–108

Ortner, D J, and Putschar, W G J, 1981 *Identification of pathological conditions in human skeletal remains*, Washington, DC

Orton, C R, 1982 The excavation of a late medieval/transitional pottery kiln at Cheam, Surrey, *Surrey Archaeol Collect* 73, 49–92

Orton, C R, 1988 Post-Roman pottery, in *Excavations in Southwark 1973–6, Lambeth 1973–9* (ed P Hinton), London Middlesex Archaeol Soc and Surrey Archaeol Soc Joint Pub 3, 295–364, London

Orton, C R, and Pearce, J E, 1984 The pottery, in A Thompson, F Grew, and J Schofield, Excavations at Aldgate, 1974, *Post-Medieval Archaeol* 18, 34–68

Page-Phillips, J, 1980 *Palimpsests: the backs of monumental brasses* (2 vols), London

Parsons, F G, 1932 *The history of St Thomas's Hospital* (3 vols), London

Paul, R W, 1912 The plan of the church and monastery of St Augustine, Bristol, *Archaeologia* 63, 231–50

Pearce, J, 1992 *Post-medieval pottery in London 1500–1700: Vol 1, Border wares*, London

Pearce, J, 1998 A rare delftware Hebrew plate and associated assemblage from excavations in Mitre Street, City of London, *Post-Medieval Archaeol* 32, 95–112

Pearce, J, in prep The greyware industries, in L Blackmore and J Pearce in prep, *Medieval coarsewares of the London area: a dated type series of London medieval pottery: Part 5, Shelly-sandy ware and the greyware industries*, MoLAS Monogr Ser

Pearce, J, and Nenk, B, in prep *Post-medieval pottery in London 1500–1700: Vol 3, Redwares*

Pearce, J E, Vince, A G, and White, R, with Cunningham, C M, 1982 A dated type series of London medieval pottery: Part 1, Mill Green ware, *Trans London Middlesex Archaeol Soc* 33, 266–98

Pearce, J E, Vince, A G, and Jenner, M A, 1985 *A dated type series of London medieval pottery: Part 2, London-type ware*, London Middlesex Archaeol Soc Spec Pap 6, London

Peers, C, 1917 *St Botolph's Priory, Colchester, Essex*, repr 1977, London

Pennant, T, 1813 *Some account of London*, 5 edn, London

Perring, D, 1991 *Roman London*, London

Pevsner, N, 1973 *The buildings of England: London 1, The cities of London and Westminster*, 3 edn (rev B Cherry), Harmondsworth

Pevsner, N, 1976 *A history of building types*, London

Pevsner, N, 1984 *The buildings of England: Leicestershire and Rutland*, 2 edn (rev E Williamson with G K Brandwood), Harmondsworth

Phenice, T W, 1969 A newly developed visual method of sexing the os pubis, *American J Phys Anthropol* 30, 297–302

Philp, B, 1968 *Excavations at Faversham, 1965: the royal abbey, Roman villa and Belgic farmstead*, Kent Archaeol Res Grp Res Rep 1, Bromley

Pipe, A, 2000 The animal bones from a Saxon deposit at 32–40 Mitre Street, 71–77 Leadenhall Street, London EC3, City of London (LEA84), unpub MoL rep

Platt, C, and Coleman-Smith, R, 1975 *Excavations in medieval Southampton 1953–69: Vol 2, The finds*, Leicester

Poole, A L, 1955 *From Domesday Book to Magna Carta*, 2 edn, Oxford

Porter, S, and Richardson, H, in prep *Charterhouse*, Engl Heritage Survey of London

Postles, D, 1993 The Austin canons in English towns, c 1100–1350, *Historical Research (Bull Inst Hist Res)* 66, 1–20

Poulton, R, 1988 *Archaeological investigations on the site of Chertsey Abbey*, Surrey Archaeol Soc Res Vol 11, Guildford

Price, J E, 1870 Medieval kiln for burning encaustic tiles discovered near Farringdon Road, Clerkenwell, *Trans London Middlesex Archaeol Soc* os 3, 31–6

Prior, E S, 1900 *History of Gothic art in England*, London

Pritchard, F, 1984 Late Saxon textiles from the City of London, *Medieval Archaeol* 28, 46–76

Pryor, S, and Blockley, K, 1978 A 17th-century kiln site at

Woolwich, *Post-Medieval Archaeol* 12, 30–85
Pye, B, nd Excavations at 12–14 Mitre Street (MIR84), unpub MoL rep
Rackham, B, 1939 A Netherlands maiolica vase from the Tower of London, *Antiq J* 19, 285–90
Rackham, D J, 1986 Assessing the relative frequency of species by the application of a stochastic model to a zooarchaeological database, in *Database management and zooarchaeology* (ed L H van Wijngaarden-Bakker), J European Study Grp Physical, Chemical, Biological, Mathematical Techniques Applied to Archaeology Res Vol 40, 185–92, Amsterdam
RCHME, 1916 Roy Comm Hist Monuments Engl, *An inventory of the historical monuments in Essex: Vol 1, North-west Essex*, London
RCHME, 1921 Roy Comm Hist Monuments Engl, *An inventory of the historical monuments in Essex: Vol 2, Central and south-west Essex*, London
RCHME, 1924 Roy Comm Hist Monuments Engl, *An inventory of the historical monuments in London: Vol 1, Westminster Abbey*, London
RCHME, 1925 Roy Comm Hist Monuments Engl, *An inventory of the historical monuments in London: Vol 2, West London*, London
RCHME, 1928 Roy Comm Hist Monuments Engl, *An inventory of the historical monuments in London: Vol 3, Roman London*, London
RCHME, 1929 Roy Comm Hist Monuments Engl, *An inventory of the historical monuments in London: Vol 4, The City of London*, London
RCHME, 1930 Roy Comm Hist Monuments Engl, *An inventory of the historical monuments in London: Vol 5, East London*, London
RCHME, 1977 Roy Comm Hist Monuments Engl, *An inventory of the historical monuments in the town of Stamford*, London
RCHME, 1980 Roy Comm Hist Monuments Engl, *An inventory of the historical monuments in the city of Salisbury: Vol 1*, London
RCHME, 1993 Roy Comm Hist Monuments Engl, *Salisbury: the houses of the Close*, London
Reilly, L A, 1997 *An architectural history of Peterborough Cathedral*, Oxford
Riley, H T (ed), 1868 *Memorials of London and London life in the 13th, 14th and 15th centuries: being a series of extracts, local, social and political, from the early archives of the City of London, AD 1276–1419*, London
Rivière, S, 1986a Excavations at 71–77 Leadenhall Street, 32–34 Mitre Street (LEA84), unpub MoL rep
Rivière, S, 1986b The excavation at Mitre Street, *Popular Archaeol* 6(12), 37–41
Rivière, S, 1986c Watching brief at Mitre Street (MIT86), unpub MoL rep
Robinson, D, 1980 *The geography of Augustinian settlement in medieval England and Wales*, BAR Brit Ser 80, Oxford
Robinson, G, and Urquhart, H, 1934 Seal bags in the Treasury of the cathedral church of Canterbury, *Archaeologia* 84, 163–211
Rodwell, W, 1989 Archaeology and the standing fabric: recent studies at Lichfield Cathedral, *Antiquity* 63, 281–94
Roffey, S, 1998 The early history and development of St Marie Overie Priory, Southwark: the 12th-century chapel of St John, *London Archaeol* 8(10), 255–61
Rogers, K, 1928 *The Mermaid and Mitre Taverns in Old London*, London
Rollason, D, Harvey, M, and Prestwich, M (eds), 1994 *Anglo-Norman Durham 1093–1193*, Woodbridge
Rosenfield, M C, 1970 Holy Trinity, Aldgate, on the eve of the Dissolution, *Guildhall Miscellany* 3(3), 159–73
Roth, C, 1950 *The Great Synagogue, London, 1690–1940*, London
Rot Hund *Rotuli hundredorum temporibus Henrici III et Edwardi I in Turr' lond' et in curia receptae scaccarij Westminster asservati* (eds W Illingworth and J Caley), 2 vols, 1812–18, London
Rubens, A, 1966 The Jews of the parish of St James Duke's Place in the City of London, in *Remember the days: essays on Anglo-Jewish history* (ed J M Shaftesley), 181–205, London
Ruempol, A P E, and van Dongen, A G A, 1991 *Pre-industrial utensils 1150–1800*, Museum Boymans–van Beuningen, Rotterdam
Rumbelow, D, 1987 *The complete Jack the Ripper*, 2 edn, London
Ryan, M, 1990 Excavations at 80–84 Leadenhall Street (LAH88), unpub MoL rep
St John Hope, W H, 1898 The architectural history of the cathedral church and monastery of St Andrew at Rochester, *Archaeol Cantiana* 23, 194–328
St John Hope, W H, 1900 The architectural history of the cathedral church and monastery of St Andrew at Rochester: II, The monastery, *Archaeol Cantiana* 24, 1–85
Salzman, L F, 1967 (1952) *Building in England down to 1540: a documentary history*, rev edn, Oxford
Samuel, E R, 1961 The first fifty years, in Lipman, 27–44
Samuel, W S, 1924 *The first London synagogue of the Resettlement*, London
Saunders, A, and Schofield, J (eds), 2001 *Tudor London: a map and a view*, London Topogr Soc Pub 159, London
Saunders, S R, 1989 Nonmetric variation, in Iscan and Kennedy, 95–108
Schmid, E, 1972 *Atlas of animal bones for prehistorians, archaeologists and Quaternary geologists*, London
Schofield, J, 1975 Seal House, *Current Archaeol* 49, 53–7
Schofield, J, 1977 New Fresh Wharf: 3, The medieval buildings, *London Archaeol* 3(3), 66–73
Schofield, J, 1985 Excavations on the west side of Mitre Square (HTP79), unpub MoL rep
Schofield, J, 1993 Building in religious precincts in London at the Dissolution and after, in Gilchrist and Mytum, 29–42
Schofield, J, 1994 Saxon and medieval parish churches in the City of London: a review, *Trans London Middlesex Archaeol Soc* 45, 23–145
Schofield, J, 1997 Excavations on the site of St Nicholas Shambles, Newgate Street, City of London, *Trans London Middlesex Archaeol Soc* 48, 77–136
Schofield, J (ed), with Maloney, C, 1998 *Archaeology in the City of London 1907–91: a guide to records of excavations by the Museum of London and its predecessors*, MoL Archaeol Gazetteer Ser 1, London
Schofield, J, 1999 (1984) *The building of London from the Conquest to the Great Fire*, 3 edn, Stroud
Schofield, J, 2003a (1995) *Medieval London houses*, rev edn, New Haven and London
Schofield, J, 2003b Some aspects of the reformation of religious space in London, 1540–1660, in *The archaeology of Reformation 1480–1580* (eds D Gaimster and R Gilchrist), 310–24, Leeds

Schofield, J, in prep *The archaeology of St Paul's Cathedral: Vol 1, Survey and excavation up to 2004*

Schofield, J, and Dyson, T, 1980 *Archaeology of the City of London*, London

Schofield, J, and Dyson, T, in prep *London waterfront tenements 1100–1750*

Schofield, J, Allen, P, and Taylor, C, 1990 Medieval buildings and property development in the area of Cheapside, *Trans London Middlesex Archaeol Soc* 41, 39–237

Schour, I, and Massler, M, 1944 *Development of the human dentition*, 2 edn, Chicago

Scott, I R, 1996 *Romsey Abbey: report on the excavations 1973–91*, Hants Field Club Archaeol Soc Monogr 8, Hampshire

Seymour, R, 1734 *A survey of the cities of London and Westminster, the Borough of Southwark and parts adjacent*, London

Shepherd, E B S, 1902 The church of the Friars Minor in London, *Archaeol J* 59, 238–87

Shoesmith, R, 1980 *Excavations at Castle Green*, Hereford City Excav 1, CBA Res Rep 36, London

Simpson, W G, and Litton, C D, 1996 Dendrochronology in cathedrals, in Tatton-Brown and Munby, 183–210

Slater, T R, 1996 Medieval town-founding on the estates of the Benedictine Order in England, in Eliassen and Ersland, 70–92

Sloane, B, in prep *Excavations at the nunnery of St Mary* de fonte, *Clerkenwell, London*, MoLAS Monogr Ser

Sloane, B, and Malcolm, G, 2004 *Excavations at the priory of the Order of the Hospital of St John of Jerusalem, Clerkenwell, London*, MoLAS Monogr Ser 20, London

Smith, C F, 1909 *John Dee 1527–1608*, London

Smith, E B, 1956 *Architectural symbolism of Imperial Rome and the Middle Ages*, London

Sowan, P W, 1975 Firestone and hearthstone mines in the Upper Greensand of East Surrey, *Proc Geol Ass* 86(4), 571–91

Spence, C, and Grew, F (eds), 1989 *Department of Urban Archaeology, Museum of London: the annual review 1989*, London

Stalley, R A, 1971 A 12th-century patron of architecture: a study of the buildings erected by Roger, Bishop of Salisbury 1102–39, *J Brit Archaeol Ass* 3 ser 34, 62–83

Stalley, R A, 1981 Three Irish buildings with West Country origins, in *Medieval art and architecture at Wells and Glastonbury* (eds N Coldstream and P Draper), Brit Archaeol Ass Conf Trans 4, 62–80, London

Steele, A, in prep *Excavations at the monastery of St Saviour Bermondsey, Southwark*, MoLAS Monog Ser

Stenton, D (ed), in prep *Qallunaat Island archaeology and oral history*, Department of Canadian Heritage, Prince of Wales Northern Heritage Centre

Stephan, H-G, 1991 *Kacheln aus dem Werraland: die Entwicklung der Ofenkacheln vom 13. bis 17. Jahrhundert im unteren Werra-Raum*, Schriften des Werratalvereins Witzenhausen Vol 23, Witzenhausen

Stephenson, R, 1991 Post-medieval ceramic bird pots from excavations in Greater London, *London Archaeol* 6(12), 320–1

Stephenson, R, with Spoerry, P, 1997 The pottery, in Thomas et al, 184–6

Stocker, D A, 1986 The excavated stonework, in Gilmour and Stocker, 44–82

Stott, P, 1991 Saxon and Norman coins from London, in Vince, 279–325

Stow, J, 1603 *A survey of London* (ed C L Kingsford), 2 vols, 1908 repr 1971, Oxford

Strauss, K, 1972 *Die Kachelkunst des 15. und 16. Jahrhunderts: Part 2*, Basel

Strype, J, 1720 *A survey of the Cities of London and Westminster from 1633 to the present* (2 vols), London

Stuart-Macadam, P L, 1989 Nutritional deficiency diseases: a survey of scurvy, rickets and iron deficiency anaemia, in Iscan and Kennedy, 201–22

Sundick, R I, 1978 Human skeletal growth and age determination, *Homo* 30, 297–333

Sutton, A, and Sewell, J, 1980 Jacob Verzelini and the City of London, *Glass Technology* 21(4), 190–2

Tait, H, 1992 The earliest dated English delftware?, in *Everyday and exotic pottery from Europe c 650–1900: studies in honour of John G Hurst* (eds D Gaimster and M Redknap), 359–70, Oxford

Tatton-Brown, T, 1995 Westminster Abbey: archaeological recording at the west end of the church, *Antiq J* 75, 171–88

Tatton-Brown, T, and Munby, J (eds), 1996 *The archaeology of cathedrals*, Oxford Univ Comm Archaeol Monogr 42, Oxford

Taylor, H M, and Taylor, J, 1965 *Anglo-Saxon architecture* (2 vols), Cambridge

Thomas, C, Sloane, B, and Phillpotts, C, 1997 *Excavations at the priory and hospital of St Mary Spital, London*, MoLAS Monogr Ser 1, London

Thompson, A, Westman, A, and Dyson, T (eds), 1998 *Archaeology in Greater London 1965–90: a guide to records of excavations by the Museum of London*, MoL Archaeol Gazetteer Ser 2, London

Thorn, J, 1976 Three medieval jugs from St Bartholomew's Hospital, *London Archaeol* 2(14), 360–1

Thurlby, M, 1985 The elevations of the Romanesque abbey churches of St Mary at Tewkesbury and St Peter at Gloucester, in Heslop and Sekules, 36–51

Thurlby, M, 1988 The Romanesque priory church of St Michael at Ewenny, *J Soc Architect Historians* 47, 281–94

Thurlby, M, 1991 The Romanesque cathedral of St Mary and St Peter at Exeter, in *Medieval art and architecture at Exeter Cathedral* (ed F Kelly), Brit Archaeol Ass Conf Trans 11, 19–34, London

Thurlby, M, 1993a The high vaults of Durham Cathedral, in Jackson, 64–76

Thurlby, M, 1993b The purpose of the rib in the Romanesque vaults of Durham Cathedral, in Jackson, 43–63

Thurlby, M, 1994a The roles of the patron and the master mason in the first design of Durham Cathedral, in Rollason et al, 161–84

Thurlby, M, 1994b The Romanesque apse vault at Peterborough Cathedral, in *Studies in medieval art and architecture presented to Peter Lasko* (eds D Buckton and T A Heslop), 171–86, Stroud

Thurlby, M, 1995 Jedburgh Abbey church: the Romanesque fabric, *Proc Soc Antiq Scotl* 125, 793–812

Thurlby, M, 1996 The influence of Norwich Cathedral on Romanesque architecture in East Anglia, in *Norwich Cathedral:*

church, city and diocese 1096–1996 (eds I Atherton, E Fernie, C Harper Bill, and H Smith), 136–57, London

Thurlby, M, 1997a L'Abbatiale romane de St Albans, in *L'Architecture normande au Moyen Age* (ed M Baylé), 79–90, Caen

Thurlby, M, 1997b Aspects of the architectural history of Kirkwall Cathedral, *Proc Soc Antiq Scotl* 127, 855–88

Thurlby, M, 1997c The Elder Lady chapel at St Augustine's, Bristol, and Wells Cathedral, in *'Almost the richest city': Bristol in the Middle Ages* (ed L Keen), Brit Archaeol Ass Conf Trans 19, 31–40, London

Thurlby, M, 2001 The place of St Albans in regional sculpture and architecture in the second half of the 12th century, in *Alban and St Albans: Roman and medieval architecture, art and archaeology* (eds M Henig and P Lindley), Brit Archaeol Ass Conf Trans 24, 162–75, Leeds

Thurlby, M, and Baxter, R, 2001 The Romanesque abbey church at Reading, in *Windsor: medieval archaeology, art and architecture of the Thames valley* (eds L Keen and E Scarff), Brit Archaeol Ass Conf Trans 25, 282–301, London

Toman, R (ed), 1997 *Romanesque: architecture, sculpture, painting*, Cologne

Toy, S, 1932 The crypt at Whitefriars, London, *J Brit Archaeol Ass* 2 ser 38, 334–7

Trotter, M, and Glesser, G C, 1952 Estimation of stature from long bones of American whites and negroes, *American J Phys Anthropol* 10, 463–514

Trotter, M, and Glesser, G C, 1958 A re-evaluation of estimation of stature based on measurements of stature taken during life and from long bones after death, *American J Phys Anthropol* 16, 79–123

Turner, D J, 1974 Medieval pottery kiln at Bushfield Shaw, Earlswood: interim report, *Surrey Archaeol Collect* 70, 47–55

Turner-Rugg, A, 1995 Medieval pottery from St Albans, *Medieval Ceram* 19, 45–65

Tweddle, D, Biddle, M, and Kjølbye-Biddle, B, 1995 *A corpus of Anglo-Saxon stone sculpture: Vol 4, South-east England*, Oxford

Tyler, K, 1991 Excavations in Dukes Place, 1977 (DUK77), unpub MoL rep

Unger, I (ed), 1988 *Kölner Ofenkacheln: die Bestände des Museums für Angewandte Kunst und des Kölnischen Stadtmuseums*, Cologne

VCH, 1905 *The Victoria History of the county of Surrey: Vol 2*, London

VCH, 1906 *The Victoria History of the county of Northamptonshire: Vol 2*, London

VCH, 1908 *The Victoria History of the county of Hertfordshire: Vol 2*, London

VCH, 1909 *The Victoria History of the counties of England: London, Vol 1*, London

VCH, 1912 *The Victoria History of the county of Bedfordshire: Vol 3*, London

VCH, 1976 *The Victoria History of the county of Middlesex: Vol 5*, London

VCH, 1994 *The Victoria History of the county of Essex: Vol 9*, London

Veeckman, J (ed), 1992 *Blik in de bodem: recent stadsarchaeologisch onderzoek in Antwerpen*, Antwerp

Veeckman, J, 1999 Maiolica in 16th-century and early 17th-century Antwerp: the archaeological evidence, in Gaimster 1999b, 113–23

Vince, A, 1981 Coarse pottery, in A Vince and G Egan, The contents of a late 18th-century pit at Crosswall, City of London, *Trans London Middlesex Archaeol Soc* 32, 162–4

Vince, A, 1982 Medieval and post-medieval Spanish pottery from the City of London, in *Current research in ceramics: thin section studies* (eds I Freestone, C Johns, and T Potter), Brit Mus Occas Pap 32, 135–44, London

Vince, A, 1985 Saxon and medieval pottery in London: a review, *Medieval Archaeol* 29, 25–93

Vince, A, 1990 *Saxon London: an archaeological investigation*, London

Vince, A (ed), 1991 *Aspects of Saxo-Norman London: Vol 2, Finds and environmental evidence*, London Middlesex Archaeol Soc Spec Pap 12, London

Vince, A, and Jenner, A, 1991 The Saxon and early medieval pottery of London, in Vince, 19–119

Vitruvius The ten books on architecture (trans M H Morgan), 1914, Cambridge, Mass

Waldron, T, 1993 The human remains from the Royal Mint site (MIN86), unpub MoL rep

Walker, D (ed), 1998 *The cartulary of St Augustine's Abbey, Bristol*, Gloucestershire Rec Ser 10, Bristol

Ward, S W, 1990 *Excavations at Chester: the lesser medieval religious houses, sites investigated 1964–83*, Grosvenor Mus Archaeol Excav Survey Rep 6, Chester

Ward, S W, 1993 The monastic topography of Chester, in Gilchrist and Mytum, 113–26

Wardwell, A E, 1988–9 *Panni Tartarici*: Eastern Islamic silks woven with gold and silver (13th and 14th centuries), *Islamic Art* 3, 95–173

Webb, E A, 1913 The plan of St Bartholomew's, West Smithfield, and the recent excavations, *Archaeologia* 64, 165–76

Webb, E A, 1921 *The records of St Bartholomew's Priory and of the church and parish of St Bartholomew the Great, West Smithfield* (2 vols), Oxford

Webb, G, 1956 *Architecture in Britain: the Middle Ages*, Harmondsworth

Webber, M, 1991 Excavations on the site of Norfolk House, Lambeth Road, SE1, *London Archaeol* 6(13), 343–50

West, B, 1986 The Late Saxon skeletons from Mitre Street (LEA84), unpub MoLAS rep

West, B, 1990 Burials from the Dominican friary: human bones, in Ward, 127–37

Wheatley, H B (ed), 1956 (1912) *Stow's survey of London*, rev edn, London

Wheatley, H B, and Cunningham, P (eds), 1891 *London past and present* (3 vols), London

White, W, 1988 *Skeletal remains from the cemetery of St Nicholas Shambles, City of London*, London Middlesex Archaeol Soc Spec Pap 9, London

Wilckens, A von, 1992 *Mittelalterliche Seidenstoffe*, Berlin

Wilkinson, D, and McWhirr, A, 1998 *Cirencester Anglo-Saxon church and medieval abbey*, Cirencester Excav 4, Cirencester

Wilkinson, R, 1825 *Londina Illustrata* (2 vols), London

Williams, N, 1964 *Thomas Howard, 4th Duke of Norfolk*, London

Williams, T D, in prep *The archaeology of Roman London: Vol 4, The development of Roman London east of the Walbrook*, CBA Res Rep

Willis, R, 1846, The architectural history of Winchester Cathedral, in *Proc Summer Meeting Roy Archaeol Inst* (repr 1972, in R Willis, *Architectural history of some English cathedrals*, Part 1, section 2, 1–70 [individually paginated sections], Chichely

Wilson, C, 1986 The Gothic abbey church, in Wilson et al, 22–69

Wilson, C, 1992 (1990) *The Gothic cathedral: the architecture of the great church, 1130–1530*, rev edn, London

Wilson, C, 1998 The stellar vaults of Glasgow Cathedral's inner crypt and Villard de Honnecourt's chapter-house plan: a conundrum revisited, in *Medieval art and architecture in the diocese of Glasgow* (ed R Fawcett), Brit Archaeol Ass Conf Trans 23, 55–76, London

Wilson, C, Gem, R, Tudor-Craig, P, and Physick, J (eds), 1986 *Westminster Abbey*, New Bell's Cathedral Guides, London

Wilson, T, 1987 *Ceramic art of the Italian Renaissance*, London

Wilson, T, 1999 Italian maiolica around 1500: some considerations on the background to Antwerp maiolica, in Gaimster 1999b, 5–21

Wittkower, R, 1974 *Palladio and English Palladianism*, London

Wood, M E, 1965 *The English mediaeval house*, London

Woodman, F, 1981 *The architectural history of Canterbury Cathedral*, London

Woods, D, Rhodes, M, and Dyson, T, 1975 Africa House sections, London, 1973, *Trans London Middlesex Archaeol Soc* 26, 252–66

Yeoman, P, 1995 *Medieval Scotland*, London

Zarnecki, G, 1972 *The monastic achievement*, London

Zarnecki, G, Holt, J, and Holland, T (eds), 1984 *English Romanesque art 1066–1200*, Hayward Gallery exhibition catalogue, London

INDEX

Compiled by Ann Hudson

Page numbers in **bold** indicate illustrations, tables and maps
All street names and locations are in London unless specified otherwise
County names within parentheses refer to historic counties